THE DEMOGRAPHIC TRANSITION

The Demographic Transition

Stages, Patterns, and Economic Implications

A Longitudinal Study of Sixty-Seven Countries
Covering the Period 1720–1984

JEAN-CLAUDE CHESNAIS

translated by
Elizabeth and Philip Kreager

CLARENDON PRESS · 1992

Oxford University Press, Walton Street, Oxford OX2 6DP
Oxford New York Toronto
Delhi Bombay Calcutta Madras Karachi
Petaling Jaya Singapore Hong Kong Tokyo
Nairobi Dar es Salaam Cape Town
Melbourne Auckland
and associated companies in
Berlin Ibadan

Oxford is a trade mark of Oxford University Press

Published in the United States
by Oxford University Press, New York

English edition (abridged) of La Transition
Demographique, Presses Universitaires de
France-INED.

British Library Cataloguing in Publication Data
Data available

Library of Congress Cataloging in Publication Data
Chesnais, Jean Claude.
[Transition démographique. English]
The demographic transition: stages, patterns, and economic
implications: a longitudinal study of sixty-seven countries
covering the period 1720–1984 / Jean-Claude Chesnais; translated by
Elizabeth and Philip Kreager.
p.   cm.
Translation of: La transition démographique.
Includes bibliographical references and index.
1. Demographic transition—History.   2. Economic development—
History.   I. Title.
HB887.C4813   1992   304.6—dc20   91-41100
ISBN 0-19-828659-7

Typeset by Best-set Typesetter Ltd., Hong Kong
Printed in Great Britain by
Bookcraft (Bath) Ltd, Midsomer Norton, Avon

Contents

Figures

Tables

Abbreviations

AER	*American Economic Review*
ASEAN	Association of South-East Asian Nations
CBR	crude birth-rate
CEHE	*Cambridge Economic History of Europe*
CICRED	Comité International de Coopération dans les Recherches Nationales en Démographie, Paris
CRR	crude reproduction rate
EDCC	*Economic Development and Cultural Change*
EHR	*Economic History Review*
EJ	*Economic Journal*
ESC	*Économies Sociétés Civilisations (Annales)*
FAO	Food and Agricultural Organization, Rome
FEHE	*Fontana Economic History of Europe*
GDP	gross domestic product
GNP	gross national product
GRR	gross reproduction rate
ICOR	incremental capital–output ratio
ILO	International Labour Organization (or Office)
IPPF	International Planned Parenthood Federation
ISEA	*Institut de Science Économique Appliquée (Cahiers)*
ISI	International Statistical Institute, La Haye
JEEH	*Journal of European Economic History*
JEL	*Journal of Economic Literature*
JPE	*Journal of Political Economy*
JSSP	*Journal de la Société de Statistique de Paris*
MBS	*Monthly Bulletin of Statistics*, UN, New York
MMFQ	*Milbank Memorial Fund Quarterly*, New York
NBER	National Bureau of Economic Research
NNP	net national product
NRR	net reproduction rate
OECD	Organization for Economic Co-operation and Development
OEP	*Oxford Economic Papers*
PDR	*Population and Development Review*
PUF	Presses Universitaires de France
QAEGN	Quantitative Aspects of the Economic Growth of Nations
RES	*Review of Economics and Statistics*
SGF	Statistique Générale de France
TFR	total fertility rate
IUSSP	International Union for the Scientific Study of Population
UN	United Nations
WFS	World Fertility Survey
YNAS	*Yearbook of National Accounts Statistics*

Introduction: The 'Theory' of Demographic Transition: Its Conciseness, Diversity, and Flexibility

DEMOGRAPHY is a science in which general theories are rare. Aside from Malthus's theory, which emphasizes constraints of subsistence on population, as a principal body of thought there is only what is called by convention the theory of demographic transition. The most important point of comparison between these two explanatory systems lies in the supposed effect of economic development on fertility. In the Malthusian view, economic development stimulates fertility, the increase in demand for work encouraging marriage and family formation.[1] In the transitional view, the relation between industrialization and fertility is inverse: industrial revolution raises the standard of living and stimulates, especially, a general aspiration towards an always greater degree of comfort, which, in turn, promotes the limitation of child-bearing.[2]

However, a close reading of certain authors, like Leroy-Beaulieu (1913),[3] makes one wonder whether this antinomy is not circumstantial and, therefore, more apparent than real. The assumptions of each model have a tendency to lead on to those of the other, so that their opposition is resolved by the crossing of specific thresholds in the standard of living: 'a first step towards improved conditions amongst primitive populations with few needs tends to stimulate prolificness; further improvements in comfort, education and democracy tend to encourage restraint'. One of the aims of this book will be to define the range and limits of this body of theory more precisely.

Harsh Criticisms, at Times Unwarranted

Malthus's theory has been criticized as ceasing to be true for Europe at the very time of its conception; a more or less similar charge has arisen against demographic transition theory, since the 1950s. Discussing the latter, however, is not easy, since it is one of those rare theses having multiple authorship (Landry, Notestein, Davis, and Thompson), and scientific discussion has never specified entirely which texts should be included in its brief. Not

---

[1] Conformity to this model has often been demonstrated through observations on the past. Thus, according to various studies, fertility in traditional peasant societies increases with wealth; similarly, England and The Netherlands experienced a rise in fertility during the Industrial Revolution.

[2] Easterlin's approach, which we consider applies to the situation of post-transitional societies, borrows elements from both of these theories.

[3] See Chapter 1 for bibliographic references to this Introduction.

infrequently one or another of these authors (Landry, especially, at least outside Europe) is excluded from the argument. And, apart from the some-times lengthy exegesis devoted to analysis of past demographic trends, considerations of transition theory are confined to a few laconic passages, strongly inspired by pre-war European experience, and often without claim to generality. The common aim is to explain why a society passing from a timeless state of quasi-stagnation to modern economic growth (in its broadest sense, as, for example, understood by followers of Kuznets) registers a decline in mortality followed by a decline in fertility; in other words, these texts offer global, liberal, non-interventionist interpretation of demographic changes assumed to have occurred of their own accord in the course of structural change in societies.

This view has been the subject of heated controversies,[4] especially during the period 1955–65,[5] since when assessments have been less extreme or exclusive. Positions have ranged from outspoken support to total rejection, although the most hostile criticisms often lack validity, as they misinterpret, and even ignore, the original texts. It is useful to review the main tenets, confining ourselves here to the original theory, which, by convention, focuses on Notestein's synthesis of 1953.

The Main Ingredients

It is possible to distinguish two approaches in these texts, the one purely descriptive, the other explanatory, which vary widely in application from one author to another. Some confine themselves entirely to established facts, from which the claim of empiricism and the frequent reluctance to admit the theoretical status of new interpretations arose.

1. *The evidence.* The demographic transition consists of a logical succession of historical phases through which every population passes in the movement towards modernity. Depending on the degree of detail in the presentation, authors distinguish three or five successive phases. With three, one is dealing with stages of pre-transition (long-standing equilibrium of high mortality and fertility), transition (destabilization), and post-transition (modern equilibrium characterized by low mortality and fertility).[6] In other words, the first ap-

---

[4] The World Population Conference in Bucharest (1974) marked the culmination of conflict between doctrines of development (whose ethic is summed up in the formula 'the most effective contraceptive is development') and neo-Malthusians (who encourage specific interventions to speed up fertility decline).

[5] Despite a considerable decline in mortality, the fertility decline in poor countries was then non-existent (or unknown), a fact which called the whole theory of transition into question.

[6] In Landry (1909, 1934), these stages are named, respectively: (1) primitive regime, (2) intermediate regime, and (3) contemporary regime; in Notestein (1945), who emphasizes the influence of age structure on population growth, they are defined as: (1) high growth potential, (2) transitional growth, and (3) potential decline. Blacker (1949) subdivides the transitional phase into two stages, the first characterized by consistently high fertility and high, but declining, mortality

proach describes an internal dynamics of populations, drawing our attention to the influence of mortality on fertility. This relationship had been seen much earlier, for example, by Guillard, inventor of the word 'demography' (1855). Using international statistics, he called attention to the close correspondence between levels (and trends) of mortality and fertility. The idea of the mechanism of the transition was thus already germinating. A century ago the statistical link between infant mortality and fertility was clearly perceived by Geissler (1885) as a replacement effect; and before the First World War authors such as Wolf (1912), analysing possible causes of the decline in German fertility, focused, in the first place, on improved trends in mortality.

This approach has aroused scarcely any controversy, aside from certain central areas of Europe, especially France, where the expected linkage in phenomena was not (according to certain theories, which we shall reject) followed. In the case of France, the response of mortality to modernization did not precede, and sometimes did not occur as rapidly, as that of fertility. The contribution of many authors such as Thompson (1929, 1946), Carr-Saunders (1936), and Davis (1945) stopped short at a basic outline of the evidence; others, in particular Landry (1934) and Notestein (1945, 1953), proposed explanatory theories.

2. *Interpretation.* Explaining the mortality decline is inevitably easier than that of fertility, although what proportion to assign to the principal contributing factors (medical discoveries, health improvements, and higher standards of living) is far from being unanimously agreed upon. For the development of fertility, which claims prime attention amongst these authors,[7] the factors appear more numerous and complex. Nevertheless, our two great precursors shared the view that fertility declines chiefly as a response, an adjustment to structural changes of economy and society. The preponderant influence of socio-economic development, considered as the very essence of transition theory, has been frequently called into question, and the primacy of the economy at times fiercely contested. Because traditional socio-economic indicators have failed to account for the diversity of demographic experiences

(thus greatly expanding the rate of natural increase), and the second by a decline both in fertility and mortality, fertility being the faster of the two (the latter being a reaction to the rapid natural increase of the preceding stage). The phase conventionally called post-transitional (characterized by low fertility; see Chapter 7, below) is also subdivided by Blacker into two stages, the first defined by an equilibrium between low fertility and low mortality, and the second by a decline in which deaths begin to outnumber births. This fivefold distinction is repeated by Davis (1950), who differs only in his definition of the final phase in which fertility, while relatively low and stable, remains higher than mortality, thus maintaining a certain growth. Of course, by this time, the first three phases were a thing of the past (at least for the most advanced countries), and apparently only the last stages of the transition were open to discussion. Thompson's threefold definition (1929, 1946), referring to 'pre-industrial', 'expanding', and 'stationary' countries, reiterates that of Landry.

[7] Social thinkers early became preoccupied by the decline in fertility especially in France and Germany. Landry, in his first demographic writings (1909), where the foundations of his major work are already apparent, reveals his affinity to Dumont (1890) and Mombert (1907).

recorded in Europe, social theories based on cultural (Leasure 1963), socio-political (Lesthaeghe and Wilson 1982), or anthropological reasoning (Caldwell 1976; Le Bras and Todd 1981) have been put forward in opposition.

A False Dichotomy

Such critiques may well be questioned, to the extent that Landry's original formulation is often deliberately ignored in favour of Notestein's schematized and almost caricatural account. To begin with, in Landry no such dichotomy between the economic and the mental or 'cultural' existed. Like most great European social thinkers of his time (Troeltsch 1911; Sombart 1913; and especially Weber, 1920–21), he places the history of ideas above that of social (or familial) organization. He advances a 'new conception of life', the principal cause of fertility decline being the 'massive movement of the liberation of minds'. And he recalls that the phenomenon in France started 'at the same time as the beginnings of the Revolution'. To sum up the essence of this new and hedonistic philosophy, Landry uses the phrase 'rationalization[8] of life'; he perceives the manifestation of this in all spheres of daily life: political, familial, industrial, etc. It is in the post-war American account, and in the increasingly condensed extracts derived from it and empirically applied, that the interpretation becomes reductionist,[9] drifting gradually into economism (see, for example, Coale and Hoover 1958); whereas the European tradition, from Levasseur and Leroy-Beaulieu to Sauvy, via Mombert and Wolf, perceives at the root of these phenomena a network of complex causes, amongst which the systems of values (culture, religion, morality) play a determining role. The connection between fertility and 'civilization' (a rather imprecise term then favoured) is none the less explicitly analysed by Bertillon *père* (1874),[10] who anticipates the later argument of 'social capillarity' (Dumont 1890): the desire for social ascent in an open society where traditional class structure, with its fixed attributes, is overthrown, and child-bearing is limited because of the family's concern for its immediate way of life, as much as by an ambition for future generations. Leroy-Beaulieu's formula 'democratic civilization lowers fertility' best sums up the thought of these writers on demographic transition. Dumont's remark that 'a society's fertility is not that of the class to which it belongs, but that of the class to which it would like to belong' anticipates Easterlin's post-transitional view, which, as we shall see, oscillates between a narrowly economic interpretation and a sociological one.[11]

[8] A phrase which Caldwell (1976) takes up in order to contest, without apparently being aware of its origin or real significance, reducing it to its economic dimension (and opposing it, moreover, to a supposed irrationality in poor societies).

[9] Notestein himself did not deny the role of culture, calling attention to the change in norms and values which occurs during the movement from agrarian to modern urban society.

[10] His son, J. Bertillon, wrote on French depopulation (1911).

[11] Except that in Easterlin's case, the frame of reference is the family, the level of aspiration being determined by the status of the family of origin.

In practice, most empirical studies intended to test the foundations of transition theory either leave to one side cultural variables (norms, traditions, family structure), thereby blatantly ignoring history and social structure, or incorporate them only in opposition to economic (or socio-economic) variables. The 'theory of thresholds' (UN 1963) is a clear illustration of this reductive tendency, since it assumes that fertility declines are due to the combined action of different socio-economic factors representative of a general level of development (life expectation at birth, infant mortality, per capita income, proportion of literate female adults, etc.).[12] In certain authors, however, like Beaver (1975) or Lesthaeghe (1983), cultural heritage is taken into account and the historical perspective re-established by means of long time series; prior to their work, tests were for the most part applied only to comparative trends in material indicators, between countries over an average period—with little real significance for the development of mentalities.

Some Real Weaknesses

Transition theory is claimed to be the direct outcome of experience (that of certain European countries), the actual observations having taken place a relatively long time ago. Not surprisingly, given its eclecticism and apparent simplicity, it has at times been denied the status of 'theory' (passing instead, as already noted, as a pure description of historical events), or dismissed as an outmoded model. Its historic rooting is, in our view, one of its strengths, and careful consideration reveals that its original definition is sufficiently open to offer a flexible frame of reference. Moreover, it has the advantage of being the only interpretative schema which reflects a synthetic and coherent view of contemporary demographic changes. But its general nature rapidly reveals its insufficiencies: it is manifestly incapable of predicting the particular pattern of historical development in any one country. Too often it has been wrongly called upon for this purpose and consequently condemned for its short-comings as applied to historical, present, or even future populations—or, at least, for failing to conform to the rigid discipline of certain models imposed upon it. But is there any theory in the social sciences which can long withstand the test of projection, whether into the past or into the future? What model today is capable of predicting the level of demographic parameters for all countries, and the date at which trends change?

In our view, the weaknesses are precisely where they are least looked for: the theory is silent about the regulative role of external migration (Friedlander 1969), which manifestly affects the interaction between mortality and fertility. It also has very little to say about the role of nuptiality (Landry makes only one brief allusion), or the mechanisms by which demographic changes diffuse from country to country.

[12] Various attempts at evaluating the synthetic indicators for world-wide development were made by different experts around 1970.

A Double Objective

The aim of this work is not to itemize the conformity of historical reality to the intellectual schema of the first authors (the field has obviously been greatly enriched since their seminal contributions), but rather, starting from as complete and accurate a picture as possible of the transition in time and space, to test the original theory in some of its central propositions and to amend it on certain points that historical fact has led us to consider essential for the comprehension of the mechanisms at work.

To start with, the accent will be solely on the description of demographic phenomena and their reciprocal linkages (the order of the stages, time lags, possible interactions); international migration will be reintegrated into the general dynamic, and the manner by which the transition is completed will also be considered. At the close of this presentation, types of transition will be distinguished on grounds of duration and rhythms of growth.

In Part II, attention will focus on the main forms of transition, throwing into relief the principal issues where fertility is concerned: for, in its different versions, whether early or more recent, European or American, transition theory is, as we have observed, above all a theory of fertility. This second section will consist both of a critical discussion of existing approaches and an investigation—always with relation to the founding texts—of the common denominator of countries entering the last phase of the transition (i.e. the decline in fertility).

In the third and final section, there will be a more lengthy analysis of the theory's most important proposition, which concerns the relation between the transition and modern economic growth. Macro-economic trends of different large countries will be reconstructed, and possible relations between these trends and corresponding types of transition, as presented in the first section, will be considered. Consequently, demographic transition will no longer be regarded (as in the theory) solely as a dependent variable arising from socio-economic changes, but as an independent variable capable in its own right of influencing economic growth, positively or negatively, and by diverse mechanisms such as the decline in mortality. The transition will, in other words, be situated not in a framework of dependence, but in a framework of interaction.

This re-examination of the original theory of the transition will take particular account of ideas and facts relating to the evolution, during the past half-century, of less developed countries, for which the validity of theoretical postulates drawn from Europe needs to be tested.

Thus, aside from the the indispensable analysis of regional or national peculiarities, the main thrust will be an enquiry into those mechanisms which establish the universality of the phenomenon, its developmental stages, and the general conditions accompanying it—in other words, the coherence of the structural changes observed. From the theoretical framework of the transition we shall identify three central propositions, the validity of which we shall then attempt to demonstrate: the priority of the decline in mortality, the existence of two phases in the control of fertility, and the influence of the context of 'modernization'.

1. *The chronological sequence: mortality decline, followed by fertility decline.* The decline in mortality precedes that of fertility, and is a prerequisite of the limitation of births. The control of life would be inconceivable without a degree of control over death, and at the very least without the disappearance of traditionally high mortality. This postulate is common to the way all the authors approach the evidence, even if not expressly stated in their reasoning. Notestein (1945) alone is explicit:

the process of modernization in the European world led to a rise in standards of living, greater control over disease and a decline in mortality. Fertility, on the other hand, was less responsive to the process of modernization . . . the reasons why fertility declined only after mortality are fairly clear. With the high mortality of the premodern era, all societies needed high fertility to survive. The organization of all these societies was finely adjusted so as to assure the necessary number of births. Their religious doctrines, moral codes, laws, education, social customs, marriage systems, and family structure were all designed to maintain high fertility. Such institutions only change gradually, and only provided they are subjected to immense pressure.

The argument that the decline in mortality necessarily precedes that of fertility was nevertheless swiftly contested: certain exceptions were noted which would constitute a fundamental flaw in the theory (Knodel and van de Walle 1967). The most significant of these—France—has been emphasized by Coale (1973). Further cases have subsequently been cited (Belgium and Germany, for example: see Knodel and van de Walle 1967). In Chapters 5 and 12 we shall attempt to show that these are not true exceptions.

2. *A model of the reproductive transition in two phases: restriction of marriages, followed by limitation of births.* While absent from most early versions of the theory, this second argument is, however, explicit in Landry (1934), even though one possible mechanism behind it (mortality decline) is scarcely alluded to. According to Landry, it is the establishment of the custom of limiting marriages which marks the distinction between 'primitive' demographic regimes (where there is no form of voluntary control over demographic behaviour) and 'intermediary' regimes (where the desire to 'maintain the accustomed level of well-being' encourages the regulation of access to marriage). The final stage, called the 'contemporary' regime, is characterized by widespread practice of birth control. Landry writes:

In the intermediary regime, technological progress will result in population increase. The decline in mortality . . . will result in further restrictions in marriage in order to adjust birth rates to reduced mortality levels.

But this stage is provisional, because marriage restriction, even if it enables certain adjustments, rapidly shows itself to be insufficient:

celibacy and delayed marriage only afford limited results as means of reducing fertility ... it is the restriction of births within marriage that has much wider effect.

Chapter 8 will explore the extent to which, after the first phase of transition (the decline in mortality), marriage restrictions produced an initial adjustment of fertility.

3. *The influence of the context of modernization on the onset of fertility decline.* Although differing from author to author, this issue is present and indeed occupies a central position in all the early versions of the theory. Thus, in Landry's view, the desire for fewer children is no longer a product of the desire to maintain particular standards of living, as in the intermediate regime, but, by means of economic progress, to raise these standards, as much for future generations as for the generation in question. Notestein, on the other hand, emphasizes structural changes which mark the transition from traditional agrarian society to modern urban and industrial society, which tends to encourage the desire for fewer children among couples. He writes (1953):

The economic organization of self-supporting agrarian communities is centred almost exclusively on the family, and the family is the principal guarantee of support and personal security ... The new ideal of the restricted family arose in industrial urban society ... It is nevertheless evident that urbanization is not the magic ingredient where the fertility decline is concerned. The ideal of the restricted family and the strong motivation towards fewer children arose in very varied conditions. It may reasonably be assumed that the following were among the main factors: the rise of the individual to the detriment of the family, and particularly the extended family; the development of a new mental attitude valorizing reason and secularity; the influence of progress in public education on knowledge of the world and modern techniques; the improvement in health; the emergence of alternatives to early marriage and procreation as means of existence and prestige for women.

The emergence of the model of the restricted family, in each of these schemas, is thus unthinkable without a prior process of complete change—in other words, without socio-economic development (in the sense of the school of Kuznets). Transition into the era of birth control, in this view, should invariably be preceded by a boost in modern economic growth, with the real product per capita being one of the most reliable measures of such change. This argument will also be put to the test in Chapters 11 to 13.

In testing each of these propositions, we shall confine ourselves to the simplest possible statistical methods, the analysis of frequency and correlation.

Finally, there are certain issues on which the original theory of transition is either weak or silent. In our view these are as follows:

1. *The notion of pre- and post-transitional equilibrium.* Before and after the transitional stage of growth, it is implicitly assumed that there is virtually no population increase. However, just as there is great diversity in the pre-transitional stage (if the concept of 'natural' fertility is misleading, so is that of 'traditional' mortality—see Chapters 3 and 4), post-transitional development

can give rise to relatively different patterns of variation which in no way preclude the possibility of significant and lasting declines among populations (Chapter 7). The variability of initial conditions of natural increase goes a long way towards explaining the heterogeneity of subsequent population increases, measured through what we shall call the 'transitional multiplier of population' (Chapter 9).

2. *The absence of international movement.* This proposition is evidently open to question. International, like internal, migration, cannot play a neutral part in demographic transition. Indeed, there is no reason why, for example, it should not considerably influence the course of natural increase by slowing down the process of transition in countries of departure, and speeding it up in countries of reception (Chapters 6 and 10). This raises the possibility of large discrepancies in the transitional multipliers of population for the countries concerned (Chapter 10). Furthermore, the supposed absence of migration means that each country is implicitly treated as a discrete unit, and factors affecting its demographic mutation are linked only to internal development. The tremendous improvement in communications and transportation suggests, prima facie, that the diffusionist thesis, although very difficult to prove, offers great explanatory potential. This will be seen on a number of occasions, through successive international comparisons (Chapters 4, 12, and 18 particularly).

3. *The exclusive concentration on fertility as a dependent variable.* This approach has not only obscured the fundamental role of mortality decline in the transition, but has also led to the neglect of the reciprocal influences between economic and demographic variables. If, for example, mortality decline results in part from economic development, it is also capable, in turn, of contributing, by various mechanisms, to economic growth, so that even in cases of rapid population growth, a significant improvement in standards of living can occur (Chapters 15 to 18).

1 Problems, Methods, and the Field of Enquiry

> The human sciences fragment everything in order that it may be understood; kill everything in order that it may be examined.
>
> (Tolstoy)
>
> The disintegration of social inquiry into specialized disciplines leads to exclusion of the most essential questions, which are relegated disdainfully to the margins of a vague social philosophy.
>
> (Hayek)

SOCIETY cannot progress without the division of labour. The growth of learning has itself necessitated an ever increasing specialization in the various branches of knowledge. In science, the segmentation of tasks has been accompanied by the ever greater partitioning of fields of study. While indispensable, the seemingly indefinite fragmentation of science is not, however, without its drawbacks. It carries a threefold risk for basic research: the loss of heuristic benefits (resulting from multiplication *ad infinitum* of more and more partial studies, which robs research of all finality); the declining unity of knowledge (consequent on loss of overall vision); and, finally, the gradual smothering of 'physiological' knowledge (i.e. of society as an organic process) by 'anatomical' knowledge (society analysed further and further into more refined, elementary categories).

Demography is no exception. On this score, nothing is more revealing than the transformation in its linguistic usage. In the area which concerns us, the semantic shifts are massive. Since fertility has become the preferred object of demographic study, the concepts of demography and fertility have gradually been assimilated, at least in France. Hence, to indicate the decline of fertility in modern Europe, one speaks of 'la baisse de la démographie européenne' (the decline in European demography). But the confusion is no less elsewhere. In English, for example, the notion of demographic transition refers nowadays to little more than the decline in fertility, and the theory of demographic transition is commonly reduced to a theory of fertility (the recently coined phrase 'fertility transition' (*circa* 1976) is, more often than not, merely a linguistic concession).

This process of fragmentation calls for a return to holistic perspectives. It is startling to observe how much intellectual energy writers have been able to devote to researching the pre-conditions of nineteenth-century fertility declines in Europe, and especially in contemporary less developed countries, without in most cases having first outlined a demographic picture of the whole. Short-term and cross-sectional analyses, without the support of a historical framework, are at once partial and misleading for the study of long-term and essentially dynamic processes. Only by relating the demographic transition, in all its ramifications, to other phenomena, may we reveal its true mechanisms. Before embarking on a quest for pre-conditions of fertility and mortality decline, it is thus appropriate to turn towards the pre-conditions of research: the complete reconstruction of the process of demographic transition in its first dimension—the historical dimension. This history is still known only fragmentarily.

1. Problems

A Double Task

One of the first tasks is to establish a spatio-temporal framework within which to evaluate the broad characteristics of the transition, in so far as they can be discerned in the current state of knowledge, and from previous findings. Only by establishing a dynamic perspective can we ensure accurate appreciation of the generality (or, on the other hand, the specificity) of the experience of this or that country. Using this framework, we hope to uncover the principal relations between the three great parameters of mortality, fertility, and external migration: their evolution, the interrelations consequent on their evolution, and the mechanisms which are the likely source of their linkage.

A second task, following the intellectual tradition which gave rise to demographic transition theory, is to attempt to reinstate demographic evolution in the global context to which it belongs. The transition is only one aspect of a process of structural transformation, the general revolution which, from Western Europe since the Renaissance, has spread by successive stages through the rest of Europe and world-wide, affecting one by one societies in their most fundamental and complex aspects.[1] The context in which demographic transition was born, developed, and matured has varied greatly, depending on the state of technical development, cultural heritage, geographical factors, etc.—in other words, according to the character peculiar to a population at a given period in history. But historically, there is no example of demographic transition occurring independently of a more general

---

[1] It is significant that in certain social spheres of advanced Western countries, birth prevention at the time of the Renaissance was already fairly widespread.

evolution, whether in the material form of socio-economic changes, or in the immaterial and less obvious form of transformation of mental outlook.[2]

Demographic transition is thus a partial evolution which needs to be elucidated with the help of other components of the general transformation of which it is part. The absence of an overall view results in an unrealistic and overly abstract picture, susceptible to the attractions of simplified historical models. Since Thompson (1946), Sweden in the period 1751 to the present has been a perennial example in textbooks of how demographic transition proceeds. Models of intellectually dominant countries are similar, as with the US since 1940 for post-transitional fertility. The idea of formal diversity in explanatory theory—which makes no a priori exclusion of the presence of unity—has been assigned a habitually negative interpretation. Its general and flexible character has, however, been emphasized above. Its application to certain propositions of transition theory, while desired, has been based hitherto on observations limited as much by the number of cases as by the temporal field considered. The results are inevitably confused and con-tradictory. Thus, in order for such tests to be valid, certain minimal conditions are essential: theoretically consistent propositions; insertion in the *longue durée*; and a dynamic perspective.

Confronted with this second task, we do not propose to take the place of the historian but, more modestly, to focus attention on phenomena which in our view have received unsatisfactory explanation. By means of comparative methods, we shall specify those salient features which, historically, have been most frequently associated with demographic transition. But before proceeding further, the notion of demographic transition itself requires clarification.

The Theoretical Vagueness of the Notion of Demographic Transition

Literally, 'demographic transition' implies the passage from one demographic state to another. In this sense, all populations could claim to be undergoing demographic transition since, even in a quasi-stationary state, populations experience fluctuations of size and structure.

In fact, as conceived by its authors, the concept indicates the passage, brought about by processes of world-wide 'modernization', and allowing for a certain time lag, from a traditional regime of demographic equilibrium with high mortality and fertility, to a modern regime of equilibrium, with low mortality and fertility. Thus, it concerns a stage of demographic evolution highly particular and radically new. In this sense, the rather neglected phrase 'demographic revolution' appears a better choice.

But, as observed, for some time now the tendency to shift and shrink the

[2] Like all slow and profound changes, those belonging to the mental sphere elude methods of statistical measurement designed for observing relations between external and concrete phenomena.

meaning of the concept has become more and more apparent in the (ever growing) literature. Most often implicitly, but sometimes explicitly, demographic transition is considered in one aspect only, the passage from 'natural fertility'—following the terminology of Henry (1961)—to controlled fertility. To stand by such a meaning is, evidently, to ignore the decline in mortality. The latter has, doubtless, seemed more certain, because more rapid and apparently less awkward to explain than fertility decline. Yet the case of sub-Saharan Africa, where life expectation is on the whole still very low, serves to remind us that the decline in mortality also has certain pre-conditions. We should not forget that the fall in mortality rates, whilst commanding a brisk acceleration in demographic growth, is checked in turn by the counter-balancing effect of fertility control. Likewise, a purely mechanical consequence of the drop in infant mortality is the decline in replacement fertility. To opt for the narrow meaning of the transition, in short, is to concern oneself solely with the retrenchment of natural increase.

Our approach being historical, we shall choose instead the second, classic, definition. Its application, however, proves difficult, in so far as its temporal parameters are ill defined.

Criteria of Delimitation

According to recent studies in most countries, and notably in the less developed world (where, that is, the evidence is clear), the decline in mortality precedes that of fertility. But for certain European countries, the further back historical demographic studies go, the more it becomes necessary to qualify and, at times, reject knowledge hitherto regarded as definitive. For example, significant falls in long-term fertility (followed, admittedly, by recoveries) were apparent in certain German states in the eighteenth century, as with England after the plague. Long-term fluctuations would thus have antedated the time series we have at our disposal, at least those based on demographic events as recorded by means of civil registration. How, in these circumstances, are we to date with certainty the period of mortality and fertility declines?

The stabilization of birth-rates over a period of decades at a level as high as 40 per 1000 can quite easily follow an earlier stage of even higher fertility. The example of Czechoslovakia, where figures exist since 1785, is highly illustrative: an analyst having access, say, only to post-1830 data, might conclude that the birth-rate, more or less stable between 1830 and 1880 at around 38 births per 1000, did not fall until the end of the nineteenth century. In fact, around 1780 the birth-rate was 45 per 1000. The contemporary decline would thus have been preceded by earlier ones, separated by successive plateaux, and linked to fluctuations in nuptiality or age distribution. This pattern is, moreover, suggested by a careful reading of the data for several countries. Hence stability, or the maintenance of fertility and mortality in a certain equilibrium, can simply indicate that several adjustments in the decline have already been effected in the past. These represent, in effect, minor transitions, preceding the large modern movement.[3]

In this study we have chosen the following criteria to fix the extreme points $T\alpha$ (beginning) and $T\omega$ (end) of the process of demographic transition:

1. $T\alpha$ marks the apparent starting-point of a continuous decline in mortality,[4] in other words, a fall which is not followed by a return to higher rates.
2. $T\omega$ indicates the point of lasting return (at least five years) to an average rate of natural increase which equals, or is less than, that of the period preceding[5] the date of $T\alpha$.

Two cases then present themselves:

1. Mortality is not yet very low, which enables us to discount subsequent improvements and to recognize that the equilibrium at a given level is only provisional (as in certain European countries at the time of the 1930s depression). We have therefore, not without arbitrariness, added a condition of minimal life expectation of 73 years, for females, at birth;

2. Mortality is very low, less than the level just cited; only then do we have the point at which the previous trend has been overcome.

Given these two conventions, one can assign a duration $D = T\omega - T\alpha$ to the transition period, and analyse the basic parameters of change in a population—fertility, mortality, and growth—during the period in question.

In addition to this general characterization of the transition, partial transitions may be defined for each of the components of demographic change: a 'health transition', a 'reproductive transition', and a 'migratory transition'. Considered in relation to the classic schema, this way of carving up the transition as a whole specifies natural increase as the criterion of the completion of the process (and it will be in relation to the profile of natural increase that specific country-types of transition are defined). But nothing guarantees the conformity of subsequent developments to this schema; in particular, it is not inconceivable that, in many cases, natural increase should become permanently destabilized. In other words, the implied condition of relative symmetry in the levels of growth between pre-transitional and post-transitional phases would not then be fulfilled. Migration could, however, play a compensating role, not envisaged in the theory of transition properly speaking, although this factor is present in the writings of several authors

---

[3] Pre-modern transitions, notably the transition dubbed, in Coale's terminology (1965), 'Malthusian' (i.e. marriage limitation: Hajnal 1953, 1965), in contrast to 'neo-Malthusian' (the limitation of births within marriage) will not be analysed as such here. The existence of two phases (and the generality of the principle) in the control of fertility will be discussed in Ch. 13.

[4] If the trend of crude mortality is uncertain (owing, perhaps, to war, disease, or changes in age structure), we will then employ, as far as possible, the series of infant mortality rates, as it is more representative of the general improvement of health.

[5] This criterion has its drawbacks: the period of reference varies in length and is often known too incompletely over the long term to provide a good approximation of natural increase in the pre-transitional phase; the levels of post-transitional growth are rather variable.

concerned with depopulation, such as Dumont (1890), Bertillon (1911), and Wolf (1912).

Since the period in which they wrote, the general approach has nowhere exhausted the historical diversity of the phenomena, which does not cease after the return to a low rate of natural increase. It is in this light that the chapters devoted to mortality, fertility, and international migration have been written—no single date of conclusion has been fixed for any of the corresponding transitions. We have, however, allowed fertility to become 'post-transitional' from the point at which the combined indicators consistently and non-accidentally (i.e. not through war) attain the level of generational replacement.

2. Methods

Demographic Statistics

In order to encompass the process in its historical and phenomenological entirety (the unfolding of events, sequential linkage of phases, etc.) the work will be based on time series which are as long as possible, priority of attention being given to pronounced trends. This choice imposes a constraint: reliance on crude indices, aggregated together. This disadvantage is, nevertheless, outweighed by several advantages, at least where demographic matters are concerned:

1. This method of description provides a faithful reflection of the historical changes in the phenomena which chiefly interest us; more sophisticated indices, in our view, provide very little more information.

2. Given the incertitude concerning the situation in certain less developed countries, which influences not only the numerators (age-specific events) but also the denominators (the corresponding populations), precision is an illusion.[6]

3. The use of simple indices allows long-term coverage and comparison between countries having reliable statistics and those in which data are defective.

4. Continuity is in this way maintained with the work of our predecessors (Landry, Thompson, Notestein, Davis, etc.), who themselves used only simple indices. Hence, it is possible to connect our observations directly with theirs and to situate them within their general framework; similarly, our results may be used to continue, or rather resume, the work on population growth curves

---

[6] Until the most recent Chinese census (1982), the margin of error in estimating the world's population was nearly 400 million. Today the uncertainty is of the order of 200 million. This uncertainty is no less pertinent to African countries: the population of Africa's most significant country, Nigeria, is still the object of the most contradictory conjectures.

undertaken by diverse authors who were convinced of the universality of logistic increase (Verhulst 1844; Yule 1925; Pearl 1925).[7]

5. At the macro-economic level, crude rates possess a significance which refined demographic indicators lack. (For policy-makers responsible to a given collective body, a summary growth rate has more implications for the management of capital than age-specific fertility or mortality rates.)

Nevertheless, more sophisticated demographic indicators (or their estimation) are sometimes retained when analysis requires them, and particularly when data permit. Thus, comparative international mortality is assessed by means of life expectation at birth, and the development of crude rates is filled out by reference to infant mortality (in view of possible implications for fertility). Similarly, most series of birth-rates have, as is well known, been profoundly—if diversely—marked by history, as, for example, in the impact of wars and mass migration on age-specific structures (in Germany, Japan, the USSR, etc.), or by variations affecting the regime of nuptiality. These series have therefore been supplemented by total fertility rates for particular periods,[8] and by nuptiality indices covering both the intensity and precocity of marriage trends. To understand the possible mechanisms of reproduction after the return to low rates of population growth, we have reconstituted series of net reproduction rates, as these appear most appropriate for rendering the long-term consequences of the current demographic situation. Finally, in the case of international migration—examined only in those developed countries most frequently alluded to—we have calculated net migration rates, obtained directly when reliable data were available, or indirectly by comparison of variations in population size (from successive censuses) and natural fluctuations (in vital registration data). By reconstituting the historical patterns characteristic of each of these phenomena (especially their mode of diffusion) and combining the indices appropriate to each by means of frequency analysis, evidence will be provided of potential patterns of behaviour (the assumed laws of demographic transition) and the predominant types of connection between phenomena such as fertility and international migration.

Economic Statistics

The third part of this study is devoted to the broad outlines of economic history, and aims to establish the relation between demographic transition

---

[7] Such an approach, first developed in connection with developed countries, now tends to raise a smile: given the upheavals experienced in Europe, the divergences from the logistic model in the 20th century have been very pronounced. Its use is far from being absurd for a considerable number of underdeveloped countries at the present time, as we shall have occasion to observe. The method, in any case, is regularly employed in the projection of individual demographic parameters of fertility and mortality.

[8] Coale's indices, which take into account the relative fertility of marriages with relation to 'natural' fertility, are only exceptionally called upon in the second part of this work to illustrate, where necessary, mechanisms capable of stimulating emigration, such as the expulsion of the younger members of a family, or the growth of towns and industry.

and long-term economic growth, demographic change being taken as an independent variable. It will rely upon two categories of data:

1. Net production statistics reconstituted in chronological series which are as homogeneous as possible. This will enable one to throw light on two issues: the connection between growth of national income per capita and the demographic parameters of fertility and mortality in the course of modernization, and the relation between economic progress and population growth.

2. Labour force statistics, presented sectorially, illustrating the possible mechanisms of demographic growth which, under given conditions, influence overall productivity.

The discrepancy between a priori models (including projections) and the historical facts will be analysed, and the reasons for such differences considered, as they arise. At this point we shall introduce into discussion the possible influence of demographic growth on investment and food production. Recourse to long time series, demographic or economic, imposes a second constraint: analysis is confined to the national level. In all instances our figures refer to the nation as a whole, without distinguishing regional subgroups. Such distinctions would of course be highly desirable for countries with large and sharply contrasting subpopulations, such as India, USSR, Brazil, and Mexico. We shall, however, furnish the requisite information which will allow an understanding of the sense in which measures may best be interpreted.

The Context of Transition

The second part of the book, especially Chapters 12 to 14, focuses more particularly on the decline of fertility. This is by far the most difficult question, for, although empirically less ambitious, it runs up against all the inevitable theoretical problems encountered in the search for causality.

From the outset it raises redoubtable questions of definition. Quantitative measurement is complicated by the rich and multiple qualitative elements of which the development process—the motive force of transition—is composed: culture (religion, language, customs), health (life expectation, climate), economy (nutrition and level and disparity of income), society (family structure and social organization and hierarchy, and especially the individual's place within society), education (including both the standard and professional and ethical content of teaching), gender (female status, role differentiation), politics (the tolerance, stability, and maturity of institutions), and so forth. In other words, one is dealing with a vast and nebulous structure, the functioning of which is difficult to discern: its recomposition, explicit or otherwise, starting from some selection of variables, is necessarily partial and arbitrary.[9] The several aspects of the phenomenon change, of course, according to country

---

[9] Development is accompanied, above all, by a complete change in personal attitudes, behaviour, and mental patterns.

and period, so that a similar pattern of urbanization and industrialization may not possess the same implications for fertility in all cases. Finally, existing 'socio-economic' data do not submit easily to analytical requirements; this is especially the case with historical sources, which are generally rare, incomplete, unreliable, and ill suited to the more refined and reliable demographic indices; such measures need, above all, comparable data from one country to the next to be truly revealing.

Where the search for causality is concerned, obviously our aim will not be to settle eternal controversies, but to reveal mechanisms at work and to stress the relativity and liability of certain propositions which, at times, may appear quite anodyne. A case in point is Beaver (1975), who sums up an entire philosophy of history, central to certain recent theoreticians of the transition: 'socio-economic development of a society causes a displacement in its system of values', which, in turn, progressively 'encourages fertility limitation'. This proposal, like many others, is so symmetrical and reversible that, not only does it appear manifest at the outset, the analyst may always interpret the play of influences as operating equally in two ways. A simple case, at least in appearance, is the relation between mentalities and mortality; it is currently accepted that the secular decline in mortality, in liberating the thrall of the flesh, awakened the mind and stimulated a taste for progress. But it is no less evident that the decline in mortality would not have been possible without the renouncement of traditional fatalism, or the slow disappearance of submission to divine decree (one need only recall the international controversies over medicine, from Harvey to Pasteur, and over demography itself, from Süssmilch to Quételet).

The aim of Part II, beginning from the demographic series established in Part I, will be to classify countries by formal types of transition (based on calculation of multipliers for comparable populations), and to provide a summary and critical evaluation of prevalent conditions of fertility decline. It is chiefly in this section that the main paradigms of the original theory of transition will be tested. The modalities of fertility decline, as presented in the best-known comparative studies and explanations, will be examined and discussed. Our aim will be to identify phenomena which have not, or have been incompletely, accounted for hitherto, notably, international differences in pre- or post-transitional fertility.

This examination of the conditions of fertility decline will be conducted in three stages: first, the most advanced countries of the eighteenth century (France and England); secondly, those countries where the transition got going in the nineteenth century (peoples in Europe, or of European origin, and Japan); and thirdly, those which waited until the twentieth century. In each case, we will attempt to show to what extent the principal postulates of the original theory are valid or not. Beyond the obvious differences which separate nineteenth-century European experience from that of contemporary less developed countries (rapidity of demographic growth, economic backwardness, contraceptive methods, the role of the State and media in promoting family planning, etc.), we shall try to throw into relief the most significant elements of similarity (or difference) between countries experiencing early transitions and those with relatively tardy ones.

3. The Field of Inquiry

If temporal limits have been imposed primarily by constraints of data, the geographical field has been restricted deliberately to countries which fit certain conditions laid down, fairly arbitrarily and for our own purposes, beforehand. To comprehend the transition in its development, mechanisms, and implications, it is necessary to use some instances in which the process is already advanced. Our model therefore encompasses countries in which not only have mortality rates fallen, but there is a clear and lasting decline in fertility prior to 1980. The choice was conditioned by the following three criteria:

1. female life expectation at birth equal to at least 50 years, in 1980;[10]
2. a sustained decline in the birth-rate equal to at least 20%;
3. a birth-rate (most recent known figures) less than 35 per 1000, or a reproduction rate of less than 2.5, in 1980.[11]

Our choice has been further conditioned by minimum population size: all countries with populations less than 500,000 in 1980 have been excluded.

Below is a list of the countries selected, with the starting date of the time series, arranged alphabetically by continent:

Europe (25 countries). Albania (1930), Austria (1820), Belgium (1830), Bulgaria (1881), Czechoslovakia (1785), Denmark (1800), Finland (1751), France (1740), Greece (1860), Hungary (1861), Ireland (1864), Italy (1862), The Netherlands (1840), Norway (1735), Poland (1851), Portugal (1886), Romania (1859), Spain (1858), Sweden (1721), Switzerland (1868), United Kingdom (1838), USSR (1860), Germany[12] (1817), Yugoslavia (1862).

Northern and Central America (10 countries). Canada (1851), Costa Rica (1885), Cuba (1820), Dominican Republic (1950), Jamaica (1844), Mexico (1885), Panama (1920), Puerto Rico (1900), Trinidad and Tobago (1886), United States (1800).

South America (7 countries). Argentina (1870), Brazil (1870), Chile (1876), Colombia (1938), British Guiana (1886), Uruguay (1885), Venezuela (1873).

Asia (17 countries). China (1931), Cyprus (1901), Hong Kong (1938),

---

[10] Values obtained by interpolation of estimations for 1975–80 and 1980–85.
[11] See n. 11, above.
[12] Since 1946, the series has been combined with that of West Germany, but the development of the two states runs parallel.

India (1871), Indonesia (1920), Israel (1923), Japan (1881), Korea[13] (1895), Lebanon (1950), West Malaysia (1911), Philippines (1950), Singapore (1910), Sri Lanka (1871), Taiwan (1907), Thailand (1950), Turkey (1935).

Africa (5 countries). Egypt (1906), Mauritius (1876), Réunion (1946), South Africa (1950), Tunisia (1945).

Oceania (3 countries). Australia (1861), Fiji (1910), New Zealand (1871).

This list comprises 67 countries, of which 38, that is, more than half, may be classed as less developed.[14] The whole of Europe and North America are included, and most of Latin America, East Asia, and Oceania. The Middle East and sub-Saharan Africa, however, are almost completely absent.

A glance at the starting date of the time series shows that nearly all those countries (even less developed ones) where fertility has declined possess relatively early data, covering a period of at least 30 years, and capable of stretching to over 250 years. For the less developed countries, taken by themselves, the mean length of series exceeds 75 years. The 'average' series, therefore, dates from 1909. Here we have probably the only truly indisputable common denominator for countries where fertility decline has occurred. Not that the early existence of statistical observation should actually cause the phenomenon! But it is in fact a powerful index of the degree of modernization and social organization.

Regional Coverage

To summarize, the population in countries affected by a significant decline in fertility, and hence engaged in that phase of demographic transition, may be distributed by continent as shown in Table 1.1, according to the total size, expressed in millions of inhabitants, and the proportion experiencing transition.[15] Thus, the population of those countries in which fertility has declined considerably represents nearly 80% of the population of the whole world,[16] and nearly three-quarters of the population of the developing world.

Since our main concern with the demographic transition, in its quantitative aspect, is to elucidate its primary formal properties, these data will be represented in the text graphically. The statistical series used are given in the Appendices, and their sources listed in the General Bibliography. The latter also gives the seminal publications for the original theory of the demographic transition. Each chapter has its own bibliography, bearing on one or other specific aspect of the transition. In the case of non-demographic data, notably

---

[13] Since 1945, the series for the whole of Korea has been combined with that of South Korea.

[14] Albania has been grouped along with the less developed countries, which is easily justifiable, at least from the demographic point of view.

[15] Data as of mid-1983 (source: UN 1985).

[16] This estimate should be treated with caution, as in numerous countries declines are still modest; they are, in any case, unevenly distributed, and it is not inconceivable that they have been overestimated for highly populated countries like Indonesia, Brazil, and Mexico.

TABLE 1.1. *Regional Coverage*

Continent	Population involved	Total population	Proportion (%)
Europe (incl. USSR)	761	761	100
North America	259	259	100
Latin America	321	389	83
Asia	2,185	2,733	80
Africa	85	520	16
Oceania	19	24	80
World	3,630	4,686	78

long-term macro-economic series, we have indicated the essentials of the statistics employed by citing the provenance of the figures, the manner in which they were obtained, and finally the treatment to which they have been subjected in order to attain the objectives we have set ourselves.

The starting dates of the demographic series presented above correspond roughly to the base dates for annual series of crude birth-rates and mortality rates. Sometimes, however, this date is simply an estimation for only one of these parameters. For a certain number of developing countries, it represents merely the earliest observation or evaluation available (and not the beginning of civil registration); in the not infrequent cases where registration data are either non-existent or too unreliable, it represents the base date of United Nations estimates.

It has not been possible to homogenize the geographical significance of economic and demographic series. Reconstructions of series on the basis of present-day territorial boundaries are, in fact, rare. In order that comparisons between the populations observed remain connected, it has been necessary to carry out analysis for almost all countries that have suffered modification of their frontiers as if they were continuous entities. This disadvantage is, however, limited by the fact that reasoning is generally based on rates and not absolute values,[17] and that the most important territorial changes (notably, in Central Europe) occurred at times when the heterogeneity of variables was not particularly marked. The time series thus reflect the territorial boundaries of each period.

The Demographic Weight of Countries Included in this Study

Table 1.2 gives the population of countries with 'advanced' transitions. They cannot be taken on par with each other. In the developed world, more often

---

[17] When economic series giving production totals are used, they are placed alongside the population which corresponds to them; the perspective thus emphasizes the active population (i.e. population structure, rather than size).

TABLE 1.2. *Population of countries with advanced transition, mid-1983* (millions)

Developed World	Population	Less developed world	Population
Europe		Europe	
Austria	7.55	Albania	2.84
Belgium	9.86	Africa	
Bulgaria	8.94	Egypt	45.92
Czechoslovakia	15.42	Mauritius	0.96
Denmark	5.11	Réunion	0.55
Finland	4.86	Tunisia	6.89
France	54.65	South Africa	30.80
Germany (East)	16.70	Latin America	
Germany (West)	61.42	Costa Rica	2.38
Greece	9.85	Cuba	9.88
Hungary	10.69	Dominican Republic	5.96
Ireland	3.51	Jamaica	2.26
Italy	56.84	Mexico	75.10
Netherlands	14.36	Panama	2.09
Norway	4.13	Puerto Rico	3.35
Poland	36.57	Trinidad and Tobago	1.15
Portugal	9.95	Argentina	29.63
Romania	22.55	Brazil	129.66
Spain	38.23	British Guiana	0.92
Sweden	8.33	Chile	11.68
Switzerland	6.48	Colombia	27.52
United Kingdom	56.38	Uruguay	2.97
USSR	272.50	Venezuela	16.39
Yugoslavia	22.80	Asia	
Overseas English-speaking countries		China (mainland)	1,021.18
Australia	15.37	Cyprus	0.65
Canada	24.91	Hong Kong	5.31
New Zealand	3.20	India	732.26
United States	234.50	Indonesia	159.43
Asia		Israel	4.10
Japan	119.26	Lebanon	2.64
		North Korea	19.19
		Philippines	52.06
		Singapore	2.50
		South Korea	39.95
		Sri Lanka	15.42
		Taiwan	14.86
		Thailand	49.46
		Turkey	47.28
		Oceania	
		Fiji	0.67

Source: UN 1985.

than not, the transition has been completed, in some cases for many years; whilst in the less developed world its evolution is at various stages. Few of the highly populated countries (having 50 million or more inhabitants) are not on the list: Bangladesh, Pakistan, and Nigeria are in fact the only ones missing. All three have in common the fact that they have been totally or partially Islamicized.

Bibliography to Introduction

BEAVER, S. E. (1975), *Demographic Transition Theory Reinterpreted* (Lexington, Mass.: Lexington Books).

BERTILLON, A. (1874), 'Natalité', in *Dictionnaire encyclopédique des sciences médicales* (Paris), 89 ff.

BERTILLON, J. (1911), *La Dépopulation de la France, ses conséquences, ses causes, mesures à prendre pour la combattre* (Paris: Alcan).

BLACKER, C. P. (1949), 'Stages in Population Growth', *The Eugenics Review*, 39(3), 88–101.

CALDWELL, J. C. (1976), *Toward a Restatement of Demographic Transition Theory, PDR*, 2(3–4), 321–66.

CARR-SAUNDERS, A. M. (1936), *World Population: Past Growth and Present Trends* (Oxford: Clarendon Press).

COALE, A. L. (1967), 'Factors Associated with the Development of Low Fertility: An Historic Summary', *World Population Conference, Belgrade, 1965* ii. 205–09.

COALE, A. J. (1973), 'The Demographic Transition Reconsidered', *IUSSP Conference, Liège*, i. 53–72.

—— and HOOVER, E. M. (1958), *Population Growth and Economic Development in Low-Income Countries* (Princeton, NJ), 10–13.

COWGILL, D. O. (1963), 'Transition Theory as General Population Theory', *Social Forces*, 270–74.

DAVIS, K. (1945), 'The World Demographic Transition', *Annals of the American Academy of Political and Social Science*, 273 (Jan.), 1–11.

—— (1950), *Population and Resources*.

DUMONT, A. (1890), *Dépopulation et civilisation: étude démographique* (Paris: Lecrosnier et Babé).

DURKHEIM, E. (1893), *De la Division du travail social, étude sur l'organisation des sociétés supérieures* (Paris: Alcan).

FRIEDLANDER, D. (1969), 'The Role of Migration in the Process of Demographic Change', *IUSSP World Conference, London, 1969*, iv. 2634.

GEISSLER, A. (1885), 'Über den Einfluss der Saüglingssterblichkeit auf die eheliche Fruchtbarkeit', *Zeitschrift des Sächsischen Statistischen Bureaus* (Dresden), 31, 23–24.

GUILLARD, A. (1855), *Éléments de statistique humaine, ou démographie comparée* (Paris: Guillaumin).

HAJNAL, J. (1953), 'Age at Marriage and Proportions Marrying', *Population Studies* (Nov.), 111–36.

—— (1965), 'European Marriage Patterns in Perspective', in D. V. Glass and D. E. C.

Eversley (eds.), *Population in History: Essays in Historical Demography* (London).

HENRY, L. (1961), 'La Fécondité naturelle: observation—théorie—résultats', *IUSSP Conference, New York, 1961*, ii. 97–108.

KNODEL, J., and VAN DE WALLE, E. (1967), 'Demographic Transition and Fertility Decline: The European Case', *IUSSP Conference, Sydney, 1967*, 47–55.

LANDRY, A. (1909), 'Les Trois Théories principales de la population', *Scientia*, Paris, 6(3), 3–29.

—— (1934), *La Révolution démographique: études et essais sur les problèmes de la population* (Paris: Librairie Sirey).

LEASURE, J. (1963), 'Factors Involved in the Decline of Fertility in Spain, 1900–1950', *Population Studies*, 16: 271–85.

LE BRAS, H., and TODD, E. (1981) *L'Invention de la France* (Paris: Coll. Pluriel).

LEROY-BEAULIEU, P. (1913), *La Question de la population* (Paris: Alcan).

LESTHAEGHE, R. (1970–71), 'Le Dossier de la transition démographique', *European Demographic Information Bulletin*, 1(4), 218–29.

—— (1983), *A Century of Demographic and Cultural Change in Western Europe: An Exploration of Underlying Dimensions*, Working Paper, Brussels.

—— and WILSON, C. (1982), 'Les Modes de production, la laïcisation et le rythme de baisse de la fécondité en Europe de l'Ouest de 1870 à 1930', *Population*, 3: 623–46.

MALTHUS, T. R. (1798), *An Essay on the Principle of Population* (London).

MAYR, G. von (1897), *Statistik und Gesellschaftslehre, Zweiter Band: Bevölkerungsstatistik* (Freiburg i.B.).

—— (1917), *Dritter Band: Moralstatistik* (Freiburg i.B.).

MOMBERT, P. (1907), *Studien zur Bevölkerungsbewegung in Deutschland in den letzten Jahrzehnten, mit besonderer Berücksichtigung der Ehelichen Fruchtbarkeit* (Karlsruhe).

—— (1920), *Ausgewählte Lesestücke zum Studium der politischen Oekonomie*, vi, Bevölkerungslehre (Karlsruhe: Braun), preface, 1–23.

NOTESTEIN, F. W. (1945), 'Population: The Long View', in E. Schultz (ed.), *Food for the World* (Chicago, Ill.: University of Chicago Press), 36–57.

—— (1953), 'The Economics of Population and Food Supplies: Economic Problems of Population Change', *Proceedings of the 8th International Conference of Agricultural Economists, London, 1953*, 13–31.

PEARL, R. (1925), *The Biology of Population Growth* (New York).

SOMBART, W. (1913), *Der Bourgeois, zur Geistesgeschichte des modernen Wirtschafts-menschen* (Munich: Duncker und Humblot).

THOMPSON, W. S. (1929), 'Population', *American Journal of Sociology*, 34(6), 959–75.

—— (1946), *Population and Peace in the Pacific* (Chicago), ch. 2, pp. 22–35.

TODD, E. (1983), *La Troisième Planète: structures familiales et systèmes idéologiques* (Paris: Seuil).

TROELTSCH, E. (1911), *Die Bedeutung des Protestantismus für die Entstehung der modernen Welt* (Berlin: Oldenbourg).

UN (1963), *Population Bulletin*, 7: 143.

—— (1985), *MBS* (Jan.).

VERHULST, P. F. (1844), *Recherches mathématiques sur la loi d'accroissement de la population* (Brussels).

WEBER, K. E. M. (1920–21), *Die Wirtschaftsethik der Weltreligionen: Gesammelte Aufsätze zur Religionssoziologie*, 3 vols. (Tübingen: Siebeck).

—— (1924), *Wirtschaftsgeschichte, Abriss der universalen Sozial-und Wirtschaftsgeschichte*, 2nd edn. (Munich: Duncker und Humblot).

WOLF, J. (1912), *Der Geburtenrückgang: Die Rationalisierung des Sexuallebens in unserer Zeit* (Jena: Fisher).

—— (1913), *Das Zweikindersystem im Anmarsh und der Feldzug dagegen* (Berlin: Hirschwald).

YULE, G. U. (1925), 'The Growth of Populations and the Factors which Control it', *Journal of the Royal Statistical Society*, 88(1), 1–58.

PART I

Stages of Demographic Transition

A PHENOMENON of the *longue durée*, the demographic transition of a country requires us to set its historical markers as precisely as possible. We have already presented the extreme limits $T\alpha$ and $T\omega$, the respective starting- and end-points of the transition process. In order to decompose this process, it is necessary to add a further index: the point at which fertility begins to decline, designated $T\beta$. The several phases of the transition may thus be distinguished clearly, and illustrated following a simplified classic presentation,[1] as in Fig. I.1. Two phases of transition occur between the stages of equilibrium:

1. a phase of inflated growth, beginning at $T\alpha$, the speed of which increases in proportion to the strength of the decline in mortality;

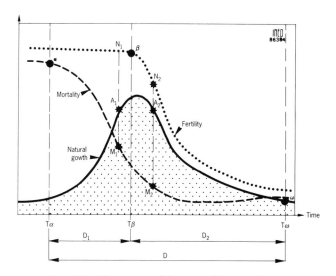

FIG. 1.1. The stages of demographic transition

---

[1] The secular decline in fertility is often preceded by a temporary increase, linked to improvements in income and hygiene.

2. a phase of contracted growth, which may begin at $T\beta$ or later, depending on whether the decline in fertility by then initiated is faster or slower than the decline in mortality.

In the course of demographic transition, a population experiences substantial growth, the importance of which is connected with three factors: the level of growth at the starting-point, the interval $T\alpha T\beta$ between the two declines, and the respective rates of decline in mortality and fertility. The following chapters will examine these factors. We shall attempt to go beyond the classic presentation by introducing external migration into the analysis, and deriving types of demographic transition, along with their corresponding age-structural implications.

2 Demographic Transition: The Current Position

Life dictates its laws to man, which are nowhere set down.

(Sholokov)

THE countries examined in this work share one characteristic, that of having begun secular declines in fertility, or in other words, of reaching point $T\beta$. The extent of transition varies greatly, however, from one case to another, some having already attained the post-transitional phase for a greater or a lesser period. By contrast, countries not included in our sample may be more or less distant from the transition, depending on their level of mortality; but some may be on the point of entry. The aim of this chapter is precisely to establish the demographic stage reached by the diverse countries of the world, which will assist comparative assessment of the international position of the different cases to be examined in the present study. The analysis will cover the quinquennial period 1975–80.

1. Rates of Population Growth

Interpreting Rates of Demographic Change

A population in the course of transition begins by seeing its rate of growth increase, gradually peak, and finally decrease until it reaches a new balance of low growth. In other words, in the absence of migratory exchanges with the outside world, it is possible, from the sequence of a given country's growth alone, to deduce the pattern of transition already undergone, and to project a plausible future trajectory. If, however, only one rate is available for a given period, interpretation takes longer, as this rate may occur at two points in the curve (A_1 and A_2, for example, in Fig. 1.1) and belong to two different demographic stages. Thus, when the growth rate is very low, one may be dealing equally with a country with high fertility and mortality, or one with low fertility and mortality—thus with two completely opposite situations. On the other hand, if the growth rates are high, this implies that the general decline in mortality is already fairly advanced (points M_1 and M_2) and that fertility has not declined, or only slightly (points N_1 and N_2). Uncertainty is clearly less in this case than in the preceding one.

TABLE 2.1. *Average population growth rates* (% per annum)

Average rate of increase (% per annum)	Europe	America	Africa	Asia	Oceania	World
<0	3 (3)	0	0	2 (1)	0	5 (4)
0.00–0.49	10(10)	0	0	1 (1)	0	11(11)
0.50–0.99	8 (8)	2 (2)	0	1 (1)	0	11(11)
1.00–1.49	3 (3)	5 (4)	1	2 (2)	2(2)	13(11)
1.50–1.99	0	2 (2)	4(2)	5 (4)	1(1)	12 (9)
2.00–2.49	1 (1)	6 (5)	6	11 (5)	0	24(11)
2.50–2.99	0	6 (3)	21(3)	7 (3)	1	35 (9)
≥3.00	0	6 (1)	15	6	0	27 (1)
TOTAL	25(25)	27(17)	47(5)	35(17)	4(3)	138(67)

In practice, however, the first case is non-existent today, since, in all less developed countries, even those which have received the least assistance, mortality has shown a marked decline since the Second World War, by at least 15 per 1000; excepting in countries subject to extreme conditions (war, famine, epidemics, etc.) life expectation at birth now exceeds 40 years, and the corresponding crude death-rate has fallen to less than 20 per 1000. Population growth rates systematically exceed 2.2%. Aside from mainland China and Indonesia, there are a number of countries which contemporary terminology defines as less developed, and which have low natural growth rates of around 2% per annum, or even less. These countries belong more properly, given their socio-economic character (life expectation, average per capita income, percentage of adults literate, etc.), to the developed world (a good example is Singapore); or, in some cases, the size and mixed composition of these countries, including a strong European component, suggests a semi-developed status (Israel, Cyprus, Argentina, Chile, Uruguay, Cuba, Trinidad and Tobago, South Korea, Sri Lanka, Taiwan). The ambiguity is important only on one side or the other of the central phase in which growth is peaking (very high growth rates exceeding 3% or even 3.5% per annum represent, without exception, the summit of the curve). Having growth rates in excess of 2%, almost all the less developed countries are currently situated around the central section of the curve.

Differences in Growth

The rates of population growth for 1975–80 are presented in Table 2.2. They have been grouped into eight levels in Table 2.1, and represented on a map in Fig. 2.1. Table 2.1 sets out, by continent, the number of countries

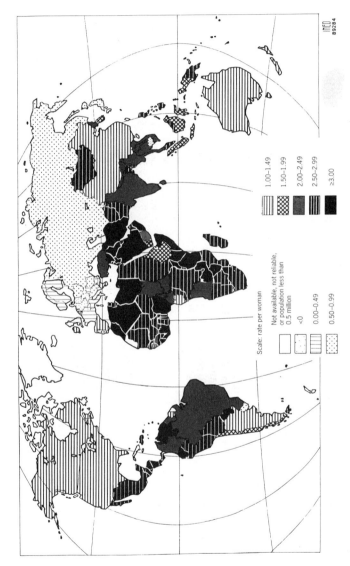

FIG. 2.1. Average population growth rates, 1975–1980 (per cent per year)

TABLE 2.2. *Estimated rates of population growth (%). Crude birth- and death-rates (per 1000) by continent and country, 1975–1980. Net migration rates (per 1000)*

Country	Growth (%)	Births (per 1000)	Deaths (per 1000)	Net migration (per 1000)
Europe				
Albania	2.40	30.9	6.4	0
Austria	-0.01	11.5	12.4	+0.8
Belgium	0.12	12.4	11.7	+0.5
Bulgaria	0.64	16.2	9.8	0
Czechoslovakia	0.68	18.4	11.5	+0.5
Denmark	0.24	12.3	10.4	-1.6
Finland	0.30	13.6	9.0	+0.2
France	0.38	13.9	10.3	-0.5
Germany (East)	-0.13	13.1	13.9	
Germany (West)	-0.09	9.6	11.7	+1.2
Greece	1.27	15.7	8.9	+5.9
Hungary	0.34	16.2	12.7	0
Ireland	1.35	21.2	10.1	+2.4
Italy	0.44	12.9	9.6	+1.1
Netherlands	0.71	12.7	8.1	+2.5
Norway	0.35	12.9	10.0	+0.6
Poland	0.90	19.2	9.1	-1.1
Portugal	0.94	17.8	10.0	+1.6
Romania	0.88	18.6	9.6	-0.2
Spain	1.01	17.3	7.9	+0.7
Sweden	0.29	11.7	10.9	+2.1
Switzerland	0.15	11.6	9.0	-1.1
United Kingdom	0.02	12.5	12.0	-0.3
Yugoslavia	0.89	17.6	8.6	0
USSR	0.86	18.3	9.7	0

Country	Growth (%)	Births	Deaths	Net migration[a]
Africa				
Algeria	3.33	47.4	14.2	0
Angola	2.46	47.6	23.1	0
Benin	2.97	48.8	19.1	0
Botswana	2.83	50.7	17.5	-4.9
Burundi	2.24	45.3	22.9	0
Central African Republic	2.18	44.3	22.5	0
Chad	2.00	44.1	24.1	0
Congo	2.56	44.6	19.0	0
Egypt	2.56	38.4	12.8	0
Ethiopia	2.56	38.4	12.8	-6.6
Gabon	1.00	31.2	21.3	0
Gambia	2.82	47.5	22.9	+3.6
Ghana	3.12	48.4	17.2	0
Guinea	2.54	46.1	20.7	0
Guinea-Bissau	1.69	40.0	23.0	0
Ivory Coast	3.45	47.5	18.2	+5.2
Kenya	3.95	53.8	14.4	0
Lesotho	2.35	39.8	16.3	0
Liberia	3.47	48.7	14.0	0
Libya	4.07	47.4	12.7	+6.0
Malagasy Republic	2.60	45.0	19.0	0
Malawi	3.20	51.1	19.1	0
Mali	2.73	49.4	22.2	0
Mauritania	2.79	50.2	22.3	0

Country	Growth (%)	Births	Deaths	Net migration[a]
Africa (cont.)				
Mauritius	1.62	26.4	7.6	-2.6
Morocco	3.19	45.4	13.6	0.0
Mozambique	2.59	44.8	19.0	0.0
Namibia	2.84	43.5	15.1	0.0
Niger	2.90	51.4	22.4	0.0
Nigeria	3.21	49.8	17.8	0.0
Réunion	1.71	24.0	6.9	0.0
Ruanda	3.04	49.6	19.3	0.0
Senegal	2.58	47.8	22.1	0.0
Sierra Leone	2.64	45.5	19.2	0.0
Somalia	7.88	46.2	19.9	+52.5
South Africa	2.77	37.9	10.3	0.0
Zimbabwe	3.38	47.3	13.6	0.0
Sudan	2.74	45.8	18.4	0.0
Swaziland	2.84	47.5	19.1	0.0
Togo	2.73	47.8	18.9	-1.6
Tunisia	2.50	35.5	11.1	0.0
Uganda	3.05	44.7	14.4	0.0
Cameroon	2.30	42.3	19.4	0.0
Tanzania	3.06	46.3	15.8	0.0
Burkina-Faso	2.58	47.8	22.1	0.0
Zaïre	2.75	46.2	18.7	0.0
Zambia	3.21	49.2	17.2	0.0

TABLE 2.2. (cont.)

Country	Growth (%)	Births (per 1000)	Deaths (per 1000)	Net migration[a] (per 1000)
North America				
Canada	1.06	15.5	7.3	+2.4
Costa Rica	2.38	29.1	5.3	0
Cuba	0.84	17.0	6.0	−2.6
Dominican Republic	2.56	36.7	9.0	−2.1
El Salvador	2.93	39.5	7.5	−3.4
Guatemala	3.03	41.1	10.9	0
Haiti	2.38	41.8	15.7	0
Honduras	3.53	47.1	11.8	0
Jamaica	1.38	28.1	6.7	−7.6
Mexico	2.89	38.3	7.8	−1.6
Nicaragua	3.29	46.6	12.2	−1.5
Panama	2.45	30.0	6.0	−0.9
Puerto Rico	2.90	22.1	5.8	+12.7
Trinidad and Tobago	1.53	22.1	5.9	−0.9
United States	1.06	15.3	8.8	+4.1
South America				
Argentina	1.27	21.2	8.8	+0.3
Bolivia	2.59	44.8	17.5	−1.4
Brazil	2.42	33.3	9.1	0
British Guiana	2.22	31.0	5.5	−3.3
Chile	1.71	25.4	8.1	−0.2
Colombia	2.14	32.1	8.2	−2.5
South America (cont.)				
Equador	3.04	41.6	10.4	−0.8
Paraguay	3.30	36.7	7.6	+3.9
Peru	2.70	38.6	11.6	0
Surinam	1.32	37.1	6.9	−17.0
Uruguay	0.57	20.3	10.1	−4.5
Venezuela	3.51	36.9	6.1	+4.3
Asia				
Afghanistan	2.54	48.5	23.2	0
Bangladesh	2.82	46.8	18.7	0
Bhutan	2.21	42.7	20.6	0
Burma	2.44	38.6	14.3	0
Cambodia[b]	−1.01	30.9	29.4	−15.0
China (mainland)	1.38	21.2	7.5	0
Cyprus	0.35	19.6	9.1	−7.0
Hong Kong	2.75	17.4	5.2	+15.3
India	2.02	35.3	15.1	0
Indonesia	1.74	33.6	16.2	0
Iran	3.04	44.4	13.6	−0.4
Iraq	3.42	47.0	13.0	+0.2
Israel	2.26	26.0	6.9	3.5
Japan	0.90	15.2	6.2	0
Jordan	3.65	46.9	10.5	0
North Korea	2.42	32.5	8.3	0
South Korea	1.72	25.3	8.1	0
Asia (cont.)				
Kuwait	6.00	43.6	4.4	+20.8
Laos	2.39	44.1	20.3	0.0
Lebanon	−0.80	30.1	8.7	−29.4
Malaysia: West	2.53	33.1	7.9	0.0
Mongolia	2.89	37.1	8.3	0.0
Nepal	2.30	43.7	20.7	0.0
Pakistan	2.81	43.1	15.0	0.0
Philippines	2.67	36.2	8.6	−0.9
Saudi Arabia	4.23	45.9	14.4	+10.8
Singapore	1.23	17.4	5.2	0.0
Sri Lanka	1.71	27.6	7.6	−2.9
Syria	3.76	46.4	8.9	0.0
Taiwan	1.97	24.3	4.7	0.0
Thailand	2.34	32.3	8.9	0.0
Turkey	2.46	34.9	10.2	−2.8
Vietnam	2.30	40.1	14.3	−5.4
Yemen, North	1.91	48.6	24.1	−3.4
Yemen, South	2.33	47.6	20.9	+3.8
Oceania				
Australia	1.21	16.0	7.7	−6.6
Fiji	1.78	28.6	4.2	+2.0
New Zealand	1.14	17.2	8.1	0.0
Papua New Guinea	2.69	42.5	15.7	

Notes: The countries belonging to our sample are in italics.
a Differential evaluation, fairly approximate. Only orders of magnitude worth retaining.
b Dubious data. For a more detailed assessment, see Ea (1981).

Sources: UN (1981), excepting countries with good registration data, for which the most recent figures available have been used (UN 1982).

belonging to each of these groups; the number of countries included in the sample used in the present study is given in parenthesis.

The distinction between developed and less developed countries is very clear, as the growth rate in the former is less than 1% (with the exception of Spain, 1.01%; USA and Canada, 1.06%; Ireland, 1.13%; New Zealand, 1.14%; Australia, 1.21%; and Greece, 1.27%), and in the latter exceeds 2%, excepting cases mentioned above. Rates for wealthy countries, no matter how low, include the incidence of past and present migration. If current migration is taken into account, natural increase is even lower, in all cases (excepting Ireland) appreciably less than 1%. In Europe, at the close of the 1970s, three countries (East and West Germany, and Austria) even experienced population decline. North-western Europe, taken as a whole, is distinguished by rates which tend to converge around zero growth, whilst countries where growth still exceeds 0.5% generally belong to eastern or southern Europe. With a rate of 0.9%, Japan has reached an equivalent stage.

In the area of intermediary growth (1% to 2%) are grouped the above-named exceptions, coming as much from the developed as from the developing world. Setting aside Gabon and Guinea-Bissau in Africa (where, for specific reasons, infertility is relatively frequent), and North Yemen (due to emigration) in Asia, the intermediary countries have all recorded a marked decline in fertility, thus falling within the scope of this study. Almost half (11 out of 24) of the countries with fairly strong growth (2% to 2.5%) are in advanced transition, for example, Albania and, to cite only the most populous, India, Brazil, Turkey, and Thailand. Further up the hierarchy of growth rates, the proportion of countries with declining fertility becomes more rare: 9 out of 35 in the section 2.5% to 3%, and only one out of 27 above 3%. In these instances demographic increase, although already rapid, is still capable of acceleration. Countries with very rapid growth rates are situated principally in Africa, the Middle East, and tropical Latin America.

2. The Components of Growth

Fertility

Of the 109 countries represented in Table 2.2, only 16 have crude birth-rates less than 30 per 1000; with the notable exception of mainland China, these are mostly fairly small countries, both in size and population. Rates exceed 40 per 1000 in the majority of poor countries: in Africa and the Middle East such rates are the rule, and it is not rare to encounter levels around 50 per 1000 or above—a phenomenon which occurs nowhere else. By contrast, the rates for developed countries[1] are consistently less than 20 per 1000; it is even possible

---

[1] Excepting Ireland: 21.2 per 1000.

TABLE 2.3. *Estimated gross reproduction rate (GRR) per woman, by continent, 1975–1980*
(years)

GRR	Europe	America	Africa	Asia	Oceania	World
<1	13(13)	2 (2)	0	2 (2)	1(1)	18(18)
1.00–1.34	10(10)	3 (3)	0	2 (2)	1(1)	17(17)
1.35–1.69	1 (1)	3 (3)	2(2)	3 (3)	0	9 (9)
1.70–2.19	1 (1)	5 (5)	1(0)	3 (2)	1(1)	11 (9)
2.20–2.69	0	6 (4)	4(2)	8 (7)	0	18(13)
2.70–3.04	0	4	13(1)	4	0	21 (1)
3.05–3.39	0	3	17	7	1	28
≥3.40	0	1	10	5	0	16
TOTAL	25(25)	27(17)	47(5)	35(17)	4(3)	138(67)

to cite a case without historical precedent of fertility less than 10 per 1000 (West Germany, 9.6‰). The difference between extreme situations is thus fivefold.

Given the importance of differences in age structure, this breakdown of birth-rates only partially reflects differences in reproduction. As it is desirable to overcome this limitation, we have listed (and sometimes recalculated) gross reproduction rates (GRR) in Table 2.3. The regrouping into eight levels, on the same principles as used above, gives the statistical classification of countries by continent shown in Table 2.4. The lowest rates (GRR less than 1) occur in North America (Canada and the USA), north-west Europe, Singapore, Japan, and Australia. In fact, of the developed countries only a minority (12 countries in 29) continued to have a GRR above 1 in the period 1975–80. Among these 12 countries, only 10 (representing 1 developed country in 3) have fertility levels sufficient to guarantee replacement over the long term (i.e. net reproduction rates at least equal to 1). Again it is necessary to emphasize that, with the exception of Ireland (GRR: 1.65), and given the narrowness of existing margins and recent downward trends in southern and eastern Europe, the situation may be entirely provisional. The countries where fertility no longer insures replacement constitute 15% of the world's population.

At a slightly higher level (GRR greater than 1, but less than 1.35) there are 15 countries, 10 of which are European, and situated in the central, eastern, and southern parts of the continent; elsewhere in these regions, two countries (East Germany and Italy) have already reached replacement level. The seven other countries in this range are: New Zealand; three small nations of Central America (Puerto Rico, Trinidad and Tobago, Cuba); and three in Asia (Hong Kong, Taiwan, Cyprus). The only European countries which do not fit into either of these two first groups are Ireland (1.65) and Albania (2.03), the latter

TABLE 2.4. *Estimated Gross Reproduction Rate (GRR) per woman and expectation of life at birth, for both sexes (in years), by continent and country, 1975–1980*

Country	GRR	Life expectation	Country	GRR	Life expectation	Country	GRR	Life expectation
Europe			Africa			Africa (cont.)		
Albania	2.03	69.3	*Algeria*	3.55	55.3	*Mauritius*	1.45	63.9
Austria	0.80	71.7	*Angola*	3.15	41.0	*Morocco*	3.35	55.4
Belgium	0.83	71.8	*Benin*	3.30	45.9	*Mozambique*	3.00	46.0
Bulgaria	1.09	72.0	*Botswana*	3.20	48.3	*Namibia*	2.90	51.2
Czechoslovakia	1.15	70.2	*Burundi*	2.90	40.9	*Niger*	3.50	42.1
Denmark	0.82	74.1	*Central African Republic*	2.90	41.8	*Nigeria*	3.40	47.5
Finland	0.80	72.7				*Réunion*	1.40	64.8
France	0.92	73.7	*Chad*	2.90	39.8	*Ruanda*	3.40	45.9
Germany (East)	0.88	71.8	*Congo*	2.95	46.0	*Senegal*	3.20	42.1
Germany (West)	0.69	71.8	*Egypt*	2.55	54.8	*Sierra Leone*	3.02	45.9
Greece	1.12	72.8	*Ethiopia*	3.30	39.0	*Somalia*	3.00	42.5
Hungary	1.03	69.9	*Gabon*	2.00	43.5	*South Africa*	2.50	60.3
Ireland	1.65	72.2	*Gambia*	3.15	41.0	*Zimbabwe*	3.25	53.5
Italy	0.90	72.5	*Ghana*	3.30	48.3	*Sudan*	3.20	46.5
Netherlands	0.78	74.8	*Guinea*	3.05	43.5	*Swaziland*	3.19	45.9
Norway	0.88	75.0	*Guinea-Bissau*	2.65	41.0	*Togo*	3.20	46.0
Poland	1.10	70.8	*Ivory Coast*	3.30	46.0	*Tunisia*	2.75	57.9
Portugal	1.14	70.0	*Kenya*	4.00	53.5	*Uganda*	3.00	52.5
Romania	1.23	70.4	*Lesotho*	2.65	50.3	*Cameroon*	2.79	46.0
Spain	1.23	72.8	*Liberia*	3.40	52.9	*Tanzania*	3.20	50.5
Sweden	0.80	75.3	*Libya*	3.60	55.4	*Burkina Faso*	3.20	42.1
Switzerland	0.74	74.7	*Madagascar*	3.00	46.0	*Zaire*	3.00	46.0
United Kingdom	0.89	72.3	*Malawi*	3.45	46.0	*Zambia*	3.40	48.3
Yugoslavia	1.06	69.4	*Mali*	3.30	42.1			
USSR	1.16	68.5*	*Mauritania*	3.40	42.1			

*Revised estimate, taking into account the rise in mortality, see M. Fesbach, 'The Soviet Union: Population Trends and Dilemmas', *Population Bulletin* (Population Reference Bureau), Aug. 1982, vol. 37, no. 3, 448.

TABLE 2.4. (cont.)

Country	GRR	Life expectation	Country	GRR	Life expectation	Country	GRR	Life expectation
North America			**South America** (cont.)			**Asia** (cont.)		
Canada	0.87	73.5	Ecuador	3.07	60.0	Kuwait	3.15	69.2
Costa Rica	1.74	69.7	Paraguay	2.54	64.1	Laos	3.00	43.5
Cuba	1.06	72.8	Peru	2.68	57.1	Lebanon	2.10	65.1
Dominican Republic	2.44	60.3	Surinam	3.00	67.2	Western Malaysia	2.25	63.3
El Salvador	2.93	62.2	Uruguay	1.41	69.5	Mongolia	2.61	62.5
Guatemala	2.77	57.8	Venezuela	2.31	66.2	Nepal	3.15	43.3
Haiti	2.89	50.7				Pakistan	3.12	50.8
Honduras	3.48	57.1	**Asia**			Philippines	2.44	60.7
Jamaica	2.00	70.1	Afghanistan	3.35	40.5	Saudi Arabia	3.55	53.0
Mexico	2.63	64.4	Bangladesh	3.25	45.8	Singapore	0.91	70.8
Nicaragua	3.20	55.2	Bhutan	3.00	43.3	Sri Lanka	1.90	65.0
Panama	1.92	69.6	Burma	2.70	52.5	Syria	3.63	64.4
Puerto Rico	1.15	73.0	Cambodia	2.00	30.2	Taiwan	1.32	71.6
Trinidad and Tobago	1.30	68.9	China (mainland)	1.52	67.2	Thailand	2.20	60.2
United States	0.88	72.9	Cyprus	1.12	72.1	Turkey	2.42	60.5
			Hong Kong	1.05	76.0	Vietnam	2.72	52.7
South America			India	2.45	49.4	North Yemen	3.30	41.3
Argentina	1.40	69.2	Indonesia	2.30	47.5	South Yemen	3.40	44.0
Bolivia	3.12	48.6	Iran	3.10	53.5			
Brazil	2.20	61.8	Iraq	3.40	55.1	**Oceania**		
British Guiana	1.92	69.1	Israel	1.66	72.0	Australia	0.98	73.1
Chile	1.51	65.7	Japan	0.88	75.6	Fiji	1.75	71.3
Colombia	2.10	62.2	Jordan	3.55	60.1	New Zealand	1.03	72.8
			North Korea	2.21	62.5	Papua New Guinea	3.05	50.3
			South Korea	1.65	62.5			

*Contestable data (war). For more information, see EA, M., *op.cit.*, 1981.

Sources: See Table 2.2.

being an exceptionally tardy case. By themselves, these two first groups comprise more than half of those countries in which demographic transition is in its second phase.

The other half exhibit a level of fertility intermediate between these low levels and the high fertility peculiar to sub-Saharan Africa and Islamic countries (see Fig. 2.1). It is composed exclusively of less developed countries, or, put the other way round, developed countries have GRRs less than 1.35, whilst the developing world, with the exception of a few island states, possesses GRRs consistently above this level. The dividing line is clear.

This second half of our selection thus comprises the following:

1. The majority of Latin American countries (of which 15 out of 25 countries meet our requirement of a population above 0.5 million). Latin America presents a very heterogeneous fertility profile, ranging from countries with levels already nearing replacement (the three islands cited above), to others such as Bolivia, Honduras, and Nicaragua where there is apparently almost no fertility regulation, the GRR exceeding 3. Similarly, in the Caribbean, where the population stood at 31 million in 1984, of which 10 million live in Cuba, the differences are enormous. Between Cuba and Haiti, for example, the levels were 1.06 and 2.89 respectively. On the continent, however, an important development has begun: the two giants, Brazil and Mexico, have experienced a decline in fertility since the mid-1960s and mid-1970s, respectively, and both probably have by now reached a level of 4 children per woman. Other fairly populous states such as Colombia, Venezuela, and the Dominican Republic have made similar, and sometimes only recently recorded, progress. Nevertheless, the contrast remains, on the one hand, between Argentina, Chile, and Uruguay, at the southern tip of the continent (together with certain relatively advanced cases in Central America: Cuba, Puerto Rico, Trinidad and Tobago, Costa Rica), where the number of children per woman is less than 3.5, and on the other, the large tropical countries of South America, where it is still closer to 4.

2. Almost half of the Asian countries (17 out of 35), the most important of which are in south and east Asia. Setting aside Japan, which began to follow Western patterns very early, the GRR of the countries with declining fertility settles fairly consistently between 0.91 (Singapore) and 2.45 (India), following a scale which appears at first glance to combine the degree of urbanization and the proportion of the population that is Chinese. Singapore and Hong Kong, which are almost exclusively Chinese and urbanized, in fact already have fertility levels equivalent to those of Europe. The only cases which do not conform, in appearance, to the hierarchy based on these two criteria are Sri Lanka (1.90) and South Korea. In the latter, the GRR is less than that of West Malaysia (1.65 and 2.25, respectively), of which a third of the population is Chinese. But it is worth bearing in mind that even if South Korea's population includes only a very small Chinese minority, the country

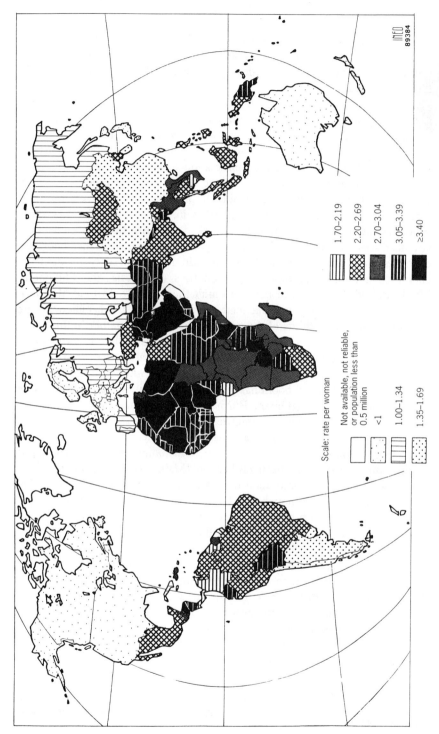

Scale: rate per woman

	Not available, not reliable, or population less than 0.5 million
	<1
	1.00–1.34
	1.35–1.69

	1.70–2.19
	2.20–2.69
	2.70–3.04
	3.05–3.39
	≥3.40

FIG. 2.2. Gross reproduction rates, per woman, 1975–1980

is in fact much more heavily urbanized and industrialized than most other Asian countries and, moreover, has been subject to a triple influence: Chinese (through tradition), Japanese (through proximity), and North American (through politics).

In the light of available estimates, the difference between China and India is considerable (1.5 against 2.5), for countries with fairly similar levels of urbanization and industrialization, and where, at least up to the mid-1950s, the demographic parameters were analogous. The Chinese pattern, which the 1982 census and the post-census enumeration show quite clearly, is the result of a vigorous country-wide policy, since 1970 focusing especially on the villages. In India, on the other hand, despite the continued efforts of 30 years, the change has been slow and uncertain; the development now seems firmly set in motion, but there is a marked disparity between some fairly advanced southern states (Kerala and Maharashtra) and less advanced northern counterparts (Uttar Pradesh, Bihar). In addition to these two continental countries, a number of other large countries (Indonesia, the Philippines, Thailand, and Turkey) have begun to limit their fertility. In total, the Asian countries where fertility has declined numbered almost 2.1 billion people, which is close to two-thirds of the populations brought together in this study.

The countries where as yet there has been no clear decline in fertility (Fig. 2.1) fall into three categories: (1) Middle Eastern states (Iraq, Iran, Kuwait, Saudi Arabia, Syria, Jordan, and the two Yemens), where Islam is a fundamental factor, and the oil boom has yet to change family structures; (2) poorer South Asian countries (Bhutan, Burma, Nepal, Pakistan, and Bangladesh); and finally, (3) Indo-Chinese countries (Vietnam, Laos, Cambodia), where political instability has long been an obstacle to modernization.

3. A small minority of African countries, including two little islands profoundly influenced by Western civilization (Mauritius and Réunion); South Africa (where there are important demographic differences between the four main ethnic groups—although the Bantu majority has a declining fertility); Tunisia, where the grip of Islam is weaker than elsewhere, and family planning has been an important concern for the past 15 years; and, finally, Egypt.[2] In the last case, the decline has had a tendency to mark time, although the results obtained are fairly remarkable. Here, too, it doubtless required the conjunction of many factors to lessen the influence of Islamic culture: the mental imprint of British rule on the urban élite and, by extension, on wider social strata; official propaganda and encouragement of birth control; and problems of overcrowding, population density standing at an average of around 1000 inhabitants per square kilometer in the main habitable area, the Nile valley.

---

[2] Egypt answers to the criteria adopted here only when these criteria are interpreted exactly; the same is true of Tunisia, but the recent trend appears sufficiently strong to justify the country's inclusion in this group.

These countries are on the whole exceptions, and elsewhere in Africa a GRR less than 3 is often the result of poor health conditions or particular practices, such as prolonged breast-feeding and sexual taboos. Strictly speaking, Black Africa, as much as the Maghreb (but with the exception of Tunisia), is not affected by the decline in fertility.

4. The island of Fiji, in Oceania.

The world-wide distribution of fertility, in outline, describes a U-shaped curve. Of 138 countries with more than 0.5 million inhabitants, 35 have a GRR less than 1.35; only 28 have a GRR between 1.35 and 2.20 (or an average number of children between 2.8 and 4.5); whilst the vast majority (the 83 remaining countries) have higher fertility. In 16 countries the GRR is equal or greater than 3.4, giving an average of 7 or more children. With the exception of Kenya, which, with an average of 8.2 children per woman, clearly stands out from the rest, these countries are generally Islamic: North and West Africa (notably Algeria, Morocco, Libya, and above all, Nigeria, with its population of 80 million in 1981) and the Middle East (Saudi Arabia, Iraq, Jordan, Syria, etc.).

Mortality

Let us first cast an eye over the crude death-rate (Table 2.2) before turning to more reliable indices. In practice, we know that the value of these rates is only indicative at the extremes, that is, if it is either very low or very high, because it depends closely on age structures. The rates range from 4.2 (Fiji) to 24.1 per 1000 (North Yemen); in Fiji life expectation at birth is 71 years (which is by no means the best national performance) whilst in North Yemen it is only 41 years. East Germany, with the highest proportion of elderly in the world (16% were 65 years or older in 1980), had a crude death-rate of 13.9 per 1000 in 1975–80, which is appreciably higher than Egypt's (12.8), and comparable to Burma's (14.3), but in the latter two countries, life expectation at birth is nearly 20 years less.

The differences in life expectation at birth are very pronounced (Fig. 2.3); almost a third of the countries sustain a mean length of life of at least 70 years (35 countries). Considerable progress has none the less been made, as an equivalent number of countries (36) now have a mean length of life of 60 to 70 years. The distribution of mortality, like that of fertility, is fairly concentrated at the extremes of the existing scale of values, but if there is asymmetry in either case, this asymmetry is towards the left for fertility, and the right for mortality, Table 2.4, then, gives the distribution of countries by groups of life expectation for the years 1975–80. The differences shown are the very image of the demographic transition: while the poorer countries as a whole have begun their health transition—a large proportion of them appearing, in this table, to be nearing the stage achieved in Western countries—a goodly number of them none the less have yet to show declining fertility; and

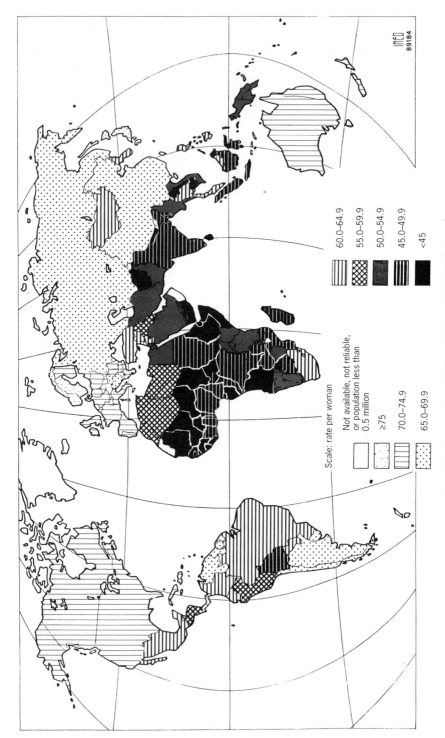

Scale: rate per woman

Not available, not reliable,
or population less than
0.5 million

≥75

70.0–74.9

65.0–69.9

60.0–64.9

55.0–59.9

50.0–54.9

45.0–49.9

<45

INED
89184

Fig. 2.3. Expectation of life at birth, 1975–1980 (years)

TABLE 2.5. *Expectation of life at birth*

Expectation of life at birth	Europe	America	Africa	Asia	Oceania	World
<45	0	0	15	7	0	22
45.0–49.9	0	1	17	3 (2)	0	21 (2)
50.0–54.9	0	1	8(1)	5	1	15 (1)
55.0–59.9	0	4	4(1)	1	0	9 (1)
60.0–64.9	0	7 (4)	3(3)	9 (6)	0	19(13)
65.0–69.9	4 (4)	9 (8)	0	4 (3)	0	17(15)
70.0–74.9	19(19)	5 (5)	0	4 (4)	3(3)	31(31)
≥75	2 (2)	0	0	2 (2)	0	4 (4)
TOTAL	25(25)	27(17)	47(5)	35(17)	4(3)	138(67)

in those areas where the change has begun, there is often a long way to go to reach the level of equilibrium.

Setting aside those countries affected by severe political troubles (Cambodia, Yemen, Ethiopia, Somalia, Angola, etc.), the persistence of high mortality is localized in two areas of the world: sub-Saharan Africa and South Asia. These are precisely where the greatest poverty occurs. In sub-Saharan Africa (separating out, for simplicity's sake, the more advanced cases of Zimbabwe and South Africa), life expectation at birth, according to United Nations estimates, is only of the order of 45 to 47 years, the most problematic areas being West and Central Africa (the Sahelian countries, and inland areas such as the Central African Republic). The contrast with North Africa is clear, the latter being credited with 53.7 years (Egypt: 54.8); Kenya, with 53.5 years, is the only large Black African country to occupy a comparable position. Contrasts in Asia are still more pronounced, especially between the east and south. Certain east Asian countries now have a mean length of life greater than that of Norway or Sweden, whose progress in this respect was achieved at a much earlier stage. Yet several South Asian countries come next in order to the worst areas of Black Africa. There is thus an enormous rift between the Far East (including Hong Kong (76 years), Japan (75.6 years), Singapore (71 years), mainland China (67 years),[3] North and South Korea (62.5 years)), or even the Middle East (Kuwait (69), Syria (64)), and their large southern counterparts like Indonesia (47.5), India (49.4), Pakistan (50.8), and Bangladesh (45.8).

In Latin America, although the differences are fairly distinct, they are less extreme, all countries, excepting Bolivia (49 years) and Haiti (51 years), having a mean length of life of at least 57. The best averages are found in

---

[3] This is without doubt an overestimate (see the ensuing chapter for a discussion).

Costa Rica (70), Puerto Rico (73), Cuba (72.8), and Jamaica (70), and in states located in the temperate southern tip, notably Argentina and Uruguay (69) and Chile (66).

Although in its general outline the map of mortality is fairly similar to that of fertility (the highest fertility, like mortality, occurring in Black Africa and South Asia), it none the less differs in one major respect: the countries with higher fertility are not *invariably* those where mortality is highest. This observation is charged with significance, for the absence of a strict parallelism between the two phenomena is what explains the presence of explosive demographic growth in certain countries, and which, elsewhere, excludes the possibility of rapid growth in the poorest countries—poverty being an obstacle to attaining very low mortality levels. Contrary to general assumption, it is not in the poorest countries, but in those with a middle income, that demographic growth is highest. This actually follows the logic of transition theory. If large discrepancies to this pattern are rare, there is one striking exception: the Muslim countries of North Africa and, especially, the Middle East, stand out with exceptionally high fertility in the context of intermediate or low mortality (Kuwait being the clearest example: $e^0 = 69$, GRR $= 3.15$). This sort of difference can be clarified by further analysis. Thus, by calculating the relation between net and gross rates of reproduction, one arrives at an index which takes into account not only the general level of mortality, but female status also. This ratio is, in fact, a measure of the probability of child-bearing for a young female not prevented by premature death (between 0 and 50 years); it provides us with the probability of survival from birth to the mean age at child-bearing. At the general level of given mortality in Muslim countries, this index tends to be relatively lower (UN 1975).

Almost all the countries in our selection (63 out of 67) fall into the first four groups (life expectancy greater than 60 years), and, as a rule, these countries display a very clear statistical link between their mortality and fertility indices. Fertility has only declined in those countries where there has been a large fall in mortality; on the whole, the lower the mortality level, the more dramatic the decline.

International Migration

In Table 2.2, by contrasting the difference between population growth in the period 1975 to 1980, and the rate of natural increase for the same period, we have established net migration rates. In the vast majority of cases, the rates observed are negligible.[4] We should not be misled into thinking that such a

---

[4] Such a conclusion is in part artificial, the population of 1980 for less advanced countries having been projected rather than observed, on the hypothesis that net migration is nil (see the notes to Table 2.2). The choice of such a hypothesis is, however, not inappropriate in states where the phenomena are well known.

result is more a reflection of our ignorance than of the real absence of an asymmetry of migratory exchanges in most countries. Migration is by nature far more difficult to establish than the fundamental and non-repetitive vital events represented by births and deaths. There are well-known exceptions to the tendency of migration flows to balance around zero: the non-socialist European countries; large-scale migration related to specific factors such as the oil boom, forced movements in wartime, or the displacement of former colonial populations towards old colonial powers; or the movement of populations from small, often insular, countries towards economically dominant neighbouring areas, for example, Caribbeans towards the USA. Verifying population movements is especially difficult in highly populated and poor countries, demographic information being rarer and less reliable due to the lack of registry offices and regular censuses. All developed countries have a non-zero net migration, whilst, by contrast, this situation is true only of 8 out of 47 countries in Africa, and 14 out of 35 in Asia. Latin America's position is intermediary; on the basis of available information, a zero net migration occurs only in 4 out of 25 cases. Our observations will thus pertain essentially to Western Europe and the two Americas.

In addition to the uncertainty of results when dealing with small orders of magnitude, one should bear in mind that migration intensity differs from fertility and mortality in its highly contingent nature, varying greatly from one period to the next. In spite of the suspension, in the wake of the first oil boom, of migrant workers heading for OECD countries, migration streams have retained a force which suggests that familial and political immigrants (refugees) are accompanied by a fairly important 'clandestine' element. Thus, with the exception of Switzerland and the United Kingdom, and despite a fairly active policy for return migration, the main countries experiencing migration in north-west Europe exhibit a positive net flow (West Germany, Austria, Belgium, Denmark, France, The Netherlands, and Sweden). Southern Europe, traditionally a net exporter, or a transit area for immigration from poorer countries to wealthier European states, has, in turn, become a net importer. This could, of course, reflect the return of expatriates as much as an influx of foreigners, although the return migration factor is probably small in older emigration countries such as Italy and Spain.

Overseas English-speaking countries retain a positive net migration, which is fairly considerable in the case of the US and Australia (0.4% per annum), and about half of this for Canada and New Zealand. Aside from Venezuela and Puerto Rico, which also have a positive net migration, and certain countries like Brazil, with an apparent zero migration, the current situation prevailing more or less everywhere in Latin America is emigration. If this is really a reversal of the traditional pattern, the phenomenon must be analysed over the long term, indeed, in the perspective of the demographic transition. This question will be resumed in Chapter 6.

Conclusion

The list of countries in advanced transition is steadily growing. The present work covers 67, amongst which 38 belong to the developing world, out of 109 countries with over 0.5 million inhabitants classed as less developed. Although this represents only 35% of the poorer countries, these contain almost three-quarters of the population concerned, since most of the demographic giants entered their transition in recent decades. If the adopted criteria are not completely free of an arbitrary element, and certain borderline countries have been included, whilst others were excluded—and despite the often fragile extimates available, revisable at any point—it none the less remains a fact that at the beginning of the 1980s an important demographic slowing down was occurring in the world's most populated countries. The only notable exceptions amongst countries with over 50 million inhabitants being, as previously demonstrated, Pakistan, Bangladesh, Nigeria, and Vietnam.

Bibliography to Chapter 2

CASSEN, R. H. (1978), 'Current Trends in Population Changes and their Causes', *PDR* (June), 331–53.

EA, M. (1981), 'Kampuchea: A Country Adrift', *PDR* 2 (June), 209–29.

GENDREAU, F. (1977), 'La Démographie des pays d'Afrique: revue et synthèse', *Population*, 4–5: 901–43.

TABAH, L. (1980), 'World Population Trends: A Stocktaking', *PDR*, 3 (Sept.), 355–90.

UN (1975), *Demographic Yearbook 1974* (New York: UN), 518–27.

—— (1981), 'World Population Prospects as Assessed in 1980' *Population Studies*, 78 (New York: UN).

—— (1982), *MBS* (Nov.).

3 The Decline in Mortality

Today two contrary laws seem locked in struggle: a law of blood and death which, in its tireless capacity to conceive new opportunities for combat, obliges people always to be ready for battle; and a law of peace, of work, of security, whose sole aim is to deliver man from his troubles. The one seeks violent conquests, the other the solace of humanity. The latter places a single human life above all, while the former would sacrifice hundreds of thousands of existences to the ambition of one alone.

(Pasteur 1888)

UNTIL the mid-twentieth century, mortality trends played a primordial role in the demographic evolution of developed countries. In fact, it is the decline in mortality, more than the factor of fertility exceeding replacement level, that has long explained the phenomenon of population increase and the maintenance of relatively young age structures. Above all, it is the unexpected extension of the average length of human life which is the motivating factor behind the demographic transition and which is at the base of one of the most monumental changes experienced by the human race in the course of its history.

In most cases the improvement of mortality in underdeveloped countries continues, and will continue for some decades yet, to play a decisive role, particularly in Africa. The reasons for this are various:

1. The past decade shows that the direction of mortality trends is not as linear (or rather logistic) as generally supposed; it is attended by acceleration, but more frequently by deceleration, and sometimes unexpected reversals.

2. Although the lag behind developed countries has on the whole lessened in recent decades, it none the less remains considerable, with a difference of life expectation at birth of around 20 years on average, and is capable of reaching 30 years between northern Europe and West Africa, for example.

3. The poorer countries present the widest mortality differences between social strata, due to the coexistence of advanced sanitary conditions in certain Westernized urban strata, together with the most primitive conditions in impoverished communities with high fertility. This inequality—insufficiently understood for lack of sufficient observation—may, on a priori grounds, be considered as inherent in the very nature of medical progress; it is quite probably even more extreme than that of nineteenth-century Europe at the height of the Industrial Revolution. It constitutes an important factor blocking the improvement of health conditions.

In light of recent information on the development and comparative state of mortality, this chapter will attempt to take stock of the mortality transition in those countries which have advanced demographic transitions, according to the definition given in Chapter 1. This is not an easy task. A large majority of developing countries lack reliable data; moreover, in the 1970s they were affected by new phenomena whose significance is still insufficiently understood. The advancement of demographic knowledge, due to more effective methods of death registration and newly conducted censuses and sample surveys, and also the development of new techniques of estimation, has made for less approximate, although by no means entirely satisfactory, evaluations of demographic parameters. Earlier evaluations have in consequence proven at times seriously questionable.

For instance, mortality tables of the 1950s and 1960s gave a false illusion of progress in many places. The striking declines in mortality observed in Sri Lanka, Mauritius, and various Central American countries were thought for a time to indicate that mortality could largely transcend the influence of levels of development. Mortality decline was, in this view, a technical phenomenon, in contrast to the essentially cultural nature of the decline in fertility. In 1962, according to a United Nations synthesis of world mortality trends, 'it [was] no longer necessary that a country should have a highly developed economy for its population's level of health to be at least satisfactory' (UN 1962: 12). Further on, they are more explicit: 'it is perhaps not over-optimistic to hope that in a decade or two, life expectation at birth will reach or exceed 65 years for the great majority of countries in the world' (UN 1962: 14). As it is, the estimation of life expectation at birth for the period 1975–80, on the basis of available statistics, stands at an average of only 55 years for developing countries; only a slender minority of small, fairly atypical countries, mostly in east Asia or Central America, exceed 65 years (UN 1981). Mortality thus responds to a system of determinants infinitely more complex than was possible to calculate with the experience of 20 years ago. This does not mean, however, that we should turn from an 'excessive optimism' to a pessimism 'equally excessive' (Tabah 1980).

The aim of this chapter is to work towards as accurate as possible an evaluation of this experience, with the benefit of an additional 20 years' observation. Section 2 will retrace the history of the health transition, with attention to pre-decline mortality levels, the date of the apparent break from traditional mortality, and the stages and rhythms of ensuing declines. But before this, Section 1 will examine the sources and quality of the data. Section 3 will then give an outline of *possible causes* of recorded trends, before concluding, in Section 4, with a swift introduction to the range of arguments on demographic and economic consequences, direct and indirect, of the decline in mortality. These arguments will be the subject of detailed analysis in Part III of this work, which is addressed to the implications of demographic transition.

1. The Data: Sources, Quality, and Indices Used

Sources and Quality

In developed countries, the registration of deaths is more or less 100% efficient. Civil registration is an established practice, following upon the earlier keeping of parish registers, and the data are of high quality; censuses, conducted periodically since the nineteenth century, now generally occur regularly, supplying very reliable measurements of mortality and its variations across time.

Developing countries present a very different situation: existing statistical information is more often than not derived from sample surveys and the analysis of census results. Data is rarely acquired directly from civil registers. As a whole, the geographic coverage of civil registration has not really progressed since the 1950s; in certain cases the degree of completeness has actually regressed.

According to Willcox (1940: 200), in 1833 the parts of the world with a system for the registration of births and deaths amounted to less than 100 million people (or 10% of world population); a century later, in 1933, registration accounted for almost a billion people, or about half of world population; a quarter of a century on (1958), according to certain estimates, 'the countries and territories for which there are registration data represent approximately 86% of world population' (UN 1962). But these data are far from being always accurate: the quality of the information gathered varies greatly from one country to the next. In conventional terms, what are considered 'complete' statistics give a 90% coverage, or more, of vital events; in 1958, such statistics existed in countries whose population represented only a little over one-third (36%) of world population, that is, the whole of the developed world, *and only a tenth of the developing world*. Table 3.1 summarizes this phenomenon.

The difference between the two figures for the existence and completeness of national civil registrations (86% and 36% respectively) gives an indication of that part of the world's population for which information is defective (50%). This figure represents countries where there is no apparent system of death registration; it has probably increased since 1958 due to the differential growth rates of the populations concerned. According to another source (Poplab 1975), in 1971 the coverage of so-called 'national' registers was 41% of the total world population. 85% of these are considered complete. This means that complete statistics would be available for only 34% of the world's population, Asia being the worst represented at 6% (by comparison with 16% for Africa, where a significant increase in coverage at least up to the 1960s seems to have been effected).

Civil registration thus remains patently deficient for an overwhelming majority of the population of poorer countries, hence the indispensable

TABLE 3.1. *Mortality statistics derived from complete registration; percentage of population covered, by major world regions, 1958*

Region	% of registered deaths
Africa	4
North America	99
Latin America	42
Asia	7
Europe	98
Oceania	76
USSR	100[a]
TOTAL	36

[a] We consider this percentage highly questionable, for various reasons: it is permissible to suspect the integral completeness for certain republics, particular in central Asia, more especially as the church registers of Imperial Russia (which preceded the civil register set up in 1923) were manifestly insufficient for the south and east of the country; the rate of coverage was only 78% in 1926; and, finally, the figures published even in 1960 remained very partial (UN 1962).

Source: UN (1962).

recourse to indirect methods of estimation. Such methods, now in wide use, are plainly no more than expedients: they are no substitute for complete civil registration data, and result for the most part in inaccurate and unsatisfactory evaluations, often differing considerably from one to the next, depending on the methods used. Their advantage lies in the production of probable orders of magnitude, matched with often fairly large confidence intervals (particularly for Black Africa).

Comparative Position of Countries with Advanced Transitions

As already remarked, the quality of demographic information for the industrial world (countries with European populations, Japan, and small countries of east Asia) may be considered perfect, whereas it remains fairly debatable for almost all developing countries. The inaccuracy of crude data nevertheless varies greatly between countries, the least problematic being those in advanced stages of transition (i.e. on the point of returning to an equilibrium of feeble growth).

   In the case of Africa, a distinction must be made between sub-Saharan Africa and North Africa, the latter yielding more reliable and complete data. Knowledge of the level and trends of mortality relies principally on surveys. None the less, in a country as densely populated as Egypt, civil registration operates fairly efficiently, since the proportion of deaths registered around the mid-1970s was estimated at 87%. The figure for countries like Algeria, Morocco, and Libya remains in doubt, but is probably 'closer to 50 than 100%' (UN 1982*a*). Civil registration statistics for deaths are still fairly incomplete for Tunisia, the proportion of undeclared deaths being estimated at around 30% for the period 1960–73 (Seklani 1974: 58). Nevertheless, Tunisia and Egypt represent the countries with easily the most reliable data of the region; these two countries are included in our selection precisely because their fertility has declined appreciably, even though somewhat hesitantly, over the last two decades. The direct measurement of mortality for sub-Saharan Africa is impossible, with the exception of a few tiny and atypical countries (Mauritius, Réunion, Cape Verde). Fertility is already relatively low and well below the African norm in these places, which are thus clearly within the scope of this study (excepting Cape Verde, due to its tiny population). Lastly, South Africa presents a more complex case: there are four large groups (Whites, Asians, Coloureds, and Bantu—in descending order of advancement[1] of demographic transition), all with very different demographic behaviour; registration is reliable only for the white minority, and to a lesser degree, the Asian and coloured minorities.

Latin America presents a far more positive situation. More accurate data covering a larger period are available for a significant number of countries. Out of 24 states numbering more than half a million inhabitants in 1980, nine can supply 'complete' data on mortality covering a reasonable period of time. (See Table 3.2) If one excludes Cuba and the countries of temperate South America having a sizeable population of European origin (Argentina, Chile, and Uruguay), once more the countries concerned are defined by their small demographic dimensions. For the two Latin American giants (Brazil and Mexico), comprising in themselves more than half of the population of the region (53% in 1980), the quality of the data is deficient; but while death registration in Mexico has been nearly complete in recent years, civil registration in Brazil only operates efficiently in the region of São Paulo. It is thus possible, for the recent period (the last, or perhaps last two, decades), to add Mexico to the list of nine countries given above. Henceforth, it will be assumed that continuous and reliable information on the development of mortality is available for almost 50% of the Latin American countries. All these countries are included in our selection. The five remaining members not on this list are Brazil, Colombia, Panama, the Dominican Republic, and

---

[1] In light of the population growth rate of the different ethnic groups, it would appear that the fertility transition is already well established in the black population, since its growth rate between censuses shows a marked decline, i.e. from 3.6% as an annual average in the 1960s to 2.7% in the 1970s (which marks a return to the level of the 1950s) (see South Africa 1982). This observation is corroborated by recent estimates of fertility; the total fertility rate for the black population drops from 6.6 to 5.2 children on average per woman between 1965 and 1980 (South Africa 1984: 30).

TABLE 3.2. *Available mortality data, Latin America*

Region	Number of countries		Countries studied
	Studied	Total in region	
Caribbean	4	6	Cuba, Jamaica, Puerto Rico, Trinidad and Tobago
Central America	1	7	Costa Rica
Tropical South America	1	8	British Guiana
Temperate South America	3	3	Argentina, Chile, Uruguay
TOTAL	9	24	

Venezuela. With the exception of Brazil, they all have long-standing but defective national civil registers.

In Asia, where over three-quarters (78%) of the less developed world's population lives, the availability of adequate data falls somewhere between that of Africa and Latin America (UN 1982a). Civil registration is incomplete or non-existent in most countries and, apart from Sri Lanka, has not noticeably improved since 1950. Only four countries possess complete civil registers: Hong Kong, Singapore, Malaysia, and Sri Lanka. Once more, these are non-representative[2] island or partly island populations, sometimes even city-states (Hong Kong and Singapore), with a strongly outward-looking attitude. The two Asiatic giants, China and India, have two kinds of registration: China uses local police registers, the content (civil registration aside) and operation of which are little known, but which one has good reason to believe were subject to serious disruption during recurring periods of disturbance including, of course, the Cultural Revolution, to mention only events in the last third of the century. India, apart from its old and very incomplete civil registration, has a permanent system of sampling procedures which, although defective, is partly supplemented by the quality and regularity of the census, thus enabling indirect estimates to be calculated. A census has been taken every 10 years since 1872. For several other large countries (Indonesia, Turkey, and Korea), the measurement of mortality, in the absence of good systems of registration, is arrived at by indirect estimation. This produces fairly diverse results; in South Korea, for example, life expectation at birth for the period 1960–65 varies, according to the methods used, from 48.1 to 59.8 years for men, and from 53.5 to 63.9 for women (UN 1982a).

All in all, complete civil registration exists in only 15 less developed

---

[2] Sri Lanka's mortality tables, for example, conform to Coale and Demeny's 'Western' model.

countries, all tending to be in the vanguard of demographic transition. Such a coincidence can scarcely be fortuitous, and we shall return to this question.

Indices Used

The measurement of mortality levels relies most often, given the data available, on three indices: the crude rate of mortality (the relation between numbers of deaths and the average·population in a given year); the rate of infant mortality (the relation between the number of infant deaths under 12 months and the number of registered live births in a given year); and life expectation at birth (the average length of life of members of a hypothetical cohort, subject to prevailing death risks at various ages). The use of one or another of these indices gives a different picture of trends, each of which has its own validity and, subject to the data and objectives of a study, gives a different characterization of mortality values. The aim of this work being to describe the principal modalities of demographic transition and economic changes pertaining to them, especially differential rates of population growth, our attention will be focused primarily, in the first instance, on trends in crude mortality rates. These data are available on an annual basis for long periods in the majority of countries having reached an advanced state of transition.

A crude rate, as its name implies, is a relatively rough aggregate index, useful where the relative importance of groups with a high probability of death (the elderly) is concerned. However, its interval of variation is so wide (from 5 to 35 per 1000 in real populations[3]) that the relative differences between individual rates becomes highly misleading where intrinsic levels of mortality have fallen, or, in other words, where crude rates have already become fairly low. The investigation will be rounded off with an outline of infant mortality trends, given their importance in respect of both their traditional populations (where they describe up to 25% of the total number of deaths, as opposed to 1% to 2% in modern populations) and their fundamental role in the decline of fertility. This index, when it is available, has the additional advantage of being calculated on a regular annual basis, whilst life expectation at birth can be used only occasionally in this study, since it is available on a more or less discontinuous basis. It is important, where countries with imperfect statistics are concerned, not to overlook its reduced reliability: it requires equally good figures for deaths as well as live births, and an accurate knowledge of the ages concerned.

---

[3] The case is different for stationary populations. Imagine, for instance, two stationary populations, each characteristic of extreme demographic regimes. One has a very high mortality (average length of life 25 years), the other a very low mortality (75 years). The corresponding crude rates would be 40 and 13.3 per 1000, respectively (these are, by definition, the inverse values of the average life expectancies).

2. Levels and Trends of Mortality

The Dating of Marked Changes

General Mortality

For the most and least developed countries alike, it is not always possible to date the period in which crude mortality rates began to decline as accurately as one would wish. This is due as much to uncertainty concerning the quality of data (sometimes very old) as to the long fluctuations affecting the rates. Also, available time series are in some cases either too short or too broken up to enable us to specify an incontestable date. With all due caution,[4] and taking due account of both such reservations and the significance of the mortality rate,[5] modern declines in mortality at the national level (or more precisely, their commencement) can be divided schematically into three periods for developed countries, and two for developing ones (on this point, see Figs. 8.1 to 8.8). The three periods characteristic of developed countries are as follows:

1. The last years of the eighteenth century and the beginning of the nineteenth century: this wave of progress affected, at minimum, the following areas: France, Czechoslovakia, and Scandinavia (Finland excepted). It could be partly linked to the discovery of smallpox vaccine, by Jenner, in 1796. The decline in mortality began slowly, but accelerated after 1870.

2. It is precisely from 1870, that is, about three-quarters of a century later, that the trend towards marked declines was simultaneously set in motion across most of Europe: in the north-west[6] (England and Wales, Belgium, The Netherlands), in central Europe (Switzerland, Germany, Austria, and

---

[4] Important declines in mortality, enabling a large increase in population, have been remarked since the second half of the 18th century in the most advanced countries of north and west Europe: England and Wales, Belgium, The Netherlands, Denmark, Norway, Sweden, the Swiss cantons, and western parts of Germany. But the estimates remain tenuous or not easily comparable with the data on which we rely. Even in England, then economically the most developed country, where civil registration was established in 1837, the data remain incomplete until around the 1860s. Nevertheless, McKeown (1965) has been able to demonstrate that population increase in England in the 18th century was due to the decline in contagious diseases, and in the 19th in great part to the gradual elimination of tuberculosis. Revised estimates of crude rates have been published in Deane and Cole (1964), and more recently in Wrigley and Schofield (1981).

[5] As a summary measure, the crude death-rate may be heavily influenced by the age-specific structure of a population. It can disguise the real trend of the level of health as shown, for example, by the average length of life. Improvements recorded in crude rates may be attributable to two other causes: (1) a rejuvenation of the population, due to immigration or a *lasting* increase in fertility. In the short term, however, such increases can produce the opposite effect, given the relative weight of infant deaths in general mortality, and the positive correlation between fertility levels and infant mortality; or (2) oscillatory effects, where excess mortality due to an epidemic reduces pressure on subsistence in the following period or, in effect, brings forward in time a certain number of deaths which would have occurred in a later period. Such fluctuations were important in the development of early populations.

[6] See n. 4, above.

TABLE 3.3. *Crude death-rates, Europe, 1800–1890* (per 1000)

Period	Western Europe	Eastern Europe	Total
1800–1820	28.0 ⎫	⎫	31.5
1821–1830	26.1 ⎪	⎪	30.0
1831–1840	27.2 ⎬ 26.7	⎬ 38.0	31.3
1841–1850	26.2 ⎪	⎪	30.5
1851–1860	26.1 ⎭	⎭	30.3
1861–1865	25.5	36.3	29.5
1866–1870	26.8	35.6	30.0
1871–1875	26.5	37.0	30.4
1876–1880	24.9	35.1	28.8
1881–1885	24.3	34.2	28.2
1886–1890	23.4	33.3	27.3

Source: Levasseur (1898) (based on an estimate by Grundbärg, no reference given).

Hungary) and even in the east (Poland and European Russia). This was followed, a few years later, by certain Mediterranean countries (Italy in 1875; and Yugoslavia in 1880). The trend extended beyond Europe, affecting countries with Latin populations (Argentina and Brazil[7]) and Anglo-Saxon ones (US). This second phase appears to correspond with Pasteur's discovery of the microbic origin of infectious diseases (1884) and, above all, the spread of its application in preventive medicine.

3. Twenty years later, the countries at the south-western end of Europe (Spain and Portugal) and the south-eastern end (Bulgaria and Romania), long outside the main sweep of modernization, benefited from this decline. Once more, certain countries to which these populations migrated were also affected.[8]

Table 3.3 shows the general development, for Europe, distinguishing between east and west. For the whole of the nineteenth century, mortality rates in the east are around 50% higher than in the west. Such a discrepancy cannot be attributed exclusively to health conditions: very high fertility, coupled with a different pattern of nuptiality—universal early marriage—would have played its role in the very high infant mortality. We will return to this question in Chapter 4.

Turning now to the developing countries, and setting aside the case of

---

[7] Estimates for this country, however, are tenuous.

[8] This, on the basis of the crude rate alone, was the case with the United States, although improvements in life expectation at birth had become manifest much earlier (roughly at the same time as France). In general, it is advisable to stress here the difficulty of establishing the decline in mortality for immigration countries solely from the crude rate. One may, however, assume that their development stands midway between those of the several principal countries of origin.

TABLE 3.4. *Annual average population growth rate by broad period and broad category of country* (per 1000)

Period	Developed countries[a]	China (incl. Taiwan)	Other developing countries[b]
1750–1800	4.2	9.6	0.9
1800–1850	*6.7*	5.2	3.5
1850–1900	*10.6*	0.3	5.6
1900–1920	8.1	*4.4*	*5.2*
1920–1930	12.0	*5.3*	*13.0*
1930–1940	8.0	*6.0*	15.2
1940–1950	4.4	5.5	15.3
1950–1960	13.1	20.5	21.2
1960–1970	10.5	20.9	24.6
1970–1980	7.6	17.3	24.0

Note: Italicized figures correspond to the period of accelerating growth (related to the decline in mortality).

[a] Europe, USSR, North America, Australia, New Zealand, temperate Latin America.

[b] Due to inadequate data, Japan has had to be included under this rubric.

Sources: Calculated from UN (1981), for the period 1950–80; UN (1975); Durand (1974), for China before 1950.

certain states in South America with a large population of European origin where the decline started around 1870 (Argentina and possibly Brazil), or at the end of the nineteenth century (Uruguay and British Guiana), the decline falls mainly into two periods:

1. Immediately after the First World War,[9] and during the inter-war period, the majority of developing countries in this study (at least 20 out of 36) experienced a sudden decline in mortality. Important instances include India, Mexico, Korea, Turkey, and probably China. The situation in several further countries remains unclear, due to population changes, lack of dependable data, or sufficiently long time series: Panama, mainland China, Israel, North Korea, Albania, Réunion, and Tunisia. However, according to estimates of life expectation at birth made around 1950 and, especially, the trends observed in their population growth rates, these countries appear to have experienced an appreciable decline in mortality since the inter-war period.

2. The remaining countries (in particular, Indonesia, and possibly Egypt) appear to have experienced the phenomenon a quarter of a century later, in the immediate post-war period. This same period is marked by an astonishing

[9] It is also at this point that the decline began to manifest itself clearly in Japan.

acceleration of the decline in mortality in certain countries where the trend had begun some decades earlier: in Japan, from 1935–36 to 1958, life expectation at birth altered from 48 to 67 years; in Mexico, from 1930 to 1949–51, it altered from 33 to 50 years. The leaps were even greater for small island countries: between the years 1945–47 to 1954, Sri Lanka registered a change from 46 to 60 years, an annual average increase of 1.75 years; on Mauritius there was a leap from 33 to 51 years between 1942–46 and 1951–53, an annual average increase greater than two years (2.25), completely without precedent (UN 1962).

The trend of population growth rates over the past two centuries follows these two large phases, at least if we assume that fertility did not appreciably alter at the start of the transition process (Table 3.4).

Thus, since the nineteenth century, and sometimes even the eighteenth century, the whole of Europe (except Albania) and, more generally, the developed world experienced a decline in mortality which spread, slowly to begin with and then more rapidly, from the north to the west, then to the centre, the east, and south. The majority of less developed countries with which this study is concerned benefited relatively early from health improvements. But, in view of the sharp change in the trend around 1920 (with the exception of China, where estimates are even more subject to caution), such improvements do not sufficiently distinguish this group of less developed countries, even if the falls in mortality were particularly dramatic in their case. The decline in mortality in these less advanced countries is much earlier than is generally credited; on the whole it precedes the advent of penicillin and antibiotics, and may go back as far as 60 years.

Infant Mortality

Before embarking on the study of individual countries, let us take a quick look at the international situation. In order to illustrate the historical and geographical spread of mortality changes,[10] and to trace the decline in countries with advanced transition, we have drawn up maps of infant mortality (Figs. 3.1 to 3.3), for twenty-five-year periods,[11] from 1850 to 1975 in Europe, 1925 to 1975 in Latin America, and from 1950 to 1975 in east Asia.[12]

The raw data are summarized in Tables 3.5 to 3.7. Everywhere, the point at which infant mortality began to decline is close to the starting date of the series and, in general, the older the series, the better the country's health conditions.

---

[10] Although there is no strict correspondence between infant mortality and general mortality, nor between their levels or patterns of temporal variation, the connection is none the less sufficiently close to illustrate the broad lines of development at the international level.

[11] The boundaries are those of the period under consideration.

[12] Data for around 1925 are available for barely half the countries studied.

TABLE 3.5. *Development of infant mortality rates, Europe, since 1850 (per 1000 live births)*

Country	Period					
	1850	1875	1900	1925	1950	1975
	1846–55	1871–80	1896–1905	1921–30	1948–52	1973–77
Austria[a]	251[b]	256	221	128	72.0	20.6
Belgium	151	153	153	97	53.0	14.7
Bulgaria[c]	—	—	(145)	(152)	107.0	24.4
Czechoslovakia[d]	254	260	233	146	75.0	20.6
Denmark	141	138	126	82	31.7	10.3
Finland	—	167	135	92	42.2	10.6
France[a]	164	172	148	92	52.0	13.5
Germany[e]	294	261	208	109	57.0	19.3
Germany (East)	—	—	—	—	80.0[f]	14.9
Greece[ac]	—	—	—	(92)	(40.3)[g]	23.0
Hungary[a]	252	—	215	180	86.0	31.4
Ireland[h]	—	(97)	102	70	47.1[i]	16.8
(N. Ireland)	—	—	—	—	(42.3)	(20.9)
Italy	—	215	168	118	68.0	21.2
Netherlands	190	203	144	59	26.4	10.7
Norway	109	104	88	51	27.0	10.6
Poland[a]	—	—	—	163[j]	107.0	24.7
Portugal	—	—	—	146	98.0	38.9[k]
Romania[a]	—	298	199[l]	197	124.0	34.1
Spain	—	195[m]	175[n]	138	69.0	(14.6)
Sweden	151	130	95	59	21.8	8.8

Table 3.5. (cont.)

Country	Period					
	1850	1875	1900	1925	1950	1975
	1846–55	1871–80	1896–1905	1921–30	1948–52	1973–77
Switzerland	—	193	139	60	32.1	11.4
United Kingdom[o]	158	149	147	72	32.3	15.6
USSR[p]	—	(266)	260	178[q]	81.0[i]	(35.0)[r]
Yugoslavia[s]	—	—	154	144[t]	120.0[g]	39.3

[a] As defined by contemporary national boundaries.
[b] The years 1847 and 1848 not included (data not available).
[c] Values probably underestimated for early periods.
[d] Czech populations (Bohemia, Moravia, Silesia) only for the first 3 periods.
[e] West Germany since 1946.
[f] 1946–54.
[g] 1949–51.
[h] Incl. values for N. Ireland given in parentheses below. Value 97 for 1875 is questionable.
[i] 1950.
[j] Average of values for the years 1922, 1923, 1927, 1928.
[k] 1975.
[l] Half total of the average annual values for 1891–95 and 1906–08.
[m] Average for the four years 1869, 1870, 1880, 1881 inclusive.
[n] Quinquennial average 1900–04.
[o] England and Wales only, for the first four periods.
[p] European Russia for 1875 and 1900. Registration area (85 government units) for 1925.
[q] 1926–27.
[r] Estimate, taking account of underregistration.
[s] Serbia only, for the period 1900.
[t] 1924–26.

Sources: Various, see General Bibliography.

TABLE 3.6. *Development of infant mortality rates, America,[a] since 1900* (per 1000 live births)

Country	Period			
	1900	1925	1950	1975
	1895–1904	1921–30	1948–52	1973–77
North America				
Canada	—	79	40.9	15.0
United States	149[b]	71	29.9	16.0
Central America				
Costa Rica	—	174[c]	92	36.3
Cuba	225[d]	142[c]	35.7[e]	26.6
Dominican Republic	—	—	(85.0)	41.5[f]
Jamaica	—	171[c]	80.0	22.2
Mexico	326[g]	213[h]	98.0	52.0[i]
Panama	—	—	61.0	32.2
Puerto Rico	—	150	70.0	21.7
Trinidad and Tobago	—	136[c]	81.0	25.6[i]
South America				
Argentina	—	114[c]	67.0	44.6[j]
Brazil	—	172[k]	149.0	92[l]
British Guiana	—	167[c]	79.0	46.4[m]
Chile	264[n]	250[c]	143.0	60.0[i]
Columbia	—	(119)	(125.0)	(47.8)[i]
Uruguay	98[g]	102	57.0	47.6[i]
Venezuela	—	159[o]	86.0	45.9

Notes: Decimals calculated only for values under 50 per 1000.

[a] Countries in which fertility declined, before 1980.
[b] Calculated from the statistics for Massachusetts for the years 1895–99.
[c] 1920–29.
[d] 1899.
[e] 1953.
[f] 1973–76.
[g] 1901–05.
[h] 1922–28.
[i] 1974–76.
[j] 1977.
[k] State of São Paulo, 1923 and 1929 not included (data not available).
[l] 1978.
[m] 1972–73.
[n] 1900.
[o] Average of the four years 1921, 1922, 1927, and 1928.

Sources: Various, see General Bibliography.

TABLE 3.7. *Development of infant mortality rates, Asia,[a] since 1900* (per 1000 live births)

Country	Period		
	1925	1950	1975
	1921–30	1948–52	1973–77
China (mainland)	—	120–160[b]	50–70[b]
Cyprus	—	64.0	26.8
Hong Kong	—	92.0	15.0
India	241[c]	164.0[d]	110–120
Indonesia	—	—	125–143[e]
Japan	148	58.0	10.0
North Korea	—	—	—
South Korea	186[f]	114.0	38.0[g]
Singapore	221[h]	76.0	15.0
Sri Lanka	183[h]	84.0	46.8[i]
Taiwan	159	46.7	13.9
West Malaysia	—	92.0	33.5

Notes: Decimals calculated only for values under 50 per 1000.

[a] Countries in which fertility declined before 1980.
[b] Author's estimate, based on data for 1975 (Banister and Preston 1981).
[c] Estimate from the 1921 and 1931 censuses, for 1921–31.
[d] Average of intercensus estimates, 1941–51, 1951–61.
[e] 1971.
[f] Infant mortality q_0 for 1925–30, North and South Korea combined.
[g] 1971–75.
[h] 1920–29.
[i] 1974 and 1977.

Sources: Various, see General Bibliography.

The gradual spread of the decline in *Europe* from north to south and west to east appears quite clearly in these materials. But if the contrasts between regions gradually diminish, the differences were no less manifest, and the current relative positions of individual countries remain as a whole highly consistent with the timing of the decline in general mortality.

The shading of the map for *Latin America*[13] around 1925 resembles that of Europe a quarter of a century earlier. There is an absence of countries either with very high infant mortality (over 250 per 1000), or relatively low (less than 80 per 1000). As a whole, countries do not yet share the pattern of southern Europe in the same period. Twenty-five years later, the change is of the same order, and the general level analogous, to that of Europe in the 1920s. In spite

[13] Analysis refers only to countries with advanced transition.

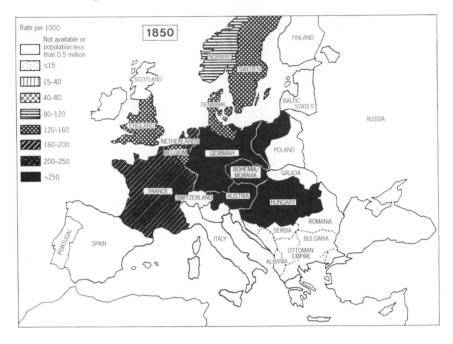

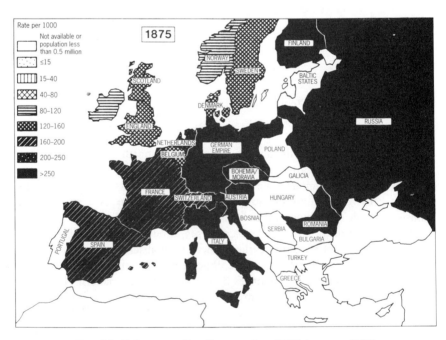

FIG. 3.1. Infant mortality, Europe, since 1850 (rate per 1000)

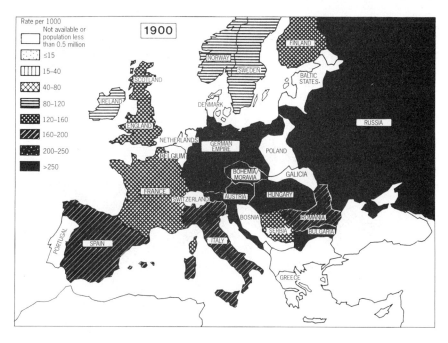

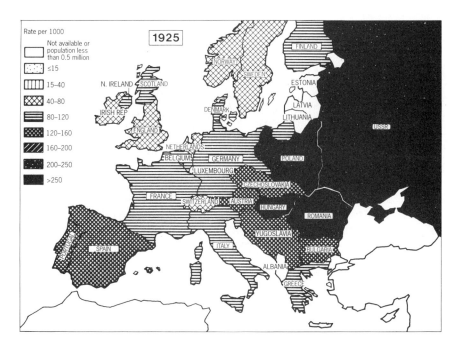

Fig. 3.1. (cont.)

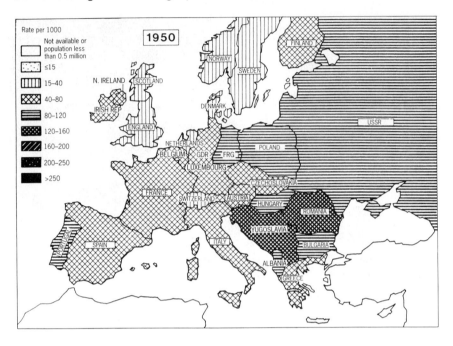

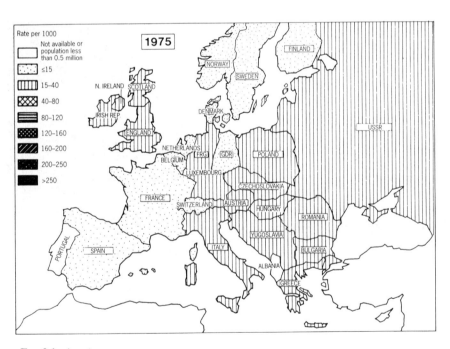

Fig 3.1. (cont.)

of significant progress, the bulk of the mortality excess, around 1975, remains to be overcome, notably in Brazil, where the rate is still close to 100 per 1000. With rates between 22 and 42 per 1000, the small Central American countries situated in range of North American influence appear to be doing fairly well by comparison with the larger countries, such as Mexico and Colombia. The countries in the southern tip (Argentina, Chile, and Uruguay), where rates vary between 45 to 60 per 1000, occupy a position intermediary but superior to their northern counterparts, especially Brazil (92 per 1000 in 1978).

East Asia likewise presents great contrasts. On the one hand, there are the small Chinese cultures of Taiwan, Hong Kong, and Singapore, in which infant mortality is already on par with the most advanced European countries. In Taiwan the rate in 1983 had fallen to 8.3 per 1000; in Hong Kong and Singapore it is steadily declining, and stood at around 10 in 1982. India, on the other hand, is comparable to Brazil of 15 years ago (110 to 120 per 1000), or Spain 50 years ago. Indonesia, with a rate calculated at between 125 and 143 per 1000 in 1971, is even less advanced. However, the Indian results should not be underestimated, as infant mortality rates have been reduced by half since the 1920s. South Korea and West Malaysia are at an intermediary stage (35 per 1000 around 1975). Mainland China would appear to occupy a level similar to these two last countries, on the basis of available data, but the quality of the latter is highly questionable. It is sufficient to note, in this respect, that the World Bank opted for an order of magnitude of 60 per 1000 for 1982; estimates based on the 1982 census, however, result in values of the order of 40 per 1000 (Calot 1984). Finally, Japan has risen in a few decades to the international forefront, vying easily with the traditionally most advanced countries of Norway, Sweden, and The Netherlands. Even if the Japanese level is a little exaggerated by a definition which understates the reality, the exceptional nature of the progress accomplished in the last half-century cannot be denied, nor can the superiority of the position currently attained.

National Retrospective Data

The reconstitution of series applies to 34 countries, chosen according to three criteria: demographic dimension, quality, and age of data (these two last being closely connected). The corresponding time series are given in Appendix 1, and represented in 12 graphs (Figs. 3.4(a) to (l)), for which the following arrangement has been adopted:

1. Northern Europe (Denmark, Finland, Norway, Sweden);
2. Ireland;
3. North-western Europe (England and Wales, Belgium, France, The Netherlands);
4. English-speaking overseas countries (Australia, Canada, the US);
5. Central Europe (Germany, Austria, Switzerland);

FIG. 3.2. Infant mortality, Latin America, since 1925 (rate per 1000)

FIG. 3.2. *(cont.)*

6. Southern Europe (Italy, Portugal, Spain, Yugoslavia);
7. Eastern Central Europe (Czechoslovakia, Hungary, Poland);
8. Eastern Europe (Bulgaria and Romania) and the USSR;
9. Africa (Egypt);
10. Latin America (Argentina, Brazil, Mexico);
11. South Asia (India, Sri Lanka);
12. East Asia (Japan, Taiwan).

Our commentary will be brief and descriptive. It will concentrate on a number of salient points, in fact raising more questions than it answers. The first of these concerns the comparative quality of data. A glance at the graphs reveals a suspect trend in several cases, in which initially low levels are shortly followed by abrupt upward movements. This appears in Figs. 3.4(*b*) and (*f*) (Ireland and Spain), and also, to a lesser degree, Figs. 3.4(*c*) and (*e*) (Austria (before 1830), Belgium, and England). Since these are nineteenth-century series, it is feasible to assume that variations reflect, in part, improvements in registration. In the cases of Belgium and England, the rise in rates may perhaps even reflect a certain deterioration in health conditions, linked to industrialization. A second question involves the extent of differences, around the mid-nineteenth century, which appear between countries sometimes very

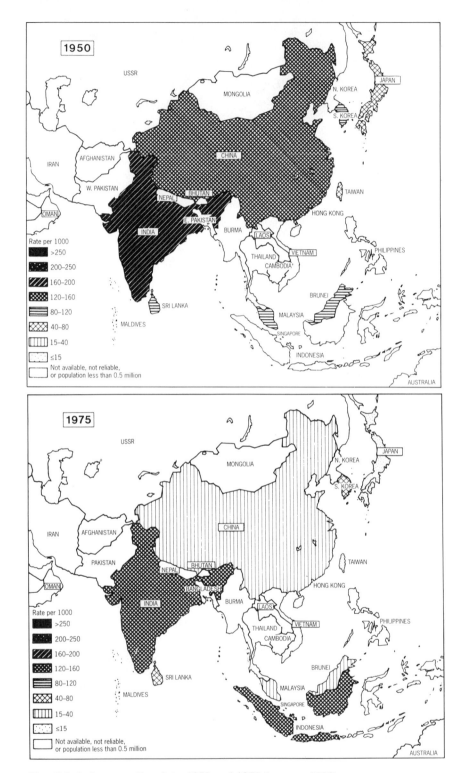

Fig. 3.3. Infant mortality, Asia, 1950 and 1975 (rate per 1000)

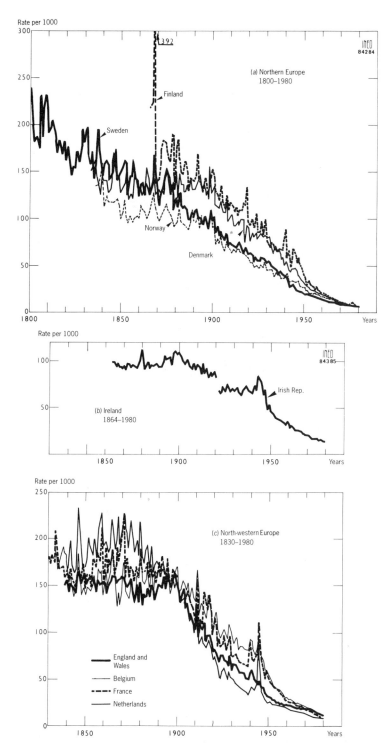

FIG. 3.4. Infant mortality rates

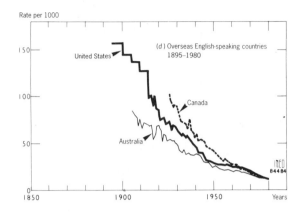

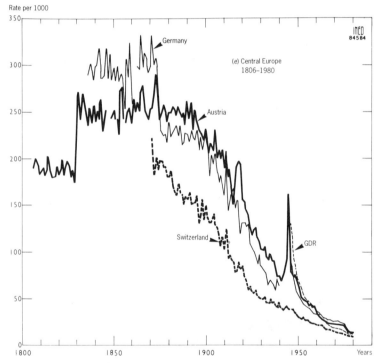

Fig. 3.4. (cont.)

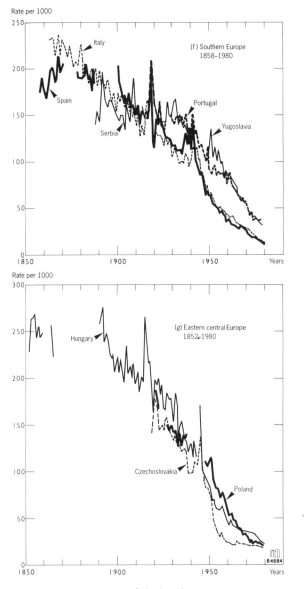

FIG. 3.4. (cont.)

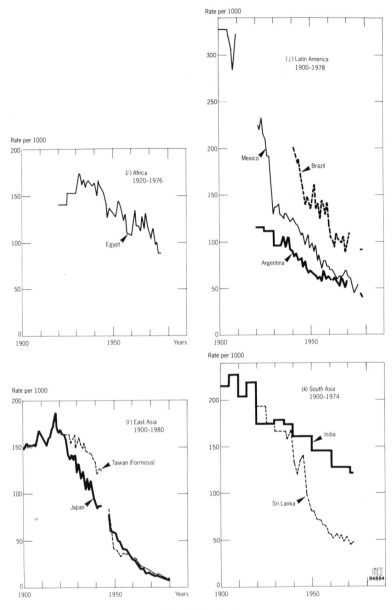

Fig. 3.4. (cont.)

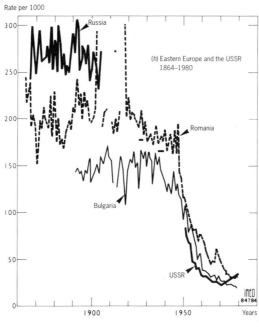

FIG. 3.4. (*cont.*)

TABLE 3.8. *Infant mortality rates, Europe, 1861–1870* (per 1000)

Country	Infant mortality rate	Country	Infant mortality rate
Norway	110	Italy	230
Sweden	130	Switzerland	(240)
Denmark	135	Finland	(250)
Belgium	160	Hungary	(250)
England and Wales	160	Austria	(260)
France	180	Russia	(280)
Netherlands	200	Germany	300

Note: Data in parentheses are orders of magnitude to which some degree of doubt is attached (insufficient, however, to invalidate the classification).

close both geographically and in their level of development. Table 3.8 gives a hierarchy of infant mortality rates in Europe between 1861 and 1870, a period which, for most European countries, may be considered to precede the modern fertility transition.

Norway already occupies the most advanced position, followed by Sweden,

TABLE 3.9. *Infant mortality rate, less developed countries,*
1921–1930 (per 1000)

Country	Infant mortality rate	Country	Infant mortality rate
Argentina	115	India	180
Egypt	150	Sri Lanka	190
Japan	150	Mexico	200
Taiwan	160	Brazil	(250–300)

whilst Russia and the central European countries come at the rear with extremely high rates; only a little over a century ago these countries registered the death of over 1 in 4 infants per annum. From the evidence, the case of Germany is the most striking, with a rate over twice as high as Denmark, and exceeding even Russia. Such differences can only be explained by factors other than the degree of socio-economic development, notably customs and techniques of child-rearing (breast-feeding, weaning, wet-nursing), or the status of children (proportion of extra-marital births, size of families, etc.).

The period 1921–30 has been chosen to reflect the comparative pre-transitional situation of the less developed countries under consideration. The corresponding order of these countries, including Japan, is shown in Table 3.9. Fifty years ago Japan and Taiwan were on a par with Egypt; by 1980 their infant mortality rate was eight times lower. These countries have emerged from the category of underdeveloped countries to take the lead of the most advanced. Such an unprecedented achievement is certainly not independent of their spectacular economic progress, but this in itself does not constitute a complete explanation, as the lag in economic development separating them from the richest countries has not in all cases been completely made up.

In developing as much as in developed countries, the diversity of international differences during the so-called 'pre-transitional' period is such that it is difficult to fix definite break points for the series. In many countries, starting levels, although sometimes very old and doubtless realistic, are comparatively so low that the beginning of the decline probably pre-dates the starting date of the series. This is principally the case for Scandinavian countries in the first half of the nineteenth century. As a general rule, the decline in European infant mortality appears to have occurred later than that of general mortality, mostly around 1900, rather than 1870. This in fact represents a new phase following a long plateau; urbanization and industrialization, as well as the improvement in registration, go some way towards explaining this absence of decline. In the less developed countries, the importance of progress recorded in the inter-war period is undeniable, confirming the earlier observation regarding general mortality, on the relative

TABLE 3.10. *Crude death-rates, selected developed countries, 1861–1870* (per 1000)

Country	Death-rate	Country	Infant mortality rate
Norway	18.0	Netherlands	25.4
Denmark	19.9	Germany	26.9
Sweden	20.2	Italy	30.9
England and Wales	22.5	Austria	31.5
Switzerland	23.0	Finland	32.6
France	23.6	Hungary	(33.0)
Belgium	23.8	Russia	(37.0)

precocity of the health transition. The scarcity and tenuousness of data earlier than the First World War, however, prevents us from distinguishing those countries where changes preceded the war from those where they occurred after it.

Are these conclusions regarding infant mortality equally applicable to mortality in general—especially the diversity of pre-transitional levels and periods at which the transition commenced? To verify this, we have summarized a selection of developed countries in Table 3.10, arranging them in terms of crude death-rates, for the period 1861–70. Here, too, the differences are considerable, the highest rate being more than double the lowest. The hierarchy is fairly similar to that established from rates of infant mortality, although Germany clearly occupies a better position.

Stages and Tempo of the Decline

The development of mortality proceeds by successive leaps which, taken together, comprise a curve of gradual improvement. The history of mortality is characterized above all by great discontinuities, of which four may be distinguished schematically:

1. the second half of the eighteenth and beginning of the nineteenth centuries, which witnessed considerable agricultural advancements, the improvement of health conditions, and the discovery of smallpox vaccine (Jenner, 1796);

2. the last third of the nineteenth century, marked by the first real medical revolution, due to the work of Pasteur, Koch, and their successors on the identification of pathogens and the prevention and treatment by vaccines and serums of the principal contagious diseases;

3. the First World War and the period immediately following it, characterized by an extension of medical techniques and the general diffusion of health education;

4. the Second World War and immediately afterwards, with the discovery of penicillin (1929) and its synthesis by Fleming (1943), and, not long after, the emergence of antibiotics such as streptomycin (1944) and aureomycin (1948) which now treat an increasingly wide microbic spectrum, from the commonest to the rarest germs.

The capacity to make use of great medical innovations varies with cultural awareness and levels of development. Up to the First World War, only European populations managed to benefit from discoveries relating to small-pox and infectious and parasitic diseases. The accumulation of knowledge and the eminently transferable nature of techniques for fighting disease and death should, on a priori grounds, facilitate the telescoping of the health transition in the less developed countries.

This phenomenon is easily confirmed by comparing the tempo of the decline in mortality between the developing and the developed countries. Given that, in 1937, the birth-rate for the developing countries (China excluded) was estimated at 42.5, and the death-rate at 31–32 per 1000, and allowing that the acceleration of population growth in these countries from 1920 through the inter-war period was due only to the decline in mortality and that this decline did not begin before 1920 (so that fertility remained the same for 1900–20 as around 1937), then one must agree that in about 15 years (1920–37) the rate of mortality declined 6 or 7 points, the rate of natural growth having advanced from 5 to 11 or 12 points (see Table 3.4). This decline is identical to that observed during the following 15 years, from 1937 to 1950–55, and even to that of the twenty-year period which follows, from 1950–55 to 1970–75 (Kuznets 1981). This not only recalls the antecedent nature of the decline in mortality, but, at the same time, calls into question the general view of the abrupt acceleration of this decline after the Second World War. Thus, at a very early stage, the speed of mortality decline was considerable, of the order of 3 to 5 points on average per decade during the period of greatest progress (1920–50), as opposed to only one point in the developed countries over the equivalent historical period (1870–1910). When measured in absolute terms,[14] the tempo of decline was 3 to 5 times more rapid.

This development may not be uniform across all age groups. As we have seen, in certain cases like east Asian countries within the Chinese cultural sphere, or Japan and countries under its economic influence, the decline has been so strong, particularly among young children, that life expectation at birth for both sexes around the late 1970s exceeded 75 years (for Hong Kong and Japan) and 70 years (for Taiwan and Singapore). These are clearly quite exceptional and spectacular cases. As a test, therefore, we thought it desirable to assess the comparative speed of declines in infant mortality after the health

---

[14] The contrast appears less striking when measured by life expectation at birth.

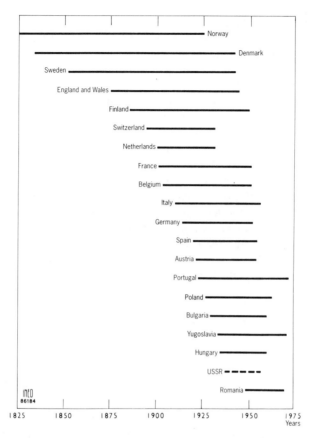

FIG. 3.5. Health transition and rate of mortality decline in developed countries: period from infant mortality rate of 150 per 1000 to 50 per 1000 (moving average of five years)

transition had begun. An indicator of duration has been used: the time t in which the rate of infant mortality passes from 150 per 1000 (in a moving average of 5 years).[15] Where Europe is concerned (Fig. 3.5), the principle of acceleration is, as a general rule, fairly clear: thus, in the most advanced northern countries (Scandinavia, Finland, England and Wales), where the rate had fallen below 150 before 1885, this duration is in the region of 75 years, compared with only 20 to 25 years for eastern Europe. (The Russian case, with an ostensible duration of less than 30 years, is clearly improbable, given the unusual demographic heterogeneity of the country: Soviet data need to be

[15] These values have been chosen to include a sufficient number of observations from the less developed countries in our selection.

reconsidered).[16] However, this first impression is misleading, and it is not possible to conclude that slowness is a corollary of precocity, since between these extremes are countries which, within our criteria, can be defined as having health transitions which were both early (reaching the level of 150 per 1000 before the end of the nineteenth century) and rapid (with a value t around 30–35 years). If one completes the analysis for the 11 developing countries for which this calculation is possible,[17] the differences in fact appear more subtle. Table 3.11 gives the average duration t according to the period when the level 150 per 1000 was reached.

If one takes into account the fact that these 11 countries constitute a selection which is both arithmetical (i.e. countries where infant mortality remains in the interval 50–150 have, a priori, a longer transition) and socio-cultural (all are more or less small countries subject to strong 'Western' influence), there appears no assurance that a similar acceleration will occur in countries where this transition did not begin until the second half of the twentieth century. Recent trends in infant mortality in numerous developing countries incline one to think rather the opposite.

3. The Causes of the Decline

A False Dichotomy: Health versus Socio-economic Development

A country's mortality level inevitably depends on multiple factors: its medical infrastructure of clinics, dispensaries, and hospitals; biomedical resources and equipment such as vaccines, serums, antibiotics, apparatus, and laboratories; the density, quality, and spatial distribution of medical and paramedical personnel; water, sewerage, transport, and communications networks; the State's authority in matters of health legislation, vaccination, the cost of medical products and services, preventive and social medicine, and urban planning; ecological conditions of climate and habitat; economic conditions, notably the level and distribution of income; and cultural attitudes towards illness, standards of education, and so forth. A complex network of factors is thus at play. In the pursuit of clarity, it is customary to separate out the socio-economic factors underlying what are, properly speaking, health conditions; the traditional debate on the causes of the mortality decline consists in determining the relative importance attributable to each of these groups of

[16] There is an obvious discontinuity—for which as far as we are aware no satisfactory explanation has been given—between the data for the pre-war period and those for the post-war period. See Chesnais 1981: 1179 n. 6.

[17] These countries, with their corresponding time sequences, are as follows: Mauritius (1942–75), Costa Rica (1935–73), Cuba (1942–45), Jamaica (1931–62), British Guiana (1934–63), Venezuela (1934–63), Cyprus (1931–53), Taiwan (1934–50), Malaysia (1937–65), Sri Lanka (1940–69), Singapore (1946–56).

TABLE 3.11. *Infant mortality, date and duration of declines*

Group of countries	Date at which rates reach 150 per 1000	Number of countries	Average duration t (years)
Developed countries			
Group I	1825–1900	6	76
Group II	1900–1925	8	41
Group III	1925–1950	6	28[a]
Less developed countries			
Group IV	1925–1950	11	26[b]

[a] 30 without USSR.
[b] 29 without Taiwan and Singapore.

factors in the improvements observed. If such a dichotomy has the advantage, for planners, of facilitating choice of investments and priorities of action in public health matters, it is at the same time too reductive at an analytical level to embrace reality effectively and, above all, to reveal the underlying mechanisms. Without doubt, health conditions are closely associated with levels of socio-economic development, and with socio-medical programmes set up by public authorities; but they are also associated with other factors, such as those just listed.

There is an obvious interdependence between 'health' and 'economic' components of mortality decline which makes any attempt to separate them somewhat artificial: health has a price which varies according to the nature of the interventions required to maintain or restore it; conversely, the decline in morbidity (a corollary of mortality decline) is attended by positive results in the productivity of labour which are both direct (reduced absenteeism, an increase in potential energy) and indirect (changes in agents' temporal perspectives, returns from certain productive investments). Strictly speaking, the distinction is valid only in the short term; otherwise, progress has to be mutually interactive. In short, both sets of factors are in large part functions of shared regional and historical heritage.

Attempts to evaluate the effectiveness of public health programmes have consequently been unconvincing, even contradictory. The same writer may be inclined to put forward very different orders of magnitude, depending on his or her assumptions and the statistical methods employed. In this way, increasing life expectation at birth due to the improvement of medical techniques and public health in developing countries has been evaluated at between 50% and 80% for the period 1940–70 (Preston 1975, 1981). Given the diversity of historical experience, one must guard against hasty and general conclusions. It is clear, moreover, that the relation of average length of life to income is not linear, and that either may change in response to the other and, hence, with successive phases of the health transition and degrees of economic development. Even certain spectacular cases of public intervention, with the massive logistical support of international organizations, have not been susceptible to definitive interpretation.

A frequently cited example is Sri Lanka, where in 1947 a campaign to eliminate malaria resulted in a massive decline in mortality. The crude rate fell from 19.8 per 1000 in 1946 to 14 per 1000 in 1947, and 9.9 per 1000 in 1956–58. It is difficult to analyse this case for an average period, and thus to apply it to other countries. One has to take into account concomitant factors, such as the considerable increase in medical services during the period under consideration: the number of inhabitants per doctor passed from 12,000 to 5,300 between 1946 and 1953. Consideration must also be given to demonstration effects (i.e. of exemplary programmes intended to show the intensity and importance of the endemic disease); and to the variability of results, depending on the amount of land brought back into cultivation by the use of insecticides, or the more or less debilitating effects of malaria, with their implications for other causes of illness and death.

General and Specific Factors

The traditional dichotomy is thus unsatisfactory. A more fruitful distinction may be made between specific, sectional factors which aim at direct action through prevention or treatment of specific diseases, and general factors having indirect repercussions on the health of a population, although not designed with that express purpose. Heavy investments (construction of hospitals, training of general practitioners and specialists, establishment of laboratories) are amongst the specific factors, along with less costly light technology (penicillin, antibiotics, sulfamides, vaccines, insecticides, etc.). The latter, introduced into developing countries via the West in the immediate post-war period, caused a new burst of demographic growth. The general factors are extremely varied and were enumerated earlier. Two in particular—nutrition and education—tend to be singled out (UN 1980). Malnutrition, particularly protein deficiency, whose incidence and effects are still insufficiently understood, can lead to diminished production of antibodies, and thus acts indirectly on infectious diseases. Increase in the general level of education manifests itself in different ways: knowledge of hygiene and medical techniques, alteration in the conditions of work and living, reduction in fertility, and so forth.

The connection with cultural determinants appears even stronger for mortality than for fertility. Average per capita income is a syncretic variable strongly correlated with these two factors; its ostensible relation to mortality indicators should also be analysed.

The Income Effect: Importance and Limits

A first method of analysing the relation between income and mortality is simply to follow out the chronological development of life expectation at birth in a given country, as a function of rising income. The results are well known: as with all aspects of the process of structural change that accompany economic growth, life expectancy tends towards a logistic progression (Chenery 1975). But the historical experience of 1930 to 1970 presents contradictory information, at least in appearance. The 1930s, characterized by a massive rise in unemployment and a marked decline in incomes, recorded no increase in general or infant mortality, even in the worst-hit countries like the United States or Germany. Conversely, the 1970s witnessed a decline in life expectation in eastern Europe, especially the Soviet Union. The apparent paradox is due, doubtless, to the difference in both levels of life expectation and social organization between the two cases. It is possible that recent economic and environmental problems in eastern Europe, visible in the growing debt to Western banks, has contributed—given the inflexibility of centralized planning systems—to a disruption of both health and food policy. To the extent that life expectation is closer to the normal maximum, its improvement will appear more tenuous.

A second method consists in comparing these variables in different countries for given years. This approach is the more frequent of the two (Vallin 1968; Preston 1975; UN 1982b). Thus Vallin, confirming the results of our historical parallel, shows that the independence of health progress from economic development is not without limits; life expectation quickly reaches a ceiling if income ceases to rise. 'Outlays on investment and maintenance continue to increase', he remarks, 'beyond the period in which the world launched its attack against the great infectious and parasitic diseases.' Economic progress may therefore be necessary. Preston, using international data for three periods (1900, 1930, and 1960), demonstrates the diminishing effect of income on life expectation at birth: medical progress over the period 1900–60 was such that considerable increases in the length of life were observable without strong economic growth. There exist, however, levelling effects, amply illustrated by the experience of the last two decades, in which there has been a marked slowing down in health progress.

The present study approaches this question, with respect to developed countries, by comparing GNP per capita y in 1978,[18] with infant mortality rates x for the same year. There is a strong correlation between the two variables ($r^2 = 0.75$), even when one eliminates the eight countries with planned economies ($r^2 = 0.65$). The scattering of points conforms to a curve for the value $x = 93{,}415.44y^{-1.055}$ (Fig. 3.6). Where very high incomes occur, the statistical relation is less close. The improvement of health organization

[18] Based on World Bank 1981.

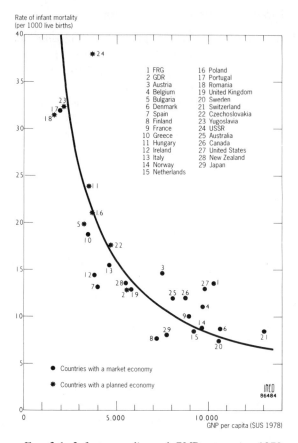

Rate of infant mortality
(per 1000 live births)

1 FRG	16 Poland
2 GDR	17 Portugal
3 Austria	18 Romania
4 Belgium	19 United Kingdom
5 Bulgaria	20 Sweden
6 Denmark	21 Switzerland
7 Spain	22 Czechoslovakia
8 Finland	23 Yugoslavia
9 France	24 USSR
10 Greece	25 Australia
11 Hungary	26 Canada
12 Ireland	27 United States
13 Italy	28 New Zealand
14 Norway	29 Japan
15 Netherlands	

● Countries with a market economy

✳ Countries with a planned economy

GNP per capita ($US 1978)

FIG. 3.6. Infant mortality and GNP per capita, 1978

and progress in medical knowledge and techniques thus probably contribute more to the possibility of renewed declines in infant mortality than does the growth of income. The cases of Japan and Finland, where infant mortality is very low despite what are closer to 'average' income levels, demonstrate this; the same is true of West Germany and the United States, which have high incomes and 'average' infant mortality. The relation between general mortality and income is less strong where socio-economic growth encourages the growth of overeating, smoking, sporting accidents, etc. (UN 1982*b*).

Variability of Influences according to the Stages of the Health Transition

The factors contributing to mortality decline have certainly varied in different periods and countries. As a very general rule, however, it can be said that in the first stages of the decline, from the eighteenth century to the revolution brought about by Pasteur's discoveries, the establishment of modern States exercised a decisive influence. When administration became powerful enough to impose social order and legal discipline, great progress was made in terms of infrastructures, transport, agriculture, and commerce, all of which contributed to the decline of famines and epidemics (e.g. agrarian reform, road building, construction of canals and hospitals, etc.). Institutional change was all the more important for facilitating both economic growth and control of natural disasters. The gradual unification of countries and institutional centralization were accompanied, in many cases, by the establishment of schools for midwives, and the erection of hospitals, faculties of medicine, and other health organizations. Germany provides a good example of this (Lee 1979).

In the second stage, when the great medical discoveries began to be applied and disseminated, specific factors tended to predominate. This in no way implies that levels of development had been a negligible influence until then. This is testified, on the one hand, by the manner in which improvements in mortality in non-European countries fell behind before the First World War; and, on the other, by the considerable increase in life expectation experienced in the 1920s by certain developing countries experiencing rapid economic growth closely connected to the West through international commerce (Taiwan, Japan, and Cuba). It was later that the role of economic factors considerably diminished, over the period 1935–60, or the time of the second health revolution. This period witnesses a universal decline in mortality. Over the last 20 years, however, the lack of any major innovation in techniques for controlling morbidity and mortality, and, more recently, the world-wide economic recession, have effected a sudden slowing down in health progress, even in relatively unadvanced countries. As a consequence, economic, cultural, and institutional factors assume a new role.

The Economy of Diverse Pathologies

The temporal variation in the role of economic variables in mortality decline may be explained partly by the stages of the health transition, particularly the order in which different groups of diseases declined (or, sometimes, increased). Thus, according to the estimates of Preston and Nelson (1974), life expectation at birth rose from 27.5 years in the *ancien régime* to 50 years in the intermediate regime, levels which correspond to crude rates of mortality of 35 and 20 per 1000, respectively. Of this fall, 33.2% was due to the decline of influenza, pneumonia, and bronchitis, which fell from 7.85 to 2.87 per 1000; 9.5% to that of respiratory tuberculosis, which fell from 3.85 to 1.42 per 1000; and 16.6% to that of other infectious and parasitic illnesses, which fell from 4.0 to 1.51 per 1000. In other words, most of the improvement was due to techniques which were relatively inexpensive and simple to apply, such as vaccines and antibiotics. Infectious and parasitic diseases, along with respiratory tuberculosis, account for almost 50% of deaths in the *ancien régime*, around 30% in the intermediate regime, and less than 5% in the modern regime (where life expectancy reaches 70 years). In the first phase of the mortality decline, it is this group of causes of death, for which medical techniques were easily transferable, that diminished sharply. Thereafter, general improvements in mortality have depended principally on the treatment of degenerative problems such as cancer, and cardiovascular diseases, which demand heavy investments and refined techniques which are much less easily transferable.

However, the picture requires further elaboration. More precisely, according to Preston (1975), a distinction should be made between two categories of illness in developing countries: the first, including malaria, tuberculosis, smallpox and measles, requires only small outlays in the health system in order to achieve immense progress; the second, which includes diarrhoeal and infectious diseases, demands more profound structural changes, and cannot really be resolved short of improvements in agriculture and infrastructure (standards of nutrition, fresh water supply, sanitation plants), and particularly education, which affects aspects of social behaviour such as fertility, child-rearing, and weaning.

The discrepancy, remarked earlier, between the very rapid tempo of mortality decline and the much slower one for infant mortality is a revealing indicator of the level of maternal education. In certain countries which have achieved low mortality despite low income levels, such as Costa Rica and Cuba in Central America, or Sri Lanka, Taiwan, Kerala (in India), Malaysia, and mainland China[19] in Asia, alteration has not been confined to specific components of the socio-medical system, such as child care, but directed to general factors (nutrition and education, especially in rural areas). These examples show that mortality, like the other components of demographic change, is far from being governed by purely technical developments, but is intimately bound up with cultural and socio-economic factors—or, in other words, to the entire structural development of a country.

Japan, Hong Kong, and Singapore, all having strong international contacts and very rapid economic growth, have achieved even more impressive results by following more indirect, and less egalitarian, strategies of development, which show that many approaches are possible, even if not all are within range of most developing countries. All of these countries are also characterized by sometimes considerable declines in fertility, especially where economic growth has been rapid. The declines recorded have nevertheless been rather im-

[19] If Kerala and mainland China were not included, one could object that the distinctive trait of these countries is not essentially their strategy of development. The other countries are effectively advantaged by their small dimensions and geographical position, and are thus better situated to benefit from international aid: they are, besides, traditionally very open to foreign influence.

pressive even where growth is slow and strongly redistributive, as with Cuba or, to a lesser degree, Sri Lanka, where policies have been addressed to satisfying basic needs of the greatest number. Thus, declines in mortality and fertility appear subject to common determinants arising from structural changes accompanying general economic development.

4. The Consequences of the Decline in Mortality

The repercussions of mortality decline are innumerable and incalculable. They modify not only the reality of the individual and the collectivity, but also images of self, time, and the universe. The indirect effects are in this way probably far more profound than direct consequences. It will suffice to enumerate a few principal effects of such a decline:

1. *The increase in the tempo of population growth.* The possible implications of this increase vary depending on the level and context in which it occurs (states of resources, institutional heritage, technological capacity, etc.).

2. *The growth of the dependency ratio.* At a high level of mortality, the risk of death takes the form of a U-shaped curve; with mortality decline, it becomes more J-shaped. Mortality decline thus affects primarily the two age extremes, but youth more than old age, except at the utmost stages, when life expectation is already very high. In practice, those under 5 years of age and those over 40 are most affected (Preston 1981). The long-term consequences are thus manifest in an increase in the proportion of individuals under 20 and over 75—or an increased pressure on adult responsibility. The phenomenon is more or less marked depending on variations in the age schedule of mortality, especially in the infant and juvenile age groups.

3. *The founding of a new system of demographic regulation.* The decline in mortality affects the totality of demographic behaviour. Its direct impact on fertility in the short term is ambiguous, given that it can lead to an increase or a decline, depending on the mechanisms we have been considering. On the other hand, the indirect effect of mortality decline over the long term is indubitably more profound: it entails a process of adjustment aligned sometimes more, sometimes less, with the decline in fertility. The linkages to international migration are less well understood, but it seems clear that the great European migrations to Australia and the New World were a response to mortality decline.

4. *Rural exodus and the transformation of social structures.* The influence of mortality decline on rural–urban migration is complex, as it depends simultaneously on the differential fertility and mortality of towns and the countryside, and on conditions of life. One notes, in particular, conditions of rural poverty in which very high fertility is perhaps compensated by excess mortality. The decline in mortality is instrumental to breaking out of the traditional self-regulating system; the older age to which parents generally

survive tends, where the transfer of property occurs at their death, to encourage the departure of excess children. This mechanism induces change in the composition of the active population, and, in a more general manner, the development of a differential demography of social classes linked to temporal fluctuations and the different phases of the transition. In the initial stage, improvements tend to be in the middle classes and the urban élite; while, in the second, it affects the labouring classes. The implications of this for income distribution and economic growth require further investigation (Kuznets 1981).

5. *Effects on economic growth.* This issue is implicit in points 1 to 4, above, and no firm conclusion can be established, since very diverse mechanisms are at work, some of which further economic growth, and some of which hinder it. For Kuznets, the decline in mortality is an indispensable prerequisite to modernization. The fall of mortality and morbidity in poor countries requires a considerable expenditure of human effort and activity. The decline, however, increases individual mobility and the rationalizing of attitudes towards life. But its effects may also cause depression where it suddenly disrupts the balance between population and subsistence, for instance, by inducing property division or an over-intensive exploitation of land. Thus it may either stimulate or depress economic growth, depending on circumstances and institutions. Part III of the present work will show that, contrary to general opinion, the second of these two possibilities has become much less frequent than in the past.

Bibliography to Chapter 3

BANISTER, J., and PRESTON, S. H. (1981), 'Mortality in China', *PDR*, (Mar.), 98–110.

BLANC, R. (1977), 'Synthèse critique de l'expérience des trente dernières années', in *L'Observation démographique dans les pays à statistiques déficientes*, Chaire Quételet 1976 (Liège: Ordina Editions), 13–32.

CALOT, G. (1984), 'Données nouvelles sur l'évolution démographique chinoise', *Population*, 4–5: 897–936, and 6: 1045–62.

CHENERY, H. B., and SYRQUIN, M. (1975), *Patterns of Development, 1950–1970* (Oxford: Oxford University Press).

CHESNAIS, J. -C. (1981), 'La Hausse de la mortalité infantile en Union Soviétique', *Population*.

DEANE, P., and COLE, W. A. (1964), *British Economic Growth, 1688–1959: Trends and Structure* (Cambridge: Cambridge University Press).

DURAND, J. D. (1974), *Historical Estimates of World Population: An Evaluation* (Philadelphia, Pa.: Population Studies Center).

KUZNETS, S. (1975), 'Population Trends and Modern Economic Growth: Notes towards an Historical Perspective', in *The Population Debate, Dimensions and Perspectives*, i, Papers of the World Population Conference, Bucharest (New York), 425–33.

—— (1981), 'Recent Population Trends in LDC's and Implications for Internal Income Distribution', in NBER, *Population and Economic Change in Developing Countries* (Chicago, Ill.: University of Chicago Press), 471–511.

LEE, W. R. (ed.) (1979), *European Demography and Economic Growth* (London).

LEVASSEUR, E. (1898), 'Mortalité', in *La Grande Encyclopédie* (Paris).

MacKEOWN, T. C. (1965), *Medicine in Modern Society* (London: Allen and Unwin).

POPLAB (Laboratories for Population Statistics) (1975), 'The Conventional Vital Registration System', *Scientific Report Series*, no. 20, University of North Carolina (Apr.).

PRESTON, S. H., and NELSON, V. E. (1974) 'Structure and Change in Causes of Death: An International Summary', *Population Studies*, 1: 19–51.

—— (1975) 'The Changing Relation between Mortality and Economic Development', *Population Studies* (July), 231–48.

—— (1981), 'Causes and Consequences of Mortality Declines in Less Developed Countries during the Twentieth Century', in NBER, *Population and Economic Change in Developing Countries* (Chicago, Ill.: University of Chicago Press), 289–341.

SEKLANI, M. (1974), *La Population de la Tunisie* (Paris: CICRED).

South Africa (1982), *Official Yearbook* (Johannesburg).

—— (1984), *Official Yearbook* (Johannesburg).

STOLNITZ, G. H. (1955–56), 'A Century of International Mortality Trends', pt. I, *Population Studies* (July 1955), 22–55; pt. II, *Population Studies* (July 1956), 17–42.

—— 'International Mortality Trends: Some Main Facts and Implications', in UN, *The Population Debate: Dimensions and Perspectives*, World Population Conference, Bucharest, 1974 (New York: UN).

TABAH, L. (1980), 'World Population Trends: A Stocktaking', *PDR*, 6(3) (Sept.), 355–89.

UN (1962), *Bulletin démographique*, no. 6 (New York: UN).

—— (1975), *The Population Debate: Dimensions and Perspectives* (New York: UN).

—— (1980), *Population Trends and Policies*, 1979, Monitoring report, i, ST/ESA/SER.A/70, (New York: UN).

—— (1981), 'World Population Prospects as Assessed in 1980', *Population Studies*, 78, ST/ESA/SER.A/78 (New York: UN).

—— (1982a) 'Infant Mortality: World Estimates and Projections 1950–2025', *Population Bulletin*, 14.

—— (1982b) *Levels and Trends of Mortality since 1950*, ST/ESA/SER.A/74 (New York: UN).

VALLIN, J. (1968), 'La Mortalité dans les pays du Tiers-Monde: évolution et perspectives', *Population*, 4: 845–68.

WILLCOX, W. F. (1940), *Studies in American Demography* (Ithaca, NY: Cornell University Press).

World Bank (1981), *World Bank Atlas: Population Per Capita Product and Growth Rates* (Washington, DC: World Bank).

WRIGLEY, E. A., and SCHOFIELD, R. S. (1981), *The Population History of England 1541–1871: A Reconstruction* (London: Arnold).

4 The Fertility Decline

In the eighteenth century France experienced its great political revolution, which erupted in 1789: but one should also speak of a demographic revolution. The political revolution was marked by sensational events, like the storming of the Bastille or the abolition of privileges; within a few years it reversed or supplanted many things. There was nothing sensational to mark the beginning of the other revolution. Its progress was inconspicuous and relatively slow. None the less, it still fully qualifies as a revolution, since where there is a change of regime there is a revolution—and this applies to the demographic field as much as to others. Abruptness of change is not a prerequisite. Indeed, speaking of a demographic revolution in which limited procreation replaced unlimited, there is every reason to adhere to this definition without adding anything further.

(A. Landry, *Traité de démographie*)

FERTILITY, whilst much more the object of research than mortality, has rarely been analysed in its interrelations, over the long term, with the other elements of the demographic system. The aim of this chapter is to contribute to the construction of as solid as possible a statistical basis for this kind of approach.

In the last 30 years, the unprecedented demographic growth in less developed countries, on a scale altogether unexpected, has stimulated the multiplication of surveys and the great improvement of demographic knowledge, particularly of fertility. The World Fertility Survey (WFS) stands as both the outcome and symbol of this interaction between changing demographic reality and our knowledge of it.

Established in 1972, the WFS represented a major undertaking in over 60 countries, including 40 in the developing world. The information resulting from its surveys provides the basis for the criteria of selection used in the present study: the inclusion or exclusion of countries in which fertility has more or less begun its historic transformation. For example, amongst those included are Indonesia, Thailand, the Philippines, and Colombia, countries in which current fertility is manifestly lower than it was in the past. Calculated on the basis of the average number of married women at the end of their reproductive life (45–49 years), these countries register a decline of the order of 21% to 42%.[1] With the notable exception of India and China, almost all

---

[1] The difference between these two figures, however, exaggerates somewhat the actual decline in fertility, since the second refers exclusively to married women, whilst the former includes all women, whether married or not.

countries included in the present study having more than 5 million inhabitants are also in the WFS, which implies that the list of countries involved in that operation has been fairly selective.[2]

Setting aside those cases where change is already profound and where the turning-point was reached some time ago (i.e. in the 1960s), there remain a number of countries such as Pakistan, Bangladesh, and Peru which have shown signs of transition (Kendall 1980). When other sources, such as censuses and national surveys, are considered, it is also possible that some countries not involved in the WFS project, like Algeria, Vietnam, and Mongolia, are experiencing similar changes. In short, our selection can only broaden in time to include, at a more or less distant date, the entire world. What we aim to show here is precisely the present state of affairs, in light of data available in 1982. The degree of uncertainty inherent in any interpretation of contemporary trends cannot be concealed, given both the tenuousness of existing data and the hesitant nature of apparent breaks in traditional equilibrium. But this information is in itself already valuable: the order and conditions of entry into the Malthusian transition are capable of throwing a singular light on the mechanisms and possible causes of the developments recorded.

The principal object of this chapter, therefore, will be to situate contemporary changes within a historical perspective which reconstructs as accurately as possible a picture of the secular patterns preceding them. The chapter will follow the same basic structure as the last, with the exception that emphasis is laid exclusively on presenting the data. Interpretation will be reserved for Chapters 11 and 12. The following breakdown has been adopted:

1. The data: sources and quality, indices used.
2. Overview of the current situation.
3. The pre-transitional situation.
4. The stages of the decline.
5. The emergence of the Malthusian transition.
6. Comparative rates of development.

1. The Data

Sources and Quality

The sources and quality of fertility data are of much the same character as for mortality, so that the general observations made in the preceding chapter need not be reiterated.

---

[2] As in our selection, the countries in Africa, the Middle East, and Indo-China are scarcely represented, or are absent, in WFS.

Developed Countries

Registration of births is more or less complete in the developed countries, the only exceptions to this near-100% coverage being Greece, certain regions of the Soviet Union, and possibly Yugoslavia. The passage to complete coverage is a long process, those countries without written traditions or an administrative heritage naturally lagging further and further behind. Geographical coverage becomes more and more restricted the further one goes back in history, the scarcity of archives adding to the problem. It is only possible to reconstruct population trends satisfactorily from civil registers and parish records in a few rare cases in northern and western Europe, such as Scandinavia, England, France, and Czechoslovakia. As a rule, not all births were declared or entered when the civil registers were first established. This was compounded by inevitable ambiguities in contemporary definitions of live birth; recent developments in observation techniques used to monitor parturition tend to modify the traditional criteria—cry, respiration—for defining life.

The number of 'live' births, therefore, cannot be compared precisely even between advanced countries, and it appears that there is an even greater likelihood of inaccurate figures for neonatal mortality. Whilst civil registration in France, for example, dates from a very early period (the 1539 edict of Villers-Cotteret), its coverage was still not complete at the mid-nineteenth century; the rate of omission for 1851 has been estimated at 0.5% (Henry and Blayo 1975), and the question of false still-births[3] has been the subject of long-standing confusion in attempts to establish homogeneous time series. In England, the vital registry was set up in 1838, but registration continued to be defective at least until around 1880. Spain's time series began in 1858, but by the turn of the century registration was still only 96% complete.

In many cases, efficient civil registration with complete geographical coverage had to await the establishment of stable political structures (realization of national unity, centralized administration). Thus, series for the German Empire date from 1817, but only by the mid-nineteenth century did omissions become scarce, reaching a point considered negligible by 1880. Italy occupies a similar situation, since registration begins in 1862; nevertheless, as with England,[4] the rate of omission was still around 4% after 30 years. Such figures are negligible compared with those of less developed countries. The quality of data in contemporary Western countries may thus be considered to have reached a high level quite rapidly.

The case is altogether different for southern Europe, particularly Greece, and especially east European states such as Bulgaria, Romania, and the USSR. Japan, the US, and Canada likewise differ. For the period 1932–38,

---

[3] That is, children born alive but dying before their registration (which was obligatory within 48 hours of birth).

[4] Underregistration in Ireland proved to be a greater and more enduring problem.

registration represented only 90.8% of births in Romania, and 95.3% of births in Yugoslavia (Notestein 1944). Underregistration in Greece was similar to Romania, and perhaps worse. Omissions in the immediate post-war period, although less common, still occurred in various east European countries, the case of the USSR being the most complex and backward on account of its relative isolation and heterogeneity. Continuous time series for the entire Soviet Union exist from only 1950 and, even today, discrepancies arise between the future implications of the last census results (1979) and current civil registration figures. Up to 1920, registration in Japan and Canada remained partial. Not until 1933 was national registration enforced in the US, and even then the deficit stood at 7.7% in 1940 (compared with Canada's 3% to 4% in 1941, and 2.1% in 1950[5]). These imperfections will, of course, be taken into account in the tables and commentary which follow.

Developing Countries

The lack of reliable time series for the majority of developing countries renders analysis of long-term trends impossible. Fertility levels are accessible only through censuses and sample surveys, and the figures are, even then, discontinuous and often contradictory. In 1963, complete registration statistics (i.e. covering at least 90% of births) existed in only 27 developing countries (UN 1965). It is necessary, therefore, to fall back on methods of indirect estimation, either by using stable or quasi-stable[6] population models, cal-culations based on the survivors of successive censuses,[7] or various methods (e.g. Brass techniques) applied to survey results. In virtue of such methods, we have had for 20 years now at least approximate figures for fertility trends in about 40 developing countries: 20 in Latin America, 17 in Asia, and 4 in Africa. These cover almost the entire range of our selection.

Before proceeding to the state of data for the developing countries which principally concern us, let us take a swift look, in Table 4.1, at the state of registration, by continent. In Asia, and Africa in particular, only a very small percentage of births were registered around 1960.[8] Latin America's position lies midway between the performance of these continents and the developed world.

[5] Less than 1% in 1960, underregistration has since slowly diminished, although illegal immigration will have retarded the process.

[6] A stable population presumes that mortality and fertility have not varied over time; in a quasi-stable population, mortality has begun to decline whilst fertility levels remain constant.

[7] Thus, it is current practice to take the number of children aged 5–9 years (more reliably represented in censuses than the under-5 age group), and apply to this number the inverse of a probability of survivorship (taken from the appropriate mortality table): from this one may calculate the number of births of which these children are the survivors.

[8] This is still the case.

TABLE 4.1. *Percentage of population covered by 'complete' registration statistics for births,* circa *1960, by continent*

Region	% of registered births
Developed countries	99
Africa	2
Asia	8
Latin America	40
TOTAL	36

Source: UN 1965: 14.

Africa

Registration in Africa is 'complete' only in peripheral and atypical countries. This applies to Mauritius, where complete series date to 1920, and also to a lesser degree to Réunion and Tunisia since the war, Algeria since the 1970s, and to the non-black minorities of South Africa over a varying period (white populations since the First World War, Asians since the Second World War, with coloured populations occupying an intermediary position). Even though registration in Egypt has been compulsory since 1912, there is only partial coverage of the country. The rate of omissions up to the 1960s has at least remained relatively low. In those areas benefiting from health departments (45% of the total population), the fertility rate in 1960 rose to 46.6 per 1000; the application of the inverse of the probability of survival to the size of the 5 to 9 age group at the 1960 census gives a rate of 45 per 1000 for the period 1950–55, which fits the pattern quite well. For the period 1925–40, Abdel-Aty has estimated (1965) that failure to register comprised only 4% for the whole country, but he relies on the assumption that registration is complete in those areas with health departments. Basing his calculations on the stability of age distributions from successive censuses, El-Badry (1955), on the other hand, infers a higher level of underregistration, yet not exceeding 11% between 1911 and 1946. At the outset of the 1960s, underregistration was estimated at 7% (UN 1977).

The population of South Africa, at 30.5 million in 1982, including Transkei, Bophuthatswana, and Venda, may be broken down as follows (in percentages):

Blacks	72.1
Whites	15.7
Coloureds	9.2
Asians	3.0
TOTAL	100.0

Data for the white population have been 'complete' since at least 1920; for the coloured population since 1960 (the series began in 1937). But for the Asian population, composed mostly of descendants of Indian immigrants who arrived at the end of the nineteenth century, underregistration was high at the outset (26% for 1946–51), although this has probably lessened considerably since. Data for the Bantu majority, however, are notoriously incomplete, and the figures put forward are based on indirect estimation.

Civil registration data for Tunisia may be regarded as reliable since 1966, the rate of omission in 1970 being of the order of 2% to 4%, at most.

The African situation may thus be summarized, once again, as follows: with the exception of Algeria, where trends are insufficiently known, the populations in which couples have begun to practise birth control are precisely those for which relatively reliable data are available. The proportion of Africa's population covered by complete systems of registration stands at only 17% in 1980.[9]

Asia

Good registration is also the exception in Asia. Only seven countries offer complete statistics, two of which are European in culture (Israel and Cyprus). In the remaining five, all influenced by Sino-Japanese culture, the usual criteria hold: they are either already highly developed (Japan) or semi-developed (Singapore, Taiwan, Hong Kong, and Malaysia). Sri Lanka's position is close to this small group, registration being adequate at 88% since 1953. The data for all remaining areas, even where there are registration systems of long standing (India, Thailand, the Philippines), are too uncertain to allow realistic reconstruction of fertility levels and trends. Registration in many countries such as Indonesia, Pakistan, Bangladesh, Korea, and Turkey—to cite only the most populous—is extremely deficient, and age data obtained from successive censuses are rendered poor and suspect by the heavy omission of young children, especially female, and the uncertainty which surrounds statements of age. This accounts for the inaccurate and questionable character of past estimates; the increase in surveys over the period 1960 to 1970 has led to the improved convergence of more recent ones.

Finally, mainland China, even though its national system of civil registration was set up at the time of the 1953 census, has experienced too troubled a recent history for this system to function smoothly. Even before the first troubles in 1957, data were fairly inadequate; despite the return of internal order for 15 years, it appears that the system has been unable to reach maturity, as implied by the absence of publications other than those based on the census and post-census survey of 1982. Uncertainty with regard to age

[9] Including Egypt; if we discount the latter, the figure would be 8%.

structures has long rendered the calculation of fertility rates problematical; even the 1953 census gave rise to too many irregularities to serve as a basis for estimates. The other Asian giant, India, has an older system of civil registration, covering the majority of states (varying geographically in different periods), but which is particularly weak in its coverage of vital events. Nevertheless, demographic surveys and, especially, the establishment of a tradition of regular censuses have guaranteed a fairly sound knowledge of population trends.

For the small number of countries with reliable data, the knowledge of trends goes back several decades, but the quality of registration deteriorates as one recedes further back in time. Underestimation is frequent for Japan and Sri Lanka, for example, in series pre-dating 1920, and in those before 1930 for Singapore, Malaysia, and Cyprus. On the other hand, in the case of Hong Kong, where the series dates from 1938, doubt attaches more to the denominator than to the numerator, estimates of the population before 1960 being regarded as inaccurate. By contrast, Taiwan appears to have reliable data very early (1910). Only the immediate post-war period, with the departure of Japanese administration (1944), seems to have marked a phase of uncertainty, albeit very brief. Similarly, with regard to Israel, registration has been obligatory in Palestine since 1920 and became efficient extremely swiftly, at least for the Jewish population; fertility trends are, moreover, fairly closely connected with those of Western populations. Lebanon, which at a cultural level is influenced equally by East and West, has a defective registration system, and even the size of the population has been uncertain for around 50 years.

Latin America

In Latin America, where migration has made European influence fairly strong, if variable from one country to another, 15 states have 'complete' statistics, of which 10 are included in our selection: Mexico, Costa Rica, Jamaica, Panama, Puerto Rico, Trinidad and Tobago, Venezuela, British Guiana, Argentina, and Chile. Three other countries have more or less defective registration: in Colombia, underregistration for the period 1951–64 was estimated at 20% at least; for Cuba, 1943–62, the figure was about half this, and since then has progressively diminished towards completeness; whilst civil registration in Brazil is practically non-existent. With the exception of Cuba, extant data thus represent relatively fragile indirect estimates derived from censuses or surveys.

The era of 'complete' registration, that is, of coverage equal to or greater than 90%, varies according to country. It begins at the end of the nineteenth or the start of the twentieth century for Cuba. Argentina's coverage is considered to have scarcely varied over time, remaining at a level close to that of 1960 (97%). For the period 1910–17, Chile's coverage has been calculated at 85%, and improvement seems to have been slow. In Uruguay, where series date from 1885, good data appear to have been achieved very early, but the absence of any census between 1908 and 1963 leaves the first half of the century rather in the dark; nevertheless, coverage for the period 1950–60, assessed at 90–95%, would imply that the quality has been maintained. Puerto Rico, within the registration area of the US since 1943, has experienced since 1950 a drop in its rate of omission to 4%; whilst, a little earlier, around 1940, birth registration figures in Cuba represented only about two-thirds of actual births. This rate is comparable to that of Mexico around 1930, and carries implications for recorded levels of reproduction: birth-rates recorded since the beginning of the century were below 30 per 1000, before rising abruptly to around 45 per 1000; yet analysis of age pyramids at successive censuses shows that the real level of birth-rates for the period 1900–30 was above 40 per 1000. Finally, Venezuela, like Cuba, only achieved satisfactory registration around mid-century, the percentage of registered births being 88% in 1940–44.

In sum, the population of Latin American countries having complete registration around 1980 represents approximately 60% of that of the whole continent (UN 1982).

Indices Used

In most cases, and particularly when comparisons between distant periods are involved, crude birth-rates will be used. This rate in fact reflects relative levels of fertility quite accurately: the proportion of women in the reproductive period, as a general rule, varies little, since the ageing of populations accompanying demographic transition affects, above all, those age groups at the two extremes, so that the age pyramid tends to pivot on its centre. A discrepancy between the crude birth-rate and total fertility rate, when it occurs, may be related to three factors: an important variation in the size of the fertile age group (15–44 years); a significant alteration of structures within this group; or an irregularity in the ratio of males, connected usually with migration or war losses. This last factor has often played a major role in certain developed countries in the post-war period, as, for instance, in the Soviet Union, East Germany, and Portugal. For this reason we shall complete our examination of fertility by considering contemporary trends, the breakdown of births according to age of the mother existing in most cases for at least the last 50 years.

Various retrospective reconstructions having been conducted by different authors in respect of certain questions arising from the analysis of census data, the time sequences do in fact cover the greater part of the period of the reproductive transition. Attention will be directed primarily to total fertility rates (TFR), that is, the sum of age-specific rates in a given year. However, for certain countries, gross and net reproduction rates will also be taken into consideration, the gross rate (GRR) being the average number of daughters born to each woman given the fertility level of a particular period, not taking into account mortality; the net rate (NRR) includes mortality, and represents the ratio between two successive generations.[10] These reproductive rates refer to periods or birth cohorts, depending on the case. In the absence of immigration and mortality decrease beyond the average age of parenthood, maintenance of net reproduction rates below unity tends, in the long run, to lead to population decline. One should not misinterpret the real significance of this measure, therefore: depending on the initial age composition of a population and the parameters of its development, sustained growth or decline are both possible with a net reproduction rate equal to unity.

2. The Current Situation

A crude birth-rate of 30 per 1000 (or a replacement rate of 2) is the level by which less developed countries are generally distinguished from developed ones: fertility control, above this level, is practised only by a very small minority of the population, at all events in countries with late and selective nuptiality. Conversely, a birth-rate below 20 per 1000 indicates that birth control is fairly widely practised throughout a society. Those countries in which fertility is in full transition are situated between these two limits. To begin with, the countries in this study may be divided very simply into three large groups: 30 per 1000 and over, 20 to 30 per 1000, and less than 20 per 1000. Fig. 4.1 shows their corresponding positions at the end of the 1970s.

From the evidence, the figure 30 per 1000 is out of date: many so-called 'developing countries' have rates below, and sometimes well below, this level. This is the case in almost 20 countries with populations above 500,000; all of these, by definition, belong to our selection. This phenomenon may be rationalized by various hypotheses, the most obvious, if not mutually exclusive, being as follows: (1) the countries in question are, for diverse reasons, such as size or ethnic composition, atypical with regard to the relation between demographic and socio-economic development; (2) these countries, at least the most advanced amongst them, no longer fit the vague 'less developed' label still habitually applied to them.

Geographically, the distortion replicates almost exactly the pattern of three large regions, previously observed with regard to mortality:

1. The Pacific rim of east Asia, within the Sino-Japanese sphere of influence: Singapore (17 per 1000 in 1975–80), Hong Kong (18.6), Taiwan (24), South Korea (25), and mainland China (21);[11]

---

[10] That is, the concept of 'generation' in its current usage of mothers/daughters.

[11] This figure is based on the UN estimate of 21.3 per 1000 in 1975–80; if it seems improbable that China's birth-rate should be lower than Taiwan's, a country in many ways much more advanced, we must bear in mind the pressure exerted on family planning by the government at the local level, i.e. the fixing of quotas.

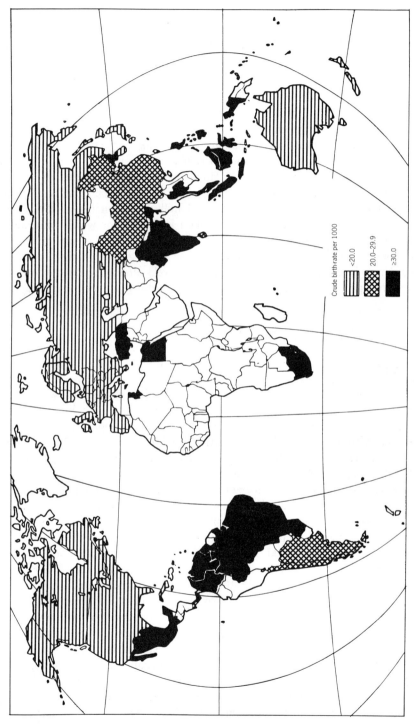

FIG. 4.1. Crude birth-rates for countries with advanced transition, 1975–1980

Crude birth-rate per 1000

<20.0

20.0–29.9

≥30.0

2. The Caribbean, within the traditional sphere of American influence: Puerto Rico (22), Trinidad and Tobago (22), Jamaica (28), and Cuba (17);
3. Temperate South America, characterized by populations of south European origin: Argentina (21), Uruguay (20), and Chile (25).

Situated outside these geographical categories are the already familiar cases of countries which are small, insular, or maritime, and with mixed populations: Mauritius and Réunion (27 and 24, respectively), Costa Rica (29), Cyprus (20), Israel (27), and Sri Lanka (28).

These countries are now in a situation comparable to that of eastern Europe around 1950 or western Europe on the eve of the First World War. With the exception of South Korea (40 million inhabitants in 1983) and, of course, mainland China (1,020 million in 1983), for which estimates—variously of American, Chinese, and French provenance—are fairly well established and relatively convergent, the demographic weight of these countries is comparatively weak. But the levels already reached show that despite a preponderance of fertile age groups, fertility can decline very rapidly.

3. The Pre-transitional Situation

High Fertility

Before the era of voluntary control, the fertility of couples was largely governed by physiological factors inherent or 'natural' to the human condition. Hence the interest in a knowledge of the theoretical upper limits of human fertility. From the time of the Industrial Revolution, there would have been a slight change in these limits, along with improvements in nutrition, sanitation, health, and living conditions. The age span of the reproductive period tended to widen due to the earlier onset of menarchy (Biraben 1982), the (apparently) delayed onset of menopause, and, above all, the likely increase in fecundability (the probability of conception per menstrual cycle). Nevertheless, since the inter-war period, there have been numerous observations on the frequency of sterile couples (Kuczynski 1938a), and on the theoretical upper limits of fertility. According to data gathered by Kuczynski (1936), the birth-rate has certainly never exceeded 65 per 1000; the highest known rates—just over 60 per 1000—belong to certain provinces of pre-revolutionary Russia. Although the age-specific structure in the United States was extremely favourable owing to immigration, and nuptiality was precocious and more or less universal, the rate in 1800 was about 55 per 1000. Differences from the historical maximum (doubtless itself lower than the theoretical maximum, given demographic structures) reflect, in addition to various checks imposed by custom (duration of breast-feeding, periods of sexual abstinence, etc.), circumstances of age composition, and, above all, nuptiality. The average age of marriage is especially important, given that fecundability increases up to 20 years, appears to level out between 20 and 30, and subsequently declines with age (Henry 1957; Leridon 1973) as a result, perhaps most notably, of reduced frequency of sexual intercourse.

Owing to certain retrospective surveys, and family reconstitutions based on the analysis of parish registers, we now have at our disposal reliable information on three cases of very high fertility: that of the Cocos-Keeling Islands (Smith 1960), the classic case of the Hutterites[12] (Tietze 1957), and the legendary first Quebecois colonies (Henripin 1968). In the Cocos-Keeling islands, for example, women married at the age of 14–15 and bore an average of 10.82 children; the figure fell to 6.6, a more normal order of magnitude for traditional populations, when the age of marriage rose to 20–21 years. Hutterite nuptiality was less precocious, but the standards of living were probably better: women married at 20 during the period 1921–30 had a completed fertility of 10.9 children. Hutterite fertility has since frequently been referred to in analyses of age-specific marital fertility, particularly in research at Princeton over the last 20 years. It is used to define an empirical upper limit to reproduction in a quasi-natural sense, which is to say, fertility not influenced negatively by culture (culture, in turn, being defined merely as social norms and individual behaviour). In practice, this usage retains the idea of maximum 'natural' fertility, in the sense of Henry, that is, fertility where no deliberate birth controls are imposed. Defined in this way, so-called 'natural' fertility is a purely *empirical* concept, which, far from referring to maximum biological capacity to procreate, represents merely the absence of voluntary and conscious birth control on the part of married *couples*. Social custom, on the other hand, retains the power to impose a limiting influence—in particular, religious prescriptions concerning abstinence. Given the variability of sexual mores, the meaning of the concept of 'natural fertility' must, by definition, vary noticeably from one society to another.[13]

Major Differences

Birth-rates in less developed countries before the reproductive transition were almost invariably higher than European birth-rates before marital fertility began to decline. Whilst pre-transitional levels in Europe were generally around 30 to 45 per 1000, in Africa levels have been almost 50 per 1000, in Latin America they ranged from 40 to 45 per 1000, and in Asia they stood at around an average of 40 per 1000.

Such differences result largely from the system of nuptiality or, more

---

[12] A religious sect of North Dakota.

[13] Though father of the phrase 'natural fertility', Louis Henry himself recognized the unsatisfactory character of the epithet 'natural', which has paradoxically ended up being applied in a narrowly cultural sense.

precisely, from the average age at which sexual relations commence.[14] Generally speaking, it remains the case (although significant changes are beginning in a number of countries) that a model of early and universal marriage characterizes less developed countries, whilst in many parts of historical Europe, an inverse pattern of late and selective nuptiality prevailed.[15] This model of nuptiality appears to have constituted an important historical exception, temporally and spatially restricted to a fairly limited area.

This first line of distinction between the developed and less developed world is a manifest over-simplification: even within the orders of magnitude cited above there exists great variation. Not only does the concept of marriage differ from one civilization to another, but our degree of knowledge concerning matrimonial practice from continent to continent is very uneven. Even if the average age of women in Africa at first marriage is known to be very early, because we do not know the actual figure, the continent remains, statistically, largely *terra incognita*. In Latin America, consensual union often takes the place of marriage. According to available data from different countries (Colombia, Costa Rica, Mexico, Panama, Peru, the Dominican Republic, etc.), singulate mean age at marriage has varied little, and stands around 18 to 20 years. It is, however, rising, and occurs much later in the southern tip of the continent. In Asia (excluding East Asia), the pattern of early marriage seems largely predominant, especially in the Indian subcontinent, with average ages at first marriage still close to 17–19 years around 1970.

Beyond this apparent diversity, however, in all cases in the less developed world, lifelong celibacy or its equivalent is very rare. It is probably this characteristic which most clearly distinguishes early modern Europe from the other continents. Many indices imply that a number of societies outside Europe, particularly in Asia (Japan, Korea, and Sri Lanka) have for some time been practising less precocious forms of marriage, yet which cannot be called delayed, and which we will therefore, for the sake of convenience, call 'semi-delayed'.[16]

As a rough guide-line, Europe itself can be divided into two distinct areas, separated by an imaginary line running from Trieste to Leningrad (Hajnal 1965). West of this line, at the time of the Renaissance, and in some cases even earlier, a system of demographic controls via nuptiality (Chaunu 1974) were established, and maintained up to the end of the nineteenth century (the period in which the decline in marital fertility takes over). The east, in

---

[14] In countries with a tradition of pre-pubertal marriage (India and Bangladesh, for example), the distinction between marriage (the rite) and sexual union (cohabitation) is important, since the shared life of spouses is often considerably delayed.

[15] With a high proportion of life-long celibacy.

[16] At an average of around 20 years, which is to say, midway between the 'early' model (around 15 years) and the 'late' (around 25).

contrast, was spared such restrictions. The proportions of lifelong celibacy,[17] around 1900, also differed markedly: 10% to 20% of single women in the west, instead of less than 5% in the east. As marriage occurred at a significantly later age in the west, around 1900 it was still the case that approximately three-quarters of women aged 20–24 years were single, whilst no more than about a quarter were still unmarried in the east. This phenomenon would explain the very high fertility and rapid demographic growth of countries like Russia, Serbia, and Bosnia.

Together with the proportion single at each age, there appears to be a fairly large variation in age at marriage from one country to another. For want of early and good censuses in the various east European countries, there remains insufficient information to ascertain precisely[18] an average age at marriage. If the average age for women in the west seems to have been on the whole above 24–25 years (more around 26–27 years), in the east it stood at an average of around 20–21 years, although certain indications from the better censuses (e.g. Romania, in 1912) suggest a later age of 22 in certain cases: a pattern corresponding, in other words, to the 'semi-delayed' marriage. The existence of such differences within the most fecund age groups has weighty implications for natality. Let us now examine the state of fertility in the different regions immediately prior to the reproductive transition.

Pre-transition Levels

Despite the correcting influence of mortality,[19] differences in fertility connected for the most part with variations in nuptiality have significant implications for levels of net reproduction. At the close of the nineteenth century,[20] eastern Europe had net reproduction rates at around 2, whilst in northern, western, and central Europe the rates were around 1.5 (Kuczynski 1936). Net reproduction in less developed countries, considered as a whole, and given both average rates of natural increase and prevailing mortality levels in the second quarter of the twentieth century, seem to have been closer[21] to the figures encountered in Western than in east European countries.

Northern Europe and Overseas English-Speaking Countries

These countries have been grouped together owing to the cultural similarity of their populations at the point at which fertility decline became apparent

[17] Amongst the 45–49 age group.
[18] Statements of age have long been held in doubt, and the reliability of statements of marital status remains unknown.
[19] There exists a strong positive correlation between fertility and mortality.
[20] At this time, the decline in fertility was still scarcely perceptible in the Western countries, and east–west comparisons remain valid.
[21] Or indeed noticeably lower, especially in China.

in Western countries, around 1870–75. Fertility levels for the preceding period are extremely variable: they range from 30–31 per 1000 in Norway, Denmark, and Sweden (1800–70), to 45–46 per 1000 in Canada (1846–76), through 36 per 1000 in Finland (1800–70), 37 per 1000[22] in England (1840–70), and around 40 per 1000 for the remaining English-speaking overseas countries (US, Australia, New Zealand, 1800–75). Canada's situation is explained not so much by its age-specific structure, which was not at the time favourable (owing to the high net emigration of women to the US), but by exceptionally high marital fertility—bordering on that of the Hutterites. Conversely, the low comparative fertility of countries like Ireland, Norway, Sweden, and Denmark relates not to the commencement of birth limitation within marriage, but to the application of the west European model of nuptiality:[23] marital fertility rates remain constant at least back to the 1870s (Festy 1979). Only the white population of the United States (and, more precisely, New England) had begun to limit their births before the last quarter of the nineteenth century.

Western and Central Europe

With the exception, on the one hand, of central Europe (the German Empire, Austria, and Czech populations), where rates were relatively high (approximately 37–39 per 1000 in the third quarter of the nineteenth century), and of France, where fertility had declined since the Revolution[24] and stood at only 25 per 1000, rates in the remaining countries of continental western Europe were relatively low, converging on 30 to 32 per 1000 in Belgium, The Netherlands, and Switzerland. This pattern suggests that, except for France, there was still no voluntary limitation of births, and that the west European model of nuptiality only truly prevailed at this time in certain countries: its existence has been ascertained, for example, in Switzerland (Festy 1979), but it seems debatable for a number of German-speaking countries. Nevertheless, even where limitation of marriages was being practised, fertility appears to have varied little before 1870 (Fig. 4.2).

Southern and Eastern Europe

Fertility decline in southern and eastern Europe occured much later than in the west, becoming manifest only from the end of the nineteenth century. Its pre-transitional levels were also appreciably higher, except of course in central

---

[22] After adjustments made for underregistration.

[23] Confronted with a decline in mortality, which began earlier in these countries, increasingly strict control of nuptiality was exercised through a rise in life-long celibacy and in the age at marriage in successive generations.

[24] The birth-rate was on the order of 40 around 1750 (Henry and Blayo 1975). Nuptiality was early.

Europe and the English-speaking overseas countries. In the second half of the nineteenth century they approximated 40 per 1000 in Italy and Spain, nearly 45 per 1000 in Hungary, Poland, Bulgaria, Romania, and Yugoslavia,[25] and around 50 per 1000 in Russia. Here, once more, the east–west divide is manifest, highlighting the particular Russian pattern where fertility is much higher than the European average. Portugal is the exception, with a rate of only 33 to 34 per 1000: its model of nuptiality is curiously similar to that of Switzerland and the Scandinavian countries. Finally, Greece, with recorded rates of less than 30 per 1000 in 1860–90, appears to be a case of heavy underregistration: given its early and frequent nuptiality pattern, the actual level is likely to be around 45 per 1000; we shall return to this.

Latin America

The period of reference varies, depending on the country. Wherever possible, data have been assembled to cover several decades, especially as, immediately preceding the onset of fertility decline, there was often a significant rise in the birth-rate more closely connected with the improvement of health conditions than with age structures or improved registration. The period covered is confined generally to the first decades of the twentieth century, with the exception of the southernmost countries. The development of fertility in Argentina and Chile stands intermediately between that of large countries whose populations are composed of immigrants (and hence reflect the effects of age structures) and those composed of native peoples (reflecting traditional cultural practices). Owing to deficiencies in civil registration, the situation is often unclear; the exact rates are significantly higher than those recorded.

Various indirect estimates, particularly those calculated using projection backwards from census figures for the 5–9-year age group, give rates around 45 per 1000 (Brazil, 1904–40; Mexico, 1900–60; Colombia, 1928–46; Venezuela, 1926–56), and sometimes as much as 50 per 1000 where immigration was involved (Cuba, 1909–14; Chile, 1876–1905; Argentina, 1870–85). Pre-transitional levels were therefore, on average, about 5 per 1000 higher than those prevalent in Europe a half-century earlier,[26] but this contrast refers chiefly to western Europe (Fig. 4.3).

Asia

The countries of east and south Asia[27] included in our selection represent in themselves almost half the total world population (2.2 out of 4.6 billion

[25] Taking into account underregistration of births, it is perfectly possible, given the age pyramids for around 1900, that east European rates had been even higher.

[26] For what are, properly speaking, the Western countries, the average is 38 per 1000 (Festy 1979).

[27] Knowledge of Middle Eastern developments, for example, in Israel, Lebanon and Turkey, is incomplete, but it has been possible to establish a rate for Turkey at around 45 per 1000.

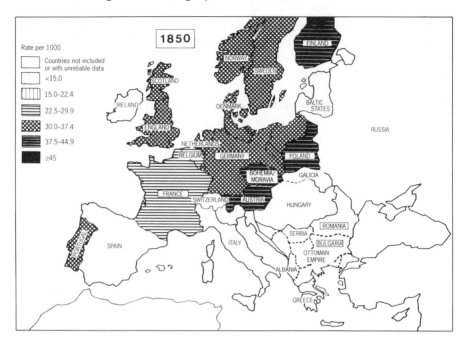

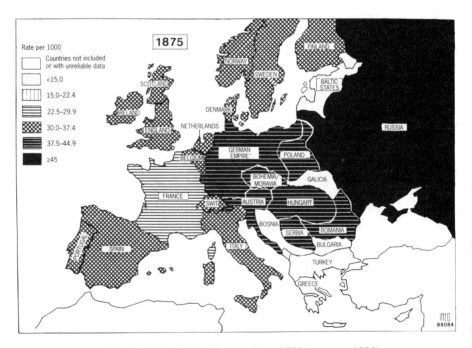

FIG. 4.2. Fertility in Europe since 1850 (rate per 1000)

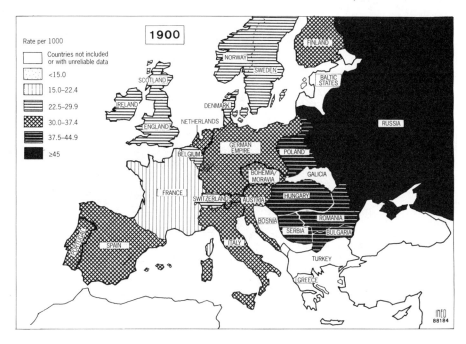

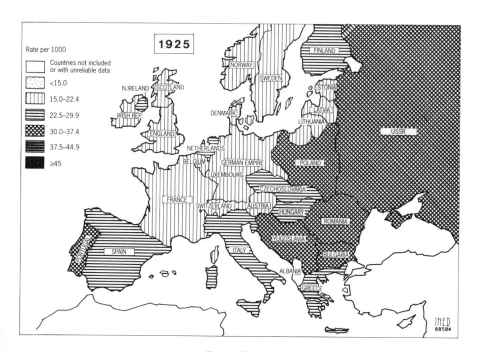

FIG. 4.2. (cont.)

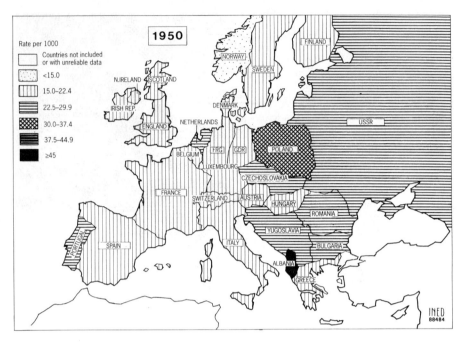

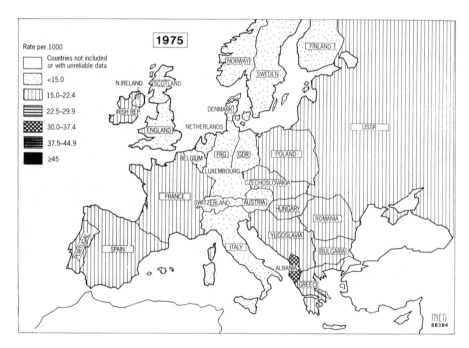

Fig. 4.2. (cont.)

TABLE 4.2. *Estimated birth-rates, selected Asian countries, in given periods* (per 1000)

Country	Period	Birth-rate
China	1929–47	37–40
India	1901–40	45–49
Indonesia	1950–60	46–47
Japan	1920–40	33–35
Philippines	1929–52	50–53
Thailand	1927–55	46–47
Korea	1920–50	42–44
Taiwan	1920–55	42–47
Sri Lanka	1921–52	36–39
Malaysia	1935–55	44–48
Hong Kong	1938–56	[30–36][a]
Singapore	1935–55	44–46

[a] This figure is approximate owing to uncertainty about Hong Kong's population during this period.

in 1983), but historical information for most of this considerable group is critically deficient. Estimates are subject to frequent retrospective revision on the basis of data arising from recent surveys or censuses. The period of reference corresponds to the second quarter of the twentieth century. Table 4.2 lists the most probable estimates for birth-rates (per 1000) and the periods to which they refer, in decreasing order of each country's population size. The quality of data sources varies greatly from one country to another. In China, for example, we have a survey conducted between 1929 and 1931 on rural households in different regions (covering approximately 200,000 people), and population censuses taken in 1942 and 1947 in certain provinces. However, the sex ratios reported and the variability of results between regions are such that it is difficult to decide orders of magnitude for the whole country. In India, on the other hand, one is dealing with intercensal estimates calculated by backward projection. In all the remaining cases, except for Japan, where civil registration has been complete since 1920, we are dealing with indirect estimates. A comparison of orders of magnitude reveals a fairly clear distinction between countries with very high birth-rate—above 40 per 1000, and more often closer to 45 per 1000—and countries with 'moderate' birth-rate—less than 40 per 1000—(China, Sri Lanka, Hong Kong, and Japan). This phenomenon could be bound up with various practices, such as female infanticide (China and Japan), prolonged breast-feeding (China), or 'semi-delayed' marriage (Japan and Sri Lanka). It is quite conceivable that such traditions of indirect fertility control facilitated the modern transition, as

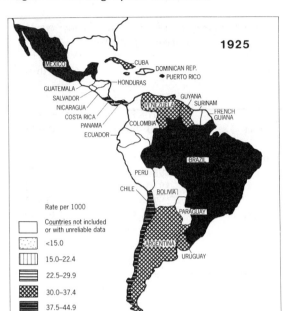

FIG. 4.3. Fertility in Latin America since 1925 (rate per 1000)

FIG. 4.3. (*cont.*)

the development of these countries is fairly atypical. Given the exceptional incidence of early marriage in India where, for example, in 1931 only 5% of women aged 20–24 were still single (and the percentage was the same for rural China in 1930, even though age at marriage was higher: 17.6 as opposed to 13 years), its fertility level appears comparatively low; this could be due, in addition to poor health conditions, to customs such as the prohibition of widow remarriage, prolonged breast-feeding, the isolation of mothers, and sexual abstinence during certain periods set by tradition (Fig. 4.4).

Africa

In all the countries studied, the traditional level of fertility seems to have been very high: around 45 per 1000 in Egypt during the first half of the century, and much the same in Tunisia during the 1950s and Réunion over the period 1946–60. But the order of magnitude is higher (up to 48 per 1000) for the Bantu majority and the coloured and Asian minorities of South Africa, around 1950. The island of Mauritius stands out as the one exception, with a rate below 40 per 1000 over the period 1900–30.

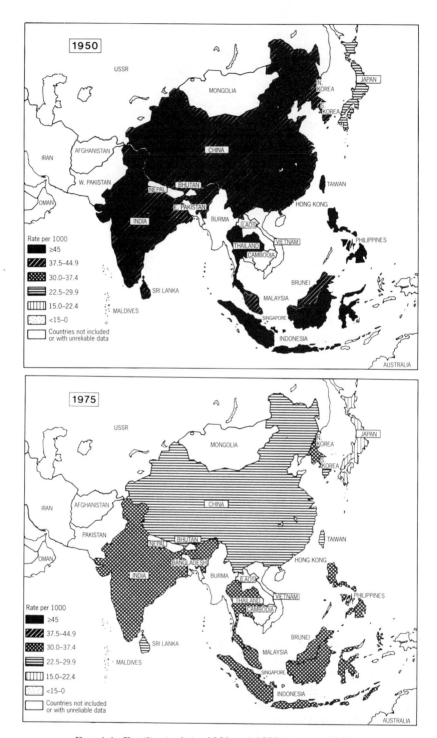

FIG. 4.4. Fertility in Asia, 1950 and 1975 (rate per 1000)

The very wide range of pre-transitional birth-rates (30 to 55 per 1000) emphasizes the diversity of traditional, or 'natural', fertility levels. For an apparently culturally unified group of countries such as Western societies, the average number of children per married woman aged 20–24 ranges from 6.61 to 9.15 (Festy 1979). This shows the extent to which, even in the absence of intentional birth limitation amongst couples, societies have managed to invent very diverse rules to avoid their excessive proliferation. Amongst these rules, the control of marriages seems to have been a decisive factor. Already described by Cantillon in 1755 and advocated (together with sexual abstinence) by Malthus in 1798, the moderating effect of nuptiality on the growth of a population has been determinant in a number of Western societies, particularly in northern Europe (Norway, Sweden, Denmark, and Ireland), a few rare cases in western (Switzerland and Belgium) and southern Europe (Portugal), and, to a lesser extent, in certain Asian countries (Sri Lanka, and especially, Japan). The comparison, following Henry's example, of strikingly different cases such as Algeria (the 1920–24 cohort) and Sweden (cohorts born around 1840), which shows a difference of almost 10 years in the average age at marriage (17.9 and 27.5, respectively) is sufficient to demonstrate the extent to which the marriage model can affect differences in marital fertility. In Algeria, the average number of children per couple, assuming there is no divorce, was 7.78, whilst in Sweden it was only 4.85. But we are dealing here with extreme situations, especially in the case of Sweden, for the 'West European model' of nuptiality, as we have seen from the data already presented, possesses neither the generality nor, especially, the frequency suggested by Hajnal's reading of 1965: its effects are in fact noticeable only in certain countries, mostly those with small populations.[28] These cases aside, the birth-rate in pre-industrial Europe was around 40 per 1000 in the west and 45 per 1000 in the east. In other words, the difference between 'developed' and 'less developed' countries before the transition is not, as generally assumed, of the order of 10 to 15 per 1000 (Noin 1983), but rather 5 per 1000, or indeed less.

4. The Stages of the Beginning of the Decline

We are interested at this stage in the first appearance—and not the spread—of a new pattern of behaviour, as manifested by crude birth-rates at the national level. It is clear that the decline in fertility assumes a completely different significance depending on whether prevailing levels are low (30 per 1000), moderate (40 per 1000), or high (50 per 1000), and according to the

---

[28] It would appear that the propensity toward celibacy is not the most common factor. Amongst those countries with delayed marriage, some—like Sweden—are even characterized by a high incidence of illegitimate births.

scale of change observed.[29] Attention will therefore be focused on the date of the apparent change in trends.

As in the case of mortality, the decline in fertility does not occur everywhere at the same time; the various starting-points are spread across a century, or even two centuries if we include some rare cases. For the most advanced countries, however, the beginning of fertility decline is easier to place than that of mortality; and it poses no problem either in less developed countries (excepting the latest arrivals amongst them, where civil registration is defective), owing to its recentness and the tremendous concentration of demographic research on the subject. In both cases, four stages may be distinguished, which, however, occur at different periods.

The Four Stages of Developed Countries

1. The first lasting declines in fertility—not followed by a sustained return to previous levels—date from the second half of the eighteenth century. Four areas are in the forefront of this movement: Finland (1750), France (1760), Czech populations (1785), and the United States (1800). The beginning dates of the decline are only indicative as, in all cases except France, the preceding pattern of development is insufficiently known. While the movement in the US reflects, for the most part, a change in age structures characteristic of countries receiving immigrants, the decline in marital fertility amongst the white population, particularly in New England (Coale and Zelnik 1963) should also be noted. Finland could be a case of very gradual recovery from the northern wars,[30] but the level recorded from 1840 to 1890 would imply that the real start of the modern contraceptive transition dates from the end of the nineteenth century. The case of Czech populations is fairly difficult to interpret, in as much as one observes a level nearly the same as in Finland: should the preceding decline be regarded as a long-term fluctuation or, conversely, as an indication of the beginning of transition? As in Finland, however, the pattern of sustained decline only gets going in the last quarter of the nineteenth century, so that in neither of these two countries can a real early decline in fertility be admitted.

2. A century later, around 1875–80, a whole group of countries become involved almost simultaneously in the decline. The first were the most advanced Scandinavian countries (Sweden and Norway), then northern (England and Wales, The Netherlands, Belgium, and Finland) and central Europe (Germany, Austria, Czech populations, and Switzerland), and the English-speaking population of Australia and New Zealand. The trend affected

[29] The decline in certain cases starts out very slowly (e.g. in Italy it begins around 1885, but only really gets going in the 1920s), and is even sometimes followed by a reversal (Egypt); the typical case is that of countries involving marked regional differences.

[30] The total female marriage rates for 1751–60 slightly exceeds unity (1.16) and this continues, although slackening, into the following decade (1.03 marriages per woman).

a smaller number of countries than did the decline in mortality, as it did not reach any of eastern or southern Europe. The decline continued uninterrupted throughout the last quarter of the nineteenth century.

If, in Spain and Ireland, the movement appears to have occurred still earlier (1865 and 1870–75, respectively), account must be taken of the extent of emigration to the Americas, which, by depriving these countries of a large portion of their young population, exercised for some time an indirect effect on reproduction.[31]

Situated further from the great centres of modernization and social change, Hungary, Italy, and Serbia were not affected until around 1885. Denmark's turn came a few years later, in this also lagging behind its neighbours, but the gap in relation to Norway and Sweden is less than shown for mortality.

3. At the periphery, declines began around 1900 in the north-east (Poland and European Russia) and south-west (Spain).

4. Finally, much later still, around 1920 or after, the decline gets going in the extremities of south-eastern Europe (Bulgaria, Greece, Romania, and Yugoslavia),[32] the south-west (Portugal, 1925), and Japan (1925).

Fertility decline in the majority of less advanced countries has generally been sudden and rapid; while this facilitates dating the break with previous levels, it opens up the problem of the indifferent accuracy of estimates, inevitably entailing reliance on period averages of varying lengths.

The Four Stages of Less Developed Countries

1. The first period is contemporaneous with that of southern Europe, and involves precisely those Latin American countries whose populations originated there. It affects, at the end of the nineteenth and beginning of the twentieth centuries, Argentina (1885) and Uruguay (1895), with Chile following around 1915–20 (estimates vary, depending on the author). The subsequent states seem, in comparison, very recent, all occurring in the last 30 years.

2. The middle to late 1950s. At the beginning of this period, or even earlier (Cyprus, 1950), the decline occurs only in small, densely populated societies which are geographically insular yet open to outside influence: the westernized African islands of Mauritius and Réunion; Asiatic islands with Chinese cultures (Taiwan, Singapore); and Sri Lanka. The People's Republic of China is still not affected at this stage.[33]

At the end of this period, the less developed countries which experience a

[31] Nevertheless, the quality of registration in such countries, especially Ireland, leaves much to be desired.

[32] Dating is somewhat approximate where Yugoslavia is concerned, owing to the lack of retrospective series before the First World War.

[33] Since the first birth control campaign in the mid-1950s, there have been periods such as the Great Leap Forward and the Cultural Revolution, during which declines have been interrupted, or even reversed (Lin Fu De 1981); up to the end of the 1960s, changes, whether proceeding via the delay of marriage or fertility regulation, essentially affected only the cities.

decline in fertility are also islands or are peninsular, or at least are fairly small maritime countries open to external influence: in Asia, once again, areas of Chinese cultural influence (Hong Kong, West Malaysia, South Korea); in Latin America, areas of American influence (Puerto Rico, Trinidad and Tobago, British Guiana, Cuba); in Europe, Albania; and in Oceania, Fiji.

3. The period 1960–70. The countries affected are larger in size and, although part of major continental land masses, are none the less all maritime.[34] They are as follows: in Latin America: Costa Rica, Panama, the Dominican Republic, Brazil, Colombia, and Venezuela; in Asia: India, Thailand, the Philippines, North Korea, and, at the end of the period, mainland China; in Africa: Egypt and Tunisia.

Thus, the 1960s see the decisive turning-point in which 3 of the 4 most populated countries of the developing world (China, India, and Brazil)— which, between them, represent more than half of the total population of countries in this group (55%)—are swept up in the contraceptive revolution. In China, urban fertility began to decline in the 1960s, and the severe governmental policy to regulate each individual's fertility was established in rural areas around 1970. There then followed a fall unprecedented, given the preceding average of 6 children per woman, to levels below 3 children per woman in rural areas, according to a sample survey in September 1982.

4. The 1970s. The period is clearly too recent for anything but a pro-visional assessment. Nevertheless, fundamental changes have appeared in two countries, Indonesia and Mexico. Two other potential cases suggest them-selves: first, very poor parts of Latin America like Paraguay, Peru, and El Salvador, where the process seems seriously intimated, even though fertility levels as estimated around 1980 did not yet meet criteria for inclusion in this study; and secondly, countries where signs of decline still require con-firmation. The latter countries are Vietnam, where traditional fertility levels seem to have been lower than in most other Asian countries; Nicaragua; and the principal Muslim countries of Morocco and Algeria in Africa, Iran and Kuwait in the Middle East, and finally, but most importantly, Pakistan, and to a lesser degree Bangladesh, in south Asia. The fertility levels for these countries remain, apparently, very high; but if declines are confirmed, we will most certainly be dealing with the major development of the 1970s in the history of fertility.

At the end of this historical overview, we shall limit ourselves to the obser-vation that the developing countries considered have all, to varying degrees,[35]

---

[34] Most of these countries already had, by around 1960, established government policies favouring fertility regulation, or at least had programmes funded or encouraged by private bodies. It would be difficult to disentangle the appearance of such policies from the particular contexts in which they arose; but, clearly, they were not the product of chance, either in time or place.

[35] Increasing interdependence is the rule in the present era, although the extent to which countries are ready to participate obviously varies.

been subject to foreign influence, be it Western, North American, or Sino-Japanese, and that most of them experienced the beginning of fertility decline at around the same period as that of the sudden renewed decline observed across the industrial world. The spatio-temporal picture of the decline suggests that some mechanism of diffusion is at play. The case of China again deserves special mention, since, according to published data, results exceed in success those of Japan for the period 1949–57. But it must be said that this is an exceptional case, in which the pressure of the authorities has played a central part (the notion of individual autonomy is not that of the Western world). The number and spacing of births are organized and planned locally, involving a highly complex system of penalties and bonuses. According to certain provisional indications, in 1984 the fertility level would have fallen to around or even below that of replacement.

Broadly speaking, outside certain enclaved mountainous countries (Afghanistan, Bolivia, and Nepal) and specific cases (Haiti, Burma, Laos, and Cambodia), the only remaining countries unaffected by the massive contemporary trend are in the Arab Middle East and Black Africa.[36]

The Adjustment of the Demographic System

Fertility decline is not an isolated phenomenon. In most countries, at least where careful study has been possible, it is accompanied by a transformation of the entire demographic system. As during the phase of demographic disequilibrium caused by mortality decline, everything proceeds as though a Malthusian reaction had set in, with multiple components, occurring simultaneously or out of phase. The case of Ireland immediately following the great famine of 1847–50 is a tragic illustration, but the phenomenon would appear to have a certain generality. Louis Henry's study of the Genevan bourgeoisie (1956) shows that life expectation increased by 15 years between the first half of the seventeenth and the second half of the eighteenth centuries. After this demographic expansion, there occurred almost simultaneously a large emigration of males, a tightening of marriage controls, and a regulation of fertility within marriage. It was as if the social difficulties resulting from increase in a densely populated and closed, or at least rigid, environment, and by extension the risks of declining social status associated with a more rapidly growing bourgeoisie, induced an adjustment of social behaviour.[37]

In the same way, in Europe, mass emigration occurred in those countries where there was an early decline in mortality. There would even appear to be a certain proportional relation, over the long term, between net reproduction and the propensity to emigrate: in those countries with the highest net

---

[36] The only known exception, on a national scale, being South African Bantu populations.

[37] This is the classic historical argument; Easterlin's thesis may be taken as a simplified modern variant.

reproduction rates amongst the generation born in the mid-nineteenth century (Norway, Germany, and Great Britain), emigration was also proportionately greatest; this relation obtained in precisely those generations where net reproduction reached a historical record. It was also at roughly the same time as this large wave of emigration that nuptiality, in many countries, became more delayed and less frequent. Sweden between 1750 and 1870 is a case in point; even more so Japan during the inter-war period. Japan was at that time actively colonizing Korea, Manchuria, and Taiwan; between 1920 and 1955, the proportion of women married at the age of 20–24 years fell by half, from 68.6 to 33.9 (Davis 1963). Similar patterns of development have been observed in a number of Western countries, notably in Scandinavia and Great Britain (Festy 1979).

To conclude, the sequence of stages for the Western world, for which our historical knowledge is greatest, may be broadly set out as follows: (1) up to the Renaissance: high mortality, high nuptiality, and high marital fertility, with an absence of migratory pressure; (2) from the Renaissance to 1870: the first tentative mortality declines, restricted marriage,[38] high marital fertility, and high migratory pressure; (3) from 1870 to 1935: decline in mortality, decline in fertility, strict control of marital fertility (at the end of the period replacement level is no longer guaranteed), and a corresponding reduction in migratory pressure; (4) 1935 to 1965: a slight but noticeable fall in juvenile mortality, increase in nuptiality and fertility,[39] and the reversal of migratory streams (net immigration); (5) since 1965: the reduction of infant and child mortality to very low levels, decline in nuptiality, decline in fertility,[40] and attempts to regulate net immigration.

Not all these stages are logically necessary. Demographic transition may, in effect, follow a course which is reduced to three, or even two, phases, proceeding directly from the first to the last. This tends to be the current pattern of most countries undergoing late transition.

5. The Unfolding of Fertility Decline

Trends in birth-rates reflect fairly accurately the development of fertility, although changes of age structure inherent in the demographic transition mean that a bias in one or other direction must be borne in mind: at first, the decline in birth-rates gives an exaggerated view of declining reproduction;

---

[38] This seems to have been pushed to an extreme in Bavaria: authorization to marry entailed very strict economic conditions, such as possession of deeds of ownership, or proof of regular income. Dating from 1616, the restrictions were not completely abolished until 1868 (Landry 1945).

[39] Where reproduction is concerned, this fourth phase may in fact amount to a historical accident, connected with the Great Depression and, especially, the war which followed. The fifth phase would therefore be partly an echo of the fourth.

[40] See n. 39, above.

subsequently, it understates it. In fact, mortality decline, which favours the youngest age groups, leads first to an expansion at the base of the population pyramid, and a relative narrowing amongst adults of child-bearing age;[41] the decline in fertility in the second phase leads to a contraction at the base of the pyramid and a corresponding expansion in adult age groups, while the proportion of elderly has not had time to increase.

The Transition to Controlled Fertility

Once more, taking the level of 30 per 1000 as a criterion of entry into the modern regime of controlled fertility, and dating the breakthrough point for each country, one gets an initial idea of the map of the maturation of fertility trends, and the time gap between various countries. In France, the level was reached in the 1830s; the first countries to follow suit, 50 years later, were two neighbours, Belgium and Switzerland (in the 1880s). Thereafter follow the countries listed in Table 4.3, and the corresponding Fig. 4.2 (as well as the sequence of figures in Chapter 8), in an order which gives a striking condensed view of the major stages of the transition. First, in the 1890s, come Nordic or English-speaking countries: Sweden, Denmark, Great Britain, Australia, and New Zealand. In the 1900s, Norway, The Netherlands, Germany, and the United States follow suit. Then, in the 1910s, come a number of countries which are either landlocked or bordering areas of decline: Austria, Hungary, Czechoslovakia, Finland, and Canada. These are followed, in the 1920s, by southern Europe (Italy, Spain, and Portugal); in the 1930s by eastern Europe (Poland, Bulgaria, and Romania); in the 1940s by Yugoslavia and the USSR; and in 1950 by Japan.

The less developed countries which have currently reached this stage are fewer in number, there being only about 20 of them. With the exception of countries with European populations (Uruguay, 1915; Argentina, 1930; Cyprus, 1949; Israel, 1954), the 30 per 1000 mark was not reached until the 1960s (see Tables 4.4 and 4.5 and Figs. 4.3 and 4.4) in Chile, Puerto Rico, Cuba, Trinidad and Tobago, Hong Kong, Singapore, Taiwan, and Mauritius; it was reached in the 1970s by Jamaica, Costa Rica, Panama, British Guiana, Fiji, Réunion, Sri Lanka, South Korea, the People's Republic of China, and, probably, Albania.

Let us now turn to the transition to 20 per 1000, which implies general control of fertility and introduces the post-transitional phase. Given its considerable start, France still comes in the lead, but the gap has closed considerably, since the major Western countries are now only 15 years behind: Sweden and Switzerland (1922), England and Wales (1923), Austria and Belgium (1924), Norway (1925), Germany (1926), Denmark and Scotland (1927). Landlocked and bordering countries come next, in the 1930s: Ireland

---

[41] Otherwise, the decline in morbidity among couples may increase their fertility.

TABLE 4.3. *Crude birth-rates, Europe, 1845–1980* (per 1000)

Country	Period					
	1850	1875	1900	1925	1950	1975
	1845–54	1871–80	1895–1904	1921–30	1948–52	1971–80
Albania	—	—	—	—	37.5	(31.0)
Austria[a]	37.5	39.0	36.5	19.8	15.9	12.5
Belgium	29.3	32.3	28.5	19.4	16.7	12.9
Bulgaria	—	—	40.8	36.0	23.4	15.9
Czechoslovakia[b]	40.0	39.8	35.2	25.2	22.8	18.3
Denmark	31.2	31.4	29.7	20.8	18.7	13.3
Finland	35.8	37.0	32.9	23.6	24.9	13.4
France	26.7	25.4	21.7	18.8	20.7	15.0
Germany[c]	35.6	39.1	35.5	20.3	16.2 (15.5)	10.2 (12.5)
Greece	—	(27.7)[d]	(25.7)[d]	—	(19.6)[e]	15.8
Hungary[f]	—	43.5	38.9	27.7	20.4	15.9
Ireland	—	30.2[g]	23.2	20.8[h]	21.6[i]	21.8[i]
Italy	—	36.9	33.5	28.1	19.6	14.2
Netherlands	33.0	36.2	32.0	24.5	23.3	13.8
Norway	31.5	31.0	29.6	20.1	19.3	14.2
Poland	—	—	—	33.5	30.1	18.6
Portugal	(33–34)	(33–34)	30.9[d]	32.0	25.2	18.9
Romania	—	(35.0)[d]	40.2	36.5	25.5	19.1
Spain	—	35.8[j]	34.8	29.2	21.1	18.1
Sweden	31.3	30.5	26.7	17.5	16.7	12.5
Switzerland	—	30.7	28.2	18.5	18.1	12.6
United Kingdom	36.8[g]	36.5[g]	29.1	18.7	16.4	13.3
USSR[k]	—	50.4	49.1	42.7[l]	26.7[m]	18.1
Yugoslavia[n]	—	40.5	40.1	34.6	29.0	17.8

Notes: for the Baltic States around 1930 (Estonia, Latvia, and Lithuania), see Kirk (1946: 264–69).

[a] Not including Venice and Lombardy, before the First World War.
[b] Czech populations only, before 1913.
[c] West Germany only, since the war; East Germany in parentheses.
[d] Underestimates; see text for corrected figures.
[e] 1949–52.
[f] Former Kingdom, not including Croatia and Slovenia, before the First World.
[g] After adjusting for underregistration of births (see Festy 1979).
[h] Ireland, incl. N. Ireland.
[i] The Irish Republic, not incl. N. Ireland.
[j] 1878–80. Underestimate: the actual rate was around 38–39 per 1000 (see Livi-Bacci 1968).
[k] European Russia, before 1928.
[l] 1923–27.
[m] 1950–52.
[n] Serbia only, before 1913.

Sources: See General Bibliography.

TABLE 4.4. *Crude birth-rates, North and South America, 1895–1980* (per 1000)

Country	Period			
	1900	1925	1950	1975
	1895–1904	1921–30	1948–52	1971–80
Argentina	44.4	34.0	26.0	21.4[b]
Brazil	43.0[a]	45.0	44.0	33.0
British Guiana	(32.0)	(32.0)	41.0	31.7[b]
Canada	30.5	25.3	27.3	15.7
Chile	47.0[c]	41.0	35.0	23.8
Colombia	—	—	48.0[d]	33.5[b]
Costa Rica	39.6	42.0	47.0	29.9
Cuba	—	37.0[e]	28.0	20.7
Dominican Republic	—	—	52.0	39.3[b]
Jamaica	39.5[f]	36.5	33.0	30.0
Mexico	47.0	45.0	45.0	38.5
Panama	—	38.0	36.0	31.6
Puerto Rico	44.0[a]	42.0	39.0	22.8
Trinidad and Tobago	(37.0)	(32.0)	38.0	25.0
United States	32.3[g]	24.3	24.6	15.5
Uruguay	33.0	25.2	22.7	20.7
Venezuela	45.0[h]	40.0[i]	42.0	37.2[b]

[a] 1900–05.
[b] 1970–80, based on UN (1981).
[c] 1901–05.
[d] 1950–55.
[e] Average of estimates for the years 1920 and 1930.
[f] 1891–1911.
[g] 1900.
[h] 1891.
[i] Average of estimates for the years 1920 and 1926.

(1930), Finland (1932), Czechoslovakia (1933), Hungary (1938). Two south European countries whose decline had been slow, Italy (1950) and Greece (1952), follow in the post-war years. Then, from the mid-1950s to the mid-1960s, come Japan (1955) and eastern Europe, where the process had gathered momentum: Bulgaria (1956), Romania (1960), Poland (1962), the USSR (1964), and Yugoslavia (1967). Finally, there are those areas where the baby boom and age structural factors had delayed the process: The Netherlands, the US, and Australia (1965), and Canada (1966). At the beginning of the 1970s, the Iberian countries, Spain (1970) and Portugal (1974), enter the post-transitional phase. At this point there are only four

TABLE 4.5. *Crude birth-rates, Asia, 1921–1980* (per 1000)

Country	Period		
	1925	1950	1975
	1921–30	1948–1952	1971–1980
China (mainland)	—	(40.0)	(25.4)[a]
Hong Kong	—	(30.0)	18.4
India	46.0	41.0	37.2[a]
Indonesia	—	(45–50)	36.5[a]
Japan	34.1	28.7	16.8
Korea	44.0	41	27.0 (34.1)[b]
Philippines	(50–55)	(50.0)	37.2[a]
Singapore	(31.0)	46.5	19.3
Sri Lanka	40.0	40.0	28.1[a]
Taiwan	43.0	47.0	24.1
Thailand	—	(45–50)	35.1[a]
West Malaysia	—	42.0	34.2[a]

Notes: Estimates involving some uncertainty are given in parentheses.

[a] 1970–80, see UN (1981).

[b] In parenthesis, North Korea 1970–80.

Sources: See General Bibliography.

cases in the developing world: Cyprus (1969), Hong Kong (1971), Singapore (1974), and Cuba (1976).

To the general but secondary deviations which we have noted in the duration and trend of fertility, and, by implication, the dynamics underlying the course of the transition, must be added specific biases associated with the individual history of each country, including international migration and war losses, which were particularly significant for European populations. In order to allow for the impact of irregularities in the age structures of populations, it is necessary to retrace the evolution of the main fertility indices over the long term, and to this end we have gathered available estimates for the period 1850–1980.

National Retrospective Data

The time series are given in Appendix 2, and represented in Figs. 4.5 to 4.10, according to the following groups:

1. Northern Europe: England, Ireland, Norway, Sweden, Finland, and Denmark;
2. Western Europe: West Germany, Austria, Belgium, France, The Netherlands, and Switzerland;

TABLE 4.6. *Gross (GRR) and net (NRR) reproduction rates for women born between 1826 and 1950, France*

Generation	GRR	NRR	Generation	GRR	NRR
1826–30	1.660	0.950	1891–1900	0.97	0.68
1831–40	1.660	0.955	1901–1910	1.06	0.79
1841–50	1.640	0.975	1911–1920	1.16	0.89
1851–60	1.540	0.920	1921–1930	1.26	1.07
1861–70	1.395	0.860	1931–1940	1.25	1.12
1871–80	1.270	0.810	1941–1945	(1.14)	(1.02)
1881–90	1.090	0.740	1946–1950	(1.02)	(0.94)

Sources: Generations, 1826–1900: Landry (1945: 332). The figures have, however, been revised to take into account the latest estimates for completed fertility (cf. Festy 1979). Generations of 1901–40: Festy (1979). Generations of 1941–50: estimates extrapolated from most recent available data, according to three parameters: completed fertility, average ages at parenthood, and the probability of survivorship at these ages (the NRR being equal to the product of the first by the third parameter, multiplied by the proportion of female births—0.488).

3. Southern Europe: Spain, Greece, Italy, Portugal, and Yugoslavia;
4. Eastern Europe: East Germany, Bulgaria, Hungary, Poland, Czechoslovakia, and Romania;
5. Overseas English-speaking countries: Australia, Canada, the US, and New Zealand; and
6. The USSR and Japan.

In most of these countries data on births according to mother's age became available fairly late: around 1870 for the Nordic countries, in 1892 for France, 1895 for Austria, and 1938 for Great Britain, for example. However, in a good number of cases, the inclusion of retrospective enquiries in censuses has made it possible to extend the series further back into the past and to reconstruct the situation from the period at which fertility began to decline.

In northern Europe, pre-transitional fertility levels appear to be relatively similar, averaging around 4.5 to 5 children per woman, and it is easy to identify the countries with delayed nuptiality—Sweden and Norway—by their position at the bottom of the range. The main part of the decline was achieved before the Second World War: thus, in the three socio-economically most advanced countries (England and Wales, Norway, and Sweden), fertility had fallen to around 1.7 by 1933–35. After the great upheaval which followed, all

TABLE 4.7. *Gross (GRR) and net (NRR) reproduction rates, England, France, Germany, Italy, and Sweden, 1826–1980*

Period	Germany[a]		England and Wales		France		Italy		Sweden	
	GRR	NRR	GRR	NRR	GRR	NRR	GRR	NRR	GRR	NRR
1806–1810	—	—	—	—	1.990	1.080	—	—	1.990	1.000
1811–1820	—	—	—	—	2.000	1.080	—	—	2.130	1.250
1821–1830	2.530	1.310	—	—	1.940	1.060	—	—	2.280	1.460
1831–1840	2.390	1.250	—	—	1.820	1.040	—	—	2.190	1.410
1841–1850	2.380	1.300	2.130	1.280	1.730	1.010	—	—	2.090	1.400
1851–1860	2.330	1.290	2.200	1.340	1.670	0.970	—	—	2.100	1.340
1861–1870	2.450	1.370	2.300	1.420	1.710	1.010	—	—	2.120	1.380
1871–1880	2.570	1.480	2.350	1.530	1.680	1.040	2.390	1.170	2.150	1.450
1881–1890	2.450	1.470	2.140	1.470	1.590	1.020	2.460	1.290	2.060	1.440
1891–1900	2.360	1.520	1.870	1.320	1.430	0.975	2.300	1.340	1.940	1.420
1901–1910	2.120	1.480	1.630	1.230	1.320	0.965	2.170	1.380	1.820	1.420
1921–1930	1.100	0.900	1.080	0.915	1.150	0.935	1.790	1.310	1.120	0.960
1931–1940	0.980	0.880	0.874	0.805	1.035	0.890	1.477	1.170	0.876	0.783
1941–1950	0.970	0.830	1.072	1.009	1.243	1.099	1.300	1.075	1.170	1.074
1951–1960	1.080	1.004	1.145	1.099	1.322	1.260	1.127	1.040	1.094	1.045
1961–1970	1.177	1.127	1.325	1.266	1.329	1.293	1.208	1.148	1.087	1.057
1971–1975	0.793	0.765	1.006	0.971	1.092	1.065	1.128	1.081	0.916	0.899
1976–1980	0.691	0.669	0.871	0.847	0.913	0.892	0.904	0.875	0.806	0.791

[a] FRG since 1931 (reconstruction for the years 1931–50): see Ch. 7.

Sources: Depoid (1941), up to 1930; various authors since.

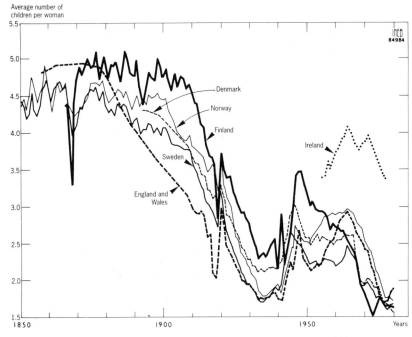

FIG. 4.5. Total fertility, northern Europe, 1850–1980

countries excepting Ireland, which remained outside the pattern, had arrived at a similar level by the end of the 1970s.[42]

In several west European countries (Belgium, The Netherlands, and Germany) there was a rise in fertility immediately preceding the decline,[43] which has been given various explanations, notably the beginning of the Industrial Revolution and the improvement of health conditions. Setting aside France, where the average number of children per woman was 3.5—a level which Germany would only reach in 1913—the situation in the third quarter of the nineteenth century enables us to distinguish clearly between countries with delayed marriage (Switzerland and Belgium) and the others (Germany and Austria). The indicator is only 4 in the former, as opposed to 5 or more in the latter. The Netherlands, before recent declines in the period 1965–77, had long maintained higher fertility than its neighbours. The position of France is exactly the reverse, as its fertility—traditionally lower—is now above its neighbours. Generations born since the period of the Revolution have

[42] However, signs of a decline in Irish fertility have existed for some time.
[43] The rising birth-rates of the German Empire do not appear to be a statistical artefact: although amplified by declines in infant and juvenile mortality, the rise is confirmed by comparative analysis of age distributions at the 1871 and 1880 censuses.

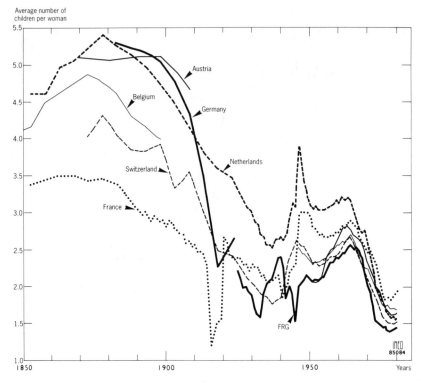

FIG. 4.6. Total fertility, western Europe, 1850–1980

ceased to ensure their own replacement (Table 4.6), with the exception only of the inter-war period—in other words, the extraordinary period of general euphoria following the First World War. If the population of France has not declined, it is because of immigration, the inertia of age structures, and, above all, the increase in life expectation. In this respect, it is important to note that net reproduction rates account for the survivorship of women up to the average age of child-bearing, and that life expectation at these ages greatly increased in successive generations.[44]

Germany experienced a very rapid change: in 33 years, its index fell by a factor of 3 (5.0 in 1900; 1.6 in 1933). Austria was similar (see our estimates for the 1930s in Chapter 7). Vienna and Berlin were the capitals of infertility: in 1936–37, Vienna recorded the historically unprecedented birth-rate of 5.4 per 1000, with net reproduction standing at 0.25; in Berlin, in 1933, the NRR was only 0.37. The average NRR for the entire inter-war period in Germany

[44] In order to assess this, in respect of demographic growth, we can calculate an NRR for the years lived, weighted according to the relation between the life expectation of girls and that of their mothers. Thus, for Swedish female generations, 1846–75, the NRR is 1.25 and the NRR for years lived is 1.45 (Festy 1979).

was lower than that of France (Table 4.7). This characteristic of German populations has re-emerged 40 years later, as, after a very rapid decline, fertility has settled at around 1.4 in West Germany, since the mid-1970s.

The series for southern Europe are incomplete up to the war; the movement belongs especially to the inter-war years, taking place slowly in Italy and Portugal, whilst in Spain it is interrupted during the period of Franco. In Yugoslavia, the movement does not get going until the 1930s, but picks up momentum very rapidly, reaching its height in the 1950s. Finally, where Greece is concerned, published data are so dubious that the pattern of development remains a matter of conjecture: for example, the reproduction rate of 2.1 recorded at the beginning of the 1960s fails to comply with both what is known of the country's level of development and the population pyramid for the 1971 census. The series of birth-rates since 1860 is consistently underestimated, and is scarcely compatible with the traditional regime of early and universal nuptiality; but it is difficult to correct owing to the poor quality of successive censuses. The size of age groups and sex ratios reported in the censuses taken in 1870, 1879, 1889, and 1907 do not comprise a sufficiently consistent sequence to serve as a basis for reconstructing the pre-transitional situation. Even the 1971 census is fraught with anomalies, as the sex ratio at 10 to 14 years is as high as 1.062, and at 5 to 9 years 1.060, as opposed to only 1.030 at 0 to 4 years.

If, as a minimal hypothesis, we assume that in the period 1860–89 absolute underregistration of births was equal to that of deaths, then the rate of natural increase recorded (8 per 1000) reflected reality; it is possible then to assess mortality by using the more reliable data of neighbouring countries, such as Serbia and Romania,[45] giving a crude mortality rate of at least 35 per 1000, as opposed to the 20.6 per 1000 registered. On this basis a birth-rate on the order of 45 per 1000 may be proposed as the pre-transitional level. If, on the other hand, as seems more likely, the underregistration of mortality and fertility bear a proportional rather than an absolute relation to each other, then the estimate becomes more like 50 per 1000.[46] This reasoning is confirmed by the retrospective estimates by Siampos. An average rate of natural increase of about 15 per 1000 may be deduced, corresponding very closely to average rates of intercensal increase (1.6 and 1.5, respectively) for the periods 1870–79 and 1889–96. On the other hand, the movement of rates over the past century is purely hypothetical, each country having had its own particular pattern; there seems good reason to think that the Greek situation could be similar, for example, to southern Italy.

Three observations deserve mention where overseas English-speaking countries are concerned: (1) the initial difference between Canada and the

---

[45] In Romania, infant mortality in the period 1871–80 was 298 per 1000.

[46] The recorded rate is 28.6 per 1000 and the coefficient of correction $35/20.6 = 1.70$; hence, by computation, $28.6 \times 1.70 = 48.6$ per 1000.

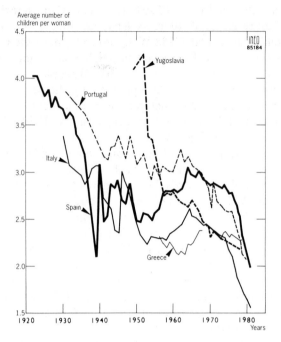

FIG. 4.7. Total fertility, southern Europe, 1920–1980

US is marked, whilst the Australian pattern, since 1920 at least, overlaps that of the US; (2) the basic trends, such as the large post-war fluctuation, are identical; and (3) with time, the levels have converged progressively, so that fertility rates have never been as close as they are today.

Where availability of data is concerned, eastern Europe in the inter-war period is much the same as southern Europe. But there is a large difference between the central European countries (Czechoslovakia, Hungary, and East Germany) and what are, properly speaking, eastern countries (Poland, Bulgaria, and Romania). Around 1925, the Bulgarian fertility level was still close to an average of 5 children per woman, whilst it was 3.3 in Hungary, and 2.8 in Czechoslovakia, and within the then boundaries of East Germany, only a few years later, it fell to the lowest ever known levels (1.2 in 1933, for the province of Saxony[47]). Romania occupies a similar position to that of Bulgaria.[48]

---

[47] Population of 5.2 million.
[48] The age pyramid for the 1912 census is sufficiently regular to allow adjustment to a quasi-stable population (only mortality has declined); the average age at first marriage, using Hajnal's method of calculation, is 22 years. For the last quarter of the 19th century, crude birth-rates were around 45 per 1000, giving, with a natural increase of 9 per 1000, a crude death-rate of 36 per 1000.

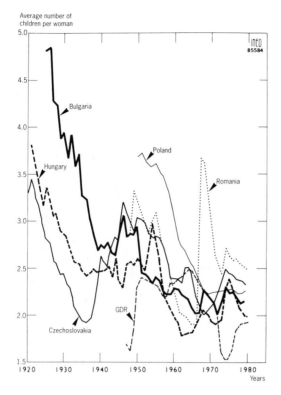

Fig. 4.8. Total fertility, eastern Europe, 1920–1980

With the exception of East Germany, whose development up to around 1975 (when a new family policy was established) was comparable to West Germany's, all these countries recorded a decline in fertility since the mid-1950s, the trend increased by liberal abortion policies.[49] This continued up to 1965–68, a period in which Hungary, Romania, and Czechoslovakia adopted outspoken pronatalist policies, causing sometimes dramatic fluctuations—the most spectacular (indeed, notorious) being Romania in 1967, as a result of the illegalization of abortion.

Finally, in the USSR and Japan, developments were late but rapid once begun. Fertility in the USSR was very high in the nineteenth century, averaging 6.7 children per woman in 1895 (Lorimer 1954). Between 1926 and 1934 fertility was reduced by half (2.9 in 1934 as opposed to 5.6 in 1926), but then increased to an average of 4 children per woman in the period up to the war, owing to sudden legislative changes. After the war, development becomes less uneven, and the decline is slower; despite the increase of Asian populations

[49] Abortion is historically the preferred method of fertility regulation in this part of Europe.

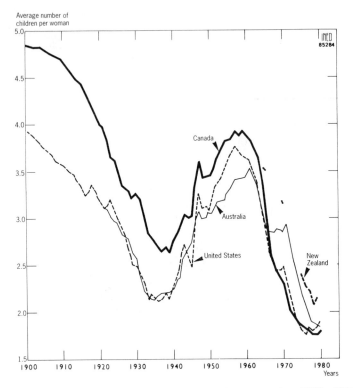

FIG. 4.9. Total fertility, overseas English-speaking countries, 1900–1980

with higher fertility, and, even with the rise in juvenile mortality, total fertility, at 2.26, has finally reached replacement level.

Japan experienced a noticeable decline in fertility in the inter-war years, as a result of a significant rise in the average age at marriage; but the period covering 1949–57 marks an even more dramatic change. Following adoption of the eugenic protection law (1948), which, revised in 1952, permitted voluntary abortion, there was a drastic and historically unprecedented decline in fertility: until then, Japan had one of the highest fertility levels in the industrial world; suddenly its fertility became the lowest in the whole world.

A Convergence nearer Equilibrium

As we have seen, pre-transitional fertility levels, far from being similar, were markedly different even within the 'developed' world, total fertility rates ranging from around 4 in Switzerland to almost 7 in European Russia. Because of the staggered nature of the Malthusian transition, the end of the nineteenth century saw an increase in international differences; and sub-sequent decades, and the inter-war period especially, have seen a reversal of

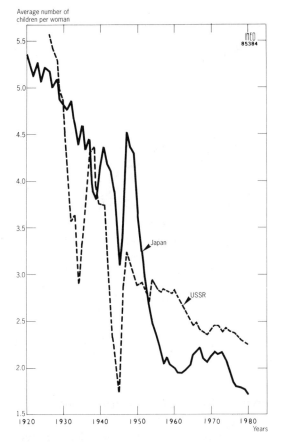

FIG. 4.10. Total fertility, USSR and Japan, 1920–1980

preceding patterns. The baby boom, although of very differing amplitude, occurred in the Western countries previously most advanced in their transitions (making here some exception for the Axis powers during the 1930s in which, owing to pronatalist policies, there was an increase in fertility); yet it did not occur in southern and eastern Europe. This recent divergence in trends was unexpected, countries with low fertility returning to higher levels not experienced since the 1920s, or even the beginning of the century. Over the last 20 years, with the progressive spread of the most recent fertility declines (North America, 1960; northern and western Europe, 1964; southern Europe and Japan, 1974), differences once again have been rapidly disappearing (Fig. 4.11): around 1980, the different areas of the developed world had average levels of 1.7 to 1.9, the variance of observations (unweighted) in western Europe falling from 0.47 in 1965 to 0.35 in 1983. Only eastern Europe, up to the present, has succeeded in maintaining fertility above demographic

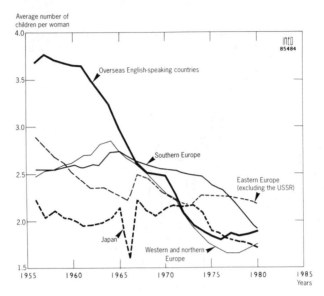

FIG. 4.11. Changes in total fertility, developed countries, by major demographic regions, 1956–1980

equilibrium—and this at the price of costly pronatalist policies with limited, and even doubtful, efficacy, at least in the very long term.[50]

6. Comparative Rates of Development

Despite differences in the periods at which declines began, and in initial fertility (levels being generally higher in countries with late transition), present-day developed countries have similar fertilities. There seems to have been a progressive acceleration of changes in fertility, a phenomenon observed some time ago by Kuczynski (1936). Several criteria for assessing such differentials are, in each case, possible. Kirk (in Behrman *et al.* 1969), for example, uses the time taken for a fertility level of 35 per 1000 to pass to 20 per 1000. In so doing, he excludes France and countries with delayed marriage, notably Sweden, Norway, Denmark, Belgium, and Switzerland. In the present study, we shall take the higher limit of 30 per 1000, although it is evident that the meaning of this index will differ strongly according to a country's starting-point.

---

[50] Detailed analysis of the policies' content, as well as their apparent results, shows that there are in fact no two similar cases. But actual efficacy is often difficult to assess because of aggregate indices which disguise contradictory trends; after analysis by social class and generation, these differences would appear more considerable than is generally admitted.

TABLE 4.8. *Changes in total fertility, developed countries, by region, 1956–1983* (weighted averages)

Years	Overseas English-speaking countries[a]	Western and northern Europe[b]	Southern Europe[c]	Eastern Europe[d]	Japan
1956	3.69	2.48	2.54	2.89	2.21
1957	3.77	2.54	2.54	2.79	2.04
1958	3.71	2.55	2.54	2.68	2.11
1959	3.69	2.60	2.57	2.60	2.04
1960	3.65	2.62	2.60	2.50	2.01
1961	3.65	2.70	2.57	2.43	1.95
1962	3.50	2.71	2.60	2.35	1.96
1963	3.37	2.83	2.60	2.36	1.98
1964	3.24	2.85	2.73	2.33	2.03
1965	2.96	2.73	2.75	2.27	2.14
1966	2.76	2.68	2.66	2.21	1.60[e]
1967	2.60	2.59	2.65	2.49	2.22
1968	2.51	2.50	2.60	2.47	2.10
1969	2.50	2.40	2.58	2.37	2.06
1970	2.50	2.30	2.53	2.29	2.13
1971	2.32	2.25	2.53	2.25	2.15
1972	2.05	2.10	2.52	2.18	2.12
1973	1.93	1.95	2.48	2.17	2.13
1974	1.87	1.85	2.48	2.28	2.04
1975	1.81	1.75	2.38	2.26	1.89
1976	1.77	1.70	2.34	2.26	1.83
1977	1.80	1.67	2.24	2.26	1.78
1978	1.77	1.67	2.14	2.23	1.77
1979	1.79	1.70	2.03	2.22	1.74
1980	1.82	1.75	1.95	2.18	1.72
1981	1.81	1.72	1.84	2.12	1.72
1982	1.81	1.69	1.81	2.10	1.74
1983	1.75	1.63	1.73	2.08	1.74

[a] Australia, Canada, New Zealand, United States.

[b] West Germany, Austria, Belgium, Denmark, Finland, France, Iceland, Ireland, Luxemburg, Netherlands, Norway, Sweden, Switzerland, United Kingdom.

[c] Greece, Italy, Portugal, Spain, Yugoslavia.

[d] Bulgaria, Czechoslovakia, East Germany, Hungary, Poland, Romania.

[e] Year of the Horse and Fire (daughters born in this year are believed fated to kill their husbands).

TABLE 4.9. *Onset of fertility decline, developed and less developed countries*

Countries	Date of transition to CBR of 30 per 1000	Number of countries	Average duration (years)
Developed countries			
Group I	1830–99	9	40 (35 without France)
Group II	1900–24	9	29 (23 without Netherlands and Spain)
Group III	1925–49	7	27 (23 without Portugal)
Less developed countries			
Group IV	1915–70	13	24–25

Let us consider the group of developed and less developed countries where fertility, at the time of writing, has reached a level of 20 per 1000, or is about to (i.e. in which the probable date of attainment can be extrapolated from current trends with little risk of error), and let us group them according to the period (or date of entry) at which the fertility rate reached 30 per 1000. The results are shown in Table 4.8. Although it holds as an average, the acceleration is far from being systematic, as, from the same starting-point at a given time, the variation in subsequent declines is very great from one case to another. Countries like Holland, Germany, and Austria, which have comparable pre-transitional levels and dates of entry, have none the less experienced radically different rhythms of transition, the time taken to pass from 30 to 20 per 1000 being 57 years in Holland, as opposed to 13 years in Austria and 16 years in Germany. The process in Spain and Portugal has also been comparatively slow (see Fig. 4.12). On the whole, the contraceptive transition appears shorter when it begins later, only the first group, including all the countries with controlled nuptiality, and thus with lower initial fertility, noticeably deviating from the norm. The differences amongst the remaining three groups are fairly slight. Nevertheless, no definitive assessment can be drawn from comparisons of crude birth-rates where the influence of age structures is important. It seems likely that the same calculations, using more sophisticated measures of fertility, would show up greater differences, but in the absence of adequate observations for less developed countries, this exercise has not been attempted here.

Conclusion

In all countries, the decline in fertility has resulted in the spread of smaller families. But the maintenance of a constant average level of births in a population may result from very different behavioural patterns, and contain

Fig. 4.12. Period of fertility transition and rate of fertility decline in developed countries: period from birth rate of 30 per 1000 to rate of 20 per 1000 (moving average of five years)

very different distributions of couples by completed fertility. A total fertility rate around 2, for example, may derive from the juxtaposition of two dominant patterns: in the first, there is a predominance of families having no children or only one child, together with a lesser number of large families with many children; the second pattern derives from concentrating on the model of the restricted family, i.e. one or, more usually, two children. The first case is that of France around the time of the First World War; the second is that of

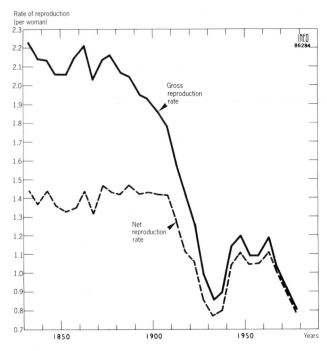

FIG. 4.13. Crude and net reproduction rates, Sweden, 1830–1980

contemporary France. The implications for the economic behaviour of house-holds, or family policy, are obviously completely different.

In other respects, which depend on prevailing levels of mortality, a single measure of fertility in no way carries the same meaning where the future development of population is concerned. In the past, declining mortality in age groups below 30 slowed down the decline in net reproduction for a long time. From now on, the degree of progress possible in either juvenile mortality or mortality as a whole is very slender; the corresponding possibilities of an increase in the net reproduction rate, or the net reproduction rate for years lived, through a further decline in mortality, are therefore negligible. In populations where transition is completed or in its final stages, subsequent changes will thus be entirely dependent on the pattern of fertility.

Certain observations, as, for example, the trend of Swedish fertility since the 1930s (shown in Fig. 4.13), suggest that, once a certain base level has been reached, fertility will fluctuate around replacement level: others believe the situation is indeterminate. This issue, which has been the subject of much controversy over the past 20 years, will be examined in Chapter 7, in light of the experience of a large number of countries during the last half-century. The question is not a novel one (see, for example, the work of Lösch 1936), but post-war fluctuations have given it renewed urgency.

Bibliography to Chapter 4

ABDEL-ATY, S. H. (1965), 'Life-Table functions for Egypt based on Model Life-Tables and Quasi-Stable Population Theory', *MMFQ*, 39 (Apr.), 350–77.

BEHRMANN, S. J., CORSA, L., and FREEDMAN, R. (eds.) (1969), *Fertility and Family Planning: A World View* (Ann Arbor: University of Michigan Press).

BIRABEN, J. N. (1982), 'L'Évolution récente du temps biologique dans les sociétés industrielles', in *Les Âges de la vie*, Travaux et Documents, Cahier no. 96 (Paris: INED-PUF), 3–10.

BLAYO, Y. (1975), 'Le Mouvement naturel de la population française de 1740 à 1860', *Population*, special number (Nov.), 15–64.

CANTILLON, R. (1755), *Essai sur la nature du commerce en général* (London: Fletcher Gyles).

CARLSSON, G. (1966), 'The Decline of Fertility: Innovation or Adjustment Process', *Population Studies* (Nov.), 149–74.

CHAUNU, P. (1974), *Histoire, science sociale: la durée, l'espace et l'homme à l'époque moderne* (Paris: SEDES).

COALE, A. J., and RIWES, N. W., Jr. (1973), 'A Statistical Reconstruction of the Black Population of the United States, 1880–1970: Estimates of True Numbers by Age and Sex. Birth Rates and Total Fertility', *Population Index* (Jan.), 3–36.

—— and TYE, C. Y. (1961), 'The Significance of Age Patterns of Fertility in High Fertility Populations', *MMFQ* (Oct.), 631–46.

—— and ZELNIK, M. (1963), *New Estimates of Fertility and Population in the United States* (Princeton, NJ).

DAVIS, K. (1963), 'The Theory of Change and Response in Modern Demographic History', *Population Index* (Oct.), 345–66.

DEPOID, P. (1941), *Reproduction nette en Europe depuis l'origine des statistiques de l'état civil* (Paris).

EL-BADRY, M. A. (1955), 'Some Demographic Measurements for Egypt based on the Stability of Census Age Distributions', *MMFQ*, 32 (July), 303.

FESTY, P. (1979), *La Fécondité des pays occidentaux de 1870 à 1970*, Travaux et Documents, Cahier no. 85 (Paris: INED-PUF).

HAJNAL, J. (1953), 'Age at Marriage and Proportions Marrying', *Population Studies* (Nov.), 111–36.

—— (1965), 'European Marriage Patterns in Perspective', in D. V. Glass and D. E. C. Eversley (eds.), *Population in History: Essays in Historical Demography* (London: Edward Arnold), 101–43.

HENRIPIN, J. (1968), *Tendances et facteurs de la fécondité au Canada* (Ottawa).

HENRY, L. (1956), *Anciennes Familles genèvoises: étude démographique: XVIᵉ–XXᵉ siècle*, Travaux et Documents, Cahier no. 26 (Paris: INED-PUF).

—— (1957), 'Fécondité et famille: modèles mathématiques', *Population*, 3: 413–44.

—— (1961), 'Some Data on Natural Fertility', *Eugenics Quarterly* (June), 81–91.

—— and BLAYO, Y. (1975), 'La Population de la France de 1740 à 1860', *Population*, Special Number (Nov.), 71–122.

HIMES, N. E. (1936), *Medical History of Contraception* (Baltimore, Md.).

KENDALL, M. (1980), 'L'Enquête mondiale sur la fécondité: situation et résultats actuels', *Population Reports*, M3 (Apr.).

KIRK, D. (1946), 'A New Demographic Transition?', in *Rapid Population Growth:*

Consequences and Policy Implications (Baltimore, Md.: Johns Hopkins University Press, National Academy of Sciences), ii. 123–47.

KNODEL, J. (1967), 'Law, Marriage and Illegitimacy in Nineteenth-Century Germany', *Population Studies*, 1 (Mar.), 279–94.

—— and VAN DE WALLE, E. (1979), 'Lessons from the Past: Policy Implications of Historical Fertility Studies', *PDR*, 2: 217–45.

KUCZYNSKI, R. R. (1928–31), *The Balance of Births and Deaths*, i: *Western and Northern Europe* (New York, 1928), ii: *Eastern and Southern Europe* (Washington, DC, 1931).

—— (1936), *The Measurement of Population Growth, Methods and Results* (New York: Oxford University Press).

—— (1938*a*), 'Childless Marriages', *Sociological Review*.

—— (1938*b*), 'The International Decline of Fertility', in L. Hogben (ed.), *Political Arithmetic* (London), 47–72.

LANDRY, A., BUNLE, H., DEPOID, P., HUBER, M., and SAUVY, A. (1945), *Traité de démographie* (Paris), 289–394.

LERIDON, H. (1973), *Aspects biométriques de la fécondité humaine*, Travaux et Documents, Cahier no. 65 (Paris: INED-PUF).

LIN FU DE (1981), 'The Status-Quo and Prospect of China's Population', *International Conference of the IUSSP, Manila, 1981*, special session 2, 15–25.

LIVI, L. (1940), *Trattato di demographia*, i: *Factori bio-demografici nell ordinamento sociale*, ii: *Le leggi naturali della popolazione* (Padua).

LIVI-BACCI, M. (1968), 'Fertility and Nuptiality Changes in Spain from the Late Eighteenth Century to the Early Twentieth Century', *Population Studies* (Mar.), 83–102; (July), 211–34.

LORIMER, F. (1946), *The Population of the Soviet Union and Prospects* (Geneva: League of Nations).

—— (1954), *Culture and Human Fertility: A Study of the Relation of Cultural Conditions to Fertility in Non-industrial and Transitional Societies* (Paris: IUSSP-UNESCO).

LÖSCH, A. (1936), *Bevölkerungswellen und Wechsellagen* (Jena: Fisher).

LOTKA, A. J. (1939), *Théorie analytique des associations biologiques: Il analyse démographique avec application particulière à l'espèce humaine* (Paris: Hermann).

MAULDIN, W. P. (1978), 'Patterns of Fertility Decline in Developing Countries 1950–1975', *Studies in Family Planning*, 9(4), 75–84.

MYRDAL, A. (1945), *Nation and Family: The Swedish Experiment in Democratic Family and Population Policy* (London: Kegan Paul).

NOIN, D. (1983), *La Transition démographique dans le monde* (Paris: PUF).

NORTMAN, D., and HOFSTATTER, E. (1980), *Population and Family Planning Programs* (New York: Population Council).

UN (1956), *Population Bulletin*, no. 7 (New York: UN).

—— (1977), *Levels and Trends of Fertility throughout the World, 1950–1970*, ST/ESA/SERA/59 (New York: UN).

—— (1982), *World Population Trends and Policies 1981: Monitoring Report*, i, ST/ESA/SERA/79 (New York: UN).

NOTESTEIN, F. W., TAEUBER, I. B., KIRK D., COALE, A. J., and KISER, L. K. (1944), *The Future Population of Europe and the Soviet Union* (Geneva: League of Nations, Office of Population Research).

RYDER, B. (1967), 'The Character of Modern Fertility', *Annals of the American Academy of Political and Social Science* (Jan.), 26–36.

SEKLANI, M. (1960), 'La Fécondité dans les pays arabes: données numériques, attitudes et comportements', *Population*, (Oct.–Dec.), 831–55.

SMITH, T. E. (1960), 'The Cocos-Keeling Islands: A Demographic Laboratory', *Population Studies* (Nov.), 94–129.

TAEUBER, I. B. (1963), 'The Conundrum of the Chinese Birth Rate', in *IUSSP Conference, Ottawa, 1963*, 221–40.

THOMPSON, W. S., and WHELPTON, P. K. (1933), *Population Trends in the US* (New York).

TIETZE, C. (1957), 'Reproductive Span and Rate of Reproduction among Hutterite Women', *Fertility and Sterility*, New York, 8 (Jan.–Feb.), 89–97.

UN (United Nations) (1981), *World Population Prospects as Assessed in 1980*, Population Studies, no. 78 (New York: UN).

WHELPTON, P. K., and KISER, C. V. (eds.) (1946–58), *Social and Psychological Factors Affecting Fertility*, v: *Concluding Reports and Summary of Chief Findings from the Indianapolis Study*, 5 vols. (New York: MMFQ).

5 Divergence and Concordance

On earth, mortals pass like leaves: if the wind blows some to the ground,
the vigorous forest, at spring's return, will put forth many others.

(Homer)

IN its classic version, as defined up to the 1950s, demographic transition
theory had as its object knowledge of the transformation of fertility and
mortality, in the historical passage from traditional to modern societies. The
transition was measured simply in terms of crude rates. In order to appreciate
the descriptive qualities of this theory, we shall draw upon the materials
presented in the two preceding chapters.

We are presented, from the outset, with a fundamental fact: Landry's
prediction of the generalization of the process of demographic transition has
fulfilled itself to a remarkable degree. Here is what he was saying half a
century ago: 'In the contemporary period, a new demographic regime has
successively taken over (or is in the process of so doing) all the countries in
Europe, and some further afield. Far from being absurd, there are reasons to
think that it will eventually take over the entire world.' Beyond this generalization it is important to enquire whether, beneath the apparent convergence
of trends, there is not a wide diversity in patterns of development and their
mechanisms. To this end, the analysis for different countries of differences in
timing between the trajectories of the two principal phenomena of fertility and
mortality is a valuable guide: it can show up the existence of conditions
statistically necessary to the emergence of particular developments. Similarly,
the analysis of differences observed between countries in one of these
phenomena, when the other is observed to maintain a level equivalent in all
cases, gives an indication of the strength of the relation between them, and
hence the degree of their independence.

This analysis of divergence and concordance is also useful in helping to
assess the appropriateness of certain theoretical presuppositions which have
become customary in most recent developments of transition theory. Focusing
attention on the most prominent historical and geographical features of the
transition effectively relativizes several recurring themes in the demographic
literature; the concentration of studies on one aspect (fertility) and on one part
of the world (western Europe) has resulted in the by now ritual reiteration
of certain questions concerning the transition and, in consequence, silence
surrounding issues no less important to our understanding.

1. Temporal Discrepancies

The Diversity of Mortalities and 'natural' Fertilities

We have already indicated the deceptive nature of the term 'natural' as applied to fertility; it is now time to elaborate on this point. According to Henry's original usage, the concept of 'natural fertility' refers not, as etymology would imply, to a theoretical level of reproduction amongst couples in the absence of cultural obstacles to child-bearing, but to the absence of voluntary birth limitation amongst couples in a given population. Consequently, the variability of fertilities in different milieux has been attributed not to the conscious choice of interested parties, but to the influence of customs governing sexual and social life in the communities to which they belong, or, in other words, to norms beyond the individual of the kinds studied by social and cultural anthropologists. From a statistical point of view, the concept is simple: the absence of conscious fertility regulation within marriage is indicated by the statistical independence of the number of children born from the number of children to come; at a given age and duration of marriage, there is no link between completed fertility and the probability of increase. In these terms, the divers ecological and social constraints on the family effectively dictate the levels fertility will reach: for young married couples, where the wife is under 20, the capacity of increase is twofold, ranging from less than 5 children for the Swiss in the mid-nineteenth century, to an average of over 10 amongst the Hutterites, in North America, in the first half of the twentieth century. The concept of a pre-transitional level of fertility would correspond better to the reality thus described; whilst 'natural fertility' seems more appropriate for the (inevitably arbitrary) upper limits now customarily used in the measurement of marital fertility (Coale's indices) or the intensity of contraception (Coale–Trussel fertility models). The concept of natural increase is less ambiguous, as it refers simply to the growth of a population, disregarding net migration.

To our knowledge, the concept of natural mortality has never been used as an analogue of natural fertility: its use is, rather, in contradistinction to violent death, which implies exterior causes and brutal acts of aggression against the individual. But let us now suppose the following analogy: natural mortality would define the existing level of mortality in the absence of 'efficient' medical techniques. What little data are available reveal, here too, that a remarkable range of observations exists even within close socio-geographic contexts. Thus, differences in infant mortality between Norway, Sweden, and Finland in the mid-nineteenth century were in a ratio of 1, 1.4, and 2 respectively; or, levels of life expectation at birth in French departments at the beginning of the nineteenth century varied from over 45 years among women in Calvados,

Manche, Lozère, and Ariège to only a little over 20 years[1] in Loiret and Loir et Cher, in 1801–05. Such contrasts are sufficient to illustrate the possible diversity, and hence the futility, of using the term 'natural' to describe situations which have nothing in common but their distance from the present.

Time did not stand still in the past, any more than it does now. Where reliable early data do exist, large fluctuations are apparent, of which Finnish fertility, between the mid-eighteenth and mid-nineteenth centuries, or the relative mortality of French departments just remarked, provide examples. Pre-transitional mortality, in the same way as pre-transitional fertility, is governed by an extremely complex and still insufficienty comprehended system of determinants, entailing not only environmental conditions (climate, resources, quality of water), but social organization (legislation, law and order, infrastructure, and communications) and local customs (nutrition, hygiene). In the face of the enormous diversity of pre-transitional contexts, the measurement of differences between 'starting' dates of mortality and fertility decline becomes somewhat relative: such points of departure may be very widely separated.

The General Priority of Mortality Declines

The time lag between mortality and fertility declines is not always easily established, since differences in age structures may be considerable, and the want of adequate retrospective studies has meant that the history of mortality remains scantily researched. If it now seems certain that, at least in north-western Europe, mortality has declined since the eighteenth century, and from 1750–60 in particular,[2] nothing precludes the possibility of progress having begun earlier. Famine tends to give way to food shortages, for various reasons: improvements in transport and grain storage; reduction of fallow land; introduction of fodder; developments in breeding; and the spread of potato cultivation, producing high yields from poor farmland which had often previously been left uncultivated. Likewise, the establishment of a mechanism of demographic leverage in which, for example, population increase stimulates a rise in food prices, in turn stimulating agricultural discovery and the cultivation of new land, would, in varying degrees, have played a role in different countries (Drummond 1957). The plague, which had been rampant in Europe

---

[1] It is currently assumed that a population in which average life expectation remains below 20 years is destined to extinction. This is generally true, since where health conditions are poor, fertility can never be very high. However, this assumption may be contested on a priori grounds: it presupposes that fertility does not exceed 50 per 1000. With birth-rates close to 60 per 1000 (such as have been observed in certain regions of western Europe during the 19th century) a life expectation of around 17 years would be sufficient to prevent population decline (mortality levels in the cases concerned were, however, not as high).

[2] In France, for example, the average life expectation for women (who are less affected by war or civil strife) rises from 25.7 years in 1740–49 to 32.1 years in 1790–99, and 40.2 years in 1851–55. Progress is thus particularly marked since the second half of the 18th century.

TABLE 5.1. *Cases of plague, Europe, 1550–1850*

Period	Number of 'cases' (outbreaks)
1550–99	1,764
1600–49	2,158
1650–99	750
1700–49	214
1750–99	61
1800–49	17

Notes: based on Biraben 1975.

since the thirteenth century, disappeared during the course of the seventeenth and eighteenth centuries. Table 5.1 gives a résumé of the total number of cases in Europe[3] from 1550 to 1850. The determining factor in this evolution seems not to have been of a climatic or 'demographic' order (certain authors claim that the population of black rats, which carried the disease, was displaced by that of brown rats which were not vectors) but of a *political* order: it was not until an international network of information and health control had been set up which could regulate maritime or other trade with infected ports that the plague could be efficiently combated. In other words, it entailed waiting for the emergence of State-controlled organizations sufficiently powerful to be respected both within and without their own territory.

Likewise, we cannot exclude the possibility that the birth of modern States actively influenced other determinants of mortality, by facilitating production, commerce, and communication. Early advances in health and hygiene, among the privileged classes, documented from archival sources (the classic examples being the British peerage and the Genevan bourgeoisie), could in such circumstances have spread to other social strata. Perhaps the extraordinary improvement of mortality in countries like Norway at the beginning of the nineteenth century should be interpreted in this way? But it is also necessary to consider factors such as the generality and duration of breast-feeding, the effects of the spread of potato cultivation on nutrition, the role of natural phenomena (climate, the geographic isolation of villages separated by hills or fiords, etc.), and the influence of religion (improvements such as the introduction of the potato—which had a better nutritive value and increased yields per acre—and the smallpox vaccine were due to the action of the clergy). The Norwegian case is to mortality what France is to fertility. And yet this Norwegian peculiarity has scarcely been studied; no precise assessment of the role of the factors cited above has been made.

[3] Not including the south-east Balkans, the Ukraine, the Caucasus, and south-east Russia.

Thus, the decline in mortality, at least in western Europe, was very early: it preceded fertility declines by at least a century, and in some cases perhaps two centuries. If, however, the time lag between mortality and fertility declines is represented by crude rates alone, without due allowance for the insufficient length of retrospective series, a false impression may result: the decline in mortality became rapid after 1870 and so the differences in the timing of the two declines appears correspondingly small. The levels reached by the third quarter of the nineteenth century should, none the less, lead one to suspect significant earlier declines; in the few countries where it has been possible to reconstruct the past back to the beginning of the nineteenth century, the *apparent* differences (still in terms of crude rates) exceed 50 years; in Denmark, Norway, and Sweden, they represent around 50 to 70 years.

In eastern Europe, mortality decline occurred much later. On average crude rates in the period 1800–60 were around 38 per 1000, as opposed to 27 per 1000 in western Europe (Table 3.3): improvement apparently did not begin until the second half of the nineteenth century.[4] The beginnings of mortality declines in eastern Europe thus followed the west by about a century, whereas only about 25 years intervened between their respective declines in fertility. Fertility, in fact, only began to decline in eastern Europe around the end of the nineteenth or the start of the twentieth century, depending on the country. Nevertheless, in both regions mortality decline preceded that of fertility, and fertility changes were more concentrated in time than those of mortality, for which developments appear, to begin with, to have been very slow, and very different between countries. This leads one to think that mortality may have been governed by a more varied and complex system of determinants than fertility.

Belgium and Germany

An analogous situation holds in less developed countries; indeed, the very inflation of their rates of natural increase, and the persistence of historically unprecedented levels of growth, leaves no doubt about the priority of mortality declines. It is precisely the tempo of the change in mortality, together with fertility's delayed response, which lie behind the demographic growth of these countries. Consequently, the argument that the decline in infant mortality in many cases came after that of marital fertility appears prima facie surprising. Even in France, where the secular decline in marital fertility was exceptionally early (a century ahead of the advanced Western countries), infant mortality had already fallen appreciably at the time couples began to practise contraception: infant mortality in 1780–89 was at a level of 278 per 1000, as opposed to 296 per 1000 in 1740–49.

---

[4] To find equivalent levels in France it is necessary to go back before 1750, i.e. before decisive improvements had occurred.

Yet some authors (van de Walle and Knodel 1980), following Scrimshaw (1978), have none the less argued the priority of declines in marital fertility. This contradicts the central assumption of transition theory that the decline in fertility cannot occur unless mortality has already regressed; or, put another way, that, without progress in health, all attempts at family planning risk failure. These authors reverse the theory by making mortality depend on fertility, the argument by anteriority, to their minds, supporting a causal relationship. Two examples where such a reversed order has been observed are called upon: that of Belgium, studied by Lesthaeghe (1977), and Germany, by Knodel (1974). We shall examine these cases in more detail.

Where Germany is concerned, as we have seen, there was scarcely any decline in marital fertility before 1880; however, between 1850 and 1875 infant mortality declined by more than 10%, falling from 294 to 261 per 1000[5] (Table 3.5). Fertility in Belgium began to decline in the same period, but declines in infant mortality appeared much earlier, as can be seen on three accounts: (1) with a rate close to 150 per 1000 in the mid-nineteenth century, the Belgian level was comparable to that of England and Sweden, where there had been a considerable decline since the eighteenth century; this level, which was half that of its German neighbour, would imply that improvements were already under way at an earlier date; (2) for the few countries with reliable long-term series, transitional levels were always considerably higher than 200 per 1000 (Sweden before 1810, Finland before 1830) or even 250 per 1000 (eighteenth-century France, Austria, and Czech populations during the first half of the nineteenth century); and (3) the Belgian rate for 1834–40 (the first years for which registration data are available) was 20% higher than the rate recorded at the outset of the fertility decline (182 per 1000 as opposed to 154 per 1000). The thesis that fertility is traditionally high in response to high mortality (there being a need to replace dying infants with new births, to ensure security in old age and continuity of the male line) cannot therefore be rejected where the argument of priority is concerned; at a national level, we have found no counter-examples. Moreover, it is known that in a number of Western countries the battle against smallpox, a cause of high infant mortality, did not have to wait until Jenner's discovery, at the end of the eighteenth century, in order to achieve results. Also, fresh-water policies were introduced in many towns before the second half of the nineteenth century.

Certainly, the possibility that high mortality could, in part, be a response to exuberant fertility cannot be precluded. The existence of a range of more or less conscious practices, from infanticide, abandonment, and exposure to wet-nursing, neglect, or other means of underfeeding, may indicate a significant level of unwanted fertility, particularly in large families. None of this, however, specifically discredits the classic thesis that fertility adjusts to mortality, or

---

[5] Given that registration improved over this period, the initial level was without doubt higher than the figures suggest and the decline still more pronounced.

TABLE 5.2. *Time differentials at which comparable life expectation at birth was reached in four developed countries*

Country	Period	Life Expectation (years)	
		Men	Women
Norway	1825	45.0	48.0
Sweden	1871–1880	45.3	48.6
France	1898–1903	45.3	48.7
Japan[a]	1926–1930	44.8	46.5

[a] Japan, in the period since 1930, has not only overcome its time lag, but now maintains the highest levels of male life expectation in the world.

would justify replacing this thesis with its opposite. As we shall show later on, the two are not incompatible, and complex mechanisms of interaction can exist between them. In our view, the question is not so much their relation, as relative intensity.

A European Perspective

The temporal difference in the onset of fertility and mortality declines remains a matter of conjecture in many countries, as efficient civil registration was established after early advances in health had been made, whether we are considering developed or less developed countries. Hence, it is often necessary to make do with orders of magnitude. Nevertheless, good data in countries with advanced transitions can help us to conceive other indicators of time differentials, for example, in terms of the dates at which a given level of development is reached. Thus, life expectation at birth in Norway—the most advanced country in terms of mortality—from 1825 exceeded the age of 45 years for males. This age is approximately midway between typical figures for pre-transitional and post-transitional societies (20 to 25 years, and 70 to 75 years, respectively). As Table 5.2 shows, the same level was not reached for another half-century in Sweden; France waited three-quarters of a century, and Japan a whole century for comparable figures to emerge.

Since life expectation data are available only for rather irregular intervals, recourse to infant mortality rates will enable us to draw up a more complete and accurate picture. Take, for example, the data at which a rate of 100 per 1000 was reached. Here, too, Norway retains the lead, with a data of around 1850; but now we are in a position to arrange all the developed countries in order of time difference. The time lags for different countries in relation to Norway are:

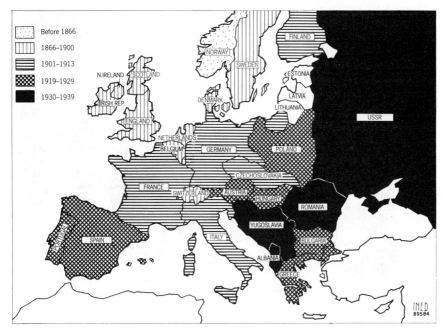

FIG. 5.1. Period in which crude death-rates fell below 20 per 1000

1. A half-century: Sweden;
2. A three-quarter century: France, Germany, The Netherlands, and Switzerland;[6]
3. A century: Poland, Romania, Yugoslavia, and the USSR.

No explanation, so far as we know, has been advanced with regard to Norway's lead, particularly over Sweden. Yet such a difference offers an exceptional opportunity for exploring the properties of pre-transitional mortality.

Turning now to fertility, as is well known, France long led the movement toward widespread birth control. A total fertility of 3.5 children per woman, which is half-way between pre-transitional and post-transitional fertility, was reached by the first half of the nineteenth century. Comparable levels did not occur elsewhere until around 1900 in England, on the eve of the First World War in Germany and the US, around 1930 in Italy, and around 1950 in Japan.

In order to illustrate these differences for the group of European countries, we have chosen simply to compare the dates at which crude rates of natality and mortality reached 20 per 1000; the results are given in Figs. 5.1 and 5.2.[7]

[6] The Netherlands and Switzerland advanced to the lead immediately after the First World War.
[7] Following convention, boundaries at the time of the inter-war period have been used.

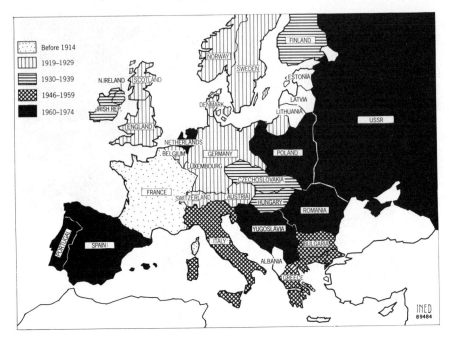

FIG. 5.2. Period in which crude birth-rates fell below 20 per 1000

Although the significance of crude data will be much clearer for natality than for mortality, owing to the distribution of chances of death according to age, a value of 20 per 1000 in the European context reflects an already well-advanced health transition, the pre-transitional rates having been of the order of 30 to 40 per 1000.

There are clear geographical divides. In 1900, with the exception of Switzerland, the only countries with mortality below 20 per 1000 were in northern and western Europe: Norway, Sweden, Denmark, The Netherlands, Belgium, Britain, and Ireland. France, Germany, Italy, and Czechoslovakia were by then fairly advanced, and joined this group in the years preceding the First World War. Not until the 1920s did several central, southern, and eastern European countries attain this level: Austria and Hungary; the Iberian peninsula and Greece; and Bulgaria and Poland. The USSR and the remaining Balkan states of Romania, Yugoslavia, and Albania were the slowest, only arriving at this position just before the Second World War.

The geography of fertility reveals similar differences, but the order sometimes varies considerably in detail. For example, in western Europe, setting aside France on account of its considerable lead, Italy, The Netherlands, and Ireland are notable for their relative lags.[8] Conversely, Austria and Hungary

---

[8] The lag in Italy and The Netherlands has dwindled in recent years.

have the lead over their southern and eastern neighbours, but the position amongst countries which were the last to enter transition differs only where Poland, Portugal, and Spain are concerned, where fertility declined relatively slowly.

Comparison of the two maps confirms the principle of the priority of mortality decline: in all cases, mortality attained the value of 20 per 1000 before fertility, the average interval of separation between the two transitions being 40 years. The interval was much larger in Scandinavian countries (except Finland), where mortality declined early: it was around 50 years earlier for Sweden, 60 years for Denmark, and 110 years for Norway, result-ing in a considerable population increase at their level of demographic devel-opment. These countries were, in fact, amongst the west European countries to experience the largest demographic growth in the last two centuries. As we shall see, Norway was characterized by a massive contribution, relative to its population size, to the great wave of nineteenth-century emigration. Conversely, the smallest apparent intervals belong to central Europe, where fertility decline was generally exceptionally fast: Austria (5 years), Hungary (13 years), Czechoslovakia (20 years), and Germany (23 years). The size of the demographic growth recorded in these countries since the mid-nineteenth century is largely a product of the cumulated growth potential in the initial age structures (and, for West Germany, the immigration following the war).

The Relation between Mortality and Fertility Levels

The extreme variability of declines which has been observed from one country to another underlines the multiplicity of historical relations obtaining between mortality and fertility. Thus, in France, when fertility began its long descent, mortality was still over 35 per 1000, until it too began to recede, the two processes thence running more or less parallel for a century and a half. When fertility turned in northern Europe, mortality was of the order of 15 to 20 per 1000; in Germany and Switzerland it was 25 per 1000; and in central Europe, notably amongst Czech populations, Hungary, and Poland, it was 30 per 1000. In other words, a wide range of mortalities were present. In less developed countries today, owing to their exceedingly young age structures, the range is smaller; around 20 per 1000 in India, 15 per 1000 in South Korea, Egypt, Tunisia, and Brazil, and 10 per 1000 in Mexico and Taiwan. Nevertheless, in relative value these differences are considerable, since the highest is twice that of the lowest.

A more detailed examination is advisable, however, bringing together countries of comparable socio-economic status, and comparing pre-transitional fertility levels with infant mortality within the same periods. This is possible only for certain countries with long-established statistical traditions. Four groups of fertility levels may thus be constituted, corresponding to an average of 4, 4.5, 5, and 5.5 children per woman—once again, taken as general orders

TABLE 5.3. *Infant mortality levels immediately preceding fertility transition, with average numbers of children per woman*

Country	Period	Fertility	Infant mortality (per 1000)
Switzerland	1870–80	4.0	193[a]
Norway			100–10
Sweden	1850–70	4.5	130–50
Finland			222[a]
France	1760–89		280–90
Germany	1870–80	5.0	261[a]
Austria			256[a]
Netherlands	1870–80	5.5	203[a]
Japan	1920–24		160[a]

[a] Average for the period indicated.

of magnitude. Table 5.3 results. There is no manifest statistical link between levels of fertility and infant mortality; for a single initial fertility level, differences in infant mortality are sometimes considerable; evidently fertility declines occur in widely different health conditions. As this selection of only nine countries shows, all the levels of infant mortality are represented, from the lowest (100–150 per 1000) to the highest (250–300 per 1000). This heterogeneity of demographic experience demonstrates the absence of rigidity in connections between phenomena, condemning in advance reductionist theories of fertility and, *a fortiori*, those laying claim to universality. Not only is it difficult to identify the nature of interactions, any statistical linkages can only be considered coincidental and, moreover, subject to great variations according to time and place.

2. Interactions

If we consider demography as the integral analysis of those three great processes of population renewal—fertility, mortality, and external migration—then a diagram of possible interrelations between these phenomena could be proposed along the lines of Fig. 5.3. Of the six relations here envisaged, transition theory, strictly speaking, only studies one: the influence of mortality on fertility. In so far as the reciprocal effects are neglected, the probable synergies between the first and second poles of natural movement are all the more difficult to understand. International migration is completely omitted as a major component of transition; we shall draw it into the picture in the

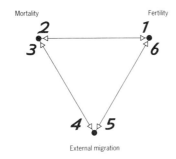

Fig. 5.3. A model of demographic interactions

following chapter. Its role in demographic equilibrium has been decisive in many cases; by altering the pressure of numbers on a given milieu, it introduces a supplementary margin for manœuvre, and there is every reason to suppose that in its absence the behaviour of mortality and fertility would have been different. In the absence of sufficient statistical data, however, only countries with European populations can be considered.

Let us now return to the interplay between mortality and fertility. If, having brought together available data, declines in mortality seem to be necessary for transition to modern regimes of controlled fertility to occur, this condition is hardly sufficient to account for the diversity of existing relations. As we have just seen, infant mortality levels themselves vary in Western countries at the start of fertility declines, over a range from 100 to 300 per 1000. This fact can be interpreted in another way: the transition to low mortality (in the historical circumstances, infant mortality below 100 per 1000) is incompatible with continuing high fertility.

A System of Demographic Flexibility: Coherence and Synergy

The diversity of contexts should not, however, obscure a basic fact: high fertility and high infant mortality generally go hand in hand: they are causally linked. Consistently high infant mortality levels encourage high fertility in various ways: by the replacement of children who have died in infancy, by the necessity to ensure posterity of the male line, and by psychological effects of death's omnipresence. Conversely, high fertility is a factor of high mortality: the shortening of the interval between successive births increases the rate of premature deliveries; repeated pregnancies in close succession weaken the mother's health, making her more vulnerable to illness and risks of death; conception shortly following the birth of a nursing infant curtails breast-feeding, thus reducing the child's chances of survival; finally, excessive expansion of the family compromises standards and conditions of living.

Nevertheless, even if there are no countries with 'low' fertility and 'high' mortality (characterized, say, by a crude birth-rate of less than 30 per 1000 and a mortality rate above 15 per 1000), the existence of high fertility cannot be explained only in terms of high mortality. The extremely selective nature of infant mortality in traditional societies—by order of birth, in particular—clearly shows that levels were not simply the product of circumstances beyond the individual; there have always existed more or less conscious and deliberate social means of dealing with unwanted births. Infanticide—whether active or passive, instant or deferred—was not exclusive to certain oriental societies. Abandonment, exposure, wet-nursing, undernourishment, neglect, abuse, and other means have been used for centuries to alleviate domestic distress: because there was no easy way of controlling births before the event, a posteriori methods were used, which also thereby enabled some control of quality. Generally, techniques were discrete, and compatible with the morality of the period and the social milieu; chances of survival were cut short without direct violence, thus leaving it to God (that is, to nature or to chance) to decide the fate of the rejected child.

Fertility was likewise actively bound up in the regulation of traditional societies: fluctuations in size were not solely the result of variations in mortality, as was believed for many years. Fertility was subject to significant changes, dictated by social rules: age at marriage, sexual taboos, periods of abstinence, breast-feeding customs, child care, and so forth. Without doubt, both the adaptability of traditional societies and the multiplicity of demographic levels immediately preceding the reproductive transition should be attributed to this exceptional normative flexibility. However, there is no evidence that high infant mortality was more an adjustment to fertility than the reverse; of course, couples can react by indifference[9] or negligence towards the birth of unwanted children, but this may reflect the generally high mortality at all ages in traditional societies, and not represent a specific mechanism pertaining to infants. High mortality and fertility are inseparable elements of traditional demographic regimes: they represent a reciprocal relationship entailing interaction, synergy, and expansion in socio-economic and institutional contexts favourable to demographic growth.

Common factors may influence the transformation of mortality and fertility. Thus, the evolution of attitudes towards children in the rising classes of the French bourgeoisie, well analysed by Ariès, may have contributed as much to the decline in infant mortality as to the start of contraception. The relative simultaneity of changes observed in many cases, such as in certain French departments or the leading families of Geneva, lead one to think that a group of common determinants may have been at work. Similarly, for Europe as a whole, especially in the west, the phases of the major decline in mortality and fertility were more or less concomitant: this is amply illustrated by the relatively controlled rate of natural increase—invariably below 2%. Profound

---

[9] One should not, however, exaggerate the significance of the attitude of indifference towards children. In France, for example, wet-nurses were very well paid.

political changes (the achievement of national unity in particular) and major economic progress (industrialization, the rise of international commerce, and an increase in the real value of wages) preceded and, as it were, prepared the ground for the demographic transformations of the last quarter of the nineteenth century. After all, the few founding texts of transition theory regarded demographic development as the result of more general transformations. This development, in reality, was probably both cause and consequence of linked structural changes, each with its own temporal scale and inhering in a system of unstable relations, resistant to observation. The few statistical indicators available to us are but the traces of a fleeting reality, difficult to decipher. Any attempt at retrospective causal reconstruction arises in part from an a priori choice.

Conclusion

It has long been agreed that demographic equilibrium in traditional societies is characterized by the coexistence of a mortality which periodically wipes out surplus population. It is now known that even if the regulatory mechanisms of death (plague, war, epidemic, famine) wields its power, fertility itself is not entirely prey to blind destiny: the customs of every society at every period mark it with a particular stamp—hence the major possibility of fluctuations in fertility over the long term. For centuries, violence has been one of the main demographic regulators: 'the Moloch states destroying themselves every 30 years, organizing the holocaust in order to arrive at an optimum of stable populations' (Le Roy-Ladurie 1978). Today, the entry of countries characterized by a very advanced state of transition into an implosive or contracting demographic regime, could herald a completely different system of control in which, once again, State intervention would be decisive (e.g. migration policy, welfare policy). But political history is even more difficult to foretell than the demographic future. A general theory of systems of demographic control remains to be invented. New indicators must be developed, allowing, for example, for the integration of international migration into the calculus of reproduction.[10]

Bibliography to Chapter 5

ARIÈS, P. (1973), *L'Enfant et la vie familiale sous l'Ancien Régime* (Paris: Le Seuil).
BADINTER, E. (1980), *L'Amour en plus: histoire de l'amour maternel (XVIIᵉ–XXᵉ siècles)* (Paris).

[10] One could, for instance, regard an individual whose marriage involves the spouse's migration into a community as a doubling of its contribution towards reproduction. Some of Keyfitz's work (1977) points in this direction.

BIRABEN, J. N. (1975), *Les Hommes et la peste en France et dans les pays européens et méditerranéens* (Paris: Mouton), i. 363–74, and ii. 183–84.

DRUMMOND, J. C., and WILBRAHAM, A. (1957), *The English Man's Food: A History of Five Centuries of English Diet*, new edn. (London: Alden Press).

HENRY, L. (1956), *Anciennes Familles genevoises: étude démographique: XVIe–XXe siècle*, Travaux et Documents, Cahier no. 26 (Paris: INED-PUF).

KEYFITZ, N. (1977), *Applied Mathematical Demography* (New York: Wiley).

KNODEL, J. (1974), *The Decline of Fertility in Germany, 1871–1939* (Princeton, NJ: Princeton University Press).

LE ROY-LADURIE, E. (1978), *Le Territoire de l'historien*, ii (Paris: Gallimard).

LESTHAEGHE, R. (1977), *The Decline of Belgian Fertility, 1800–1970* (Princeton, NJ: Princeton University Press).

LEVASSEUR, E. (1919), *Salariat et salaires* (Paris: Doin), ch. 7.

REBAUDO, D. (1979), 'Le Mouvement annuel de la population française rurale de 1670 à 1740', *Population*, 3: 589–606.

SCHULTZ, T. P. (1976), 'Interrelationships between Mortality and Fertility', in R. Ridker (ed.), *Population and Development: The Search for Selective Interventions* (Baltimore, Md.: Johns Hopkins University Press).

SCRIMSHAW, S. (1978), 'Infant Mortality and Behavior in the Regulation in Family Size', *PDR*, 4: 383–403.

VAN DE WALLE, E. (1978), 'Alone in Europe: The French Fertility Decline until 1850', in C. Tilly (ed.), *Historical Studies of Changing Fertility* (Princeton, NJ), 257–88.

— and KNODEL, J. (1980), 'Europe's Fertility Transition: New Evidence and Lessons for Today's Developing World', *Population Bulletin*, 34(6) (Feb.).

6 The Migration Transition

The majority of English people 'go overseas' when they visit Canada or Australia, and 'go abroad' when they cross the Channel.

(W. H. Auden)

THE history of international migration is, in certain respects, a digest of universal history; it is one of the liveliest, but also most complex, chapters in population history. It stands at the meeting-point of all the forces—political, economic, cultural, institutional—which define relations between countries.

After its first voyages of discovery and conquest, Europe, having established its naval capability, continued its epic expansion up to the end of the nineteenth century. Industrial and demographic revolution ensured its means and power. Up to the First World War, the planet was under the exclusive dominion of a few west European nations. This process of expansion had been long in the making: since the sixteenth century, European peoples had been sending colonists in all directions in search of new territories; at the beginning, this entailed only the occasional adventurer, but in the nineteenth century, with technical progress and transport facilities, these expeditions gave way to a mass exodus of populations, and acquired a demographic dimension. The populations in question settled in the virgin lands of America and Oceania. This resulted in an unprecedented expansion of effective living space: the territory occupied by populations of European origin increased eight- or ninefold. In a century, from the Congress of Vienna to the First World War (1815–1914), over 60 million Europeans (over 20% of the population in 1850), left their continent of origin. But successive failures in the attempt to settle in the interior of central China marked a first crack in this process of Europe's indefinite expansion. Inherent in the demographic dynamic itself, the process of decolonization began in the First World War, and accelerated with the Second. One by one, the great empires that had been built up over the centuries crumbled; European dominion withdrew, and other civilizations re-emerged to establish themselves.

A Neglected Mass Phenomenon

Emigration is thus one of the outstanding features of nineteenth-century European demography. However, curiously, migratory movements are absent from the theory of demographic transition, which is supposed, none the less, to be grounded precisely in European experience of this period. Moreover, migration is overlooked repeatedly in demographic and economic analysis: formal demography concedes only a token place for the study of external migration, whilst economic analysis 'ignores international mobility of factors' (Tapinos 1974). Although interdependence between countries is nowadays increasingly evident, the hypothesis of a closed field (whether an economy or a population) in fact always underlies current theories. To what are we to attribute this neglect? To the sheer difficulty of incorporating the international environment, with its uncertain future, and its manifold influences, into the study of any given setting? To insufficient appreciation of long-term historical processes? To a fundamental refusal to consider non-linear factors in history? To unconscious fears of violence, war, disaster, depopulation? Probably all of these, and more.

Migration is a mechanism of demographic regulation. When populations expand, threatening the traditional equilibrium with subsistence, a number of adjustments are possible. As in Europe from the mid-nineteenth century, under the effects of prolonged mortality decline, there may be increased pressure on resources, fertility control, expulsion, and departure of young adults, or the 'positive check' described by Malthus: the removal of population surplus by increased mortality. Nineteenth-century Europe witnessed the coexistence of all these responses, each to a greater or lesser degree depending on place, period, and circumstance. But emigration from Europe rapidly played a major role; once started, the flow of departures responded to an internal logic far more complex than that of mere repulsion, and capable of assuming unanticipated dimensions, as long as the contributing forces manifested themselves. The demographic consequences in countries of reception is evident, as whole continents were populated in this way, growing from very small to mass dimensions; but countries of departure themselves could also be greatly affected. This last point has given rise to endless controversy, stemming basically from differences of opinion on the fundamental causes of migration.

Demographic Potential and Migratory Potential

My intention in this chapter is not to reconstruct migration statistics detailing population exchanges between the several countries with advanced demographic transitions; such an undertaking, in addition to its excessive weight, would in most cases yield results too imprecise on this problem (see Chapter 2) to permit sound observations, particularly where less developed countries are concerned. Instead, after brief presentation of the main theses on causes and effects of European emigration, the large waves of migration will be situated in the history of the demographic transition, in order to establish possible relations between trends in natural increase and the intensity of emigration. This objective will be carried out solely on those countries which, at the time of writing, have completed the different phases leading to very low fertility and an ageing or implosive population. The age composition in such countries, in which the number of places left vacant by retiring workers tends to be greater than those available in the rising generation, is the opposite of historical patterns hitherto. The current trend of natural increase means that, sooner or later, this type of age composition will extend across the entire Western world (Chesnais 1982); the tremendous contrast between this situation and that of the less developed world may eventually bring about a major reversal in migration streams. We shall concentrate, therefore, on how migratory flows affecting countries with European populations have altered in dimension and direction, in relation to successive phases of demographic transition.

1. Causes and Consequences of the European Exodus

The Reasons for Departure

International migration arises from multiple causes. Two sorts of explanation are generally put forward where labour migration is concerned: the first, borrowed from physics, refers to factors of attraction and repulsion; the second (not only complementary to the first but in fact subsumed by it) refers to differences in pay between country of origin and country of destination. Different schools take different lines on these issues: certain authors, like Böhning (1977), for example, drawing on contemporary experience, suggest that employment opportunities count more than differences in pay, and that migration flows are determined more by the demand for jobs than by their supply; others, like Tapinos (1981), advance far more complex mechanisms, including not only the obvious issue of labour regulations, but the operation of job markets, policies of host countries, international specialization, industrial policy, and so forth.

Opinion on the mass European exodus to the New World likewise has its divisions. Writers who witnessed the event, in Europe at least, tend to emphasize the impetus of depressed conditions in countries of origin, whereas twentieth-century economists, especially trans-Atlantic ones, emphasize the attraction of America. Plainly it is vain to want to separate these influences, since both factors existed; it is their combined force which influences decisions to migrate: one leaves one's country for the reason both that one is experiencing difficulties at home and that, from what one hears, one hopes for a better life abroad. Furthermore, it is inevitable, historically speaking, that effects attributed to the one or the other should vary widely, depending on the country or period under consideration. In other words, we must situate the debate in the historical light of prevailing economic and demographic conditions.

Let us take, by way of illustration, the case of European emigration to the

US. What were the economic conditions? It must be said that, except in rare instances (or for certain peasant populations attracted by free land), the full force of America's attraction could not have been felt until circumstances combined to its advantage. In other words, until a strongly rising American economy had begun to acquire its powerful reputation, which could scarcely happen until after the Civil War. On the other hand, the effects of over-crowding in Europe would have gained force at the time when countries concerned experienced simultaneously a large demographic increase and an insufficient economic growth. This conjunction of circumstances occurs at very different periods in different countries (see Chapter 17). Consequently, each case must be treated in its own right, without underestimating the variety of circumstances in a given country, according to particular characteristics (profession and religion, especially of migrants). Push factors remained significant in areas of the Iberian peninsula, where demographic growth attained relatively high levels, and social and economic changes did not occur until the twentieth century.

The Role of Economic Cycles

The relation between the intensity of European emigration and levels of economic activity in the US was first analysed by Jérôme (1926); he established that, on the whole, factors of attraction associated with American prosperity tended to prevail over the impetus resulting from European crises. Bearing in mind the preliminary observations above, this conclusion is hardly surprising, as the period covered by his study begins in 1870. Kuznets (1958) and Easterlin (1961) have studied a longer period, but begin from the same date, and reach similar conclusions. Schumpeter (1912), however, leaves the issue more open to discussion, remarking that migration is 'conditioned by economic cycles associated with industrialization'. Comparable studies have been conducted by Winsemius (1940) on Italian migration, by D. S. Thomas (1941) on Swedish migration, and by Forsyth (1942) on emigration to Canada and Australia, which arrive at a more subtle conclusion. This is especially the case with Thomas's study: migration is envisaged in a system of inter-dependence between the overall economic situation in Sweden and that in the US; emigration only becomes high when the difference between the cyclical trends of the two economies is weighted in favour of the US. Conversely, when the Swedish economy compares favourably, the country experiences a decline in migration, and an increase in return migration.

Population Pressure, or the Black Year of 1847

However, studies such as these never seem entirely convincing. To begin with, migration involves a dynamic interaction in which, while economic inertia weighs heavily at home, and prosperity encourages immigration abroad, the combined effect may be to maintain growth in both places. Moreover, considering cycles in the medium term may help to clarify the temporal pattern of migration between successive periods, but it manifestly fails to clarify two fundamental issues: the date at which the process began and the scale it attained. More complex structural variables must be brought into play, such as demographic development, political changes (the creation of nation-states), agrarian structure, and customary law pertaining to inheritance of property. In certain areas of central Europe, the practice of equal division of land, along with declining rural mortality, led to the parcelling out of farms and the total pauperization of the peasantry. The subsequent rural exodus, of considerable proportions, was reinforced by the attraction of cheap and virgin farmland in the US (Von Der Goltz 1893).

Historians are in agreement that, in the first half of the nineteenth century, population pressure was the determining influence in rural areas of western Europe. The exodus dates from the start of the century in Germany, for example. In Ireland, Germany, and Scandinavia, and also—to a lesser degree—in Great Britain, with the decline in mortality, which was often more pronounced in the country than the city, agricultural areas became over-populated in relation to the state of productive techniques. A succession of climatic reverses rapidly led to dramatic food shortages. The local spread of industrialization was irregular in its initial stages and highly susceptible to disruption by unbalanced urbanization, declining living standards, intermittent unemployment, and the wiping out of small agricultural enterprises and traditional crafts. In other words, industrialization could itself play a part in driving out the victims of the restructuring it entailed. General economic development remained, in consequence, tributary to the agrarian sector, and the size of the waves of migration was dictated by fluctuations in harvests.

The Irish famine is a familiar example, but because of its extreme character it has too often been treated as exceptional and, consequently, encouraged underestimation of the general influence of agricultural conditions on emigration. Nevertheless, Irish emigration was significant well before famine in the 1840s; moreover, annual patterns of migration to the US coincided with the pattern of harvests, not only in Ireland, but in the major emigration countries of the period (Germany, England, and Scandinavia). If 1847 was a bad year, this was the case more or less everywhere: it precipitated a great wave of Irish migration, as well as in the other advanced countries of north-western Europe, except for France. Table 6.1 presents various data on this subject. Between 1847 and 1854, 20% of Ireland's population (1,630,000 people) emigrated, and the country also experienced high mortality (985,366 deaths registered between 1847 and 1851), and a marked decline in fertility. Between 1845 and 1851, the population fell from 8,295,000 to 6,552,000, an unparalleled process of depopulation, emigration being consistently higher than natural increase. In Germany, at the same time and for largely similar

TABLE 6.1. *North-west European emigration to the United States, 1842–1858*

Period	Annual number of emigrants, Ireland ('000s)	Annual number of immigrants arriving in the US from north-west Europe ('000s)				
		Ireland	G. Britain	Germany	Scandinavia	Other countries
1842–46	73	40	17	29	1.3	7.2
1847	215	106	23	74	1.3	24.0
1848	178	113	35	58	1.1	10.0
1849	214	159	55	60	3.5	8.0
1850	209	164	51	79	1.6	11.0
1851	250	221	51	72	2.4	21.0
1852	220	160	41	146	4.1	11.0
1853	193	163	38	142	3.4	14.0
1854	150	102	59	215	4.2	23.0
1855–58	82	58	45	70	2.0	9.6

Bracketed averages: emigrants 204; Ireland 149; G. Britain 44; Germany 106; Scandinavia 2.7; Other countries 15.1.

Source: Ferenczi, in Willcox (1929).

reasons,[1] a wave of emigration swept over the country: between 1853 and 1855 almost a million people emigrated each year. Great Britain experienced a food crisis, but of a lesser order: for the period 1847–54, over 300,000 arrivals were registered in the US (for these three countries, see Harkness, Burgdorfer, and Snow, respectively, in Willcox 1931). Emigration was also considerable in the other countries in north-west Europe.

Irish emigration continued despite considerable improvements: the disappearance of non-viable smallholdings; departure from slums; departure of the uneducated, beggars, and the desperate poor; a 9% increase of land under cultivation between 1841 and 1851; a 30% decline in rural density; but also a series of good harvests at the beginning of the 1850s. This pattern was also manifest in Germany[2] and Great Britain, but the proportions were of quite a different order; Germany's migration rate, for example, was at its highest at 6.6 per 1000, whereas the Irish maximum was six times this figure, at 38 per 1000 in 1851. Migration is by nature cumulative: emigrants save money, send funds to their family or friends still remaining, and help them to leave the country; the initial force of the exodus thus sets in motion a process which continues at its own rate. Hence the depression in England in the 1880s resulted in high emigration, a phenomenon which continued, albeit with less intensity, into the prosperous pre-war period of 1901–11.

Industrial Revolution, Social Destabilization, and Demographic Boom

With industrialization in western Europe, emigration became less dependent on the hazards of climate than on economic cycles connected with industry. Migration only truly became a mass phenomenon after the economic boom had occurred. Entry into a period of general growth in fact created the conditions favourable to mass exodus: the disappearance of traditional enterprises; alienation connected with urban and industrial concentration; development of infrastructure and communication networks; and the creation of a demographic surplus brought about by declines in mortality, rises in productivity, etc. The poorest areas of southern and eastern Europe did not contribute to the pattern of emigration to the US until the Industrial Revolution and its attendant demographic revolution. Their turning-point came several decades later than the rest of Europe, but migration was more intense: there was a higher level of demographic increase, and economic growth was not sufficient to absorb the surplus. Without doubt the rhythm inherent in the demographic revolution (connected with the discovery of vaccination) was more rapid than that of the Industrial Revolution, the latter

---

[1] The political troubles of 1848 also played a part.

[2] The abolition of restrictions on marriage and household formation which applied in certain German states up to the 1860s, notably Bavaria, made it easier for young couples to establish homes for themselves, and diminished the tendency to emigrate.

being less easily transferred: this adumbrates the recent experience of the less developed world. Migration is thus not solely influenced by differences of demographic potential as writers like Leroy-Beaulieu or Bertillon were inclined to think. (The former even spoke of 'endosmosis', as if population movement back and forth across national boundaries was a process with its own internal regulation.) However, migration calls into play more complex relations, both between population and economy within a country of departure, and between economic situations in each of the countries concerned.

The Demographic Influence of Migration

International migration will be considered here first of all in its relation to mortality. The clearest and most immediate connection is that of possible substitution of mortality by migration, the latter providing means to escape crises. In an over-populated rural economy, emigration provides a safety valve whenever agrarian population pressure is not compensated by sufficient growth in employment opportunities in industry or the tertiary sector. It alleviates economic stress, thus averting a fall in living standards and any excess mortality that might thereby arise. It is therefore an alternative solution to the rationalization of agriculture or industrial development as ways of reducing risks of subsistence crisis. If in Ireland, for example, emigration had been less, there is no reason to think that population size would not ultimately have been reduced to the same level, although the adjustment, through famine or restriction of marriages, would doubtless have been slower and more painful—and of course the countries of reception would not have experienced the same growth.

In addition to this observation, there is the legitimate question of whether migration did not actually entail certain demographic consequences, especially if we consider the selective nature of emigration. The selection of migrants could not have been entirely spontaneous; the migrants quite probably had lower mortality than their countrymen who remained at home, but it is not known to what degree this advantage was reinforced by settling in a more advanced country. Furthermore, by contributing in various ways to improved living standards among the still-resident population, migration would be capable of accelerating mortality decline. (This aspect, although difficult to establish from the evidence, could then reasonably be expected to act as a counterbalance to the possible negative effects which migration had on fertility; but this is not a usual line of reasoning.)

On the other hand, the interaction between migration and fertility forms a conventional part of analysis. For the country of departure, the immediate effects result from the volume and selectivity of migration, usually con-centrated in the cohort aged 15–24 (a cohort with high 'reproductive poten-tial', to use Keyfitz's concept (1977): see Table 6.6). The effect on fertility is strongest through marriage where migration is sex-specific, as with Italian emigration, which was 80% male before the First World War. But these effects are not free of ambiguity: the establishment of a tradition of migration can help maintain or even increase local fertility, by virtue of slowing down permanent rural exodus, by the advantages of financial support expected from children sent abroad, and by the correlative reduction of local demographic pressure, both on jobs and lines of descent, in the long term, however, it is likely that the gradual transition to a monetary economy and modern growth associated with emigration accelerate more than retard the demographic transition.

Debate is more frequently centred on fertility in the country of arrival. If one assumes generally that migrants adopt a pattern of behaviour midway between that of their country of origin and country of destination, and that they gradually incline towards that of the latter, the only problem is the length of the period of adjustment. This is in fact often much shorter than is generally allowed, as Livi Bacci (1965) has observed regarding the Italian population in the United States. The question of the effect of immigration on the fertility of native populations is, in contrast, subject to heated argument. Walker's thesis (1891), according to which 'instead of constituting a new contribution to the population, immigration merely results in a replacement of natives by foreign elements', has remained famous. In this view, immigration has a depressive effect on indigenous fertility, which cancels out the addition of new numbers. This thesis has been contested by various authors. In the case of the US, Walker's argument[3] is clearly inadmissible on account of the sheer volume of migration: growth due to immigration far outweighs the effect of the decline in fertility. In 1790, the population of the US was only 3.9 million; if we were to suppose an extreme demographic development, on a par with that of French Canada, there could have been a maximum of 37 million inhabitants a century later, when Walker was writing; whereas the population had by then risen to 63 million. Fifteen million immigrants, at a minimum,[4] arrived between 1820 and 1890 (see Table 6.11).

This argument has antecedents, already discernible in outline in the writings of Benjamin Franklin (1775). It has sometimes been advanced in another form, notably by Bertillon (1873), for France; while less easy to refute in French circumstances, it has, however, also been rejected (Levasseur 1892; Gonnard 1928), for two reasons. First, fertility decline precedes immigration by a considerable period (see Table 6.14), the latter only becoming truly significant after the war of 1870. Second, departments with low levels of immigration experienced fertility declines no different from those in which immigration was a major factor.

If Walker's argument is rejected or, at least, is considered not to have the

---

[3] Advanced in an attempt to prohibit immigration; in this it anticipates the restrictive measures later adopted.

[4] Registration for the start of the period is incomplete.

importance attributed to it, then immigration has a strong and positive effect on the demographic growth of countries of arrival. This influence operates by direct or indirect effect on mortality as much as on fertility. Migration would appear to have a less negative effect than expected on the demographic growth of the country of departure. All things considered, immigration should therefore contribute to a boom in demographic growth.

2. European Emigration and the Stages of Demographic Transition

Although European emigration dates from an early period, it did not become a mass phenomenon until technology (with its implications for the cost and safety of transport) and demographic and economic conditions had developed. It is easily the largest migration of the modern period. In this section we shall trace the temporal outline of overseas emigration for the principal countries concerned.

However, we need to be wary about the quality of data, from the outset: statistics for legal migration are 'the least reliable and least comparable of all demographic statistics' (Golini 1982). There is no universally accepted definition of what constitutes an emigrant, and data are collected on the basis of different criteria in different countries. As a general rule, knowledge of migration overseas is superior to that over land; but not infrequently, even in countries bordering the sea, nineteenth-century migrants left by land in order to embark from a port in a neighbouring country.[5] The comparative quality of registration remains unknown and, even if we concede that we are less in the dark about overseas migration than other sorts, the usual discrepancies are none the fewer.

For instance, in the period 1846–1932 the number of migrants, according to their countries of departure, totalled 53.5 million; but in countries of arrival they totalled 59.2 million, a figure which Carr-Saunders further increased to 65 million. This sort of uncertainty is slight compared with that which surrounds figures for return migration. These appear to have long been underestimated, and may have increased at the end of the nineteenth century, when virgin land began to become rarer in the US, and several west European countries entered the second phase of their industrialization. It is thus necessary to develop indirect measures from census data: this is how Kuznets and Rubin (1954) were able to calculate the rates of return migration for the US prior to 1908—the date from which returning migrants were officially registered.

---

[5] Harbour statistics generally indicate nationality (Ferenczi 1929).

The Geography of Transatlantic Migration

The significance of migratory flows demands to be assessed in its true dimensions, that is, over a long period. Table 6.2 gives the crude statistics of emigrants and immigrants for those countries in which the cumulative flow exceeded 500,000 people in 1932. The countries have been arranged in descending order, according to numbers of migrants. The percentages represent these totals in relation to total populations at the beginning of the particular periods under consideration: this gives us an index of average overall propensity to emigrate.

The British Isles come first by a long way amongst countries of emigration, with 18 million departures for the period 1846–1932. Italy follows, with 11 million, then Austria-Hungary, Germany, and Spain, each with a contingent of around 5 million; Russia and Portugal are well behind, with around 2 million, and last come Sweden and Norway, with around 1 million.

The relative significance of this phenomenon, as measured by proportions migrating, provides an index of propensity; this reflects the role of migration in demographic transition, at least as a first approximation,[6] and gives quite a different picture. With an overall index of propensity to emigrate of 64%, the British Isles easily have the lead, but this is partly—and only partly—due to Irish emigration. Almost 5.5 million Irish emigrated between 1846 and 1932, whilst in 1845 the Irish population was 8,295,000; hence the Irish index of 66%, in comparison to Great Britain's 64%.[7] Norway presents a similar value (63%). In light of this index, the legendary emigration from Ireland loses its sensational edge. What has marked Irish emigration out in particular is, of course, the disaster of the years 1846–50; but in the longer term, what is more significant was the sudden conversion of its regime of nuptiality, causing an extraordinary fall in natural increase to less than 1%, as opposed to 2% or more over the preceding decades. Emigration was thus consistently greater than natural increase.

With an index bordering on 50%, Italy and Portugal occupy a similar position to their three Nordic counterparts; but Sweden and Spain—also maritime countries—are well below this (around 33%), whilst Germany and Austria-Hungary fall back into a middle position (16%), and Russia comes last, along with countries like Japan and France, where the effects of emigration were negligible.

Where immigration is concerned, the leading position is clearly occupied by one country, the United States, which received 60% of the European

---

[6] As the initial date is identical for all the countries, the method of calculation tends to overestimate the role of emigration in transition where the latter has been delayed.

[7] It should be remembered, however, that during the preceding period Irish emigration largely dominated British emigration: from 1815 to 1845, the number of Irish emigrants is calculated at 1.9 million; this is over three times that of the figure for the English and Scots combined (Ferenczi 1929: 99).

TABLE 6.2. *Overseas migration, 1821–1932*

Emigration			Immigration			
Country	Number of emigrants 1846–1932[a] ('000s)	% of initial population	Country	Period	Number of immigrants ('000s)	% of initial population
British Isles[b]	18,020 (5,443)	64.0 (66.0)	United States	1821–1932	34,244	320
Italy	11,092	48.0	Argentina	1856–1932	6,405	500
Austria–Hungary	5,196	17.0	Canada	1821–1932	5,206	(550)
Germany	4,889	15.0	Brazil	1821–1932	4,431	110
Spain	4,653	31.0	Australia	1861–1932	2,913	290
Russia	2,253[c]	4.0	Cuba	1901–1932	857	54
Portugal	1,805	48.0	South Africa	1881–1932	852	24
Sweden	1,203	36.0	Uruguay	1836–1932	713	(800)
Norway	854	63.0	New Zealand	1851–1932	594	(475)
Poland	642[d]	2.4	Mauritius	1836–1932	573	(433)
France	519	1.5				
Japan	518	1.6				

Notes: Only taking into account the countries for which the estimation of the cumulative flow of emigrants or immigrants exceeds 500,000 during the period indicated.

[a] Unless stated otherwise.
[b] Irish data in parentheses.
[c] 1846–1924.
[d] 1920–32.

Sources: Calculated from Ferenczi, in Willcox (1929), Carr-Saunders (1936); and national censuses.

emigrants. The next country in line, Argentina, received only one-fifth as many immigrants (6.4 as opposed to 34 million). With 5.2 and 4.4 million respectively, Canada and Brazil follow close on Argentina, whilst Australia (2.9) rather takes the back seat. In total, these five countries received more than 90% of European immigrants; the remaining countries received less than a million immigrants in the periods of registration indicated. Except for South Africa, and to a lesser degree Cuba, where white immigration remained a minority factor, the proportional effect of these population transfers was far greater on countries of reception than departure, since these places were relatively unoccupied. Brazil alone had, at the start of the period, a population comparable to its migratory intake. The other countries registered inflows 3 to 8 times greater than their 'initial' population: thus, in the US, the total volume of immigration from 1821 to 1932 is 3.2 times greater than the population in 1821.

The Spatio-temporal Profile of Migration

As we have seen, intercontinental emigration, with the exception of Austria-Hungary, affected primarily the Western maritime powers. Confined initially to small numbers of adventurers or deportees, migration ceased to be marginal during the 1830s; progressively, through the second half of the century, as structural changes swept across the old continent, it assumed quite extra-ordinary dimensions. The first waves were confined to north-western Europe, mainly Ireland, whose demographic growth was then unequalled, proportion-ately, except by England and Russia. By mid-century, overseas migration began in Germany, spreading 30 years later to the rest of central Europe, and finally reaching southern and eastern Europe. Intercontinental emigration by decade (1851–1960) is summarized for the principal European countries in Table 6.3. The corresponding rates of emigration (Table 6.4) have been calculated from data in this table and presented in Figs. 6.1(a) to (d). In this way, by comparing the profiles of natural increase examined in Chapter 8, it is possible to establish that in each country, the peak of emigration in most cases coincided, within a margin of a few years, with the peak in natural increase. Migration is at its highest during the period when, following the decline in mortality, the curve of natural increase approaches its apex; and the size of the wave of departures is closely connected with the level of natural increase and hence with patterns of demographic transition. The traits of migration are inseparable from the profiles of transition, and vice versa. We will return to this relationship in subsequent analysis.

   In France, where fertility decline more or less paralleled the decline in mortality—the characteristic transition profile therefore being low and flat—there was a rise in fertility during the Second Empire. The outline for migration reflects this pattern exactly: it is low and flat and has a small peak during the 1880s, or about 20 years after the recovery of fertility.

TABLE 6.3. *Volume of emigration from Europe by decade, 1851–1960* (per 1000 inhabitants)

Country	Period										
	1851–60	1861–70	1871–80	1881–90	1891–1900	1901–10	1911–20	1921–30	1931–40	1941–50	1951–60
Austria-Hungary[a]	31	40	46	248	440	1,111	418	61	11[b]	—	53[c]
France	27	36	66	119	51	53	32	4	5	8	155
Germany[d]	671	779	626	1,342	527	274	91	564	121[e]	618	872
Italy	5	27	168	992	1,580	3,615	2,194	1,370	235	467	858
Norway	36	98	85	187	95	191	62	87	6	10[f]	25
Portugal	45	79	131	185	266	324	402	995	108	69[g]	346
Russia	—	—	58	288	481	911	420	—	—	—	—
Spain	3	7	13	572	791	1,091	1,306	560	132	166	543
Sweden	17	122	103	327	205	324	86	107	8	23	43
Switzerland	6	15	36	85	35	37	31	50	47	18[h]	23
United Kingdom	1,313[jk]	1,572[k]	1,849[k]	3,259	2,149	3,150	2,587	2,151	262	755[f]	1,454

a Austria only, since 1921.
b 1931–37.
c 1954–60.
d West Germany, 1941–50, 1951–60.
e 1932–36.
f 1946–50.
g Incl. emigration to European countries, 1941–49.
h Incl. emigration to European countries, 1941–49.
i And Ireland.
j 1853–60.
k Not incl. emigration directly from Irish ports.

Source: Woodruff (1966).

TABLE 6.4. Rates^a of emigration from Europe by decade, 1851–1940 (per 1000 inhabitants)

Country	Period								
	1851–60	1861–70	1871–80	1881–90	1891–1900	1901–10	1911–20	1921–30	1931–40
Austria–Hungary^b	0.10	0.12	0.13	0.60	0.98	2.26	0.80	0.93	0.23^c
France	0.08	0.10	0.18	0.31	0.13	0.14	0.08	0.01	0.01
Germany^d	1.97	2.04	1.46	2.85	1.00	0.45	0.14	0.89	0.31^e
Italy	0.02	0.10	0.61	3.37	5.03	10.79	6.06	3.47	0.55
Norway	2.42	5.75	4.67	9.66	4.48	8.25	2.46	3.19	0.21
Portugal	1.16	1.88	2.96	3.83	5.08	5.72	6.70	15.43	1.50
Russia	—	—	0.06	0.27	0.38	0.63	0.25	—	—
Spain	0.02	0.04	0.08	3.29	4.39	5.67	6.34	2.49	0.54
Sweden	0.47	3.04	2.36	7.00	4.10	6.09	1.51	1.77	0.13
Switzerland	0.24	0.58	1.31	2.94	1.11	1.05	0.82	1.27	1.14
United Kingdom	4.63^{gh}	5.22^h	5.64^h	9.05	5.44	7.69	5.77	4.78	0.56

^{a} It should be remembered that rates are calculated on an annual basis

^{b} Austria only, since 1921.

^{c} 1931–37.

^{d} West Germany, 1941–50, 1951–60.

^{e} 1932–36.

^{f} And Ireland.

^{g} 1853–60.

^{h} Not incl. emigration directly from Irish ports.

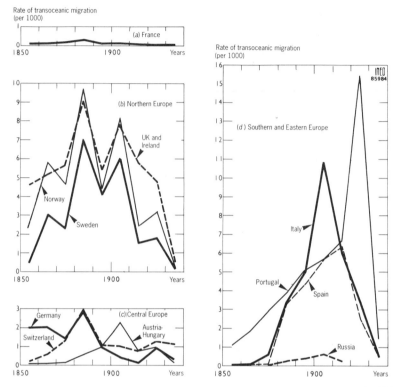

Fig. 6.1. Rate of transoceanic migration in Europe, by main regions, 1850–1940

North European countries having early transitions from fairly 'high' rates of natural increase (UK, Ireland, Norway, and Sweden), experienced rates of emigration which peaked relatively early (in the 1880s), as well as at relatively high levels (between 5 and 10 per 1000), whilst their central European counterparts (Germany, Switzerland, and Austria-Hungary), where the transition exhibited similar characteristics, but where maritime access was nil or slight, experienced a peak in emigration at the same period, but at a much lower level (only 2 to 3 per 1000).

The transition in southern and eastern Europe was slower, and natural increase correspondingly higher; migration streams only begin to peak in Italy, Spain, and Portugal after 1900, at levels comparable to those of northern Europe (over 5 per 1000); but the rates tend to continue to rise, and the general trend suggests that had if it not been for the tragic upheavals of subsequent decades (the First World War, restriction of non-Anglo-Saxon immigration to the US, the Great Depression, establishment of dictatorships in the east and south of the continent, and the Second World War), transatlantic migration would have continued, and even increased. Here, too, the

TABLE 6.5. *Number of births and emigration*

Age groups (years)	Period of migration	Birth cohorts	Linear correlation coefficient
15–19	1863–1906	1845–88	0.665
20–24	1863–1906	1840–83	0.732
25–29		1835–78	0.556

unavoidable distinction between maritime and land-locked countries holds: even if Russia, for example, also recorded an increase in migration, the rates remained very low (the country, it should be said, offers immense virgin tracts for colonization).

It was thus at precisely the time when the proportion of young adults was exceptionally large that there was a surge in overseas emigration. This relation between emigration and demographic pressure becomes all the stronger when large cohorts of young people coincide with rigid social structures which hinder their advancement, or economic innovations which make their man-power redundant. This statistical link between rates of emigration and natural increase was established by Ravnholt (1937), on the basis of observations on Sweden and Norway from 1850 to 1930, which showed the existence of a very strong correlation.

The observation was extended to the whole of Europe by B. Thomas (1954). According to him, the temporal pattern of European emigration cannot be explained solely by the demand for labour in the United States. It depends on demographic developments in the countries of departure; and, in this, less on reproductive cycles, as would be expected, than on the decline in mortality. Each of the four main waves of emigration was connected with a peak in natural increase which preceded it by 25 years.

Thomas also begins his argument with an analysis of Swedish emigration statistics, which possess the double advantage of being of good quality and of including the age distribution of emigrants. By comparing the number of emigrants per cohort with the size of the corresponding generations, he reveals a strong correlation between the two series: the larger the number of births, the more significant emigration tends to be. The calculation is conducted on the three quinquennial groups aged 15–19, 20–24, and 25–29 years, which at the time of highest emigration in the second half of the nineteenth century in themselves comprise two-thirds of the emigrants (65.6% over the period 1851–1900; Sundbärg 1907). The development may be followed using moving averages for 5-year periods, as shown in Table 6.5. The correlation is highest for the age group 20–24 years; this is followed by the 15–19- and then the 25–29-year age groups. The result is hardly surprising; it is the very image of the pattern of age-specific rates character-

TABLE 6.6. *Emigration rates by age, Sweden, 1891–1900 (per 1000)*

Age (years)	Emigration rate		Age (years)	Emigration rate		Age (years)	Emigration rate	
	Male	Female		Male	Female		Male	Female
0–4	2.15	2.19	25–29	10.78	10.24	50–54	1.48	1.36
5–9	2.37	2.32	30–34	6.63	5.75	55–59	1.12	1.45
10–14	2.11	2.37	35–39	4.57	3.39	60–64	0.86	1.23
15–19	11.44	12.82	40–44	3.04	2.07	⩾65	0.56	0.62
20–24	19.07	16.18	45–49	2.08	1.58	All ages	5.22	4.79

Source: Sundbärg (1907: 100).

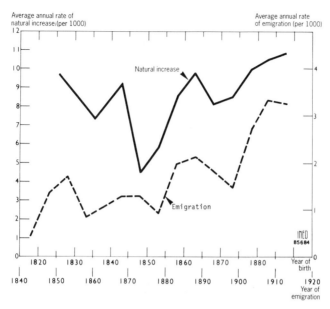

FIG. 6.2. Natural increase and emigration, Europe, 1820–1915

istic of international migration; the 20–24 age group is in fact easily the most affected by the departures (Table 6.6). An argument thus may be found here for specifying an optimum time lag between time series of births and those of overseas emigration.

Data for other countries are not as rich as Sweden's. Thomas was none the less able to demonstrate, for Europe as a whole, a correspondence between an excess in natural increase and the emergence of streams of emigration 25 years later: the four great waves of 1844–54, 1863–73, 1878–88, and 1898–1907 thus echo high points of natural increase of 1820–29, 1840–45, 1860–65, and 1880–90 respectively. These observations, which refer to the period 1815–1907, are summarized and extended up to 1915 in Table 6.7. Fig. 6.2 highlights the close relation between fluctuations in the two series. The linear correlation coefficient arrived at is 0.740 (value significant at 5%).

This pattern may now be examined more generally in Europe, by region, but excluding France, which was not a major participant in the development. Europe may be divided into three large areas, where nineteenth-century overseas migration is concerned: the north-west, which supplied the 'older generation' of migrants; and then the south and east, where migration occurred later but in much greater numbers. In the latter areas, emigration streams did not become really large until the 1880s, but they quickly overtook the north-western European movement in size: annual average departures around 1910, for the south and east, exceeded 500,000, whereas during the decade of

TABLE 6.7. *Natural increase and emigration, all of Europe, 1821–1915 (per 1000)*

Period	Emigration rate	Period	Natural increase	Period	Emigration rate	Period	Natural increase
1841–45	0.56	—	—	1881–1885	1.98	1856–1860	8.6
1846–50	1.35	{1821–30	9.6	1886–1890	2.13	1861–1865	9.8
1851–55	1.69	{1831–40	7.4	1891–1895	1.86	1866–1870	8.1
1856–60	0.86	1841–45	9.2	1896–1900	1.49	1871–1875	8.5
1861–65	1.04	1846–50	4.6	1901–1905	2.72	1876–1880	10.0
1866–70	1.30	1851–55	5.8	1906–1910	3.35	1881–1885	10.5
1871–75	1.30			1911–1915	3.04	1886–1890	10.8
1876–80	0.96						

Sources: Sundbärg (1908), except for emigration after 1906, for which see Ferenczi, in Willcox (1929), and Kirk (1946).

TABLE 6.8. *Natural increase and emigration, north-western Europe excluding France, 1801–1915* (rates per 1000)

Natural increase		Emigration		
Period	Rate[a]	Period	Annual total ('000s)	Rate
1801–15	4.5	1826–1840	78.3	0.95
1816–20	11.0	1841–1845	143.0	1.59
1821–25	12.3	1846–1850	254.3	2.74
1826–30	9.0	1851–1855	331.3	3.46
1831–35	7.2	1856–1860	184.7	1.87
1836–40	8.8	1861–1865	202.9	1.98
1841–45	10.2	1866–1870	308.4	2.90
1846–50	6.8	1871–1875	310.1	2.79
1851–55	8.3	1876–1880	192.8	1.65
1856–60	10.5	1881–1885	480.7	3.94
1861–65	10.3	1886–1890	407.2	3.21
1866–70	10.0	1891–1895	273.9	2.06
1871–75	11.3	1896–1900	137.5	0.98
1876–80	11.7	1901–1905	253.0	1.71
1881–85	11.1	1906–1910	322.3	2.07
1886–90	11.2	1911–1915	325.6	2.01

[a] Western Europe (north-west and south-west), excluding France, to 1850, inclusive.

Sources: Calculated from data in Sundbärg (1908) and Kirk (1946).

the 1880s which was the period of highest emigration among 'Western' populations (mainly British, German, and Scandinavian), the annual average flow of emigrants remained below 450,000. Unfortunately, comparative rates of return for the different regions are not known.

In north-west Europe, as we have seen, average annual rates of emigration were relatively low, ranging between 1 and 4 per 1000 for the entire period 1801–1915. They do not reach or exceed 3 per 1000 until the periods 1846–55, 1866–70, and 1881–90, that is, a quarter of a century after natural increase had crossed a threshold of 10 per 1000 (in 1816–25, 1841–45, and 1856–60, respectively). The only exceptions are the last decades studied, following the last quarter of the nineteenth century, when the rates of natural increase had reached their peak (11 to 12 per 1000; see Table 6.8): by this time the economies of the countries concerned had reached a rhythm of industrial growth sufficient to absorb demographic increase.

Similarly, in southern Europe, emigration only becomes considerable after a surge in natural increase, but the respective levels and rates of departure are quite different. From the point at which natural increase exceeds a level of

TABLE 6.9. *Natural increase and emigration, southern Europe (Italy, Spain, and Portugal), 1851–1915* (rates per 1000)

Natural increase		Emigration		
Period	Rate	Period	Annual total ('000s)	Rate
1851–55	(3.7)	1876–1880	46.2	0.94
1856–60	(3.8)	1881–1885	128.5	2.53
1861–65	7.9	1886–1890	230.9	4.39
1866–70	6.5	1891–1895	259.1	4.86
1871–75	6.1	1896–1900	268.1	4.85
1876–80	7.1	1901–1905	418.2	7.27
1881–85	7.9	1906–1910	587.8	9.93
1886–90	8.5	1911–1915	532.4	8.66

Sources: Calculated from data in Sundbärg (1908) and Kirk (1946).

6 per 1000, the rate of departure becomes very high, equalling and then exceeding, at the beginning of the century, the rate of natural growth in the relevant earlier period (1876–90)—even though the latter had not yet reached its highest point (Table 6.9). This phenomenon reaches its climax in Italy: in 1906–10, for example, the number of departures is a third higher than the natural increase for the years 1881–85.

Finally, in eastern Europe, where developments occurred even later, emigration likewise became important only when natural increase manifested itself in marked demographic pressure, which is to say, from the beginning of the twentieth century. Here, too, the correspondence between demographic pressure resulting from a progressive increase in surplus fertility, from the 1880s onward, and the expansion of migratory streams, 20 years later, is clear[8] (see Table 6.10). As with southern Europe, the curve of natural increase had not yet reached its limit when the associated migrations were interrupted, first by circumstances of war, then by politics: the introduction of very strict quotas by the American government. If emigration rates, compared with those of southern Europe, look low (barely 3 per 1000 as opposed to 9 to 10 per 1000, just before the First World War), the number of migrants by the end of the period, owing to the volume of the demographic reservoirs concerned, are entirely comparable; analysis of trends would suggest that, had it not been for the American policy suspending migration in the early 1920s, Slavic emigration would not only have ranked first, but easily exceeded in volume, the Anglo-Saxon and even Latin emigrations.

---

[8] The case of eastern Europe is distinguished, however, by the emigration of prosecuted peoples (Jews, Armenians, White Russians).

TABLE 6.10. *Natural increase and emigration of east European populations,[a] 1841–1915* (rates per 1000)

| Natural increase | | Emigration | | |
Period	Rate	Period	Annual total ('000s)	Rate
1841–60	7.0	⌠ 1861–1870	4.4	0.04
		⌡ 1871–1880	17.3	0.15
1861–80	10.6	⌠ 1881–1890	75.9	0.57
		⌡ 1891–1900	139.7	0.94
1881–90	13.5	1901–1910	447.1	2.64
1891–95	13.8	1911–1915	507.1	2.78

[a] Russia, Poland, Romania, Serbia, Bulgaria, Hungary, Galicia and Bukovina, Bosnia-Hercegovina, Balkans.

Sources: Calculated from data in Sundbärg (1908) (natural increase) and Kirk (1946) (emigration).

If in the analysis of factors affecting the size, direction, and timing of migratory movements, attention is (rightly) focused on the influence of economic cycles, then demographic factors in the determination of long trends have a more important role than is generally allowed.[9]

The Peopling of the United States

The history of US immigration reflects the successive phases of the migratory transition. The official registration of immigrants began in 1820, following an Act of Congress in 1819, but records of repatriation and return migration date only from 1908. Table 6.11 reconstructs the migratory flows according to country of origin. Four periods may be distinguished: 1820–89, 1890–1914, 1915–45, and 1965–79.

1. Up to 1890, one is dealing with the old Anglo-Saxon Protestant migration (except for Ireland), which was a continuation of that of the original settlers. The flows from countries other than northern Europe and Germany were negligible (see, for example, Johnson 1913, Carrothers 1929, and Walshaw 1941, on the British Isles).

[9] It is significant that a writer like B. Thomas should see in the demographic transition the major phenomenon underpinning the economic history of the last century; but his prime concern being the analysis of business cycles, which is to say, variations around central tendencies, he gives little place to the study of long-term movements.

TABLE 6.11. *Number of immigrants by national origin, United States, 1820–1979* ('000s)

Region and country	1820–89	1890–1914	1915–45	1946–79	Total
Europe	13,280	15,739	3,658	3,746	36,267
North-west Europe[a]	7,797	3,482	1,263	1,223	13,765
British Isles[b]	6,119	1,995	748	781	9,638
(Ireland)	(3,432)	(888)	(273)	(135)	(4,724)
Scandinavia	1,017	1,059	284	138	2,498
Central Europe[c]	4,848	4,842	1,078	1,302	12,070
Germany[d]	4,413	1,069	547	956	6,985
Poland	57	108	251	104	520
Southern Europe[e]	406	4,138	1,065	1,103	6,712
Italy	337	3,639	745	579	5,300
Eastern Europe[f]	229	3,277	252	77	3,835
Russia and Baltic countries	221	3,055	152	44	3,472
America	1,176	822	2,513	4,737	9,248
Canada	1,048	456	1,556	1,066	4,125
Mexico[g]	27	120	649	(1,375)	2,177
Asia, Oceania	316	451	224	2,025	2,161
Africa	2	13	13	114	142
Others or unspecified	206	46	1	28	309
All countries	14,980	17,071	6,409	10,664	49,124

Notes: Discrepancies in the totals may be due to the use of round figures or changes in classification.

[a] Benelux, Denmark, France, Great Britain, Iceland, Ireland, Norway, Sweden, Switzerland.

[b] Incl. data for Ireland in parentheses below.

[c] Austria, Czechoslovakia (since 1920), Germany, Hungary (since 1861), Poland, Yugoslavia (since 1920).

[d] Incl. Austria, 1938–45.

[e] Greece, Italy, Portugal, Spain.

[f] Baltic States, Bulgaria, European Turkey, Finland, Romania, Russia.

[g] Given the number of illegal entries, estimates for Mexico are questionable, especially in the latter period.

Sources: Calculated from: *Historical Statistics of the US*, Washington, 1975; *Statistical Abstract of the US* (recent edn.).

2. From 1890 to 1914, immigration increased in force. European emigration averaged nearly 1 million per year, as opposed to under 400,000 from 1846 to 1890. But the earlier flows, as remarked before, were replaced by a new Latin and Slavic migration. Southern and eastern Europe took over from north-west Europe, in waves which appear to have been uncontrollable: in

1913 and 1914, for example, 1.2 million people arrived each year in the US. The Italian rate of emigration reached a record level of 20 per 1000 in 1913, comparable to the Irish peak in the years 1847 to 1854; and in this same year, 85% of the arrivals in the US came from places outside of the original Anglo-Saxon countries of departure.

3. The following decades are marked by the events which combined to reduce the number of entries, and even encouraged repatriation of recent immigrants (notably, the Great Depression). By fixing extremely restrictive quotas based on the population distribution by nationality at the time of the pre-war censuses (3% of the current population in 1910, and 2% in 1890, respectively), the laws of 1921 and 1924 introduced a drastic reduction in the flow of entrants, and more specifically, selective policies to the disadvantage of east and south European immigrants, who were deemed undesirable. Asian populations, however, had found their reception barred a good deal earlier: in California, a law hostile to Asians had already been passed in the mid-nineteenth century (Commons 1907); it was reinforced by general restrictions applied in 1882 to the Chinese, in 1907 to the Japanese, and so forth. This marked the end of the period of mass migration: from 1921–29, the rate of European emigration was half that of 1846–90. Ethnic composition continued to change, European predominance gradually giving way. Mexican immigrants, previously very small in numbers (10%), began to prevail over German and Scandinavian immigrants, almost equalling the intake of British and Italians. This restructuring reflects the history of the demographic transition.

4. If one discounts German refugees in the period 1949–52, the few subsisting European contingents in the post-war period come from England and Italy. This flow is little more than an effect of inertia: the European contribution to American population becomes marginal (less than one-sixth of total immigration, 1975–79), whilst that of less developed countries becomes increasingly predominant. Asia and Latin America (with 37% and 31% of the flows, respectively), being more advanced in their transition and geographically proximate, occupy the most important position; but African migration (2%) gets going, with over 10,000 people per year by the end of the 1970s. Given the scale of illegal migration, the size of Latin American flows has in fact been considerably greater, and the 1970s appear to represent the period of highest permanent immigration (in absolute value) in all of American history. Taking into account the size of the demographic reservoirs in question, and the level of density already reached in the US, migration can only be highly selective, confirming a trend begun in the inter-war period.

Thus, the main sources of emigration to the developed New World have changed as demographic transition has proceeded. But where developed countries of long-standing habitation are concerned, not only does emigration tend gradually to wane, as demographic surpluses disappear, but immigration from less advanced countries acquires a new significance, coming from

TABLE 6.12. *Estimated net migration ('000s) and its place in population growth (per cent), European regions, 1950–1980*

Period	Region				
	North[a]	West[b]	South[c]	East[d]	All regions
1950–60 Balance ('000s)	−501	3,643	−3,529	−2,766	−3,153
% of variation	−14	+31	−41	−35	−10
1960–70 Balance ('000s)	−260	4,912	−3,464	−902	286
% of variation	−6	+36	−38	−14	+1
1970–80 Balance ('000s)	−205	2,335	2,591	−718	4,003
% of variation	−13	+48	+20	−11	+18
1950–80 Balance ('000s)	−966	10,890	−4,402	−4,386	1,136
% of variation	−10	+35	−14	−21	+1

[a] Denmark, Finland, Ireland, Norway, Sweden, United Kingdom.
[b] Austria, Belgium, France, FRG, Luxemburg, Netherlands, Switzerland.
[c] Albania, Greece, Italy, Malta, Portugal, Spain, Yugoslavia.
[d] Bulgaria, Czechoslovakia, GDR, Hungary, Poland, Romania.

Sources: UN (1980: 66), for 1950–60 and 1960–70; our own estimates thereafter.

southern and eastern Europe, and then from Third World countries either geographically close or linked historically from the colonial period.

3. The Migratory Transition: Net Reproduction and Net Migration

For long an area of emigration, Europe has in its turn become a locus of immigration. In the post-war period, the traditional flow of migrants from western Europe was reversed (Sauvy and Moindrot 1962), and the phenomenon gradually spread to the other European areas: during the 1970s southern Europe recorded a substantial positive net migration (of 2.6 million people)[10] in the other regions, the figures progressively dwindle with each decade (Table 6.12).

European migration was, up to the inter-war period, mostly external; it became predominantly internal between the end of the war and the 1960s, before embracing African and Asian populations. Levasseur's (1892) reasoning at the time of the great European migration has become appropriate to other continents: 'Every year Europe produces a surplus of births which,

[10] Where the east European countries are concerned, the persistence of a negative balance may well result for the most part from the political division of Europe.

under the present state of agricultural, industrial and commercial productivity, and with current average individual consumption, she cannot support.'

Table 6.12 retraces the general dynamic. It has been obtained by the so-called equation method, in which the difference between variations in a total population are evaluated from one census to the next and the corresponding intercensal changes noted. As with all estimates based on net changes, it is of course not exempt from error,[11] but the development of orders of magnitude is sufficiently clear to speak for itself.

The turning-point in western Europe occurred just before 1960: emigration gave way to immigration in most countries, accompanied by large waves of return migrants from old colonial areas of Africa and Asia. In the early 1960s, Italy, in its exchanges with Latin America, particularly Argentina, registered more returns than departures. In 1964, western Europe employed only 3 million migrant labourers, 1 million of which were in France, a country where the end of demographic growth had become evident much earlier. In 1973 this figure was above 6 million. Because of the attraction created by its prosperity, and on account of the shortage of young manpower caused by the decline in fertility during the 1930s depression and the war, north-western Europe managed to compete with overseas English-speaking countries in the international labour market. It attracted workers from south European countries with agricultural economies, and from the other side of the Mediterranean. At the same time overseas emigration diminished. For the period 1960–70, migration in the whole of Europe was positive (adding some 286,000 people); in western Europe it rose to almost 5 million, the movement being substantially fed by south European countries. In spite of the economic recession, western Europe remained a net importer of migrants for the next decade: almost two-thirds of the balance is credited to the account of West Germany, where the supply of entrants to the labour market was insufficient to meet the demands of production. Countries with traditionally high migration, like Ireland and Norway, are characterized even today by net immigration, the negative balance for northern Europe being attributable to Great Britain, whose relative position in the international economy deteriorated markedly during the post-war period.

In sum, over the general period 1950–80, immigration prevailed over emigration across the whole of Europe; the traditional divide between the countries of the north-west and those of the south—still very strong at the start of the period—gradually dwindled, all countries now being characterized in varying degrees by net immigration.

[11] Any error in the calculation of one of the components has repercussions on the quality of the results. Nevertheless, we have an accurate knowledge of natural increase, and there is generally little variation in the comparative quality of successive censuses (except, perhaps, in certain southern countries with high emigration). Even in the case of countries with uninterrupted records, the accuracy of results obtained by this method is none the less very much superior to those derived from an account of flows.

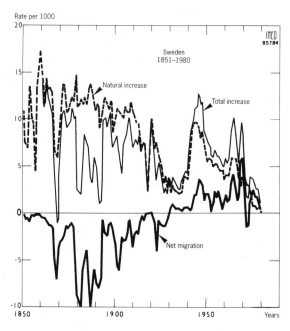

FIG. 6.3. *Net migration and natural increase, Sweden, 1951–1980*

Figs. 6.3 and 6.4 illustrate this inversion of migratory streams, along with the decline in natural increase, in Sweden and Italy. In both cases, net migration, which is negative and maximal at the time of highest natural increase, falls back when the latter declines. This inversion in fact occurs when net reproduction rates have fallen below replacement level (see Figs. 7.3 and 7.4). Migration thus exercises a moderating influence on demographic growth, slowing it down when it is very rapid, and boosting it when it is weak.

4. The Influence of Migration on Demographic Growth

Bearing in mind the disproportionate size of the populations in question, especially in the nineteenth century, the relative influence of migration was for a long time more limited in countries of emigration than in countries of immigration. Thus, over the peak period of 1891–1900, the average rate of immigration rose to 0.7% per year in the five big immigration countries (the United States, Canada, Australia, New Zealand, and Argentina) whilst the corresponding rate of emigration for Europe was below 0.2%.

We shall not return at this point to the theoretical discussion on this subject given at the beginning of the chapter; we shall confine ourselves, instead, to presenting a few interesting results, in such a way as to emphasize the

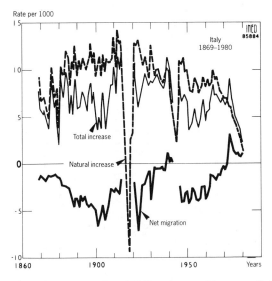

Fig. 6.4. Net migration (estimate before 1921) and natural increase, Italy, 1869–1980

complexity of the facts compared with the relative simplicity of certain theories. The reality is composed of a wealth of different cases, of which the calculation of indices of propensity to migrate has already given us a foretaste.

Countries of Immigration

The role of immigration in population growth has varied greatly from one case to another: over the period 1840–1940, net immigration was equal to almost 60% of the natural growth in Argentina, about 40% in the US, and only 20% in Brazil or Canada. Between 1851 and 1951 net immigration in Canada was only 0.7 million, whilst demographic increase rose to 11.6 million (Keyfitz 1961). Canadian emigration to the US was considerable, and natural increase rapid; likewise, in Brazil, the share of immigrants was slight in relation to sustained natural growth (Mortara 1954). Conversely, immigration over the entire history of the United States has played a decisive part in its demographic development: from 1820 to 1979 the country received almost 50 million immigrants; even very recently (1971–79) the annual flows of incomers exceed an average of 400,000 (probably by a long way, given illegal migration). Net immigration has become a rapidly increasing proportion of total population growth owing to the several factors leading to the decline in natural increase: the slump in fertility; the consolidation of improvements in life expectation; and the shift of age structures towards older generations. Net migration accounted for 11% of total American growth in the 1950s; 17% in the 1960s; and 38% in the 1970s. Since the beginning of the last century,

TABLE 6.13. *Net migration as a proportion of total population growth, United States, 1801–1980*

Period	Share in population growth (%)	Period	Share in population growth (%)	Period	Share in population growth (%)	Period	Share in population growth (%)
1801–10	3.7	1851–1860	27.3	1901–10	28.5	1950–60[a]	10.8
1811–20	5.8	1861–1870	26.1	1911–20	22.8	1960–70[a]	17.2
1821–30	4.7	1871–1880	18.2	1921–30	15.5	1970–80[a]	20.5
1831–40	13.7	1881–1890	29.4	1930–40[a]	–15.7		
1841–50	26.9	1891–1900	18.4	1940–50[a]	9.5		

[a] From 1930, for each 10-year period, calculation is based on the average population (instead of the initial population) of the first year of the period under consideration. The natural balances for the outside dates ending with 0 have therefore been divided by 2.

Sources: Landry (1945: 427), for the period 1801–1930; our own estimates thereafter.

this contribution has never been as high as it is at present (see Table 6.13). This is because, until now, natural growth has maintained an exceptionally rapid rhythm, attributable to the age composition bequeathed by earlier immigration.

On the other hand, where natural increase is traditionally low, as in France up to the Second World War, immigration has managed to exert a determining influence on the country's demographic future, by pre-empting population decline through its direct, and especially indirect, effects. Under the Third Republic, from 1872 to 1931, immigration consistently accounted for at least a fifth of population increase in each decade (Table 6.14); it represented more than half at the end of the nineteenth century, and more than three-quarters immediately after the First World War (in compensation for war losses).

More generally, Landry (1945) has estimated (without, however, clearly explaining his method) that over the period 1801 to 1936 immigrants and their descendants contributed more than a third of France's population increase. This contribution has lessened in the post-war period despite repatriation from Indo-China and, especially, North Africa. From the mid-1960s, the force and length of the baby boom tended to check both the decline in natural increase and the demand for foreign labour. If, since the economic recession which began in 1973, net migration has become relatively small, the contrast with a country like West Germany is nevertheless striking; there, as a result of sustained very low fertility, population growth for the last 10 years has been entirely dependent on migratory development. It is also highly significant that France, whose position in the international hierarchy of fertility rose immediately following the war, has since that time had a migration coefficient appreciably lower than other west European countries (27% as opposed to 38% in 1950–80),[12] whereas the opposite was the case for almost a century and a half. During the last decade this coefficient (15%) in France is out of all proportion to that of its western counterparts (90%) and is even less than that of southern Europe (20%).

Countries of Emigration

At the time of the great demographic expansion in Europe, emigration exercised an undeniable moderating effect on population growth. According to Citroen (1948), a fifth of Europe's natural increase was counterbalanced by emigration in the nineteenth century. None the less, even during the period of mass migration around 1900, emigration rates for the continent did not exceed 3 per 1000. But discrepancies from one region to another were considerable, southern Europe having experienced rates above 5 per 1000 (and even 15 per 1000 for Italy, just before the First World War).

According to Ravnholt (1937), during the period 1850–1930, the pro-

[12] The period for France refers to 1946–82.

TABLE 6.14. *Net migration as a proportion of total population growth, France, 1801–1982*

Period	Share in population growth (%)	Period	Share in population growth (%)	Period	Share in population growth (%)	Period	Share in population growth (%)
1801–21	5.5	1861–1872[a]	−100.0	1911–21[ab]	22.1	1962–68	35.1
1821–31	13.7	1872–1881	26.9	1921–31	74.4	1968–75	30.5
1831–41	16.4	1881–1891	19.8	1931–46[b]	−82.4	1975–82	14.4
1841–51	5.8	1891–1901	57.5	1946–54	13.4		
1851–61[a]	4.3	1901–1911	33.3	1954–62	39.4		

Net migration and corresponding total increase in population ('000s)

Period	Net migration	Total population variation (constant territory)
1851–1861	−36	+840
1861–1872	−300	+300
1911–1921	+495	−2,240

Notes: From 1931, calculations are based on the average population of the first year of the period indicated, and proceed by the same method as in Table 6.8.

[a] For these periods, calculations refer to contemporary natural boundaries (incl. Nice, Savoy, and Alsace-Lorraine).

[b] During these periods the population declined, but net migration was positive for 1911–21, and negative for 1931–46.

Sources: Landry (1945: 455), for the period 1801–1931 (with the exception of 1851–72 and 1911–21); our own estimates thereafter.

portion of the flow of entrants to the job market lost through emigration, for the whole on Europe, oscillated between 12% and 30%. For northern and western Europe this percentage varied between 30% and 55%. For southern Europe, where the loss was generally much greater, it ranged between 19% and 107%, whilst eastern Europe's percentage was relatively low (1% to 15%).

In Ireland, emigration was consistently greater than natural growth for almost a century; other countries, such as Italy in 1905–07 and 1913, experienced a similar if not lasting situation; East Germany after the war provides another example of special circumstances. Aside from these extreme cases, the long-term picture in countries experiencing mass emigration involved proportions of up to one-third of natural increase. Scandinavia in the period 1861–1910 is an instance. Nevertheless, after taking into account repatriation and the rapidity of natural growth, the UK (1871–1931) and Germany (1841–1910) lost only one-sixth to one-seventh of their natural increase through net migration, respectively.

Finally, estimates have sometimes been made of the total impact of migration on European population. By applying laws of mortality and fertility to the population of emigrants, Novitsky and Tolokonsky (1929) calculated what the European population would have been in 1910 had there been no emigration since 1800. According to them, Europe could have claimed 88 million more people than there actually were. The reality, however, is more complex than these authors supposed, as much due to our ignorance of the number of returns as to the interactions enumerated above. In Malthus's view, emigration actually stimulates growth rather than depleting a population; by averting a fall in living standards, it releases people from traditional checks on reproduction; losses to migration are then compensated by earlier, more frequent, and more fertile marriages. However, it is not possible to concur with Malthus's view that, because of the continuous pressure of population on subsistence, migration must ultimately fail to have an effect on population size, whether in the country of departure or arrival. The Novitsky–Tolokonsky method appears likewise exaggerated. It is highly likely that emigration reduced demographic growth a little in European countries, but, in relieving poverty, it doubtless also helped in the longer term to encourage the decline in fertility. An exact assessment of its influence is inevitably fairly arbitrary. The situation for countries of immigration, in contrast, is far less ambiguous: through its direct and indirect effects, immigration was the principal factor in the peopling of the New World. At the same time, it brought with it the Industrial Revolution and massive economic development—the first migrants having originated from the most advanced countries.

Conclusion

Migration is a mechanism for relieving population pressure: it encourages the levelling of demographic and economic conditions between countries. In the past it helped Europe solve its social problems; in the present age, it relieves (but to a much lesser degree) the poverty of certain poor countries having large demographic surpluses. When migration is possible, the onset of crisis or catastrophe may be avoided, or the effects of such disasters palliated after the event. In this sense, it serves to redress imbalances in demographic history, and on the whole ensures, by an opening up of frontiers, a cumulative growth of numbers greater than if it had not occurred.

However, the European demographic situation in 1880 and that of less developed countries in 1980 shares little common ground: transition has assumed entirely new forms in the latter, and there remain scarcely any new territories to colonize. The characteristics of the migratory process itself have altered with time; the multiplicity and interweaving of factors by which it is determined are such that any forecasts involve a much greater degree of uncertainty than would be necessary for any other demographic parameter. The analysis of demographic trends can only reveal the existence of migratory potentials; these potentials may or may not materialize, in larger or smaller proportions, depending on the overall international economic situation, or on political circumstances. Forecasts like Just's (1948), which reckoned on high European emigration, show just how much the future may differ from a simple extrapolation of the past, or from intuitions suggested by present problems (a case in point being the question of German refugees). The only historically consistent factor to have been established until now, where Europe is concerned, is the connection between natural increase and net migration; but the strength of this connection has varied from one case to another, and even more so the factors which compensate for migratory losses.

Bibliography to Chapter 6

BERTILLON, J. (1873), 'Migration', in *Dictionnaire encyclopédique des sciences médicales* (Paris), vii. 637–63.

BÖHNING, W. R. (1977), 'The Migration of Workers from Poor to Rich Countries: Facts, Problems, Policies', in *Congrès International de la Population, Mexico, 1977*, ii. 307–18.

—— (1979), 'Faits et chiffres sur les migrations internationales', *Population*, 6: 1130–1137.

BORRIE, W. D. (1948), *Population Trends and Policies: A Study in Australian and World Demography* (Sydney).

CARROTHERS, G. A. B. (1929), *Emigration from the British Isles with Special Reference to the Overseas Dominions* (London: King), 328.

CARR-SAUNDERS, A. M. (1936), *World Population: Past Growth and Present Trends* (Oxford: Clarendon Press).

CHESNAIS, J.-C. (1982), 'La Baisse de la natalité et ses conséquences pour la planification sectorielle dans les pays capitalistes développés', *Population*, 6: 1133–1158.

CITROEN, H. A. (1948), *Les Migrations internationales: un problème économique et social* (Paris: Médicis).

COMMONS, J. R. (1907), *Races and Immigrants in America* (New York: Macmillan).

DAVIE, M. R. (1947), *World Immigration with Special Reference to the United States* (New York: Macmillan).

EASTERLIN, R. A. (1961), 'The American Baby-Boom in Historical Perspective', *AER*, 51: 869–911.

FAIRCHILD, H. P. (1925), *The Melting Pot Mistake* (Boston: Little, Brown).

FAZIO, E. (1948), 'Sviluppi e caratteri del movimento migratorio dei paesi mediterranei', *Annali di Statistica*, Rome, 2: 215–41.

FERENCZI, I. (1929a), 'A Historical Study of Migration Statistics', ILO, *Revue Internationale du Travail*, 3, 356–84.

—— (1929b), 'International migrations', in Willcox 1929.

FORSYTH, W. D. (1942), *The Myth of Open Spaces (Australian, British and World Trends of Population and Migration)* (Melbourne).

FRANKLIN, B. (1755), *Observations concerning the Increase of Mankind, Peopling of Countries* (Boston).

GOLINI, A. (1982), 'Effectif et accroissement des populations immigrées', in Council of Europe, *Conférence démographique européenne, Strasbourg*, 1982.

GONNARD, R. (1928), *Essai sur l'histoire de l'émigration* (Paris: Librairie Valois).

HANSEN, M. L. (1940), *The Atlantic Migration 1607–1860* (Cambridge, Mass.: Harvard University Press).

ISAAC, J. (1947), *Economics of Migration* (London).

ISHII, R. (1937), *Population Pressure and Economic Life in Japan* (Chicago, ILL.: University of Chicago Press).

JÉRÔME, H. (1926), *Migration and Business Cycles*, NBER Occasional Paper, no. 9 (New York).

JOHNSON, S. C. (1913), *A History of Emigration From the United Kingdom to North America, 1763–1912* (London: Routledge).

JUST, O. (1948), *Au-dessus des mers et des frontières...* (Rio).

KEYFITZ, N. (1961), 'The Changing Canadian Population', in S. D. Clark (ed.), *Urbanism and the Changing Canadian Society* (Toronto), 3–19.

KIRK, D. (1946), *Europe's Population in the Interwar Years* (Geneva: Princeton University Press).

KULISCHER, E. M. (1948), *Europe on the Move: War and Population Changes, 1917–1947* (New York: Columbia University Press).

KUZNETS, S. (1958), 'Long Swings in the Growth of Population and in Related Economic Variables', *Proceedings of the American Philosophical Society*, 102: 25–52.

—— and RUBIN, E. (1954), *Immigration and the Foreign Born*, NBER, Occasional paper no. 46, (New York).

LANDRY, A., BUNLE, H., DEPOID, P., HUBER, M., and SAUVY, A. (1945), *Traité de démographie* (Paris: Payot).

LEVASSEUR, E. (1889–92), *La Population française. Histoire de la population avant 1789 et démographie de la France comparée à celle des autres nations au XIXe siècle*, 3 vols., (Paris: Rousseau).

LIVI-BACCI, M. (1965), 'Caratteristiche demografiche ed assimilazione degli Italiani negli Stati Uniti', *Studi emigrazione*, Rome (Oct.), 17–31.

LORIMER, F., and OSBORN, F. (1934), *Dynamics of Population: Social and Biological Significance of Changing Birth Rates in the United States* (New York: Macmillan).

MAUCO, G. (1932), *Les Étrangers en France: leur rôle dans l'activité économique* (Paris: Colin).

MÖNCKMEIER, W. (1912), *Die deutsche überseeische Auswanderung, ein Beitrag zur deutschen Wanderungsgeschichte* (Jena: Fischer).

MORTARA, G. (1954), 'The Development and Structure of Brazil's Population', *Population Studies*, 2: 121–39.

NOVITSKY, R., and TOLOKONSKY, N. (1929), 'Vliianie emigratsii na usloviia sushchestvovaniia proletariata europy, v.XIX i XX vekakh', *Statisticheskoe obozrenie* (Moscow), 91–103.

RAVNHOLT, H. (1938), 'A Quantitative Concept of the International Mobility of Population and its Application to Certain European Countries in the Period 1851–1935', in *Théorie générale de la population*, International Conference on Population, Paris, 1937 (Paris), i. 224–29.

SAUVY, A. (1944), *Richesse et population* (Paris).

—— (1949), 'European Migrations: Regulations and Treatises', *Annals of the American Academy of Political and Social Science*, 262 (Mar.), 22–30.

—— (1950), 'Besoins et possibilités de l'immigration française', *Population*, 2: 209–28, and 3: 417–34.

—— and MOINDROT, C. (1962), 'Le Renversement du courant d'immigration séculaire', *Population*, 1: 51–64.

SCHUMPETER, J. A. (1912), *Theorie der Wirtschaftlichen Entwicklung* (Leipzig: Duncker und Humblot).

SÜNDBARG, G. (1907), *Bevölkerungstatistik Schwedens, 1750–1900* (Stockholm).

—— (1908), *Aperçus statistiques internationaux* (London: Gordon and Breach).

TAPINOS, G. (1974), *L'Économie des migrations internationales* (Paris: Colin, Fondation Nationale des Sciences Politiques).

—— (1975), *L'Immigration étrangère en France, 1946–1973*, Travaux et Documents, Cahier no. 71, (Paris: INED-PUF).

—— (1981), *European Migration Patterns: Economic Linkages and Policy Experiences*, Winespread Conference Centre, Racine, Wis.

THOMAS, B. (1951), 'Migration and the Rhythm of Economic Growth, 1830–1913', *The Manchester School of Economic and Social Studies*, 19(3) (Sept.), 215–71.

—— (1954), *Migration and Economic Growth: A Study of Great Britain and the Altantic Community* (2nd edn. 1973 Cambridge: Cambridge University Press).

THOMAS, D. S. (1941), *Social and Economic Aspects of Swedish Population Movements 1750–1953* (New York: Macmillan).

UN (1950), *Immigration in Brazil* (Mass), E/CN.12/169/Add. 1 (New York: UN).

—— (1953), *International migration statistics, organisation and operation recommended standards, samplings* (Sept.), ST/STAT/Ser, M/20 (New York: UN).

—— (1975), *Economic Survey in Europe*, pt. II: *Post-war Demographic Trends . . .* (New York: UN).

—— (1978), *Demographic Yearbook 1977* (New York: UN).

—— (1980), *L'Offre et les migrations de main-d'œuvre: dimensions démographiques (1950–1975) et perspectives* (New York: UN).

United Kingdom Royal Commission on Population: Report (1949) (London: HMSO).

VARLEZ, L. (1930), *Les Migrations internationales et leur réglementation*, Académie de droit international, Recueil international, Recueil des cours (Paris), v. 167–348.

VON DER GOLTZ, J. (1893), *Die landliche Arbeiterklasse in dem preussichen Staat* (Jena: Fisher).

WALKER, F. A. (1891), 'Immigration and Degradation', *Forum*, New York (Aug.), 822–29.

WALSHAW, R. S. (1941), *Migration to and from the British Isles: Problems and Policies* (London).

WILLCOX, W. F. (1940), *Studies in American Demography* (Ithaca, NY: Cornell University Press).

—— (ed.) (1929–31), 'International Migrations', NBER Occasional Paper, nos. 14 and 18, i. *Statistics*, ii *Interpretations* (New York).

WINSEMIUS, I. (1940), 'Wanderungen und Verbrauch: Ein Beitrag zur Theorie der Raumwirtschaft', *Weltwirtschaftliche Archiv*, 1: 38–73.

7 The Notion of the Cycle in Demography: Is Post-Transitional Fertility Cyclical?

> The predominant factors in history, in the last instance, are the production and reproduction of the immediate conditions of life.
>
> (Engels)

THE demographic transition, according to its principal theorists, represents a phase of temporary population disequilibrium. After this phase a new equilibrium emerges through the adjustment of fertility to mortality. The idea of lasting or permanent disequilibrium is, however, excluded.

Easterlin's hypothesis refers specifically to the pattern subsequent to transition. It assumes that post-transitional fertility oscillates cyclically around a level which ultimately guarantees the replacement of generations. It is still too early to confirm with any certainty the validity of this assumption, as the final stage of transition has only been reached by a small number of countries and, relatively speaking, only very recently. Any attempt at generalization would thus appear premature. Nevertheless, there exist some 20 countries in which the net period reproduction rate has bordered on unity for almost half a century. A preliminary study is thus possible, from which a provisional typology of patterns of post-transitional fertility may be derived.

The notion of fertility cycles has not long been a feature of demographic thinking. Following the sustained recovery of fertility after the war, declining reproductive rates in the industrial world have in the last two decades produced an oscillating pattern which suggests a cyclic form. The idea of population cycles was first applied to total population growth by Pearl and Gini.[1] More explicitly, Cowgill (1949) distinguished several theoretical types of cycle of population growth. He divided them into historical stages, as follows:

  1. 'primitive' or early cycles, caused by mortality crises[2] characteristic of pre-industrial societies;

---

[1] See, especially, Pearl 1930: 22; Gini 1929.

[2] Certain historians speak of 'thirty-year waves' (see e.g. Goubert 1960: 653; Dupaquier 1979: 440), but these appear to be simply fluctuations in the number of births, the mechanism of which is unknown and the universality of which is far from proven; nothing similar has been observed in early modern England, for example (cf. Wrigley and Schofield 1981: 779).

2. 'modern' cycles, associated with the priority and greater rapidity of mortality declines, in relation to fertility declines during the demographic transition;

3. 'future' cycles[3] (which could be called 'current'), determined by a successive rise and fall in fertility within a more or less stable context of mortality.

These three types of cycle, which we shall call 'pre-transitional', 'transitional', and 'post-transitional' respectively, respond to completely different realities, as much in their temporality as in their underlying mechanisms. The second, for example, describes a unique secular phenomenon in which a traditional equilibrium is upset, giving rise to unprecedented demographic growth. The other two are recurrent phenomena, less long-lasting, the first of which relates to fluctuations in mortality, and the second, to fertility variations. In other words, in the 'post-transitional'[4] phase, it is primarily fertility which is responsible for fluctuations in the rate of population growth. Easterlin's theory, which postulates the existence of fertility cycles and describes their mechanisms, thus refers to a post-transitional context: after the major period of decline, fertility undergoes cyclical fluctuations.

The Origin of Easterlin's Notion of Demographic Cycle

It was at the time of his work on economic history, while attempting to prove the existence of Kuznets cycles[5] in the post-war American economy (up to 1958), that Easterlin (1961) came to formulate his idea of fertility cycles. Kuznets (1958), by using long-term macro-economic series (1870–1955), had shown the close connection between aggregate demand and the intensity of net migration. In this way he was able to account for the waves of American population growth up to the First World War, migration then being the principal determinant of the rhythm of demographic growth. For the following period, Kuznets established that the mechanisms had changed: with the restriction on immigration in 1924, migratory flows lost their determining role in demographic growth, and fertility gradually took over. Easterlin, likewise

---

[3] Cowgill also mentions a fourth type of cycle, which may be regarded as a variant of the third: it concerns fluctuations in population size, in which an increase in fertility is followed by either an immediate or a delayed increase in crude mortality (due respectively to pressure on resources and the ageing of the generations concerned).

[4] The expression 'countries with completed demographic transition' is often used in studies on fertility, without being precisely defined. For convention's sake, we shall assume that what is called 'post-transitional' fertility represents a return to levels which are equal to replacement, or below it.

[5] An economic cycle of the length of approximately 20 years. Where establishing long-term links between economy and demography is concerned, the use of Kondratieff cycles (50–60 years) would have been more appropriate, especially if the determining demographic variable is fertility (this would not be the case with international migration, however), which is known to have begun to recover at the beginning of the 1940s. According to various writers, a new Kondratieff cycle would have emerged precisely around 1940.

basing his observations on American experience, hypothesized the existence of fertility cycles which he believed to be already present in the nineteenth century:[6] fluctuations in the fertility of the white population were, at that time, not very pronounced, and often echoed migratory waves.[7] But the post-war cycle appeared to have a different amplitude and nature from preceding ones, which Easterlin considered connected to Kuznets cycles. Easterlin therefore sought to establish his own explanation but, unlike Sauvy (1948), he failed to grasp that the completed fertility of generations had now become an inevitable implication of entering the post-transitional stage of controlled fertility. Sauvy writes in 1948:

having become very low, fertility manifests great elasticity. Here we have a new fact, appearing for the first time in observations of the period 1925–1950, and which depends on the disproportion between the duration of a woman's reproductive period (over 30 years) and the time required to complete a family. If each couple decides to have only two children over the course of their procreative period, they then have a considerable margin in which to achieve this programme. Fertility can be extremely low in difficult periods and exceedingly high in periods of optimism and full employment.

Explanation of the Post-War Fertility Cycle

In its initial stages, Easterlin's approach is fairly explorative. In searching for the origins of the fertility increase of the 1940s, he brings into conjunction three favourable circumstances: strong economic expansion, immigration control, and the low rate of entrants to the job market. In other words, he calls attention to the inversion of the overall economic situation, thus giving precedence, as did Kuznets, to the basic patterns of economic history. The argument is then progressively refined and narrowed. Easterlin explicitly singles out the *relative* economic status of *young adults* as the determining variable of fertility (Easterlin 1968 and, particularly, 1973); he then proceeds to a definition of endogenous demographic fluctuations (Easterlin 1976, 1980) as the exclusive product of generational effects, capable of infinite repetition.[8] In particular, the fertility of a given generation is assumed to be an inverse function of the relative size of that generation. From this point the model becomes somewhat mechanical[9] since the relative size of generations is assumed to determine not only their fertility, but their nuptiality, divorce rate,

[6] In 1906 Yule made a similar observation on the existence of fertility cycles in 19th-century England.
[7] The results are unconvincing for two reasons: first, because the author uses crude birth-rates, thereby ignoring the possible effects of variation in age structure; and secondly, because he uses a statistical method which may prove misleading (recourse to quinquennial averages, whose variations are studied over the following quinquennial period, between 1855–59 and 1955–59).
[8] The only question is then that of the initial impulse.
[9] But, curiously, Easterlin also develops a parallel thesis, in collaboration, which attempts to reconcile his theory of relative income with the micro-economic theory of time allocation (Easterlin *et al.* 1980: 81–149). The mechanical and blind nature of the exercise becomes

suicide rate, criminality, and so on. In other words, Easterlin sees in this variable one of the keys to the functioning of modern societies; even stagflation is a product of the effect of particularly large cohorts entering the adult age group. In short, he defines a general theory of social equilibrium. As such, Easterlin's hypothesis seems far too schematic to be used in the following analysis. We shall address ourselves, instead, to Easterlin's more subtle, intermediary formulation of 1973.

Easterlin postulates that the fertility of a couple is a function of the comparison of two elements: the level of consumption desired (itself dependent on the living standards experienced during adolescence, within the familial milieu) and the earnings achieved a few years later within the professional world (as measured by the income[10] of young adults). In other words, fertility depends not on absolute income. but *relative* income.[11] Easterlin writes: 'we may consider the balance between the income potential of young adults and their desired living standards to depend, to a considerable extent, on comparison of the income (or profession) experienced by these young adults and that of their parents … We shall call this comparative situation the "relative economic status" of young adults.'

Consequently, in large generations where competition is keener and job prospects less favourable, a discrepancy between income and expectation occurs, which manifests itself in frustration and thereby a lessened propensity to marry and have children. Conversely, the children born into the resulting smaller generations, with happier prospects, will tend to marry more and at an earlier age, and to produce larger families, giving rise to cyclical fluctuations in the size of birth cohorts, capable of repetition over long periods.

1. Tests of the Easterlin Hypothesis

Before presenting an account of the nature of fertility trends since 1930 and the possible mechanisms behind them, we shall give a rapid critical presentation of existing studies on the subject, including those inspired by Easterlin's reasoning, and those revising or rejecting it. Two types of analysis have been carried out, the first applying demographic tests, and the second econometric ones.

---

apparent in certain projections: how, for example, is a Dutch fertility four times greater than a Swiss fertility, by the year 1995, to be justified? This is none the less the authors' result (cf. Artzrouni and Easterlin 1982: 81–99).

[10] The idea of the adjustment of fertility to real income variations is not new. It is present in Ricardo (*Principles of Political Economy*, 1817), according to whom 'the natural tendency of individuals to give themselves up to the delights of domestic society' is only checked by the intervening forces of reality.

[11] The notion of relative income appears in Brady and Friedman (1947), and is more specifically applied to fertility in Banks (1954), and especially in Grauman (1960); the latter, transposing the law of supply and demand, was the first to postulate explicitly a direct relation between the relative size of a generation and its fertility.

Demographic Tests

The first studies were addressed to the period since the war, and confined to the US alone (Easterlin 1961, 1968) or English-speaking countries including the US, Canada, Australia, England and Wales (Easterlin and Condran 1976). The authors compare trends in the birth-rates or period fertility measures (sometimes using rates for five-year age groups, sometimes synthetic measures) to trends in the number of young adults[12] aged 15 to 35 years, related to the number of mature adults aged 35 to 65. This ratio (15–34/35–65) is then considered as a proxy for relative economic status. The same work has more recently been done on France by Leridon (1978), for the period 1946–76. Boyer *et al.* (1979) have likewise analysed eight countries in the period 1948–72; the US, Canada, and England (already studied by Easterlin and Condran), France, Belgium, The Netherlands, Sweden, and Finland. In most cases, the authors indicate a strong correspondence between the series studied, at the same time as admitting (as have Easterlin and Condran) that the correspondence may sometimes be a matter of 'pure coincidence'. The range of analysis is enriched by O'Connell (in Simon 1978), who studied 16 countries (including 7 of the 8 above, but excluding The Netherlands) for a longer period beginning in 1930, and introduced time lags between series. His method is somewhat different, as he uses only the 20–24-year-old age group, comparing the fertility rate of women and the absolute number of men at this age. He establishes a negative relation between the two variables in 10 countries (all of which, except France, were covered by the preceding authors, but including Denmark, Norway, and New Zealand as well). A positive relation in 3 countries (Austria, Switzerland, and Japan), and no significant relation in the 3 others (France, Portugal, and Hungary). The situation is thus far from being conclusive.

Limitations of the Tests

Two major questions are posed by such studies: the theoretical salience of the arguments put forward, and the empirical validity of the methods used.

Theoretical Salience

The proposition that a connection exists between the size of a generation and its fertility is, in itself, no more than orthodox economic reasoning.[13] It is not difficult to see that, all things being equal, a decrease in job opportunities in the working-age population may make it difficult to integrate young people into society; and that, in order to safeguard their standard of living, these

---

[12] The calculation relates either to males only, or to both sexes.

[13] Demographic projections none the less usually begin from the hypothesized independence of fertility and age structure.

young people may, in such circumstances, react by controlling the only variable available to them, the choice over numbers of children. The assumption
that the development of the relation between age groups 35–64/15–34 is a
determining factor in current fertility presupposes, of course, that future
fertility is dependent not only on past fertility,[14] but also (to an extent which
Easterlin leaves unspecified) on comparative variations in mortality within
these two generation groups. Particular attention also needs to be given to
international migration, since it played a significant part in the development
of age structures in the adult age groups of many European countries in
the post-war period; consequently, given the predominance of young adults
among the migrants, immigration should act as a check on fertility, whilst,
conversely, emigration should contribute to its increase.[15] This remains to be
verified. Moreover, if the job market is the place where expectation confronts
reality, then it is the age-specific composition of the working population,[16]
rather than of the total population, which should be taken into account. The
demand for renewal of manpower, and variations in rates of labour force
participation, will be determined in part by age-specific factors. Whenever
these rates tend to rise, in a context of insufficient general demand, they can
contribute to increased competition and the sense of overcrowding, thereby
encouraging delay or restriction of family formation. This logic also prevails,
supplemented by a number of different micro-economic arguments, in the
economic analysis of female labour force participation.

Thus the determinant role in this sort of model comes down to the supply
of jobs, but the argument presupposes (following the convention of 'all things
being equal') two essential conditions: the absence of variations in aggregate
demand, and constant rates of age-specific labour force participation. This is
far from being the case. There have been very varied rhythms in economic
activity since the war; and it is also not unusual for compensation—at least
partial—to occur between rates of labour force participation at different
ages.[17]

Empirical validity

As we have seen, the testing of Easterlin's theory was carried out, in the first
instance, within the Atlantic economy—that is, within the sphere of influence
of the American English-speaking cultural community. That the results
should be relatively consistent is not particularly surprising; but the moment

[14] Again, the parameters of the relation remain to be defined, only the general idea having
been indicated, and in a purely qualitative manner.

[15] If, that is, the country of departure has itself entered the post-transitional phase of fertility
control—which is rarely the case.

[16] And also the job-specific composition.

[17] This is what has been observed in OECD countries during the recent economic recession: a
significant decline in rates above 55 years, with the emergence of large cohorts and an increase in
female labour.

the field of study departs from this sphere, as with O'Connell or Boyer, conclusions become more ambiguous. It would appear that the countries selected were arrived at by a process of exclusion based more on available means (which is to say, the requisite statistics) than objective ends. The latter, while escaping the tyranny of means, may require recourse to indirect estimates to make up for absent data. By their means of selection, the authors define a biased universe. Countries with irregular or incomplete statistics have particular characteristics which represent potential deviation from the international norm—if indeed such a norm exists—and which one cannot ignore in a theory which claims to give a general account of post-transitional fertility trends.

Finally, the adequacy of the temporal field chosen by the authors, although essential to the credibility of the demonstration, often leaves much to be desired. This choice varies from author to author, even regarding periods analysed for the same country, and is only rarely explained, despite its decisive role in the interpretation of empirical results. The one clear justification we have found occurs in an article by Easterlin et al. (1978): 1940 is taken as the starting-point for the ensuing observation as the Second World War, according to the authors, introduced a radical break in economic history, at least, in the US; until the war, economic growth was, in their view, controlled by development of aggregate demand, whereas since then, it has depended more on job supply.[18]

Examination of the Results

The primary question, with regard to studies in which the role of cycles is paramount, is simply whether their existence is actually established. 'Cycle' here is understood in the full sense of the term: the alternation of phases of expansion and contraction according to a certain temporal pattern. Either cross-sectional or longitudinal indices may be used, but since the latter are more stable,[19] analysis of the completed fertility of generations is the preferable test. Whether one is dealing with amplitude or periodicity (or merely the interval separating minima from maxima), the statistical pattern constituting a cycle is difficult to work out. Table 7.1 presents some of the observations gathered on various Western countries from one of the studies cited. Despite the small number of examples given, the variations are striking. In addition to cases of 'long' fluctuation, which correspond to the expected model, a number of instances of 'short' fluctuation emerge (an interval of less than 20 or even 10 years between minimum and maximum). The existence of such cases runs

---

[18] Although this argument can hardly be regarded as established, we consider it necessary, since fertility is itself even more susceptible to variations in job supply, and hence may be regarded as controlled entirely by such factors.

[19] Since longitudinal indices are weighted averages of period measures for 25–30 year periods, they describe a more regular, smoother development.

TABLE 7.1. *Cohort fertility, selected countries in Europe and North America, 1913–1935*

Country	Cumulative fertility (minimum)		Cumulative fertility (maximum)		Difference	Interval (years)
	Cohort	Rate	Cohort	Rate		
Belgium	1913	2.07	1930	2.30	0.23	17
Canada	1911	2.75	1931	3.35	0.60	20
Finland	1906	1.90	1919	2.64	0.74	13
France	1895	1.98	1928	2.64	0.66	33
Netherlands	1905	2.70	1914	2.88	0.18	9
Sweden	1905	1.81	1935	2.16	0.35	30
United Kingdom	1907	1.78	1936	2.43	0.65	29
United States	1909	2.23	1933	3.36	1.03	24

contrary to the implicit logic of Easterlin's model, in which the interval separating extremes should be of the same order as the average age at maternity. In other respects, the tempo and extent of oscillations are so varied for countries sometimes geographically very close, like Belgium, France, and The Netherlands, for example, that one may legitimately ask in what the notion of fertility cycle consists—the sole common denominator being the reversal of trends.[20]

The second question is whether, even in cases where it has been possible to demonstrate a covariation with Easterlin's demographic ratio, there are alternative explanations for the cause of the fluctuations. For example, in the case of France one will observe that the fertility minimum corresponds to the generation of 1896, and the maximum to that of 1928. These generations, as it happens, were disturbed by unprecedented events: the first reached the age of 18 in 1914 and suffered particular disruption to its marital regime through war losses among the corresponding male age group; and conversely, the generation of 1928 was 18 years old in 1946 and was in the reproductive period during the post-war reconstruction and the extraordinary economic expansion of the ensuing 30 years. We shall return to this point.

Econometric Tests

Econometric tests present greater problems than do demographic ones, since they may entail many qualifications and refinements the justification of which

[20] Festy's analysis (1979), covering a larger number of countries, confirms this heterogeneity. In Italy, for example, the minimum completed fertility was achieved in the same generations that, in France, experienced the maximum (1929–30); the interval separating the minimum from the maximum is only around 4 to 5 years.

inevitably remains more or less open to question. We shall first give Easterlin's definition of the concept of relative income, before presenting its possible variants, without departing from the author's theoretical framework.

For Easterlin, the notion of relative income consists in a comparison between parents' standard of living during the adolescent's period of dependence and that of the first years of his working life. Measures of income may be derived in various ways: one, addressed to age groups of potential parents, compares the real income of young heads of family aged 14 to 25 years to that of the corresponding 35–44-year-old age group five years later; another, omitting the time lag, compares the real income of men in the 20–24 age group to their counterparts aged 25–34.[21] This presupposes that fertility is a positive function of relative income thus defined, or, in other words, that it may be routinely derived from comparison between the trend of economic growth, as given by the rate of increase in national income, and the improvement of personal income by age.[22] Let us observe in passing that consumption levels are defined in consequence everywhere solely with reference to the earnings of family heads, taking into account neither the size of the family (original or current, hence taking in a number of units of consumption), nor the possibility of other income, particularly from working mothers. Moreover, since fertility, in this logic, results from the confrontation of objective circumstances (current income) and subjective expectations (the consumer level desired), certain authors have introduced psychological variables into their tests, such as subjective income (the idea one has of one's own income) or expectations of future economic conditions.

Still using the United States as the field of study, both macro-economic and micro-economic tests (Thornton and McDonald respectively, in Simon 1978) have been made using real income data. Both show the absence of positive effects on fertility by income. Other and more thorough studies, like Seiver's (in Simon 1978), introduce an important distinction of income effects by parity: the husband's income exercises a positive effect on the first two children, but negative thereafter.

Easterlin's own results are themselves scarcely more convincing. We shall limit ourselves here to two main criticisms, levelled by Sweezy (1971). First, the proposed model fails to account for the pattern of inter-war fertility: the 1920s in particular were marked by both a strong economic expansion[23] and a decline in international migration, and should therefore have shown a recovery in fertility, yet there was a rapid drop;[24] indeed, the relative decline

[21] It should be remarked that this choice of age groups is not consistent with his theory of trends, and is completely at odds with the demographic test, as the two age groups compared belong to the same part of the population (young persons under 35 years).

[22] Assuming one takes the rate of economic growth and the pattern of earnings by age to be independent of each other.

[23] And probably an improvement in the relative status of young people.

[24] Such a pattern brings out particularly clearly the fundamental difference between transitional and post-transitional (controlled) fertility behaviour.

was greater before the economic crisis (1925–29) than during it (1929–33). Secondly, the relative income of young people continued to increase after 1962[25] and up to 1968, during the very period in which fertility was in sharpest decline.

One cannot fail to be struck, therefore, by the arbitrary nature of the choices used to establish the evolution of relative income. The possible terms of reference are manifold; the diversity of applicable tests goes some way to explain the often contradictory nature of the results obtained. It should be stressed, moreover, that the notion of relative income which has been seized upon from amongst the several indices of measurement ignores certain phenomena which have played a considerable role in determining the comparative status of age groups over the last few decades: the development of credit and of intergenerational transfers.

2. Some Developments

Easterlin's work has served as a focus of economic research on post-war American fertility for more than a decade. Its seductively simple character, conforming to a prevailing neo-Malthusian spirit, and the relative ease with which it could be applied to the post-war American situation—during the 1940s and 1950s, at least—have meant that his hypotheses have excited extensive discussion. Both elaborations of the original analytic framework and alternative models based on opposing theoretical foundations have emerged. We will concern ourselves here only with those propositions that can be tested empirically by comparison of time series in different periods.[26]

Oppenheimer (1974), for example, considers Easterlin's measurement of expected living standards inappropriate, since it fails to take into consideration either the number or the age of children (adolescents being considered as adult consumers), or the greater flexibility which the contributions of working mothers gives to the domestic economy. The new factor in this argument,[27] which distinguishes it from the traditional and somewhat stereotyped view of the link between fertility and female labour, is that it admits the possibility that the two phenomena are not connected solely by the obvious negative relation which present fertility, but also by a positive effect of fertility levels current about 15 years earlier. In this argument, the increase in rates of female labour force participation since the 1960s (which both reflected the impact of the

---

[25] Conceived in 1961, Easterlin's theory adapts fairly well, up to that date, to the observed situation; but despite repeated contradictions, its principles have not been revised since.

[26] The propositions put forward by the new household economics have—where they have been tested at all—generally been examined using only very incomplete survey data. The reverse of many such propositions can often be maintained.

[27] Easterlin does in fact use this line of reasoning (1968), but fails to draw on all its implications.

baby boom, and aggravated competition for jobs) contributes to the deterio-rating relative economic status of young couples and, thereby, encourages them to lower their fertility. Far from contradicting Easterlin's analysis, this view represents only a revision of his hypothesis.

Butz and Ward (1979), however, pursuing the micro-economic approach to the family laid down by the Chicago school regarding opportunity costs on the mother's time (Becker, Mincer, and especially Willis), arrive at a very different argument. In their view there is a fundamental dichotomy between households in which the wife has a professional job and those in which she does not. In the case of the latter, fertility would represent a positive function of the husband's income, whereas, in the former, fertility would always be positively connected with the husband's income, but negatively with the wife's.[28] Although it appears, by definition, more consistent with the model of economic behaviour characteristic of contemporary nuclear families in an urban setting—at least for young couples both in salaried employ—we do not consider this hypothesis to have been convincingly demonstrated by its authors. Their calculation is confined solely to the 20–24-year-old age group (which provides only about a third of total births) and to the period 1947–75:[29] by excluding the years 1940–46 they evidently cannot claim to explain the post-war increase.[30] This model has been tested for England by Ermisch (1979), but here again the choice of period (1955–75) removes all interest from the exercise: it is precisely a matter of comprehending the alternation of two opposing trends, and not solely the recent decline.

Often guided by a blind empiricism, econometric studies of the adjustment of fertility—which we have touched on only briefly—have tended to multiply and become increasingly complicated, leaving an impression of theoretical confusion. It is also no secret that the success of estimates obtained by this approach rests on examination only of those results consistent with the hypothesis tested, the others being discarded. It is for this reason that we consider a return to the basic issues to be essential, by examining, for the largest possible number of cases, whether trends conform to Easterlin's schema and whether there exists an alternative model to the one already advanced.

[28] By giving a privileged role to the relative position of women in the job market as the main explanatory variable influencing fertility, this type of analysis arrives at projections which run counter to those of Easterlin's school: they suggest a condition of sustained low fertility, and even of further decline.

[29] Furthermore, the resulting adjustment in the graph of fertility and income trends is far from convincing. Since 1975 the development of fertility has failed to conform to what Butz and Ward expected.

[30] At least where the US is concerned, contrary to the implications of this model, there was no more a fall in rates of female labour during the 1940s than there was a rise in the 1930s.

3. Fifty Years of Net Reproduction

Instead of using total fertility rates, we will take the net period reproduction rate as dependent variable, designated by the symbol R_0. By comparison, this measure has the advantage of integrating the possible influence of mortality on fertility,[31] which was probably still considerable during the 1930s and 1940s, at least in the poorer parts of certain countries. In consequence, comparisons between countries or periods should be less misleading: from the point of view of reproductive behaviour, only the number of surviving children is at issue where couples are concerned. The use of a synthetic measure makes possible less cumbersome presentation, while avoiding the problem of different fertility distributions across time and space. Like all such measures, R_0 is subject to the vicissitudes of history, which it registers as differentials in the timing of events; there is thus good reason to think that the variations it records are linked to general economic conditions—a recession producing a predicted level of completed fertility, reflecting delayed family formation, and, conversely, favourable conditions encouraging couples in earlier child-bearing. It thus lends itself to the line of analysis proposed by Easterlin.

The beginning date has been set at 1930. It is around this time that most of the Western countries entered the regime of controlled or post-transitional fertility—net reproduction rates then tending towards unity. With the exception of eastern Europe, where rates since the war bear the imprint of wilful and changing demographic policies, all the developed countries with sufficiently reliable vital and age-structural data to justify the reconstruction of series for the entire period 1930–82 have been included (see the Appendix to this chapter).[32] This results in a selection of 18 countries.

Several Distinct Paths

If the current state of fertility in the developed world is striking for the relative homogeneity of levels, the paths followed none the less vary greatly. The pre-war period was marked by a definite convergence of trends, which was followed, in the post-war period, by a very clear divergence; then came the massive international convergence observed since 1960. Analysis of the trends for net reproduction (heavily outlined in Figs. 7.1 to 7.4) enables us to distinguish, with a little simplification, five types of development.

1. *A very long full undulation around replacement level, having a regular cyclical appearance.* This type is only truly present in the three overseas English-speaking countries. These, in order of decreasing regularity of the 'cycle' are: the US, Canada, and Australia (Figs. 7.1(*a*) to (*c*)). The regular sinusoidal

---

[31] Through the replacement of children dying in infancy.

[32] Greece and Yugoslavia are excluded on account of defective data; also, countries with small populations like Luxemburg and New Zealand have been left out.

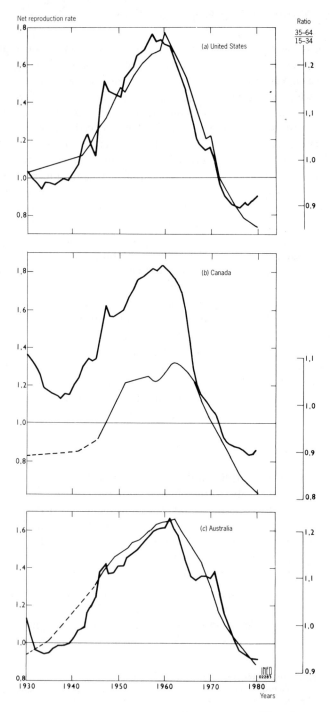

FIG. 7.1. Net reproduction rate and age structure. Type 1

shape of the curve is satisfactory, although current values are far from confirming a return—as a strict definition of the cycle would imply—to the initial
minimal values, or rather, in this instance, to the central intermediary minimal
values. Thus, in Canada, for example, the value of R_0 at the close of the
1970s is considerably lower than what it was at the end of the 1930s (0.85 as
opposed to 1.15).

2. *A long and fairly ample undulation, having a quasi-cyclic character.* The
trend line is less smooth in this type, and less sinusoidal, there being considerable asymmetry between ascending and descending phases. The following countries may be classed under this second type: Norway, England and
Wales, France, The Netherlands, Finland, and Denmark. All are characterized by marked unimodal curves, if one ignores the steep recovery of the years
1946–47 (Figs. 7.2(*a*) to (*f*)). The difference between the post-war maximum
and the current minimum values is of the order of 0.5 to 0.7 children per
woman, as opposed to 0.7 to 1.0 in the case of the overseas English-speaking
countries.

3. *An oscillation which is slight, uneven, and generally long.* This third type
occurs in Sweden and Switzerland, where R_0 describes a curve with a
bimodal, fairly flat trajectory; it also occurs in West Germany, Austria, and
Belgium (Figs. 7.3(*a*) to (*e*)), where the curve is late unimodal (maximum
fertility around 1960 rather than 1950). The range of variation is only 0.4 to
0.5.

4. *Slight, erratic variations, with no marked trend,* except since the mid-
1970s, when there is a sudden decline. This pattern is characteristic of
southern European countries with recent demographic transitions: Italy,
Spain, and Portugal (Figs. 7.4(*a*) to (*c*)).

5. *An abrupt downward trend,* with no apparent cyclical undulations since
reaching replacement level. Japan alone in this selection represents this type.[33]

In addition to this analytical demonstration of the diversity of post-
transitional development, an examination of Figs. 7.1 to 7.4 leads to four
general observations: (1) In almost every case, the existence of long cycles in
the strict sense (that is, symmetrical fluctuations in which the same processes
are repeated) appears not to be established. (2) Post-war fertility presents an
apparently new phenomenon, which is more than a mere recovery following
the 'crisis plunge' of the 1930s, since its developments are asymmetrical.
Thus, around 1960 marriage is more general and occurs at an earlier age than
around 1930; this difference necessarily contradicts the idea of repetition
inherent to the notion of the cycle. (3) At the time of writing, no complete
cycle has been observed in any country—only, at the most, half a cycle, or the
beginning of a cycle. (4) Finally, where developments do appear to have a
cyclical character, the size and periodicity of patterns is rather variable. Even

---

[33] It may, however, well illustrate the case of many developing countries currently in rapid
transition.

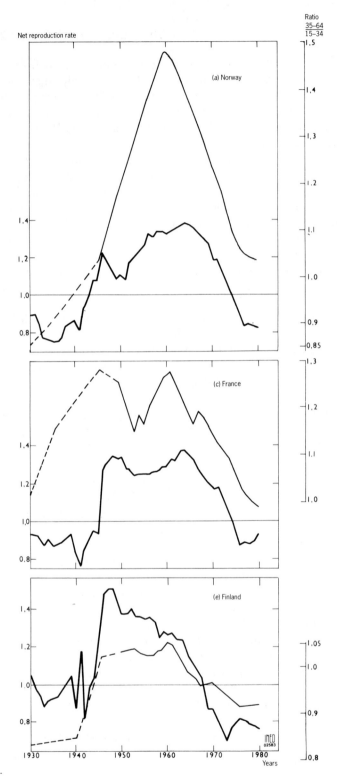

Net reproduction rate

Ratio $\dfrac{35\text{–}64}{15\text{–}34}$

(a) Norway

(c) France

(e) Finland

Years

FIG. 7.2. Net reproduction rate and age structure. Type 2

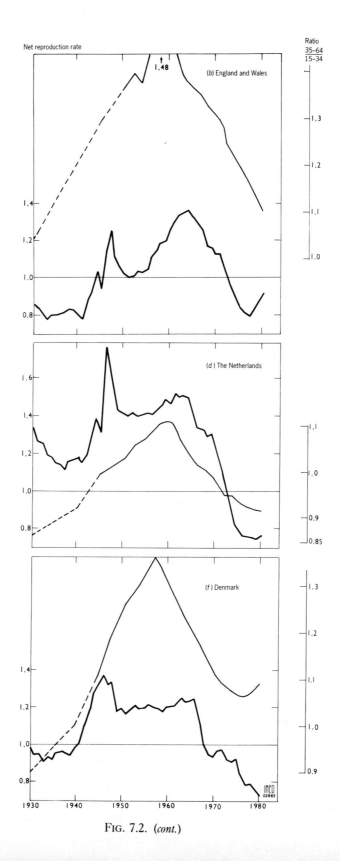

Net reproduction rate

(b) England and Wales

1,48

Ratio
$\frac{35-64}{15-34}$

(d) The Netherlands

(f) Denmark

INED
02883

FIG. 7.2. (cont.)

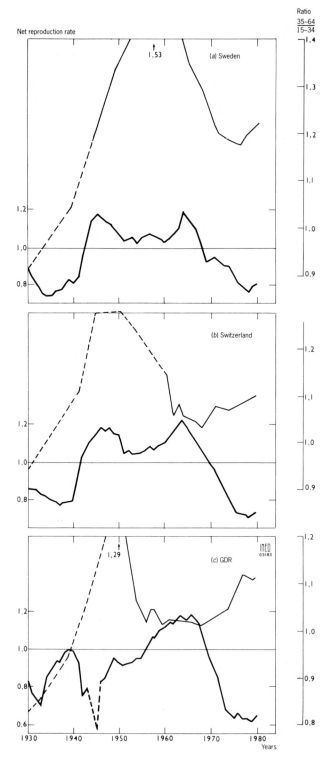

FIG. 7.3. Net reproduction rate and age structure. Type 3

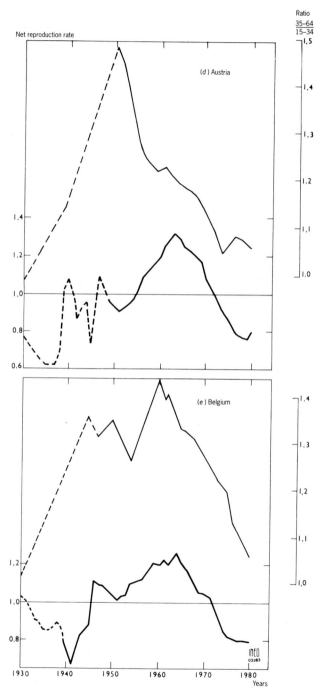

FIG. 7.3. (*cont.*)

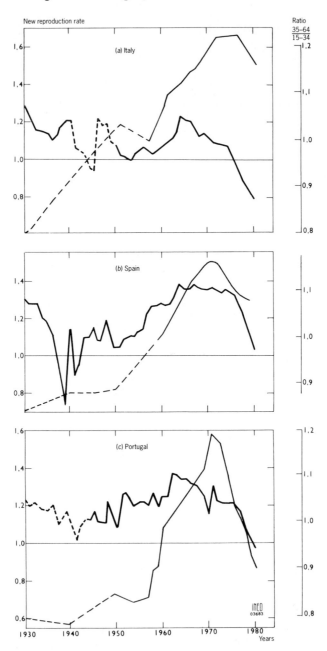

FIG. 7.4. Net reproduction rate and age structure. Type 4

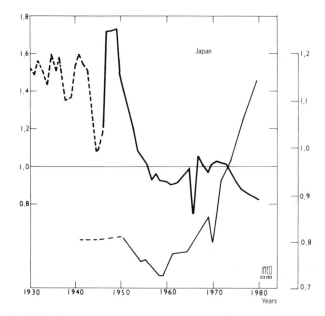

FIG. 7.5. Net reproduction rate and age structure. Type 5

the duration of changes, as measured by the interval between the two extreme points of the fertility curves, often differs too much from the average inter-generational interval to be explained by Easterlin's model.

Because we do not have sufficiently long time series, covering a century or more for post-transitional populations, it is premature to conclude that long fertility cycles exist. At most, we can detect the beginnings of a pattern of cyclical appearance in some countries experiencing earlier transitions, notably in North America, Australia, and northern Europe. But there is no evidence assuring its continuation.[34]

We shall now examine whether variations in fertility are related to differences in the relative status of young people, using as a proxy (designated r) for the proportion of 'mature' to 'young' adults,[35] the ratio of the sizes of the age groups 35–64/15–34 years.

Fertility and Age Structure

The development of this ratio is outlined in the several figures just presented. The case of the US, which inspired the hypothesis linking the evolution of age structures and reproductive patterns, has been used as a gauge. The very

[34] In the US, for example, where the decline began over 25 years ago, there is still no sign of a lasting and significant reversal of trends commensurate with the recorded decline.

[35] Both sexes.

close correspondence between the two curves (Fig. 7.1(a)), and especially the considerable elasticity of fertility (coefficient equal to 2) in relation to age distribution, will come as no surprise. Each variation in relative numbers of mature adults is accompanied by a variation in the same direction, twice as large, of net fertility. The same scale, corresponding to an elasticity of the order of 2, has been used for our entire selection; in so doing, the comparative responsiveness of fertility to age composition can be apprehended.

We thus arrive at the following account:

1. The covariation between the two series. Positive correlation (above 0.6, significant at 5%) is fairly satisfactory in seven cases: the US, Canada, Australia, France, Belgium, Finland, and The Netherlands. The reversal of the two curves, for these countries, is more or less synchronic, the differences, in either direction, being less or equal to four years. On the other hand, in a fair number of cases the development is completely the reverse: Austria, Switzerland, West Germany, and Japan especially. The main conclusion in the remaining seven cases is either the absence of any apparent link between the two phenomena (in England, for example), or a relationship which is erratic and unstable.

2. The apparent responsiveness of fertility varies considerably. Thus, for the same level of fertility, the number of mature adults, depending on the case, may sometimes be appreciably less than the number of young adults, and sometimes considerably greater; hence, when R_0 reaches replacement level, the variable r extends over a continuum ranging from 0.78 to 1.09; moreover, the same variation in R_0 may correspond to very different variations in r—the most striking example being the case of the US and Canada (Figs. 7.1(a) and (b)).

Thus, in cases where the covariation between the two phenomena is evident, the elasticity of R_0 in relation to r is so diverse (very strong in The Netherlands, but very slight—almost 4 times less—in Norway, for example: Figs. 7.2(a) and (d)) that there is reason to doubt an explanation in which changes in fertility are determined by changes in age structure, especially for those countries where the elasticity is very weak. Finally, regarding countries in which net reproduction in the half-century covered may be called 'cyclic' or 'quasi-cyclic' (types 1 and 2, as defined above), it must be said that the covariation in the timing of developments is evident only in a limited number of cases, chiefly the US and Australia, and less clearly in Canada, France, and The Netherlands. There is no evidence that the parallelism then observed is not merely fortuitous and that the undulation of fertility does not rely on causal mechanisms other than those advanced.

As an outcome of this fairly negative reassessment, one is tempted to propose some alternative explanation, subject, again, to the test of evidence.

A Return to History

Fertility, because so sensitive to many simultaneous historical factors, as well as the chance element of wars and crises, represents a fundamental stratum of human behaviour. One is therefore astonished by the mechanical, ahistorical character of Easterlin's schema: the great events which have shaped the twentieth century, manifest in the age structures of its populations, are absent. His reasoning implicitly supposes a definite symmetry between the recent and radical decline in fertility and the post-war recovery, and an analogy between the experience of the 1930s and contemporary experience, despite fundamental differences in social context (such as income levels, the status of women, and attitudes towards contraception and the techniques available) and economic context (standards of living, social security, the international linkage of economy, stagflation, etc.). A return to less partial explanations would thus appear desirable.

The most problematic issue is, evidently, interpreting the recovery of fertility in the 1940s. Looking at the rates of the 1940s and 1950s, it is impossible not to be struck immediately by the negative statistical link between the size of the economic crisis of the 1930s and the size of the post-war fertility increase. If one discounts the Axis powers (where pronatalist policies were implemented before the war), the higher the rate of unemployment, the stronger the fertility increase,[36] notably in the US, Canada, The Netherlands, Norway, and Belgium. In all these countries,[37] the rate of unemployment[38] exceeded 20%, often over a span of several years. Given that social security was more or less non-existent, unemployment was synonymous with poverty, and it may well be imagined that the memory of these dark years, swiftly followed by the war, could make a lasting impression on collective consciousness. In consequence, the profound contrast provided by a return to full employment would have contributed to a radical change in outlook—to the extent that the increase meant more than merely making up for the births prevented or delayed by circumstances. In the US, particularly, the psychological shock of the depression would have been all the more profound; the economy—long predominantly agrarian, having experienced strong and steady growth with the enlargement of the home market, had until then been fairly immune to crises, and the 1920s had given an illusion of indefinite expansion, to the point of total elimination of poverty.

The collapse of fertility over the last 10 to 20 years has brought about a marked and rapid convergence between countries, in which the previously diverse character of the immediate pre-war years has come to an end. As the

---

[36] France suggests another explanatory approach, i.e. political (the adoption of the Code de la Famille and the ordinances of 1945–46 on social security).

[37] Except Canada, where the rate reached 17.3% and 18.8% in 1932 and 1933.

[38] As a proportion of the total civilian labour force in the US and Canada, and a proportion of assured or unionized labour elsewhere.

geographic diffusion of the decline (beginning in North America, and then spreading to western and finally southern Europe) seems to indicate, this transformation has arisen from the percolation of profound changes in life-style through national frontiers: there is neither simultaneity nor a simple and uniform time lag between the break in fertility trends and the break in long macro-economic series. Such convergence, despite the continuation of considerable differences in living standards, rates of economic growth, rates of female labour force participation, and the degree of exposure to international crises, would appear to relegate purely economic explanations to the background. In any hypothesis, it seems unlikely that a single logic could have been operating in both the recovery and the subsequent decline.

Conclusion

In the current state of research, it would be premature to conclude that fertility conforms to cycles or even self-regulating mechanisms: nothing precludes the possibility that current trends end in permanent disequilibrium. History does not repeat itself, but consists in successive changes and ruptures. Fertility is governed by a complex and shifting matrix of factors which extend far beyond the narrow analytic frameworks into which some writers seek to confine them. In the case of the US alone, which has produced the greatest abundance of studies, we have seen that Easterlin's model, in its most detailed version,[39] gave a relatively good account of the post-war fertility increase, but failed to account sufficiently for the period of decline;[40] and that, in contrast, the alternative model of Butz and Ward proved appropriate for the period of the decline, but inappropriate for comprehending the increase. In other words, there exists no simple and generally applicable explanation of the development of fertility. Its ramifications, for the most part, resist rationalization, and doubtless its movements will not cease to surprise us.

[39] If, in Easterlin's simplified version (based on the ratio of the 35–64/15–34 age groups), the correlation of trends for the whole period 1940–75 is strong, this owes in part to his construction of the data: Easterlin acknowledges that the choice of age groups was reached by repeated trial and error.

[40] Even though adhering to the same basic premiss, Easterlin's logic across his various publications since 1961 is far from being constant, reflecting the author's hesitations in the face of the changing realities before him.

Appendix.   Net Reproduction Rates (Per Woman), 1930–1982

Sources: United Nations, *Demographic Yearbooks*, *1954*, *1965*, *1978*.
The most recent years represent the author's estimates based on the values for total fertility rates (see *Population* 4–5 (1981)) and probabilities of survival S_a, up to the average child-bearing age. These figures take into account the recent comparative development of infant mortality rates and of probabilities of survival in the latest published tables.

Data marked with the symbol α are derived by methods of indirect estimation. These generally concern pre-war data. Three sorts of data have been used: age structures at successive censuses, the series of crude birth-rates, and the series of infant mortality rates t_i. By comparing the first two of these, it is possible to produce a fairly reliable reconstruction of the series of total fertility rates. Secondly, the estimates for the probability of survival S_a (equal to the ratio R_0/R, i.e. the net rate to the crude reproduction rate) have been obtained by applying a linear regression to the development of the ratio t_i/S_a in countries with mortality developments similar to those studied.

Various additional data have been used:

Austria: the value of R_0, published for the years 1934–55 (*Statistisches Jahrbuch* 1980).
Spain and Portugal: the series of total fertility rates, published in Monnier 1980. And for Spain alone, the values of R_0 for the periods 1930–31, 1935–36, and 1940–41, published in Saez 1979.
The United States: the value of R, published for the year 1935 and the periods 1930–35 and 1935–40 (*Historical Statistics of the US*, Washington DC, 1975).
Italy: the series of total fertility rates (see Festy 1979).
Japan: statistical tables published in Japanese by the Tokyo Institute of Demographic Research, giving R and R_0 for 1930.

Bibliography to Chapter 7

ARTZROUNI, M. A., and EASTERLIN, R. A. (1982), 'Birth History, Age Structure and Post World War II Fertility in Ten Developed Countries: An Exploratory Empirical Analysis', *Genus* (July–Dec.), 81–99.
BANKS, J. A. (1954), *Prosperity and Parenthood* (London).
BECKER, G. S. (1960), 'An Economic Analysis of Fertility', in *Demographic and Economic Change in Developed Countries* (Princeton, NJ: Princeton University Press).
BOYER, P., CAILLOT, P., RICHARD, A., and ROMIER, G. (1979); *L'Autorégulation de la fécondité dans les pays industriels*, Paris, report for the Commissariat Général du Plan.
BRADY, D. S., and FRIEDMAN, R. D. (1947), *Savings and Income Distribution: Studies in Income and Wealth* (New York: National Bureau of Economic Research).
BUTZ, W. P., and WARD, M. P. (1979), 'The Emergence of Countercyclical US Fertility', *AER* (June), 318–28.

TABLE 7.2. *Net rate of reproduction, 1930–1986* (per woman)

Years	Australia	Austria	Belgium	Canada	Denmark	England and Wales	Finland	France	Germany (West)
1930	1.130	0.800[a]	1.030[a]	1.356	0.980	0.857	1.047	0.930	0.850
1931	1.034	0.750[a]	1.000[a]	1.326	0.949	0.834	0.986	0.930	0.770
1932	0.963	0.710[a]	0.970[a]	1.285	0.950	0.812	0.947	0.920	0.730
1933	0.959	0.680[a]	0.910[a]	1.201	0.907	0.773	0.875	0.880	0.700
1934	0.941	0.650	0.900[a]	1.184	0.930	0.795	0.904	0.900	0.860
1935	0.945	0.650	0.860[a]	1.171	0.922	0.793	0.925	0.870	0.890
1936	0.975	0.660[a]	0.850[a]	1.147	0.962	0.800	0.930	0.880	0.930
1937	0.989	0.650[a]	0.860[a]	1.132	0.968	0.808	0.964	0.890	0.930
1938	0.984	0.700[a]	0.890[a]	1.163	0.956	0.829	1.011	0.910	0.980
1939	0.995	1.040[a]	0.860	1.152	0.940	0.822	1.040	0.930	1.000
1940	1.017	1.100[a]	0.750	1.206	0.987	0.788	0.868	0.820	0.990
1941	1.068	1.020[a]	0.670	1.240	1.002	0.778	1.179	0.770	0.930
1942	1.072	0.860[a]	0.730	1.296	1.116	0.873	0.813	0.850	0.750
1943	1.167	0.930[a]	0.830	1.342	1.188	0.922	0.993	0.900	0.800
1944	1.198	0.960[a]	0.850	1.328	1.263	1.021	1.036	0.940	0.740
1945	1.244	0.740[a]	0.879	1.338	1.322	0.936	1.245	0.930	0.560
1946	1.379	0.930[a]	1.112	1.510	1.370	1.138	1.486	1.277	0.830
1947	1.416	1.090[a]	1.089	1.621	1.318	1.244	1.512	1.319	0.850
1948	1.376	1.040[a]	1.084	1.557	1.232	1.107	1.514	1.343	0.900
1949	1.382	0.960[a]	1.056	1.564	1.177	1.054	1.449	1.329	0.960
1950	1.415	0.940[a]	1.041	1.571	1.182	1.017	1.379	1.330	0.935
1951	1.409	0.911	1.013	1.600	1.162	1.001	1.385	1.267	0.922
1952	1.468	0.919	1.029	1.663	1.182	1.009	1.408	1.265	0.928
1953	1.477	0.930	1.033	1.713	1.205	1.033	1.361	1.240	0.930
1954	1.497	0.947	1.097	1.765	1.186	1.031	1.359	1.247	0.951
1955	1.532	0.997	1.104	1.774	1.196	1.038	1.350	1.242	0.953
1956	1.546	1.081	1.115	1.789	1.215	1.107	1.361	1.246	0.997
1957	1.598	1.109	1.127	1.822	1.197	1.149	1.334	1.261	1.071
1958	1.603	1.135	1.164	1.805	1.190	1.182	1.255	1.258	1.068
1959	1.614	1.163	1.208	1.835	1.173	1.190	1.284	1.284	1.106
1960	1.613	1.187	1.193	1.817	1.207	1.252	1.270	1.290	1.110
1961	1.668	1.254	1.233	1.795	1.203	1.303	1.275	1.341	1.141
1962	1.605	1.277	1.208	1.766	1.206	1.336	1.246	1.316	1.134
1963	1.567	1.320	1.251	1.735	1.251	1.347	1.246	1.370	1.170
1964	1.475	1.296	1.260	1.660	1.226	1.361	1.197	1.380	1.184
1965	1.395	1.252	1.218	1.497	1.231	1.329	1.135	1.346	1.176
1966	1.355	1.243	1.179	1.319	1.239	1.294	1.105	1.325	1.190
1967	1.342	1.220	1.131	1.217	1.115	1.243	1.058	1.266	1.169

TABLE 7.2. (*cont.*)

Years	Australia	Austria	Belgium	Canada	Denmark	England and Wales	Finland	France	Germany (West)
1968	1.360	1.201	1.082	1.145	1.000	1.160	0.981	1.219	1.121
1969	1.360	1.167	1.052	1.124	0.944	1.160	0.873	1.194	1.039
1970	1.349	1.073	1.060	1.085	0.927	1.126	0.870	1.168	0.947
1971	1.386	1.034	1.042	1.026	0.965	1.124	0.813	1.178	0.901
1972	1.277	0.982	0.986	0.955	0.970	1.029	0.751	1.139	0.806
1973	1.177	0.915	0.918	0.911	0.915	0.955	0.709	1.090	0.725
1974	1.123	0.905	0.862	0.892	0.908	0.901	0.776	0.999	0.711
1975	1.023	0.869	0.818	0.880	0.921	0.848	0.798	0.917	0.680
1976	0.983	0.804	0.815	0.873	0.829	0.818	0.823	0.872	0.686
1977	0.958	0.781	0.803	0.868	0.794	0.797	0.808	0.887	0.659
1978	0.937	0.773	0.804	0.842	0.797	0.830	0.789	0.879	0.654
1979	0.928	0.769	0.804	0.839	0.766	0.882	0.784	0.892	0.656
1980	0.910	0.799	0.799	0.820	0.732	0.906	0.775	0.932	0.689
1981	0.930	0.814	0.790	0.810	0.689	0.877	0.789	0.934	0.686
1982	0.930	0.810	0.762	0.800	0.684	0.852	0.820	0.910	0.667
1983	0.930	0.760	0.740	0.800	0.660	0.850	0.830	0.850	0.630
1984	0.900	0.740	0.720	—	0.670	0.850	0.810	0.860	0.610
1985	0.940	0.710	0.710	—	0.700	0.860	0.790	0.870	0.600
1986	—	0.690	0.730	—	0.710	—	—	0.880	0.630

COWGILL, D. O. (1949), 'The Theory of Population Growth Cycles', *The American Journal of Sociology* (Sept.), 163–70.

DUPAQUIER, J. (1979), *La Population rurale du Bassin parisien à l'époque de Louis XIV* (Paris).

EASTERLIN, R. A. (1961), 'The American Baby-Boom in Historical Perspective', *AER*, 51: 869–911.

—— (1968), *Population, Labor Force and Long Swings in Economic Growth: The US Experience* (New York: NBER), ch. 4 and 5.

—— (1973), 'Relative Economic Status and the American Fertility Swing', in E. B. Sheldon (ed.), *Family Economic Behavior: Problems and Prospects* (Philadelphia, Pa.: Lippincott), 166–223.

—— (1976), 'The Conflict between Aspirations and Resources', *PDR* (Sept.), 417–26.

—— (1980), *Birth and Fortune: The Impact of Numbers on Personal Welfare* (New York: Basic Books).

—— and CONDRAN, G. A. (1976), 'A Note on the Recent Fertility Swing in Australia,

TABLE 7.2. (*cont.*)

Italy	Japan	Netherlands	Norway	Portugal	Spain	Sweden	Switzerland	United States
1.280	1.520	1.330	0.890	1.230[a]	1.300	0.878	0.890	1.040[a]
1.220	1.490	1.270	0.890	1.210[a]	1.280	0.818	0.850	1.000[a]
1.160	1.560	1.257	0.845	1.220[a]	1.280	0.800	0.850	0.970[a]
1.160[a]	1.500	1.188	0.773	1.190[a]	1.280[a]	0.747	0.830	0.940[a]
1.150[a]	1.430	1.175	0.758	1.180[a]	1.210[a]	0.742	0.820	0.980[a]
1.140	1.600[a]	1.145	0.746	1.170[a]	1.190	0.739	0.800	0.975
1.110	1.510[a]	1.140	0.750	1.200[a]	1.140	0.766	0.790	0.960[a]
1.130	1.580[a]	1.119	0.767	1.100[a]	1.030	0.772	0.760	0.970[a]
1.180[a]	1.350[a]	1.158	0.832	1.130[a]	0.910[a]	0.802	0.780	1.000[a]
1.210[a]	1.360[a]	1.168	0.849	1.170[a]	0.740[a]	0.830	0.790	0.980[a]
1.210[a]	1.520[a]	1.181	0.858	1.100[a]	1.150	0.812	0.800	1.027
1.060[a]	1.600[a]	1.155	0.813	1.020[a]	0.890[a]	0.843	0.910	1.075
1.050[a]	1.540[a]	1.196	0.936	1.090	0.950[a]	0.960	1.020	1.185
1.020[a]	1.510[a]	1.319	0.995	1.130	1.100	1.063	1.080	1.228
0.950[a]	1.410[a]	1.382	1.073	1.120	1.100	1.140	1.120	1.163
0.940[a]	1.080[a]	1.309	1.075	1.170	1.150	1.176	1.160	1.132
1.220[a]	1.196[a]	1.758	1.221	1.123	1.080	1.161	1.180	1.344
1.180[a]	1.718	1.642	1.164	1.108	1.080	1.133	1.170	1.505
1.190[a]	1.722	1.504	1.126	1.216	1.190	1.124	1.180	1.462
1.100[a]	1.729	1.429	1.088	1.129	1.100	1.079	1.150	1.446
1.042	1.516	1.417	1.107	1.082	1.040	1.056	1.145	1.435
1.031	1.382	1.405	1.081	1.256	1.040	1.032	1.053	1.519
1.013	1.292	1.421	1.174	1.265	1.090	1.042	1.060	1.563
0.999	1.176	1.396	1.212	1.239	1.100	1.055	1.039	1.599
1.034	1.076	1.411	1.231	1.201	1.100	1.018	1.043	1.657
1.053	1.045	1.420	1.259	1.216	1.130	1.055	1.047	1.676
1.066	0.998	1.412	1.324	1.214	1.140	1.061	1.063	1.729
1.042	0.926	1.439	1.321	1.200	1.230	1.073	1.083	1.765
1.027	0.960	1.453	1.334	1.262	1.260	1.049	1.076	1.736
1.060	0.920	1.486	1.336	1.200	1.260	1.041	1.092	1.742
1.071	0.920	1.459	1.329	1.310	1.242	1.023	1.100	1.715
1.094	0.900	1.518	1.341	1.360	1.264	1.046	1.140	1.704
1.110	0.910	1.500	1.357	1.390	1.282	1.064	1.160	1.633
1.141	0.930	1.505	1.375	1.350	1.319	1.097	1.210	1.564
1.225	0.950	1.500	1.383	1.390	1.387	1.177	1.220	1.507
1.205	1.000	1.430	1.370	1.360	1.349	1.147	1.191	1.376
1.153	0.745	1.380	1.359	1.350	1.352	1.121	1.152	1.288
1.157	1.050	1.333	1.325	1.330	1.382	1.083	1.110	1.213
1.134	0.994	1.292	1.298	1.300	1.355	0.992	1.070	1.166
1.140	0.976	1.302	1.275	1.280	1.348	0.919	1.026	1.161

TABLE 7.2. (cont.)

Italy	Japan	Netherlands	Norway	Portugal	Spain	Sweden	Switzerland	United States
1.123	1.010	1.225	1.183	1.230	1.348	0.924	0.981	1.168
1.118	1.020	1.122	1.188	1.260	1.355	0.939	0.954	1.075
1.090	1.010	1.026	1.136	1.240	1.348	0.916	0.914	0.956
1.091	1.010	0.909	1.057	1.210	1.335	0.896	0.859	0.897
1.083	0.970	0.843	1.026	1.200	1.354	0.899	0.822	0.879
1.023	0.900	0.793	0.949	1.190	1.330	0.851	0.763	0.853
0.976	0.880	0.776	0.892	1.200	1.321	0.804	0.730	0.840
0.910	0.860	0.753	0.835	1.160	1.259	0.785	0.723	0.869
0.869	0.856	0.754	0.846	1.070	1.198	0.766	0.710	0.856
0.824	0.847	0.745	0.837	1.020	1.106	0.795	0.716	0.875
0.790	0.840	0.770	0.823	1.000	1.029	0.804	0.731	0.880
0.746	0.840	0.746	0.815	0.960	0.950	0.780	0.737	0.870
0.748	0.850	0.750	0.820	0.940	0.900	0.775	0.742	0.870
0.730	0.860	0.710	0.790	0.920	0.820	0.770	0.720	0.860
0.720	0.870	0.720	0.800	0.900	0.790	0.790	0.730	0.870
0.680	—	0.730	0.810	0.810	—	0.830	0.730	0.860
—	—	—	—	—	—	0.860	—	—

[a] Estimate.

Canada, England and Wales and the United States', in H. Richards (ed.), *Population, Factor Movements and Economic Development: Studies Presented to Brinley Thomas* (Cardiff: University of Wales Press), 140–51.

——, and POLLACK, R. A., and WACHTER M. L (1980), 'Toward a More General Model of Fertility Determination: Endogenous Preferences and Natural Fertility', in *Population and Economic Change in Developing Countries* (Chicago: University of Chicago Press).

——, and WACHTER, M. L., and WACHTER, S. M. (1978), 'Demographic Influences on Economic Stability: The US Experience', *PDR*, 1: 1–22.

ERMISCH, J. (1979), 'The Relevance of the "Easterlin Hypothesis" and the "New Home Economics" to Fertility Movements in Great Britain', *Population Studies* (Mar.), 39–57.

FESTY, P. (1979), *La Fécondité des pays occidentaux de 1870 à 1970*, Travaux et Documents, Cahier no. 85 (Paris: INED-PUF).

GINI, C. (1929), *Population*, Harris Foundation Lectures (Chicago).

GOUBERT, P. (1960), *Beauvais et les Beauvaisis de 1600 à 1730* (Paris).

GRAUMAN, J. (1960), 'Comment', in *Demographic and Economic Change in Developed Countries* (Princeton, NJ), 275–84.

Historical Statistics of the US.

KUZNETS, S. (1958), 'Long Swings in the Growth of Population and in Related Economic Variables', *Proceedings of the American Philosophical Society*, 102: 25–52.

LE BRAS, H. (1971), 'Éléments pour une théorie des populations instables', *Population*, 3: 525–72.

LERIDON, H. (1978), 'Fécondité et structures démographiques: une hypothèse sur l'évolution de la fécondité depuis 1940', *Population*, 2: 441–47.

MONNIER, A. (1980), 'L'Italie, l'Espagne et le Portugal: estimation démographique', *Population*, 4–5: 927–59.

OPPENHEIMER, V. K. (1974), 'The Life Cycle Squeeze: The Interaction of Men's Occupational and Family Life Cycles', *Demography* (May), 227–45.

PEARL, R. (1930), *The Biology of Population Growth* (New York).

SAEZ, A. (1979), 'La Fécondité en Espagne depuis le début du siècle', *Population*, 6: 1007–22.

SAUVY, A. (1948), 'La Reprise de la natalité dans le monde', *Population*, 2: 249–70.

SIMON, J. L., (ed.) (1978), *Research in Population Economics*, (Greenwich, Conn.: Jai), i.

SWEEZY, A. (1971), 'The Economic Explanation of Fertility Changes in the US', *Population Studies* (July), 255–67.

WRIGLEY, E. A., and SCHOFIELD, R. S. (1981), *The Population History of England, 1541–1872* (London).

YULE, G. U. (1906), 'On the Changes in the Marriage and Birth-Rate in England and Wales during the Past Half Century; with an Enquiry as to their Probable Causes', *Journal of the Royal Statistical Society*, 69: 88–132.

PART II

Forms of Demographic Transition

THE demographic transition is an ineluctable phenomenon resting on universal underlying principles. If the secular fertility decline is not yet manifest world-wide, the mortality decline, on the other hand, is. Further, there is no country in which natural increase retains a steady level of 3% or more following declines in mortality, without fertility having declined, in its turn. Of course one runs across instances—to raise Malthus's famous example—of the doubling of population size within 25 years (annual average growth = 2.8%), but this has never occurred across two consecutive twenty-five-year periods. If we must choose mathematical law, it is more to logistic models than geometric progressions that modern demographic growth is related. In other words, the general appearance of the profile of natural growth is a bell-shaped curve.

But the common denominator stops there: the variety of pre-transitional levels of mortality and fertility, the diverse paths followed in their downward curves, the variability of time lags between corresponding declines, the history of international migration—all these combine to multiply possible differences. However, beyond the accumulation of individual cases, it is possible to outline a typology which is more or less robust, depending on the degree of maturity of the transition (Chapter 8).

With these different types of transition are associated successive transformations in age pyramids. At the time of writing, the rhythm and degree of the final ageing of populations appears, in the light of existing data, to promise profound variations (Chapter 9).

The universal character of the demographic transition may, at first appearance, suggest that the phenomenon occurs independently of the context in which it first emerges: religion, social organization, agrarian regime, family structures, level of socio-economic development, and so forth. But, looking solely at the reproductive transition, one finds that it began in France over two centuries ago, while still being almost non-existent in an entire continent today: Black Africa. The historical lags are thus considerable. The main issue, then, is to establish the origin of such differences and, thereby, to assess the degree to which fertility decline depends on the contextual elements mentioned. The comparison between France and England is, in this respect, rich in information (Chapter 11).

Moreover, if the process of demographic transition is general in principle, it may well be asked how comparable instances are to be established, and what explanatory mechanisms then underlie them. By way of a test, the applicability of certain observations drawn from European experience, and present in most theories of the transition, may be measured against contemporary trends in less developed countries. Put in other terms, beyond the many and well-known differences, are there any common points between the demographic development of pre-Revolutionary France, that of Europe in the last third of the nineteenth century, and that of the poor countries of the second half of the twentieth century? A primary general pre-condition of the decline in fertility has already been examined: the decline in mortality. Two others—the limitation of marriages, and socio-economic development—are advanced more or less explicitly as part of transition theory. We will endeavour to see here (Chapters 11 to 13), using as many observations as possible, if these two additional conditions are as relevant to contemporary transitions as to earlier ones. This process of validation will be conducted within a larger framework of critical discussion addressed to the most prominent studies on the context of transition.

8 The Types of Demographic Transition

> There is no such thing as mankind. There are only bipeds as different from each other as elephants and giraffes.
>
> (S. I. Witkiewicz)

BY type or form of demographic transition, we understand, in the first instance,[1] not different possible combinations[2] of variations in crude birth- and death-rates, but their effective yields: the modalities of development manifest in natural balance.

A Priori Types

This balance may, for example, remain above pre-transitional levels for an extended period, in which case we are dealing with a long transition. Conversely, it may remain higher only briefly, at least on the time-scale with which we are concerned: this would be a short transition. But this criterion of total duration is hardly sufficient. It is necessary to take into account further aspects, including: height (i.e. poor countries may be said to have 'high' transitions, whilst wealthy countries experienced 'low' ones); the duration of the phase of maximal growth (where this extends across several decades, and the decline in birth-rates takes time to manifest itself, a country may experience severe tensions, such as the anarchic growth of shanty towns, aggravation of urban unemployment, increased dependence, etc.); and, finally, asymmetry (when natality remains at a much higher level than mortality over a prolonged period, owing, for example, to age distribution requiring sustained investment in housing, schools, infrastructure, technology—and also job creation).

Let us imagine an example. If, as an extreme case, the decline in crude mortality is very rapid, and birth-rates only start falling at the point at which mortality has ebbed, then the transformation described is an acute-angled transition; such a high and sharply pointed figure immediately recalls certain less developed countries with very strong demographic growth. In theory, this

---

[1] Migration will be taken into consideration in Chapter 10, which deals with the transitional multiplier of population.

[2] The possible variants are manifold: R. Mackensen presented a theoretical study of these at the World Population Conference in Sydney, 1967 (see final bibliography). The terminology which follows, however, is our own.

extreme case should result in increases close on 4% per year, since the traditional level of natality is often around 45 to 50 per 1000 and the crude mortality rate—bearing in mind the large proportion of young people in the population—declines to around 5 to 10 per 1000. This transition type has in fact only rarely been encountered up to the present. Even where mortality has declined exceptionally rapidly, as in Sri Lanka or Taiwan, it took 50 years for the traditional level of life expectation (25 to 35 years) to reach the modern level (over 70 years, for women). However, as we have seen, the decline in birth-rates generally begins after a shorter delay, and this delayed reaction— of a more or less long duration—and the force of the decline in the birth-rate, determines the contours of the second phase of the transition. This phase, the duration of which has been set fairly arbitrarily as $T\omega - T\alpha$, had already been completed by most developed countries, including Japan, by the end of the 1970s, and Iberia by the beginning of the 1980s (but not Ireland). If it has begun in all the less developed countries considered here, it has not been completed, however, in any of them. Therefore, it would be premature at present to concern oneself with *symmetry* or types of *asymmetry* in these two phases of transition in the less developed world.

Not all forms of transition are equally possible, and some occur much more frequently than others. We shall see that a diagrammatic presentation combining the geographical diffusion of mortality declines with those of fertility enables specific types to be isolated for developed countries, at the very least. The classification of European countries by two criteria—the period of highest population growth and the corresponding rate of growth— shows that these two criteria are very closely related; the resulting classification fairly accurately reflects existing geographical divisions in Europe associated with modernization, as seen through indicators such as the size of the agricultural sector or the percentage of illiterate adults in the population.

This contrast, for the less developed countries in our study, is less clear, and appears to rest on neither a geographical nor even a historical criterion. It is hazardous as yet to sketch a typology for a phenomenon whose development generally belongs more to an unknown future than to the known past.[3] We have therefore classified these countries simply by level of maximal growth, the corresponding period being still too recent to be taken as definitive. Three groups have been identified:

1. 2 to 2.5% per year;
2. 2.5% to 3% per year;
3. over 3% per year.

---

[3] For countries with delayed transitions, the reliability and precision of our information diminishes proportionately with the degree of delay: on the whole, estimates for several-year periods are all that is available, and these are often subject to doubt.

Here, then, for the ensemble of countries in our selection, are the groups adopted:[4]

1. European developed countries and Japan:
   (a) France (Fig. 8.1);
   (b) Northern Europe: Sweden, Norway, Finland, the UK, Denmark, and The Netherlands (Figs. 8.2(a) to (f));
   (c) Western Europe: Belgium, Switzerland, Germany (Figs. 8.3(a) to (c));
   (d) Central Europe: Czechoslovakia, Austria, Hungary, Poland (Figs. 8.3(d) to (g));
   (e) Southern Europe: Italy, Yugoslavia, Spain, Portugal, and Greece; and Japan (Figs. 8.4(a) to (f));
   (f) Eastern Europe: USSR, Bulgaria, Romania (Figs. 8.4(g) to (i));
   (g) Ireland (Fig. 8.5).
2. Countries with overseas European populations: Canada, Australia, New Zealand, the US, Argentina, and Uruguay (Figs. 8.6(a) to (f)).
3. Less developed countries:
   (a) Fairly high maximal growth peak: Cyprus, Chile, China, India (Figs. 8.6(a) to (d));
   (b) High maximal growth peak: Puerto Rico, South Korea, Sri Lanka, Hong Kong, Cuba, Egypt, and Tunisia (Figs. 8.8(a) to (g));
   (c) Very high growth peak: Europe and Africa: Albania, Mauritius, and Réunion (Figs. 8.9(a) to (c)); Latin America: British Guiana, Jamaica, Panama, Trinidad and Tobago, Brazil, Costa Rica, Mexico, and Venezuela (Figs. 8.9(d) to (k)); Asia: Formosa, Singapore, West Malaysia, and Fiji (Figs. 8.9(c) to (o)).

In order to highlight long-term trends, all figures conform to the same condensed time-scale. We shall only comment briefly on their broader outlines and particularities. A synthesis of this account of national profiles will then be presented, in order to isolate the characteristics of the principal types of transition.

1. Transition Profiles: The National Cases

European Developed Countries and Japan

France

France holds a special place for two reasons: (1) its fertility decline was very early; and (2) the profile of natural increase during the transition period was

---

[4] Those countries with short retrospective series (dating from 1950 only, for example) consisting largely of five-yearly estimations are not represented. They are: Colombia, the

fairly flat and maintained at around zero growth. Not only did fertility and mortality decline at about the same pace, but they tended towards permanent equilibrium, except over a period of slight increase (1815–45), when natural growth reached the level of 6 per 1000 per year: this is the lowest 'peak' ever observed at the height of a transition process. On a number of occasions, in peacetime, and since the end of the nineteenth century, negative growth has prevailed. The sharp rise in the birth-rate in the immediate post-war period is all the more remarkable. But by 1950, a downward trend in the birth-rate curve, followed by a brief break in 1972, has returned growth to its habitual level of less than 5 per 1000. The French profile, in sum, is completely atypical, its demographic history differing from that of all other European countries.

Northern Europe

After France, northern Europe was the first area to complete the several stages of demographic transition, decades ahead of the rest of Europe. Discounting post-war fertility increases, Sweden corresponds almost perfectly to the theoretical model presented in demographic handbooks[5]—a pattern which, as we shall see, is generally little respected, if at all, in actual transitions. In Sweden the war created, as it were, a historical parenthesis of 30 years where fertility is concerned, without the slightest disruption of the continuing improvement of mortality: crude death-rates continued to decline up to about 1960, but have since then slowly increased as health improvements have failed to compensate for the effects of demographic ageing. As a result, natural increase is at its lowest since 1810.

Norway's development is similar. In both countries, the long time taken for fertility to respond, and the initial slowness of its decline, appear as a wide plateau of increased growth, extending over more than half a century, at twice the height of the average level of pre-transitional growth. With the accelerated fertility decline to around 1935, the contour of natural increase takes the form of an asymmetric dome.

Finland differs from its two Scandinavian neighbours, first, by its markedly earlier (1750)[6] and generally much stronger declining fertility; and, secondly, by the considerable delay in the onset of declines in crude mortality (1870).

Dominican Republic, Indonesia, Israel, North Korea, Turkey, and South Africa. Colombia and the Dominican Republic belong to group 3(c), described below (very high levels of growth); North Korea, South Africa, and Turkey to group 3(b) (high levels of growth); Indonesia to group 3(a) (moderately high levels of growth); and Israel more to group 2 (countries of immigration). See the statistical appendix for detailed data, and Tables 8.1 and 8.2 for the quinquennial series.

[5] See e.g. Keyfitz and Flieger 1971: 101. Sweden is also most frequently used as a model.

[6] This could also be a long-term fluctuation connected with the previous period's historical set-backs (epidemics, wars, Russian occupation) and the disruptions in age structure caused by them (See Chapter 4).

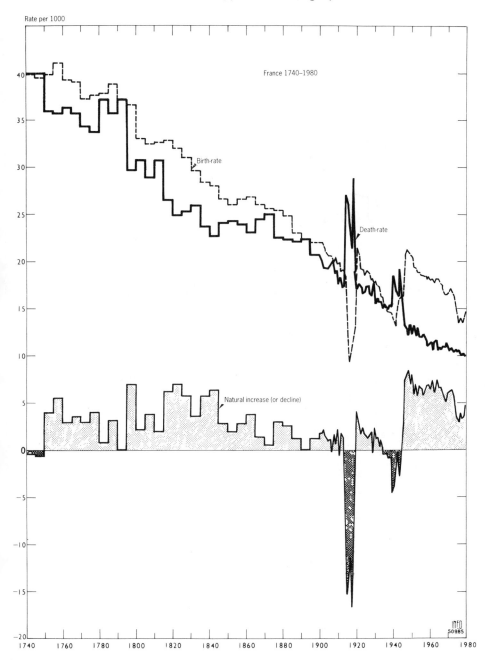

FIG. 8.1. Natural increase of the French population since 1740

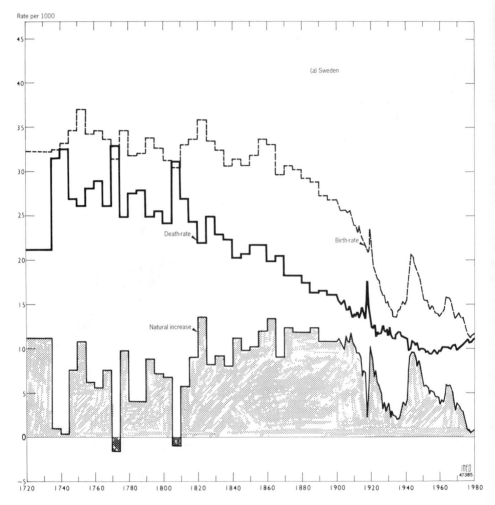

FIG. 8.2. Natural increase in northern Europe, 1720–1980

This resulted in a very extended decline in natural growth, over the long period 1750–1870, after which the Finnish pattern was comparable to its neighbours.

Birth-rates, and mortality rates especially, were already relatively low in England and Wales around 1840, and may be compared (allowing for some underestimation) to Sweden's for the same period; the crude mortality rate had certainly dropped well before the apparent date (1875) in Fig. 8.2(d). There are a few specific differences, however: (1) the surge of growth during the middle phase of the transition is due not to declining mortality, but to strong increases in fertility at the height of the Victorian era; (2) mortality has

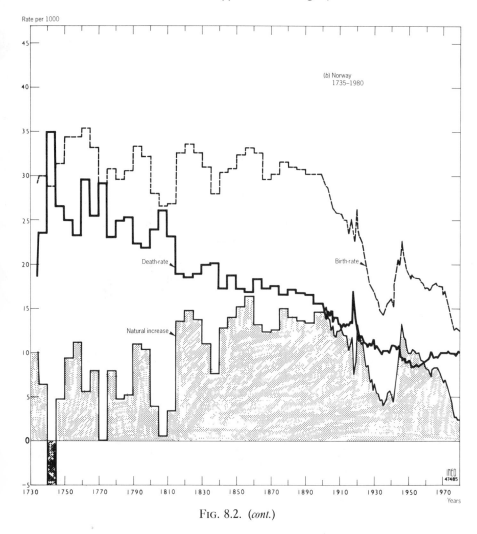

Fig. 8.2. (cont.)

remained almost stationary since 1920, which fits the pattern of early declines,
just noted; and (3) the baby boom is even shorter-lived than in Sweden after
the war.

Altogether, these four countries are characterized both by a very long
transition (a century to a century and a half), with maximum growth occurring
around 1870–80 (or 1855–60 in Norway). They define what we shall call the
Nordic model of demographic transition.

With a shift of about a quarter-century, at least for the rising phase of the
transition (maximal growth around 1900), Denmark's pattern conforms closely
to the Nordic type. This is also the case with The Netherlands, but its fertility

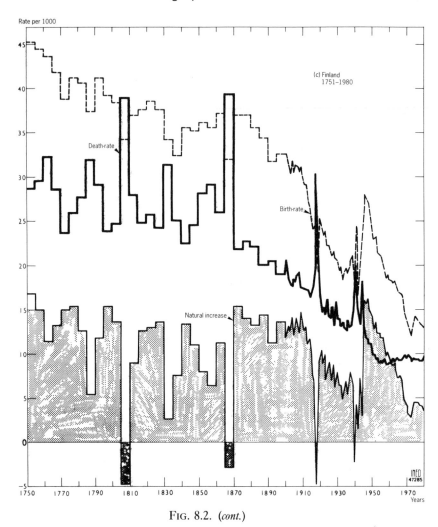

FIG. 8.2. (cont.)

and mortality levels were higher at the outset, producing a sort of hybrid between the north European and west European countries.

Western Europe

Up to 1940, in Belgium and Switzerland the parameters developed at fairly similar levels and followed comparable trends. Around 1870, on the eve of the transition, fertility was a little above 30 per 1000, and mortality was just over 25 per 1000. By 1900, at the time of maximum growth, crude mortality was

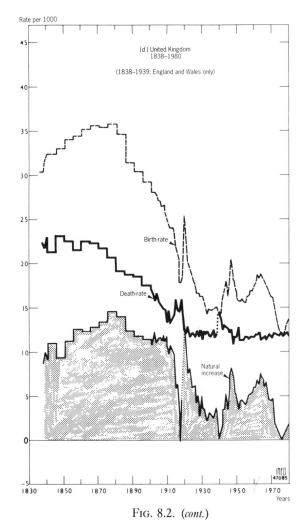

Rate per 1000

(d) United Kingdom
1838–1980

(1838–1939: England and Wales only)

Birth-rate

Death-rate

Natural
increase

INED
47085

1830   1850   1870   1890   1910   1930   1950   1970
Years

FIG. 8.2. (cont.)

no more than 18 per 1000. But the decline slowed down, especially in
Belgium, producing a rapid contraction in natural growth, which fell in the
space of 40 years from 1.1% (1900) to 0.3% per year (immediately prior to
the war). The modest increase in Belgium's population since the war would
appear to be due more to changes in mortality than to changes in fertility.

Germany is similar in its broad outlines, but maximum growth was higher
(close on 1.5% per year, around 1900), owing to stronger fertility. This made
the collapse in growth all the more spectacular: without Hitler's brusque
populationist policies, German demographic growth (as in France, but later)

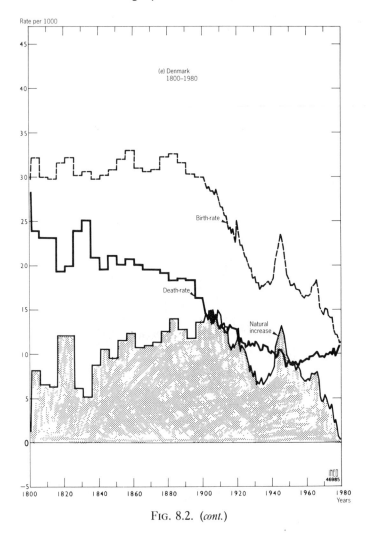

FIG. 8.2. (*cont.*)

could well have fallen to zero or below.[7] By comparison with the increase in
births in the years 1934–41, and a second and consequent wave between
1957 and 1967, the post-war baby boom scarcely stands out. Since 1965,
fertility has again declined drastically, and much faster than in Belgium and
Switzerland; since 1975, total fertility has been confined to a historically

---

[7] Economic policy may have played an even greater part than actual demographic measures.
According to Kirk (1942), in the light of the relation observed between employment and fertility
in various European countries, the recovery of German fertility may account for three-fifths of the
gradual eradication of unemployment.

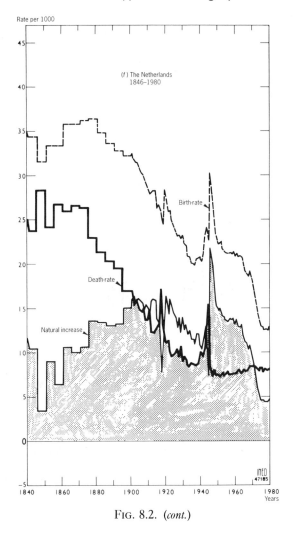

FIG. 8.2. (*cont.*)

unprecedented level for a large country: an average of 1.4 children per woman.

Central Europe

Similar to the countries of western Europe during their transition period, the countries of central Europe experienced a plateau of maximal growth which was: (1) later than in northern Europe; (2) centred around 1900; and (3) relatively brief (only 10 to 20 years). However, history intervened heavily, revising national boundaries, provoking mass population transfers, and (in

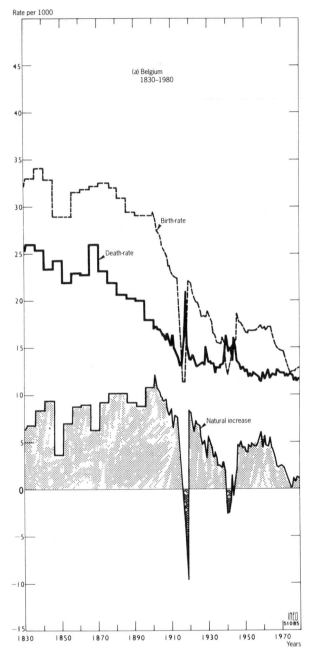

FIG. 8.3. Natural increase in western and central Europe, 1785–1980

b

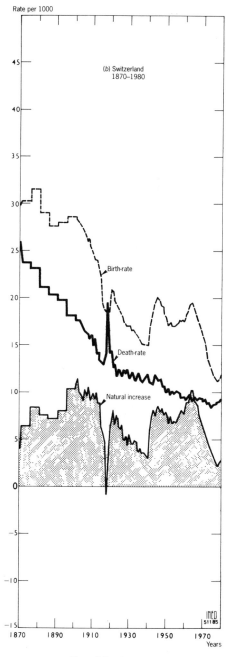

Rate per 1000

(b) Switzerland
1870–1980

Birth-rate

Death-rate

Natural increase

FIG. 8.3. (*cont.*)

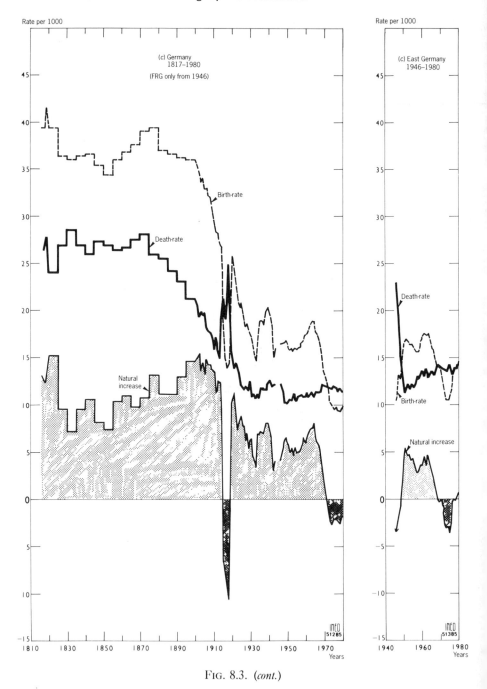

Fig. 8.3. (cont.)

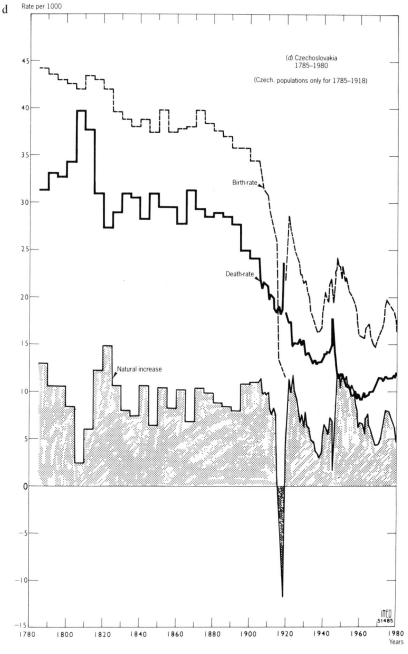

FIG. 8.3. (*cont.*)

e

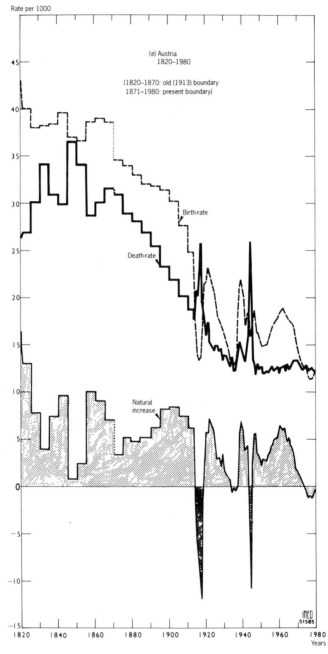

Rate per 1000

(e) Austria
1820–1980

(1820–1870: old (1913) boundary
1871–1980: present boundary)

Birth-rate

Death-rate

Natural
increase

FIG. 8.3. (cont.)

f

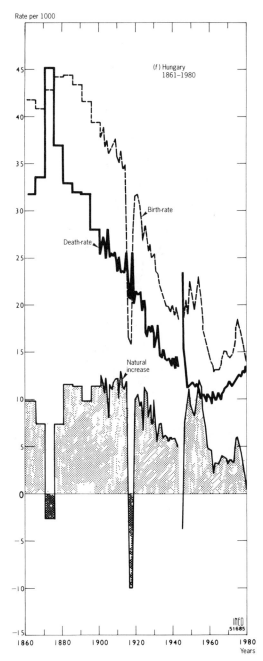

Rate per 1000

(f) Hungary
1861–1980

Birth-rate

Death-rate

Natural
increase

INED
51685

FIG. 8.3. (*cont.*)

g

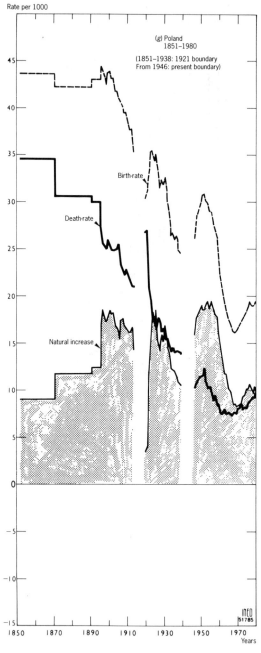

FIG. 8.3. (cont.)

three cases) installing different political systems. The result is a turbulent demographic profile, attenuated none the less by certain traditional resemblances between the countries.

The Czech countries[8] stand out with a relatively flat profile up to the end of the nineteenth century. Their growth up to the 1940s then resembles other central European countries, in which a more or less dramatic fall in fertility occurred. The pattern has subsequently been governed largely by political changes: an increase in fertility during the Nazi occupation; a post-war population policy at first liberal (in the 1950s), then conservative regarding birth control, leading to the introduction of pronatalist measures (around 1970); and, towards the end of the 1970s, a slight downward trend in fertility.

For over a century Austria, within its present boundaries, has maintained a low rate of growth, its development remaining very close to Germany's. Although heavily declining fertility in recent years has lead to a birth deficit, Austria during the *Anschluss* (1938) experienced a fertility peak lasting several years; there was then an echo of this peak a generation later, between 1956 and 1969. Even though recent fertility declines have been less rapid than West Germany's, the slight rise in the crude mortality rate, connected with ageing, has brought Austria to the level of negative natural increase.

Fertility and mortality in Hungary during the second half of the nineteenth century were higher than in Austria, and although fertility also fell by 50% between 1900 and 1940, mortality—which had lagged behind—fell faster than in Austria, producing a much more rapid decline in natural growth. The similarities lessen just after the war: as in other east European countries, developments lose their spontaneity, becoming a balance between relaxed governmental attitude (notably to abortion in the 1950s, when natality fell to the lowest level in the world, despite a relatively young age structure and a high agricultural percentage of the population) and recent strictness (a recovery in the last 10 years, of uncertain durability,[9] associated with the launch of social programmes promoting the increase of families).

At the beginning of the demographic transition, both of Poland's parameters occupied a fairly similar position to Hungary's. But while the mortality decline occurred at the same time, the fertility decline began later and was less decisive. Maximum growth was thus higher and longer lasting: just before

[8] The period 1785–1918 covers Czech populations only, owing to a lack of Slovak data, but from 1919 onwards refers to Czechoslovakia. The countries comprising the Czech populations—Bohemia and Moravia—have fairly close connections with the western sphere; their populations show characteristics similar to those of German populations, while Slovakia belongs more to the eastern sphere of delayed transition.

[9] The superimposition of different fertility schedules (a catching up of deferred births together with an anticipation of future births) is rather like a process of accumulating stock. If the existence of such a mechanism which concentrates births is undeniable, and if, consequently, declines fluctuate, this fluctuation does not at all mean that policies have had no effect. Only trends in the long term or, in other words, the generational pattern of completed fertility, can tell us their meaning.

the Second World War, the rate of natural increase was still over 1% per year. The post-war fertility increase was proportionate to war losses[10] (not given here, owing to lack of annual distribution of births and deaths), but as in Czechoslovakia and Hungary, it was rapidly replaced by dramatic declines, which were also checked, but more slowly, and without draconian measures or fundamental revisions in family policy. Demographic growth nevertheless remained very high (almost 1% per year) compared with the European norm; if towards the end of the period it has fallen, this is due more to an increase in mortality than to reduced fertility.

As a general principle, the countries of western and central Europe, represented in the series of Fig. 8.3, experienced a transition which differs in two respects from the Nordic model: (1) it occurs later (maximum growth around 1900, as opposed to 1870–80); and (2) it is shorter: a century or less, as opposed to a century and a half (e.g. 130 to 160 years in Scandinavia).

Southern Europe (and Japan)

Crude mortality rates in the south of Europe differ relatively little from those of the west and centre, either in starting dates or persistently downward trends. But fertility declined more slowly over a long period, the length of which increased in proportion to more general delays in development.

For 60 years between 1880 and 1940, Italy maintained a natural growth of at least 0.9% per year (war years excluded, although Mussolini's populationist policy had scarcely any noticeable effect on the trend). Yugoslavia over the same period sustained growth rates of at least 1.1%; it is only in the last few years that its rates have fallen slightly below 1% per year, following a renewed decline in fertility which, as in other Communist countries, curtailed the baby boom from the start of the 1950s; the recent interruption in this decline has not brought about its reversal. In the past 15 years Italian fertility has declined on the pattern of western Europe, starting in the north and rapidly spreading, with the result that its natural growth has gradually contracted. By contrast, Yugoslavian fertility is currently maintained at around 17–18 per 1000, doubtless on account of its heterogeneous population; natural increase stands at around 1%, which is to say, at levels similar to those of other east and south European countries.

Spain is distinguished by a very noticeable anomaly: an interruption in its natality decline lasting over 30 years, as if the process had been put to sleep under Franco. With the recent reawakening, the curve has begun to head downwards once more. Aside from periods of war, the rate of natural growth since 1900 has stood mainly at around 1% per year, and at times somewhat above this figure (close on 1.3% during the period 1955–65).

---

[10] Poland was the country most affected by changes in boundaries and ethnic composition, leading to a greater homogeneity; this makes comparison with the pre-war period problematical.

a

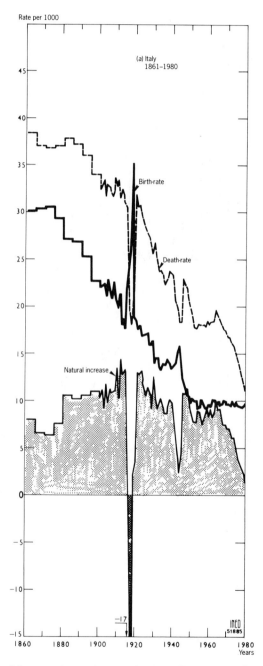

FIG. 8.4. Natural increase in southern and eastern Europe, and Japan, 1858–1980

b

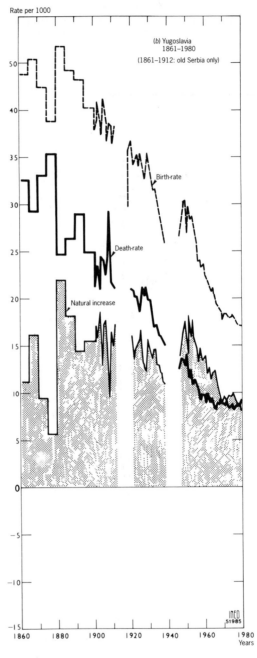

FIG. 8.4. (*cont.*)

c

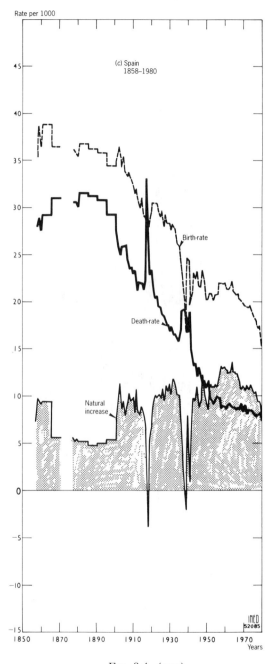

Rate per 1000

(c) Spain
1858–1980

Birth-rate

Death-rate

Natural
increase

INED
52085

1850   1870   1890   1910   1930   1950   1970
Years

Fig. 8.4. (cont.)

d

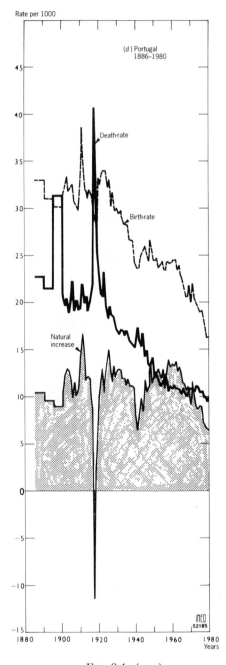

Fig. 8.4. (cont.)

e

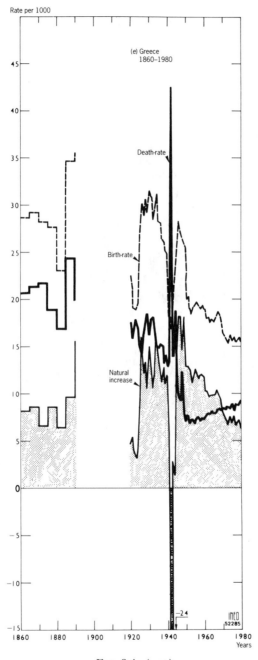

Rate per 1000

(e) Greece
1860–1980

Death-rate

Birth-rate

Natural
increase

−2 4

INED
52285

1860   1880   1900   1920   1940   1960   1980
Years

FIG. 8.4. (cont.)

f

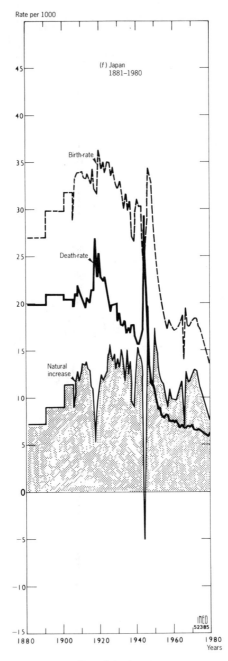

Fɪɢ. 8.4. (cont.)

g

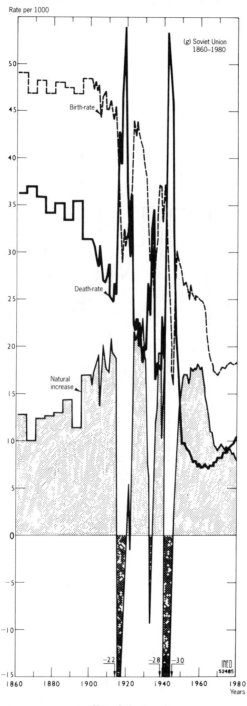

Rate per 1000

50

45

40

35

30

25

20

15

10

5

0

−5

−10

−15

(g) Soviet Union
1860–1980

Birth-rate

Death-rate

Natural
increase

−22   −28 −30

IИED
52485

1860   1880   1900   1920   1940   1960   1980
Years

FIG. 8.4. (cont.)

h

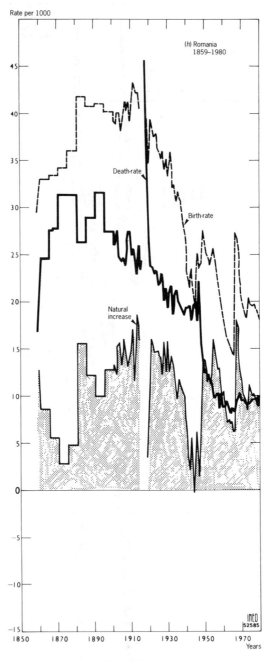

FIG. 8.4. (*cont.*)

i

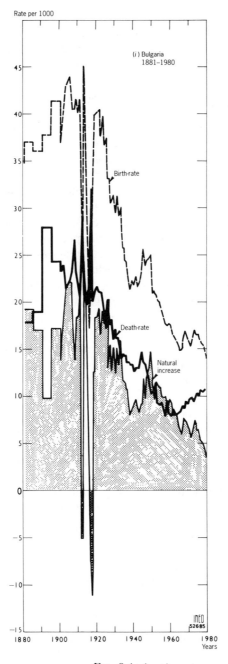

FIG. 8.4. (cont.)

A similar anomaly existed in Portugal under Salazar, albeit at a higher level, but over a similar length of time (1932–62). Fertility declines recorded since then are significant but gradual when compared to the rapid fall in Poland or Hungary during the 1950s, or with the 10 years up to 1975 in Austria, Germany, The Netherlands, and even Canada.

In both cases, mortality[11] declined consistently from 1900 and again from around 1920. This produces transition profiles characterized by a very wide plateau of maximal growth (three-quarters of a century), rising slightly in Spain's case, and ending only as recently as 1969 at a level of around 1.3% per year, for both countries. According to our criteria, the demographic transition has thus not quite been completed, but looks as if it will be very shortly, as mortality has stopped declining (and may be likely to rise slightly) whilst fertility has fallen below 15 per 1000. An Iberian type is thus fairly easily distinguished from the Mediterranean type, by its later character.

The analysis of Greece must be circumspect, owing to lack of data for a period of more than 30 years and unreliable figures (on mortality especially). Even though available series are somewhat fragile,[12] they may without question be considered within the southern type, similar but distinct from the Mediterranean and Iberian species: maximum growth is still recent, of the order of 1 to 1.5% per year; transition is heading towards completion, but is still in the future.

Japan, finally, presents curious similarities to Portugal: (1) demographic variables at the same level around 1880: mortality a little over 20 per 1000, fertility around 30 per 1000 (a low value for the period, which may be due in part—at least in Japan's case—to underestimation[13]); (2) sustained growth of 1.2% to 1.4% on average per year for about 50 years up to 1955. Differences emerge only after this date. Rapid fertility decline in the period 1949–56 was consequent on the adoption of an eugenic population policy in 1948, at which time the country appeared to be threatened by overpopulation. The decline was largely compensated, in terms of natural growth, by a significant fall in mortality. There followed a fairly long period of stability (1956–72), which itself was followed by a modest decline, reflecting a new downturn in fertility. Here, too, dominant trends show a demographic transition in process of

[11] Pre-1920 mortality in Portugal is probably underestimated. Fertility, on the other hand, is extremely low owing to the considerable marriage limitations (age at marriage very late, high incidence of lifetime celibacy).

[12] Data on the natural increase are generally much better than on each of its components, and where errors occur, these are always in the same direction. Corrected data have been published by Siampos (1973) for the period 1821–1970: the level of pre-transitional fertility is very high (early and almost universal marriage) and comparable to that of many east European countries.

[13] This seems to be a well-established fact: otherwise, it is difficult to explain the surge in fertility between 1880 and 1920. Corrected figures exist, however, year by year since 1900 (Shinozaki 1982). The size of the underestimation should not, however, be exaggerated, in that the practice of late marriage was very widespread.

completion: Japan has returned to a rate of natural increase comparable to that of the end of the nineteenth century (0.8 to 0.9% per year).

To summarize, all the countries grouped under the southern type, and illustrated in Fig. 8.4, are characterized by the following features:

1. relatively high levels of natural increase prior to transition;
2. a very extended plateau of maximal natural increase from 1900, only a little above traditional levels, and unaffected by fertility declines during the 1930s depression; and a transition all but completed, or near the end of its term, in 70 to 90 years (beginning in northern provinces in both Italy and Spain, for example).

Eastern Europe

In spite of the exceptionally troubled nature of Soviet history between 1917 and 1945, with deep gashes cut in the line of natural increase by mortality, and despite the ruthlessness of legislative changes regarding fertility, it is possible, by means of J. N. Biraben's (1958) reconstruction, to sketch a profile of the transition in the Soviet Union since 1860 (within its current boundaries). The principal features are as follows:

1. a very high level of pre-transitional growth, consequent on high rates of fertility;
2. a very rapid mortality decline, comparable to that of contemporary less developed countries (falling from a rate above 30 per 1000 in 1900 to 8 per 1000 in 1925), resulting in:
3. fairly high maximum levels of natural increase (almost 2% per year) occurring relatively early (around the First World War); and
4. an exceptionally short demographic transition of 70 years. Natural increase has fallen below the pre-transitional level, since 1965, while female life expectation at birth has reached 74 years.

The Soviet Union, however, is a case unto itself, as much on account of its extraordinary ethnic diversity (each population having its own demographic stage of development) as to the significant decline in health and hygiene since the mid-1960s.

In Bulgaria, and to a lesser degree Romania, the basic pattern of transition is, at least before the war, fairly similar to that of the Soviet Union (setting aside the upheavals of famine, civil war, purges, mass deportation, etc. characteristic of Russia in that period). The fertility decline between the First and Second World Wars was also more rapid than mortality declines, and the period of maximum growth spans the First World War. Pre-transitional levels of fertility and mortality, whilst lower than the Soviet Union's, are certainly underestimated, especially for the beginning of the time series.

Since the war, population policies and demographic trends generally have tended in the same direction as elsewhere in eastern Europe, changing more or less at the same time, if in some cases more violently (as in Romania after the prohibition of abortions in 1966). There are, however, subtle differences in the substance of policies which are bound to affect the pattern of fertility. But while demographic transition in Bulgaria, as in Russia, may be considered complete since about 1965—female life expectation at birth then being 73 years—the transition in Romania will not finish for some years yet. This delay will confer on it a longer transition (close on 90 years, compared with about 70 years in Russia and Bulgaria), which, combined with a lower plateau of maximal growth, represents a variant half-way between the east and south European types.

Ireland

Like France, but at the opposite end of the history of demographic transition in Europe, Ireland stands out: its transition is still in the early phase of sustained natural increase.[14] Since the failure of the potato crop in 1845–48, and subsequent famine, demographic trends unique to Ireland (above average celibacy, very late marriage) have fixed the country in what may be called a protective regime which calls to mind the system of marriage and family formation in early modern western Europe. Such a regime is in contrast to the preceding century's absence of demographic checks, in which early, universal, and fertile marriage prevailed. Natality at rates of 21 to 23 per 1000 from the end of the nineteenth century onwards (except during the inter-war period) appear, in retrospect, very low; to begin with, such levels were due as much to mass emigration as to marriage restriction. But by now they are considerably higher than the European norm. In terms of mortality, however, the country has clearly kept pace, so that natural increase has risen from 0.5% per year around 1900 to over 1% around 1960. Fertility, on the other hand, has been absolutely constant for decades, and still showed no sign of declining by 1980, although important developments are currently in process.

   But a closer examination reveals that this profile is ambiguous. Apparently, Ireland experienced a double transition. Up to 1880, it traced the same course as other north European countries (notably, England and Wales), reaching a maximum growth around 1870. It then diverged—very high emigration (in spite of its natural growth, Ireland lost a third of its population in 60 years from 1851 to 1911) first of all causing a noticeable decline in natality and, subsequently, a more lasting check on the decline of the crude mortality rate, through effects of age structure.

   In addition to the several regional patterns traced in the preceding pages, it is important to remember that the world powers experienced their demo-

---

[14] Ireland is the only case, in this phase, in which a modern regime of mortality (female life expectation at birth above 72 years since 1970–72) has coexisted with an archaic fertility regime, governed by access to marriage.

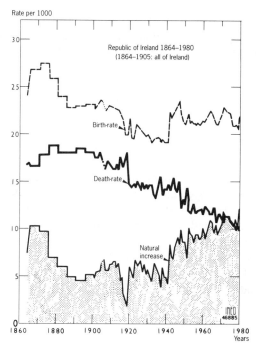

FIG. 8.5. Natural increase in Ireland, 1864–1980

graphic peak during the last third of the nineteenth century—a phenomenon which announced the end of an era of expansionism. The relative demographic expansion of Europe as a whole culminated just before the First World War: in 1750, a fifth of the world's population was composed of Europeans; by about 1910, a third of the world was populated by people of European descent. The slow decline of Europe begins at this point, coupled with the gradual emergence of other populations.

Countries of Immigration

It is not possible to assign fixed dates for the demographic transition in the principal countries populated predominantly by immigrants, using the criteria adopted up to now. Only the finishing date can be set precisely, with any ease, and this is possible only if a criterion of fertility is used in place of the return to pre-transitional growth levels. The latter device cannot be used here since, according to mechanisms explained earlier, natural increase tends over the long term continually to decrease. We have chosen a gross reproduction rate of 1.25.[15] It would be possible, although somewhat artificial from a formal point of view, to fix starting dates using estimations for life expectation or infant mortality. On these principles, a transition period of around 75 years could be assigned to the US, and 70 to Canada (which, following the European norm, would place these countries in the 'short' transition group), and a duration of 90 to 95 years for Australia and New Zealand. The finishing date for Argentina and Uruguay is situated in the future, but a duration part way between that of North America and Oceania seems likely. The possibility of longer durations is not excluded, particularly in Argentina, given that trends recorded in the last decade have tended to fall behind.

The actual shape the transition assumes is in all cases that of a line of gradually decreasing slope. In other words, it assumes the form of a half-transition, in which only the descending phase is apparent. The slope varies according to country and period, as a function of the relative intensity of migratory streams. In the US and Australia, it is very steep in the second half of the nineteenth century and up to the First World War, which corresponds to the period of highest immigration. Thus, in Australia, 60 years after the discovery of gold (1851), the population increased tenfold, the greater part of immigration having occurred at the beginning of the period.

Less Developed Countries

For a considerable number of the less developed countries considered here, the accuracy of fertility and mortality rates is doubtful, because underestimated. However, uncertainty concerning balances between these rates is less problematic,[16] and the specific forms of transition are not affected, at least in their general outline. The most recent UN estimates (1985), published separately for the period 1950–85, give an idea of the degree of underestimation.

Moderate Levels of Growth

Cases in which growth rates during transition have peaked below 2.5% per year are relatively rare. These are either semi-developed countries, like Cyprus and Chile, or very large ones, like China and India, where differences in regional development reduce overall variation.

[15] There is an inevitable random element in this choice. It is based on certain empirical observations and a theoretical consideration: in a stable population characterized by the values GRR = 1.25; e_o^f = 73 years and m = 27 years (average age of motherhood), demographic growth will be of the order of 0.7% per year, which is the average figure for pre-transitional growth in the countries which supplied the New World with its population.

[16] For two reasons. Errors can be compensated in part because successive censuses provide a reasonably accurate picture of the development of natural increase; and also because the quality of birth and death registration (as indicated in preceding chapters) tends to improve progressively. There are usually several series of estimates for countries with unreliable data, often revised in light of new information. We have therefore used mainly the most recent results published by the UN (Tables 8.1 and 8.2, for example).

a

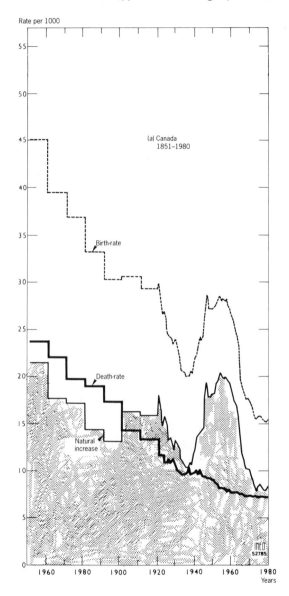

FIG. 8.6. Natural increase in countries of immigration, 1820–1980

Even amongst these countries, rates of growth vary significantly. The time taken to pass from a 'traditional' level (around 0.5% in China and India, and slightly over 1% in Chile and Cyprus) to peak growth (nearly 2.5% per year) was: 45 years in India, 30 years in Chile, 20 years in Cyprus, and, it would appear, only about 20 years in China, as a result of outstanding advances in

b

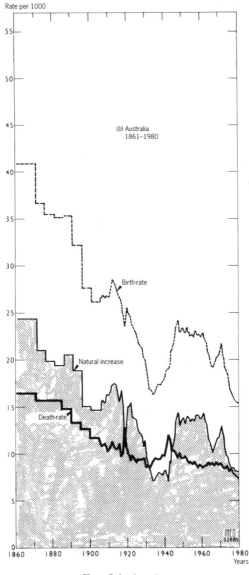

FIG. 8.6. (cont.)

reducing mortality.[17] According to UN estimates (1985), natural increase in China would have fallen from an average of 2.4% per year during the period

---

[17] Chinese data for the period before 1953 are not only rare but unreliable. The publication of age composition data from the 1982 and 1964 censuses has contributed vastly to our

c

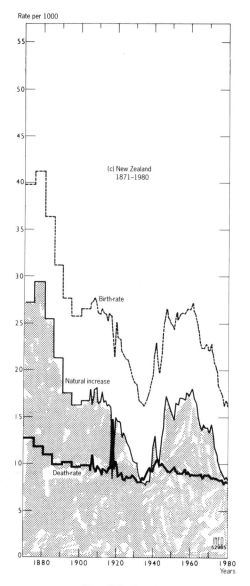

Rate per 1000

55

50

45

40   (c) New Zealand
      1871–1980

35

30

25   Birth-rate

20

      Natural increase
15

10   Death-rate

5

0
      1880   1900   1920   1940   1960   1980
                                              Years

INED
52985

FIG. 8.6. (*cont.*)

1970–75 to scarcely 1.5% in 1975–80, and 1.2% in 1980–85. This is hardly
surprising, given the laws and social pressures on reproduction. In India, at

understanding of developments over the last decades. But a number of doubts remain, given the
many continuing inconsistencies.

d

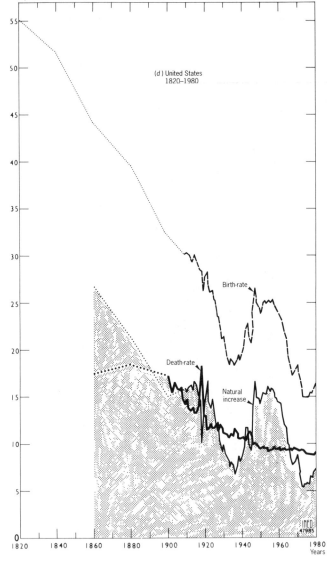

FIG. 8.6. (*cont.*)

the beginning of the 1980s, growth was still close on 2%; however, it appears that a decline is emerging, fertility beginning to fall faster than mortality. Maximum Chinese growth must have occurred during the period 1955–74 (despite 'accidents' such as the black years of 1959–61, which were followed by a recovery of deferred births (Calot 1984)). China's peak growth thus

e

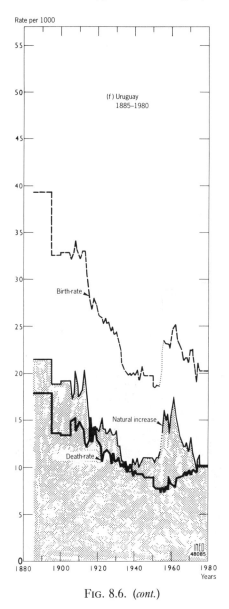

FIG. 8.6. (*cont.*)

occurred about 10 years earlier than India's. The ensuing decline was so steep that, according to existing estimates, between 1971 and 1977 growth was cut by half (1.3% as opposed to 2.6%). The force of ideology, coupled with a rigorous family planning system at the local level, makes such reversals entirely credible. India, in contrast, shows no fertility decline up to the mid-

f

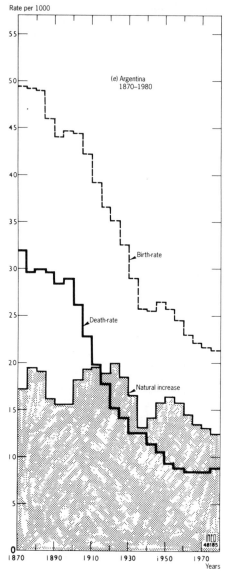

FIG. 8.6. (*cont.*)

TABLE 8.1. *Development of crude birth-rates in less developed countries with advanced transition, 1950–1980* (per 1000)

Country	1950–55	1955–60	1960–65	1965–70	1970–75	1975–80
Europe						
Albania	38.2	41.7	39.9	34.8	31.9	30.3
Africa						
Egypt	46.9	45.6	45.9	41.8	38.4	41.1
Mauritius	47.3	44.7	42.5	32.2	26.1	26.7
Réunion	45.4	45.6	43.1	37.2	28.6	24.0
South Africa	41.3	41.5	41.4	41.2	39.5	38.2
Tunisia	46.4	46.7	46.5	41.8	37.1	35.6
Latin America						
Argentina	25.4	24.3	23.2	22.6	23.4	25.0
Brazil	44.6	43.3	42.1	36.4	33.6	32.0
British Guiana	48.1	43.9	40.4	35.4	32.5	31.5
Chile	35.2	37.5	35.7	30.0	26.0	25.4
Colombia	47.6	45.9	44.6	39.6	33.3	32.1
Costa Rica	47.6	48.3	45.3	38.3	31.0	30.7
Cuba	29.7	28.2	35.3	32.0	25.8	17.0
Dominican Republic	49.1	49.5	47.7	45.5	41.9	34.6
Jamaica	34.8	39.2	39.6	37.3	32.5	28.2
Mexico	46.7	45.8	44.9	44.2	42.7	37.6
Panama	40.3	41.0	40.8	39.3	35.7	31.0
Puerto Rico	36.6	33.5	31.3	26.8	24.4	23.8
Trinidad and Tobago	38.2	38.0	36.3	27.8	26.0	26.0
Uruguay	21.2	21.9	21.9	20.5	21.5	20.3
Venezuela	47.3	46.9	45.2	40.9	37.5	36.9
Asia						
China[a]	45.5	45.5	37.2	40.6	34.1	22.0
Cyprus	27.4	26.4	25.2	21.0	18.3	19.6
Hong Kong	33.1	36.3	33.1	23.5	19.5	18.6
India	46.3	48.3	47.1	43.2	39.7	36.1
Indonesia	43.0	45.4	42.9	42.6	41.4	36.4
Israel	32.5	27.9	25.5	25.5	27.4	26.7
North Korea	37.0	42.5	39.5	38.8	35.7	32.5
Singapore	44.4	41.6	34.0	24.9	21.2	17.2
South Korea	37.0	45.9	39.6	31.9	28.8	25.3
Sri Lanka	38.5	36.6	34.7	31.5	28.6	27.6
Thailand	46.6	44.3	43.5	41.8	35.1	31.4
Turkey	44.9	44.7	41.0	39.6	37.0	34.9
West Malaysia	45.2	45.4	43.2	38.5	32.9	30.8
Oceania						
Fiji	44.3	44.7	39.4	32.0	25.0	28.6

[a] Incl. Taiwan.

Source: UN (1985).

TABLE 8.2. *Development of crude death-rates in less developed countries with advanced transition, 1950–1980* (per 1000)

Country	1950–55	1955–60	1960–65	1965–70	1970–75	1975–80
Europe						
Albania	13.9	12.2	10.1	8.0	6.9	6.4
Africa						
Egypt	23.1	20.6	19.8	18.1	16.2	14.2
Mauritius	15.7	10.6	9.1	7.8	7.0	6.3
Réunion	14.6	13.0	11.2	9.3	7.7	6.9
South Africa	24.0	22.1	20.3	18.6	16.8	15.2
Tunisia	22.6	20.3	17.9	15.5	13.0	11.0
Latin America						
Argentina	9.1	8.6	8.8	9.1	9.0	8.8
Brazil	15.1	13.6	12.3	10.8	9.7	8.9
British Guiana	13.5	10.7	8.6	7.7	7.6	6.7
Chile	13.6	12.8	11.9	10.0	8.4	8.1
Colombia	16.5	14.2	12.2	10.4	9.0	8.2
Costa Rica	12.3	10.7	9.1	7.2	5.8	4.6
Cuba	11.0	9.6	8.8	7.4	6.4	6.0
Dominican Republic	21.8	18.5	15.4	13.1	11.0	9.1
Jamaica	11.5	9.8	9.1	8.0	7.4	6.7
Mexico	16.2	13.2	11.3	10.3	9.2	8.0
Panama	13.2	10.9	9.6	8.4	7.3	6.0
Puerto Rico	9.0	7.0	6.9	6.6	6.6	6.4
Trinidad and Tobago	11.3	9.3	7.3	6.9	6.8	6.8
Uruguay	10.5	10.1	9.6	9.6	10.1	10.2
Venezuela	14.9	12.3	10.1	8.3	6.8	6.1
Asia						
China[a]	23.9	30.0	19.7	14.8	10.5	7.6
Cyprus	10.5	10.5	10.5	9.9	9.7	9.1
Hong Kong	8.9	7.2	6.2	5.4	5.1	4.4
India	27.5	25.5	22.2	19.1	16.6	14.6
Indonesia	26.1	24.3	21.5	19.3	17.3	15.1
Israel	6.9	6.2	6.0	6.7	7.1	7.3
North Korea	32.0	13.3	12.2	11.2	9.4	8.3
Singapore	10.6	8.6	7.1	5.6	5.1	5.1
South Korea	32.0	14.9	12.5	10.4	8.8	8.1
Sri Lanka	11.5	9.9	8.5	7.5	6.3	7.6
Thailand	19.2	15.9	13.4	11.4	9.3	8.4
Turkey	17.5	16.2	15.0	13.6	11.7	10.2
West Malaysia	19.9	16.5	13.3	10.4	8.0	6.9
Oceania						
Fiji	14.1	12.9	7.0	5.0	4.3	4.2

[a] Incl. Taiwan.

Source: UN (1985).

1960s, according to several studies and sample survey registrations, and there was only the tentative beginnings of a decline, around 1970, for urban areas alone. Despite delays due to excesses committed by some family planning zealots (i.e. forced sterilization campaigns in some states), the Indian programme has achieved appreciable results; according to most recent available estimates (1985) growth rates from now on should be about 2% per year. In sum, demographic declines in the two great Asian giants accounting for almost 40% of the world's population have begun in earnest.

High Levels of Growth

The seven countries in this category are grouped together in view of their period of maximal growth. Looking at only the first five of them (i.e. up to Fig. 8.8(e): Cuba), one might be tempted to conclude that the more recently this maximum occurred, the shorter the phase of peak growth. The reality is not so simple, as Egyptian and Tunisian examples will show.

In Puerto Rico, where growth peaked early, the rate of natural increase remained above 2.5% per year for over 20 years, whereas in Hong Kong, whose maximum was of the same order (3%) but occurred 10 years later, the peak was more acute and the period of growth above 2.5% per year lasted only around 10 years. Hong Kong is also the only less developed country in which the transition is close to completion: female life expectation at birth crossed the threshold of 73 years 15 years ago; by 1980, natural growth was no more than 1.2%, compared with 3% in 1960. This is the shortest transition yet observed, since, according to recent trends, its duration should barely exceed 40 years. Its representativeness and significance should, however, be qualified to the extent that a number of exceptional factors are involved: Hong Kong is at once a small country, an island, a city, a Chinese cultural centre, and a territory with insurmountable spatial limitations. Demographic growth since the beginning of the nineteenth century has been staggering, and population density at the time of writing exceeded 4,000 people per km^2.

In Egypt, where, since the beginning of the century, natality remained between 40 and 45 per 1000 with few exceptions, the beginnings of a decline emerged in 1967; the decline in mortality which immediately followed the war produced a sudden and considerable increase, from 1.5% to over 2.5% in a few years. If the series used here appear underestimated from the point of view of a recent assessment (Fargues 1986)—particularly for pre-war mortality—the profile as whole seems hardly affected. Since 1967, the almost linear progress of the fall in mortality combined with the reluctant decline in fertility has prevented natural increase from falling appreciably. The rapid rise in fertility after 1972, largely connected with the entry of the 1945−54 baby boom generation into its reproductive period, and reinforced by the post-war mortality decline among younger age groups, caused a sudden leap in growth

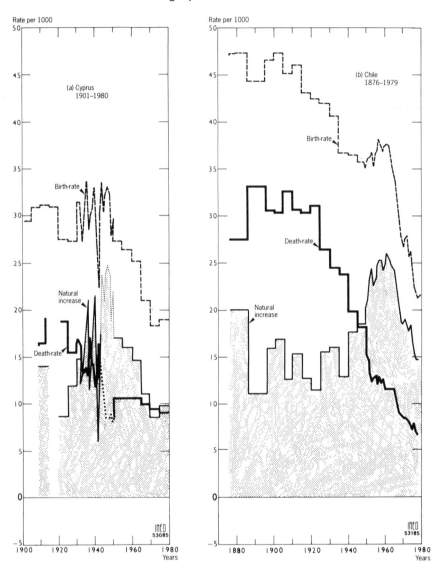

FIG. 8.7. Natural increase in less developed countries with moderate growth levels, 1871–1980

to around 3%—an unprecedented level, which may imply a second period of maximal growth. With a crude mortality rate over 10 per 1000 in 1980, and a very young age structure, there is high growth potential, and the possibility that future declines in fertility will be insufficient to reduce rates of natural

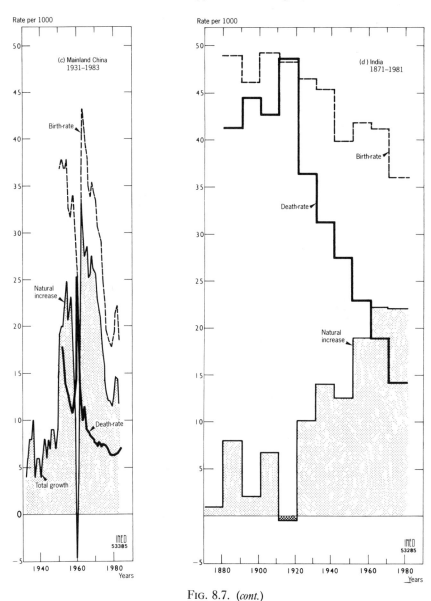

FIG. 8.7. (*cont.*)

increase below 2%, for some time—perhaps 50 or even 60 years. Egypt's period of sustained growth would then be three times longer than Hong Kong's (18 years), and twice as long as Sri Lanka's. The fertility decline in the latter two countries did not begin until mortality was low (10 per 1000 in

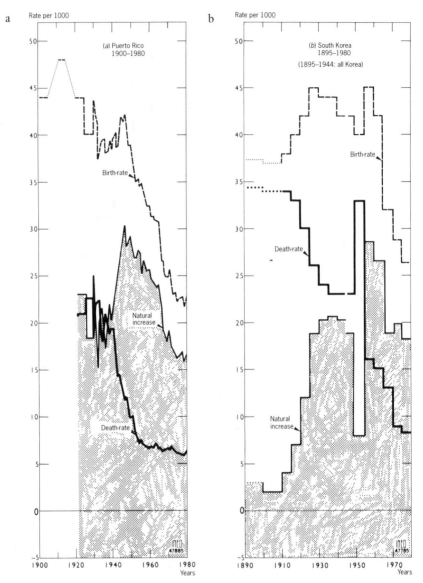

Fig. 8.8. Natural increase in less developed countries with high growth levels, 1820–1980

Sri Lanka) or very low (6 per 1000 in Hong Kong), whilst Egypt's mortality rate for 1966–68 was still close on 16 per 1000.

The situation in Tunisia at the beginning of the 1970s was fairly similar to Egypt's, but has subsequently differed with a continuing if moderate decline in fertility.

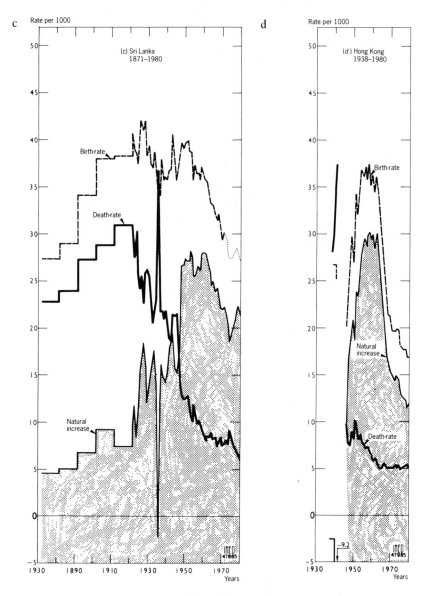

FIG. 8.8. (*cont.*)

Very High Levels of Growth

The number of countries in which growth has surpassed 3% per year represent half of the less developed countries studied (17 out of 35). Their common features are:

e

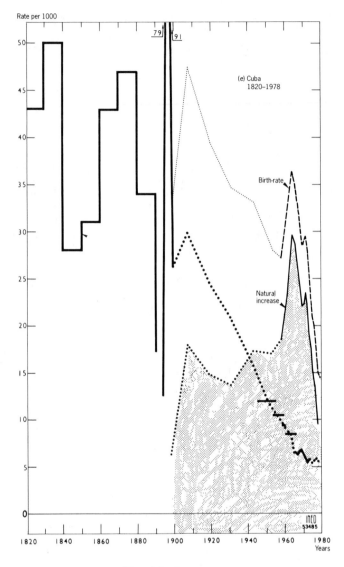

FIG. 8.8. (*cont.*)

1. a fairly long phase of ascending growth (15 to 30 years);[18]
2. maximum growth occurring after 1950;
3. a peak growth of about 3% per year and, in a few extreme cases, almost

[18] In most cases with reliable series.

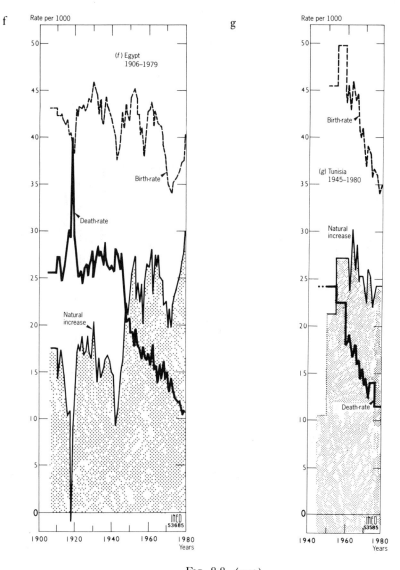

FIG. 8.8. (*cont.*)

3.5% or even 4% per year (for example, in Costa Rica over a ten-year period)

4. a fairly short period of maximal growth (rarely over 20 years, and generally around 15); but of course

5. a longish phase of high increase (over 2% per year).

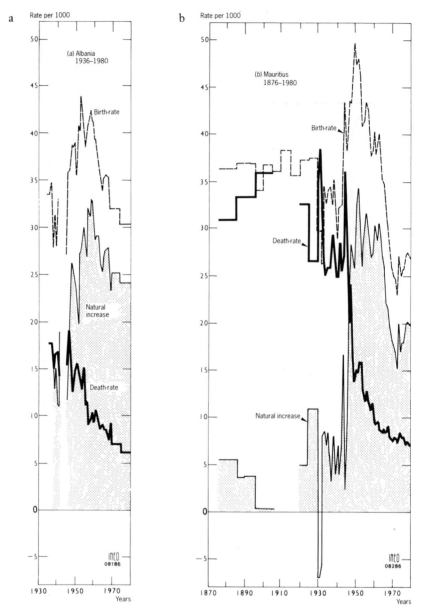

FIG. 8.9. Natural increase in less developed countries with very high growth levels, 1844–1980

c

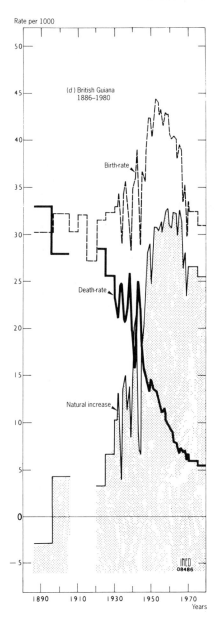

d

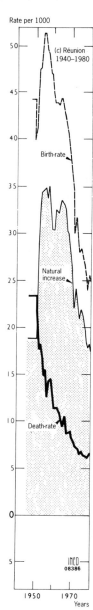

FIG. 8.9. (*cont.*)

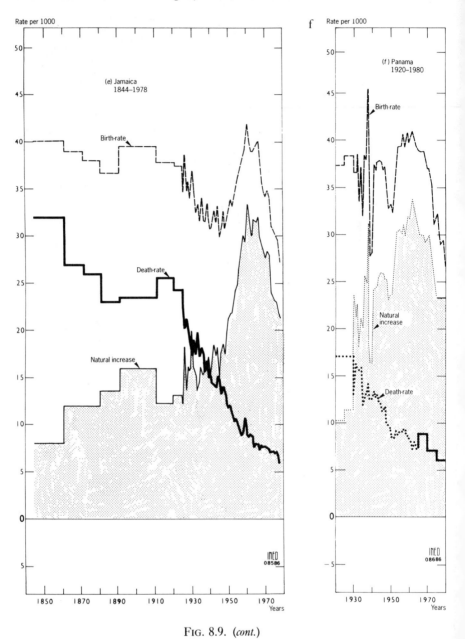

FIG. 8.9. (*cont.*)

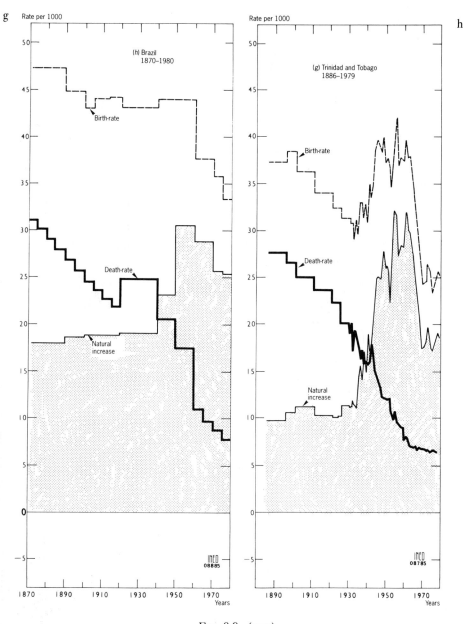

FIG. 8.9. (*cont.*)

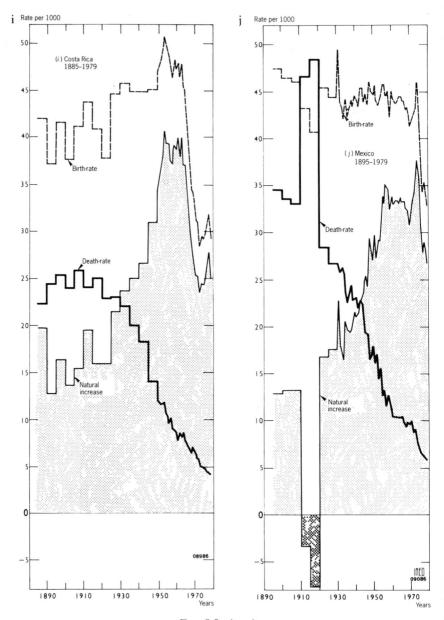

FIG. 8.9. (cont.)

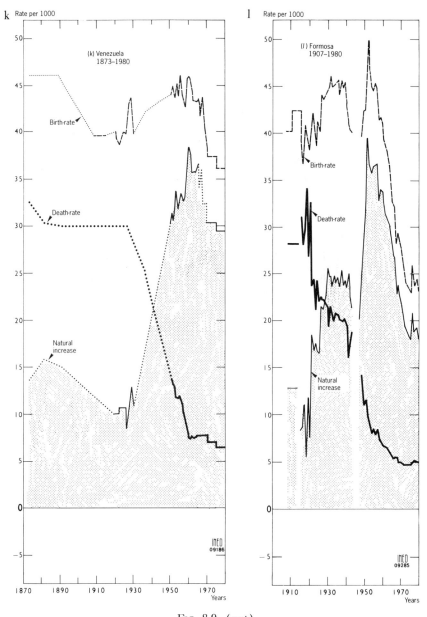

FIG. 8.9. (*cont.*)

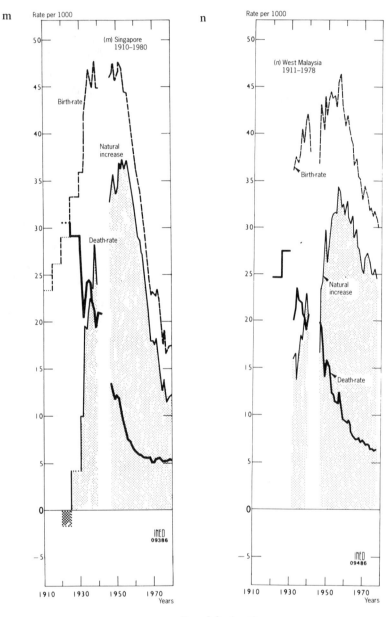

FIG. 8.9. (*cont.*)

O

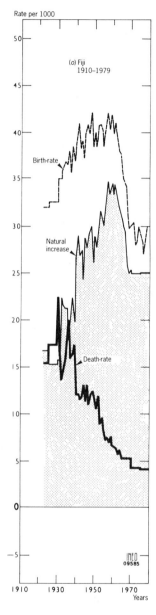

Fɪɢ. 8.9. (*cont.*)

The countries described by the last point comprise two different types. First come seven small countries belonging to Europe, Africa, and Latin America, depicted in Figs. 8.9(a) to (g): the phase of maximal growth in these countries ranges (or will range) between 20 and 30 years. Secondly, there are the Latin American countries with faster growth rates (Figs. 8.9(h) to (k)), together with four Asian countries (Figs. 8.9(l) to (o)). The duration of their growth phases will be appreciably longer: 40 to 55 years, or more, with the exception of Singapore (35 years). In certain cases (Jamaica, Panama, and Costa Rica) the period would appear to have already ended, around 1980 or soon after. The phase is already complete in Taiwan, and Singapore especially, where the transition was earlier. In other cases, such as Brazil, Mexico, and Venezuela, the process seems likely to continue for some time. As these are already fairly populous countries—especially Brazil[19] and Mexico—the latter will have populations amongst the largest in the world.

6. A phase of generally very rapid decline in population growth reflecting the fact that, in most cases, fertility started downwards at a point when mortality was already almost at its lowest levels.

This last point, however, requires careful handling. Even if the phase of declining growth has begun in all cases, it is still at very different stages, between 1.2 and 2.5% per year. Of course, a certain symmetry between descending and ascending trends of growth is frequently observable. Moreover, in certain cases where transition is very advanced, as in Singapore and, to a lesser degree, Taiwan, the descent is more rapid than the ascent. But one should not be misled in this: a closer analysis shows that just before the war a first growth peak occurred (or its intimation, in the case of Taiwan). In both cases, the considerable post-war decline in mortality pushed this level a notch higher, and fertility responded even more dramatically. One should not therefore base one's reasoning on these exceptional cases. Whether fertility declines will be as rapid as those of mortality is not yet known, but the recent slowing down, as a result of the accumulated inertia in age structures which is noticeable in a number of cases, would imply the contrary.

We shall complete these general observations with a few remarks that are more specific in character:

1. From a demographic point of view, Albania's classification amongst the less developed countries is incontestable: its transition profile is perfectly analogous to that of the African countries, alongside which it has been placed.

2. The very intense character of the transition in Mauritius and Réunion

---

[19] From its transition profile, Brazil cannot be grouped with the countries of immigration: whilst immigration was high in the last decades of the 19th and first decades of the 20th centuries, most of it occurred before the transition. Mortara (1954) has thus been able to establish that 81% of the demographic growth over the period 1840–1940 was attributable to the then native population of Brazil.

implies a total duration unlikely to last more than 40 years, and thus as short a transition as Hong Kong's.

3. Latin America experienced relatively slow rates of increase, especially to begin with, in those countries where mortality began to decline in the same period as in Europe.

4. There are some obvious anomalies. First, the low value of pre-war fertility and mortality rates in Albania; and, likewise, fertility rates in British Guiana. Secondly, the steplike movement of the Brazilian decline between 1870 and 1920, which was followed by an astonishing rise between 1920 and 1940.

5. Finally, and most importantly, there is the apparently good conformity of the transition to mathematical laws. In many cases, in which profiles take a bell-like shape, one thinks immediately of a Gaussian curve. The famous logistic growth curve for changes in population size is thus vindicated, at least for the transition period—and with it, a number of mathematical developments. One should not, however, race ahead in rash generalization; this chapter has demonstrated the multiplicity of forms of which demographic history is capable. Well-known debates have already been occasioned, in the 1920s, by the approximation of population trends in developed countries to logistic curves, used as instruments of projection. Pearl (1924), in particular, is noted for his exposition of this approach, and Knibbs (1925) for its discussion and refutation. In the light of recent trends, the frequent tendency amongst less developed countries towards asymmetrical profiles of natural growth implies that attempts to resurrect such an approach would only produce similarly approximate results (that is, confined to the general appearance of population curves over very long periods).

2. Some Profile Types

The foregoing presentation of the several profiles of transitional growth may have seemed long and somewhat dense, but we have been breaking new ground. It may therefore help to retrace our steps and sketch an outline of some specific transition forms, using typical cases. To identify these types it will suffice to recall the grouping used at the beginning of this chapter; this procedure will only give a very provisional picture for the poor countries—only a few small countries and perhaps continental China, within the less developed world, being at present close to the end of the transition.

Type I: Developed Countries in Europe

These are distinguished by two characteristic features: (1) natural increase peaked at rates below 2% per year; and (2) demographic transition was very long, lasting from 75 to 200 years.

Setting aside the two special cases of France (with its flat profile) and Ireland[20] (a U-shaped profile),[21] the European group divides schematically into three subgroups of countries which share a common evolution. These may be called: the Nordic model, the Western model, and the Southern model, and their respective characteristics are as follows:

1. Nordic model: a very long transition period, lasting almost a century and a half, with maximum growth occurring around 1870–80. Example: Sweden.
2. Western model: a long transition period of approximately a century, with maximum growth occurring later (around 1900). Example: Germany.
3. Southern model:[22] a fairly long transition period of 70 to 90 years, with a relatively broad plateau of maximal growth occurring after 1900. Example: Italy.

The forms which the demographic transition has taken in Europe are thus related to historical and geographical patterns of development: progress in health and birth control spread from the north-west to the south and east of the continent.

Type III: Less Developed Countries

Those countries where fertility has declined perceptibly are characterized both by a plateau of maximal growth consistently above 2%, and sometimes considerably above (up to 4%), on the one hand, and, on the other, by a transition period which—given the sudden and rapid fertility decline in the largest countries—seems likely in most cases to be relatively short (from about 40 to 80 years). The fertility decline is still too recent in these countries to enable us to establish their characteristic differences. We have thus used the simplest method, which consists of grouping countries according to levels of maximum growth. This produces three groups: fairly high growth (from 2% to less than 2.5% per year, for example, India); high growth (from 2.5% to less than 3% per year, for example, Egypt); and very high growth (3% and above per year, for example, Mexico). It thus emerges that maximal growth in

---

[20] Both countries have a point in common: they were both at their highest population density at the point at which their demographic histories began to diverge from other European countries (around 1770 for France and three-quarters of a century later for Ireland). But each one responded in its own way to the threat posed by pressure on resources: France chose to practise birth control within the family; Ireland let its sons leave for America. *It thus appears that density is a decisive factor in determining the transition profile.* The rapidity of the fertility decline in countries like Japan and China tends to confirm this view.

[21] Unlike the others, this form is not definitive since Irish fertility is still very high.

[22] The east European profile is fairly closely related to the southern type, as much in duration as in the extended and late nature of the peak period of natural growth (either spanning the First World War or the inter-war period). Japan's profile, on the other hand, has properties analogous to Portugal's, as we have seen.

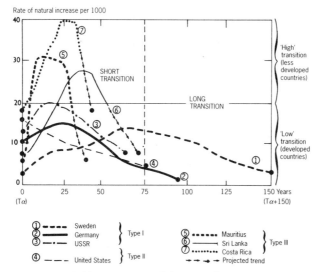

FIG. 8.10. The types of demographic transition

the majority of countries levelled off in the neighbourhood of 3% and, in all countries with advanced transition, this peak lasted less than 20 years.

Type II: Principal Countries of Immigration

Between the two clear major types given above, there is an intermediary type comprising what we have called countries of immigration: the United States, Canada, Australia, New Zealand, Argentina, and Uruguay. Owing to age-specific selective migration and the inevitable ageing of populations, the transition profile no longer takes a bell-shaped form, but a line of steadily decreasing slope; on a graph the appearance is of a demi-transition, in which only the declining phase is shown, indicating a contraction of growth.

Table 8.3 summarizes these observations, and Fig. 8.10 represents them schematically[23] for several typical cases. It should be remembered that only net growth is under consideration. However, it is clear, particularly for European populations, that patterns have been influenced to varying degrees by international migration, and not only countries belonging to Type II. The extreme situation of Ireland, depopulated through emigration, may be contrasted with other less pronounced cases in which considerable declines in natural increase were related to large waves of emigration amongst young adults, such as Italy, where natural increase in consequence only reached the

[23] The figure is much simplified, in order to eliminate certain more or less short-term historical 'accidents'.

TABLE 8.3. *The types of demographic transition*

Type of demographic transition	Onset $T\alpha$	End Tw	Duration $T\alpha - Tw$ (years)	Period of maximal natural increase	Rate of natural increase (corresponding %)
I Europe and Japan					
Nordic Model[a]					
Sweden	1815	1965	150	1855–1865	1.6
Western Model[b]					
Germany[c]	1875	1965	90	1896–1905	1.5
Southern Model[d]					
(and Eastern[e])					
Italy	1875	1965	90	1911–1913 and 1921–1930	1.2
II Countries of immigration[f]					
United States	(1895)[g]	1959	(64)	n/a	n/a
III Less developed countries					
Moderate growth:[h]					
<2.5% per year					
India				1961–1971	(2.2)
minimum hypothesis	1920	2010	90		
maximum hypothesis		2040	120		
Level of High growth:[i]					
maximal 2.5–3% per year					
increase Egypt				1958–1967	(2.6)
minimum hypothesis	1946	2010	65		
maximum hypothesis		2025	80		
Very high growth:[j]					
>3% per year					
Mexico				1954–1974	3.4
minimum hypothesis	1920	2000	80		
maximum hypothesis		2020	100		

Notes: France and Ireland are atypical cases. n/a = not applicable.

[a] Sweden, Norway, Finland, United Kingdom, Denmark, Netherlands.
[b] Belgium, Switzerland, Germany, Czechoslovakia, Austria, Hungary, Poland.
[c] West Germany only, since 1946.
[d] Italy, Yugoslavia, Spain, Portugal, Greece (USSR, Bulgaria, Romania).
[e] The demographic transition type for east European countries is fairly similar, as much in duration as in the extended and late nature of the peak period of natural growth (either spanning the First World War or during the inter-war period). Japan's profile, on the other hand, is fairly closely related to that of Greece or Portugal.
[f] Canada, Australia, New Zealand, United States, Argentina, Uruguay, Israel.
[g] Massachusetts only.
[h] Cyprus, Chile, China, India.
[i] Puerto Rico, Turkey, South and North Korea, Sri Lanka, Hong Kong, Indonesia, Cuba, Egypt, Tunisia, South Africa.
[j] Europe, Africa: Albania, Mauritius, Réunion; Latin America: British Guiana, Jamaica, Panama, Trinidad and Tobago, Costa Rica, Colombia, Brazil, Venezuela, Mexico, Dominican Republic; Asia and Oceania: Taiwan, Singapore, West Malaysia, Thailand, Fiji.

relatively low average level of 1.2% per year, as opposed to 1.6% in Sweden, and 1.5% in Germany.

Conclusion

There is no single model of demographic transition, but, on the contrary, an astonishing diversity of situations; this chapter has given only a foretaste of possible variants for less developed countries. As great as this variety is, it is nevertheless possible to apply an initial criterion of classification: the earliness of the process, related to the geographico-cultural sphere to which it belongs. As a general rule, in the countries studied, the more recent the transition, the shorter the overall duration and the higher the levels of natural increase tend to be.[24] But nothing indicates that the future will replicate the past: countries with less advanced transitions differ profoundly in numerous aspects of culture and economy from their counterparts with advanced transitions.

Bibliography to Chapter 8

BIRABEN, J. N. (1958), 'Essai sur l'évolution démographique de l'URSS', *Population*, Special Number, 41–4.

CALOT, G. (1984), 'Données nouvelles sur l'évolution démographique chinoise', *Population*, 4–5: 897–936, and 6: 1045–62.

FARGUES, P. (1986), 'Un Siècle de transition démographique en Afrique méditerranéenne, 1885–1985', *Population*, 2: 205–32.

KEYFITZ, N., and FLIEGER, W. (1971), *Population: Facts and Methods of Demography* (San Francisco, Calif.: Freeman).

KIRK, D. (1942), 'The Relation of Employment Levels to Births in Germany', *MMFQ*, 20(2) (Apr.), 126–38.

KNIBBS, G. H. (1925), 'The Growth of Human Populations and the Laws of their Increases', *Metron*, 5(3) (Dec.), 147–62.

MACKENSEN, R. (1967), 'Theoretical Considerations regarding Differential Transition', *World Conference of the IUSSP, Sydney, Aug. 1967*, 37–46.

MORTARA, G. (1954), 'The Development and Structure of Brazil's Population', *Population Studies*, 8.

PEARL, R. (1924) *Studies in Human Biology* (Baltimore Md.: Williams and Wilkins).

SIAMPOS, G. (1973), *Demographic Evolution of Modern Greece* (in Greek; Athens), 20.

UN (1985), *World Population Prospects as Assessed in 1982* (New York: UN).

YULE, G. U. (1925), 'The Growth of Populations and the Factors which Control it', *Journal of the Royal Statistical Society*, 88(1) (Jan.), 1–58.

---

[24] This is particularly the case with less populated countries.

9 Chronology and Typology of the Ageing of Populations

Only the sun keeps its youth and beauty.

(C. F. Meyer)

THE age pyramid of a population is the preferred tool of the population economist. The study of variations in age composition therefore warrants a chapter of its own. This chapter will focus exclusively on variations in the *relative* size of different age groups, the preceding chapter having dealt with variations in absolute numbers.

An age pyramid informs the trained eye of the dynamics of a population being studied, including levels of mortality, levels of fertility, and, where they are sufficient to alter the general profile, the potential size of migratory exchanges with other populations. It thus provides a schematic summation of the main assertions in the preceding chapters, a synthetic illustration of nearly a century of history. But at the same time, it offers the economist an index not so much of the past, but of the future.

Segmentation of the ages of life, by providing the numerical size of successive generations, indicates the *potential* development of certain socio-economic needs in future decades: today's babies will enter the school-age population in about 5 or 6 years, the working population in about 15 or 20 years, and the retired population in about 60 years' time. But in addition to its value in forecasting the life trajectories of those already born, the particular form of a pyramid is rich in implications for future generations—today's children being tomorrow's parents.

1. Components and Trajectories of Ageing Populations

Components

International migration has, of course, the capacity to encourage or reduce the ageing of populations, depending on the ages at which it occurs. But setting aside this important factor for the moment, the development of an age pyramid over the course of demographic transition may be said to depend on three factors:

1. the initial potential of an age structure;
2. the temporal pattern of mortality decline by age; and
3. the temporal pattern of developments in fertility.

The initial potential implied by a population pyramid at the point at which transition begins (i.e. the date of the census nearest to Ta) depends on the nature of demographic regulation in the population considered, and in particular on its marriage type. At a given level of mortality, early and universal marriage (or consensual union), such as exists in Asia or Latin America,[1] results in a pyramid dominated by much younger age groups than in a population with late marriage and frequent lifetime celibacy, as in early modern Europe[2] and contemporary Ireland.

Depending on the way in which it affects different age groups, mortality decline may contribute to either a reduction or an increase in the average age of a population. Let us assume, for simplicity's sake, that it acts on its own. The *first* stage of decline entails eliminating contagious and parasitic diseases, which requires only fairly light and non-costly investments (addressed to sanitation and public vaccination of children, for example), and which usually results in a more than proportionate decline in infant mortality. The base of the pyramid accordingly expands (rejuvenation). If progress continues— probably somewhat more slowly—there follows an inevitable period in which sizes of the older rather than younger age groups benefit; in this *second* stage mortality declines contribute more to the ageing than to the rejuvenation of a population. When the residual mortality consists mostly of illnesses of old age and cancer, any improvement in mortality rates will benefit older age groups almost exclusively, thus acting in the full sense of ageing. This represents the *third* or final stage.

Albeit somewhat schematic, this presentation corresponds broadly to the historical development of Western countries. The completion of the first stage occurred just after the Second World War, and the last stage commenced in the 1960s. Given that the risk of dying becomes very low from the point at which life expectation exceeds 70 years—under 0.5% in each age group from 1 to 50 years—*the effect of the decline in mortality on age composition can only be very strong in the final stage.*

The demographic transition is accompanied by a change in fertility models, from an average of 5 or more children per woman to 2 or less children, or a more than 50% reduction, which produces a corresponding contraction at the base of the pyramid. Any decline in fertility thus has the immediate effect of reducing the supply of young persons to the pyramid, and all the more so if the decline is rapid. By operating in such a selective way on each new successive generation, a fertility decline considerably alters the overall profile.

---

[1] The African case is more complex due to polygamy, but the resulting age pyramids are analogous.

[2] i.e. in western Europe.

It produces an ageing both at the base (i.e. decline in the proportion of young people) and at the apex (an increase in the proportion of old people). Its effects continue well beyond the period of the fertility transition: still assuming that mortality is static, if we suppose that fertility ceases to decline, ageing would continue for another 60 years beyond this date. It will only stop and give way to a rejuvenation when the less numerous generations in their turn arrive at a mature age.

In reality, mortality and fertility can only act independently in the short term. An undeniable long-term interaction exists between them: mortality decline brings in its train an eventual fertility decline, the two movements working together in a complex interplay. The relative decline in infant and juvenile mortality may, for instance, partly counterbalance fertility declines while they are still small. But as soon as declining fertility gains momentum, and most of what can be accomplished in terms of combating juvenile mortality has been achieved, the base of the pyramid rapidly contracts. After all, birth control within families tends to be adopted when the number of children, owing to the progressive elimination of the chances of infant mortality, becomes too costly to support. Moreover, if such fertility declines occur in smaller generations (as in West Germany during 1966–78, and Japan since 1975), the contraction at the foot of the pyramid is reinforced by an echo effect (as successive small generations reach reproductive age) and ageing is more rapid.

Finally, precisely because of its age- and sex-specific selectivity, international migration has a significant effect on the ageing process. It tends to rejuvenate host countries and produce an ageing effect in countries of departure. The case of north-west Europe (and, more recently, southern Europe) in which countries were first suppliers and then receivers of migrants, is interesting in this respect: ageing initially accelerated, up to the inter-war period, and then slowed down after the war.

Sequences of Development

According to the mechanisms just described, all age pyramids inevitably go through several successive phases in the course of demographic transition. A considerable number of different shapes are conceivable, depending on the initial situation and the modalities of decline. This diversity apart, age composition most commonly falls into four main phases:

Phase 1: a rejuvenation, connected not only with a big drop in infant mortality, but sometimes also with short-term rises in fertility. The duration and intensity of this phase depends on prevailing levels of infant and juvenile mortality, and the interval between the beginning date of mortality decline and that of fertility (interval $T\alpha$ $T\beta$).

Phase 2: ageing principally at the base of the pyramid. This occurs when fertility decline in turn becomes palpable and lasting.

Phase 3: ageing, mainly at the centre and then at the top. Once fertility has stabilized around its new regime of post-transition equilibrium, the larger generations resulting from the transitional regime progressively move up the age ladder.

Phase 4: stabilization, possibly preceded by a certain decline in ageing, with the death of the last transitional generations, which were larger.[3]

Starting with a basically *triangular* profile, the age pyramid passes in the course of Phase 1 through an inverted *V-shape*, and then gradually, in Phase 2, through what is sometimes, although not very appropriately, called an *ace of spades* profile (perhaps the image of a Chinese lantern, with a narrow base and a bulging centre, better describes this movement of a population's centre of gravity towards its mean age). Finally, having passed through a *mushroom-shaped* profile (Phase 3), it tends, according to the average fertility level of post-transitional equilibrium, towards one that is *rectangular* or urn-shaped.

This chronology is of course only illustrative: quite apart from the diversity of parameters influencing the course of natural growth, historical phenomena such as migratory exchanges and wars are capable of speeding up or delaying the pattern described.

2. The Profiles Observed

We shall consider only a few representative cases of the types of demographic transition presented in the previous chapter:

1. France (a unique case characterized by an early and very long transition, and a flat profile of growth);
2. Sweden (north European model);
3. Germany[4] (west European model[5]);
4. Italy (south European model[6]);
5. USSR (east European model);
6. the United States (the model for countries of immigration); and
7. three less developed countries (Egypt, Mexico, and India), representing the type of transition in countries with high levels of growth.

Pyramids are given at thirty-year intervals,[7] dating from the beginning of the transition, since such a period is sufficient to show structural change. In

---

[3] Because the process takes much longer, this last phase has not yet been remarked in any of the countries.

[4] From 1946 onwards this refers only to West Germany.

[5] What is true for the whole is not necessarily true in detail. Thus, within Germany there have coexisted different models of nuptiality; and similarly, Northern Italy's transition profile would imply a closer affinity to the western model than the southern, but we have not introduced regional distinctions.

[6] See n. 5, above.

[7] The sole exception to this rule is Mexico, where we have juxtaposed the pyramids for 1930 and 1950, having been unable to locate the pyramid for 1920.

order to avoid unnecessary detail, and to keep to fundamental changes, we have adopted the following division into five large age groups:[8] 0–14 years (children), 15–34 years (adolescents and young adults—the mobile and active population in which potential demographic changes are especially manifest), 35–64 years (mature adults), 65–74 years (young pensioners), 75 years and over (old pensioners).

The initial contrast between pyramids[9] is very clear, particularly within the youngest age group, as this accounts only for a third at most of the total population in western Europe (31.9% in Sweden, 1810; 32.2% in Italy, 1881; 33.3% in France, 1775), and a little more as one moves eastwards (35.5% in the German Empire, 1880; 38.6% in European Russia, 1897). The order of magnitude in European Russia is akin to that of the less developed countries (38.2% in Egypt, 1947; 39.2% in Mexico, 1930; and 39% in India, 1921). Here one is encountering *the difference between two historical models of nuptiality*.

A marked difference emerges between the development of the pyramids for developed countries and less developed countries during the first decades of the transition. Owing to differences between both starting levels of infant mortality and initial rates of decline, the increase in the proportion of young people in developed countries was fairly low (an additional 2 to 3 percentage points in Italy or Sweden, for example), whilst it is sometimes very pronounced in less developed countries (an additional 7 percentage points in countries such as Mexico), thereby reinforcing an already considerable growth potential, and mortgaging the future even more heavily to the past.

In the middle of the pyramid, differences between countries and periods progressively lessen. During the process of maturation and ageing the pyramid gradually pivots around its central age groups, as though the young were being replaced, *in proportion*, by the old. Thus the fraction for the 15–34-year-olds is maintained between the limits of 30% to 35%, except in western Europe since the last war, as a historical consequence of the war and the economic depression which preceded it. For the 35–64-year-olds, there is a pronounced difference between western Europe (excepting Germany) and elsewhere: the corresponding proportion at the beginning of the transition reaches 30% or more in the former, but less than 25% in the latter (Russia thus belongs to this category, with Germany situated between the two). The elderly (65 years and over) represent 5% of Western populations, and 3% or even less in less developed countries.

The ageing process already described emerges with the declining fertility

---

[8] No distinction is made between sexes. The arbitrariness of this division depends on the period and country under consideration; distinction into large age groups carries the advantage of overriding most errors of age declaration.

[9] The precision of census data on the age of individuals varies between countries and censuses, but the quality of the statistics improves proportionately to economic development. In spite of the adopted grouping, distortion is still possible, particularly underestimation in older age groups in the first censuses.

TABLE 9.1. *Age-structural development according to transition type* (per 1000)

Country and year	Age group (complete years)					Population size (millions)
	0–14	15–34	35–64	65–74	≥75	
France						
1775[a]	333	332	291	34	10	25.6
1811[a]	326	321	296	41	16	29.3
1841[a]	304	322	310	45	19	34.4
1872	271	315	340	54	20	36.1
1901	257	318	340	60	25	35.5
1931	226	321	357	67	29	41.3
1962	264	266	354	74	44	46.4
Sweden						
1810	319	328	301	38	14	2.4
1840	339	331	283	34	13	3.1
1870	347	304	294	38	15	4.2
1900	324	305	287	56	28	5.1
1930	248	339	320	61	32	6.1
1960	220	263	398	77	42	7.5
Germany						
1880	355	320	277	36	12	45.2
1910	341	335	274	37	13	64.9
1938	233	323	366	56	22	69.4
FRG						
1970	232	280	356	90	42	60.7
Italy						
1881	322	326	301	38	13	28.5
1911	340	311	284	47	18	34.6
1936	306	322	298	51	23	42.9
1971	244	283	360	74	39	54.1
Russia						
1897	386	323	249	30	30	93.4
USSR						
1926	372	353	234	29	12	146.9
1959	308	342	288	42	20	208.8
United States						
1880	381	350	235	34		50.2
1910	321	362	273	44		92.0
1940	250	344	337	69		131.0
1970	285	297	319	99		203.2
Egypt						
1947	382	315	270	22	11	18.5
1976	399	325	240	26	10	36.6
Mexico						
1930	392	353	226	19	10	16.6
1950	419	323	226	23	9	25.8
1979[a]	462	326	180	21	12	69.4
India						
1921	390	336	249	17	8	315.3
1951	376	338	249	24	13	356.8
1980[a]	396	341	229	23	11	663.6

[a] See Sources.

Sources: National censuses except years marked[a], for which see General Bibliography.

and advancing age of generations born before fertility stabilized. The decline in fertility produces an ageing at first more noticeable at the base than the summit of the pyramid. Germany is a particularly good example: its fertility transition was the most rapid in Europe, taking around 30 years for the modern regime (2 children or less per woman) to replace the traditional (an average of at least 5 children per woman); period fertility was 2.10 in 1926–30, as opposed to 5.04 in 1896–1900. The proportion of young people fell by over 10 points[10] (23.3% for the under-fifteens in 1939, as opposed to 34.1% in 1910), and the elderly cohorts increased by just under 3 points (65-year-olds and above represented 7.8% of the whole in 1939, as opposed to 5.0 in 1910). But thereafter, although fertility changed relatively little when compared with preceding patterns, a massive ageing phenomenon is apparent at the top of the pyramid (Table 9.1): the proportion of young people remains static, whilst the elderly increase by over two-thirds, reaching a level above 13%. This phenomenon is all the more remarkable in that this proportion refers to West Germany alone, and, for 1970, well before fertility had reached its base level (1.4 from 1975). The transformation of the pyramid in the course of the decades reflects this change: on the eve of the war, only the base was rectangular; by 1970, the rectangular structure extended to the older age groups (Fig. 9.1). Only the immigration of East German refugees and guest-workers has played a moderating role.

In France, where birth control began almost a century earlier, this rectangular configuration was nearly established by 1900. In Italy, where fertility transition occurred a little later than in Germany but had long been less dramatic, a similar profile to France's was not attained until around 1970. In countries like the USSR and the US, a mature profile still appears to be well in the future (Fig. 9.2). The position of these last two countries is due to the initial structure's high proportion of young people, but also, in Russia's case, to the presence of prolific subpopulations, and in America, to the post-war fertility boom.

The proportion of older people tends everywhere to grow more or less constantly, except during Phase 1, when the base of the pyramid expands. The percentage of 65-year-olds and over in Sweden more than doubled between 1870 and 1960, as in Italy from 1881–1971 (the proportion of 75-year-olds alone tripled). On the other hand, this group has scarcely altered in the less developed countries under consideration (Fig. 9.3), fertility having only just begun its historical descent. The consequences of demographic change only emerge slowly; in multiplying the number of potential parents, the post-war development built up a powerful inertia at the base of the pyramid. Pronounced ageing can only be brought about by rapid fertility decline, which brings in its train slow rates of growth: smaller cohorts of

---

[10] The pronatalist policies promoted by Hitler evidently weakened this decline, without, however, changing the basic development.

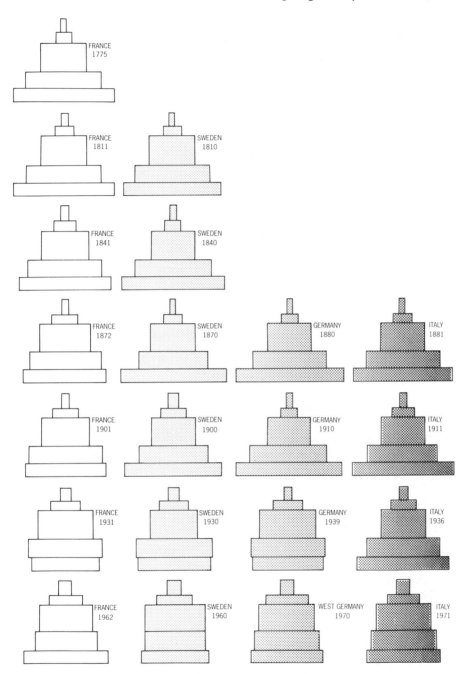

FIG. 9.1. Age-structural development during demographic transition, Europe

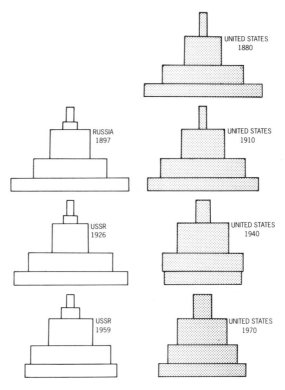

FIG. 9.2. Age-structural development during demographic transition, USSR and USA

children become parents whilst earlier, larger cohorts of parents, entering into older age groups, increase the number of deaths.

The case of Japan, whose reproductive transition was late, coming between those of countries with European populations and the Third World, gives an idea of what can occur in extreme cases. Fertility fell by half in the space of only 8 years (1949–57), the health transition was extremely rapid, and migratory exchange was negligible. In consequence, between 1950 and 1980 Japan gained over 30 million people, during which the proportion aged 65 or over moved from 4.9% (in 1950) to 8.9% (in 1980). On the hypothesis that current fertility (1.7) is maintained, and that the average life extends slightly, this proportion would rise to 15.4% in the year 2000 and 22.0% in 2030; in this period the proportion under 15 years old will fall from 35.4% in 1950 and 24.0% in 1980 to 14.2% in 2030. The final impact of fertility decline on age structures is slow to appear, as populations continue to age for more than half a century afterwards. The effects are none the less spectacular: still taking Japan as our example, by the year 2030 the number of old people (fairly simple to predict as it involves people already born) will be seven times the figure for 1950 (26.9 and 4.1 million respectively), whilst within the same

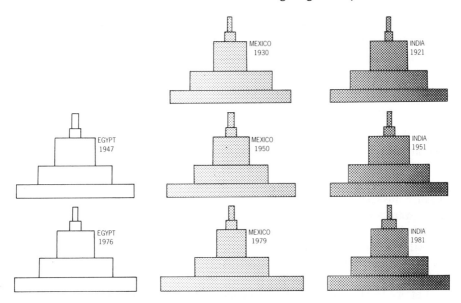

FIG. 9.3. Age-structural development during demographic transition, less developed countries

period the number of young people will be reduced by almost half (17.4 as opposed to 29.5 million). In other words, old people will vastly outnumber children, in a ratio of 3 to 2, instead of 1 in 7 or 8 three-quarters of a century earlier. The ratio of old to young will thus increase elevenfold. Japan perhaps represents a limit case, but it is worth bearing in mind as a measure of possible changes over the course of coming decades.

With the exception of certain Latin American and Asian countries, fertility declines in most of the less developed world are not yet dramatic. Up to now, developments even in mainland China remain tentative, as indicated by the reversal at the beginning of the 1980s—doubtless partly linked with decollectivization. As a result, age structures have changed little, and ageing is consigned almost completely to the future. In those countries permitting it, the retrospective study of age structural transition at the extreme ends of the scale deserves to be developed, for it can provide valuable information on possible trends.

3. Transition in Extreme Age Groups

Each period of life has its own transition: that of the youngest age group is bound up with fertility transition (give or take a slight time difference, measured by age); that of the oldest is capable of registering, aside from changes in fertility, the effects, at a given age, of temporal variations in mortality and international migration. For purposes of illustration, we have chosen the age groups 5–14 years, and 65 and over, which by convention correspond to school-age children and retired people respectively.

The School-Age Population

With the exception of the post-war era, characterized by the recovery of fertility and the rapid increase in young people, notably in France and the US (but not Germany) (see Fig. 9.4), the number of children 5 to 14 years old was at its highest as early as the second half of the nineteenth century in France, just before the First World War in the UK and Germany, during the inter-war period in Italy, and only in 1969 in the US. The school-age population of India did not increase appreciably until the 1920s, but the growth rate swiftly overtook that of countries with early transition. The timing of the fertility transition and its associated growth rates are readily apparent in this pattern.

Let us briefly examine the economic implications of this pattern. The French situation differs widely from the others on account of its lack of growth, which meant that up to the Second World War, the country had little difficulty in schooling its children. At the beginning of the 1880s, when compulsory education was introduced, the number of children 5 to 14 years old reached about 6.5 million (Table 9.2), and it was not until the mid-1950s that this figure was exceeded and demographic change created a significant demand. Up till then, only the enrolment ratio was capable of affecting development of student numbers, but in fact, enrolment in primary and secondary education remained almost constant: 5.6 million in 1885, and 5.7 million in 1935. The education system was thus in equilibrium, although the stagnation of numbers did not stimulate democratization.

The situation of neighbouring countries is completely different: during the four decades of greatest increase in numbers of young people (1851–91 in the UK, 1871–1911 in Germany, 1861–1901 in Italy) growth reached about 60%, or an average rate of about 1.2% per annum, which in effect stimulated the spread of schooling. In Italy, the number of pupils enrolled during the period 1871–1901 increased by an average of 1.6% per year, whilst the school-age population only increased by 0.7%. The UK is even more outstanding, as, between 1851 and 1891, school numbers increased more than tenfold, rising from 387,000 to 4,410,000: there annual growth represents an average of 6.3%. Demographic increase during the Victorian era did not prevent educational democratization: the two phenomena occurred simultaneously.[11]

---

[11] The UK has been substituted for Sweden as a northern model, its aggregate numbers being closer to those of the other countries studied, and thus easier to represent graphically.

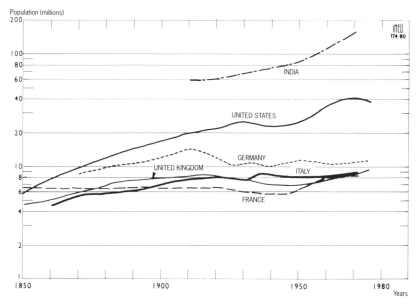

Fig. 9.4. Changing population size, school-age children

In the United States, however, where general education occurred earlier, school numbers were governed primarily by the demographic factor: the number of pupils between 1871 and 1931 rose from 5.6 to 24.6 million. The case of India, which is fairly typical of poor countries with late transition, is unlike the French situation for 1880–1930, although similar to English experience in the second half of the nineteenth century: the increase in young people and the spread of education have occurred simultaneously. But as India has a recent and, therefore, rapid transition, it is not surprising that the demographic factor is twice as great as in England, even though the latter was exceptional, at least in Europe.

The Elderly Population

For countries with simultaneous and similar health transitions, as was more or less the case for the five basically European populations singled out here, the differences in numbers of elderly people relate, for the most part,[12] to differences in fertility at the time the generations concerned were born, i.e. at least 65 years before the dates we are talking about. Amongst these five countries, France had the greatest number of elderly people in the mid-

---

[12] In countries such as England, Italy, and the US migration streams influenced the size of generations born between 1830 and 1900, which became 65 from the end of the 19th century.

TABLE 9.2. *Changing population size, children 5 to 14 years old ('000s)*

Year	France	United Kingdom	Germany[a]	Italy	United States[b]	India
1851	6,447	4,663	—	—	6,132	—
1861	6,522	5,136	—	4,486	7,892	—
1871	6,413[c]	5,909	8,896	5,606	9,601	—
1881	6,546	6,803	9,847	5,719	12,195	—
1891	6,682	7,549	10,993	—	14,608	—
1901	6,461	7,790	12,244	6,949	16,954	—
1911	6,627	8,201	14,318	7,421	18,868	(58,140)
1921	6,421	8,146	10,199	8,240	22,039	(61,070)
1931	5,868	7,411	11,044	7,669	24,613	(69,192)
1941	5,844[d]	—	10,173	8,303[e]	22,431	(76,670)
1951	5,540	6,759	11,564	8,090	24,319	(85,695)
1961	8,152	7,858	(10,318)	8,208	35,465	113,937
1971	8,414	9,123[f]	12,507[f]	8,800	40,746	151,147
1981	(8,250)	(8,000)	(10,800)	(8,300)	(34,000)	(171,500)

Notes: Figures in parentheses are estimates.

[a] For 1890, 1900, 1910, 1925, 1933, 1939; and the two Germanies, incl. Berlin, from 1946.

[b] All dates ending in 0.

[c] 1872.

[d] 1946.

[e] 1936.

[f] 1975.

Sources: National censuses and annual statistical reports.

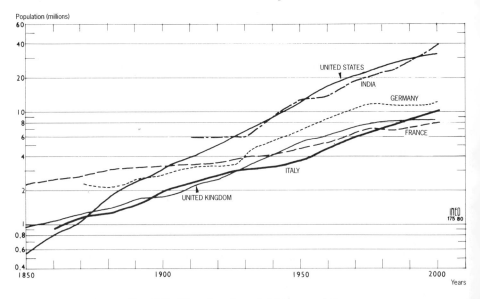

FIG. 9.5. Changing size of elderly populations

TABLE 9.3. *The changing size of elderly populations (aged over 65)* ('000s)

Year	France	United Kingdom	Germany[a]	Italy	United States[b]	India
1851	2,317	969	—	—	575	—
1861	2,502	1,080	—	911	809	—
1871	2,677[c]	1,248	2,274	1,369	1,154	—
1881	3,031	1,377	2,132	1,461	1,723	—
1891	3,160	1,577	2,522	—	2,417	—
1901	3,244	1,734	2,570	1,972	3,080	—
1911	3,367	2,136	3,268	2,365	3,950	5,915
1921	3,570	2,584	3,593	2,748	4,933	6,153
1931	3,946	3,318	4,636	3,018	6,634	5,986
1941	4,440[d]	—	5,387	3,199[e]	9,019	9,229
1951	4,796	5,333	6,792	3,895	12,270	12,799
1961	5,347	6,045	(8,687)	4,827	16,560	13,598
1971	6,591	7,345	10,651	6,102	20,065	18,346
1975	7,115	7,845	11,572	6,755	22,422	17,942
1985	6,728	8,308	11,086	7,834	27,247	24,048
2000	8,053	8,444	12,170	10,007	31,766	38,357

Notes: Figures in parentheses are estimates.

[a] For 1890, 1900, 1910, 1925, 1933, 1939; and the two Germanies, incl. Berlin, from 1946.

[b] All dates ending in 0.

[c] 1872.

[d] 1946.

[e] 1936.

Sources: National censuses and annual statistical reports, and UN (1981).

nineteenth century: 2.3 million (Table 9.3), as compared with 575,000 in the US, for example. Yet both countries had about the same number of 5–14-year-olds (6 million). This was still the case around 1900, but by the year 2000, in consequence of low French fertility up to the late 1930s, France will have the smallest elderly population (Fig. 9.5).

All countries have experienced an increase in numbers of elderly people, but not at the same time or rate.[13] The average French rate of increase for the entire period 1850–2000 works out to 0.8% per year, or about half that of neighbouring countries: 1.3% in Germany,[14] 1.5% in the UK and 1.7% in Italy. The latter is currently undergoing its highest increase in elderly

[13] Whilst it is not possible to be entirely certain about the number of elderly people by the year 2000, the doubt is minimal, as this number only depends on mortality—which up to now has only improved very slowly.

[14] Had it not been for the war losses (especially the generations of 1915–29), the German rate would have been appreciably higher.

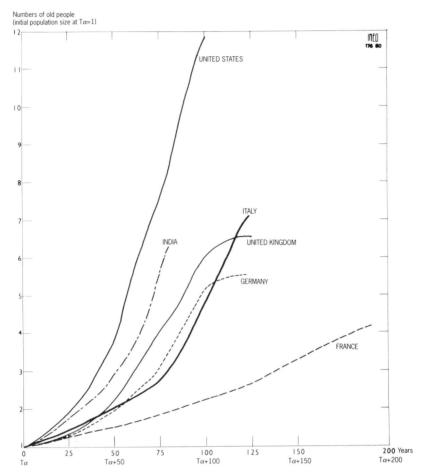

Numbers of old people
(initial population size at $T\alpha=1$)

FIG. 9.6. Changing size of elderly populations in the course of demographic transition

people, with a rate of nearly 2% for the second half of the twentieth century. This thrust of growth in the numbers of old people occurred half a century earlier in the UK (1900–50), and quarter of a century earlier in Germany (1920–70). These are only slight differences, however, compared with those separating countries of immigration, like the US, from developing countries such as India, or, again, from the French. In Fig. 9.6, the number of elderly people at the beginning point of the transition is set at unity, for all of these countries, which permits striking illustration of their subsequent development. A century after the date $T\alpha$, there are 12 times as many elderly people in the US, but only twice as many in France, and 5 to 6 times as many in the other European countries.

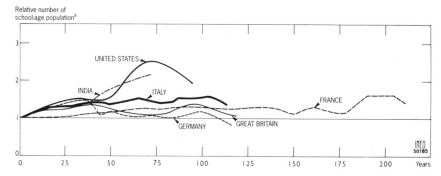

FIG. 9.7. Changing size of school-age populations in the course of demographic transition

[a] This number is considered as 1 at the beginning of the transition, in year 0.

Fig. 9.7, which refers to young people, is constructed on the same principle, using the same scale , and shows how much slighter the differences between countries are at the younger ages.

The strikingly different development of elderly populations in these countries reflects marked disparities in the growth of expenditure on health and retirement; hence, long-term demographic changes play a major role in the evolution of social budgets. An analysis of State expenditure reveals that, in 1975, India allotted a fraction of its budget seven times smaller than that of Italy to health, social security, and social services. More generally, at a given date, budgetary composition and the employment situation of a country are closely connected with its present form and phase of demographic transition (Chesnais 1981).

The consequences of demographic trends, such as pressure on educational requirements, net job creation, and financial support for the aged, are for the most part relatively mechanical, and do not require complex analytical treatment. Indeed, the differences in institutional context from one period to the next, and especially between countries, make attempts at detailed comparison hazardous. The following chapters, therefore, will concentrate on less visible but more decisive interactions influencing aggregate and national development.

Conclusion

The demographic transition involves a great diversity of types. Characteristic variations in age pyramids across time are associated with these different types, and in this chapter we have reconstructed a number of typical cases by retrospective analysis. Such changes in age distribution have obvious economic implications; they are accompanied by modification of collective needs, and hence a restructuring of public expenses and of priorities for social policy. From such information the broad outlines of a schedule of development may be sketched: if the type of demographic transition in a given country is known, and its degree of advancement in the transition process, it becomes possible to infer and evaluate the future direct influence of demographic factors in spheres such as education, employment, housing, and retirement homes. This provides an instrument which both throws light on the future and may serve as a guide to long-term planning, but which is ultimately constrained by changes of political and institutional context.

The present work, however, only gives a provisional survey of the transition types now in process and yet to come; new developments are possible in many less developed countries, on which a study of the past throws very little light. The mortality transition is still far from being completed, whilst the fertility transition in most cases is just beginning, and is likely to continue for several decades yet. The process of demographic ageing which follows and completes the transition will continue about a further 60 years; this process has not yet ended in developed countries, and will probably go on for another half-century. Consequently, the study of demographic ageing in the less developed world as a whole, where this process has barely begun, depends not on history but demographic projections. 'The 21st century', Sauvy has written, 'will be the century of ageing.'

Bibliography to Chapter 9

BOURGEOIS-PICHAT, J. (1951), 'Evolution générale de la population française depuis le XVIIIᵉ siècle', *Population*, 4: 635–62.

COALE, A. J. (1972), *The Growth and Structure of Human Populations: A Mathematical Investigation* (Princeton, NJ: Princeton University Press).

CHESNAIS, J. -C. (1981), 'Aspects socio-économiques de la transition démographique', in *Atti del Seminario su: 'La transizione demografica': Interrelazioni tra sviluppo demografico e sviluppo economico*, Collana di Studi e monografie, no. 7 (Bari).

—— (1982*a*), 'La Baisse de la natalité et ses conséquences pour la planification sectorielle dans les pays capitalistes développés', *Population*, 6: 1133–58.

—— (1982*b*), 'The Problem of Aging and Possible Strategies to Deal with it in Modern Societies: The Case of France, Germany (F.R.) and Japan', in *Japanese–German–French Symposium on Comparative Study of Declining Fertility Trends between Western Europe and Japan, Tokyo, 1981*, in *Sekai to Jinko* (in Japanese).

FREJKA, T. (1973), *The Future of Population Growth: Alternative Paths to Equilibrium* (New York: Wiley).

Institute of Developing Economics (1976), *Age Pyramids of World Population 1950– 1970* (Tokyo).

MACKENROTH, G. (1953), *Bevölkerungslehre: Theorie, Soziologie und Statistik der Bevölkerung* (Berlin: Springer Verlag), 20–25.

NOTESTEIN, F. W., TAEUBER, I. B., COALE, A. J., KIRK, D., and KISER, L. V. (1944), *La Population future de l'Europe et de l'Union Soviétique: perspectives démographiques 1940–1970* (Geneva: University of Princeton, League of Nations).

SAUVY, A. (1981), *Mondes en marche* (Paris: Calmann-Lévy).

UN (1956), 'Le Vieillissement des populations et ses conséquences économiques et sociales', *Études Démographiques*, New York, 26.

UN (1981), *World Population Prospects as Assessed in 1980* (New York: UN).

VILLEY, D. (1956–57), *Cours de démographie* (Paris: Monchrestien), i. 173.

10 The Transitional Multiplier of Population

Sciences are built of facts, like houses are built of stones... but an accumulation of facts is no more a science than a heap of stones is a house.

(H. Poincaré)

ONE of the characteristics of demographic transition is that it does not everywhere manifest the same rhythm and periodicity. Its temporal displacements and differences of scale are evident in the growing diversity of national population profiles. In the eighteenth century, all countries shared a comparable situation of high mortality, compensated to a greater or lesser degree by high fertility. Progressively, a differentiation emerged between the developed and less developed worlds, and, since the 1950s and especially the 1960s, the latter has itself split into two or three subgroups, each distinguished by given changes in fertility. This accentuation of demographic disparity has resulted in some new and complementary trends, but also in tensions and imbalances, number being one of the props of power.

Each type of demographic transition possesses its own growth potential. Chapter 8 demonstrated that in countries with advanced transition, as a general rule, the more recent the transition, the more it tends to be short in duration and high in its maximum level of natural increase. There is just reason, therefore, to enquire whether, in the end, very high rates of growth are not compensated by shorter durations of transition; in other words, are the implications for population growth at the conclusion of the transition process similar (and in what conditions) or, conversely, very different? This is one question that this chapter will tackle. In the first instance, enquiry will be addressed solely to European countries where we already have the results, the transition being completed. We shall also attempt to assess the possible role of international migration,[1] which, by its direct or indirect effect on components of natural increase, may influence the structuring of the transition profile in both countries of departure and arrival. Consequences deriving from the development of population numbers will then be tackled. Turning to the less developed countries, we shall consider expected variations in the number of inhabitants between the beginning and end of the transition, and the obstacles

---

[1] Emigration's role as a safety-valve is bound to be considerably less—at least proportionately—for less developed countries.

these countries are bound to come up against. Their experience relative to the Western countries can then be assessed, bearing in mind our prescriptions for criteria of temporal delimitation.

Choice of Representative Countries

In order to draw up a balance sheet of the different forms of transition, according to total natural increase, we will use each of the representative countries given at the end of Chapter 8, supplemented by certain cases selected for their particular features. Eleven countries are used, 5 of which belong to the developed world (Sweden, Germany, Italy, USSR, and France) and 6 to the less developed world: 4 of these are Asian (including China and India), 1 African (Egypt), and 1 Latin American (Mexico). In this way we not only maintain geographic coverage, but also address the different forms of transition—from the longest (Sweden and France) to the less long (USSR and China),[2] and from the 'highest' (Mexico) to the less 'high' (France), via intermediary types such as India. For each of these countries we shall begin by delimiting the period of transition, before dividing it into broad phases.[3] It is possible to calculate indices of natural growth for each European country, since the several stages are all completed. The product of these indices defines what is called the 'transitional multiplier of population'.

1. The Rise of European Population

Natural Increase

Everywhere in Europe, after the period of initial growth, natural increase was relatively low. Without doubt, emigration, but also the upheavals of European history, have played a large part in this slowing down: over the period 1911–40, average rates in Sweden and Germany were 0.6% per year, and 0.9% in Italy. The case of the Soviet Union, which compounded the classic scourges of famine, epidemics, and civil war with the evils of modern dictatorship (massacres, mass deportation, control of sexual mores) is even more striking. Taking only the period 1911–50, the average rate of increase over this particularly disturbed period of 40 years is only a third of what it was during the beginning phase, even though it includes the first years of post-war recovery. This asymmetry in the transition profile, which is more pronounced in countries with late transition, is related both to historical circumstance and

---

[2] Based on the probable development.

[3] Owing to insufficient data, the delimitation of these phases does not always correspond to population movements, especially in the case of less developed countries: a cut-off date of 1950 has been adopted.

the rapidity of fertility declines; the noticeable decline in population growth makes the post-war baby boom appear even more dramatic. In the USSR in particular, the last phase of the transition (1951–65), while marking a return to pre-transitional growth levels, none the less shows a rate of growth three times higher than that of the period 1911–50. This demonstrates the extent to which the transition process was shaken up, and the abnormal levels reached by excess mortality.[4]

In sum, with a transition period of around 70 years, the transitional multiplier of population for Russia (2.05) is nevertheless fairly close to Germany's (2.11) and Italy's (2.26), where the transition lasted 90 years. The orders of magnitude are thus very comparable.[5] As the phrase 'transitional multiplier' suggests, the population in these three countries, which are fairly representative from this point of view of most European cases, has a little over doubled in size.

The result for Sweden, where the transition dates back to the beginning of the nineteenth century, is completely different: for over a century, natural increase exceeded an average of 1% per year, which was sufficient to multiply the population by almost three. This example illustrates how long the first phase of the transition lasted, and thus the length of the interval between mortality decline and fertility decline (see Table 10.1).

The Role of International Migration

The peak of European demographic growth coincided with unprecedented migration. Conversely, as the transition drew towards its end in Europe and

[4] Assuming that the Soviet Union, whose form of transition resembles Italy's fairly closely, had suffered fewer disturbances and, after the pre-1911 period of high increase, had experienced a similar relative decline in natural growth to Italy's (14.5%) during the period 1911–40, its population in 1982, all things being equal, would be on the order of 325 million inhabitants, not 270 million. The difference would therefore easily equal the population, say, of France. The demographic record of political disturbances is a sobering one. By 1925, the population was reduced to its 1910 level: in accounting for this reduction, war losses, properly speaking, add up to only 2 million persons; additional mortality over and above the norm totalled 14 million, due mostly to famine, and diseases and epidemics following the Civil War; and the birth deficit was 10 million. In addition, 2 million people emigrated. Stalin and the Second World War blacken the record further. Under Stalin, from the early 1930s, the population of labour camps, where mortality was appalling, consistently exceeded 2 and even 3 million—the equivalent of the Norwegian population around 1950—with a peak of 15 million at the end of the 1940s—almost the equivalent of Yugoslavia's population at that period (Labin 1948; Shifrine 1980; Rosefielde 1981; Heller and Nekrich 1982). The phenomenon assumes a demographic dimension which remains to be studied. The war would have claimed 10 million victims among soldiers (many of whom were prisoners who did not survive captivity or were reported as missing); excess mortality among civilians is estimated at 15 million, and the birth deficit at 20 million. The population of European Russia in 1950 stood at its level of 1905 (110 million).

[5] The Soviet multiplier is in fact very low compared with what might have been expected, given the momentum gathered, and the age structure at the beginning of the century, which was very favourable to rapid growth. The Russian population grew by 200% during the 19th century, a rate which was so firmly established that Mendeleyev, in 1900, did not hesitate to predict a population of 800 million inhabitants by the year 2050, for the Russian Empire.

TABLE 10.1. *Natural increase during demographic transition, with corresponding transitional multipliers, Sweden, Germany, Italy, USSR, France*

Country	Period of demographic transition[a]	Principal phases	Average annual rate of natural increase (%)	Index of natural increase at the end of the phase (base = 100 at the beginning of transition)	Transitional multiplier of population[b]
Sweden	1810–1960	1810–1910	1.05	284.2	
		1911–1940	0.61	119.9	
		1941–1960	0.59	112.5	3.83
Germany (FRG since 1946[c])	1876–1965	1876–1910	1.32	157.2	
		1911–1940	0.60	119.8	
		1941–1965	0.45	111.9	2.11
Italy	1876–1965	1876–1910	1.03	143.1	
		1911–1940	0.88	130.0	
		1941–1965	0.78	121.6	2.26
USSR	1895–1965	1895–1910	1.73	129.3	
		1911–1950	0.55	124.5	
		(1911–1940)	(0.91)	(131.2)	
		1951–1965	1.62	127.3	
		(1941–1965)	(0.76)	(120.9)	2.05
France	1785–1970	n/a	0.26	n/a	1.62

Notes: n/a = not applicable.

[a] These dates are intended to be fairly approximate and conservative, especially with regard to starting-points of transition; as noted in Chapter 3, much earlier dates could be chosen.

[b] The product of indices in previous column, divided by 100.

[c] Demographic changes in the two Germanies were fairly similar, at least with regard to fertility up to 1975; this was not the case, however, for crude mortality rates and external migration.

started in other continents, Europe gradually, from 1950, became an immigration area: the transformation began in the northern and western countries of earliest transition,[6] and then, from the 1970s, spread to southern and eastern countries.[7]

There are very few European countries where migration has played a negligible role. Its real significance is difficult to evaluate in so far as certain elementary questions remain unresolved:

[6] Immigration began in France during the second half of the 19th century.
[7] Although it is very low and highly clandestine (unrecorded), immigration to the USSR and east European countries none the less occurs. It originates from satellite countries and allies (Vietnam, Algeria, China).

1. Migration is not defined uniformly from country to country, and the temporal criterion most often used to specify permanent displacement—residence of at least a year—is both difficult to apply and far from being universal. This was even more the case in the past.

2. Migration statistics come from diverse administrative sources, each with their own particular concerns.

3. Migration data are affected by an asymmetry of information, in which countries of departure are fairly well informed on emigration but badly or not at all on immigration, or at least, on return migration; conversely, countries of arrival tend to have data on the immigration which affects them, but are ill informed on departures.[8] Consequently, very little is known about return migration, despite its frequent occurrence. In the US, for example, at the height of immigration, 1890–1910, the proportion of returns has been estimated at 40%; and another large wave occurred at the time of the Great Depression.

External migration is a manifestly strategic variable in the process of a population's adjustment to its milieu. The British Isles, with 18 million emigrants for the period 1846–1932, represent the country most affected: demographic growth had been exceptionally rapid during the two preceding centuries, in which the population had quadrupled; also there were considerable demands on limited space. (European Russia had experienced a population increase of almost the same dimension during the same two centuries, but its initial density was almost five times less.) But each of the representative countries—Italy, Germany, and Sweden—with contingents of 10, 5, and 1.2 million respectively over the same period (1846–1932), were seriously involved. Russia alone was comparatively unaffected, doubtless both because of the possibilities of colonization offered by Siberia, and due to historical circumstances: at the point at which the country could have continued to provide large numbers of emigrants—on account of its late transition—American legislation in 1921 and 1924 undertook to limit Slav immigration (Willcox 1940), while the new Soviet regime sought permanently to prohibit departures. With this exception, and that of France, where immigration began a century earlier in conformity with the relative precocity of its fertility decline, emigration helped, at a time when the competition of young adults on the job market was at its highest, to reduce the threat of over-population. This correspondence between migratory waves and the transition has been analysed in Chapter 6.

---

[8] In addition, the incompatibility of the results supplied by different sources and by the countries in question (owing to conflicting methods of record-keeping) is a well-known problem in migration statistics. Thus, the number of emigrants from country A travelling to country B recorded in A for a given year generally fails to tally with the number of immigrants recorded in B coming from A for the same year.

A Complex Interdependence

Since migration behaves as a form of demographic regulation which may take the place of, for example, increased mortality or birth control, any mechanical assessment of its influence on the development of demographic transition is hypothetical, if not illusory, at least for countries of departure. It is in fact quite impossible to calculate what would have happened if the migration safety-valve had not been available. The implications of the transitional multiplier of population, set out above, can thus be estimated only at the price of more or less hazardous assumptions.

Thus, if N people leave territory A for territory B, the change in population size of both A and B depends on three factors, one of which evades all possibility of measurement.

1. in the *short term*, the volume N of migration, which adds to B and subtracts from A;

2. in the *middle and long term*, the consequences on A and B of the degree of age- and sex-specific selectivity of migration, which increases the numerical effect of the transfer;

3. in the *very long term*, the demographic repercussions of migration on non-migrant parts of the populations, both in the country of departure and arrival. In this, the argument invoked earlier, already clearly explicated by Malthus, is re-encountered: there is nothing to disprove the notion that (3) might counterbalance the direct effects of (1) and (2).[9] It is possible, then, that migration was only a short-term expedient, having no permanent effect on population size. Malthus had in mind early modern European experience, in which mortality was high and marriage delayed owing to pressure on resources; but this logic could easily be applied to populations in transition, even in the case of countries of arrival.

This line of reasoning is in fact supported in the case of the US, where it has been established that immigration, by accelerating urbanization and industrialization, facilitated the upward mobility of the population already resident, which in turn accelerated their fertility decline. Although this supports the general argument that, when migration is of enduring character and in mass proportions, its effect on growth may be considerable, the implication is that its impact is probably less than its sheer volume might seem to suggest. This role as accelerator of the transition in countries of arrival, and regulator in the countries of departure, requires more extensive analysis, since our argument does not sort out the actual complexity of the matter.

---

[9] Malthus 1798, bk. III, ch. 7. Since migration is caused by poverty, 'a certain degree of emigration is beneficial to the population of the country of origin' (p. 107)—enabling it, paradoxically, to acquire new growth.

Some Extreme Cases

There is a further uncertainty pertaining to migrants. It cannot be proven, a priori, that the demographic (and, especially, fertility) behaviour of migrants has differed from what it would have been had they remained in their countries of origin. The too frequently underestimated influence (in B. Thomas, for example) of deterrent facts such as poverty or persecution implies that candidates for departure were in a marginal position (or considered themselves to be), and in consequence, would have experienced a completely different demographic dynamic from the dominant population. Confronted with such an inevitable theoretical quandary, which affects equally the behaviour of migrants (and their descendants) and the possible adjustment of non-migrant populations in countries of departure and arrival, we are forced to resort to simplified calculations and an examination of comparative history, using examples as unambiguous as possible.

The majority of countries affected by high overseas migration prior to transition experienced sustained population growth, resulting in historically unprecedented densities. Around 1875 these densities, at about 100 inhabitants per km^2, or even more, were far higher than average in other countries.

The case of Ireland is the clearest. The introduction of the potato at the end of the sixteenth century enabled unparalleled population growth, which, despite fairly high rates of emigration by the beginning of the nineteenth century (1.5 million Irish left before 1845, or approximately 30% of the total population in 1800), increased almost fivefold in two centuries, from 1650 to 1845. Such demographic exuberance (curiously ignored by Malthus, even in the last versions of his *Essay*,[10] which amply document the situation elsewhere) was brought to a halt by the potato crop failure and its well-known consequences. Famine and cholera were responsible for a frightening death-toll, causing an excess mortality of about 800,000 people, and 1 million inhabitants left the country between 1846 and 1851, followed by a further 3 million in the remaining half-century. In spite of natural increase which continued to be quite positive (from 0.5% to 1% per year), between 1845 and 1914 the population was reduced by half. Since that date, despite considerable declines in mortality and emigration, the island's population has scarcely changed. Ireland began to practise a characteristically Jansenist mode of birth control (likewise recommended by Malthus, in conformity with nineteenth-century morality): abstinence, lifetime celibacy, and delayed marriage.

Ireland is the only country in which the economic challenge of modern population growth has required a disruption of the entire demographic system: an acute crisis of mortality (immediate), the establishment of a continuing flow of emigration (very intense at first, then slower), and a gradual

---

[10] In the 7th edition, published 1872 and written in 1825, he devotes only a few lines to the Irish development, although he dwells at length on the Scottish case.

transition to a method of birth control which limits access to marriage (still in force). Without the historic impact of the years 1845–51, it would not be possible to understand the singularity of Ireland: if, according to the usual criteria, the transition is not yet completed, this is probably due less to actual migration than to the disaster which precipitated it. Today, the Irish population is no larger than it was two centuries ago.

For other countries experiencing high rates of emigration, such as Italy or Sweden, the classic definition of demographic transition by its exclusive reference to natural surplus is equally misleading, although in a completely different way than in Ireland. The transitional multiplier of population for Italy over the period 1876–1965 works out at 2.26, although the population in fact increased by a multiplier of 1.87. In Sweden, similarly, the corresponding values are 3.83 and 3.13. In both cases, the transitional multiplier over-estimates the actual growth of the population by a proportion equivalent to 21% to 22%.

Conversely, in France, for example, where immigration dates to the nineteenth century, the transitional multiplier underestimates real growth of population at 1.6; whereas in the period 1785–1970 population actually multiplied by 2 (taking France as a territorial constant, including Nice and Savoy). Here again, the relative difference between the two indices is about 20%. But if, in order better to assess the impact of migration, we consider actual *flows* of population rather than measures of the changing *stock* of people, then these developments appear markedly different: actual growth is over-estimated by 33% in Sweden and 45% in Italy; it is underestimated by 40% in France. As rough as these figures are, this difference gives a first indication of the comparative influence of *net* migration on population. However, measurement of the difference between an observed multiplier and a transitional multiplier in this way yields, a priori, an underestimate of the order of magnitude of the influence of migration. It is an underestimate because it incorporates only component (2); and it is underestimated, a priori, because it is not known whether effect (3) might counterbalance effect (1) via fertility increases in non-migrant populations in countries of departure, and declines in countries of arrival. More-detailed estimates of migration effects, including element (1), have regularly been used in statistical studies of most countries of immigration. (The calculation has little meaning for countries of departure, as shown in the limit case of Ireland.) Yet the effects of (3), although fairly certain over the very long term, are not considered, even hypothetically. Thus, the contribution of migration to population growth in France for the years 1800–1940 has been estimated at 40%, the main increase being via extension of the average length of life. Likewise, the contribution of migration to post-war population growth (1950–70) as calculated from component (1) alone (population transfers) has been estimated at 45% for West Germany, 35% for France, and 30% for Sweden (UN 1975). Such orders of magnitude, and especially those noted previously—all of which tend to be conservative

TABLE 10.2. *Estimate of the number of people speaking different European languages, 1800–1935* (millions)

Year	English	German	Russian	French	Spanish	Italian	Polish	Portuguese	Total
1800	20–40	30–33	25–31	27–31	26	14–15	9	6	157–91
1900	116–123	75–80	70–85	45–52	44–58	34–54	26	24	434–502
1935	195	78	160	62	80	41	32	47	695

Source: Willcox (1940: 14).

estimates—demonstrate the extent to which omission of migration from explanatory frameworks distorts reality and conceals the extraordinary complexity of demographic change. In the case of Europe, it was precisely in the attempt to account for such change that transition theory was formulated.

Implications

Migration introduced greater flexibility into the demographic mechanism; in becoming a mass phenomenon after the Irish disaster, it reduced risks of similar crises in other places. All things considered, emigration to America and Australia permitted an effective expansion of numbers in population of European origin. A glance at the growth of the population in the US since the mid-nineteenth century is a graphic illustration, as one is dealing with a tenfold increase, from 23 million in 1850 to 238 million in 1985.

Such redeployment of populations has had incalculable consequences:

1. *The development of European languages and of corresponding technical culture.* As the following data show, however, this development has encouraged considerable inequality between languages, which reflects differential fertility. In less than a century and a half, the number of people speaking one of these eight languages has quadrupled. Just before the Second World War, they included one-third of the world's population, as opposed to one-tenth around 1700. The progression is easily the most significant for English and Russian, whereas the spread of German and, especially, French have marked time from an early period, French dropping from first place around 1700 to fourth by 1935. Spanish and Portuguese have enjoyed an intermediate development.

2. *Increase and restabilizing of population densities.* If the existence of a minimal density is, as Boserup (1981) argues, a fundamental pre-condition of economic viability, then, with the transition, numerous countries reached levels of human concentration sufficient for the emergence of certain economic activities. This view is given undeniable credence by the rapidity of secular economic growth (see Chapter 17) which, in addition to characterizing countries of immigration, has sometimes been called a 'miracle' in densely

populated countries like Germany, Japan, and Italy (150, 160,[11] and 130 inhabitants on average per km², respectively by 1925), and, more recently, Taiwan, Singapore, and South Korea (449, 3,500, and 350 respectively by 1975).

2. Rapid Population Growth in the Less Developed World

The importance of the first phase of the transition is even more evident in less developed countries than it was in the developed; the decline in previously very high crude mortality rates has been both dramatic and rapid, with levels of growth generally achieving rates two or three times higher. The transition in these countries is often far from reaching its term, even though, in the cases studied, the phase of most rapid growth and the plateau of maximal growth passed some years ago (more or less, depending on the case, and with the exception, perhaps, of Egypt). It has thus been necessary to extrapolate growth trends into the future, to the point at which they meet pre-transitional levels, generally assuming there is a symmetry between ascending and descending phases. In most cases this presupposes that fertility declines will be as rapid as were falls in mortality in the period of rising population growth; and this, in turn, implies that fertility will fall sufficiently rapidly to compensate for the effect of the relative size of child-bearing cohorts, which would normally slow down the decline (an audacious hypothesis, as seen above in Chapter 8). Since mortality has not yet reached its lowest point, we have incorporated into our projection the probable development of mortality and fertility. By this method we arrive at a date of 1990 (or 2000) for the end of the transition in the three Asian countries of Taiwan, mainland China, and Sri Lanka; India's turn will come in 2010;[12] and the process should end earlier in Mexico, mainly because of a higher starting level (1.2% before 1910, compared with an average of barely 0.5 per year in India). The latter applies to Egypt for the same reason.[13]

By combining the various rates of natural increase for the whole of the transition period we arrive at the multipliers given in Table 10.3. In all cases, the transitional multiplier of population exceeds 2 (Fig. 10.1). Between the case of mainland China where, only a few decades after the mortality decline,

---

[11] If only the arable area is taken into consideration, Japanese density then amounts to almost, 1,000.

[12] Comparison, in the case of the Asian countries considered here, is worth while in so far as levels of pre-transitional growth are of the same order.

[13] This is where the criterion of return to pre-transitional growth is clearly insufficient. Even though highly revealing when each country is examined separately, it becomes misleading in international comparisons. These criteria might possibly come in useful at a later stage in analysing countries of immigration, although the latter also present ambiguities.

TABLE 10.3. *Natural increase during demographic transition, with corresponding transitional multipliers, India, China, Sri Lanka, Egypt, Mexico, Taiwan*

Country	Period of demographic transition[a]	Phases[b]	Average annual[c] rate of natural increase (%)	Index of natural increase[c] (base = 100 at the beginning of the phase)	Transitional multiplier of population[d]
India	1920–(2010)	1920–1950	1.20	145	
		1951–1975	2.10	169	
		1976–(2010)	1.20	154	3.67
China	1930–2000	1930–1949	0.60	112	
		1950–1973	2.10	161	
		1974–(2000)	1.20	136	2.46
Sri Lanka	1920–(1990)	1920–1950	1.70	169	
		1951–1975	2.40	182	
		1976–(1990)	1.30	121	3.71
Egypt	1946–(2010)	1946–1950	2.15	111	
		1951–1975	2.40	181	
		1976–2010	1.90	193	3.88
Mexico	1920–(2000)	1920–1950	2.10	191	
		1951–1975	3.30	227	
		1976–(2000)	1.95	162	7.02
Taiwan	1920–(1990)	1920–1950	1.80	174	
		1951–1975	2.90	204	
		1976–(1990)	1.35	122	4.35

[a] The starting dates for China and Egypt are uncertain, since an initial decline in mortality had already begun around 1920. Taiwan actually recorded a considerable decline at this time. Egyptian levels of fertility, and especially of mortality, are probably underestimated prior to the Second World War.

[b] Dates for the conclusion of demographic transition are hypothetical. They have been derived according to our criteria (see above) and by extrapolation of rates of natural increase, taking into account the degree to which transition has already advanced, and its type. This none the less presupposes a rapid decline in fertility in each case.

[c] Rounded to the nearest decimal point.

[d] The product of indices in previous column, divided by 100.

fertility appears to have received an abrupt check—thereby producing a low multiplier—and the Mexican case of simultaneously high and fairly long transition, where the multiplier exceeds 7, the results are otherwise fairly homogeneous. That is, between these two extreme cases, the values in all

TABLE 10.4. *Population at the end of the transition* (millions)

Hypothesis	India	China	Sri Lanka	Egypt	Mexico	Taiwan
Low variant	940	1,250	17.5	66.1	96.6	19.5
High variant	1,210	1,550	20.9	93.9	142.0	23.9

instances revolve around 4—an appreciably higher figure than that of Europe. This order of magnitude is of particular note in so far as the levels of pre-transitional growth in 4 of the 5 intermediate cases were similar to European levels.

A set of alternative perspectives has been attempted for the six less developed countries considered in Table 10.3. We have, to begin with, varied the assumptions for rapid fertility decline, according to the criteria just cited, and added to this another projection which, in contrast, supposes that demographic transition takes 20 years longer, or even 30 years in the case of India. Clear differences emerge between their population sizes (see Table 10.4).

The cumulative population of China and India would exceed 2 billion, and perhaps approach 3 billion, but the proportionate growth in these countries is slight compared with what one observes in countries such as Mexico. The size of the relative differences in population growth during the transition process between France and Mexico, for example, amply illustrates this point.[14] The combined effect of three factors determines the level of the transitional multiplier of population: the speed of the decline in mortality rates (four times faster in Mexico than in France); the time lag between the two declines (from a few years to a quarter of a century in most European countries, but over half a century in Mexico); and the speed of fertility decline (depending on whether natural growth comes down to pre-transitional levels within 25 years, or only after 45 years, the Mexican transitional multiplier of population will be 7 or 10).

Thus, it is the 'height' even more than the duration of a transition which determines the volume of the population at the end of the process. A fairly simple theoretical example is sufficient to illustrate this. Let us imagine a country with a transition profile similar to that of Sri Lanka (cf. Chapter 8), and characterized by the following parameters:

1. annual average rate of pre-transitional growth: 0.5%;
2. duration of Phase 2 (increase of rates): 25 years;
3. duration of Phase 3 (stabilization of rates): 20 years;
4. duration of Phase 4 (decline of rates): 40 years.

---

[14] Natural increase only; the difference is less for total growth, on account of immigration to France and Mexican emigration to the US.

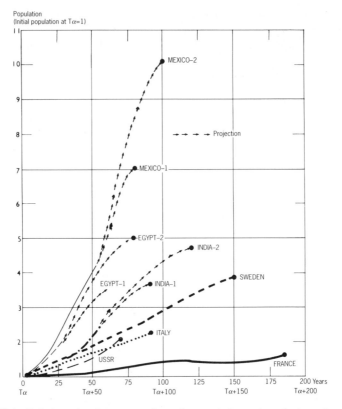

FIG. 10.1. Relative development of total population size during demographic transition, various countries

TABLE   10.5. *Transitional   multipliers   of   population according to the value of parameters* H, D, *and* r_α

r_α	H	D		
		20	40	60
$r_\alpha = 0$	2.5	1.65	2.72	4.48
	3.0	1.82	3.32	6.05
	3.5	2.01	4.06	8.17
$r_\alpha = 0.5$	2.5	1.82	3.32	6.05
	3.0	2.01	4.06	8.17
	3.5	2.23	4.95	11.02
$r_\alpha = 1.0$	2.5	2.01	4.06	8.17
	3.0	2.23	4.95	11.02
	3.5	2.46	6.05	14.88

If we assume that the development through Phases 1 and 3 is linear, and that the rate of natural increase is constant during Phase 2, then by merely fixing maximal growth at 4% instead of 3%, without altering any other variable, the transitional multiplier of population reaches a value of 9.3 instead of 5.5, an increase of two-thirds (Chesnais 1979a). To obtain an equivalent change while maintaining the plateau of maximal growth at 3% per year, the period of transition would have to be extended by several years—between 25 and 35, depending on whether this extension relates to the central phase, or the two phases on either side. The hypothesis of linearity means that the total growth in phases 1 and 3 corresponds to an arithmetical progression. Consequently, in our example, with a maximal growth of 3% per year, the final total (designated A) of recorded increases works out at:

$$A = 25 \times 0.005 + (25 \times 24 \times 0.001) \div 2 \qquad \text{(Phase 1)}$$
$$+ \ 20 \times 0.03 \qquad\qquad\qquad\qquad\qquad \text{(Phase 2)}$$
$$+ \ 40 \times 0.005 + (40 \times 39 \times 0.000625) \div 2 \quad \text{(Phase 3)}$$

hence

$$A = 1.713$$

giving

$$e^A = 5.5$$

equally, with 4%, the result is

$$e^{2.228} = 9.3.$$

A Generalization

Similar calculations have been made by Keyfitz (1977), but using simpler hypotheses: the pre- and post-transitional rates of natural increase are assumed to be nil; the curves of crude mortality and fertility rates are identical, and thus more or less superimposable. In these conditions, Keyfitz (1977) shows that if—to resume our own terminology—H is the 'height' of the transition (the maximal difference between the two trends) and $D = T\alpha \ T\beta$ (the interval between the start of the two declines), the transitional multiplier of population, designated M, would be written: $M = e^{HD} = e^A$.

It is thus possible to measure the influence of either the interval or the 'height' of trends on subsequent population growth, by constructing a table of the values of M following variations in parameters H and D. The effect of pre-transitional growth levels, or of the degree of asymmetry in the transition, on the final values of M may, moreover, be assessed without resorting to Keyfitz's simplified hypotheses. The values of M are illustrated in Table 10.5. Three hypothetical levels are given for each parameter: the length of interval $D =$ 20, 40, or 60 years; the height of the transition $H = 2.5\%$, 3%, or 3.5%; and

TABLE 10.6. *Influence of the forms of demographic transition on the value of multiplier* M (D = 60, r_α = 0.5)

Phase	Duration (years)								
1 (increase)	40								
2 (peak)	10			20			30		
3 (decline)	40	50	60	40	50	60	40	50	60
Transitional multiplier of population	5.34	6.36	7.58	7.21	8.58	10.23	9.73	11.59	13.80

(keeping Keyfitz's second hypothesis) the rate of pre-transitional growth r_α = 0%, 0.5%, or 1% per year.

The importance of interval D, the influence of delayed fertility decline, is manifest. Thus, with zero pre-transitional growth, an extension of the time lag by 20 years (to 60, as opposed to 40 years) has a greater influence on final growth levels than an increase by 0.5% in the height of transition (if D = 60 and H = 2.5, then M = 4.48; whereas M = 4.06 for D = 40 and H = 3.0). This sort of calculation supports the sense of urgency attached to efforts to reduce fertility in many poor countries.

The level of pre-transitional growth also has a significant effect on the final value of M: as it increases, it pushes the multiplier up to very high values—considerably higher than those calculated for the European countries. A multiplier in double figures may thus be reached very rapidly. For the values D = 60 and H = 3, for example, a change in pre-transitional growth from zero to 1% raises the multiplier to a value close on 11, instead of 6.

We can now turn to Keyfitz's second hypothesis, and examine the influence of different forms of transition. The cases considered to this point assume that the ascending and descending slopes of the curve of natural increase are symmetrical. However, there is good reason to think that for many countries the contraction of growth in the final phase may be longer than the initial period of increasing growth, owing in particular to the slowing down of fertility declines by continued young age structures. The period of the transition may be divided, as in the previous example of Sri Lanka, into three phases (expansion, peak, and contraction), and varying durations assigned to each phase. In order to simplify calculation, the hypothesis of linearity in the development of the growth rates will be retained.

Below, we give an example for the values D = 60, H = 3% and r_α = 0.5%. We assume that the relative durations of peak growth can be assigned values of 10, 20, and 30 years, and that the duration of declining growth (the return to pre-transitional levels) attains the values 40, 50, and 60 years. This results in the range of transitional multipliers given in Table 10.6.

At a given value of height H, interval D, and pre-transitional growth r_a, the total duration of transition only has to be extended by 40 years (20 for phase 2 and 20 for phase 3) for the multiplier to increase from 5.34 to 13.80. The duration of the peak growth phase, when it combines with time lag D, is evidently the most significant factor, but the duration of the final phase of contraction is far from being unimportant. Thus, when a symmetrical transition with relative durations of 40, 20, and 40 years turns an asymmetrical 40, 20, and 60 years, the multiplier increases from 7.21 to 10.23.

Kenya, where increases in already very high rates of fertility have brought about the most rapid growth in the world, offers a good example. With peak growth at 4% per annum for almost 20 years, the population can be expected to increase sixfold in 50 years (Chesnais 1979*b*): this represents a growth rate greater than the limit envisaged by Malthus, and Verhulst after him. Medium projections (UN 1981) indicate that when growth returns to a pre-transitional level in 2025, the population will be nearly 100 million; in 1950, when the transition began, the figure was only 6.4 million. In other words, the multiplier could reach a completely unprecedented value of around 15 or more. This sort of scenario presupposes that limited resources will not intervene to check growth. The fundamental question remains, for the several countries with late transition likely to experience similarly explosive growth: Is it possible that such growth could really occur? Migration can only play a marginal role, owing to the sheer numbers involved, the want of large virgin territories for colonization, and the erection of legal and political barriers in the dominant countries, etc. In the absence of very rapid economic progress, it is probable that demographic checks will intervene, either via radical and enforced reductions in fertility, or crisis mortality (or some combination of both). The trajectories predicted thus remain purely theoretical.

A New Dynamic of Rich and Poor Countries

The implications of the transition, in terms of the final growth of population, plainly differ considerably between poor and rich countries. Whilst the transitional multiplier of population in Europe is generally between 2 and 5, it can be as much as 10 (Fig. 10.1), and sometimes more, in those less developed countries undergoing late transitions which will take several decades to complete.

To bring this situation into clearer focus, we can assume that the transitional multiplier is 4 for the developed world, and 8 in the less developed, and that average post-transitional natural increase is zero. The changing distribution of the world's population between the beginning and end of transition is then given in Table 10.7, following current classification of developed and less developed countries. The developed world according to these assumptions will see an almost 50% drop in its relative population size. The transformation is less dramatic than it might appear, if we assume that the Western

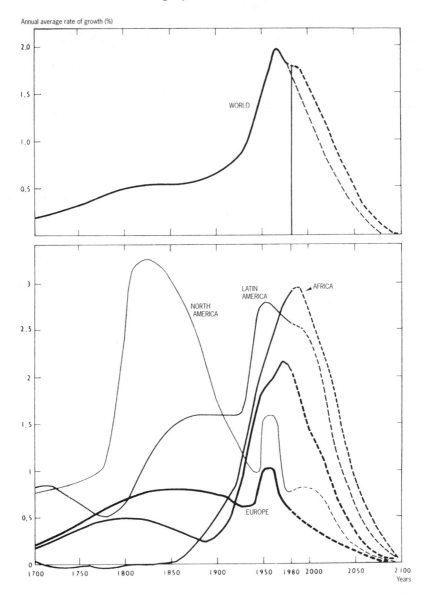

Annual average rate of growth (%)

FIG. 10.2. Retrospective development of population growth rates, 1700–1980, and projections for 1980–2100, the world and its continents

mortality transition in fact began in the eighteenth century; as Fig. 10.2 illustrates, Europe and North America experienced their main demographic peak after a very long period of growth, a century or more ahead of other continents. This long-term global picture nevertheless conceals profound

TABLE 10.7. *The changing distribution of the world's population, on certain assumptions* (%)

Type of country	Initial state (around 1850)	Transitional multiplier	Final state (around 2050)	
Developed countries	25	4	100	(14.3)
Less developed countries	75	8	600	(85.7)
TOTAL	100	7	700	100

disparities, and a considerable geographic redistribution is to be expected (Frejka 1973; Tabah 1979) to the advantage of countries with late transition, particularly where population density in relation to arable land is fairly low.

Conclusion

The diversity of modern demographic experience is clearly reflected in the extent to which transitional multipliers vary: below 2 in Ireland; barely 2 in France; almost 4 in Sweden; probably 4 to 5 in India; 7 to 10 in Mexico; 15 or more in Kenya. To this diversity of growth we must add the variety of ways in which the several parameters add up to the multiplier in question; the same index reflects completely different variations of mortality, fertility, and external migration, as the cases of India and Sweden, both with multipliers close on 4, demonstrate. Evidently, the development of populations is infinitely more complex than Malthus and the first theoreticians of the transition (Landry and Notestein) envisaged. Who, nowadays, would look for a population living in exceptionally favourable conditions (possessing a vast and rich territory, the most advanced technical resources, etc.) in order to prove a hypothetical law of geometric progression—as Malthus did in the early editions of his *Essay*, and likewise Verhulst and his disciple Quételet (all referring to the US)? And who now would follow Verhulst when, to prove his hypothesis of logistical growth, he selected the long-established populations of Belgium and France, in which each population describes a different curve which none the less conforms to a mathematical model? The notion of a law of population and, perforce, a unique law, dissolves before the abundance of facts. Even if there are incontestable analogies between types of demographic transition and different countries, there are no two countries—even geographically and historically similar ones—that have traced the same course of transition, so numerous are the possible interactions between mortality, fertility, and migration across the successive phases of transition. History yields a rich catalogue of different experiences by which demographic expansion has been checked, from those where emigration is the dominant solution (Ireland), or birth control (France), to those where mortality remains the principal factor (Soviet Union, tropical Africa).

Bibliography to Chapter 10

BIRABEN, J. N. (1979), 'Essai sur l'évolution du nombre des hommes', *Population*, 1: 13–25.

BOSERUP, E. (1981) *Population and Technology* (Oxford: Blackwell).

CHESNAIS, J. -C. (1979*a*), 'L'Effet multiplicatif de la transition démographique', *Population*, 6: 1138–44.

——— (1979*b*), 'Un Exemple de sextuplement en cinquante ans: la population du Kenya', *Population*, 1: 206–11.

FREJKA, T. (1973), *The Future of Population Growth: Alternative Paths to Equilibrium* (New York).

HELLER, M., and NEKRICH, A. (1982), *L'Utopie au pouvoir: histoire du l'URSS de 1917 à nos jours* (Paris: Calmann-Lévy).

KEYFITZ, N. (1977), 'On the Momentum of Population Growth, *Demography*, 8(1), 71–80.

LABIN, S. (1948), *Panorama de la Russie Soviétique* (Paris: Self), 438–50.

MALTHUS, T. R. (1798), *Essay on the Principle of Population as it Affects the Future Improvement of Society with Remarks on the Speculation of Mr. Godwin, M. Condorcet and Other Writers* (London: Johnson; 7th edn. London: Reeves and Turner, 1872).

MAKSUDOV (1977), 'Pertes subies par la population de l'URSS, 1918–1958', *Cahiers du Monde Russe et Soviétique*, 18(3) (July–Sept.).

ROSEFIELDE, S. (1981), *Soviet Studies*, 51–87.

SHIFRIN, A. (1980), *The First Guidebook to Prisons and Concentration Camps of the Soviet Union* (Seewis: Stephanus).

TABAH, I. (1979), 'The Changing Demographic Balance', *Populi*, New York, 6(2).

VERHULST, P. F. (1844), *Recherches mathématiques sur la loi d'accroissement de la population* (Brussels).

UN (1973), 'World Population Prospects beyond the Year 2000', *Symposium on Population and Development, Cairo, 1973*, E/CONF.60/BP/3/Add.1 (New York: UN).

——— (1975), *Economic Survey in Europe in 1974*, pt. II: *Post-war Demographic Trends in Europe and the Outlook until the Year 2000* (New York: UN).

——— (1981), *World Population Prospects as Assessed in 1980* (New York: UN).

WILLCOX, W. F. (1940), *Studies in American Demography* (Ithaca, NY: Cornell University Press).

11 Industrial Revolution and Demographic Revolution in the Eighteenth Century: The French–English Paradox

> Glory be to the French! They have laboured for the two great needs of humanity: good living and civil equality.
>
> · (Heine)

IN England, the Industrial Revolution[1] begins in the eighteenth century and the demographic revolution[2] in the nineteenth. Conversely, France has its demographic revolution in the eighteenth century and its Industrial Revolution the century following. In both cases, demographic and economic chronologies are largely dissociated. These facts, at first sight, would appear immediately and seriously to compromise transition theory. The theory was itself derived from European experience: yet apparently it is incapable of accounting for the two countries which dominated the European scene up to the last third of the nineteenth century. The French–English parallel—full of manifest paradoxes—does, however, lead to less damning conclusions when examined more circumspectly. Once social organization and certain institutional factors specific to each country are incorporated, the theory may even be strengthened.

The central question remains why demographic development was so late in England and so early in France, relative to economic improvements. Of course, no pretension can be made to settling such an issue definitively; our aim is only to advance discussion by presenting materials which are as coherent and convincing as possible.

Political arithmeticians were obsessed with the comparative economic state of the two nations, a theme belaboured for three centuries, since it was a question of assessing the strength of two rival powers. The first attempts at

---

[1] In the sense of entering a process of sustained and irreversible growth. Whatever the country or period, the character and effects of this process are fundamentally similar: population increase, the application of scientific discoveries in industry, the transformation from rural to urban societies, the rise of new social classes, more intensive and extensive use of capital, unprecedented accumulation of wealth, etc.; the pattern of growth, however, is affected by circumstances of time and place.

[2] In the limited sense of the beginning of the fertility transition.

sustained quantitative history, however, are really only more than 20 years old (Deane and Cole 1964; Markovitch 1966). Interestingly enough, the demographic picture at that time remained incomplete; it has been necessary to wait until more recently for valid comparisons of trends describing both sides of the Channel since the middle of the eighteenth century.[3]

The facts and their possible interpretation will be considered in three stages:

1. a description of fertility trends and the growth of per capita income[4] in the two countries;
2. an analysis of possible reasons why the Industrial Revolution in England, instead of encouraging birth control, led to a considerable fertility increase lasting several decades;
3. an examination of particular causes underlying early fertility regulation amongst the French peasantry, at the time of the Revolution.

1. The Data

Fertility

Recent estimates for early periods reconstructed from parish records (before 1830 for France: Henry and Blayo 1975; before 1879 for England: Wrigley and Schofield 1981) are presented in Table 11.1 alongside modern series derived by analysis of census and civil registration data; these are compared over almost two centuries, from 1750 (when the first aspects of the Industrial Revolution began to emerge in England) to 1940 (when fertility had already entered the post-transitional phase).

For France, four distinct phases emerge (see Fig. 11.1):

1. the pre-revolutionary period (1750–90): although somewhat hesitant, the movement nevertheless shows a downward trend from the years 1760–70;
2. the revolutionary period and the first half of the nineteenth century (1790–1855): this is marked by a profound change in total fertility, which falls from 5 to 3.5 children per woman. In other words, by around 1850, although there is no sign of national declines in other countries (excepting the US), fertility transition is already half-way through its course;
3. the period of modern industrialization and capitalism (1855–80): this is marked by a plateau;[5]

---

[3] Wrigley and Schofield (1981) point out that their reconstruction of English population history is robust only for the 18th and 19th centuries.

[4] Used here as an index of the stages of modernization.

[5] This plateau conceals significant local increases in regions affected by the rise of heavy industry, especially in the north and east. The phase marks what we shall refer to as the fertile crescent.

TABLE 11.1. *Total fertility: France and England, 1750–1940 (per woman)*

Period	France	England	Period	France	England	Period	France	England	England and Wales	Period	France	England and Wales
1750–1754	5.35	4.79	1800–1804	4.46	5.52	1850	3.48	4.92		1896–1900	2.90	3.62
1755–1759	5.48	4.75	1805–1809	4.41	6.01	1851–1855	3.38	4.93		1901–1905	2.79	3.40
1760–1764	5.20	4.86	1810–1814	4.39	5.88	1856–1860	3.46	5.01	4.82	1906–1910	2.60	3.14
1765–1769	5.21	4.90	1815–1819	4.36	6.26	1861–1865	3.50	5.23	4.91	1911–1915	2.25	2.84
1770–1774	5.03	5.13	1820–1824	4.23	6.11	1866–1870	3.50	5.20	4.93	1916–1920	1.65	2.40
1775–1779	5.10	5.29	1825–1829	4.13	5.85	1871–1875	3.42		4.94	1921–1925	2.42	2.39
1780–1784	5.08	5.10	1830–1834	3.82	5.31	1876–1880	3.45		4.88	1926–1930	2.30	2.01
1785–1789	5.18	5.38	1835–1839	3.71	5.19	1881–1885	3.38		4.55	1931–1935	2.16	1.79
1790–1794	4.93	5.67	1840–1844	3.64	5.11	1886–1890	3.12		4.16	1936–1940	2.07	1.79
1795–1799	4.90	5.67	1845–1849	3.50	4.87	1891–1895	2.97		3.90			

Notes: The English series 1750–1875 results from the application of the coefficient 2.05 (i.e. the inverse of the sex ratio at birth) to the series provided by Wrigley and Schofield (1981) for five-year periods from 1749–58 to 1869–73.

Sources: Blayo (1975), for France, 1740–1829; Depoid (1941), for France, 1830–50; Festy (1979), for France, 1851–1940; Festy (1979) for England and Wales, 1856–1940; Wrigley and Schofield (1981), for England, without Monmouth, 1750–1870.

4. the consolidation of modern economic growth (1880–1940): fertility declines consistently, reaching the last stage of transition, with an average level of 2 children per woman.

This chronological breakdown is noteworthy because there is every reason to think that the mechanisms at work change from one period to another, and that the opposition that different authors have perceived between certain arguments may, by this fact, be misleading, if not entirely artificial.

The development in England is clearer: the first decades of the Industrial Revolution are accompanied by an extraordinary increase in fertility which reaches its historical maximum around 1815 with an average of more than 6 children per woman: before the Industrial Revolution the long-standing and relatively low level was only around 4 to 4.5. With the mass exodus of village communities and young labour in the mills, traditional checks on marriage were released. Celibacy became rarer and marriage occurred at a significantly earlier age: the average age at first marriage between those born from 1675–99 and 1775–99 fell by almost 3 years (from 26.8 to 24.1) (Wrigley and Schofield 1981: 424). The consequent increase in fertility was then matched by a decline in the years 1820–30, giving the impression of a large fluctuation. Fertility transition did not, however, begin until much later, at the end of the 1870s, when the change was sudden and the trend steep.

Fertility and the Stages of Modern Economic Growth

Any comparison of standards of living between countries (usually expressed in terms of real per capita income) is complex and somewhat arbitrary. The problems confronting attempts to compare France and England are no different. However, Marczewski (1965) has shown how comparisons may be carried out systematically; and Bairoch (1976),[6] by reducing all values to a single scale of relative prices (based on the United States in 1960) has been able to reconstruct the historical development of real per capita income in Europe, as expressed in terms of this unit. This is the series we have adopted for the period beginning 1830, extending it further back in time in light of available retrospective estimates (Table 11.2), with adjustments for territorial changes. Because of the inaccuracy of estimates for earlier periods and the artificial nature of comparison over very long durations, only orders of magnitude and particularly marked trends are worth retaining.

The French fertility decline became apparent almost half a century before modern economic growth began; economic historians generally date the latter around 1830,[7] as Fig. 11.1 suggests. The standard of living was then 3.5

---

[6] Bairoch bases his work on the method and observations of Gilbert and Kravis (1954).

[7] While this question is hotly disputed (see Chapter 17), there is agreement on certain basic facts: on the eve of the Revolution the standard of living was still very low, and equivalent to or slightly below that of England.

TABLE 11.2. *Estimates of real product per inhabitant, France and Great Britain, 1750–1938 (gross domestic product at market prices, in 1960 $US)*

Year[a]	France	Great Britain	Year[a]	France	Great Britain	Year[a]	France	Great Britain	Year[a]	France	Great Britain
1750	—	181	1800	—	243	1850	333	480	1900	610	911
1760	—	198	1810	196[b]	249	1860	365	584	1910	685	934
1770	—	181	1820	230	288	1870	(437)	655	1913	695	996
1780	197[c]	196	1830	264	360	1880	470	708	1925	893	970
1790	—	204	1840	302	412	1890	520	814	1938	936	1,181

[a] The values indicated are triennial averages for the period spanning the year in question, except for 1913 and 1938.
[b] 1803–12.
[c] 1781–90.

Sources: Period beginning 1830: Bairoch's estimates (1976), for the dates 1830, 1860, 1913, 1925, 1928. For all other dates Bairoch's estimates have been adjusted to conform to present-day national boundaries. Period after 1830: the retrospective series of Deane and Cole (1964), for Great Britain; the retrospective series of Markovitch (1966) and Henry and Blayo (1975) (population), for France.

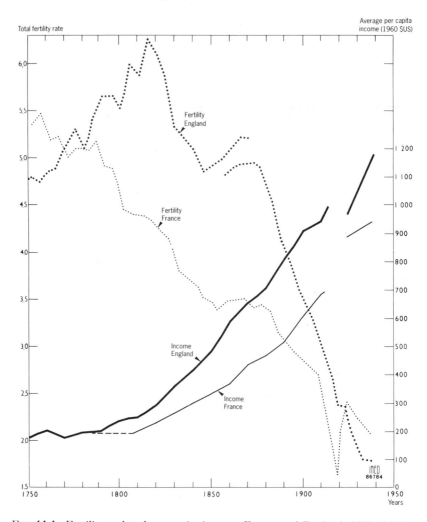

FIG. 11.1. Fertility and real per capita income, France and England, 1750–1940

times lower than it was in England at the start of its transition.[8] With a French fertility/income ratio, the English transition would have begun in the mid-eighteenth century; conversely, with an English fertility–income ratio, French fertility would not have fallen until just before the First World War. Owing to the absence of series for the eighteenth century, it is difficult to assess economic growth during the decades preceding fertility decline, but it is not unlikely that a degree of agricultural progress had been made.

[8] Or, more exactly, Great Britain excluding Ireland.

2. Industrial Revolution without Demographic Revolution: The English Case

Controversy over English Priority

The population of France on the eve of the Revolution was four times that of England, but it remained essentially an agricultural nation. The place of industry in its economy has, however, long been underestimated. At the beginning of the nineteenth century the total industrial production of France was equal to its English counterpart, and according to Markovitch's data, industrial production would have overtaken that of agriculture before 1789. Conventional estimates, however, have dated this equalization a century later, around 1885. Industrial production in Great Britain overtook agricultural production between 1811 and 1821 (Deane and Cole 1964). In fact, estimates of British national income prior to 1841 understate industrial production, many activities now regarded as belonging to industry such as those connected with retail trade or cottage industry (Marczewski 1965) being omitted. Conversely, French estimates are based on a wider definition, production being measured from consumption of raw materials; industrial activity therefore embraces not only products of light and cottage industry (very important in the French countryside), but domestic production and consumption among the peasants. After correction (i.e. by returning to current definitions), the equalization of agricultural production and industrial production seems to have occurred in France around 1830, representing 20 years' delay on England, but a considerable advance on the other great industrial powers such as Germany and the US (1850–60), Japan (1925), or Italy (1930) (Kuznets 1966). By this criterion, demographic history appears more consistent with economic history.

As just noted, the industrial power of England and France was comparable immediately before the Revolution; but because of differences in population size, per capita production was far higher in England. Arthur Young (1769) sums this up admirably: 'in a word, England is more prosperous; France richer and more powerful'. The following 25 years were to be disastrous: Revolution and Empire stopped the expansion of industry and compromised foreign trade. By 1820, England's share of world trade was double that of France (approximately 40% compared with 18%); its per capita income was henceforth appreciably higher, and this difference increased over the next four decades. Political unrest broke the industrial impetus of France, leaving England beyond competition.

The nature of industrialization in the two countries also differed considerably: from the beginning of the nineteenth century, big industry played the fundamental role in England, whilst in France production was split into numerous small traditional enterprises of a fairly exclusive kind. While this makes comparison problematic, the British industrial lead can scarcely be contested.

The British Advantage on the Eve of the French Revolution

The language of aggregates used up to now merely gives us outcomes, while concealing fundamental causes of movement. Contemporary observers were well aware that a new dynamic had developed in England in the seventeenth and eighteenth centuries. In 1691, Petty argued that Britain was a rival to France, and enumerated the factors which would ultimately enable it to take the lead; commerce, shipping, and the colonies. In 1769, Young saw the two countries as equals, refused to decide between them, and confined himself to composing a descriptive table of their respective strengths and weaknesses. By the beginning of the nineteenth century reference to France, which had been *de rigueur* from King to Chalmers, through Davenant and Young, began to disappear. Colquhoun (1814), for example, assigned England the role of dominant power, destined to conquer the entire world. With time, the country had acquired or consolidated its decisive advantages: scientific discovery, agricultural revolution, urbanization, industrial concentration, maritime and financial strength, and social stability.

Scientific Discoveries

The years 1760 to 1770 were rich in crucial inventions; the steam-engine, spinning jenny, and other devices mark the beginning of an ever increasing succession of patents. This burst of creativity boosted certain industries like textiles and metallurgy, which resulted in turn in soaring profits, falling production costs, and the liberation of manpower for new industries. Such developments, despite the handicap of scale,[9] brought about the differences noted between France and England. There was no doubt about such a technical lead: French engineers and contractors crossed the Channel in order to observe the English model.

Agricultural Revolution

A substantial change seems to have emerged in the first half of the eighteenth century: England became a regular exporter of foodstuffs. But from 1760 the process of land enclosure encouraged a restructuring, in which small tenant farmers were ousted to the advantage of large landowners, through confiscation of previously shared property. With population increase from the mid-1770s, England changed to a net importer of cereals, whilst more profitable industrial exports, facilitated by the massive transfer of labour, were beginning

---

[9] Compensated, however, by greater exploitation of the foreign market.

to take over. French agriculture around 1750–60 was peppered with examples borrowed from the pioneering English models; by the eighteenth century, the area cultivated in wheat had increased by a third and the yield per hectare by a tenth. Yet according to Young (1792), the aggregate production per working farmer in England was about 30% higher than that in France. The structural change in the working population is in this respect quite telling: by the beginning of the nineteenth century the portion of the work-force employed in the 'farming, forestry, and fishing' sector was about half that of France (35.9% in England in 1801 as opposed to almost 70% in France: Deane and Cole 1964; Toutain 1961).

In other words, all things being equal, and discounting international trade, one English farming family was sufficient to feed two other families, whereas in France it took two families of farmers to feed one non-farming family; the increase in agricultural productivity was negligible before 1830–40. Thus, the sectoral redistribution of the English working population was by that time accomplished, and the process of concentrating land was also very advanced; the accompanying development of the first large-scale farming enterprises facilitated an accumulation of capital and the implementation of new techniques of production. Moreover, the difference in average income between industry and agriculture according to figures produced by Colquhoun (1814) was around 50%;[10] in France, by way of contrast, this difference, assessed in terms of current market prices, was of the order of 5 to 1 (Marczewski 1965). This illustrates both the agricultural underproductivity[11] of France and its relative industrial backwardness.

Urbanization

The growth of cities was another aspect of the structural changes which spread through English society. With the spread of enclosures, and displacement of village communities, there emerged a mobile proletariat without ties (the notorious 'reserve army' of capitalism), which brought with it a new market for building, food, textile, and other industries. At the beginning of the nineteenth century the proportion of town-dwellers in Britain was over half as much as in France (approximately 35% lived in towns of 2,000 or more inhabitants, as compared with 22%); by the beginning of the fertility transition, three-quarters of the population were urban dwellers, whereas in France the movement began with a 75% rural population.

---

[10] The income of the 6,129,000 members of families employed in agriculture or mining, in 1812, amounted to £107,248 million (or £17.50 per head), whereas that of the 7,072,000 members of families employed in industry, commerce, or shipping amounted to £183,908 million (or £26 per head).

[11] Contemporary accounts are unanimous on the fact that the French peasant classes were by comparison extremely poor, especially in certain regions.

Industrial Concentration

The development of industry and commerce near to mining areas opened up the era of mass production, in sharp contrast to the French world of small ateliers and shops; this, in turn, stimulated the spread of technical innovations, as well as the capacity for expanding exports.

Maritime and Naval Power

Britain's superiority at sea guaranteed its commercial advantage, which, along with the fall in the cost of shipping, proved crucial. But a political event also accrued to its advantage: the invasion of The Netherlands by Napoleon's army, which caused Amsterdam to cede its financial supremacy to London.

Social Climate

The English Revolution occurred a century before the French Revolution. French political life was a good deal more unstable: the religious persecutions, notably the forced departure of the Huguenots, were economically very damaging and still recent in memory; it took little to spark social unrest. In England, on the other hand, the great social disturbances seemed to be over: whilst society was rigidly stratified, there was a greater acceptance of social order. Contrary to all expectation (Marx's included), the working class accepted its condition without rebellion, despite its numbers and the extent to which it was exploited. This difference in social climate became crucial during the period of the French Revolution, since it was then that England moved noticeably ahead.

Britain's Spectacular Progress Matched by its Considerable and Lasting Increase in Fertility

At the end of the eighteenth century, England experienced simultaneously a decline in mortality and a relaxation of fertility regulation, as its nuptiality regime became more flexible. The persistence of a type of traditional fertility behaviour—contrary to the model of demographic transition—may be surprising at first, but numerous reasons combined to facilitate this. Since all of them are more or less specific to British history, let us examine them chronologically:

1. The first was a loosening of constraints on subsistence connected, to begin with, with the agricultural revolution, and then furthered by the importation of foodstuffs.

2. Second, the Poor Laws, condemned by Malthus in his *Essay* (1798), had in 1795 introduced a new clause establishing a sliding scale of allowances, pegged on the price of bread. This clause was rigorously maintained until

TABLE 11.3. *The spread of enclosures*

Period	Average annual number of hectares
1727–1760	887
1761–1792	6,047
1793–1801	12,313
1802–1815	21,379
1816–1845	2,688

1834. Under the English system of poor relief established by Queen Elizabeth in 1601, assistance was decentralized and carried out by individual parishes; such a system proved to be of great help given the rapid spread of enclosures, which drove the poorer peasantry off the land. Table 11.3 gives the progress of enclosures of common land. The movement reached its peak at the turn of the century. According to a parliamentary report in 1803, over a million persons were then dependent on parish subsidies. More precisely, 1,040,716 were in receipt of relief, deriving from the solidarity of 9,343,561 of their fellow citizens (Colquhoun 1814). One in ten people were thus being maintained by public charity.

In times of stress, reflected in the high price of bread, neither abject poverty nor total ruination could occur: the system guaranteed subsistence. But there was another view of the matter, which considered that as good as the Poor Law might be in relieving hardship, it led to a lack of concern, prolificness, and even immorality. The scale of allocation was arranged such that allowances for children of large families were high in proportion to the adult allocation; in short, 'the more children a man had, the better off he would be' (Leroy-Beaulieu 1913). Moreover, children born out of wedlock and other illegitimates gained the right to larger allowances than their legitimate counterparts. No wonder Malthus, as an advocate of forethought and moral constraint, was concerned.

3. The third factor underlying Britain's sustained high fertility was the growth of large industry, with its concomitant effects on employment and social structure. The multitudes uprooted from the countryside to work in the cities, and swelled by the enclosure movement, were, as a contemporary expression put it, 'divorced from the land'. This confounding of time-honoured customs opened a wide thoroughfare for change. The appetites of the new industry were enormous: men, women, and (particularly from 1810 to 1820) children[12] were engulfed; salaries were low, hours long, the demand for hands

---

[12] At the 1851 census, the number of children under 10 years in the working population was around 50,000. This is of course a conservative estimate, and probably well below the actual figure.

seemingly limitless. In the factory towns, people married young and had large families:[13] children found employment from the earliest age; as young as 6–7 years they ceased to be wholly dependent on their parents and began to contribute to the family income.

4. Fourth, emigration came to play the role of safety-valve, especially from the 1840s onwards, when population increase amplified by the decline in mortality began to put pressure on economic structures. The Englishman was spontaneously outward-looking, and the venture of emigration was facilitated by progress in shipping and the creation of networks and organized aid for emigrants. The Frenchman was, in contrast, inclined to be home-loving, while Paris answered to all the attractions represented by the New World. Everything was geared to dissuading departure, and French law had been set against emigration for centuries.

5. The final factor was the relative delay in the decline of infant mortality. Particularly in industrial towns, housing and nutrition were problematic, alcoholism was rife, large families proliferated, and mothers—absent and exhausted by factor work—were unable to look after their children.

The turning-point in marital fertility came only in 1877, when England was at its peak. By this time profound social changes had occurred, and the long chapter of unfettered liberalism was over. For several decades, threatened by the revolutionary disturbances which had repeatedly shaken France, and then Europe, the ruling classes had been steadily reviewing social legislation. Compulsory schooling was introduced in 1876, and a sensational lawsuit (the Bradlaugh–Besant trial) publicized the availability of contraceptive information, and in 1875 independent workers' organizations were established and recognized legally. This meant that henceforth the working class—which already composed over half of the working population and thus a large part of the body of English society—was put on corresponding terms with other social groups. By one of those characteristic quirks of history, English industrialism—the veritable nightmare of early nineteenth-century social thinkers—produced a model of social legislation. This probably owed precisely to Britain's excesses; the improvements Bismarck, for example, introduced in Germany were made out of fear of workers' revolt. At the end of the nineteenth century, English labourers had the highest salaries and the shortest working day in Europe. From the law of 1819, which was then considered a great step forward (it fixed the lower age limit for signing on in the mills at 9 years, allowing a maximum working day of 12 hours), to the law of 1833 which introduced stricter regulation of child labour, hours, and pay, and then that of 1847 on female labour (maximum of 10 hours per day), to compulsory schooling, the ground covered was immense. This

---

[13] France experienced a similar phenomenon during its period of capitalist industrialization, under the Second Empire. In northern and eastern areas affected by the boom in the steel industry, traditional checks on marriage and procreation relaxed.

development marked the beginning of the modern age: with it fertility ceased to be instrumental, and procreation—which had become somewhat more restrained—began gradually to respond to new motivations.

The logic animating the English experience would therefore appear to hold no fundamental differences from that of other Western countries; rather, certain specific economic and institutional factors were responsible for delaying transition to the limited family. The French case, however, is clearly atypical.

3. Demographic Revolution without Industrial Revolution: The Case of France

Strictly speaking, there is no disagreement on the issue of French demographic priority. Early instances of marital fertility regulation have of course been detected elsewhere here and there in certain regions or social milieux, but this is not surprising, since, with a few rare exceptions, we know that all human societies have practised a degree of birth control—and under the most varied forms, with an intensity proportionate to the pressure of circumstances. What is new about the French case is that the phenomenon is not reversible, and it applies on the scale of a large country within a traditional agrarian context. The origins of the French pattern in the last third of the eighteenth century may be traced to three domains: the revolution of ideas, the political climate, and the agrarian question.

The Revolution in Ideas

The demographic revolution, like its political counterpart, issued from a long process of intellectual maturation as well as a spontaneous uprising in collective feelings. The signs were perceptible several decades earlier, both in philosophical writings—especially the success which they met—and through more profound indications, such as religious practice and attitudes to life.

The Decline of Religious Sentiment

The seventeenth century witnessed a scientific revolution which shook accepted beliefs. At the same time, religious unrest encouraged biblical criticism and a questioning of dogmas, likewise exciting the general appetite for learning. There was a ubiquitous sense of cultural ferment, even among the peasantry— which, it is true, remained poorly educated, but none the less made significant progress over the course of a century.[14] Enlightenment spread, increasingly

[14] For the whole of France, the proportion of spouses capable of signing the marriage register doubled amongst women and increased by two-thirds amongst the men (27% and 47% in 1786–90, compared with 14% and 29% in 1686–90, respectively: Fleury and Valmary 1957).

penetrating outside urban centres. In the name of Reason—the goddess of the century—folklore and obscurantism were combated. The clergy, which had worked so hard for Enlightenment's progress, was, in turn, itself denounced as a locus of privilege. Such intellectual ferment doubtless contributed to the weakening of religious belief; on the eve of the Revolution, the signs of indifference were multiplying, and spreading beyond even the agnostically inclined bourgeoisie to previously devout quarters (Le Bras 1942).

None the less, following the persecutions, 'religious sentiment' gained a new strength, at least in so far as may be assessed from indicators of religious practice. Other aspects of changing mental attitudes seem, however, to have been more permanently affected.

An Individualist and Libertarian Revolution

Amongst the principles of 1789, individualism in its modern definition attained the highest importance: the individual's quest for success and happiness, his rejection of constraints, his inalienable rights were all affirmed. This upheaval went to the deepest level, overturning tradition, authority, and hierarchy. In short, all established things were weighed, discussed, and subjected to sacred Reason. Philosophical ideas spread all the more easily because the nobility—abused by the monarchy, alienated from the peasants, and humiliated by the rising bourgeoisie—had lost its prestige. The emerging improvements in daily life stirred great hopes, and these were further excited by the promise of the *philosophes*, who became custodians of the new spirit. Class structure based on hereditary rights had been rejected for some time, and the Revolution would further break down the barriers between social classes. It would increase the thirst for equality and stimulate the social ambition of families, both for themselves and for their progeny. Social promotion existed under the *ancien régime*, but it was weak and required the efforts of several generations. A century before Dumont's coinage of the singularly apt term of 'social capillarity' (1890), a consciousness of social stratification and of strategies for getting around it were more or less an obsession. Restriction of births appeared to be one of the chief instruments of these strategies: the revolutionary discourse opposed number to happiness, and populationist doctrines were fought against. At the same time, in certain social strata at least, new sentiments emerged, which were interpreted well in Rousseau's *Émile* (1762). Children soon became objects of interest and then of special attention; maternal feeling developed (Ariès 1948), and fathers themselves discovered new responsibilities with regard to their offspring. France was moving towards the 'rationalization of sexual life' (Wolf 1913).

The Political Context

The early part of the decline in French fertility was slow and limited, reflecting the adaptation of fertility to mortality decline. Between 1795–99 and

1800–04, total fertility fell from 4.90 to 4.46. The first real swing in fertility occurred somewhat later, in the middle of upheaval, that is, after the Reign of Terror and the massacres, but before Napoleon's military exploits. Increasing regulation of fertility within marriage gained precedence over nuptiality control; the latter was rapidly becoming insufficient as the mortality decline continued, and the peasant economy was threatened with imbalance. The wars which followed, coming after almost a century of more or less unbroken peace, had devastating effects: they killed over a million men,[15] ruined entire regions, and isolated the country. Above all, they created a sense of deadlock, demoralization, and pointless suffering. The nation emerged weakened and, as was sometimes said a century later, after the First World War, the best part of its population had been lost. There was scarcely any sign of a recovery in fertility once the hostilities ceased. In a third of a century, average family size would decline by almost a full point: from 1815–19 to 1851–55, total fertility fell from 4.36 to 3.38. The situation in this respect recalls the case of Germany under the Third Reich.

The Agrarian Issue

The similar estimates of Ganilh (1806) and Young (1792) show that, at about the time of the Revolution, 78% of the population lived in the countryside and 68% off farming. Anything that affected the conditions of the peasantry or the pattern of landholding was thus a determining factor. But France had for some time been a populous land, cultivated and cleared to its last corners. High demographic growth during the whole of the eighteenth century only exacerbated the food problem, whilst the interest in agronomy from 1750 onwards did nothing to improve the lot of the peasant. Food production failed to really get going, and many provinces had to await the mid-nineteenth-century development of railways and the rise of commerce before anything could be done to assist their isolation and agricultural progress. Added to this sense of overcrowding in the French countryside was an extraordinary landholding and agrarian system—which the Revolution would only extend and consecrate—also entirely favourable to Malthusianism.

The Over-Population of the French Countryside

Braudel (1967) has remarked that France was 'prematurely over-populated'. The state of over-population in the eighteenth-century countryside has some-times been compared with that of rural China. In addition to the criterion of relative density, there is no shortage of measurements of over-population. For example: the impoverishment of diet by increased consumption of potatoes, maize, and buckwheat, to the detriment of the main cereals (Morineau 1974);

---

[15] Houdaille (1970) estimated the losses through the Revolution and the Empire at 1.3 million.

or the increase in agricultural prices from 1760 to 1820 (after which the relative price of wheat fell). The absence of agricultural revolution is manifest: cereal production was at a standstill, fertilizers were scarcely used, and what slight progress in production was achieved occurred at the price of intensive labour—mostly by clearing more land for cultivation (Augé-Laribé 1955): the fact that the country did not experience more famine owed more to improvements in storage and the circulation of supplies of grain than to improvements in production techniques. Basically, farming remained primitive; neglected by the authorities, and incapable of investment for want of capital (properties were often very small), it seemed condemned to poverty. Hence voluntary control of population growth seemed the only means of avoiding the removal of surplus by mortality[16]—all the more for the fact that emigration was not only impeded by the failure of colonial policy (in 1763, at the outcome of the Seven Years War, France surrendered Canada to England and Louisiana to Spain), but prohibited by laws dating from the Middle Ages and resuscitated in the eighteenth century (Blacker 1957).

The Small Family Property

In addition to the geographical diversity of inheritance systems, the development of the French agrarian system appears unique in Europe. By the eighteenth century, serfdom, whilst still prevalent in most of Europe, no longer existed in France: the peasants were personally free, and generally property-holders. This phenomenon was the result of a slow development which had been accomplished since the Middle Ages, the great wave of liberation dating to the fourteenth and fifteenth centuries. With time, lands were increasingly parcelled out, resulting in a predominance of small and medium-sized farms. Whilst the peasants in England also had their freedom, the property system there was completely different: farm holdings tended to be consolidated over time as small farmers who were victims of the enclosure system were dispossessed. There were two important historical periods of enclosure: 1470 to 1530 and especially, as we have seen, 1730 to 1850. This was one of the determinants of Britain's Industrial Revolution and without doubt one of the causes of the delay of its demographic revolution. Conversely, in France the division of property was codified by the Revolution of 1789, both by the abolition of the rights of the eldest child in 1790–91, and by the replacement of primogeniture by equal partition under the Napoleonic code.

---

[16] Disasters of this sort occurred in several European countries in the 19th century: Ireland, Russia, and even Prussia. Around 1775 the aggregate density of the population of France was 50 people per km^2—a considerable figure for the period. This density was higher than that of England and Germany, and comparable to that of The Netherlands. If other important characteristics are taken into account—in particular the geographic relief of the country with reference to agriculturally serviceable land—the French situation is utterly unique.

Such changes contributed to the delay of France's Industrial Revolution,[17] while precipitating its demographic revolution.

'The *ancien régime* produced the eldest son; the new, the only son.' This formula is familiar enough. It has been defended by Le Play and his followers (including Cheysson), and, from the end of the nineteenth century, modified if not opposed by writers such as Levasseur and Leroy-Beaulieu, Le Play's position was clear: 'A direct consequence of our system of inheritance is the systematic sterility of marriages.' No longer having, as in the past, the power to dispose of family property, the only way a father could consider himself able to ensure his children's happiness was by limiting their number. The loss of an inheritance would, for his descendants, amount to the loss of liberty[18] and would, in consequence, signify their downward social mobility. After centuries of struggle for liberty and the acquisition of land, any unplanned birth could ruin the efforts of the family line.

With the sale of national property and the sharing of common land, peasant landholding increased. The Revolution certainly improved the situation of well-off peasants who were already landowners, and increased the number of proprietors enormously. However, many small peasant farmers were in fact ruined by such purchases, despite the abolition of feudal rents: hence their relentless efforts to preserve the integrity of their holdings, generation after generation. This redistribution of lands represented the final revenge of the small family holding on the large estate, whether noble or ecclesiastical: the 'triumph of the small', as Le Roy-Ladurie (1975) has put it. Although the vast majority of peasants were landowners, their tenures were tiny and not easily divisible. The comparison with Great Britain is illuminating: in France, in 1830, landowners and their families represented 20 million persons out of 32 million inhabitants; the comparable figures for Great Britain were 3.4 million out of 23.5 million inhabitants (7.5 million of which were in Ireland[19]).

It was in this nation of small rural landowners that the modern demographic transition began. In 1850, whilst urbanization was still at its earliest stage (only 25% of the population were living in towns), fertility had already crossed the half-way mark between the traditional regime (an average of 5 or more children per woman) and modernity (2 or less). Around 1860, rural fertility was below that of provincial towns; 27 departments, mostly rural, even had a fertility below that of Paris (Tugault 1975). The peasant landowner had followed the example of the pre-Revolution noble.

As attractive as it may seem, this view is not entirely convincing. Various arguments can be put forward against it:

---

[17] By slowing down both the rural exodus towards industry and the agricultural demand for industrial products.

[18] It effectively forced them to hire themselves out to other landowners.

[19] Where property was more widely distributed.

1. The first signs of fertility decline were evident in certain provinces before the Revolution, from around the 1770s or 1780s.

2. According to Henry's survey, the south-west of France—where primogeniture was customary under the *ancien régime*—had lower fertility than other regions; despite the maintenance of this custom throughout the nineteenth century, fertility adhered to the same pattern of development as experienced in other regions.

3. The Revolution was not the definitive source of fundamental change. For example, in northern France, where common law was the norm, primogeniture hardly existed except among the aristocracy: the common people were already accustomed to more or less equal sharing. And in the south, where written law was practised, primogeniture continued, as we have noted, into the nineteenth century. The letter of the law even accorded a certain latitude to the testator: the disposable portion of an estate was not in fact as small as Le Play and his followers implied, since the testator could dispose freely of at least a quarter of family assets, and thus could act effectively on the part of one or another child. In other words, if he had two children, nothing prevented him legally from bequeathing two-thirds of his fortune to the eldest, or preferred, legatee; and if he had three children, he could bequeath half to the eldest, and only a quarter to the other two. He could therefore allocate twice as much to a preferred heir as to either of the others. Nevertheless, with the exception of the Midi, where preference for the eldest long continued, this disposal was scarcely ever carried out by lawyers since the general consensus favoured equal sharing (Leroy-Beaulieu 1913). In this, law was but the product of custom.

4. Many countries (Belgium, Italy, The Netherlands, Austria, and Prussia) adopted similar prescriptions[20] to that of France without experiencing the same drastic drop in fertility.

5. Finally, from a theoretical point of view, nothing rules out the possibility that the right of the eldest could itself have been a factor in fertility decline, through the limits it imposed on marriage. This, at least, was Montesquieu's opinion. Conversely, by facilitating marriage, equal partition might have resulted in increased fertility. Thus, on a priori grounds, the effects of a given method of partition on marital fertility could have worked contrary to its effects on the formation of marriages: on the one hand, with primogeniture, you have late but very fertile marriages; whilst, on the other, equal partition favours early but not very fertile marriages. There is no certain conclusion. The actual situation, in consequence, would be a matter of proportion, depending on the distribution of the farming population by landholding rules and the way property was divided.

---

[20] England is the most notable exception: it is the only country which allows absolute freedom to the testator.

Although Le Play's thesis has scarcely been subjected to empirical test, a considerable if none the less insufficient body of evidence may still be brought to bear on it. Pingaud's historical study of a village in Bourgogne (1971) shows, for example, that birth control was used effectively to avoid the division of lands, but that, far from being general practice, the phenomenon was restricted to a small number of well-off peasants. Study of aggregate data on 67 predominantly agricultural departments at the time of the second half of the nineteenth century has established that indivisibility of inheritance (very closely related to family structure) was indeed significantly and positively associated with marital fertility, and negatively related to nuptiality and net immigration (the departure of the younger children). However, where small farming was relatively more intense, the phenomenon did not appear to be statistically connected with inheritance practices, but was related to a low presence of stem families and to low nuptiality (Berkner and Mendels 1978). Apart from the fact that the calculation refers to a later period (the model of the 'restricted' family was by then generally widespread at a national level, and furthermore, agricultural progress and the rise of industry was tending to reduce demographic pressure on the countryside), the role of certain other fundamental variables should be considered, such as the density of habitation, soil fertility, the nature of cultivation, and differential mortality. The omission of such variables could easily ruin the finest theoretical edifice.

It is thus not so much the law in itself, but the significance of the particular socio-economic contexts in which it occurs (demographic pressure, the rise of individualism, revolutionary conflict), which left such an imprint on French population history. Of course, the fertility decline had begun before the Napoleonic code was introduced; but the security and, more significantly, the legitimization it brought to certain aspects of social behaviour very probably accelerated the tendency of peasant families to limit their issue. In this sense, differences in social structure may have an important role to play in explaining the different way in which fertility responded to the decline in mortality. In one case—France—one is dealing with a nation of small entrepreneurs, owners of smallholdings preoccupied with the lack of new land to cultivate; in the other—England—one is dealing with salaried labourers and merchants, and therefore a more varied and open—and hence flexible—economic structure. As Reinhard wrote (1946), summing up the French Revolution:

The most important consequences were in no way derived from laws pertaining to the family, or inheritance, but from the new structure and the new social climate. In short, social capillarity and the demographic revolution. . . . The relation between the demographic revolution and the political revolution was not a matter of cause and effect. Both proceeded from a common and profound transformation of ideas, but the success of the political revolution encouraged that of the demographic revolution.

It is thus pointless to search for simple, single causes with which to explain the uniqueness of French demographic history. Many countries present one or another, and sometimes several, of the characteristics described above: individualism, a prevailing concern with population density, progressive division of property, and so forth. It was the combined action of these various, inseparable factors which resulted in such a unique development.

Consequently, the opposition often made between the theory attributed to Le Play and 'modern' theories appears purely artificial. The latter, which owe to precursors of transition theory writing at the end of the nineteenth and beginning of the twentieth centuries, like Levasseur and Leroy-Beaulieu, for example, have emphasized the effects of structural changes such as urbanization, industrialization, increased education, material comforts, and leisure activities. Granted, Le Play's theory is hardly modern, but then how modern was France in 1789? The more appropriate 'modern' theories seem to be in accounting for the final phase of the transition (i.e. the last half of the fertility transition, begun in the 1880s), the more incongruous they look for rural France before the middle of the nineteenth century.

Conclusion

This comparative picture of two national demographies will have failed to satisfy the requirements of rigorous analysis. Owing to insufficient retrospective data on differential fertility amongst the professional classes of each country, a point-for-point comparison of their experiences remains impossible. The two trajectories we have traced are, none the less, so divergent, and the institutional differences so considerable, that it appears that our observations could only be slightly modified or restated in greater detail.

In addition to differences, however, there also exist, across great distances of time and space, powerful similarities and, perhaps, historical interactions. The eighteenth century was in many respects a French epoch. France held sway in its population, its ideas, and its political life: it became the pioneer of the moral and demographic revolution. The nineteenth century was English: England exported its technical inventions and conquered the world. But are these two experiences so independent? The excesses of the French Revolution disgusted the English ruling classes, and, in so doing, may have delayed by several decades certain beneficial social reforms—perhaps thereby accelerating the initial British industrialization and deferring certain socio-political changes. In a similar vein, the excesses of English industrialism were shocking as viewed from across the Channel, and may thereby have served to justify agricultural protectionism and opposition to heavy industry.

These are only conjectures. Turning once again to interactions, we shall examine not only contrasting or counterposed national experiences, but developments linking periods in individual countries. If the excessive density of the eighteenth-century French population contributed without doubt to emerging French Malthusianism, is it not likewise plausible that today's relatively low densities, which owe no less to different national experiences, may help to explain less depressed levels of current fertility?

Bibliography to Chapter 11

ARIES, P. (1948), *Histoire des populations françaises et de leurs attitudes devant la vie depuis le XVIIIe siècle* (Paris: Self).

—— (1953), 'Sur les origines de la contraception en France', *Population*, 3: 465–72.

AUGÉ-LARIBÉ, M. (1955), *La Révolution agricole* (Paris: Michel).

BAIROCH, P. (1976), 'Europe's Gross National Product: 1800–1975', *JEEH*, 2: 273–340.

BERKNER, L. K., and MENDELS, F. F. (1978), 'Inheritance Systems, Family Structure, and Demographic Patterns in Western Europe, 1700–1900', in C. Tilly (ed.), *Historical Studies of Changing Fertility* (Princeton, NJ: Princeton University Press), 209–23.

BERTILLON, J. (1911), *La Dépopulation de la France: ses conséquences, ses causes, mesures à prendre pour la combattre* (Paris: Alcan).

BLACKER, J. G. C. (1957), 'Social Ambitions of the Bourgeoisie in 18th Century France and their Relation to Family Limitation', *Population Studies* (July), 46–63.

BLAYO, Y. (1975), 'Le Mouvement naturel de la population française de 1740 à 1860', *Population*, Special Number (Nov.), 15–64.

BRAUDEL, F. (1967), *Civilisation matérielle et capitalisme*, i (Paris: Colin).

BURET, E. (1840), *De la misère des classes laborieuses en Angleterre et en France: de la nature de la misère, de son existence, de ses effets, de ses causes et de l'insuffisance des remèdes qu'on lui a opposées jusqu'ici, avec les moyens propres à en affranchir les sociétés* (Paris: Paulin).

CHALMERS, G. (1786), *An Estimate of the Comparative Strength of Great Britain during the Present and Four Preceding Reigns and the Loss of her Trade from Every War since the Revolution* (London).

COLQUHOUN, P. (1814), *A Treatise on the Wealth, Power and Resources of the British Empire* (London).

DEANE, P., and COLE, W. A. (1964), *British Economic Growth, 1688–1959: Trends and Structure* (Cambridge: Cambridge University Press).

DEPOID, P. (1941), 'Evolution de la reproduction en France et à l'étranger depuis le début du XIXe siècle', *JSSP* (June), 206–24.

DUMONT, A. (1890), *Dépopulation et civilisation: Étude démographique* (Paris: Lecrosnier et Babé).

DUPAQUIER, J. (1973), 'De l'animal à l'homme: le mécanisme autorégulateur des populations traditionnelles', *Annales ESC*, 28: 177–211.

FESTY, P. (1979), *La Fécondité des pays occidentaux de 1870 à 1970*, Travaux et Documents (Paris: INED-Puf).

FLEURY, M., and VALMARY, P. (1957), 'Les Progrès de l'instruction élémentaire de Louis XIV à Napoléon III d'après l'enquête de Louis Maggiolo (1877–1879)', *Population*, 1: 71–92.

FURET, F., and SACHS, W. (1974), 'La Croissance de l'alphabétisation en France, XVIIIe–XIXe siècle', *Annales ESC* (May), 714–37.

GANILH, C. (1806), *Essai politique sur le revenu public des peuples de l'Antiquité, du Moyen-Age, des siècles modernes, et spécialement de la France et de l'Angleterre depuis le milieu du XVe siècle jusqu'au XIXe* (Paris: Guiguet et Michaud).

HENRY, L., and BLAYO, Y. (1975), 'La Population de la France de 1740 à 1860', *Population*, Special Number (Nov.), 71–122.

HOUDAILLE, J. (1970), 'Le Problème des pertes de guerre', *Revue d'Histoire Moderne et Contemporaine* (July–Sept.), 413–22.

INED (1959), *La Prévention des naissances dans la famille: ses origines dans les temps modernes*, Travaux et Documents, Cahier no. 35 (Paris: INED-PUF).

KINDLEBERGER, C. P. (1964), *Economic Growth in France and Britain, 1851–1950* (Cambridge, Mass.: Harvard University Press).

KING, G. (1936), *Natural and Political Observations on the State of England*, ed. G. C. Barnett (Baltimore, Md.).

KUZNETS, S. (1966), *Modern Economic Growth: Rate, Structure and Spread* (New Haven, Conn.: Yale University Press).

LABROUSSE, C. E. (1943), *La Crise de l'économie française à la fin de l'Ancien Régime et au début de la Révolution* (Paris: PUF).

LE BRAS, G. (1942–5), *Introduction à l'histoire de la pratique religieuse en France*, (Paris: PUF), i, 1942; ii, 1945.

LE BRAS, H., and TODD, E. (1981), *L'Invention de la France: atlas anthropologique et politique* (Paris: Le Livre de Poche, Coll. Pluriel).

LE PLAY, F. (1855), *Les Ouvriers européens, étude sur les travaux, la vie domestique et la condition morale des populations ouvrières de l'Europe, précédée d'un exposé de la méthode d'observation* (Paris).

LEROY-BEAULIEU, P. (1913), *La Question de la population* (Paris: Alcan).

LEVASSEUR, E. (1892), *La Population française: histoire de la population avant 1789 et démographie de la France comparée à celle des autres nations au XIXe siècle* (Paris: Rousseau), iii.

—— (1893), *Les Prix, aperçu de l'histoire économique de la valeur et du revenu de la terre en France, du commencement du XIIIe à la fin du XVIIIe siècle* (Paris).

MARCZEWSKI, J. (1965), *Le Produit physique de l'économie française de 1789 à 1913*, Cahiers de L'ISEA (Paris).

MARKOVITCH, J. (1966), *L'Industrie française de 1789 à 1964, analyse des faits*, Cahiers de l'ISEA (Paris).

MORINEAU, M. (1974), 'Révolution agricole, révolution alimentaire, révolution démographique', *Annales ESC*, 29: 335–71.

O'BRIEN, P., and KEYDER, C. (1978), *Economic Growth in Britain and France 1780–1914* (London: Allen and Unwin).

PETTY, W. (1691), *Political Arithmetick; or a Discourse concerning the Extent and Value of Lands, People, Buildings . . . As the Same Relates to Every Country in General, but more particularly to the Territories of His Majesty of Great Britain and his Neighbours of Holland, Zealand and France* (London).

PINGAUD, M. C. (1971), 'Terres et familles dans un village du Châtillonnais', *Études Rurales*, 42: 52–104.

REINHARD, M. (1946), 'La Révolution française et le problème de la population', *Population*, 3: 419–27.

ROGERS, J., and T. (1884), *Six Centuries of Work and Wages: The History of English Labour*, 2 vols. (London: Sonnenschein).

——— ——— (1902), *A History of Agriculture and Prices in England, from the Year after the Oxford Parliament (1259) to the Commencement of the Continental War (1793), Compiled Entirely from Original and Contemporaneous Records* (Oxford: Clarendon Press), vol. vii, pts. I and II.

SEE, H. (1921), *Esquisse d'une histoire du régime agraire en Europe au XVIIIe et XIXe siècles* (Paris: Girard).

THOMPSON, E. P. (1964), *The Making of the English Working Class* (London: Gollancz).

TOCQUEVILLE, A. de (1856), *L'Ancien Régime et la Révolution* (Paris: Michel-Lévy Frères).

TODD, E. (1983), *La Troisième Planète: structures familiales et systèmes idéologiques* (Paris: Seuil).

TOUTAIN, J. C. (1961), 'Le Produit de l'agriculture française de 1700 à 1948, 2: La Croissance', in *Histoire Quantitative de l'Économie Française*, Cahiers de L'ISEA, no. 115 (Paris).

TUGAULT, Y. (1975), *Fécondité et urbanisation*, Travaux et Documents, Cahier no. 74 (Paris: INED-PUF).

YOUNG, A. (1769), *Letter concerning the Present State of the French Nation, Containing a Comprehensive View of the Political States, Agriculture, Trade and Commerce, Revenues; with a Complete Comparison between France and Great Britain* (London: Nicoll).

——— (1792), *Travels during the Years 1787, 1788 and 1789, Undertaken more particularly with a View of Ascertaining the Cultivation, Wealth, Resources and National Prosperity of the Kingdom of France* (Bury St Edmund's).

WOLF, J. (1913), *Das Zweikindersystem im Anmarsh und der Feldzug dagegen* (Berlin: Hirschwald).

WRIGLEY, E. A., and SCHOFIELD, R. S. (1981), *The Population History of England 1541–1871: A Reconstruction* (London: Edward Arnold).

12 European Transitions: From Malthus to Pincus

> It is painful to be a woman. When you become a woman, it hurts. When you become beloved, it hurts. When you become a mother, it hurts. But the most intolerable pain in the world is that of the woman who has not experienced all these pains, down to the very last.
>
> (Blaga Dimitrova)

EXCEPT for a few places like Ireland and Albania, on the eve of the First World War Europe had embarked upon the modern fertility decline. The system of fertility regulation drew upon much earlier sources. From the time of the Renaissance, in those densely populated areas of western Europe where the dominant countries which would be future colonial powers were gathering strength, a regime of delayed and restricted marriage based on a degree of sexual asceticism (of religious inspiration) was establishing itself. This phenomenon has no known historical equivalent. Marriage restriction as a means of birth control[1] is capable, as already seen, of reducing fertility considerably. It is more or less intense depending on the pressure of subsistence.[2]

However flexible this homeostatic system of adapting human numbers to the environment may have been, it still had its limits. It ceased to be sufficient when the mortality decline reached a certain level, thus giving a new boost to demographic growth. For example, in the third quarter of the nineteenth century, despite emigration, the rate of population growth in a country like Sweden was two or three times higher than a century earlier. The transition from a regime of early and universal nuptiality, with a singulate mean age at marriage of 17.5 years and lifetime celibacy practically nil, to a regime of delayed and restricted nuptiality, with marriage deferred by an average of 10 years and prohibited to almost one-fifth of the population, would result, assuming an age-specific fertility schedule like the Hutterites',[3] in a 50% reduction of the aggregate fertility level. Fertility would then average around 5.6 children per woman as opposed to 11.2.[4] China before 1930, with a

---

[1] In western Europe illegitimate fertility was censured by the Church, and was traditionally rare, except in Sweden and Germany.

[2] In the 19th century certain mountainous countries (Switzerland and Portugal) and those with dense populations (Belgium) experienced later marriage and more frequent celibacy.

[3] The fertility rate at 15–19 years is assumed to have been 300 per 1000.

[4] Whether married or unmarried; extra-marital fertility is presumed nil.

singulate mean age at marriage of 17.6 years, and 0.1% lifetime non-marriage, provides a classic example of the starting situation. Sweden at the end of the nineteenth century provides a contrasting case of the operation of the restricted regime: singulate mean age at marriage 27.5 years; proportion non-marrying 18.7%. But even with such restriction, fertility still remained at such a level that demographic growth could only be checked by continuing and very high mortality: the system presumes only a 0.366 chance of survival from birth to the mean child-bearing age.[5] If we assume fertility and mortality equal to that of France just before the Revolution,[6] the proportion of women destined to remain unmarried would, in order to maintain demographic equilibrium, reach a quarter of the population, and the singulate mean age at marriage for the remainder would be close on 30 years.[7] Such a solution presents manifest social difficulties. The privilege of sex being reserved solely for married couples, it is difficult to imagine—however much the state of chastity was then revered—a population barred from sexual relations to this degree. By the end of the nineteenth century this early type of delayed and non-universal marriage system was receding in western Europe whilst in the east a decline in legitimate fertility was spreading.

The role of mortality has been considered fundamental by all theorists of the transition. That mortality decline precedes the decline in fertility remains the primary postulate, with the decline in infant mortality then appearing as a necessary condition of a reduction in the number of wanted children. However, the usual frame of reference for explaining fertility decline is much broader, introducing the most diverse factors. The accent has generally been placed on the influence of industrial and urban civilization, and the corresponding transformations in the system of values. The arguments put forward in a long line of writers from several countries—as much in Landry (1934, 1949) as in Notestein (1946, 1953)—cover a very wide spectrum. Notestein himself (1953) admits that it is 'impossible to be precise about the various causal factors' behind the phenomenon.

It was only subsequently, with Grauman's narrower account of the circumstances of fertility decline in terms of socio-economic measures (1960)—

---

[5] $1 \div (5.6 \times 0.488) = 0.366$.

[6] Between 1750 and 1780, the population increased by an average of 0.39% per year. Between the mortality tables for 1740–49 and 1780–89, the number of male survivors to the average age at first marriage increased by 10%, producing an additional threat of fragmentation of family farms. With fertility at an average level of 5.4 children per woman, the coefficient of inheritance would have increased from 1.1 to 1.2 between these two generations. In other words, all things being equal, in a century (or, rather, in the space of four generations) the size of farms was reduced by 50%. If the initial and the ultimate size of the farm property are designated by P_0 and P_1, and the probability of survival to average age at marriage by S_m, the average fertility of a couple as F, and the number of intergenerational intervals under consideration as I, the equation is: $P_1/P_0 = 1 \div (F \times S_m/2)^I$.

[7] More precisely, 28.3 years. Celibacy and a higher marriage age were the only methods of birth control acknowledged by the Church.

the 'theory of thresholds'—that the explanatory framework became the object of quantitative evaluation, along with the simplification, or even schematization, that this type of exercise entails.

This chapter has four main objectives:

1. to give a more precise verification of the central assumption of transition theory—the principle of priority with regard to mortality decline—which, as already seen (Chapter 5), has been disputed for some years;
2. to examine the possible relation between fertility and a general measure of development (increase in real per capita income), through time series spanning the phase of transition in several important Western countries;
3. to discuss the significance of certain results from studies which highlight the diversity of socio-economic and cultural conditions of fertility transition;
4. to present a few propositions which may help clarify the facts, in particular the pattern of international diffusion of the phenomenon, and which may help to render the universality of the process compatible with the variety of circumstances in which it occurs.

1. Demographic Disequilibrium, or the Priority of the Decline in Mortality

Between traditional and modern society—which is to say, during transition—the role played by death is gradually replaced by that of the voluntary prevention of births. High mortality and high fertility are inseparable, but the mechanism of their association is complex. The influence of morbidity and mortality on fertility works through different factors. The duration of breast-feeding, the frequency of sexual relations, the felt need for replacement of generations all vary with how long an infant survives. Under these conditions, when mortality declines the number of desired children also inevitably falls, but the adjustment does not occur immediately since couples do not know what the infant mortality rate will be; hence the greater or lesser duration of the interval between the two declines. From the opposite point of view, the influence of the number of children on the probability of survival is no less manifest: the standard of living,[8] sexual mores, a mother's health, and other demands on her time or the availability of other family members are all closely connected with reproductive levels. In this sense, the high infant mortality of certain traditional populations is also a response—in part voluntary—to excess fertility, many births in fact being unwanted. By reducing the birth-rate to the desired level, any decline in fertility can thus reduce existing methods

---

[8] In modern and contemporary society, the effect of the number of children on the standard of living is negative; but it could be positive in early societies.

of elimination. A fertility decline which precedes (or occurs simultaneously with) mortality decline thus also has its own logic.

Belgian and German Exceptions

In 1973, Coale drew attention to the apparent synchronicity of the French and German declines. More recently, Knodel and van de Walle (1979) have observed that, in a number of Belgian and German provinces, the decline in marital fertility emerged *before* that of infant mortality.[9] This is a difficult fact to establish, however, since for both countries the absence of long and reliable time series renders any discussion of their mortality history to some extent hypothetical. But there exist numerous statistical data which suggest that these two cases are in no way exceptions, but, on the contrary, conform to a general pattern.

Belgium: Quételet's Provincial Tables (1841–1845)

The decline in Belgian infant mortality is generally assumed to have begun very late, towards the end of the nineteenth century (Duchène and Lesthaeghe 1975; Poulain and Tabutin 1977; Lesthaeghe 1977); the comparison is sometimes drawn with the French series, where a *sustained* decline in rates did not occur until the same period (Poulain and Tabutin 1977). But this analogy in itself gives grounds for doubt, precisely because, if French infant mortality stabilized around 160–70 per 1000 during the last decades of the nineteenth century, this was a result of a century-long phase of decline: in the mid-eighteenth century, the rates were about twice as high (around 300 per 1000—the probability for both sexes being, for example, 296.5 per 1000 for 1740–49). Consequently, there is no reason that a similar development did not occur in Belgium, or the Walloon-speaking areas at least, which is where the Industrial Revolution on the continent first got going.[10] Three types of data appear to illustrate this: the national series, the provincial series, and comparison of intercensal growth.

1. The *national series* reveals a decline at the end of the 1830s, which is a third of a century before the beginning of the decline in marital fertility. Table 12.1 presents the development from 1834 to 1910.[11] From 1840 onwards, infant mortality rates stabilized around 150–60 per 1000, a relatively low level for the period. The first mortality tables calculated by Quételet (1849) confirm the decline of the 1830s. The adjusted infant mortality rate developed as in Table 12.2.

2. The *provincial series*. Mortality was very high in all regions during the

---

[9] Without distinguishing between legitimate and illegitimate births.

[10] These areas experienced an industrial boom as early as the period 1800–30.

[11] Without adjusting for false still-births (which would account for about a 5% increase).

TABLE 12.1. *Infant mortality rates, Belgium, 1834–1910* (per 1000)

Period	Infant mortality rate	Period	Infant mortality rate
1834–38	181.4	1861–1870	153.4
1839–40[a]	183.5	1871–1880	153.2
1841–45	148.8	1881–1890	158.4
1846–50	153.8	1891–1900	161.0
1851–60	153.4	1901–1910	144.9

[a] From this date, not including the parts of Limburg and Luxemburg surrendered to The Netherlands in 1839 (around 7% of the total population of Belgium). As these regions were more advanced, the national average was *raised* slightly by the territorial shift.

TABLE 12.2. *Adjusted infant mortality rate, Belgium, 1827–1847*

Period	Infant mortality rate
1827	224.9[a]
1832	224.7[a]
1841–45	205.5[b]
1846–47	195.2

[a] Such orders of magnitude match the figures in various local studies of the 17th and 18th centuries (Brunéel 1977; Meeus 1980).

[b] This figure and the figure for the series preceding it do not tally: perhaps Quételet made an adjustment to account for underregistration (however, he makes no mention of this).

first half of the nineteenth century. According to Table 12.3, the proportion of infants that died before their first birthday ranges from 17% (Limburg) to 24% (Western Flanders); half the population died before reaching the age of 20.

About 40 years later, Walloon couples had begun to regulate their fertility, and geographical differences disappeared as the Walloon departments began to record significant progress; in their Flemish counterparts, however, where voluntary birth control was sometimes not appreciable until the twentieth century, the situation remained as before (see Table 12.4).

3. *Population growth.* The average annual population increase is shown in Table 12.5. The increase in the rate of growth is very pronounced. As the

TABLE 12.3. *Belgian juvenile and infant mortality, by province, 1841–1845* (survivors per 1000 births at the age of 1, 5, 10 and 20 years)

Province	Survivors			
	S_1	S_5	S_{10}	S_{20}
Anvers	814	652	604	550
Brabant	783	602	555	498
West Flanders	759	591	548	487
East Flanders	787	627	580	517
Hainaut	822	657	609	545
Liège	817	639	591	535
Limburg	826	680	625	563
Luxemburg	799	640	595	544
Namur	799	655	619	563
Whole kingdom	794	628	582	523

Source: Quételet (1849).

TABLE 12.4. *Probability of female infant mortality, Belgian provinces 1841–1845 and 1878–1895* (per 1000)

Province (department)	1841–45[a]	1878–95
Dyle—Brabant	188	175
Deux-Nèthes—Anvers	161	159
Lys—West Flanders	209	203
Escaut—East Flanders	185	198
Ourthe—Liège	159	147
Sambre et Meuse—Namur	174	119
Forets—Luxemburg	174	118
Jemmape—Hainaut	155	125

[a] It has been assumed that the ratio of excess male infant mortality did not vary between provinces (Quételet only gives a breakdown by sex for the whole of Belgium).

Sources: Quételet (1849); Duchène and Lesthaeghe (1975).

TABLE 12.5. *Annual average population increase Belgium, 1846–1880* (%)

Period	Increase
1846–56	0.44
1856–66	0.64
1866–80	0.96

birth-rate increased only by 3 per 1000 from the first to the last period, the mortality decline appears responsible for about half of the overall increase.[12] Under these conditions, it is highly probable that the lack of significant progress in infant mortality rates from 1841 to 1900 is more apparent than real, owing to underregistration at the beginning of the period.[13] It is curious that the works cited do not mention this hypothesis.[14] Whatever the level, this plateau was preceded by a significant decline in the decades leading up to it.

German Differences: The Prussian and Bavarian Cases

Similarly, there appears to be no substantive proof for the view that the order of mortality and fertility declines was reversed in Germany. Here, too, there are several convergent arguments:

1. From the outset, such a proposition appears inconsistent with the increase in rates of demographic growth: it would entail a doubling of the German population between 1800 and 1880—that is, within 80 years— whereas the previous doubling took three centuries. The increase in demographic pressure was related, in the main, to the mortality decline, and was such that fears of over-population were considerable. In several principalities, harsh measures were introduced by the authorities to prevent young and poor marriages, whilst in others emigration was encouraged.

2. The steady increase in infant mortality rates, which was proportionately more pronounced the lower their initial level, could hardly be accounted for other than by a gradual improvement in registration. The contrast, up to 1875, between Bavaria, characterized by very high infant mortality which increased only very slightly, and Prussia, with low but rapidly increasing infant mortality, is particularly suggestive—unless one assumes that industrialization and urbanization had disastrous effects on public health, particularly by way of a decline in breast-feeding:[15]

(a) This hypothesis of omission is confirmed by a statistical breakdown by age of nursing infants: the *proportion* stillborn amongst infant deaths is appreciably lower in Prussia than in other areas (particularly in neighbouring Saxony), and it increases regularly up to 1880; mortality within the first week of life shows a heavy increase disproportionate to other infant deaths, since the corresponding rate as much as doubles and sometimes triples

---

[12] International migration being negligible.

[13] In certain French departments underregistration of infant deaths was still occurring in 1880 (Levasseur 1892).

[14] It is no less curious that the writers apply themselves to explaining the high mortality (in Flanders particularly) which was normal for the period, and not the low mortality (in Walloon-speaking areas) which is precisely what calls for attention.

[15] The Prussian rate rose from 169 to 224 per 1000 between 1816–20 and 1871–75 (i.e. an increase of 0.51% per year), and the Bavarian rate from 284 to 327 per 1000 between 1826–30 and 1871–75 (or 0.31% per year).

TABLE 12.6. *Infant mortality rate, Leipzig, 1751–1870* (per 1000)

Period	Infant mortality rate	Period	Infant mortality rate	Period	Infant mortality rate
1751–60	355	1791–1800	376	1831–40	233
1761–70	366	1801–1810	340	1841–50	224
1771–80	317	1811–1820	308	1851–60	206
1781–90	328	1821–1830	235	1861–70	233

(von Bergmann, in Neumann 1883). It is, however, well known that under-registration traditionally tends to affect the youngest infants.[16]

(*b*) Contemporary statisticians admitted that underregistration affected rates recorded during the first decades of the nineteenth century. Thus, Prinzing (1899), following on von Fircks (1879), wrote that during its first 50 years (1816–66) the Prussian series could only include the deaths of children born and deceased within the same calendar year, and not the deaths of all children under 1 year of age.[17]

(*c*) The few rare and reliable retrospective observations which allow comparisons to be made over long periods imply that a considerable mortality decline had occurred well before marital fertility began to decline. Thus, in Breslau, a flourishing town at the end of the seventeenth century (1687–91), life expectation at birth, according to Halley's observations (1693), was 20 years, and infant mortality 281 per 1000. According to Süssmilch (1741), eighteenth-century infant mortality in the German provinces could reach 250 to 350 per 1000, according to various cases cited. The national rate of 239 per 1000 in 1867, and 244 per 1000 in 1872–75—the earliest official data published—would thus be intermediate between traditional and modern levels. The value of 37 years for life expectation at birth in 1871–80 tends to confirm this; and in all the countries for which we have both reliable registers and series covering a number of centuries (Sweden, Norway, France, Italy, and Czech populations) a similar level was reached only after a long process. The pre-transitional level is generally only around 25 to 30 years (Hecht 1980). In the case of Leipzig,[18] where the registers were particularly well kept owing to the quality of the education of the clergy, we are able to go back to the mid-eighteenth century, with the aid of Knapp's studies (1874). This series is shown in Table 12.6. If the disturbed period of 1790–1810 is set to

[16] In Protestant countries there was often a fairly long interval between birth and baptism; where children survived for any period before dying, but remained unbaptized, there would be no indication in the registers.

[17] If true, as much as 40% to 50% could be added to the series. The error is doubtless confined to certain localities.

[18] A town in no way atypical: in the 19th century, rates obtained from civil registration were close to the regional average.

TABLE 12.7. *High rates of infant mortality in two German provinces: Upper Bavaria and Swabia, 1835–1935* (per 1000)

Period	Upper Bavaria		Swabia	
	Urban	Rural	Urban	Rural
1835–1841	389		398	
1841–1848	394		402	
1848–1855	395		405	
1855–1862	420		409	
1862–1868	420		412	
1862–1870	407	421	426	408
1871–1875	*408*	*415*	*449*	*406*
1876–1877	*372*	*387*	*413*	*381*
1878–1882	362	373	369	372
1883–1887	336	361	340	351
1888–1892	317	344	314	321
1893–1897	295	327	290	298
1898–1902	271	311	264	276
1931–1935	74	105	72	90

Note: Italicized figures correspond to the period of the beginning of the decline in fertility.

Sources: Prinzing (1899); Knodel (1974).

one side, the first advance seems to have occurred during the second half of the eighteenth century, and a second, much more marked improvement during the 1810s and 1820s—to the extent that infant mortality rates just before the fertility transition were only slightly above 200 per 1000, as opposed to 350 per 1000 or more for the previous century.

(*d*) Last, but not least, the argument suggests that if the usual demographic order is reversed, this tends to occur, a priori, in the most backward provinces,[19] where, in contrast to most other north-west European regions, no progress in the struggle against death would have been made in the eighteenth century.[20] Let us therefore examine the two most backward provinces in the period around 1870—Swabia and Upper Bavaria—where infant mortality rates around this date exceeded 400 per 1000. As elsewhere, there was a steady, but slow, increase in rates up to around 1870, which gave way to a sharp decline from 1876, both in rural as well as urban areas (Table 12.7). The adjustment of nuptiality to the fertility decline occurred almost

[19] The decline in marital fertility occurred at approximately the same time in all German provinces.
[20] An exceptionally early decline in marital fertility, as in France, is the other extreme hypothesis which would make the reversal of the sequence more plausible.

TABLE 12.8. *Marital fertility* $(I_g)^a$ *in two German provinces experiencing high infant mortality: Upper Bavaria and Swabia, 1866–1935*

Period	Upper Bavaria	Swabia	Germany
1866–1868	0.842	0.948	0.761
1869–1873	0.839	0.942	0.760
1874–1877	*0.838*	*0.934*	*0.791*
1878–1882	*0.786*	*0.880*	*0.735*
1883–1887	0.762	0.845	0.726
1888–1892	0.732	0.814	0.706
1893–1897	—	—	—
1898–1902	0.680	0.782	0.664
	—	—	—
1931–1935	0.275	0.345	0.264

^{a} I_g is a measure of marital fertility based on that of the Hutterites, which is taken as unity. If the proportion of married women aged 15–49 years is designated by I_m, the measure of general fertility by I_f, and the measure of illegitimate fertility by I_h, the following equation is obtained: $I_f = I_g I_m + (1 - I_m)I_h$. See Coale (1965).

Source: Knodel (1974).

immediately—only two years later[21]—but the fertility decline occurred well after the decline in infant mortality had been set in motion.

Even if, in both cases, marital fertility was very high,[22] it declines here, too, at the same time as in the rest of the country (Table 12.8). The effect of the decline in infant mortality on the decline in marital fertility was apparent to contemporary statisticians. As early as 1883, Geissler was studying this phenomenon, and its role appeared so crucial that in the following decades it became the subject of considerable controversy, certain authors, like Wurzburger (1912, 1931), going so far as to claim that declining fertility rates were no more than the result of declining infant and juvenile mortality, and that the actual number of desired (or surviving) children had not altered. Whilst acknowledging the fundamental role of this factor, other more subtle authors (Wolf 1912, in particular; Geissler 1885) looked to structural and moral changes which accompanied the Industrial Revolution, thus heralding transition theory.

To conclude, it appears that the only national case in which declining rates of mortality and fertility proceeded, if not in reverse order, then at least simultaneously, could be France, owing to the exceptional earliness of its fertility decline. However, we have seen (footnote 6 of the present chapter)

[21] According to the annual figures for population growth.
[22] The regulation of marriage in these regions had been very strict up to the 1860s, and extra-marital fertility fairly high.

that juvenile and infant mortality had already declined considerably before the Revolution, when couples began to limit their fertility; between 1740 and 1780, average life expectation increased by about six years. Thus, the first postulation of transition theory emerges from this test not only unscathed, but strengthened, its universality once more established.

This result was to be expected, on three counts: (1) the historical disappearance of plague and especially of smallpox, which had hitherto killed off so many children,[23] together with the relative rareness of cholera and other epidemic diseases in the West in the period up to the mid-nineteenth century; (2) the profound political and moral changes which accompanied the growth of the modern State from the Renaissance onwards, including governmental institutions regulating public order, the erection of infrastructures (canals, sewers, roads, and from the 1830s, railways) and social institutions (schools, including nursing and maternity schools; hospitals, and schools of medicine), development policies for trade and agriculture, the gradual undermining of dogma and traditional fatalism, the emergence of the idea of equality—all of which contributed more or less to the success of the battle against death; (3) and, finally, in addition to the several determinants common to the diffusion of mortality and fertility decline, the reduction in mortality was both the object of a general consensus (regarding its desirability) and subject partly to factors beyond individual control. Whilst the level of general fertility remained dependent on decisions made by the majority, thus reflecting the mentality of the rural masses, mortality levels derived in part from improvements accomplished by the educated or governing élite, and thus tended naturally to be more advanced.

2. Fertility and Modern Economic Growth

The circumstances of European transition have often been approached with the aim of eliciting information which could help us understand the situation of contemporary less developed countries. Such studies have emphasized in particular the development of statistical indicators which identify preconditions of the onset of fertility decline. As most countries in question (except in Africa) have currently passed this stage, this approach is now scarcely used. Interest has turned more towards knowing what sort of course to expect, especially where rates of decline are concerned.

Various attempts at constructing aggregate indicators of development, in varying combinations, were made during the 1970s. But they enjoyed hardly any success—presenting more problems than they solved—and were only

---

[23] Between 1791 and 1800, smallpox still accounted for over 10% of Swedish infant mortality; in Copenhagen, the crude mortality rate for smallpox between 1751 and 1801 was 3 per 1000. The incidence of smallpox became negligible at the beginning of the 19th century (Drake 1969).

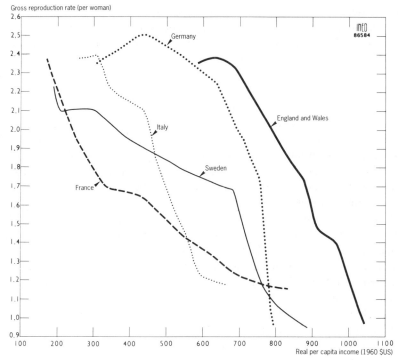

Gross reproduction rate (per woman)

FIG. 12.1. Fertility and real per capita income, Western countries, 1780–1938

applied in synchronic international comparisons, and not to national time series. Despite the widespread criticism—often unjustified[24]—to which these approaches have been subjected, we shall re-examine the use of measures of GNP per capita here, using Bairoch's series of real per capita GNP (1976), and tracing fertility variations over time in terms of income growth.

Five countries have been selected for illustration in Fig. 12.1: Germany, England, France, Italy, and Sweden. The fertility–income ratio is analysed on the basis of pre-1950 series. In Sweden, as in France, where rural society long predominated, the income flexibility of fertility was slight in comparison to other countries; but the rate of decline according to income level differed greatly between these two cases. In France, the first phase of transition was confined to a narrow margin of very low incomes ($US180–330 at 1960 values) at which no other country experienced a fertility decline. Subsequent economic growth during the Industrial Revolution was accompanied only by a very slow fertility decline: at an income level of around $800, French fertility remained higher than that of Germany or Sweden. In the latter country,

[24] Production for home consumption, for example, is included in GNP.

fertility declined slowly in the early stages of economic growth, and then speeded up once the $650–700 per capita threshold was reached.

Allowing for differences in the scale of incomes, the three cases of Germany, England, and Italy are similar: fertility transition occurred for the most part over a relatively brief period and within an income range of only about $350. The income ranges were as follows: Italy, $350–650; Germany, $450–800; England, $650–1,000. The first figure corresponds to the point of entry into fertility transition, and the second to the level at its end.[25] Each country thus had its own levels, but, once started, fertility decline was in each case concentrated into a brief phase of economic history. These few observations would imply that analogies are to be sought less in levels than in trends of independent variables. Nevertheless, if we regard the English case as one extreme (in which initial industrialization delayed demographic change) and take the French case as the opposite extreme (in which fertility decline began without industrialization), the levels of entry in between appear fairly similar, ranging on the whole between $300 and $450.

Let us now take a quick look at the experience of countries with late transition. At the point at which fertility enters modern levels, per capita income is either within this bracket, but around the lowest end of the range (Spain, Portugal, Hungary, Romania), or below it (Russia and Japan). In other words, the phenomenon seems, a priori, to proceed as if income levels gradually fell with the geographic spread of the transition, the rejection of traditional behaviour being, as it were, facilitated by the spread of the example.

3. The Diversity of Underlying Circumstances

The relation between improvements in living conditions and trends in fertility is complex: the factors involved are manifold[26] and the indicators used sometimes misleading. The relationship is also ambiguous. Certainly the increase in income enables larger families to be coped with, but as a corollary it introduces a change in tastes, a growing demand for higher-quality goods, and especially a rise in the cost of children (Heer 1966). Moreover, it is not sufficient merely to identify variables at work; we must determine their hierarchy, their respective importance, and the relations which exist between them. There are still few attempts at an overall approach which have produced convincing results in terms of explained variance.

Aside from demographic variables (mortality level, nuptiality regime), the factors most generally invoked are either socio-economic (degree of urbanization and industrialization) or cultural (level of education, language, religion).

---

[25] When GRRs were below 1.2, and the NRR around 1 or less.
[26] Sauvy (1966) identifies a dozen factors, other writers as many as 20.

The first—and static—approach generally employed in international comparisons, tends naturally to focus on geographical differences. The other method consists in analysing a given territorial unit, divided into uniform areas, whose respective evolutions are followed over time; this allows statistical treatment to be adapted to each case studied and the introduction of variables appropriate to particular historical continuities such as the maintenance of relative differences between cultural zones. The two approaches admirably complement each other, the first serving as an indispensable frame of reference for the second. We will only discuss here certain aspects of each, in the light of observations suggested both by the demographic series analysed above, and the economic series given later in Chapters 16 to 18, as well as certain underlying historical factors.

Static International Comparisons

Illustrated primarily by the studies of Knodel and van de Walle (1967, 1979), this approach relies on the use of measures of modernity, particularly the percentage of urban population, the proportion of the male working population in farming, and the rate of literacy.

Degree of Urbanization

Rural society is opposed by convention to the urban industrial world, according to the following assumption: because rural society is entrenched in traditionalism, it tends to delay transition, in direct proportion to its population size. We have already observed two considerable exceptions: France and England. But these are not isolated cases, since, in the nineteenth century, fertility began to decline first in rural areas in the US (Yasuba 1962), and in various regions of Hungary (Demeny, in *Historical Population Studies* 1968; Andorka 1972). In the Hungarian region of Ormansag, and in Massachusetts, as in France, rural populations, confronted by the scarcity of land, gave the signal for 'modernization'. In addition, the nineteenth-century rural–urban dichotomy is often artificial: many towns situated in the countryside were in fact merely large villages, while many rural settlements were rich in cottage or small industries. Likewise, the ethnic or religious composition of town populations often makes direct comparison with rural contexts misleading: in eastern Europe, many urban areas included large Jewish communities which were very outward-looking; in Germany, the more educated Protestant element predominated.

Underlying its apparent simplicity, the index of urbanization measures very different realities. Sometimes, given the population it groups together, it is as much an index of levels of industrialization as of education, or of the degree of development in trade and communications; at other times, it merely signifies the greatest concentration of settlement. The percentage of the population living in large urban concentrations is, on the other hand, more easily assessed, since large towns engender diverse constraints which are inimical to the survival of large families (e.g. anonymity, overcrowding, the segmentation of social roles).

Level of Industrialization

Measures of industrialization by sectoral distributions of manpower are similarly open to criticism, since the most significant factor is the nature of the industrialization. Depending on whether men or women are employed,[27] whether industry is concentrated or not, and whether manufacture lends itself to domestic modes of production, fertility may be influenced in different ways. The first forms of industrialization, often in textiles, were mostly rural-based with high female participation; rather than encouraging fertility regulation, they tended to stimulate reproduction. English and Japanese history provide clear examples. The development became more complex in the countries affected with the advent of the coal-mining industry: sexual division of labour among mining families was clear-cut, early marriage was the norm, and marital fertility high, although premature death (from silicosis) served as a counterbalance. But in the long term, indirect influences which were equally if not more powerful had the opposite effect: the rise of the iron and steel industry resulted in the proliferation of associated activities in industry, commerce, and banking, and was directly connected with other structural transformations such as the growth of large towns, the rise in living standards, the decline in religion, and the alteration of sexual and familial life. In subsequent stages of industrialization, from the advent of the motor car to robotics, a still different context has prevailed, characterized by effective medical treatment, the growth of conurbations, widespread compulsory education, the elaboration of social legislation, job specialization, social atomization, the information and telecommunications boom, changes in female status, and the introduction of contraceptive methods following the early researches of Pincus and others. Each of these factors, taken on its own, is favourable to fertility regulation,[28] and their intimate association in modern history has worked synergistically.

In other words, contrary to a common assumption, the influence of industrialization does not work only in one direction. The fact that European industrialization coincided with a demographic boom linked to mortality decline makes interpretation particularly delicate. It is possible to observe, at one and the same time, a tightening up and a relaxation of fertility regulation

---

[27] And sometimes children.

[28] The considerable fluctuation in fertility that occurred between 1940 and 1960 in most Western countries appears to constitute a kind of historical departure, linked to the moral climate created by the depression and the Second World War. One could cite the restoration of traditional values and the decline of individualism in this period (see Chapter 7).

(Chambers and Mingay 1966); whence the surprising nature of certain demographic developments, and the often considerable discrepancies which have appeared in intervals between the mortality and fertility declines. Such discrepancies are very slight in eighteenth-century France and late nineteenth-century eastern Europe, owing to the scarcity of non-agricultural employ. On the other hand, there is a considerable time lag in England, The Netherlands, and doubtless also in Walloon areas of Belgium, where the incentive to reduce rural fertility was checked by the emergence of new occupational openings. These last cases may also help us to understand certain less developed countries, such as Mexico, where, in spite of very rapid demographic growth and high urbanization, several decades elapsed before fertility began to decline.

Broadly speaking, however, the connection between the modernization of economic structures and demographic transition cannot be denied. In diverse instances such as Japan, Spain, and eastern Europe at the end of the nineteenth century the picture is very striking: industry was non-existent (aside, in some cases, from certain adjacent areas), peasant property was very unevenly distributed, and feudalism not abolished until very late. Fertility did not decline (or scarcely), but its subsequent development was extremely rapid. If the important exceptions already cited and discussed are set to one side, there is a fairly strong correlation, at least in the main outlines, between the stages of the Industrial Revolution described by Hirschmann (1932, 1953), Rostow (1960) and particularly Reynolds (1985), and the historical sequence of fertility declines. Both were first experienced in north-west Europe before spreading to other parts of the continent—the centre first, and then the south and east.

The Level of Education

It is not sufficient to rely on a rudimentary index such as aggregate rates of literacy. In everything which pertains to demographic behaviour (infant mortality, marriage, family constitution), differences between the sexes must be taken into account, as they are often crucial. Quality of education and its ethical content are also significant.

Aside from these limitations, the explanatory power of this factor, as measured, for example, by the proportion of women at child-bearing age having passed primary education, is great, and usually exceeds that of the income effect. But this is as might be expected, since cultural variables encompass income effects; the spread of female education occurred historically after male education, and its continuation beyond compulsory level presupposes a minimum affluence. The consequences of education are compound, including a demographic effect (delay of age at marriage), a social effect (greater likelihood of employ, and increased status), and a psychological effect (the selection of certain personal dispositions toward regularity and rationality). All of these effects tend to reduce fertility.

It is impossible to give a single quantitative measure of modernity, as it varies so much in time and space. In this sense, the theory of thresholds rests on an illusion of stasis, denying history. It is in fact the theory of thresholds—which represents a reductive deviation from transition theory—and *not transition theory itself* which Knodel and van de Walle attempt to test. In its early versions, whether European or North American, transition theory merely provided a general frame which was as loose as possible, and consequently sufficiently flexible to accommodate the indispensable nuances peculiar to various individual cases. The extraordinary diversity of demographic and socio-economic conditions of transition—unsuspected by the first writers— which has come to be regarded as a weakness in the theory, should rather be counted among its strong points: despite the multiplicity of historical, geographical, and institutional contexts, it remains the case, as Landry predicted, that all countries have experienced similar demographic changes flowing from largely similar mechanisms. The phenomenon's universality is in no way irreconcilable with the diversity of forms it can assume in different places.[29] Common denominators do exist: efficiency, prosperity, mobility, liberty, and security become increasingly evident in all places. Compared with the similarities, the differences are slight, but they do exist; and it is these particularities—cultural for the most part—which constitute powerful factors capable of accelerating or delaying demographic transition, which itself is ineluctable.

The National Historical Approach

Detailed analysis of particular national demographies does not lend itself well to generalities or schemas derived from other countries or periods: the selection of variables must always be carefully tailored, and new elements often must be added into the analysis, according to local circumstances. We have already given the example of a factor such as land availability, which is likely to play an important role in predominantly rural countries of high population density. Some authors have emphasized the influence of social structure (Dumont 1890), or the degree to which social and cultural entities cut across the administrative boundaries of states (van de Walle 1975). At a time when both economic growth and demographic development are the object of interventionist policies in less developed countries, a systematic and close analysis of east European as well as west European experience would be beneficial.

As national studies in Spain, Belgium, and Germany make clear, analysis has to go beyond the material factors which constrain society. Differences between regions largely reflect differences in fertility trends within them,

---

[29] Hence the heterogeneity of explanatory frameworks in the national monographs of the Princeton study.

returning us to the preponderant role of cultural factors, such as language, religion, and tradition.

Reproduction is bound up with man's idea of himself and his descendants, and so with systems of belief and collective representation. Religion occupies a prime position amongst these systems, since it has without doubt the greatest powers of structuring experience: in early societies, it was religion which defined notions of good and evil, thereby giving direction to individual conduct. Since Weber, the role of the Protestant ethic in the rise of capitalism has become common knowledge; its influence on demographic development could have proceeded via economic interactions, but there exist more likely direct mechanisms. By cultivating the value of self-denial, of conscious calculation, and of individual responsibility, the Protestant ethic has effectively promoted similar socio-economic values, including fertility regulation, which occurred earlier amongst Protestants than Catholics in the US and northern Europe. Of course, both Catholic and Protestant Churches have for centuries condemned contraception and abortion, but for several decades now (1930 for the UK) Protestantism has maintained a more flexible attitude in the name of individual freedom. The role of the several religious confessions, including many variant forms from region to region, is doubtless dwindling within the Christian West, as current German and American data testify. But there remain two countries in Europe in which the strength of Catholicism, whether Marian or Jansenist, helps to explain the maintenance of above-replacement fertility, even in close proximity to principal centres of Western modernization. These countries are Poland and Ireland, both characterized by a national Catholicism closely bound up with popular identity. In both countries, Catholicism is traditionally associated with combat against external oppressors, in which the clergy plays a prime role.

The influence of religion and its modern negation,[30] secularization, have indisputably played a major role in demographic history. And although this argument occurs in all post-war studies on fertility decline, we owe to Lesthaeghe (1977) the statistical measurement of its importance in relation to traditional socio-economic variables. Using Belgian data, Lesthaeghe showed that secularization—or the rejection of traditional ways of thinking—is as important as economic and cultural change in the explanation of fertility decline. The difference between the Flemish measure of marital fertility (around 0.9 in most areas) and the Walloon (generally 0.7 to 0.8 at the 1866 census) disappears when secularization is taken into account, since, at an equal level of industrialization, Walloon areas have a higher level of secularization. This process of emancipation affects the political as well as the religious sphere: it is the general attitude towards authority and knowledge which changes. The religious parties' share of the vote gradually gave way to

---

[30] In the 19th century it was no longer heresy, but indifference and unbelief, which were fought against.

the socialist vote, and marital fertility changed accordingly: individualism, in the Durkheimian sense, was making its mark. 'All civilization', Hugo wrote long ago, 'begins with theocracy and ends with democracy.'

4. A Diffusionist Model of Innovation

Each in its own way, the several national monographs on the demographic transition have demonstrated the complexity—not easily articulated because constantly changing—of the constellation of factors involved. All, however, suffer from the same flaw: by reasoning within a national frame of reference, they take each experience in isolation, independently of others. But the facts show that national experiences are closely related. In less than two centuries, capitalism—private, mixed, or State—has spread over the entire world, but who would think of undertaking a detailed national analysis without referring to the antecedents or external influences? The same goes for the formation of the modern State, the disappearance of major diseases, or technical innovation. A theory of fertility decline, like any theory of these related transformations, cannot but be historical. It must locate each development within a historical process affecting different countries at the same time.

It is no coincidence that the pattern shown by American and Australian fertility in this century should—despite the immense geographical distances separating the two countries—resemble each other, even overlapping at several points (see Fig. 4.9). If the resumption of the secular fertility decline from the 1960s began in North America, spreading subsequently to northwest Europe, and then southern Europe and Japan, is this not the route that most moral and cultural innovations over the last century have taken? The Piedmont, as the most 'continental' region of the young Italian kingdom, and Catalonia, similarly French-orientated, experienced a fertility decline before the rest of the nations to which they belonged. The eastern Baltic countries, under Germanic influence since the Middle Ages, recorded demographic trends similar to Germany. In central Europe, the model of the restricted family moved down the Danube, which was the route taken by all large migrations. Romanian Banat and Transylvania, where Saxon colonies had existed for centuries, had a Western outlook and became modernized earlier. Yugoslavia, where Balkan cultural particularisms crystallized, embodied equally contrasted developments such that the Slovenes and Croats, who converted early to Roman Catholicism, and were long governed by the Habsburgs and accustomed to looking towards Vienna, had a lower pre-transitional level and were closer to the Austrian model; whilst the Orthodox Serbs, long under Ottoman rule and amongst whom a small minority were even Islamic, followed later. Neighbouring Albania, itself massively converted to Islam and cut off amidst its mountains, has been closer demographically to Turkey or Syria than any other European country. And finally, Russia—

inward looking and paralysed by poor communication—was the last to enter into the process. The list goes on and on. Around 1930, regional fertility rates gradually increase the further one goes from the centres of communication and the main pathways of movement (Kirk 1946).

It is sometimes necessary to go a long way back into the past in order to understand the present. The medieval world was composed of small autonomous societies; the individual was attached to a trade or to the soil, and it was practically impossible for him to change that point of departure. Not to speak of the peasant, reduced from generation to generation to the condition of a serf—the moment any crisis arose, the town labourer himself had difficulties finding work in another town. Behaviour was codified; experience was carefully partitioned and entirely regimented. Customs houses formed a wall around each important compartmentalized political and economic unit, protecting against the infiltration of foreigners. This medieval fortress began gradually to disintegrate from the Renaissance onwards. Internal migration expanded, rites and traditions slackened, and the feudal barriers fell one by one; intolerance receded, and the idea of equality progressed. Individualism then embarked on its centuries-long journey. But the suppression of feudalism, which began in the fifteenth century in Europe, was not accomplished until the second half of the nineteenth century; in other continents there are still countries where the process is not yet fully achieved: these countries are of course among the less demographically advanced.

In order to understand these historical transformations, at the centre of which lies the demographic transition, we think it is necessary to define some indicators of openness to external influence and cultural penetration. It is a question of establishing a matrix of exchanges with other countries—mainly dominant ones. We consider that nineteenth-century Europe could be suitably represented by the density of means of communication, and the intensity of exchange, measured through indices such as the number of kilometres of road suitable for motor traffic or of railway line per inhabitant, the per capita volume of trade, postal traffic, and the intensity and direction of migratory flows—both internal and external. Contact with more advanced countries, and the installation of transport and communication networks, determine the spread of those factors of modernization underlying demographic transition: industry, trade, urban development, education, sanitation, and above all the traffic of men and the movement of ideas. We have already, at different points, underlined the backwardness of land-locked countries—both in their mortality and in their fertility declines.

Conclusion

The proposed course of investigation is doubtless highly ambitious, but it is certainly a promising one, since, despite the avalanche of articles on the subject, the essence of the profound mechanisms governing fertility remains remarkably mysterious. A reconstruction of routes of cultural diffusion, starting from points of origin, can only add to our knowledge of the phenomenon. There is every reason to think that demographic change involved innovation from above—in other words, that the matrix of exchanges listed in the preceding paragraph measure the density of traffic between the peaks of social pyramids, and thus the probability of social innovation within privileged milieux. The question which then arises is the spread of new models of behaviour to other sections of the social body. In this sense, although somewhat crude owing to constraints imposed by the quality of available statistics, a historical analysis of fertility by cohort and social class, located within the international context of the period, would seem necessary to comprehend the schemas of internal diffusion. In the absence of such information—precisely because of our distance from past events—the causal models inspired by intellectual fashions of the day become more concerned about coherence than knowledge; they fall into the trap of anachronism, bearing no relation to historical truth.

Finally, if applied to less developed countries (assuming the necessary adjustments), such indicators would very likely help to predict how receptive different societies will be to family planning: the numerous studies devoted to this issue have a tendency to consider each country as a closed vessel.

Bibliography to Chapter 12

ANDORKA, R. (1972), 'Un Exemple de faible fécondité légitime dans une région de la Hongrie', *Annales de Démographie Historique*, 3: 25–53.

BAIROCH, P. (1976), 'Europe's Gross National Product: 1800–1975', *JEEH*, 2: 273–340.

BEAVER, S. (1975), *Demographic Transition Theory Reconsidered: An Application to Recent Natality Trends in Latin America* (Lexington, Mass.: Lexington Books).

BEHRMAN, S. J., CORSA, L., and FREEDMAN, R. (eds.) (1969), *Fertility and Family Planning: A World Overview* (Ann Arbor, Mich.).

BELLETTINI, A., and SAMOGGIA, A. (1982), 'Premières Recherches sur les tendances de longue période de la mortalité infantile dans la campagne de Bologne (XVIIᵉ–XIXᵉ siècle)', *Genus*, 1–2: 1–25.

BRUNÉEL, C. (1977), *La Mortalité dans les campagnes: le Duché de Brabant aux XVIIᵉ et XVIIIᵉ siècles* (Louvain), i.

CALDWELL, J. C. (1976), 'Towards a Restatement of Demographic Transition Theory', *PDR*, 3–4: 321–66.

CARLSSON, C. (1969), 'The Decline of Fertility: Innovation or Adjustment Process?', *Population Studies* (Nov.), 149–74.

CHAMBERS, J. D., and MINGAY, G. E. (1966), *The Agrarian Revolution, 1750–1880* (London: Batsford).

COALE, A. J. (1965), 'Factors Associated with the Development of Low Fertility', *UN World Conference on Population, Belgrade, 1965*, 205–09.

—— (1973), 'The Demographic Transition Reconsidered', *IUSSP Conference, Liège, 1973*, i. 53–72.

—— ANDERSON, B. A., and HARM, E. (1979), *Human Fertility in Russia since the 19th Century* (Princeton, NJ: Princeton University Press).

DEMERATH, N. J. (1976), *Birth Control and Foreign Policy: The Alternatives to Family Planning* (New York: Harper and Row).

DRAKE, M. (1969), *Population and Society in Norway, 1735–1865* (Cambridge: Cambridge University Press).

DUCHÈNE, J., and LESTHAEGHE, R. (1975), 'Essai de reconstitution de la population belge sous le régime français; quelques caractéristiques démographiques de la population féminine', *Population et Famille*, 3: 1–47.

DUMONT, A. (1890), *Dépopulation et civilisation* (Paris: Lecrosnier et Babé).

GEISSLER, A. (1885), 'Über den Einfluss der Saüglingssterblichkeit auf die eheliche Fruchtbarkeit', *Zeitschrift des Sächsischen Statistischen Bureaus* (Dresden), 31: 23–24.

GLASS, D. V., and EVERSLEY, D. E. C. (1965), *Population in History: Essays in Historical Demography* (London: Edward Arnold).

GRAFF, H. J. (1979), *Literacy, Education and Fertility, Past and Present: A Critical View*, *PDR*, 1: 105–40.

GRAUMAN, J. (1960), Comment, *Demographic and Economic Change in Developed Countries*, Princeton, 275–84.

HAJNAL, J. (1953), 'Age at Marriage and Proportions Marrying', *Population Studies*, 7: 111–36.

HALLEY, E. (1693), 'An Estimate of the Degree of the Mortality of Mankind Drawn from Curious Tables of the Birth and Funerals of the City of Breslaw', *Philosophical Transactions of the Royal Society of London*, 17.

HECHT, J. (1980), 'L'Evaluation de la mortalité aux jeunes âges dans la littérature économique et démographique de l'Ancien Régime', in P. M. Boulanger and D. Tabutin, *La Mortalité des enfants dans le monde et dans l'histoire* (Liège: Ordina Éditions), 29–79.

HEER, D. (1966), 'Economic Development and Fertility', *Demography*, 2: 423–44.

Historical Population Studies (1968), *Daedalus* (Journal of the American Academy of Arts and Sciences), Spring, 353–635.

HÖHN, C., and MACKENSEN, R. (eds.) (1982), 'Determinants of Fertility Trends: Theories Re-examined', *Proceedings of a Seminar held in Bad Homburg* (GDR) (Liège: Ordina Éditions).

KIRK, D. (1946), *Europe's Population in the Interwar Years* (New York).

KNAPP, G. F. (1874), 'Die Kindersterblichkeit in Leipzig 1751–1870', *Mitteilungen des Leipzigen Statistischen Bureaus*, 8.

KNODEL, J. (1974), *The Decline of Fertility in Germany, 1871–1939* (Princeton, NJ: Princeton University Press).

—— and van de Walle, E. (1967), 'Demographic Transition and Fertility Decline: The European Case', in *IUSSP Conference, Sydney, 1967*.

—— *(1979)*, 'Lessons from the Past: Policy Implications of Historical Fertility Studies', *PDR*, 5: 217–45.

LANDRY, A. (1934), *La Révolution démographique* (Paris: Sirey).

—— (1949), *Traité de démographie* (Paris: Payot).

LANGER, W. H. (1974), 'Infanticide: A Historical Survey', *History of Childhood Quarterly*, 1(3), 353–65.

LASLETT, P., DOSTERVEEN, K., and SMITH, R. M. (1980), *Bastardy and its Comparative History: Studies in the History of Illegitimacy and Marital Nonconformism in Britain, France, Germany, Sweden, North America, Jamaica and Japan* (London: Edward Arnold).

LEA, H. C. (1884), *An Historical Sketch of Sacerdotal Celibacy in the Christian Church*, 2nd edn. (Boston).

LEASURE, J. (1963), 'Factors Involved in the Decline of Fertility in Spain, 1900–1950', *Population Studies*, 17: 271–85.

LEE, W. R. (ed.) (1979), *European Demography and Economic Growth, 1750–1970* (London: Croom Helm).

LESTHAEGHE, R. (1977), *The Decline of Belgian Fertility, 1800–1970* (Princeton, NJ: Princeton University Press).

LEVASSEUR, E. (1892), *La Population française*, iii (Paris).

LIVI-BACCI, M. (1977), *A History of Italian Fertility during the Last Two Centuries* (Princeton, NJ: Princeton University Press).

McGRANAHAN, D. V. (1971), 'Analysis of Socio-economic Development through a System of Indicators', *Annals of the American Academy of Political and Social Sciences*, 393: 65–81.

MEEUS, M. (1980), *L'Évolution et les caractéristiques de la mortalité dans la région de Diest de 1651 à 1815* (Louvain).

MYRDAL, A. (1945), *Nation and Family* (London: Kegan Paul).

NEUMANN, F. J. (ed.) (1883–1903), *Beiträge zur Geschichte der Bevölkerung in Deutschland*, 7 vols. (Tübingen), esp. vols. i, iv, and v.

NOTESTEIN, F. W. (1945), 'Population: The Long View', in E. Schultz (ed.), *Food for the World* (Chicago, Ill.: University of Chicago Press).

—— (1953), 'The Economics of Population and Food Supplies: Economic Problems of Population Change', in *Proceedings of the 8th International Conference of Agricultural Economists, London*.

—— and STIX, R. K. (1940), *Controlled Fertility: An Evaluation of Clinic Service* (Baltimore, Md.: William and Willkins).

OHLIN, G. (1961), 'Mortality, Marriage and Growth in Preindustrial Population', *Population Studies*, 3: 190–97.

PIERS, M. (1978), *Infanticide* (New York: Norton).

POULAIN, M., and TABUTIN, D. (1977), 'La Mortalité aux jeunes âges en Belgique de 1840 à 1870', *Population et Famille*, 3: 49–86.

PRESTON, S. H. (1978), *The Effects of Infant and Child Mortality on Fertility* (New York: Academic Press).

PRINZING, F. (1899), 'Die Entwicklung der Kindersterblichkeit in den Europäischen Staaten', *Jahrbücher für National Ökonomie und Statistik* (Jena).

QUÉTELET, A. (1849), 'Nouvelles Tables de mortalité pour la Belgique', *Bulletin de la Commission Centrale de Statistique* (Brussels), iv. 1–16.

—— (1853), 'Sur les tables de mortalité et de population', *Bulletin de la Commission Centrale de Statistique* (Brussels), v. 1–24.

REYNOLDS, L. G. (1985), *Economic Growth in the Third World, 1950–1980* (New Haven, Conn.: Yale University Press).

ROSTOW, W. W. (1960), *The Stages of Economic Growth* (Cambridge: Cambridge University Press).

SAUER, R. (1978), 'Infanticide and Abortion in Nineteenth Century Britain', *Population Studies*, 32: 81–92.

SAUVY, A. (1966), *Théorie générale de la population*, 3rd edn. (Paris: PUF), ii.

SCRIMSHAW, S. (1978), 'Infant Mortality and Behaviour in the Regulation of Family Size', *PDR*, 3: 383–403.

SHORTER, E. (1973), *The Making of the Modern Family* (New York: Basic Books).

STYS, W. (1957), 'The Influence of Economic Conditions on the Fertility of Peasant Women', *Population Studies*, 2: 136–48.

SÜSSMILCH, J. P. (1741), *Die Göttliche Ordnung* (Berlin: Spener).

TILLY, C. (ed.) (1978), *Historical Studies of Changing Fertility* (Princeton, NJ: Princeton University Press).

VAN DE WALLE, E. (1975), 'Les Enseignements de la transition démographique européenne, *Culture et développement*, 3–4: 575–85.

WESTERGAARD, H. L. (1901), *Die Lehre von der Mortalität und Morbidität*, 2nd edn. (Jena: Fischer).

WOLF, J. (1912), *Der Geburtenrückgang: Die Rationalisierung des Sexuallebens in unserer Zeit* (Jena: Fischer), 254.

—— (1913), *Das Zweikindersystem im Anmarsh und der Feldzug dagegen* (Berlin: Hirschwald).

WURZBURGER, E. (1912), 'Ist die Besorgnis über der Geburtenrückgang begründet?', *Zeitschrift des Sächsischen Statistischen Bureaus*, 3–4: 575–85.

—— (1931), 'Die Ursachen des neueren Geburtenrückganges', *Schmollers Jahrbuch 55* (Berlin).

YASUBA, Y. (1962), *Birth Rates of the White Population in the US, 1800–1960: An Economic Study* (Baltimore, Md.: Johns Hopkins University Press).

13 Contemporary Transitions:
The Strength of the Model

> The most beautiful thing that we can experience is the mystery of things.
>
> (Einstein)

DEMOGRAPHIC transitions in Europe are sometimes thought an unsuitable source of lessons on demographic change in less developed countries. This view takes as its starting-point the relatively disadvantaged situation of the latter. The argument proceeds thus: following the introduction of Western medical techniques, Third World mortality declined very rapidly after the Second World War, thereby bringing about the demographic revolution, but without a parallel industrial revolution. Precipitated from without, and independent of economic level and the state of institutions (Davis 1967; Petersen 1969), mortality decline took place in societies which were not prepared for economic modernization and even less so for the changes in mental attitude demanded by family planning.

We have already demonstrated that the presumed fully exogenous nature of the mortality decline is an error. The spectacular breakthrough in life expectation in newly industrialized Latin American and, especially, Asian countries, is the most striking manifestation of this, together with the deterioration of the state of health in eastern Europe since the 1960s (Chesnais 1983). It will be shown in Chapter 18, using long time series, that the assumed delay of the industrial revolution relative to the demographic revolution itself resides on a misapprehension of the history of the countries involved.

Handicap or Relative Advantage?

The relatively advantageous position of contemporary less developed countries in respect of demographic transition is as arguable as their disadvantage. Aside from the fact that transition is highly advanced in certain cases, numerous points may be put forward to suggest that less developed countries are better equipped for achieving rapid changes than their European or North American counterparts at a similar stage of development. Here are a few of them: the accumulated experience of the nature of the development process in an increasing number of countries; the motivation and sense of urgency created by hitherto unknown demographic rates; the existence of effective technology both for successful demographic innovation, as well as rapid diffusion of information about it via modern media; the presence of concerted international support, including that of specialized bodies such as the UN, World Bank, Population Council, IPPF, etc; and, finally, governmental encouragement of the implementation of birth control services.[1] The growing interdependence of national experiences has tended to support the view that social history is accelerating rather than slowing down.

The object of this chapter is to show that, aside from frequently stressed differences of context or rates, the demographic transition in poor countries in reality conforms fundamentally to the same mechanisms as operated in Europe, and that analogies between the two are more important than they first appeared. Of particular note are: the presence of a two-phased reproductive transition, passing from a regime of early and universal nuptiality[2] to one of semi-delayed or delayed and non-universal fertility; the precedence of this change in regime with respect to the decline of fertility in unions;[3] a mortality decline which anticipates fertility declines, and, finally, profound socio-economic transformations accompanying the progressive extension of life expectation and preceding voluntary birth control. These transformations include a substantial and lasting increase in real per capita income, urbanization, industrialization, higher educational standards; and so forth. In other words, through the close links it emphasizes between socio-economic development and demographic change, the logic of demographic transition theory applies equally well, and sometimes even better, to the case of developing countries than to Western history.[4]

1. Demographic Precursors

Mortality Decline

The long-standing hypothesis that the mortality decline in less developed countries owes to exogenous factors called into question the validity of tran-

---

[1] In European history, the State was often apprehensive about fertility decline, and sometimes fought openly against it.

[2] In most Asian countries until recently, adult celibacy has remained practically unknown, while the proportion of women remaining unmarried is often only 0.1% to 1.2%.

[3] Given the diversity of sexual and marital practices, the term 'union' seems preferable to 'marriage'.

[4] The experience of intermediate countries such as Japan and the USSR also conforms very closely to the theory's predictions. The secular fertility decline in Japan began around 1930, when mortality had already declined appreciably, per capita income had greatly improved (it was $US450, at 1960 values, or 2.5 times higher than pre-industrial levels); and education reached levels comparable to those of the West, as well as being the most advanced in Asia. In the USSR, the most heterogeneous state now extant, fertility only began to decline in the European section (the Russia of 50 provinces) from 1900 onwards. It followed a significant mortality decline (the crude rate being 32 per 1000 between 1898 and 1902, as opposed to 38 per 1000 between 1867 and 1873) and four decades of rapid industrialization. The Caucasian and central Asian republics with high Muslim populations waited until the 1960s or 1970s for their major changes, much in the manner of less developed countries.

sition theory. In this view, considerable health improvements appeared to be under way—contrary to what had been observed in Europe—without internal structural transformations. The suggestion, therefore, was that social and institutional maturation prior to the introduction of modern contraception was not as necessary as the theoretical model had implied. Indeed, if such a transformation really was necessary, several decades would have to elapse before vital rates improved. There was thus a pressing need to precipitate change by setting in motion intensive family planning programmes. Although, unlike Europe, no modernization had prepared the ground for fertility decline, exogenous processes would be equally effective, at the cost of considerable efforts of persuasion and encouragement.

This postulate of the implicit immobility of poor societies does not stand up to analysis: all long-term comparative studies indicate, to the contrary, that changes have proceeded with extraordinary rapidity, the spectacular decline in mortality being, like the tip of an iceberg, merely the most visible aspect of this process. Far from being independent, these changes are interdependent and mutually related, both in intensity and in temporal development (Chenery and Syrquin 1975).

In all less developed countries with declining fertility, mortality has already reached a fairly advanced stage. With the exception of India and Indonesia, where average life expectation at the end of the 1970s was still only around 50 years, the average length of life now generally exceeds 60 years—a level not reached by the industrial world until the mid-twentieth century. On the whole, only four or five decades were needed, as opposed to seven or eight in the developed world, and more in north-west Europe, for the traditional level of 30 years or less to change to current levels of over 60 years. Moreover, these societies are already characterized by fairly high excess male mortality, and sometimes even, in the case of East Asia, by rates comparable to that of wealthy countries (Table 13.1): this sort of development is inconceivable without fundamental changes in the relative status of the sexes in conditions of daily life.

Whilst it is possible to date the beginning of the fertility decline with some precision, despite deficiencies in civil registration, the start of the mortality decline, which generally post-dates the Second World War, is difficult to date precisely owing to the lack of reliable observations on the less recent past. The interval between the two declines, which thus tends to be underestimated, is fairly considerable, since it appears to be generally around 30 to 50 years. Moreover, fertility levels and trends appear closely correlated with those of mortality. The relation between pre-transitional levels has already been studied (Chapter 5), but the relation between the rate and timing of adjustments warrants emphasis: broadly speaking, *the more rapid the decline in infant mortality, the shorter the interval between the beginning of that decline and that of fertility* (as shown, for example, by east Asia and Central America). Conversely, where infant mortality declined slowly, particularly in densely

TABLE 13.1. *Life expectation at birth by sex in less developed countries with advanced transition, 1975–1980*

Country	Males	Females	Country	Males	Females
Africa			Asia		
Egypt	53.9	55.6	China (mainland)	62.6	66.5
South Africa[a]	49.8	53.2	Taiwan	69.0	74.0
Mauritius	62.6	67.3	Cyprus	72.0	75.5
Tunisia	57.6	58.6	Hong Kong	68.8	75.5
Central America			India	51.2	50.0
Costa Rica	69.0	74.0	Indonesia	48.7	51.3
Cuba	71.1	74.4	Israel	71.4	74.9
Jamaica	67.0	71.0	Lebanon	63.1	67.0
Mexico	61.9	66.3	Korea (North)	60.5	64.6
Panama	67.6	70.9	Korea (South)	62.4	68.8
Puerto Rico	70.3	77.1	Malaysia	63.5	67.1
Dominican			Philippines	60.9	64.3
Republic	58.4	62.2	Singapore	68.6	73.1
Trinidad and			Sri Lanka	63.5	66.5
Tobago	66.5	71.0	Thailand	59.3	63.2
Latin America			Turkey	58.3	62.8
Argentina	65.4	72.1			
Brazil	59.5	64.3			
Chile	62.4	69.0			
Colombia	60.0	64.5			
British Guiana	64.1	68.9			
Uruguay	66.4	73.0			
Venezuela	63.6	69.0			

[a] According to UN estimates (1985), South African life expectation at birth for 1979–80 was only slightly over 50 years, in contrast to estimates obtained hitherto. See the *Demographic yearbook, 1980*, which gave a figure close to 60 years; given what has already been observed regarding developments in these countries, the UN revision is perhaps somewhat excessive.

Sources: UN 1985 (except for Taiwan).

populated and heterogeneous countries like India, Indonesia, Brazil, and Egypt, it took a considerably longer period before fertility responded.

Once a fertility decline gets under way, its rate seems related to that of mortality; however, there are still too few observations on less developed countries, owing to the recent nature of the fertility decline, to permit a general and definitive account. At least, we may note that European data conformed substantially to this pattern. And similar facts have emerged from a statistical analysis of the transition covering 53 countries over the

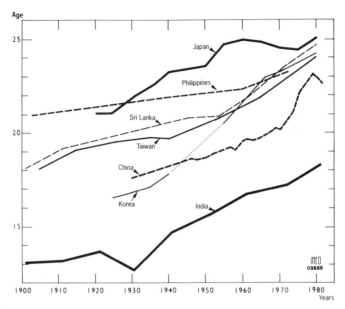

FIG. 13.1. Singulate mean age at marriage since the turn of the century, females, Asia

period 1945–70. The hypothesis that fertility trends are linked to those of mortality—which is central to transition theory—thus finds full confirmation.

The Restriction of Marriage

Fertility declines in many less developed countries were often, to begin with, merely the result of younger age structures (an increase in the proportion of children), and of an increase in the singulate mean age at marriage. In the few countries where marriages were subject to registration and of which, with the help of census data,[5] we know ages at marriage for at least half a century, the trend toward later marriage emerges even before the Second World War, and in some instances at the beginning of the century (Sri Lanka, Taiwan). Thus, in India, in 1941, singulate mean age at marriage was approximately 15 years, whereas the traditional age was around 13 years. At the same time, in Taiwan and Sri Lanka—whose developments are more or less identical (Fig. 13.1), despite cultural differences—it was already 20 years, in contrast to a figure around 18 years in 1900; by the 1970s, singulate mean age at marriage had exceeded 23 years. The rise is even more striking in Korea: between 1935 and 1970 age at first marriage rose by an average of 6 years (Blayo 1978). In

---

[5] And also Hajnal's method (1953), i.e. from the proportion of celibates (it being assumed that this has changed little over time).

all cases the increase in age at marriage preceded the fertility decline by several decades, so that even in the Philippines, where age at marriage was already comparatively high (21 years) owing to the influence of Christianity, a similar trend emerged, converging around the same value of 23 years. Concomitantly, in all these countries the proportion of lifetime celibates has generally increased from practically nil to figures ranging from 3% to 5%. This pattern occurs very widely, spreading well beyond the limits of the few Asian countries mentioned.

Hajnal (1965) has shown that it is possible to distinguish roughly three traditional systems of nuptiality: a west European, an east European, and a non-European regime. Summarized according to its main statistical characteristics (derived from measures of the unmarried female population), these regimes are as follows:

1. West European regime: late marriage, occurring on average after the age of 25, with a high incidence of lifetime celibacy (10% to 20%);
2. East European regime: 'semi-delayed' marriage (according to our terminology, see Chapter 4) at an average age around 20 years, with a low rate of lifetime celibacy (1% to 5%);
3. Non-European regime:[6] early and universal marriage, with a singulate mean age at marriage generally under 18 years, and lifetime celibacy around 1% or less.

Figure 13.2 illustrates this typology.

As the time series suggest, adoption of the West European model of late marriage from the seventeenth century onwards could have been a means of adjusting to mortality declines which owed to increasingly rare outbreaks of plague; late marriage also began earlier amongst the aristocracy or bourgeoisie (where mortality declines had started earlier) than amongst the lower classes. This regime of restricted marriage, which Coale (1965) has called the 'Malthusian transition', continued up to the period when couples began to restrict fertility within marriage, around 1870. Although pressure on subsistence in the US was in no way comparable to what it was on the old continent, the average age of females at first marriage in the US rose steadily throughout the nineteenth century:[7] in the white population it increased from 20 years in 1800 to 23.9 years in 1890 (Coale and Zelnik 1963). Table 13.2 summarizes the situation for the last generation of females who practised the regime of delayed marriage (generations born around 1840). Only Spain and Italy show an age at first marriage below 25 years: the south of each of these countries eludes the 'West European' model.

Data for eastern Europe are not so readily available. In Table 13.3 we have,

---

[6] Clearly, a more refined classification would be desirable. The description as it stands applies particularly to Asia.

[7] The persistence of this trend in the later decades of the 19th century owed in considerable part to a disequilibrium in the sex ratio consequent on the Civil War.

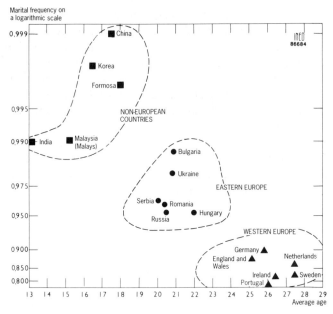

FIG. 13.2. Three nuptiality regimes: singulate mean age at marriage and marital frequency, females, before the transition of marital fertility

however, brought together some information which seems to prove that the control of marriages likewise preceded declines in marital fertility, which had scarcely begun in eastern Europe before the inter-war period. But in contrast to western Europe, this control was slight and hardly affected marital frequency, which remained very high (except in intermediate countries such as Czechoslovakia and Hungary); it mainly consisted of a slight delay in unions (1 to 3 years on average, as opposed to 5 to 10 years, probably, in the west).

The percentage of women already married at the age of 20–24 years declined appreciably in all places. Whilst the figure was as high as 70–80% around 1900, it fell to 50% and sometimes less by around 1930. The phenomenon was more marked in countries closer to north-west Europe, notably Poland, Hungary, and Czechoslovakia. In European Russia the proportion of women married at child-bearing age (Coale's index of I_m) fell from 0.696 to 0.628 between 1899 and 1926; given the effect of the First World War on the marriage market, the change is very slight (Coale et al. 1979).

Statistics for non-European countries must be read with considerable caution, on account of the relative heterogeneity of marriage practices. An initial distinction seems necessary between the countries of Latin America and the Caribbean, where consensual unions are frequent and cohabiting couples are recorded as unmarried, and Asian or African countries where the prob-

TABLE 13.2. *Singulate mean age at marriage and proportion of women married at 50 years; female generations born around 1840, Western countries*

Country	Average age at first marriage (years)	Proportion married at 50 years of age (%)
Europe		
Austria	25.1	84.9
Belgium	27.7	82.5
Denmark	27.1	88.4
Finland	25.5	85.6
England and Wales	25.2	87.6
France	24.7	86.9
Germany	25.8	89.5
Ireland	26.4	81.5
Italy	24.0	88.3
Netherlands	27.5	86.3
Norway	27.2	83.0
Portugal	26.0	78.0
Scotland	26.0	81.3
Spain	24.6	89.4
Sweden	27.5	82.4
Switzerland	27.5	81.6
Overseas English-speaking countries		
Australia	—	76.3
Canada	25.0	89.7
United States		
White women	22.6	92.7
Black women	22.1	95.2

Sources: Festy (1979).

lems of misinterpretation are of another nature: faulty age declaration (due to ignorance or, in many Islamic countries, the tendency to push up the age of young women in order to conform to laws regulating minimum age at marriage), and early marriages in which spouses do not cohabit (India in particular). Underlying this diversity of marital customs, which are often connected with the practice of dowry (Westermarck 1925), similar long-term trends are clearly visible. In order to illustrate this for the group of countries belonging to our sample which have a majority non-European population,[8] we have drawn up a comparison between two different periods. The first is prior

[8] Argentina, Uruguay, and Chile are, in consequence, excluded; their evolution appears to have followed that of southern Europe.

TABLE 13.3. *Development of female nuptiality at the beginning of the twentieth century, east European model* (percentage never married)

Country	Year	Age (years) 20–24	25–29	45–49
Bulgaria	1900	24.0	3.0	1.0
	1926	32.0	8.0	1.0
Czechoslovakia	1930	61.9	30.3	9.8
Greece	1907	44.0	13.0	4.0
	1928	55.8	25.5	3.8
Hungary	1900	36.0	15.0	4.0
	1930	51.6	24.4	6.3
Poland	1931	61.0	30.4	7.1
Romania	1899	20.0	8.0	3.0
	1912	35.0	13.0	(5.0)
Russia	1897	23		5.0
USSR	1926	27.9	8.9	3.6
Yugoslavia	1931	35.0	14.9	4.7

Sources: ISI (1916, 1939); UN (1950).

to 1950, when the secular mortality decline began;[9] the second is around 1970, when sustained fertility declines began to occur (Table 13.4). In each period we have contrasted the percentage of non-married aged 20–24 years and 25–29 years with the percentage non-married at 45–49 years. The latter may serve as an index of the frequency of lifetime celibacy; the former as an index of early marriage.

The age at entry into union has risen more or less sharply in all the countries, and yet it is not possible to identify any uniform trend for the frequency of lifetime celibacy, which rises or falls according to case. Data from the Chinese census of 1982 shows that age at first marriage has risen considerably in recent decades, giving a female average of 22.8 years (24.9 in urban areas and 22.1 in rural areas, compared with 17.5 in 1930). A similar trend applies to India, although less pronounced: the average age in 1931 was 13 years, and in 1971, 17.7 years. The custom of pre-adolescent arranged marriage is still so common that even today women in rural areas may marry earlier on average than their Chinese counterparts 50 years ago. Where the remaining Asian countries are concerned, areas of Chinese cultural influence, broadly speaking (Taiwan, Singapore, Hong Kong, Korea, Japan), and Sri

---

[9] The dates are approximate: they vary from country to country and are in part dictated by the availability of data.

TABLE 13.4. *Development of female nuptiality, Non-European model 1925–1982* (percentage never married)

Country	Year	Age (years)		
		20–24	25–29	45–49
Africa				
Egypt	1947	19.9	6.4	1.0
	1980	35.4	13.8	1.5
Tunisia (Muslims)	1946	27.6	12.6	4.3
	1975	45.5	14.5	1.6
South Africa (not incl.				
European populations)	1946	44.4	18.7	3.8
Asia				
Japan	1920	31.4	9.2	1.9
	1940	53.5	13.5	1.6
China[a]	1929–31	5.2	0.5	0.1
	1982	95.4	45.7	0.2
Hong Kong	1931	26.1	12.4	3.6
	1961	48.6	15.5	7.4
India	1931	4.7	1.8	0.8
	1971	9.1	2.0	0.4
Indonesia	(1964–65)	(14.2)	(3.6)	(1.0)
	1973	22.9	5.4	1.0
Korea (South)	1930	2.3	0.6	0.0
	1966	51.6	7.7	0.1
Malaysia	1947	7.0	2.0	1.0
	1970	32.0	9.0	1.0
Philippines	1939	36.2	18.0	5.4
	1973	55.9	24.8	6.8
Singapore	1931	24.8	13.5	—
	1966	55.8	19.9	3.0
Sri Lanka	1921	28.4	13.5	7.7
	1971	53.1	24.6	3.6
Taiwan	1905	8.4	1.8	0.3
	1965	41.4	9.7	4.0
Thailand	1947	30.0	10.9	2.9
	1970	37.9	15.6	3.0
Turkey	1935	17.6	5.5	2.5
	1980	27.1	7.3	1.5

[a] Rural China only, in 1929–31.

Sources: Population censuses, various countries; WFS (1980, 1982, 1983: 18); Blayo (1978: 984–85).

Lanka have experienced the most marked change, female age at first marriage currently approaching values characteristic of the traditional west European model of 25 years or over. Female age at marriage in the three African countries of Egypt, Tunisia, and South Africa has clearly risen, currently exceeding 20 years; for instance, Egypt in 1980 recorded an average age of 21.3, compared with 19.8 in 1947. Changes in Latin America and the Caribbean[10] are less pronounced than in Asia, which is not surprising given that unions were traditionally not formed at such early ages; but the trends have been similar at least since 1960, age at first marriage currently being around 20–22 years (Costa Rica, 1976: 22.7 years; Colombia, 1973: 22.3 years; Mexico, 1976: 21.7 years; Dominican Republic, 1975: 20.5 years; and Venezuela, 1971: 20.2 years).

This picture fully conforms to our second proposal concerning marriage restriction at the time of the health transition, since out of all the cases examined—which include virtually all countries where fertility has started to decline—we have failed to find a single exception. Moreover, certain countries are entering a regime of 'late' marriage (where unions occur on average above 25 years of age) and, aside from a few special cases, such as India (18.3 years in 1981), almost all countries are characterized by an intermediate regime in which age at first marriage averages just over 20 years. A certain convergence of models of nuptiality has thus begun, at least regarding age of entry into union: this age is increasing in places where it was hitherto young (non-European countries) while falling in those Western countries where it was previously older; as the two extremes are moving towards each other, western Europe has experienced minimal variation.

This pattern of nuptiality carries cultural and social implications which extend far beyond their immediate demographic consequences, indicating a slow transformation in relations between the sexes, in family life, and, more generally, in the status of women. Rising age at marriage in Islamic countries like Bangladesh, Morocco, Algeria, and Syria over the last two decades would appear to indicate both the power of structural changes currently in process and the generality of a two-phase transition.

2. Socio-economic Conditions

The second crucial and certainly most controversial proposition of demographic transition theory concerns the influence of economic development on demographic trends: the assumption that fertility can only decline once a

---

[10] Given the considerable instability of unions, and lack of comparability between different periods due to the changing nature of unions, these countries do not figure in our table. General observation shows a tendency for the number of legal unions to be increasing over consensual unions. Thus at the time of the 1970 census, the percentage of women in Brazil and Mexico still (legally) unmarried at the age of 50 was only 8.8 and 7.1, compared with 15.1 and 10 in 1940.

sufficiently advanced level of development has been reached. Let us situate ourselves for a moment in the mid-1960s. With the exception of those Latin American countries having considerable populations of European descent (Cuba, Argentina, Chile, and Uruguay), fertility declines had scarcely penetrated into poorer areas. The few countries which had been affected were exceptions which transition theory entirely explains: Taiwan, South Korea, Sri Lanka, and Puerto Rico. In the first three, for example, all the indicators of modernity—whether infant mortality, degree of urbanization, average age at marriage, or level of education—were very advanced in comparison to the regional average. Similarly, all the Puerto Rican indicators were very postive, and the territory, which had recently moved into the orbit of US influence, had entered a phase of large-scale emigration, which apparently accelerated its demographic transition. Birth control policies, where extant, were still at an embryonic stage, and experts admitted that fertility declines were mainly due to socio-economic changes. The success of birth control programmes appeared so dependent on the level of development that the notion was hardly debated (Freedman, in Greep 1963). It was only in subsequent years, with the apparent absence of fertility declines in the most populous countries, that criticism began to grow and was reflected in a growing number of demographic publications.

After a brief theoretical résumé, we shall examine the pattern of the main indicators of 'socio-economic development' in countries where fertility declines have begun since the 1960s.

The Transition: The Ninth Dimension of Development

The concept of development is a broad one, embracing the most varied aspects of health and economic, social, educational, cultural, and political transformations. In the most detailed study to our knowledge made on the subject (Chenery and Syrquin 1975), the phenomenon is broken down into 10 basic processes,[11] each of which may be further classified according to one of three groups: (1) accumulation (rate of investment, the proportion of national budget in the GNP, educational effort); (2) allocation of resources (structure of internal demand, sectoral distribution of production, breakdown of trade); (3) demography and distribution (sectoral distribution of the working population, degree of urbanization, stage of demographic transition, income distribution). Each one of these variables may be analysed according to its basic trends, and related directly—both in its immediate structure and in the historical sequence of changes it undergoes—to characteristics and structural changes affecting the others. At successive stages of development, measured

Within the same period, the singulate mean age at marriage rose from 16 to 22 years in Mexico, and from 22.5 to 23.3 in Brazil. Hajnal's method is inappropriate here. Finally, marital practice varies widely between countries.

[11] Defined by 27 variables.

by the growth of per capita income, the pattern of these several phenomena as a whole adheres to a typical and consistent form: in their temporal course the variables studied all show a characteristic adjustment to an S-shaped curve (or logistic function). Chenery and Syrquin's observations are equally valid for synchronic international comparisons and for national historical series, even if their method leads them in practice to concentrate on the former. Owing to the range of the field covered—101 countries in the period 1950–70, each case and each variable being considered for an interval of 2 to 20 years, their conclusions have the widest significance.

Of course the uniformity of economic behaviour disclosed by the authors is relative, much space being given to national particularities which, under the circumstances, are regarded as deviations from the average schema.

All aspects of a country's type of development may be described in terms of three components: (a) the normal effect of universal factors connected with income level, (b) the effect of other general factors such as the size of the market or national resources, and (c) the effect of the country's individual history and of its developmental policies.

Development thus described is a 'multidimensional transition', of which demographic transition is an integral part; demographic evolution is inseparable from those other basic processes which constitute development, the general pattern of structural change forming a coherent, indissociable whole.

More specifically regarding fertility, most existing studies (Adelman and Morris 1966; Beaver 1975; Oechsli and Kirk 1975; Mauldin 1981; etc.) concur in recognizing the preponderant role of four factors: health, economy, education, and urbanization. The corresponding variables are generally: the infant mortality rate (or life expectation at birth), per capita income, the literacy rate, and proportion urbanized (or the non-agricultural working population). Many studies employ a considerable number of explanatory variables—around 15 or sometimes more—but so many of them are interdependent that statistical redundance is inevitable. For example, side by side in the same analysis one finds variables like the circulation of printed media, the density of telephone networks, the proportion illiterate, attendance ratios for primary and secondary education, and so forth. Consequently, in analysing the manifold aspects of modernization, we shall use here only the most synthetic variables, referring to stocks rather than to flows, and we shall adopt a historical approach by concentrating on long time series.

The relation between fertility and health having been considered in previous chapters, let us now turn to the three other main points.

Real GNP Per Capita, or Purchasing Power

As per capita income levels are supposed to reflect stages of economic development, precision in their statistical evaluation is of the greatest importance. If, contrary to the correspondences established by Chenery and Syrquin, demographic variables are not necessarily dependent on levels of development (and hence transition theory does not hold), then fertility decline can occur at any stage of development, including the lowest income levels. Rather than give priority to economic development as the agency of fertility declines in the more or less long term, one might consider more optimistically the effect of demographic factors[12] on development, namely those which proceed through policies of family planning. This philosophy has inspired an entire school of American neo-Malthusian thought. A number of examples, notably that of Sri Lanka, have regularly been cited to support the thesis.

The support for this position remains tenuous, however, because of an error of diagnosis: *the measure of GNP per capita was calculated by conversion, using rates of exchange in dollars.* Evaluation of GNP by rates of exchange is, however, misleading because it does not necessarily reflect relative purchasing power. Such rates are based on the price of goods and services subject to international trade, yet these represent a minority of exchanges in less developed countries. Such a procedure consequently exaggerates to a great degree the real differences in income that separate developed and less developed countries. Since the introduction of floating exchange rates in 1973, giving rise to erratic fluctuations in the value of the nominal GNP as converted into dollars, correction to the level of purchasing power has become even more necessary. Work carried out on a large range of countries over the last ten years by Kravis *et al.* (1975–1982) responds directly to this issue. The divergence between nominal (or apparent) values and real (or adjusted) ones, once a common price system representative of the structure of world prices is applied, is of the order of three to four times.

Table 13.5 gives the ratio obtained (which we shall call the index of exchange rate distortion) in major less developed countries with declining fertility, alongside corresponding values, in descending order, for major developed countries. The index of distortion in exchange rates declines as GNP increases, or, in other words, the lower the income, the more methods of conversion which rely directly on exchange rates tend to underestimate real incomes. This phenomenon is due to considerable differences of price structure. Thus, in India, for example, the price of goods and services destined for exchange is half what it is in the US, while that of goods and services not exchanged is 7.5 times less. In such circumstances, at a given income, the distortion tends to decrease as national economies become more open to international trade. Sri Lanka is the absolute prototype of countries where distortion is at its highest: low income, low propensity for exchange. At a value of 3.65 the measure of distortion is the highest amongst the 18 less developed countries studied by Kravis *et al.* (1982); after correction, real per capita income in 1975 stood at $US668. When the fertility decline began, just

---

[12] Which had been thought to hinder economic growth.

TABLE 13.5. *Nominal and real gross national product (GNP) per capita in major developed and less developed countries, with a corresponding measure of exchange rate distortion*

Less developed countries	GNP per capita		Index of distortion	Developed countries	GNP per capita		Index of distortion
	Nominal	Real			Nominal	Real	
Sri Lanka	183	668	3.65	Poland	2,586	3,598	1.39
India	146	470	3.23	Spain	2,946	4,010	1.36
Colombia	568	1,609	2.83	Italy	3,440	3,861	1.12
Thailand	359	936	2.61	United Kingdom	4,134	4,588	1.11
South Korea	583	1,484	2.54	United States	7,176	7,176	1.00
Philippines	376	946	2.51	France	6,428	5,877	0.91
Mexico	1,465	2,487	1.70	West Germany	6,797	5,953	0.88
Brazil	1,149	1,811	1.58	Belgium	6,298	5,574	0.88

Source: Kravis, Heston, Summers (1982)

before 1960, this income was around $400. Adjusted to the same monetary[13] unit as used in the preceding chapter (US dollars and prices for 1960), this value is slightly above $200. In other words, in a country where fertility decline began at the lowest known level of apparent income, real GNP per capita was not very different from what it had been in European countries experiencing late transitions; and it is analogous to that of France at the same demographic stage. Indeed, it is not impossible that, in addition to the steep mortality declines experienced in many Third World countries, the factor of rural density, as in France, is playing a definite role in couples' decisions to restrict their fertility. In India and Indonesia—other examples of transition in conditions of extreme poverty—the order of magnitude at the critical period (around 1970) is similar: $200 to $250, at 1960 values. The downward trend in all the other countries cited began at appreciably higher income levels: around $300 (South Korea, Thailand, and the Philippines), $400 (Egypt), $500 (Brazil and Turkey), and even $1,000 (Mexico). The totally exceptional case of Mexico has already been remarked, in comparison with that of nineteenth-century England; earliness of industrial revolution seems to have the effect of delaying fertility decline. Aside from the two extreme points on the continuum represented by Sri Lanka and Mexico, which appear to refer to very special circumstances, the cases analysed for the most densely populated countries generally fall within the range encountered in European history: $300 to $500 ($US for 1960).

Furthermore, less developed countries experiencing marked fertility de-clines tend mostly to be distinguished by income levels appreciably higher than average in the region to which they belong, and to have embarked earlier on their economic development. In every case, even at the lowest economic levels, fertility declines were preceded by substantial rises in average incomes. Fig. 13.3 illustrates this, giving the annual increase in real per capita income (corrected) since 1950 for five countries. It should be observed, however, that there are considerable differences in initial conditions prevailing in these countries, the income bracket within which fertility begins to decline being fairly wide. It is likely that the low income thresholds in countries like Egypt, South Korea, and Sri Lanka[14] are a function of less inegalitarian income distributions and rural development policies, often accompanied by intensive family planning programmes. A similar case is that of the state of Kerala in India, where the birth-rate fell to around 25 per 1000 before 1980.

Product per capita in the main countries having advanced transitions is given in Table 13.6. The 17 countries cited represent almost 95% of the total population in our selection. In all of them except India and Indonesia real per capita income exceeds $300. However, for the chosen monetary unit, traditional levels prior to the beginning of economic development were within

---

[13] The foreign exchange value of $1 in 1975 was the equivalent of $0.534 in 1960.
[14] And, doubtless, also mainland China.

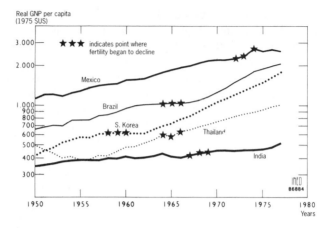

Fig. 13.3. Development of real GNP per capita in dollars, less developed countries

TABLE 13.6. *Real product per capita in less developed countries with advanced transition, 1970* (1960 $US prices)

Country	Real product per capita	Country	Real product per capita
Africa	307	Asia[a]	286
South Africa[b]	961	China (mainland)	306
Egypt	380	India	215
Tunisia	486	Indonesia	182
Latin America	886	Korea (South)	469
Costa Rica	827	Philippines	353
Mexico	923	Singapore	1,125
Puerto Rico	2,069	Sri Lanka	338
Brazil	816	Thailand	329
Colombia	621	Turkey	653

[a] Not incl. China.
[b] Incl. Namibia.

Sources: Calculated on the basis of the crude data given in Kravis *et al.* (1978: 232), except China: Bairoch (1979: 14).

the $150–200 bracket (Bairoch 1976). In the period when fertility began to decline, all the countries to a greater or lesser degree were well above this early level, and hence marked economic progress must therefore have already occurred. According to Bairoch's (1979) estimates, therefore, real per capita income in western Europe in 1870 was about double its value of a century earlier; the increase in eastern Europe at the time of the fertility decline was

TABLE 13.7. *Annual average rate of growth of the gross national product (GNP) per capita, less developed countries with advanced transition 1950–1970* (%)

Country	Rate of growth	Country	Rate of growth	Country	Rate of growth
Hong Kong	5.6	Panama	3.3	Dominican Republic	1.8
Taiwan	5.3	Venezuela	3.0	Tunisia	1.7
Jamaica	4.8	Brazil	2.7	Colombia	1.6
Korea (South)	4.5	Philippines	2.6	Chile	1.5
Trinidad and		Costa Rica	2.4	Indonesia	1.5
Tobago	4.0	West Malaysia	2.3	British Guiana	1.4
Thailand	3.8	Argentina	1.9	Egypt	1.3
Turkey	3.5	India	1.8	Uruguay	1.0[a]
Mexico	3.5	Sri Lanka	1.8		

Notes: The growth rate of living standards per capita in mainland China for the period 1952–82 amounts to an average of 2.9% per year (*Statistical Yearbook*, Peking, 1984).

[a] Figure taken from OECD Development Centre (1971).

Sources: Morawetz 1978, annex 1, except for mainland China and Uruguay

relatively of the same order, albeit with a lower starting level. Similarly, in 1970 real per capita income in China would have been over two-thirds higher than just before the Second World War; and in other less developed countries having market economies, average growth over the same period would have improved in the order of a third to half in Asia and Latin America, and by even more in Africa (the effect of economic recovery).

A detailed breakdown is given in Table 13.7 for the period 1950–70—which in most cases precedes the fertility transition—based on national accounts published by the World Bank (Morawetz 1977). None of the countries records a fall in living standards over the period concerned; indeed, the rise is fairly considerable, since, in spite of an unprecedented demographic increase, real per capita income rises generally by at least 1.5% per year. There is thus no ambiguity about the matter: the secular fertility decline occurs only after profound economic changes. Possible interpretations of these data will be considered later, in Chapters 16 and 18.

Given that fertility declines had already begun or were imminent in almost all less developed countries with over 20 million inhabitants, these conclusions are of interest more for the past than for the future. The real question for the future is to predict patterns of fertility decline, for demographic growth rates remain very high, and crude mortality is still in some cases fairly far from its base level. The relation between income growth and fertility transition can at present be studied really only in a few advanced cases in eastern Asia or

Central America, where fertility has declined considerably. However, precisely because these cases have benefited from a conjunction of favourable circumstances (their smallness, lack of ethnic conflict, openness to external influence, strategic economic position), questions arise about the degree to which their experience is transferable. We shall remark here only that the rate of mortality decline remains, in itself, a valuable indicator, since, as we have already seen, this rate tends to herald the subsequent trend of fertility decline amongst couples.

Female Education

In analysing results of differential fertility studies, it is customary to observe that the variable most closely correlated with family size is the educational level of mothers—a distinction being clearest between women educated to a standard above primary level, and those who are not. We have already remarked that logically such a relation is inevitable, owing to the selectivity of education, especially regarding women in traditional contexts. Such measures owe their discriminatory power to being indicators simultaneously of female status and of the presence of more or less long-established literate cultures.

We have used a simple measure for changes in levels of female education: the proportion of women able to read and write at various ages, as recorded in census data arranged to reflect the generations concerned. Data have been assembled for all the large countries in our selection, including China. In this way it has been possible to establish not only levels of literacy, but of the comparable rapidity of development over time. The trends for the most populous countries in each of the three continents of the less developed world are given in Fig. 13.4(a) to (c). Broadly speaking, the data cover generations born between 1900 and 1960. Every country witnessed a massive increase in education during later decades;[15] this was certainly a phenomenon of the utmost importance, and the strongest common denominator in all countries where fertility transition has become established. The second pronounced feature is that the spread of female education has generally not been a new phenomenon, but belongs to a very early movement, sometimes dating from the end of the nineteenth century.

The proportion of adult illiteracy is about one-third among generations of South African Bantu women born around 1915; they represent the most advanced non-European population in Africa in this respect. This suggests that remarkable efforts were made to promote adult literacy, beginning apparently as early as the second half of the nineteenth century; the literacy rate amongst generations born around 1940 is above 50%. Tunisia had not

---

[15] Even if the consistency of results from one census to the next leaves much to be desired (particularly where Egypt is concerned), the progress in female education over the generations remains, in all cases, relatively rapid.

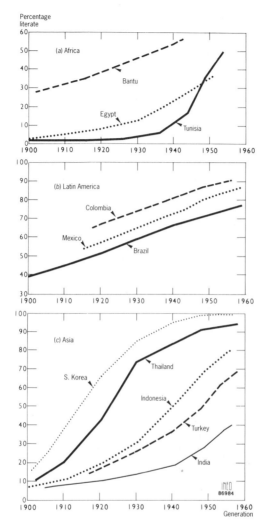

Fig. 13.4. Development of the proportion of women able to read and write, by generation, in the main less developed countries with advanced transition

reached a similar level even amongst generations born in 1950, and yet it represents the most advanced country in the Maghreb, a region much more favoured than Black Africa. In Egypt, progress started earlier but advanced more slowly than in Tunisia; the level of 10% literate females was attained among generations born around 1925. Assuming that reading and writing skills are acquired by the age of 10, the educational system would have reached this level in the mid-1930s, whereas in Tunisia this did no͏t occur until the immediate post-war education policies had borne fruit in the 1940 generation; however, the gap rapidly closed by the time of the generation born in 1948, and the youngest generations even began to take a considerable lead. The comparative slowness of the spread of elementary education in early stages of development perhaps helps to account for the difficulties later encountered by family planning programmes, and the reversibility of demographic trends which has characterized Egypt. However, there can be no doubt that a prevailing tide of religious fundamentalism has played a principal role.

Levels in the main Latin American countries of Brazil, Mexico, and Colombia are considerably higher, and fairly similar to each other, the trends themselves running parallel. The proportion of women able to read and write amongst generations born at the beginning of the century was already over 40%; in terms of historical time lags, this corresponds to a fifty-year lead over countries like Egypt or Tunisia, and implies a more rapid transition to restricted fertility. Amongst generations born around 1960, and currently of child-bearing age, the percentage of illiterate women was no greater than 10% to 20%.

The contrasts in Asia are much more marked. There is a wide gap between India, where the trend recalls that of Egypt, and the countries bordering the Pacific. Turkey occupies an intermediate position. The ASEAN countries are all distinguished by their outstanding results, which have often been the consequence of considerable efforts during the last decades represented in the figure. Nothing better illustrates this than the comparison of illiteracy percentages between age groups 55–64 and 15–24 years; Table 13.8 gives some quantitative data, derived from 1970 censuses. The ratio of the two illiteracy measures gives an idea (exaggerated on account of the forty-year gap between the two age groups) of the different abilities characterizing mothers and daughters at adult ages; and it tells us especially about the differences in human capital between candidates entering the job market and their elders at retirement age. In other words, this measure[16] is as informative about probable rates at which fertility will reach modern levels as it is on the potential for economic development.

The ASEAN countries are distinguished from the general pattern by indices consistently above 3, the record being held by South Korea, which occupies a similar position to Japan 20 years earlier. The countries with

---

[16] The slope of the trends to which this index implicitly corresponds gives a minimal and a priori idea of the speed at which literacy progresses. It is still possible in fact for the youngest generations to catch up during adulthood; also, the oldest generations tend to declare a higher level of education than they actually possess. This index has not been standardized to take into account the distance from the asymptotes of the percentages which comprise the fraction under consideration. The same index therefore does not possess the same significance, but must be interpreted according to the starting-point of trends. Thus, the Philippines and Singapore have comparable indices (5.2 and 5.4 respectively), but in the first case the percentage of illiterates only declined by 30% compared with 70% in the second. The same holds for Sri Lanka and Malaysia.

TABLE 13.8. *Proportions illiterate and indices of progress between female generations, less developed countries, 1970 (unless otherwise stated)*

Contemporary Transitions   389

Country	Proportion illiterate (age in years) 15–24 (a)	55–64 (b)	Index of intergenerational progress (b/a)	Country	Proportion illiterate (age in years) 15–24 (a)	55–64 (b)	Index of intergenerational progress (b/a)
Egypt, 1960	76.5	97.1	1.3	Indonesia	26.2	88.0	3.4
India, 1971	67.5	92.5	1.4	Sri Lanka, 1971	15.7	56.6	3.6
Turkey	45.0	89.8	2.0	Malaysia	25.5	92.5	3.6
Brazil	25.3	55.4	2.2	Philippines	7.6	39.3	5.2
China (mainland), 1982	38.0[a]	92.0[b]	2.3	Singapore	15.7	84.6	5.4
Mexico	18.2	50.0[a]	2.75	Thailand	8.2	79.8	9.7
				South Korea	1.2	61.5	(51.2)

[a] Generations born around 1950.
[b] Generations born around 1910. In the case of China, data are for 'illiterate' and 'semi-illiterate' (knowledge of less than 1,500 words).

Sources: National censuses, special sections; UN (1980).

highest economic growth and strongest demographic declines thus tend to lead the way. The combination of an educational boom, demographic revolution, and economic ascendancy can hardly be a random event: each of these three forces acts as both cause and effect on the others, a veritable cycle of excellence.

Even in the poorer countries considered earlier (India, Indonesia, Sri Lanka) remarkable progress has been achieved: within a context of low income and slow growth, fertility declines may owe largely, all things being equal, to declines in illiteracy. In each country, whatever the income level, the rate of progress is swift and the process already has a long history behind it; literacy amongst adults of child-bearing age is often greater than that which prevailed in southern or eastern Europe in the period 1880–90, at a similar stage of development. And despite the marked differences in demographic growth between these regions, the increase down generations has been considerably faster in the Asian cases. Even in India (1971), whose comparative situation is unfavourable, the trend in literacy by generation compares very favourably with that of Italy a century earlier.

Of course, in a country as vast and diverse as India the social landscape varies considerably: aggregate female literacy rates range from 1 to 6 persons out of 10, depending on the state. As Table 13.9 shows, birth-rates appear to be more closely connected with the degree of literacy than income level or population density. The states with birth-rate below 30 per 1000 have female literacy levels markedly higher than the national average (25%), the clearest example being that of Kerala, with a birth-rate of 25.7 per 1000 (compared with 33 per 1000 for the whole of India) in 1977–79, and a 65% female literacy level. Conversely, with the exception of the very poor and densely populated state of Bihar, those states with low female literacy (below 20%) have very high natality, ranging between 35 and 40 per 1000: Rajasthan, Madya Pradesh, and, especially, Uttar Pradesh, with 111 million inhabitants.

The Urban Context

With regard to urbanization, fertility transition appears to occur in very different contexts. With reference to the period around 1970, when fertility began to decline in the majority of cases, Latin American countries were characterized by a high urban population percentage (50% to 60%), whilst Asian countries were still preponderantly rural; the latter includes 20% of the population in China, India, Thailand, and Sri Lanka, about 30% in the Philippines, and 40% in South Korea, where, however, per capita income was relatively high and literacy extraordinarily advanced. These examples show that sensitivity to different developmental factors can vary from one region to another, depending on local constraints, historical background, and random circumstance. In Egypt, for example, where conventional indicators of modernity are very unfavourable, the density of its agricultural population is

TABLE 13.9. *Fertility and socio-economic characteristics, by state: India, 1977–1981*

State	Population, 1981 (millions)	Natality[a] 1977–79 (per 1000)	Mortality[a] 1977–79 (per 1000)	Density (per km^2)	Annual income per inhabitant, 1979–80 (rupees)	Percentage literate women, all ages, 1981
Andhra Pradesh	53.4	32.6	13.4	194	1,176	20.5
Assam	19.9	31.1	12.5	254	960	—
Bihar	69.8	31.2	12.8	402	773[b]	13.6
Gujarat	34.0	35.9	12.5	173	1,623	32.3
Karnataka	37.0	28.1	11.2	193	1,267	27.8
Kerala	25.4	25.7	7.0	654	1,091[b]	64.5
Madhya Pradesh	52.1	37.8	16.0	118	828[b]	15.5
Maharashtra	62.7	26.8	11.3	204	1,903	35.1
Orissa	26.3	31.7	15.2	169	843	21.1
Punjab and Haryana	29.5	32.0	11.6	314	2,100	28.9
Rajasthan	34.1	34.8	14.4	100	913	11.3
Tamil Nadu	48.3	28.9	12.9	371	1,350	34.1
Uttar Pradesh	110.9	40.1	18.5	377	981[b]	14.1
West Bengal	54.5	30.8	11.7	614	1,330	30.3
Union of India	683.8	33.1	13.9	221	1,379	24.9

[a] Sample Registration Survey.
[b] 1978–79.

Sources: Statistical Outline of India, Bombay, 1982; Lardinois (1982); Kumar and Krishnamurty in Bairoch and Lévy-Leboyer (1981).

such that the country appears relatively urbanized (42%). In its case the strategic factors determining fertility decline are likely to be of a totally different nature from those in Korea or Colombia.

The explanatory power of the urban factor is, in itself, relatively feeble. Chenery and Syrquin (1975) have shown that when one controls for the influence of per capita income, infant mortality, and educational level, urbanization plays a negligible role.

Conclusion

Even if patterns of fertility decline differ from one case to another in the developing as in the industrialized world, the same general causes appear to have been at work: improvement in health conditions, higher educational standards, increase in income, a change in female status. And this appears to hold regardless of the diversity of cultures, family structures, and social organizations, ethnicity, clan, caste, sect, and so forth. There is good reason for the close relation between the degree of advancement in demographic transition and indicators of socio-economic development: the demographic transition is itself an aspect of the general development of societies. In this sense, demographic measures are themselves indicators of development, and are used as such by experts of all disciplines, as a matter of course. As these measures relate to one of the most fundamental aspects of development—the perpetuation of life—their connection with other aspects of development cannot but be close; in consequence, it has been impossible to avoid querying the somewhat tautological nature which has characterized some attempts at empirical validation of such linkages.

Having now established the role of those classic motors of development which underlie demographic transition, it remains to consider what has fuelled this process. This brings us back to the preoccupations of the preceding chapter. A long historical perspective is, more than ever, indispensable, progress being essentially a kind of sedimentary process in which various 'deposits' or local innovations are laid down, transposed, and imitated.

The Latin American countries most permeated by European culture, through migration, language, religion, and customs, are precisely those in which socio-economic and demographic modernization began earliest; indeed, the greater the cultural influence, generally the earlier the whole process began. Conversely, demographic lags are often in direct relation to the absence of openness to external influences, together with the relative importance of the Amerindian population. Similarly, in Asia, those countries traditionally most open to the assimilation of foreign models were in all respects the most rapidly modernized. The emergence of the Japanese sphere of influence speaks eloquently of this process: Japan and its early colonies are now in the forefront, whether from the point of view of health, economic, or cultural vari-

ables. The extent and length of exposure to modernizing influences are
similarly reflected in Africa by differing mortality levels, particularly the excess
mortality of subtropical regions. The case of South African Bantu populations
is, in itself, a sufficient illustration: their educational level, life expectation,
and incomes are far superior to those of any other Black African people.

Present demographic trends in less developed countries can only be truly
understood in light of colonial history and its continuing effects. This could
not be a more delicate issue, owing to the passion which it continues to
excite, but the time has come to confront it in good conscience, and to aim
to evaluate its various effects as objectively as possible, whether 'positive'
or 'negative'. Otherwise, we shall be confined to rehearsing the data and
repeating the same clichés on the influence of this or that variable, without
being able to understand in depth what determines demographic changes.

Our conclusions on the relation between stages of development and phases
of demographic transition also contain a lesson which may add a helpful
perspective on debates about choices between economic development priorities
and family planning as means of accelerating fertility decline. From the
evidence, this represents a false choice. Whether we consider eighteenth-
century France, or the Indianapolis survey, fertility decline remains, above all,
a matter of motivation. The regime of the only child has prevailed in certain
Hungarian provinces since the nineteenth century without the aid of any
modern contraceptive. Fertility decline can occur without family planning, but
it cannot occur without socio-economic development: the repeated failures of
family planning in India during the 1950s and 1960s, despite the colossal
budgets allocated to it, are the most convincing testimony of this. There is
therefore no question of choosing between the two 'solutions' to the demographic 'problem': we should not confuse the motive force of a car with the
spinning of one of its wheels.

Family planning is only an adjunct, destined to have a greater or lesser
force depending on the general context and appropriateness of the means
chosen. As in all policies of State intervention, whether pro- or antinatalist, it
acts only marginally in itself,[17] given the many determining factors which
precede it. A World Bank study (Faruqee 1979), which in its methodological
and analytical incisiveness stands out from most others, separates the respective influences of family planning and socio-economic development and
shows, by factorial analysis of 56 less developed countries, that the effectiveness of birth control programmes is dictated by factors preceding such efforts,
and not by the characteristic methods applied in this sector. The study
emphasizes four independent dimensions. The first of these—corresponding
to the four independent variables represented by life expectation at birth,
GNP, urbanization, and density of medical services—describes the level of

[17] Short of actually violating individual freedom by recourse to authoritarian methods of
demographic control.

development; the second, which relates to the size of State budgets, particularly where education and health are concerned, describes the role of the public sector in economy. It is only with the third dimension that family planning policy appears, with its diverse contributions. The part of the variance explained by such policies is considerably less than that of development of the role of the State: 15% compared with 30% and 19%, respectively.[18] The technical vision of family planning as a universal remedy to the ills of the Third World is put in its place, whilst due prominence is given to the more weightly reflections of authors like Kuznets (1967) or Leibenstein (1974).

The incentive to adopt contraception cannot exist unless couples have already freed themselves of the fears of the past: the repeated deaths of their children, chronic malnutrition, the inability to understand or control destiny for want of personal rights and basic education—all of which can scarcely change before moderate levels of development are attained. The history of development leads us to the *histoire des mentalités*.

Bibliography to Chapter 13

ADELMAN, I. (1963), 'An Econometric Analysis of Population Growth', *AER*, 53: 314–39.

—— and MORRIS, C. T. (1966), 'A Quantitative Study of Social and Political Determinants of Fertility', *EDCC*, 14: 129–57.

BAIROCH, P. (1976), 'Europe's Gross National Product: 1800–1975', *JEEH*, 2: 273–340.

—— (1979), *Annales* (Paris).

—— and LÉVY-LEBOYER, M. (eds.) (1981), *Disparities in Economic Development since the Industrial Revolution* (London: Macmillan).

BEAVER, S. E. (1975), *Demographic Transition Theory Reinterpreted* (Lexington, Mass.).

BLAYO, Y. (1978), 'Les Premiers Mariages féminins en Asie', *Population*, 4–5: 951–86.

BONGAARTS, J. (1978), 'A Framework for Analysing the Proximate Determinants of Fertility', *PDR*, 4: 105–18.

CHANG, C. WARREN, R., and PENDLETON, B. (1979), 'Testing and Clarifying a Macromodel of Socio-economic Change and Fertility', *Social Biology*, 1: 30–50.

CHENERY, H., and SYRQUIN, M. (1975), *Patterns of Development, 1950–1970* (Oxford: Oxford University Press).

CHESNAIS, J. -C. (1983), 'La Durée de vie dans les pays industriels', *La Recherche* (Sept.), 1040–48.

CHO, L. J., and RETHERFORD, R. D. (1973), 'Comparative Analysis of Recent Fertility Trends in East Asia', *General Conference of the IUSSP, Liège, 1973*, ii. 163–78.

---

[18] The fourth dimension is economic growth, measured by rates over an average period, which accounts for 13% of the variance.

CIPOLLA, C. M. (1969), *Literacy and Development in the West* (London).

COALE, A. J. (1965), 'Factors Associated with the Development of Low Fertility', in *UN World Population Conference, Belgrade, 1965*.

—— and ZELNICK, M. (1963), *New Estimates of Fertility and Population in the US* (Princeton, NJ: Princeton University Press).

—— ANDERSON, B. A., and HÄRM, E. (1979), *Human Fertility in Russia since the Nineteenth Century* (Princeton, NJ: Princeton University Press).

DAVIS, K. (1967), 'Population Policy: Will Current Programs Succeed?', *Science* (Nov.), 730–39.

FARUQEE, R. (1979), *Sources of Fertility Decline: Factors Analysis of Intercountry Data*', World Bank Staff Working Paper no. 318, Feb. (Washington, DC).

FESTY, P. (1979), *La Fécondité des pays occidentaux de 1870 à 1970*, Travaux et Documents (Paris: INED-PUF).

FICHET-BARRE, M. D. (1980), *L'Influence de la baisse de la mortalité sur la fécondité dans la transition démographique*, Thèse de 3ᵉ Cycle (Paris: IEP).

FREEDMAN, R. (1954), *Human Culture and Fertility* (Paris: UNESCO).

GREEP, R. O. (1963), *Human Fertility and Population Problems* (Cambridge).

HAJNAL, J. (1953*a*), 'Age at Marriage and Proportions Marrying', *Population Studies*, 7: 111–32.

—— (1953*b*), 'The Marriage Boom', *Population Index*, 19(2), 80–101.

—— (1965), 'European Marriage Patterns in Perspective', in D. V. Glass and D. E. C. Eversley, *Population in History* (London: Edward Arnold), 101–43.

HARBISON, F. H., MARUHNIC, J., and RESNICK, J. R. (1970), *Quantitative Analysis of Modernization and Development* (Princeton).

ISI (1916), *Annuaire international de statistique*, i: *État de la population* (The Hague: ISI).

—— (1939), *Aperçu de la démographie des divers pays de monde, 1929–1936* (The Hague: ISI).

KING, T. (ed.) (1974), *Population Policies and Economic Development* (Baltimore, Md.: Johns Hopkins University Press).

KIRK, D. (1971), 'A New Demographic Transition', in *Rapid population growth* (Baltimore, Md.: National Academy of Sciences).

KOCHER, J. E. (1973), *Rural Development, Income Distribution and Fertility Decline* (New York: Population Council).

KRAVIS, I. B., KENESSEY, Z., HESTON, A., and SUMMERS, R. (1975–82), Phase 1: *A System of International Comparisons of Gross Product and Purchasing Power* (Baltimore, Md.: Johns Hopkins University Press, World Bank, UN, 1975). Phase 2: *International Comparison of Real Product and Purchasing Power* ... (Baltimore, Md.: Johns Hopkins University Press, 1978*a*). Phase 3: *World Product and Income: International Comparison of Real GDP* ... (Baltimore, Md.: Johns Hopkins University Press, 1982).

—— —— —— —— (1978*b*), 'Real GDP Per Capita for more than One Hundred Countries', *EJ* (June), 215–42.

KUZNETS, S. (1967), 'Population and Economic Growth', *Proceedings of the American Philosophical Society*, 111: 170–93.

—— (1972), 'Problems in Comparing Recent Growth Rates for Developed and Less Developed Countries', *EDCC* (Jan.).

LARDINOIS, R. (1982), 'L'Inde: conjoncture démographique', *Population*, 6: 1045–64.

LEIBENSTEIN, H. (1974), 'Socio-economic Fertility Theories and their Relevance to Population Policy', *International Labor Review*, 109 (May–June).

McCARTHY, J. (1982), 'Differentials in Age at First Marriage', *Comparative Studies: Cross National Summaries* (London: WFS, ISI).

McGRANAHAN, D. C. et al. (1970), *Contents and Measurement of Socio-economic Development: An Empirical Enquiry*, Report no. 70.10 (Geneva: UNRISD).

McNICOLL, G. (1980), 'Institutional Determinants of Fertility Change', *PDR*, 6: 441–68.

MASON, K. O., DAVID, A. S., et al. (1971), *Social and Economic Correlates of Family Fertility: A Survey of the Evidence*, AID contract report (Durham, NC: Research Triangle Institute).

MAULDIN, W. P. (1981), 'The Determinants of Fertility Decline in Developing Countries: An Overview of the Available Empirical Evidence', *IUSSP General Conference, Manila, 1981*, i (New York).

—— BERELSON, B., and SYKES, S. (1978), 'Conditions of Fertility Decline in Developing Countries, 1965–1975', *Studies in Family Planning*, 90–147.

MORAWETZ, D. (1977), *Twenty-Five Years of Economic Development: 1950 to 1975* (Baltimore, Md.).

NOIN, D. (1983), *La Transition démographique dans le monde* (Paris: PUF, Le Géographe).

OECD Development Centre (1971), *Latest National Accounts of LDCS* (Paris: OECD, Feb.).

OECHSLI, F. W., and KIRK, D. (1975), 'Modernization and the Demographic Transition in Latin America and the Caribbean', *EDCC*, 3: 391–419.

PETERSEN, W. (1969), *Population*, 2nd edn. (New York: Macmillan), 576.

ROBINSON, W. C. (1965), *Socio-economic Preconditions for a Successful Family Planning Scheme* (Karachi: Pakistan Institute of Development Economics).

SATIN, M. (1969), 'An Empirical Test of the Descriptive Validity of Demographic Transition on a Fifty-Three Sample', *Sociological Quarterly*, 190–203.

SWEEZY, A. (1976), 'Economic Development and Fertility Change', in *New Perspectives on the Demographic Transition* (Washington, DC: Smithsonian Institution).

TEITELBAUM, M. (1975), 'Relevance of Demographic Transition Theory for Developing Countries', *Science*, 420–25.

TSUI, A. O., and BOGUE, D. J. (1978), 'Declining World Fertility: Trends, Causes, Implications', *Population Bulletin*, Population Reference Bureau, Washington, 33(4), 3–55.

TURCHI, B. (1975), 'Microeconomic Theories of Fertility: A Critique', *Social Forces* (Sept.), 107–25.

UN (1950), *Demographic Yearbook 1949–1950* (New York: UN).

—— (1976), *Multivariate Analysis of WFS Data for Selected ESCAP Countries: New Perspectives on the Demographic Transition* (Washington, DC: UN).

—— (1977), *Compendium of Social Statistics 1977* (New York: UN).

—— (1983), *The Relationship between Fertility and Education: A Comparative Analysis of WFS Data for 22 Developing Countries* (New York: UN).

—— (1985), *World Population Prospects as Assessed in 1982* (New York: UN).

WEINSTEIN, J. A. (1979), *Demographic Transition and Social Change* (University of Iowa).

WESTERMARCK, E. (1925), *The History of Human Marriage*, 6 vols. (London).

WFS (1980), *Age at First Marriage*, Comparative Studies, no. 7.

—— (1982), *Differentials in Age at First Marriage*, Cross-National Summaries, no. 19.

—— (1983), *The Egyptian Fertility Survey 1980* (Cairo: WFS), ii.

World Bank (1978–84), *Report on World Development, 1978–1984* (Washington, DC).

14 The Revolution
in Mental Attitudes and
Demographic Revolution

Christianity in the Middle Ages had so firmly impressed upon people's minds the ideal of renunciation as the basis of personal and social perfection, that it was long impossible to follow the other path, which led to the conscious improvement and perfecting of the world.

(J. Huizinga)

The world is in no way a machine. I mean it is not like a motor run by personal interests, checks, balances; that there is something quite different in it than the racket of the spinning jenny and of parliamentary majorities; and, in short, that it is not a machine at all.

(T. Carlyle)

DEMOGRAPHY, like other disciplines, but certainly more than most social sciences, is subject to a law of development which gradually becomes more and more manifest: the growing imbalance between the accumulation of statistical data and the significance of the lessons that can be extracted from them. Does the refinement of analysis constitute an obstacle to understanding? And does the diversity of methods and results discourage all attempts at synthesis?

It is in fertility studies that this imbalance is strongest. Reading the innumerable works addressed to possible causes of secular fertility declines, one is impressed by the great confusion which exists on the subject. 'The map of fertility [in France, in 1861] recalls no known economic, cultural or religious struture,' write Le Bras and Todd (1981). Originally intended as a systematic approach which would at last sort out the historical circumstances leading to individual control of fertility, the massive Princeton study, addressed to 700 European geographic units covering six countries, certainly drew attention to the significance of cultural boundaries: but it did not lead to a unitary treatment of data, and above all, 'failed to establish precise relations' (Bolton and Leasure 1979). The phenomenon studied is indeed subject to a very complex play of changing factors, but the apparent imbroglio also seems connected with the growing proliferation of fields of study. To economics, sociology, anthropology, history, etc. are added all their possible combinations: economic anthropology, economic history, social history, and so forth. On any given problem the possible perspectives multiply. The arguments of major writers of the early twentieth century (J. Bertillon, Bohac, Leroy-Beaulieu, Landry, Wolf, Notestein), or even of the nineteenth century (Le Play, Dumont, L. A. Bertillon, etc.), often resurface, divided and reappropriated according to specialization. But they are now disguised beneath more or less obscure jargon. Theoretical disputes, when they occur, often seem more like ethnic rivalries than real exchanges of view. What *is* new is that evidence is much more rigorously scrutinized, and recently some writers have begun the attempt to overcome rifts between disciplines. The incompatibility of approaches is in fact more artificial than real.

This chapter is intended to draw attention to the unity of the subject. The first part presents a résumé, in the form of simple propositions, of the main conclusions which may be drawn from the tests carried out in preceding chapters: demographic transition theory is confirmed by them, but also updated and clarified. The second part analyses the theoretical limitations of certain studies which, by giving priority to political or religious development, attempt to play down the role of economic factors in fertility decline.

1. The Laws of Demographic Transition

Between pre-modern and modern society, populations shifted from a regime of 'high equilibrium' (high mortality and fertility) to one of 'low equilibrium' (low mortality and fertility). The demographic transition corresponds to this period of disequilibrium. The analysis of long time series leads to the following formulation of the laws that characterize this transition:

(1) The initial disequilibrium is precipitated by a mortality decline. A decline in mortality is a necessary pre-condition of fertility decline.

In all countries, the decline in infant and juvenile mortality pre-dated fertility regulation. This contradicts Scrimshaw's argument (1978) that the presence of very high levels of infant mortality indicates a population ready to adopt family planning, and thus that it is not necessary to wait until health conditions improve before implementing birth control programmes. Even if there were a real urgency to launch such a programme, it would be unlikely to succeed unless prior public health improvements had been made.

(2) Mortality decline appears consistently to have been accompanied by a spread of mass literacy, particularly among females. The decision of couples to limit their fertility thus seems inconceivable without a significant increase in basic education among women.

These two first propositions would have seemed banal in the nineteenth century; they are less so in the West at the end of the twentieth century because the real meaning of poverty, unhealthiness, and illiteracy escapes those who study them. The best predictors of fertility decline are in fact the presence of declines in mortality and of progress in mass education. Through a complex and retroactive liaison, these two multifaceted phenomena encourage individuation (in the Durkheimian sense), which is to say, the liberation of the individual from old codes of behaviour, whether familial, religious, political, or economic. Individual liberty is fundamental to innovation.

(3) As a corollary to points 1 and 2, marriage occurs later and less frequently. In all countries having the relevant statistical data, the limitation of marriages precedes the practice of fertility regulation by couples.

(4) Economic development, which may assume a variety of forms, seems generally necessary to the emergence of a decline in fertility.

Assertions such as 'economic change has not always occurred at the time of fertility decline' or 'economic development rarely suffices and is not necessary to determine a decline in fertility' (Bolton and Leasure 1979) are not confirmed, at least on a national scale. Understanding and, in particular, measurement of past economic growth has long been inadequate, but recent advances in economic history now afford us a more accurate assessment: it is thus possible to assert that demographic change is consequent on a more or less long period of economic development. In all the countries examined, at the point at which fertility among couples began to decline, economic progress, as measured by the growth of the corrected real per capita GNP, was at least 50%[1] compared with the pre-modern period: moreover, the standard of living was double or triple its level before the onset of modern economic growth. This aspect will be analysed at greater length in Chapters 17 and 18.

(5) The influence of 'urbanization' in precipitating fertility declines appears, as a general rule, to leave little room for doubt. It is, however, difficult to isolate, and has not been the subject of very detailed analysis here. All the countries in which fertility declines are manifest have reached a certain population density or a certain degree of urban concentration, varying from one case to another.

When fertility began to decline in Europe during the last third of the nineteenth century, large towns grew considerably in number and absorbed an increasing proportion of the rural demographic surplus. In the developing world with advanced transition, urbanization has become anarchic or uncontrolled, assuming unparalleled proportions; but it is also the case that rates of development—demographic, economic, educational, and cultural—have been considerably faster than in European countries at a similar stage, so

---

[1] Except perhaps in France, where growth during the pre-revolutionary period was fairly weak.

that the significance of the notion 'urban' differs profoundly from what it represented in developed countries at an equal population level. Initially urban migration may have the effect of increasing fertility by diminishing certain regulatory customs, such as maternal breast-feeding or sexual abstinence.

(6) In addition to these factors, which are common to all countries, others, such as pressure on the land or inheritance systems, can also intervene here or there. But it would be impossible to give an exhaustive list of factors, given the variety of contexts arising from historical circumstances.[2]

(7) International migration and natural increase are intimately linked. The intensity of the nineteenth-century European exodus was a direct function of the net reproduction rate experienced at the time; conversely, when the NRR falls below unity, migratory streams tend to reverse directions, after a time lag of about 20 years; immigration is then furnished by countries with late transitions.

2. The Limitations of Anti-Economic Approaches

Given the number of factors influencing procreative decisions, the possible covariations of fertility trends with the development of other phenomena is endless—hence the variety of existing analytical frameworks. Of course it is easier to handle quantifiable factors such as increasing chances of survival, rates of literacy, or income levels, but the role of qualitative factors such as the decline of 'religious feeling' or the democratization of political structures cannot be overlooked. In the preface to the article by Bolton and Leasure (1979), Le Bras writes,

Because [these authors] refuse to quantify what is called democracy, individualism, and liberty, are they condemned solely to expressing an opinion? The reader of this text should come to the opposite conclusion. They certainly do not employ statistical formulae, and confine themselves to observing the coincidence and succession of events. But there is nothing to prevent subsequent quantification of these undertakings, and further refinement of discussion.

This has now been done: both Leasure (1982) and Lesthaeghe (1982, 1983) have made quantitative evaluations of the influence of the development of mental attitudes.

---

[2] Historical disasters such as the Irish famine, the Thirty Years War in Germany, the Northern War in Scandinavia, the plague, and the Hundred Years War in England and France have had decisive effects. English population was reduced by half, only regaining its 1340 level by about 1550; two centuries later, with a population of 6 million, its numbers had only increased by half and density was fairly low. In contrast, France repopulated more quickly, and appears to have reached saturation level: the French population was then four times that of England.

Political Development and Fertility Decline

The desire for liberty, the ideal of democracy, and the questioning of monarchical and other traditional forms of authority such as the Church, the Army, and landed aristocracy, have all been put forward in opposition to economic changes as explanations of fertility decline. Although seductive at first appearance, this approach strikes us as logically debatable and unproven historically, since political and economic development are not independent of each other and, indeed, are highly interdependent. Economic growth pre-supposes both the disappearance of various taboos governing many aspects of everyday life (including many traditional social roles), and liberation from medieval tutelage and statutes, the organization of internal and foreign trade, and the shedding of certain beliefs concerning the way in which money is handled. In other words, it presupposes a new ideology based on trust and tolerance: a common currency should apply to the whole land, replacing old currencies; a common authority, endowed with policing powers, should be recognized by all social forces. The birth of the modern State could only occur after this kind of collective mental maturation, of which the motto 'Reason, Tolerance, Humanity', belonging to the philosophy of the Enlighten-ment, is the clearest illustration. The liberal State, in the Lockean sense of an arbiter of individual passions and guarantor of fundamental liberties, gradually became the incarnation of certain republican ideals.

The existence of a regulatory State and political stability acts as a guarantee for economic development. As a reciprocal function, the increase in wealth helps to reinforce the State: the growth of the budget and of a class of civil servants (who were amongst the first to practise 'contraception') assists the promotion of education, health, and security as estimable values which act, in turn, as major stimulants to economic development. What could be more symbolic of this process than the idea of economic policy, which, under the influence of Keynes, assumed such force in the everday life of nations from the 1930s.

Bolton and Leasure (1979) stress parallels between France and the United States.[3] For both countries, the eighteenth century represented the emerg-ence of the Republic and the rights of man; and fertility regulation was adopted at an early stage by both. The similarities are doubtless not fortu-itous: liberty and family planning are two faces of modernity. The authors consider that political development contributed to the precocity of demo-graphic modernization, which, at least in principle, can hardly be contested. But they pass over in silence the common factor of pressure on the land which, as already seen, seems to have played a crucial role in New England, as well as France. Above all, they fail to comment on the case of England, where

[3] In the US the total fertility rate fell from 7.0 in 1800 to 5.2 in 1860; much of the decline may be attributed to controls on nuptiality.

the Revolution occurred a century earlier and fertility only began to decline in 1878. Why, then, didn't England—the cultural womb of America—experience movement towards fertility regulation at the same time,[4] or even before, given that individualism had a long history in England (Macfarlane 1978)? Moreover, why did similar developments not occur in most European countries immediately following the 1848 revolution? Could this not happen until a critical mass had been reached?

The influence of individual emancipation, estimated from the proportion of votes attributed to non-religious parties, was measured for the first time by Lesthaeghe (1977), using Belgian data. The analysis was subsequently extended, with some adjustments, to five other Western countries: The Netherlands, Denmark, Germany, Switzerland, and Italy (Lesthaeghe and Wilson 1982). Aside from the fact that fertility declines emerged in the most diverse political contexts, including essentially monarchical or dictatorial regimes, and that the explanatory framework is only applicable to the old pluralist democracies of the West, the pertinence of this line of reasoning may be questioned. Owing to the absence of a strong State and social legislation, liberal capitalism in its early forms was a crude affair; working conditions in the first half of the nineteenth century are notorious, and strikes and uprisings were bloody affairs. The first workers' unions were formed in mining areas; their national audience depended largely on the type and degree of industrialization. In the elections at the time of the First World War, progressive or reformist votes were significant only in countries where industry occupied an important place within the economic structure (England, Walloon parts of Belgium, Czechoslovakia, Germany, and France). Consequently, the intensity of the non-traditional vote as a variable explaining fertility decline, in opposition to the level of industrialization, is not convincing, precisely because the force of the labour movement was determined by the excesses of industrialism. In mining areas, industrial capitalism was the 'catalyst of secularization'. This is not to say that the *actual* explanatory power of changes in political attitude is minimal: it is undeniable. We simply wish to relativize the scope of such arguments.

Writers like Wolf (1912), who, at the beginning of the century, connected the size of the socialist vote in German provinces in the 1907 elections with the decline in the birth-rate between 1876–80 and 1908, emphasized the difficulties of interpretation. He settled finally for the influence of a common determinant, the transformation of world-view (*Weltanschauung*). In fact, the fertility decline was most pronounced in regions where social democratic votes held a majority. Isolating the role of political attitudes was difficult in so far as socio-democratic majorities belonged to heavily urbanized and industrialized

---

[4] Could this be a function of the centralized character of the Anglican Church, in which respect it resembles Roman Catholicism? The first American couples to practise contraception emerged from amongst the followers of the Nonconformist churches (Quakers, Calvinists).

Protestant areas (Saxony in particular). The social democratic vote would thus represent the expression of a general difference in attitudes towards life.

Religious Change and Fertility Decline

Chronologically, modern economic growth followed the rise in educational standards and the mortality decline, both of which brought a powerful stimulus to innovation: they encouraged the questioning of old forms, facilitated individual mobility and institutional change, and, finally, encouraged self-reliance. Improvement in personal circumstances reduced dependence on others, thereby contributing to the growth of individualism and the calculating attitude on which not only the birth of modern capitalism and the Malthusian revolution, but secularization, rest. It is thus quite plausible to regard the decline in 'religious feeling', in so far as it can be measured,[5] in the same way as fertility decline, that is, as an indication of moral change, rather than a cause in itself of fertility regulation.

Given this theoretical limitation, let us turn to the principal studies relating to the issue. Leasure (1982), in an analysis of the fertility decline in the US between 1800 and 1860, examines the comparative effect of five variables: religiosity, percentage of the population in agricultural employment, literacy rates, the sex ratio,[6] and the availability of land. He shows the predominance of the religious factor. The selection of variables, however, may be questioned.

To begin with, the index of religiosity is not independent of economic levels and related influences. More specifically, the question comes down to the seating capacity of churches per unit of population, and not the actual frequentation of places of worship. Of course, a church's capacity may reflect intensity of religious practice; but this depends, in turn, on how early a community was established. In areas of early settlement, churches were built in proportion to original need, and seating capacity may not reflect subsequent religious attendance. North-eastern states take a considerable lead with indices above 40%, and even 58.5% in Massachusetts, whilst in the South and West—areas in many respects more conservative—indices were around 20% or less. The wealth of inhabitants will also influence crude measures of religiosity, since poor communities with church facilities equal in number to better-off areas may experience a higher rate of church-going.[7] Finally, the average cost of land corresponds fairly closely, according to the data, to the index of religiosity.

---

[5] This argument is more applicable to Catholic than Protestant countries, but is difficult to gauge since the substance of religious feeling differs according to the period. It seems more appropriate to speak in terms of the dwindling influence of the Church or clergy. In Protestant countries modernization tends rather to be associated—by Weber in particular—with religious recrudescence.

[6] Owing to imbalances caused by immigration.

[7] Because they could not raise the necessary resources for building additional churches.

The American case is exceptional, like France, in so far as in some regions fertility declined earliest in rural areas. Under the circumstances, the variable 'agricultural proportion of the working population' would no longer appear appropriate as a means of measuring the extent of economic modernization. Up to a point, it may simply reflect duration of settlement. Thus, where there was no effective communication network, the only way early settlers could feed themselves was by cultivating virgin lands; only subsequently could new activities grow up around agriculture. This sequence of establishment and occupational diversification of communities may be argued on a priori grounds, as well as being a historically typical sequence: in Massachusetts at the time when the percentage of working farmers reached a level of 18.9%, Georgia and Mississippi had levels close to 70%. Since all of this pertains to establishing the influence of economic variables, an approach using income levels would seem more appropriate.

Finally, the dependent variable (fertility decline) indicates the variation, by state, of the ratio between the number of children and the number of women, taken from Yasuba's calculations (1962); it therefore measures a change in overall fertility and does not allow a distinction to be made between the respective influence of nuptiality controls and fertility regulation within marriage. However, such a distinction is essential, since, whether Catholic or Protestant, Christianity encouraged nuptiality control (abstinence) and condemned birth control (vice), as the very clear position of Malthus on these questions reminds us. If, as is highly probable, early fertility declines were largely the result of nuptiality controls, one should expect a positive correlation between fertility variation and indices of religiosity; conversely, there should be a negative correlation where declines were very marked. This would appear to be supported by the data. Consequently, any comparison between the American pattern and those derived from studies of marital fertility in Europe are to be rejected.

Familial Mode of Production and Secularization

In a detailed analysis which takes into account the possibilities of multiple relations between economic and politico-religious variables, Lesthaeghe and Wilson (1982) distinguish four social groups pertaining, in their view, to reproduction: (1) the rural proletariat; (2) landowning farmers and small craftsmen; (3) the bourgeoisie and aristocracy; and (4) the urban proletariat and workers in large-scale agricultural concerns. The two first groups continue to live according to the 'familial mode of production' in which work and family life are united in a single setting; but in the latter two groups, family and work sites come to be separated with the development of schooling and the prohibition of child labour. Consequently, the period and rate of marital fertility decline must be related to the importance of the familial mode of production in economic life—the predominance of this mode increasing pro-

TABLE 14.1. *Fertility by social class*

Year of marriage	Farm operators	Agricultural labourers	Artisans	Manual workers
1890–99	4.30	4.71	3.70	5.11
1900–09	3.50	3.88	2.96	4.45
1915	2.69	2.74	2.13	3.54
1925	2.22	2.62	1.82	3.05

portionately with the delay and slowness of the decline. This is the authors' first hypothesis. The second refers to moral and ethical constraints, of which the distribution of votes in elections at the time of the emergence of universal suffrage gives a good indication.

The empirical test of these hypotheses is based on a study of administrative units in the six countries named above, between 1870 and 1930. The variance common to both the economic factor (familial mode of production) and the ethical factor (choice of vote) is ascribed to the economic factor. The object of the exercise thus consists in evaluating the extent to which economic considerations explain voting patterns, and in isolating the specific influence of secularization.

In practice, owing to insufficient data on home-based industry, half of the cases (Italy, Denmark, and The Netherlands) are analysed in terms of the percentage of the population in agricultural employment. In the remaining countries, the use of the variable 'familial mode of production' in preference to the proportion of agricultural workers improves the results noticeably only in Switzerland: the correlation with the decline in marital fertility increases from −0.78 to −0.89, whilst in Germany and Belgium it increases from −0.68 to −0.71, and −0.76 to −0.81 respectively. Furthermore, the pertinence of the breakdown, although attractive in theory, requires confirmation by statistical data on differential fertility. In general, French and English experience may be seen to have run counter to the proposed schema, as in Table 14.1, which presents changes in the number of children per family in Great Britain according to occupational status.[8] Whether or not English fertility changed independently of economic status, its levels and trends contradict the author's postulate. Assuming the data in Table 14.1 represent the impact of nuptiality changes on fertility—farm operators and artisans having lower fertility partly due to their pattern of delayed marriage—then the main issue is occupational differentials in the rate of decline. It is precisely within the *non*-familial mode of production that declines occur latest and proceed most slowly.

The possibility remains that changing fertility reflects less the character of a

---

[8] Based on the *Royal Commission on Population*, vol. vi, pt. 1, p. 110.

given socio-economic structure than a dynamic in which such structures are propelled by the effects of mortality declines. With the rising cost of land and farms, an increase in fertility amongst landowning peasant families multiplies the potential of proletarianization. This is clearly illustrated by the case of Sweden (Heinsohn *et al.* 1979) even in the context of very low densities: from 1775 to 1870, the number of landless labourers increased almost fivefold, and tripled as a proportion of the agricultural population (rising from 6% to 18%); the proportion of peasants owning only their house increased by almost half (16.2% as opposed to 11.4%), whilst the proportion of landowners decreased correspondingly. Clearly, the inverse proposition to that maintained by Lesthaeghe and Wilson seems to hold here: as observed in England, the restriction of births begins within the context of the familial mode of production, while free employees have the greater number of children.

Finally, the influence of the degree of economic modernization, far from being secondary, appears from the results of the proposed test as absolutely central, any additional variance being explained by the religious factor. Religion in itself appears to have only relatively marginal influence, in view of the last table in the authors' article: in Catholic areas, except in the Italian case, it is slight, and in Protestant countries, negligible.

Even today many Belgian institutions are organized according to a quadri-partite model, involving a double divide: cultural (Flemish–Walloon) and religious (public–private). Our discussion shows that, if the influence of secularization on contraception seems evident in many cases, a priori, it is none the less extremely difficult to pin down statistically. It does not appear to be universal. Amongst Western cultures, Poland, for example, recorded the most spectacular fertility decline with the least fall in Church influence: the birth-rate, beginning from a level around 60 per 1000 in the Duchy of Warsaw in the first quarter of the nineteenth century, reached 19 per 1000 around 1980.[9] Poland adhered to the typical two-phase trend we have noted: nuptiality control prevailed up to the First World War, the crude nuptiality rate decreasing by half, and reducing the birth-rate to the region of 35 per 1000; then, as in other countries at a similar stage of development, the decline proceeded via reduced marital fertility from the 1920s onwards. The need to be wary of rash generalization remains. It is necessary to examine not only the conflicting influences on marriage and fertility regulation, but also the social and national role of religion. In the West, before the emergence of the modern State, the Church was the principal agent of social change. Custodian of consciences, it was also custodian of hospitals and schools, and there played a major role in the first progress made in the struggle against mortality[10] and

---

[9] The average number of children per woman would have fallen from a rate of around 8–10 to 2.

[10] In Norway, the most advanced country in health matters from the beginning of the 19th century to the 1960s, the clergy were responsible for the introduction of the potato, which became a crucial factor in demographic development (Drake 1969).

illiteracy. In this way it indirectly helped prepare the conditions for the Malthusian revolution.

Adequate evaluation of secularization is all the more desirable as such an approach will without doubt have important applications to Islamic countries.

•

A Glaring Omission: Mortality Decline

The causal models which have been put forward to explain demographic transition consider only combinations of variables from amongst a multitude of possible explanatory frameworks, any of which might prove compatible. Among these variant models, a larger and technologically minded view which emphasized improvements in average life expectation would, to our mind, be of special value. Clearly, the history of technological development lies behind the history of changing behaviour. It is known that net reproduction rates over the long term tend to converge around unity. One could thus take the view that fertility, after an interval of greater or lesser length, merely adjusts to mortality, and that the economic, social, and political imbalances caused by the consequent demographic explosion were such that the old moral barriers had, in turn, to crumble. What if, in other words, it was simply mortality declines which, more than anything else, lay behind secularization, changing economic attitudes, and the growth of learning?

If this were the case, all explanatory constructs could be founded on the causes of secular mortality declines. This is a tempting view, capable of marshalling much conviction. And yet, on reflection, if the causes of mortality decline rest on complex and elusive interactions, it is scarcely more satisfactory than the myriad other approaches. In the human sciences, trying to pin down a cause is like the labours of Sisyphus: the moment one cause is isolated, it becomes necessary to go further back in order to discover another, and so on until one is balked by the inexplicable. The great motor forces of history belong more to philosophy than to science.

Conclusion

Three complementary observations can be made from this general review:

1. In all that pertains to understanding the morals, manners, and customs of a people or country, it is absurd to isolate one principle and focus exclusively upon it, since all of these matters are interconnected. Historically, the 'civilization' of manners (to use Elias's (1939) marvellous expression) emerges as a phenomenon in the Renaissance: the way people ate, how they lived, the way they spoke and loved, all changed. The family began to individualize itself and the life ethic itself, as expressed through suicide and homicide rates, embarked on its modern transformation (Chesnais 1981).

2. We have found no single model amongst those put forward to explain fertility declines which fully integrates those factors which there is every reason to think are central, both to developed and to less developed countries. Of particular note are the role of the State and sexual relations:

(*a*) The influence of State intervention, whose importance in less developed countries Faruqee has demonstrated (1979), may be analysed not only, as the author does, on the basis of budgetary expenditure on social (health, education, housing) or economic (public investment) matters, but also from the legislative standpoint (compulsory schooling, age at marriage, minimum wages, social security, etc.);

(*b*) Is it not curious that, with regard to reproduction, sex should be absent from the discussion? The image of sex in the Christian religion, for example, long remained that of the forbidden fruit, transgression, promiscuous pleasure. Obsessed with the dogma of the Virgin Birth the clergy raged against the flesh. Sexuality was legitimized only by the imperative of procreation. Until recently, woman herself was not regarded as a person, and for centuries certain theologians wondered whether she possessed a soul. It is possible that the image of woman and sexuality played an important role in the degree to which certain areas were advanced or backward in matters of fertility regulation.

3. We have already had occasion (Chapter 7) to point out the limitations of purely economic interpretations of post-transitional fertility, and in the present chapter we have taken the opposite tack, exposing the inadequacies of anti-economic models. There is nothing contradictory in this, simply a concern for balance and coherence. Fertility, like all other areas of human behaviour, cannot be resolved into an equation composed of a few quantifiable parameters. The failure of fertility forecasts stands as a sharp reproof of this.

Bibliography to Chapter 14

BOLTON, C., and LEASURE, J. W. (1979), 'Évolution Politique et Baisse de la Fécondité en Occident', *Population*, 4–5: 825–43.
CHESNAIS, J. -C. (1981), *Histoire de la Violence* (Paris: Laffont, 1981; repub. Pluriel, Hachette, 1982).
DRAKE, M. (1969), *Population and Society in Norway, 1735–1865* (Cambridge: Cambridge University Press).
ELIAS, N. (1939), *Über den Prozess der Zivilisation*, 2 vols. (Frankfurt).
FARUQEE, R. (1979), *Sources of Fertility Decline*, World Bank Staff Working Paper, no. 318 (Washington, DC: World Bank).
FLANDRIN, J. L. (1976), *Familles, parenté, maison, sexualité dans l'ancienne société* (Paris: Hachette).
HEINSOHN, G., KNIEPER, R., and STEIGER, O. (1979), *Menschensproduction: Allgemeine Bevölkerungslehre der Neuzeit* (Frankfurt: Suhrkamp).

LEASURE, J. W. (1982), 'La Baisse de la fécondité aux États-Unis de 1800 à 1860', *Population*, 3: 607–23.

LE BRAS, H., and TODD, E. (1981), *L'Invention de la France* (Paris: Livre de Poche, Coll. Pluriel).

LESTHAEGHE, R. (1977), *The Decline of Belgian Fertility, 1800–1970* (Princeton, NJ: Princeton University Press).

—— (1983), *A Century of Demographic and Cultural Change in Western Europe: An Exploration of Underlying Dimensions*, Working paper (Brussels).

—— and WILSON, C. (1982), 'Les Modes de production, la laïcisation et le rythme de baisse de la fécondité en Europe de l'Ouest de 1870 à 1930', *Population*, 3: 623–47.

MACFARLANE, A. (1978), *The Origins of English Individualism* (London: Blackwell).

RUSSEL, J. C. (1969), *Population in Europe, 500–1500*, in *FEHE*, i. 25–70.

SCRIMSHAW, S. (1978), 'Infant Mortality and Behaviour in the Regulation of Family Size', *PDR*, 3: 383–403.

TODD, E. (1983), *La Troisième Planète: structures familiales et systèmes idéologiques* (Paris: Seuil).

WOLF, J. (1912), *Der Geburtenrückgang: Die Rationalisierung des Sexuallebens in unserer Zeit* (Jena: Fischer).

PART III

Economic Implications of Demographic Transition

THE demonstration in Part I of the diversity of patterns followed by the main components of demographic change enabled us to establish significant differences in the types of transition experienced in different parts of the world. The variability in transitional multipliers of population is itself a reflection of the multiplicity of cases observed. Such diversity tends to call into question the simplicity of the original schema proposed by the authors of transition theory; while being the product of very different historical circumstances, it does not exclude the existence of common features which conform to the theory's propositions, as shown in Part II. These features relate as much to the demographic dynamic itself as to its connections with economic development. Just as secular fertility decline was preceded by a decline in mortality and a correlative reduction in nuptiality (particularly by way of a rise in the average age at first marriage), so it was also preceded by an increase in real per capita income.

Because transition theory was put forward at a time when measures of economic activity were relatively less developed than measures of demographic phenomena, only a very summary account of their connections could be envisaged. Demographic changes were perceived simply as the result of socio-economic changes, without regard to possible interactions. Part III of the present study will attempt to improve on this state of affairs, by resituating transition theory within the main terms of theoretical debates about economy and population. We shall show the necessary character of relations between economic and demographic growth, especially as influenced by mortality declines. And, drawing on available long term macro-economic series, we shall examine whether the different types of demographic transition are associated with particular patterns of economic growth.

15 Economic Stagnation and Neo-Malthusianism: Two Falsely Opposed Models

Men have a need to count and recount themselves to know their numbers.
They would do better to know their natures.

(Max Aub, *Contes certains*)

BEFORE embarking on an analysis of the data, it is well to review a number of theoretical issues which arise consistently in studies of economy and population. Theoretical presuppositions will be discussed and tested empirically wherever possible. Fortunately, the work of economic historians since Colin Clark and Simon Kuznets has resulted in considerable breakthroughs, including recent efforts to harmonize national accounting systems, particularly in less developed countries.

Taking a somewhat simplified view, we can distinguish two opposing theoretical perspectives on the nature of demographic influences. Both are in their own fashion basically deterministic. The first sees in demographic growth a major obstacle to economic improvement, whilst the second perceives it as an indispensable stimulant. The first is prompted by fears of excess, the second by fears of insufficiency. In reality, they are not as incompatible as they may at first appear, because they do not refer to the same universe. One begins from the static or declining populations of the industrial world, whilst the other focuses on rapid demographic growth in less developed countries. The polarization which has characterized debates on these two issues has left little room for subtlety, the adherents of each theory tending to generalize propositions willy-nilly and set them up as systems; the notion of degree, or critical threshold, is absent from most of the usual arguments. However, as we have seen, demographic transition theory, while prima facie loose and compelling, becomes highly reductive the moment it is applied to developments in this or that country. However, theories that are more precisely defined and easily quantifiable—such as those to be considered in this chapter—open themselves, *a fortiori*, to strong criticism.

We shall consider first the theory of stagnation, illustrated by the works of Keynes (1937) and Hansen (1939), and then the neo-Malthusian theory represented by the model which Coale and Hoover (1958) applied to India. Both accord a strategic role to the same factor—the formation of capital—and are at present enjoying an extraordinary revival in view of continuing low fertility in the industrial world and the growing debt of less developed countries. Moreover, because each theory was formulated several decades ago from an explicitly predictive standpoint, each may now be tested against the course of recent historical trends. The stagnationist theory is addressed to post-transitional development, although it may appear as a kind of historical refrain to the pre-transitional stage. Just as traditional societies in accordance with the self-regulating mechanism described by Malthus are supposed inevitably to be reduced to a subsistence level and condemned to the absence of any lasting economic growth, so post-transitional societies are destined to stagnation, with secular economic growth intercalated with the protracted completion of demographic transition. This approach, old as it is, has not lost its pertinence. It has just been revived for purposes of empirical application to the most advanced current instance of demographic decline—West Germany (Neal 1983).

The neo-Malthusian theory finds its usual application in the intermediate period of rapid population growth. The postulates of the Coale–Hoover model certainly appear to have retained their relevance to the present day: the intensive birth control programme in China derives from the same logic in which accelerated accumulation of capital is coupled with fertility decline; in addition, contemporary economic thought continues to assign a very privileged (but questionable, as will emerge) motivating role to investment amongst the determinants of economic growth (Denison 1980).

1. Stagnation Theory

The Sources of Long-Term Growth

The theory of stagnation was developed during the 1930s and belongs to the same body of ideas as the West's preoccupation with population decline. Hansen, noting that 'economists raised in the tradition of Malthusian theory think in static terms and have tended to give the cessation of demographic growth an optimistic interpretation', conceded that the continuation of nineteenth-century growth rates would have given rise to insoluble problems; but he argued, in opposition to Malthusian interpretations, that it would be falling into 'ill-founded optimism' to ignore the structural imbalances which would have to be faced in the case of prolonged decline. Hansen here relies on Adam Smith, who regarded population growth as both a cause and a consequence of economic progress. For Smith, the mechanism of this interaction was as follows: population growth stimulates the division of labour, leading to increased productivity; this produces a rise in income and an additional accumulation of capital; and these factors, in turn, bring about a rise in rates of pay, thereby tending to promote further population growth. Thus, a spiral of growth is set in motion: a growing population, by extending the market and stimulating creativity, facilitates the division of labour and production of wealth; this in turn encourages population growth (through mortality decline and the incentive to marry).

The theory of long-term stagnation is justifiable only if economic activity is not subject to long cycles. According to Hansen, such cycles certainly exist, but they refer to the nineteenth century. The main concern of the twentieth century, in his opinion, is full employment, because the forces which might ensure a recovery of the economy have become exhausted. Demographic factors enter his argument at precisely this point, as he considers them fundamental in the long term. Economic progress, for Hansen, consists in three elements: (1) inventions; (2) discovery and exploitation of land and new resources; and (3) population growth.

In the absence of a policy for stimulating demand, full employment of productive resources is essentially secondary to investment. The volume of investment is a function, in the short and middle term, of factors such as profit or real interest rates, but in the longer term it depends more on structural factors like the three just listed. Increased investment assumes the form of either an intensification of capital (the greatest use of capital per unit of final product), or its extension (increases by economies of scale). Basing his study on the dominant economies of England and the US for the period 1890–1939, Hansen shows that stocks of capital grew at more or less the same rate as real income, and therefore no intensification of capital occurred. (According to Keynes, however, such a process may be detected in the first stages of modern capitalism, especially in the second half of the nineteenth century.) In other words, the accumulation of capital is effected almost entirely by extension. Consequently, as demographic growth slows down, the process of extensive accumulation is itself bound to slow down. The precise influence of population increase on the formation of capital is difficult to quantify in so far as interdependence exists between the determinants of accumulation. It is none the less possible to evaluate an apparent contribution by analysing the development of orders of magnitude pertaining to some of the considered phenomena. This method reveals that the growth of production during the second half of the nineteenth century and up to the First World War produced an annual average close on 3% in western Europe, and 4% in the United States. However, in the same period, work availability increased at about half the rate of the above (a little less in Europe, and a little more in the US). It is thus possible as a first approximation to regard the balance—at an annual average of either 1% or 1.5%—as an indication of the effect of technological progress and the exploitation of new natural resources on the rate of growth. Hansen further notes that, as the 'formation of capital progressed at about the same rate as the total product . . . demographic growth in the second half of the 19th century is responsible for approximately 40% of the total volume of the formation of capital in Western Europe and 60% in the US.' With the advent of stationary populations, these economies could therefore lose half of their investment incentives.

Thus—and on this point the analyses of Keynes and Hansen are in complete agreement—population decline (or at least the slackening of rates of growth), by reducing investment opportunities, tends to aggravate unemployment and economic depression as demand falls below what investors had expected. In the analysis of long-term economic growth prospects, Keynes attributes a crucial role to demographic growth, which represents, in his view, the principal determinant of demand.

Population's role within the demand for goods is particularly important in the construction and housing sector, which in less developed countries may represent up to a third of gross investment. Kuznets (1965), for example, in his reconstruction of American growth over the long term (1870–1955), stresses the relation between long fluctuations in rates of population growth and corresponding fluctuations in housing construction. Oscillations in net or gross housing construction reflect—either immediately or after a slight interval—variations in net population growth. The same applies to other aspects of capital outlay, for example, infrastructure. Still with reference to Kuznets's series, the relation between a variable such as railway construction and demographic change proves to be very close. It is not unreasonable therefore (even though it remains to be tested) to think that this conclusion holds for a large number of investments both public (schools, crèches, hospitals, sporting facilities, administrative buildings, etc.) and private (industrial and commercial institutions).

Limitations of the Stagnation Thesis

Both by its force of logic and in the quality of its empirical supports, the thesis of long-term stagnation possesses an undeniable capacity to reflect the course of events. However, the extraordinary recovery of demographic growth in the industrial world immediately following the war brought about not only an increase in fertility, but also, as is often forgotten, considerable declines in mortality and the emergence of large migratory streams. Post-war reconstruction thus confounded all speculations on the consequences attending stagnation or the effective reduction in population. We can only observe that, for almost two centuries, modern history has tended to conform more to the reverse of this theory's argument. As we shall see in Chapter 18, demographic growth and economic growth generally share a positive relation.

There are a number of points in this thesis, however, which we consider to have received insufficient attention: the role of internal migration, foreign trade, international migration, the possibility of variation in the intensity and efficiency of capital, and finally the possible influence of the different types of transition that have been experienced.

1. *The role of internal migration.* The strategic influence of demographic variables on the formation of capital is most clearly perceived through its effects on the activity of building and public works sectors. If the population's aggregate growth rate is an incontestable force in the health of this sector, it also depends on other matters such as the development of real income, the degree of cohabitation, the durability of housing stock and equipment, and especially internal migration (mainly, in the form of rural exodus). Rural exodus was without doubt the result largely of demographic pressure in the countryside during the transition, but the growth of urbanization went well beyond simple absorption of rural surplus, and this massive population transfer provoked heavy demands for housing and the development of infrastructure. More recently, however, it appears that saturation level has been reached.

2. *Foreign trade.* By enlarging the scope of the national market, population increase enables economies of scale and a reduction of costs favourable to an improved competitive position. Such a position may be achieved equally well by greater recourse to international trade. Although inevitably more hazardous given the multiplication of risks it implies, the latter strategy may carry an added bonus of avoiding some of the diseconomies which usually accompany sustained population growth, such as urban overcrowding and the hypostasis of social organizations.

3. *International migration.* As was demonstrated in Chapter 6, there is a fairly close correlation in the long term between sustained low fertility and migration intensity. The historical contrast often remarked between French fertility and that of its neighbours is no less material to patterns of migration: during the Second Empire immigration began to predominate in France at the very time that other European states experienced mass emigration. Luxemburg is an equally telling example: since the 1930s fertility has been maintained at the lowest rates in the world whilst the proportion of foreigners has been the highest in the industrial world. The history of migratory transition, taking, for example, movements to the US by country of origin, provides further examples. If we consider the significance of income differences, and the growing demographic disequilibrium between developed and less developed countries, the hypothesis of zero net migration where there is sustained below-replacement fertility seems highly dubious. Differences in age at entry into the labour force between more and less developed countries compounds this situation. In the 1970s, even in the face of growing unemployment and the restriction of legal immigration, migration streams to European countries remained significant (Golini 1982). Various sources (Sauvy 1982; OECD 1979) stress the strong likelihood of high immigration continuing into the next decades, since there is no longer any assurance that the replacement of generations will be able to keep pace with the demands of the job market. In other words, the familiar hypothesis of stagnation accompanied by population decline seems rather unrealistic. A backward glance at early predictions shows

TABLE 15.1. *Evolution of rates of investment (accumulation of gross fixed capital in relation to national income) in various countries* (%)

Period	Country				
	Germany[a]	Italy	France	Great Britain	United States[b]
1861–65	10.7	7.8	20.5[c]	8.1	23.1[d]
1905–13	15.2	16.2	21.0[e]	6.9	22.3[f]
1935–38	12.9	19.3	19.2	10.3	20.0[g]

[a] Net accumulation of capital (including stocks).
[b] Accumulation of gross fixed capital/gross national product.
[c] 1855–64.
[d] 1869–73.
[e] 1906–13.
[f] 1907–11.
[g] 1922–31.

Sources: Calculated from the sources cited for each country in Ch. 17, and in the General Bibliography on long-range macro-economic time-series.

that, even when very slow growth rates in the number of young adults were assumed, the migratory factor was consistently overlooked (see, for example, Notestein's prognosis for Europe (1944)) or underestimated (as in French projections during the last half-century: Calot and Chesnais 1978).

4. *Variations in the intensity and efficient use of capital.* In emphasizing the role played by population growth in the accumulation of capital, Hansen relies on the fact that the average coefficient of capital is almost invariable in the case of the Atlantic economies. But the question is the extent to which this observation applies elsewhere; Table 15.1 gives a few data on the issue. In Italy and Germany, where economic growth began later, there was a very marked increase in capital intensity.

Of course, it is not impossible that certain future technological changes (robotics, information science, or biotechnology) may be such that capital accumulation will bear no relation to the increases in production they make possible.

5. *The type of demographic transition.* The ageing of population structures is favourable to the growth of personal savings, since rates of personal savings tend generally to increase with age, at least up to retirement. This expansion, often reinforced by age-related salary scales, coincides with a declining demand for property investment consequent on the smaller cohorts at the base of the age pyramid. This brings us to the heart of the stagnation problem. But the potential extent of this dampening process is related to both the institutional network for the mobilization and channelling of savings and the degree of demographic change. Moreover, as we have seen, the sequence of changes

in age structure differs greatly from one country to another. Two criteria must therefore be taken into consideration: the duration of the transition and the pattern of post-transitional fertility. There is no common measure which will accommodate rates of ageing at the base and peak of age pyramids, allowing us to compare countries which have experienced rapid transitions and non-cyclic post-transitional fertility (such as Japan or West Germany) and countries with less rapid transitions and cyclical tendencies in their post-transitional fertility (such as France and The Netherlands).

2. The Coale–Hoover Model

The aim of the Coale–Hoover model is to measure the influence of fertility declines on economic growth. It draws its inspiration from the work of Harrod (1959) and Domar (1957), which assumes that rates of income growth are determined by rates of personal savings (the former being equal to the latter divided by the rate of the earning capacity of capital). Various reasons lead us to single out this model: (1) its pioneering nature (the work of Coale and Hoover was the starting-point of a veritable industry of simulation approaches in population economics); (2) its influence on the adoption of family planning policies during the 1960s; (3) its renewed relevance for the new international economic context (Coale himself, towards the end of the 1970s took up his pen to reaffirm the virtues of the model); and, finally (4), the possibilities of empirical verification, given that we have now reached the end of the period (1956–86) which the model projected.

   Keynesian in approach, the Coale–Hoover model centres on savings and investment functions; in the role it assigns to labour it draws heavily on Lewis, who is repeatedly cited.

Formal Presentation of the Model

This model, like all its counterparts in the 1950s, singles out the accumulation of capital as the principal determinant of economic growth. A simulation of Indian economic development is put forward in five-yearly periods for 1956–86, varied according to alternative hypotheses regarding fertility rates. The basic equation is as follows (Coale and Hoover 1956, ch. 17; 1958: 259 ff.):

$$Y_{t+2.5} = Y_t + 2.5G/R, \tag{1}$$

where Y represents national income; $t + 2.5$ is the middle of the five-yearly period following the starting date of the projection; G is 'growth expenditure' or total investment; and R is the incremental capital–output ratio: $G/R = \Delta Y$.

   In conformity with contemporary observation, the authors consider the coefficient to increase over time, giving

$$R = m + nt,$$

where R is the initial value (set at 3.0) and n the annual rate of increase (assumed equal to 2%).

The formulation of G, the motor element of growth, is more complicated; it involves a distinction between 'direct growth' outlays or productive investment, and investment in human resources, the latter in turn being subdivided into per capita investments corresponding to the needs of the initial population I, and per capita investments required by the additional population I_{pi}. This is not altogether unlike Sauvy's distinction between demographic and economic investments, although the two notions are not completely interchangeable (Sauvy 1963). The value of G is written:

$$G = I_c + (e_c I_{pc} + e_i I_{pi}) L + (e_c w_c + e_i w_i)_{t-15} (1 - L)_{t-15}, \qquad (2)$$

in which L is the total activity ratio, or ratio of labour force to population; I_c represents investments in production goods; I_{pc} and I_{pi} are investments in human resources (the two categories designated above); and the coefficients e_c and e_i represent the productivity of these investments when compared to that of equivalent investments in material factors. The authors assign the values 0.5 and 0 respectively to these coefficients.

The last term, L, which also figures in the second part of the equation, represents in a similar way the weighted volume of social investments 15 years earlier, multiplied by the proportion of the economically inactive population. In other words, investments in human resources are presumed to influence economic production 15 years later, assuming that working life begins around the age of 15 years.

The problem, then, is how to assess the values I_{pc} and I_{pi}. The authors assume that I_{pc}, which corresponds to the needs of the existing population, represents a constant fraction, designated h, of national income Y. If P is population and W_c the corresponding per capita income, the following equation results:

$$I_{pc} = hY = W_c P. \qquad (3)$$

Where I_{pc} is concerned, it is agreed that satisfying the initial needs of a new member of society equals 10 times the permanent cost of maintaining W_c. Therefore:

$$I_{pi} = 10W_c \Delta P. \qquad (4)$$

The ratio of these two components of social investment is, in consequence

$$I_{pi}/I_{pc} = 10W_c \Delta P/W_c P = 10r,$$

where r is the population growth rate, and the sum of these components, designated I_p, is

$$I_p = I_{pc}(1 + 10r).$$

The total investment in expenditure, $I_c + I_m$, thus becomes

$$I = I_c + (1 + 10r)hY.$$

The volume of investment depends, in reality, on available savings E, through the postulate $I = E$.

According to Keynesian theory, there is a linear connection between the function of savings and of income; per capita savings is equal to savings or investments per head[1] at the beginning of the period (indicated I_0/P_0) increased by the fraction produced by the variation of per capita income, written $Y/P - Y_0/P_0$. Whence, the total savings function

$$E = P[I_0/P_0 + a(Y/P - Y_0/P_0)] = aY - (aY_0 - I_0)P/P_0,$$

or

$$E = aY - bP = I. \tag{5}$$

Under these assumptions investment is clearly a linear function of a population's income.

Compared with the apparent complexity of some of its more recent successors, this model has the virtue of simplicity. In addition, it possesses the advantage of stressing the importance of age structure, which had scarcely been considered up to that point, even though Lotka's work (1925) had established the relation between the development of the number of inhabitants and that of age distribution. Finally, the aim of the model is to give quantitative illustration of a central proposition of economic demography, hitherto not established arithmetically: a decline in fertility accelerates total income growth and, especially, the growth of per capita income. The authors give three possible explanations of this mechanism: the improvement in productivity per worker; the resources freed by a decline in the ratio of dependants; and the savings increase resulting from a rise in average income. Given the fundamental role attributed to the accumulation of capital, they consider this fertility variation unlikely to affect other determinants of growth, such as basic resources, or even job availability itself. Here one recognizes the heritage of Lewis's observations on unlimited labour supply: the work-force being considered in surplus, it is assumed that its growth could not affect total product.

From these premises, the authors show that a fertility decline of 50% produces considerable differences in per capita income within 30 years; income is 40% higher in populations with hypothetically low fertility than in populations in which the hypothesis specifies high fertility.

Problems Inherent in the Model

We shall begin will a critical examination of each of the principal equations of the model before embarking on a more general discussion.

---

[1] For the adult population, or its equivalent.

Equation 1 makes macroeconomic growth depend on a single factor: the injection of certain specific forms of expenditure into the economy which are designated G and endowed with a given effectiveness R. These expenditures are called 'the costs of growth'. This view, consonant with the dominant thinking of the 1950s, presupposes that there are other sorts of expenditure which would not have the same impact on growth. This becomes evident in the following equation.

Equation 2 requires a division between investments in production goods and investments in human resources, the latter being presumed fairly un-productive and in all events less profit-earning than material investments to the same amount. Yet, over a century ago, Cournot (1863) had warned against the automatic tendency to minimize the productive capacity of educational expenditure:

What could be more uncertain or more vague [he wrote] than our evaluation of pleasure and privation? . . . values which seem to disappear in those kinds of consump-tion mistakenly considered unproductive may none the less be maintained in a latent state; they serve to create skills, to develop physical, intellectual, moral, individual and collective powers which at a later date, once placed in favourable and appropriate circumstances, regenerate the value previously consumed, and even increase it . . . A father may spend a significant portion of his income, even part of his patrimony, in order to give his children an education and training: in the economist's eyes, he is doing the right thing by procuring skills for them which will make them richer than the inheritance he could leave them.

Schultz (1960) and Denison (1969) have more recently demonstrated the merits of Cournot's argument.

Equation 2 contains two further assumptions which we consider subject to criticism. The first is that the average age of starting work is 15 years; however, in light of school attendance ratios by age, and the studies carried out by the ILO (1980) on child employment, this figure is probably closer to 5 or 10 years than 15, depending on the different periods under considera-tion (1956–86). The second debatable assumption is that the profit-earning capacity of investments in human capital, in contrast to material investments, does not grow but remains constant, and by comparison very low (equal to only 50% of production goods for the living population, and zero for the future population).

Equations 3 and 4 rely on a debatable choice of conventions which do not appear to us to have been determinant; in addition, the coefficient 10 used in equation 4 appears exaggerated in the absence of empirical proof.

As it stands, equation 5 assumes that savings are a growing linear function of income, and a decreasing linear function of population. According to Myrdal (1968), an authority on the Indian economy, the Keynesian view of the function of savings may be inapplicable in the Indian case, for a variety of reasons, including conspicuous consumption, peculiarities of the tax system, and tax evasion. In short, the rate of savings does not inevitably increase with per capita income in the way Keynes envisaged. Myrdal further demonstrates that it is sufficient in the terms of this model to assume that the savings rate is constant, whatever the assumption concerning fertility, in order to reduce the total difference in income attributed to the fertility decline by two-thirds. Finally, as we shall see in Chapter 18, the presumed relation between family size (or population growth rate) and the volume of savings is not as simple as it may at first appear: in assuming that this relation is negative, the model further reveals the assumed Malthusianism evident in its arithmetical structure.

The Malthusian Bias

This Malthusian bias, which sometimes gives the model a teleological aspect, becomes even more apparent on close examination of its basic characteristics: its temporal perspective, the definition of investment, its main hypothesis, and the monolithic nature of the analysis.

1. *Temporal perspective.* The economic consequences of the birth of an individual may make themselves felt over a very long interval—say, equal to the length of his or her life—which even in a country like India means probably over 50 years on average, for generations born in 1956. Given the differences between profiles of production and consumption according to age, the economic implications of a birth are at first negative, then gradually become positive as the cumulative balance since birth is cancelled out. According to Sauvy (1963), this will occur in around 40 years in the case of a stationary population and economy; in India it would doubtless occur earlier. If, however, the average length of life is not used,[2] but an interval shorter than the age at which the balance cancels out, the result of the simulation is bound to be systematically predetermined against population growth. Choosing an interval longer than life expectation would produce a correspondingly more favourable result. Thus, a highly misleading picture is given when the parameters are set at 30 years for the initial generation (1956); this means, in fact, a horizon of 15 years on average for the generations 1956–86, that is, for those generations affected by the birth control policy which the model envisages.

2. *The definition of investment.* Investment as a generator of growth is understood by the authors in a restricted sense, since they make a clear distinction between investment in material production and social investment, the latter in fact being treated as a form of consumption, at least where added population is concerned ($e_i = 0$). The logic is as follows: rapid population growth requires a large portion of investment to be devoted to social expenditure, to the detriment of 'direct growth outlays'; hence costs are bound not to have any

---

[2] A secondary simulation is carried out over 55 years (up to the year 2011), but given the assumption that the increase in labour supply and the growth of capital are independent—which are the terms of reference used—the result is predetermined (Coale and Hoover 1958, ch. 12).

positive effects on the rate of capital formation. The model fails to consider State expenditure on infrastructure, schools, and so forth, and the role of investment in the construction industry. Housing construction is a vital link in the chain of return effects of demographic growth on economic activity: in India, the value added by the building sector corresponds, in an average year, to about one-tenth of the total added value (OECD 1975, 1980). If, however, public expenditure on education and health required by the additional population are included in savings, then public investment shows an expansion capable of compensating the reduction of private savings from households or firms (Leibenstein 1975). On this score, the model raises another crucial point: savings are determined independently, and, in consequence, it is the savings rate which sets the volume of investment; however, according to equation 5, all population increase reduces savings to a greater or lesser degree; the resulting investment will be proportionately reduced. As investment in its turn commands growth, the final result is tautological. Moreover, all one has to do to reverse the model's conclusions is to take a broader conception of savings and to adjust the weightings used in the equations to conform more with reality. The parameters e_c and e_i in equation 2, and the coefficient 10 in equation 4 are the most affected by arbitrary assumptions. Thus, the moment $e_i > e_c > 1$ occurs, the advantage will be taken over by the more rapidly growing population.

3. *The hypothesis of the zero marginal productivity of the additional worker.* The authors assume a priori that population growth does not bring any increase in average inputs into production, even in the form of an improvement in the quality of work[3] (for instance, via the renewal of generations). Therefore, they maintain that the slackening growth of the working population will have a positive effect, not only on unemployment, but even more so on productivity.

The reality is not so simple, however. The Indian economy remains predominantly agricultural, encompassing over 50% of the total added value at the end of the 1970s (OECD 1981). However, data from the detailed survey of Indian agriculture, conducted in 1954–56 by Farm Management Studies, show that, contrary to received opinion, there is no surplus labour with a zero marginal productivity. Owing to irrigation, work input may increase at the same time as an improvement in agricultural productivity is registered (Paglin 1965). The period 1950–80 conforms to this schema, and Indian writers such as Swamy (1975) have remarked that the acceleration of demographic growth and the slow expansion of the Indian economy occurred simultaneously at the beginning of the 1950s. We shall come back to this point in Chapter 18, with reference to Mukherjee's studies on economic history.

4. *Single factor analysis.* Rather than being based on at least two factors, like the Cobb–Douglas production function, that is, L and K, the basic equation

---

[3] This recalls Chevalier's notorious squib (1844) demonstrating the paradox of this sort of hypothesis: it results, in effect, in rejoicing at the birth of a calf (because this increases national income) and regretting the birth of a child (as this reduces per capita income).

only entails the single variable K. The work-force L is considered surplus, and the growth of the economy is determined by the marginal coefficient of capital. Whilst the importance of the latter factor cannot be ignored, it should not be overestimated: the role of work in the south Asian economy is very great (Myrdal 1968), and its development is a very complex process involving a quantity of interdependent parameters.[4] To isolate a single strategic factor is a great oversimplification, and one which exposes the analysis to error since not all countries follow the same type of development. Chenery (1960) has shown that those less developed countries experiencing high rates of growth during the 1950s benefited from a massive input of capital, intensive exportation of primary products, self-sufficiency in agriculture and manufacture, and a reduction in foreign dependence. Furthermore, examination of the experience of countries for which long time series are available reveals that the accumulation of capital itself is not one of the elements which most determines growth (Ohlin 1975). The choice of priorities in the allocation of resources is more influential than the volume of capital invested; the capital–output ratio varies widely from one sector to another. Finally, as illustrated by Gourou's (1966) observations on the tropical world, certain variables not included in the model, such as technological progress, the spread of knowledge and abilities, economies of scale, the flexibility of personal work, and the influence of demand on the investment function, can play a crucial role over the long term.

General Limitations of the Model

Several technical criticisms, although at times less important than the foregoing, warrant mention, if only for the sake of fidelity to historical fact. These criticisms warn us against certain mechanical aspects of the model, especially as Coale's second presentation (1979) does not really offer much in the way of revision. The critique focuses on three points: specification of the model's main component, the treatment of time, and the functional account of how the economy works and is articulated with demographic factors.

1. *Specification of the main component.* The dualism or heterogeneity manifest in the vast discrepancy between incomes makes the interpretation of aggregate data difficult. To treat the Indian economy as a whole can be misleading, for we know that over the long term, with its given rate of demographic growth, the differential between rural areas and towns has manifested itself variously in the increasing rural exodus, the accumulation of capital, and the growing productivity of non-agricultural sectors—all of which promote overall growth. This is indeed what has been observed in India during recent decades

---

[4] The rate of development is related to the combined effect of a matrix of production factors and not to each one separately; the Cobb–Douglas production function is characterized by a strong colinearity.

(OECD Development Centre 1981), in spite of an actual demographic growth much higher than the authors anticipated.[5] Furthermore, one wonders how the main component, savings, has been evaluated, since it remained something of an unknown quantity at the national level in the late 1960s (OECD Development Centre 1981); national accountants have only been publishing series—and irregularly at that—for the last 15 years. On examination, rural savings (which are very difficult to evaluate) prove to be higher than was generally assumed (Sinha 1978). The total capital–output ratio thus differs greatly in reality from the values ascribed to it in the model.

2. *The treatment of time.* The notion of investment is inseparable from that of duration, for the capital invested in different areas of the economy realizes its value over a greater or lesser period (houses last longer, for example, than machines). There is thus an interdependence between periods, in so far as the growth in a given period results from investments made during previous periods. However, this interval between the realization of investment and its contribution to production is not taken into account in the model, except very crudely in equation 2. The fifteen-year time lag introduced by this equation is, however, rather peculiar, since it merges three broad categories (women, children, and old people) which comprise the economically inactive population—60% of the total, in this case.

3. *Economic functions and their interaction with population.* In the absence of any credible theory of economic growth—existing formulations are as numerous as they are contradictory—recourse to arithmetical exercises is an attractive alternative. But this inevitably entails a certain arbitrariness, and above all grossly oversimplifies mechanisms which are extremely complex by nature. At best, the great economists have managed to take into account satisfactorily only five or six parameters at once (e.g. labour, capital, technological progress, prices, interest rates, and expertise) without necessarily comprehending the innumerable interactions involved. Their explanatory frameworks consistently prove inadequate to account for the growth observed in this or that conjunction of geographic and historical phenomena (Malinvaud 1984). Doubtless it would be necessary to incorporate dozens of parameters, or at least, failing this, to fully explain the manner in which supply and demand operate, and their equilibrium.

However, the economic limits of the model remain to be elaborated, and one cannot fail to be surprised by the absence of demand, even though shortly after its original publication, one of its authors (Coale 1960), in an article on the relation between demographic change and the development of overall demand, established a positive value for this relation. In so doing, he implicitly contradicts the model's very foundations. It is here that one of the principal weaknesses of the proposed analytic framework emerges, for *the demographic*

---

[5] The starting-point is also inaccurate: the growth rate was assumed to be 1.72% per year at the outset, whereas the values observed for the intercensal period 1951–61 exceeded 2%.

variable, while determinant, influences neither supply nor demand. In addition, while the authors claim to accept the premises of demographic transition theory—in particular, the connection between the mortality and fertility transitions on the one hand, and between the development of fertility and socio-economic development on the other—they present, in opposition to these two highly contrasting hypotheses regarding fertility, a single hypothesis of rapidly declining mortality.[6] Over and above this, they suggest that fertility declines are due to exogenous factors, when 30 years of repeated difficulties experienced by the Indian family planning programme would strongly suggest that endogenous forces are at issue (the first official birth control programme dates to 1952: Chesnais and Vallin 1976). Fertility declines, after all, can be both cause *and* consequence of improvements in living standards. The logical incoherence of the model, on this score, is manifest.

Conclusion

Although proceeding via an unconvincing route (there are plenty of alternative arguments supporting their thesis), the Coale–Hoover model shows that a reduction in rates of demographic growth is desirable in poor countries, but they do not answer the real question: How? This is a crucial matter for India, where colossal sums have been spent in specialized campaigns, without convincing results. Rather than confronting central problems such as the way in which social and caste structures operate, the distribution of power and property, or the nature of institutions, customs, cultural heritage, etc.—all of which remain capable of impeding both fertility declines and economic progress—the authors succumbed to the intellectual attitude of the day. According to prevailing opinion, the development of poor countries appeared purely a matter of financial transfusion; a few years later, the predominant view would return to the notion of according a key role to investment in human capital.

History can never give a definitive answer to the authors' question concerning differential living standards, occasioned by the contrasting hypotheses of reduced fertility or continuing high fertility. There is ultimately no way of knowing. We have gained only a certain cautiousness, as the cases of India and Mexico, both studied by the authors, show: fertility has remained more or less stable during the 1950s and 1960s in both countries, while substantial socio-economic progress has none the less been made in areas such as schooling, industrialization, and modernization of rural areas.

The theory of stagnation and the Coale–Hoover model have an undeniable pedagogical value, apart from the criticisms they invite. They remind us of the

---

[6] Although a large fertility decline is only compatible with a marked mortality decline (which tends itself to produce certain positive effects on income—studied in Chapter 4).

potential stress which too small a population—or, conversely, excessive growth associated with sustained high fertility—can place on an economic system. To this extent, both models are inevitable points of departure. The future holds too many unknown quantities, however, for the first approach to claim to describe the future economies of wealthy countries where transition has been completed, or for the second to claim it explains the situation of poor countries where fertility remains high. The reasoning of this chapter would imply that there is no a priori determinism of demographic structures. The following chapters are devoted to establishing a connection between long-term macro-economic and macro-demographic series: their aim is precisely to illustrate why, in conformity with transition theory, demographic and economic growth are historically associated, even though it appears to be impossible to establish any strict historical relation between rates of variation in the two phenomena.

Bibliography to Chapter 15

ANKER, R., and FAROOQ, G. M. (1980), 'Démographie et développement socio-économique: une nouvelle perspective', *Revue Internationale du Travail* (Mar.–Apr.), 159–73.

ARTHUR, W. B., and McNICOLL, G. (1975), 'Large-Scale Simulation Models', in Population and Development: What Use to Planners?, *PDR* (Dec.), 251–65.

CALOT, G., and CHESNAIS, J. C. (1978), 'La Prévision démographique', in A. C. Decouflé, *Traité élémentaire de prévision et de prospective* (Paris: PUF), 155–207.

CHENERY, H. (1960), 'Patterns of Industrial Growth', *AER* (Sept.), 624–54.

CHESNAIS, J. -C. (1981), 'Le Modèle économique de l'Allemagne Fédérale est-il compatible avec son modèle démographique?', *Revue d'Économie Politique*, 2: 163–77.

—— and VALLIN J. (1976), 'La Question démographique dans le sous-continent indien', *Tiers-Monde*, 67 (July–Sept.), 675–98.

CHEVALIER, M. (1844), *Cours d'économie politique fait au Collège de France* (Paris: Capelle).

COALE, A. J. (1960), 'Population Change and Demand, Prices and Level of Employment', in *Demographic and Economic Change in Developed Countries* (Princeton, NJ: Princeton University Press, NBER), 352–76.

—— (1979), 'Population Growth and Economic Development', *Foreign Affairs*, 415–29.

—— and HOOVER, E. M. (1956–58), *Population Growth and Economic Development in India, 1956–1986*, Office of Population Research, Princeton University, Preliminary draft (July 1956), and final version: *Population Growth and Economic Development in Low-Income Countries: A Case Study of India's Prospect* (Princeton, NJ: Princeton University Press, 1958).

COURNOT, A. (1863), *Principes de la théorie des richesses* (Paris: Hachette).

DENISON, E. F. (1969), 'The Contribution of Education to the Quality of Labor: Comment', *AER*, 59: 935–43.

—— (1980), 'The Contribution of Capital to Economic Growth', *AER*, 70: 220–4.

DOMAR, E. (1957), *Essays in the Theory of Economic Growth* (New York: Oxford University Press).

GOLINI, A. (1982), 'Effectif et accroissement des populations immigrées', in *Council of Europe, European Conference on Demography, Strasbourg, 1982*.

GOUROU, P. (1966), *Les Pays tropicaux: principes d'une géographie humaine et économique*, 4th edn. (Paris: PUF).

HANSEN, A. H. (1939), 'Economic Progress and Declining Population Growth', *AER*, 29: 1–15.

HARROD, R. (1955), 'Les Relations entre l'investissement et la population', *Revue Économique* (May).

—— (1959), *Towards a Dynamic Economics* (London: Macmillan).

KEYNES, J. M. (1937), 'Some Economic Consequences of a Declining Population', *Eugenics Review*, 29: 13–17.

KUZNETS, S. (1965), *Economic Growth and Structure* (Norton).

LEIBENSTEIN, H. (1975), 'Population Growth and Savings', in L. Tabah (ed.), *Aspects Économiques de la croissance démographique* (Paris: Ordina Éditions, IUSSP).

LEWIS, W. A. (1955), *The Theory of Economic Growth* (London).

LOTKA, A. J. (1925), 'On the True Rate of Natural Increase', *Journal of the American Statistical Association*, 26 (Sept.), 305–9.

MALINVAUD, E. (1984), 'La Science économique aujourd'hui', *Revue Économique et Sociale*, Lausanne (Jan.), 35–45.

MEIER, G. M. (ed) (1970), *Leading Issues in Economic Development: Studies in International Poverty*, 2nd edn. (Oxford: Oxford University Press).

MENDERSHAUSEN, H. (1938), 'On the Significance of Prof. Douglas's production function', *Econometrica*, 6: 143 ff.

MYRDAL, G. (1968), *Asian Drama: An Inquiry into the Poverty of Nations*, 3 vols. (London: Lane), esp. app. 7.

NEAL (1983), 'Slowing Population Growth and Investment Demand: The West German Case', *Conference on Economic Effects of Slowing Population Growth, Paderborn, 1983*.

NOTESTEIN, F. W., TAEUBER, I. B., KIRK, D., COALE, A. J., and KISER, L. K. (1944), *La Population future de l'Europe et de l'Union Soviétique: perspectives démographiques 1940–1970* (Geneva: League of Nations).

OECD Development Centre (1981), *Comptes nationaux des pays moins développés 1959–1968* (first pub. Paris, 1970, 156–65; repr. *Bulletin*, 14, 1981).

OECD (1979), *Interfuturs face aux futurs* (Paris: OECD).

OHLIN, G. (1975), 'La Théorie économique en face de la croissance de la population', in L. Tabah (ed.), *Aspects économiques de la croissance démographique* (Paris: Ordina editions, IUSSP), 59–73.

PAGLIN, M. (1965) 'Surplus Agricultural Labor and Development', *AER* (Sept.), 815–34.

ROBINSON, W. C., and HORLACHER, D. E. (1971), 'Population Growth and Economic Welfare', *Report on Population and Family Planning*, New York, 6.

SAUVY, A. (1962), *Théorie générale de la population*, 2nd edn. (Paris: PUF), vol. i, ch. 25.

—— (1982), *Mondes en marche* (Paris: Calmann-Lévy).

Schultz, T. W. (1960), 'Capital Formation by Education', *JPE*, 68(6).

Sinha, J. N. (1978), 'Population Pressure, Rural Labor Force and Employment: An Overview of the Problem', *Proceedings of the IUSSP Conference, Helsinki, 1978*, ii. 149–64.

Swamy, S. (1975), 'Population Growth and Economic Growth', in *Population in India's Development*, (Delhi: Indian Association for the Study of Population).

UN (1954), *Proceedings of the World Population Conference, Rome, 1954*, v.

16 Economic Progress and Demographic Transition in Poor Countries: Thirty Years of Experience, 1950–1980

> There are two kinds of problem in life. Politics are insoluble and economics are incomprehensible.
>
> (Sir Alec Douglas-Home, *Essays*)

THE preceding chapter stressed the dangers of unfounded theory. In the present chapter, an examination of the experience of development in poor countries since the war is intended to go beyond this manifest insufficiency to a more systematic comparison of theory with observation. This leads, in turn, to enquiry into the limits of our knowledge of the real processes of development, particularly with regard to economic and demographic interactions. The less developed countries are clearly the main issue since it is there that unprecedented rates of demographic growth have been reached during the last decades. Has this exceptional demographic boom impeded the rise of living standards, or has it been accompanied more by an acceleration in economic progress?

The simplest experimental approach to the relation between population and economic growth (although its use requires some care) is to calculate the correlation between population growth and increases in per capita income at constant prices over a given period. This is undertaken in the first section, where we bring together some statistical observations on these two phenomena; the second section presents a critical synthesis of the main works relating to such calculations; the final section demonstrates the limitations of the exercise, and offers an interpretation of results.

1. The Data

We shall take the beginning of the 1950s as our starting-point, as much for historical reasons as on account of statistical constraints. The general picture of population growth in poor countries from the 1950s onwards is one in which, beginning from a rise in preceding decades, rates move gradually towards a peak in the 1960s, followed by a slight decline in the 1970s. The period 1950–80 thus marks a distinctive historical phase of maximum population growth in the less developed world. Furthermore, national accounts for most of the less developed countries only became available in the last 30 years. Before presenting the results for countries with advanced transition, we shall provide a few general observations on the overall development during these last decades.

General Trends

For many poor countries there are no homogeneous macro-economic series covering the entire period under consideration. China is an especially notable example in this respect, as are Indonesia and Iran. However, the OECD Development Centre regularly undertakes to reconstruct and render comparable such series, and this makes possible a complete account of the periods 1960–70 and 1970–80. We shall also rely on some World Bank data.

In order to correlate indices of population increase and of growth in real per capita income, it is essential to include as many cases as possible, whilst taking care to set aside those countries which do not fulfil minimum conditions of comparability. We have felt it necessary to eliminate the following:

1. Less populated oil-producing countries such as Libya, Venezuela, Saudi Arabia, and the Gulf States where oil incomes were confined to a minority, greatly reducing the significance of average per capita income measurements.
2. South Africa and Rhodesia, in which there was a very uneven distribution of national income between the several populations (Whites, Coloureds, Asians, and the great mass of impoverished Blacks).
3. Vietnam, Laos, Cambodia, Algeria, Iran, and Iraq,[1] which for all or part of the last decades have experienced abnormal conditions or disturbing conflicts.
4. Countries with planned economies, where national accounts have been constructed on a different basis.

With these precautions, we have assembled observations for 58 countries for the period 1950–52 to 1967–69, and 77 countries for the period 1960–80. By way of indication, Table 16.1 gives for the first period the comparative developments of real per capita product (GDP)[2] at constant market prices according to rates of population growth.

In most countries for which we have past estimates of macro-economic series, population growth rates exceed 2%; amongst these, half are characterized by rates above or equal to 3%, indicating that the population approxi-

---

[1] The list could easily be extended, since political instability is a characteristic feature of the poorest countries.

[2] We shall return to this notion and the problems it raises in Chapter 17, which is devoted to long time series.

TABLE   16.1. *Demographic   and   economic   growth   in   less   developed   countries*
1950–1952 to 1967–1969

Annual average rate of population growth (%)	Number of countries	Annual average rate of growth of real per capita product (%)
<2	10	1.7
2.0–2.4	10	1.1
2.5–2.9	14	1.8
≥3.0	24	2.8
TOTAL	58	

Note: For certain countries the period covered is a little shorter than that indicated in the title. *The notion of real product is not the same in all countries.*

Source: Calculated from basic data provided by the OECD (1968 to 1971).

mately doubled during the period in consideration. However, *it is precisely in this subgroup of countries with very rapid population growth that the increase in GDP per capita proves to be considerably higher*: on annual average it rises 2.8% as opposed to 1.1 to 1.8% in the other groups of countries. This evidence might at first appear paradoxical, unless we accept without question the thesis of Boserup (1981) according to which increases in population density, by stimulating technological advance, hasten the removal of traditional obstacles to economic growth. This thesis, however, will need to be tested against a larger number of observations before it can be accepted.

At first reading, Table 16.2, which refers to a greater number of countries in the period 1960–70, would tend to support this conclusion. It shows that the *weighted* annual average rate of increase in real product per capita, in countries where population growth exceeds 3% per year, is close on 4%; in contrast, countries with growth rates between 2.6% and 3% experience a level of only 2.5%, and where growth does not exceed 2.5%, the figure falls to around 1.5%. According to these data, therefore, the more rapid the demographic growth, the more significant economic progress tends to be. But this empirical observation does not hold *as the general rule*, for in the following decade, the results reverse—and in a very unambiguous way: countries with rapid population growth experience the lowest growth in per capita product (1.7% per year), whereas their counterparts, whose population growth rate does not exceed 2% per year, experience a rise to over 4.5%. This sort of result in contiguous periods is somewhat disconcerting. But the explanation—to which we shall return at length—is in fact simple: the composition of each group of countries has changed in relation to the history of demographic transition. This being the case, the coefficient of linear correlation between

TABLE 16.2. *Demographic and economic growth in less developed countries, 1960–1980*

Annual average rate of population growth (%)	Period 1960–70		Period 1970–80	
	Number of countries	Weighted[a] annual average rate of increase in real per capita product[b] (%)	Number of countries	Weighted[c] annual average rate of increase in real per capita product[b] (%)
⩽2.0	18	1.65	14	4.55
2.1–2.5	24	1.48	23	1.95
2.6–3.0	24	2.48	27	3.04
>3.0	11	3.95	13	1.67
TOTAL	77		77	

[a] Weighting factor: mid-1965 population.
[b] Gross domestic product at constant market price.
[c] Weighting factor: mid-1975 population.

Source: Calculated from basic data provided by the OECD Development Centre (1981).

the two series of growth indices, from one period to the next, passes from +0.185 (non-significant) to −0.287 (value significant at 15%). A brief look at the 22 countries with advanced transition—members of the selection of 77 studied—will enable us to understand this reversal.

Economic Growth in Countries with Advanced Transition

Table 16.3 gives the rates of increase for both series (population and GDP per capita) in each of the two decades.

Population growth is rapid, but very uneven. It ranges from 1% (Uruguay) to 3.6% (Mexico) for 1970–80; two out of three countries have rates between 2% and 3%, corresponding to rates of increase 1.5 to 2 times that of European populations at the beginning of nineteenth-century industrialization. Aside from certain South or South-East Asian countries (Sri Lanka; South Korea, Hong Kong, Singapore, and Taiwan), there are very few countries showing a marked fall in demographic rates.

Differences in economic growth are much greater than demographic differences: during the 1970s, half of the countries, although marked by world-wide economic recession, had growth rates in real per capita product greater than those of Europe in its period of greatest progress during the 1960s (+4.1% on average per year, in countries having a market economy: Chesnais and Sauvy 1973). In contrast, certain Latin American countries with rates around only 1% or less, experienced near stagnation over the same

TABLE 16.3. *Population increase and growth of real per capita product in countries with advanced transition* (as an annual average percentage)

Region[a] and country	Population		Real product per capita	
	1960–70	1970–80	1960–70	1970–80
Africa	2.5	2.9	2.1	1.6
Egypt	2.5	2.5	2.0	5.1
Tunisia	2.1	2.5	2.3	5.1
Latin America	2.8	2.7	2.5	2.8
Argentina	1.4	1.3	2.8	0.7
Brazil	2.9	2.8	2.4	5.5
Chile	2.1	1.6	2.3	0.7
Colombia	2.9	2.5	2.1	3.2
Costa Rica	3.5	2.5	2.9	3.3
Cuba	2.0	1.5	−1.0	4.5
Dominican Republic	2.9	3.0	1.5	3.5
Jamaica	1.5	1.6	4.0	−2.9
Mexico	3.4	3.6	3.7	1.6
Panama	3.1	3.1	4.6	1.0
Trinidad and Tobago	2.1	1.3	2.1	4.2
Uruguay	1.3	1.0	−0.1	2.5
Asia[b]	2.4	2.3	3.1	4.0
Hong Kong	2.7	2.2	7.2	6.8
India	2.2	2.1	1.4	1.4
Indonesia	2.1	2.4	0.8	5.0
Malaysia	3.0	2.7	2.8	5.1
Singapore	2.3	1.4	6.3	6.9
South Korea	2.6	1.7	5.9	7.7
Sri Lanka	2.4	1.6	2.8	4.7
Taiwan	3.1	1.9	6.6	7.2

[a] Developing countries within the continent.
[b] Not incl. China.

Source: OECD Development Centre (1981: 8–13).

period (Argentina, Chile, Panama), and sometimes even an economic decline (Jamaica: −2.1%). The countries are thus fairly evenly spread across a wide range of rates. As a whole, however, countries with advanced transition are distinguished by markedly higher economic growth than their counterparts with continuing high fertility. This is clearly illustrated by comparing Tables 16.2 and 16.4 (Table 16.3).

Let us now compare demographic growth with economic growth. By grouping the countries according to their demographic expansion, we arrive at Table 16.4. The economic advantage enjoyed by countries with high popula-

TABLE 16.4. *Demographic and economic growth in less developed countries with advanced transition, 1960–1980*

Annual average rate of population growth (%)	Period 1960–70		Period 1970–80	
	Number of countries	Weighted[a] average annual rate of increase in real per capita product[b] (%)	Number of countries	Weighted[c] average annual rate of increase in real per capita product[b] (%)
≤2.0	4	1.72	10	4.58
2.1–2.5	8	1.38	7	2.27
2.6–3.0	6	3.13	3	5.39
>3.0	4	4.28	2	1.58
TOTAL	22		22	

[a] Weighting factor: mid-1965 population.
[b] Gross domestic product at constant market price.
[c] Weighting factor: mid-1975 population.

Source: Calculated from basic data provided by the OECD Development Centre (1981).

tion growth in the 1960s is replaced by the opposite phenomenon in the 1970s: *this inversion occurs in an even more pronounced form within the group of 77 countries* (at least in the two extreme groups). What happened, then? One observes instantly that there are 10 countries with relatively 'moderate' population increase (2% or less) in the decade of the 1970s, as opposed to only 4 in the decade of the 1960s. It is precisely in those countries of South-East Asia with an unrivalled economic growth of 7% to 8% per year—and which even experienced a slight increase in the 1970s as compared with the 1960s— that the addition occurs. Taiwan, which in the 1960s belonged to the group of countries with the highest population growth and the most rapid economic growth (after Hong Kong), thus moved into the group with the lowest population growth. It is therefore the displacement of such countries with exceptional economic performance into groups with lower population growth which produces the change observed. If one looks at the four countries in question, all within the sphere of Japanese influence, the contrast between the two periods is almost entirely removed, and the rate of population increase does not appear to have had any notable effect, either for or against, on the development of living standards. It would therefore seem that differences in population growth were not an important variable in explaining contrasting patterns of economic growth. In other words, the general view that rapid population increase is inimical to the country concerned has not been proven. Even in countries with the highest levels of demographic growth, economic growth remains clearly evident—even during the 1970s.

2. Synthesis

Comparative empirical analyses of relations between population growth and economic development are recent and, compared with the general proliferation of studies on population and economy, are still relatively few in number.

The General View: No Significant Relation

The first studies to employ statistical correlation date from the 1960s. As with Kuznets (1967), they refer mainly to developed countries. Kuznets devoted most of his scientific attention to the statistical reconstruction of Western economic history since the Industrial Revolution; the range of his knowledge confers his judgements with particular weight. In previous works (1954 and 1965, for example), he also adds some useful considerations for comparing European developments with other continents. His calculation of rank correlation between short-term population change and the growth of per capita income in 40 poor countries revealed no significant association between the two phenomena.

Most subsequent studies have also compared population growth to that of average per capita income, but in some cases the economic variable employed is average per capita savings (e.g. Conlisk and Huddle 1969) or food production per capita (e.g. Klatzmann 1975; Bairoch 1981). The earliest studies (Easterlin 1967; Stockwell 1962, 1966, 1972; Thirlwall 1972, etc.) relate only to a small number of countries (maximum 40) covering relatively short periods of at most 15 years. The authors were constrained by the availability of data, and the countries studied are in consequence hardly representative of the less developed world as a whole. With the exception of Kuznets's and Easterlin's work, calculations tend to show significant but incompatible results, positive in some cases (Thirlwall 1972) and negative in others (Stockwell 1962, 1966). Subsequently, where sufficient methodological precautions have been taken and certain artificial assumptions avoided,[3] such divergences have become increasingly rare, or even non-existent. Regular publication of crude data on the national accounts of less developed countries by the OECD and the World Bank has widened considerably the number of cases available, which now cover almost all countries for which comparison of series is desirable.

A synoptic table of the principal studies up to 1978 has been drawn up by Sagnier (1979). With the exception of Stavig (1979), whose analysis curiously compounds developed and less developed countries, as well as countries with market and planned economies, all the authors—from Sauvy (1972) to Bairoch (1981), through Chesnais (1975) and Chesnais and Sauvy (1973), Lefèbvre (1977, 1978), Bara and Guillaumont (1978), Hagen (1975), and

---

[3] By way of example, see Stockwell's first studies, discussed in *Population* (Chesnais and Sauvy 1973).

Simon (1977)—arrive at the same conclusion; the absence of any significant linear correlation. This unanimity of results should not, however, be attributed merely to the geographical diversity of countries selected, which represent more and more varied demographic and economic contexts. Consideration must also be given to the standardization of data and methods of treatment. The gradual shift in Stockwell's arguments from significance[4] to non-significance, in a series of calculations published at different intervals since 1962, is indicative.

For some authors, like Bairoch (1981), the negative effect of rapid population growth on economic development is 'more than just an assumption'. The absence of a significant correlation between the two is thus considered inadmissible, a 'paradox' related partly to imperfect economic data. This line of reasoning cannot be totally dismissed. However, study of a large number of countries, which are also very diverse as to density, natural resources, social organization, political heritage, etc., is likely to point to different mechanisms. As we shall see, the mode of analysis leads a priori to indeterminate results. But before embarking on this discussion, an important empirical problem affecting this genre of studies should be considered: the question of duration, including the related issue of the appropriate interval in which series are thought to act on each other.

Temporal Criteria

Demographic phenomena occur slowly. Even in a country with a rapidly growing population, age distributions only change very gradually and their particular characteristics carry consequences that may take decades to play themselves out. Economic development, on the other hand, is subject to multiple and fluctuating influences of the moment, such as the flow of raw materials, weather conditions, rates of interest, etc. The relation between the two series thus presents special comparative difficulties. Thus, if we wish to assess the economic effect of a demographic change, two conditions seem necessary: first, whether the change is sufficiently large; and secondly, whether the period under consideration is long enough for expected effects (positive or negative) to emerge. Periods of 10 years, as used in most existing studies, are relatively short on the demographic time-scale; there is every possibility that an indicator like GNP per capita, for a given period, might be more sensitive to the demographic growth of preceding periods than to that of its own.

The criteria on which the interval operating between series is selected are evidently not neutral. If we postulate that population growth is beneficial to economic development, then the period of demographic observation has to precede that in which the economy is studied. If we assume, moreover, that

[4] To begin with, for 16 countries only, and covering a very short period.

demographic increase is determined mainly by an increase in the number of births (or a decline in infant mortality) and that the marginal productivity of labour exceeds average productivity—premisses which are not generally clarified—then the interval can be taken as the average age of accession to the labour force or, at least, the age at which services rendered by a child exceed its cost of upbringing. In other words, given the size of the non-market sector, the interval should be around 7 to 15 years. Similarly, and still under the same conditions, if a negative statistical link is expected, the most appropriate interval would be the age of a child's maximum net costs. In reality, there is a certain arbitrariness in this choice, because we are ill informed about the economic contribution made at different ages. In consequence, writers tend to proceed cautiously: in search of the best correlation, they select the most favourable interval for which neither the stability of series over time nor the legitimacy of a posteriori theoretical justification can be assured. In the studies of Simon (1975) and Sagnier (1979), for example, this interval is 16 and 11 years respectively.

Limitations of the Exercise and Interpretation of the Results

On account of its simplicity, statistical correlation is a frequently used tool, but one whose limitations are often overlooked. Its calculation is more frequently an instrument of invalidation than validation of a hypothesis. It cannot be said too often: correlation does not imply causality.

Limitations

In addition to the difficulty of interpreting results, the first limitations are immediately imposed by the variables and method used. These are as follows:

1. *Recourse to aggregate variables like GNP or the natural increase of a population.* If the latter is relatively well measured, it can be determined by an infinite number of possible variations and combinations of variations in age structure. Such variations may be directly connected to phases of demographic transition. However, such combinations have different implications for the growth of production. Where GNP is concerned—the inadequacies of which, particularly for less monetized economies, are well known—it is mainly levels and trends which are affected by bias. Geographical comparisons consequently concentrate on certain periods, rather than comparing historical sequences in a given country. In choosing trends[5] as our variables, we should thereby reduce objections to the use of these aggregate variables.

---

[5] However, one cannot deny the existence of bias in a rising market, with the progressive modernization of an economy, as previously unpaid services acquire market value. But there is no proof—contrary to Bairoch's assumption (1981)—that this bias is stronger for countries with faster demographic growth.

2. *Comparison of phenomena subject to different historical developments obscures calculations of linear regression.* Whilst the trend of real product per capita tends to follow a rising pattern (see Chapter 17), the trend of population increase describes a bell-shaped curve, at first rising, then falling (see Chapter 8). Consequently for a given country over time the correlation will tend to be positive in the first phase of transition, and negative in the last. If one includes the entire period of transition, the correlation coefficient will tend towards zero. Similarly, there is scarcely any greater chance that a correlation will be significant when calculations combine countries at different stages of transition within the same slice of time.

3. *The absence of weighting.* This refers particularly to the demographic size of a country. In consequence, India, for example, may appear as more important in a calculation than, say, Panama. However, because the internal heterogeneity of a country increases with its size, trends—all things being equal—tend to follow the norm rather than the extremes.

Interpretation

Where a correlation exists, it may still contain ambiguities; all historical interactions between two phenomena A and B may in fact be given five different interpretations which are not mutually exclusive. One could be dealing with either the influence of A on B, or that of B on A, or the interaction between A and B, or the action of a third phenomenon C on A and B,[6] or finally a pure coincidence. Conversely, in addition to certain reasons already mentioned, the absence of any significant correlation may arise from the action of opposing forces which tend to cancel each other out.

It is possible to construct a list (not an exhaustive one) of factors which impel a correlation in one direction or the other.

1. *Factors tending towards negative correlation.* This heading embraces the familiar neo-Malthusian arguments according to which rapid population growth hinders economic development. As some of these arguments were presented in the previous chapter, we shall only review them briefly here:

(*a*) Population growth increases the pressure on natural resources, for instance, limited land or space. In the agricultural sphere, particularly, this means a decline in the average surface area of arable land per labourer, according to the law of diminishing returns. Because of the time it takes for institutions to adjust, such pressure constitutes an obstacle to the process of breaking with traditional forms (Brown 1963).

(*b*) Continuing high fertility forces most of the population to devote its time

---

[6] Thus, demographic growth and economic growth may respond to the same external impetus, such as institutional change or technical progress: in this way, the growth of technical knowledge and ability is accompanied by a greater control over public health and economic production, whence the possibility of the two phenomena emerging simultaneously (as in 19th-century Europe).

and energy to bringing up children. Productive labour outside the home is noticeably reduced, particularly among women.

(*c*) The degree of investment necessary to guarantee additional members of the population the same standard of living (which is to say, demographic investments, in Sauvy's parlance) is such that the potential for private and public capital formation is seriously reduced. A 3% rate of demographic increase, for example, will absorb from 9% to 12% of the national income, where the incremental capital–output ratio is 3 or 4. This results in a decline of investment in plant per worker, which in turn affects improvements in productivity. Conversely, a decline in fertility releases resources for the accumulation of capital: it has been demonstrated that, in the US, for example, the contraction in education costs, on the one hand, and the increase in human and non-human capital, on the other, have been almost symmetrical.

(*d*) Economic development tends, over a greater or lesser span of time to result in a greater decline in the crude birth-rate than in the crude death-rate (i.e. the third phase of demographic transition), causing population growth to slow down.

(*e*) The less developed world begins with an already considerable handicap: per capita income is many times less than it was in the currently developed countries just before their industrial revolution (Kuznets 1954); current rates of demographic growth are 1.5 to 2 times higher in the developing world than they were in the Old World when its growth rates were at their peak.

2. *Factors tending toward positive correlation.* These factors may arise equally from the effect of income on population, or vice versa.

(*a*) Economic growth may stimulate population growth by raising fertility (through reducing certain forms of sterility, intra-uterine deaths, etc.); by encouraging immigration (which, in turn, stimulates further economic growth); and above all by reducing mortality. The positive effect of improvements in health conditions, already noted in Chapter 4, is probably less fundamental in its direct influence, which could include: the gradual disappearance of economic losses connected with early death; a reduction of the destabilizing effects of death on family organization; and an increased psychological and physiological capacity for work. It is estimated that in certain tropical countries the proportion of people with malaria may have been as high as three-fifths. The indirect influence of better health on socio-economic change proceeds via its capacity to transform the environment. Thus, in early modern Europe, as much as in contemporary poor countries, malaria long caused the neglect of vast tracts of arable land; control over death promoted the emergence of rational attitudes, encouraging the decline of traditional fatalism, and facilitating the birth of the idea of progress. The decline of the immemorial tyranny of disease was a historical turning-point with incalculable and far-reaching implications. It represents a pre-condition to the modernization of societies or, so to speak, the first face of progress. It was accompanied by an increase in the quantity and—even more so—the quality of labour.

In this sense, there is a cumulative interaction between access to greater prosperity and the improvement in a population's state of health: they constitute a mutual exchange which sets in motion highly complex mechanisms in which the growth of income enables higher standards of nutrition and education, which in turn are capable of feeding back into further increases in income itself and population.

Different authors (Adelman 1963; Weintraub 1962; Krishnamurty 1966; Demeny 1974) have established that the (negative) correlation of average per capita income with mortality levels in less developed countries during the 1960s was very pronounced; and they show that such correlations were very slight or almost non-existent with fertility levels. But this stronger negative link with mortality is, a priori, only in evidence at the beginning of the transition. As we have seen, the link between income and life expectation at birth in rich countries weakened progressively. It is thus perfectly plausible that the temporal variability of income effects is precisely what lies behind the positive correlation of the 1950s and 1960s—the majority of less developed countries at this time experienced the beginning of the transition—and similarly the absence of correlation in the 1970s. In the future, the correlation could become clearly negative once fertility declines are sufficiently advanced in a number of countries. This sort of result is merely the logical consequence of transition theory's main proposition, according to which socio-economic development acts on mortality before its effects are perceived in fertility.

(b) The influence of demographic increase on economic growth. Under favourable circumstances industrialization may turn demographic growth into a valuable stimulant to the rise in standards of living, both by procuring labour to exploit natural resources and by widening the markets necessary to absorb and make profitable the fruits of mass production. Nineteenth-century America is one example. In other words, demographic increase can affect the supply and demand of economic agents.

The potential impact of such increases on the bulk of national income is as follows. An increase in the number of inhabitants is accompanied by an increase in needs and consumption; this mechanism, while obvious, is complicated by the degree to which it actually operates. Investment, for instance, may increase with population growth; in India, the net rate of capita accumulation more than doubled in relation to national income between the beginning of the 1950s and the beginning of the 1970s. Such an expansion of needs facilitates realization of economies of scale and the intensification of productive efforts by mobilizing labour capacity and underexploited resources and by changing methods of cultivation (e.g. reduction of fallow land, use of fertilizers, irrigation, mechanization, multiple harvesting practices: see Boserup 1965, 1981).

Changes in employment opportunities are the source of two mechanisms which generate gains in productivity:

1. Geographic and sectoral migration, connected with demographic pressure in rural areas. The transfer of the working population from low productivity agriculture to sectors with high productivity—even in countries with too large a surplus agricultural population to be absorbed—is generally the result of an improvement in average productivity (Fisher 1935). As a general rule, growth of the non-agricultural work-force has a strong positive relation with that of real productivity per head (Clark 1967). The economic history of Japan best illustrates this process. This mechanism relates largely to differences in incomes between the agricultural and other sectors.

An increase in the non-agricultural population can also cause a rise in food prices which is capable of reducing the rigidity of agricultural supply; by affecting wage costs such an increase can facilitate the adoption of industrial strategies relying on intensive labour to manufacture goods.

2. The replacement of generations of illiterate or semi-literate labourers by new and better-educated generations more open to modernity. This process is all the more important because, despite regular exposure of gaps in the educational process, considerable progress has been made in the last few decades. While slow and imperceptible, like all structural phenomena, such developments can prove decisive in the long term (Leibenstein 1969).

Conclusion

There is a clear contradiction between the paradigms prevailing in the economic literature and historical reality. Dominant theories are unable to account for economic development over the last few decades. A singular fact remains to be explained: in developing countries the growth rate of GNP per capita between 1950 and 1975, according to World Bank estimates, was higher[7] than that of developed countries (an annual average of 3.4% compared with 3.2%), a pattern recently confirmed for the period 1973–83.[8] This finding is all the more astonishing given that the industrialized nations, with considerably fewer demographic constraints, experienced an annual increase in per capita income of only around 2% during the phase of their greatest expansion, up to the mid-twentieth century. A considerable number of the less developed countries had, moreover, been at zero growth for centuries. The disasters forecast in the post-war period were not realized, in

[7] Even if there are considerable differences between countries, the findings are sufficiently surprising to warrant attention.

[8] Growth measurements are not free of bias. As a result of the rapid expansion of market activities and foreign exchange, there is a greater tendency to overstatement where less developed economies are concerned, and the difference in growth compared with developed economies may in consequence be exaggerated. The growing debt to Western banks should also be borne in mind (about $1,000 billion at the end of 1985, half of which is owed by Latin American countries).

spite of a larger demographic boom than was expected: the first demographic projections of the United Nations (1951) reckoned population growth at an annual rate of around 1% in Africa and Asia over the period 1950–80, whereas the actual rate was closer to 2.5%. Even the economic projections made from the early 1960s to the mid-1970s by renowned experts like Rosenstein-Rodan and Chenery erred in the direction of excessive pessimism: growth proved, after the event, to be much higher than the prognostications in the majority of cases (Morawetz 1977). It is thus advisable to avoid focusing exclusively on the single factor of demographic growth, a factor whose role within the process of economic development is difficult to predict given the many circumstances and parameters at work. The maxim 'There are no poor countries, merely badly run ones' doubtless conveys more than a modicum of truth.

Bibliography to Chapter 16

ADELMAN, I. (1963), 'An Econometric Analysis of Population Growth', *AER*, 53: 314–19.

ALUKO, S. A. (1971), 'Population Growth and the Level of Income: A Survey', *Journal of Modern African Studies*, 4: 561–75.

BAIROCH, P. (1964), *Révolution industrielle et sous-développement* (Paris: Mouton), 201.

—— (1981), 'Population Growth and Long Term International Economic Growth', *IUSSP International Conference on Population, Manila, 1981*, 141–63.

BARA, M. F., and GUILLAUMONT, P. (1978), 'La Croissance démographique optimale: à la recherche d'une vérification empirique', *Population*, 6: 1207–16.

BLARDONE, G., and PARISOT, M. T. (1973), *Progrès économique dans le tiers-monde: population active, productivité, croissance et développement* (Paris: Librairie Sociale et Économique).

BOSERUP, E. (1965), *The Conditions of Agricultural Growth: The Conditions of Agrarian Change under Population Pressure* (London: Allen & Unwin).

—— (1981), *Population and Technology* (Oxford: Blackwell).

BROWN, L. R. (1963), *Man, Land and Food* (Washington, DC: US Dept of Agriculture).

CHESNAIS, J. -C. (1975), 'Croissance démographique et développement économique dans les pays peu développés de 1960 à 1972', *Population*, 6: 1150–55.

—— and SAUVY, A. (1973), 'Progrès économique et accroissement de la population: une expérience commentée', *Population*, 4–5: 843–57.

CLARK, C. (1967), *Population Growth and Land Use* (London).

CONLISK, J., and HUDDLE, D. (1969), 'Allocating Foreign Aid: An Appraisal of Self-Help Model', *Journal of Development Studies* (July), 245–51.

DEMENY, P. (1974), 'The Population of the Underdeveloped Countries', *Scientific American* (Sept.), 149–59.

EASTERLIN, R. A. (1967), 'The Effects of Population Growth on the Economic Development of Developing Countries', *Annals of American Academy of Political and Social Science*, 369: 98–108.

FISHER, A. G. B. (1935), *The Clash of Progress and Security* (London: Macmillan).

GLOVER, D., and SIMON, J. L. (1975), 'The Effects of Population Density upon Infrastructure: The Case of Road-Building', *EDCC*, 23: 453–68.

HAGEN, E. E. (1975), *The Economics of Development* (Homewood, IU.: Irwin), 180–95.

KLATZMAN, J. (1975), *Nourrir dix milliards d'hommes?* (Paris: PUF).

KRISHNAMURTY, K. (1966), 'Economic Development and Population Growth in Low-Income Countries: An Empirical Study of India', *EDCC*, 70–75.

KUZNETS, S. (1954), 'Underdeveloped Countries and the Preindustrial Phase in the Advanced Countries', *Proceedings of the World Population Conference, Rome, 1954*, V. 947–70.

—— (1965), 'Demographic Aspects of Modern Economic Growth', *World Population Conference, Belgrade, 1965*.

—— (1967), 'Population and Economic Growth', *Proceedings of the American Philosophical Society* (June), 170–93.

LEFEBVRE, A. (1977), 'Croissance démographique et progrès économique dans les pays en développement de 1960 à 1974', *Population*, 6: 1287–93.

—— (1978), 'Croissance démographique et progrès économique dans les pays en développement de 1960 à 1975', *Population*, 6: 1221–27.

LEIBENSTEIN, H. (1969), 'Pitfalls in Benefit–Cost Analysis of Birth Prevention', *Population Studies*, 23: 161–70.

MORAWETZ, D. (1977), *Twenty-Five Years of Economic Development: 1950 to 1975* (Baltimore, Md.: World Bank), 77–79, 90–92 (French trans.: Paris: Economica, 1977).

OECD Development Centre (1968–71), *Comptes nationaux des pays moins développés* (Paris: OECD).

—— (1981), *Informations récentes sur les comptes nationaux des pays en développement*, final bulletins, esp. no. 14 (Paris: OECD).

SAGNIER, C. (1979), 'Une Hypothèse de décalage en démographie économique', *Population*, 3: 718–23.

SAUVY, A. (1972), 'Les Charges et les avantages de la croissance de la population', *Population*, 1: 9–26.

SIMON, J. L. (1975), 'The Positive Effect of Population on Agricultural Savings in Irrigation Systems', *RES*, 57: 71–79.

—— (1977), *The Economics of Population Growth* (Princeton, NJ: Princeton University Press), 165.

STAVIG, G. R. (1979), 'The Impact of Population Growth on the Economy of Countries', *EDCC* (July), 735–50.

STOCKWELL, E. G. (1962), 'The Relationship between Population Growth and Economic Development', *American Sociological Review* (Apr.), 250–52.

—— (1966), 'Some Demographic Correlates of Economic Development', *Rural Sociology*, 31(2) (June), 216–24.

—— (1972), 'Some Observations on the Relationship between Population Growth and Economic Development during the 1960s', *Rural Sociology* (Dec.), 628–32.

—— (1980), 'A Note on the Association between Population Growth and Economic Development in Low-Income Countries', *Rural Sociology*, 1: 132–38.

THIRLWALL, A. P. (1972), 'A Cross-section Study of Population Growth and the Growth of Output and Per Capita Income in a Production Function Framework', *Manchester School of Economics and Social Studies* (Dec.), 339–56.

UN (United Nations) (1951), 'Étude d'ensemble de l'accroissement de la population mondiale dans le passé et dans l'avenir', *Population Bulletin*, 1 (Dec.), 1–14.

WEINTRAUB, R. (1962), 'The Birth Rate and Economic Development: An Empirical Study', *Econometrica*, 4: 812–17.

17 Secular Growth in the Industrial World

> The miracle of the 1960s was one of the marvels of history. The question should not be, Why are things so bad today?, but, Why were they so good then?
>
> (Samuelson)

MODERN economic development has a long history. From the eighteenth century onwards, Western countries experienced a lasting increase in their rates of demographic growth. While admitting a degree of impoverishment, it appears that already in that period increases in agricultural production were at least equal to population growth.[1] For over two centuries there was a considerable population increase, but, in contrast to past increases, this wave of growth was not interrupted by famine. Moreover, instead of a resulting fall in living standards, which had been the case hitherto via the well-known mechanisms described by Malthus and illustrated for England by Lee (1980), there was a rapid economic expansion. A new demographic and economic system emerged, characterized by unprecedented growth in both sectors. Such was the upheaval that it was soon termed a 'revolution'.

The key to understanding these changes has sometimes been sought in the historical sequence in which the several revolutions—agricultural, industrial, and finally demographic—occurred. Formidable obstacles have, however, been encountered. There was little doubt about the massive demographic increase in the eighteenth century, even though it is difficult to assess precisely, except in a few countries.[2] But the very existence of an agricultural revolution in the eighteenth century has been seriously questioned, at least in certain countries like France, where progress in agricultural productivity does not seem to have occurred until the mid-nineteenth century. We are far from unanimous agreement on the date at which the process of industrial revolution began in different countries,[3] and the descriptive term has itself been ques-

---

[1] An alternative and complementary hypothesis would be the reorganization of commerce and the accumulation of food stocks, which also enable a larger population to be fed.

[2] Owing to the lack of censuses, even in France where data sources of good quality are abundant, traditional estimates have come to be contradicted by more detailed research: the number of inhabitants around 1740 was generally estimated a 21 or 22 million, but Henry's studies (Henry and Blayo 1975) have resulted in a figure of 24.6 million.

[3] The beginnings of economic growth in England, the seat of the first industrialization, are placed by Toynbee (1884) and Kuznets (1966) around 1760, while other writers, such as Nef,

tioned: it is now recognized that the phenomenon was not entirely new, but a continuing process prepared by a long period of rural proto-industrialization.

The definitive feature is, rather, the fact of acceleration consequent on important technical innovations in the harnessing of energy.[4] The nature of this phenomenon extended well beyond the industrial sphere, simultaneously transforming the realm of ideas, social structures, and political institutions. Really, one is dealing here with a general acceleration in history. In western Europe, change escalated from 1840 onwards: European prosperity became manifest, population growth increased, and domination over other continents was established. Mass migration, encouraged by falls in the cost of sea travel and the development of railways, commenced.

This chapter considers the possible influence of demographic growth on secular economic development through an examination of rates of population increase, the changing occupational composition of populations, and the phenomena underlying them. In the first place, we shall recall certain questions raised by the analysis of growth. This will be followed by a brief overview of national experiences based on a reconstruction of long series of national accounts. In this way it is possible to show that the two main phases in the rise of the modern world economy (1870–1913 and 1946–73) coincide with particular periods of demographic transition in the leading countries, and that, in a more general way, secular demographic growth and economic development went hand in hand in all the countries. The aim of the third section, using certain cases, is to explain the possible mechanisms behind this coincidence.[5]

1. Problems, Methods, and Concepts

The first evaluations of national income and its growth in an international perspective were written relatively early, from King in the late seventeenth

push the origins further back into the past. There are also disagreements in the case of France, where the pattern of development—still not sufficiently understood—appears to have been slow and fluctuating: an initial widespread increase spreading beyond open areas such as harbours became manifest between 1715 and 1720 (Marczewski 1963), that is, at about the time of the first signs of mortality decline, and after the first great troubles of the preceding period. But the real breakthrough is attributed more to the second half of the 19th century (Lévy-Leboyer 1968). Each country experienced its own chronology of 'revolutions', the first signs of development often being imperceptible and the apparent order varying with the criteria adopted. This accounts for the controversial nature of certain antecedent relations supposed necessary between the agricultural and industrial (or demographic) revolutions (Bairoch 1963). Because sequences of cause and effect are interconnected, the same element may be cause or effect in turn, depending on the way stages evolve.

[4] Between 1820 and 1880, the world supply of energy increased over 20 times; between 1880 and 1938, the figure increased another sixfold (Woytinski 1953). The process is cumulative: once a certain critical minimum level is passed, the more energy one produces, the more means one has to produce it. The very close correlation between the development of energy consumption and that of production is a well-known phenomenon.

[5] Emphasis will be given to long-term trends, since it is only over considerable stretches of time that large-scale demographic and economic interactions become perceptible.

century (1696) to the more detailed account by Mulhall at the end of the nineteenth century. But it is during the period between the wars, and particularly since then, with the works of Clark, Kuznets, Abramovitz, Denison,[6] and others, that such studies have assumed real importance and evolved a systematic approach relying on the statistical framework provided by national accounts. The reconstruction of time series presented here will refer only to the industrial world. Twenty countries have been included (see Figs. 17.1 to 17.6 and Appendix 3). Small countries have been excluded because their economic growth is more dependent on external factors; countries having planned economies have likewise been set aside because of the social and institutional practices peculiar to them.

The Nature of Growth

From a quantitative point of view, growth in real per capita income suffices as a rough initial measure of economic growth. In contrast to the pattern of past times, in which growth was uneven and dominated by complex fluctuations around what are termed 'subsistence' levels, modern economic growth is characterized by the permanent long-term rise of material prosperity. The increase in incomes is only the most visible aspect of this phenomenon; at a much more profound level it entails complete structural change. The composition of demand alters as per capita income increases, through a progressive shift in the structure of consumption which conforms to Engels' laws. The distribution of manpower changes, assisted more or less by the differential growth of different parts of the population. This process is slower than the sectoral redeployment of production, since industrialization is based on the intensive use of capital, and can attain higher levels of labour productivity in industry than in agriculture. The development of the sectoral composition of the working population in a given period is very closely connected with the shift of economic activities from a rural to an urban milieu, and thereby with the relative size of the agricultural labour reserve and the differential increase of demographic pressure in rural areas.

  While this schema of development appears much the same for each country, the course of structural change does vary; and it should be remembered that structural changes extend well beyond the economic sphere, first affecting mental outlook and social institutions (Kuznets 1954). Indeed, it is this long series of structural alterations which best characterizes modern economic growth in the most diverse fields of individual and collective life, of which demographic transition is one of the most manifest aspects (Chenery and Syrquin 1975).

---

[6] An immense literature is relevant to this topic and has been referred to in this chapter; the bibliography cites only those references which we considered most salient.

Measures of Growth

Aside from the problems inherent in establishing early series, any attempt at measuring growth by volume over the long term is complicated by the very nature of growth, which presupposes a profound change in economic variables and hence reduces the possibility of comparison. A number of factors preponderate:

1. variations in the system of relative prices: the rate of growth at constant prices can vary enormously depending on the base year selected, especially during periods of great change;[7]
2. the improvement in the quality of existing goods and services;
3. the appearance of new products; and
4. the extent to which the economy is monetized.

Finally, in the international perspective which concerns us here, any comparison involving standards between countries for a given date requires a common rate of conversion and a common monetary unit: a coefficient other than the rate of exchange is necessary, and this will entail defining scales of equivalence for the purchasing power of national currencies. Thus, in the absence of a sufficient observational basis, the moment enquiry involves the less recent past, differences between authors' estimates are likely to become extremely pronounced. For this reason we shall have little recourse to such estimates.

Growth Factors

The overall theoretical framework for analysing growth is still embryonic. Malinvaud (1984), for example, admits that 'we lack a theory of economic development. Even in the case of contemporary industrialized countries, we are able to give a clear explanation neither of the origins of their respective patterns of growth, nor of increasing or decreasing rates of growth.' However, all studies refer to three central points: the growth of the labour factor, the accumulation of capital, and technological progress. Differences occur only in the nature and importance of the role accorded to each.

The analysis of growth factors is a fairly recent phenomenon, which dates from the 1960s and refers to the most recent decades.[8] It should not be confused with study of the causes which set in motion forces of more fundamental kinds.

---

[7] The most familiar case is that of the Soviet Union from 1928 to 1937: depending on the estimate, the average annual rate of macro-economic growth ranges from 5.5% to 8% or from 8% to 16%!

[8] The studies of Solow (1957) and Denison especially (1962, 1967) show to what extent the increase in physical capital and labour account for American growth. A residual factor, related in part to improvements in the level of technical skills (a general increase in the amount and quality of education) occupies a predominant place.

On the whole, explanations of the beginnings of industrialization have tended to concentrate on one variable. Following Adam Smith's formulation of the theory that low interest rates encouraged the birth of an English capitalist class, emphasis was long placed on the crucial role played by the accumulation of capital.[9] The 1950s were entirely dominated by this view, which found its typical presentation in the Coale–Hoover model discussed in Chapter 15. Otherwise, emphasis has been placed on the role of innovation in connection with the emergence of an entrepreneurial class[10] (Schumpeter 1912 and 1939), on demographic pressure and its influence on technological progress (Dupréel 1928; Boserup 1965, 1981), or, more simply, on the endowment of natural resources (coal in England, for example)—in sum, the inevitable components of a total system of production. Nevertheless, certain authors do focus on other elements generally not included in these models which remain very important to historians and social thinkers. These include political changes such as the birth of the modern State and the rise of nationalism,[11] and changes in culture (such as attitudes to profit-making) and mental outlook (the birth of individualism and the rights of man). These changes are part of a sequence which begins in the Reformation and Counter-Reformation, with the gradual emergence of a new spirit favourable to matters long regarded as heresy: *laissez-faire*, profit, and innovation; the questioning of religious beliefs, philosophical developments (revolutionized by scientific discovery), and the gradual growth of literacy. All these phenomena contributed to the emergence of new values centred on the individual and reason. Hence alongside historians of English industrialization who emphasize the role of technological variables and inventions (Ashton 1948), there are others like Polyani (1944) who stress sociological change: the emergence of a market *society*,[12] as traditional obstacles to the free circulation of men and capital disappear.[13]

These diverse theories are in fact more complementary than contradictory; none of them, taken on its own, accounts sufficiently for the complexity of developments observed. Few attempts have been made to determine strategic variables and their functional relations; even less is known about endogenous and exogenous factors controlling the dynamics of the crucial trinity of demographic growth, the formation of capital, and technological progress. The notion of industrial revolution itself has not been defined operationally, either in terms of minimal rates of growth in real per capita income, or of structural

---

[9] The ratio is, moreover, easily reversed: the accumulation of capital may itself result from growth.

[10] On this subject, see the series of publications Explorations in Entrepreneurial History.

[11] The emergence of England in the 18th century has sometimes been interpreted as a nationalistic reaction to the claims of Holland and France to hegemony.

[12] However, according to Braudel (1967), the market economy has always existed.

[13] The decline in earlier forms of State assistance, and the revision of the Poor Laws which was completed in 1834, would have made the individual independent of his parish of origin—which was necessary to the growth of a mobile and available proletariat.

indicators such as the proportion of total income represented by industrial revenues. Moreover, even confining discussion to these three classic factors, to isolate variables relating to the one or the other over long periods of time seems arbitrary, given the degree to which they are interdependent: it is impossible to separate technological progress from the accumulation of capital and population growth; demographic increase, related essentially to the mortality decline, can only occur in its turn where there has been progress in medical, economic, and organizational techniques; sustained increases in the average length of life result, in turn, in a new economic outlook favouring the development of long-term savings and decisions to invest in human capital, not to mention the potential for undermining traditional fatalism which improvements in health and living conditions represent.

No system of principles deserving the name of a theory of economic growth in fact exists. Not even the definition of growth factors is beyond debate: aside from the increase of labour (which can assume varying economic importance depending on its origin and socio-demographic composition), not one of the terms has a simple and universal meaning. The notion of the accumulation of capital, even in an enlarged sense which includes human capital, is only very imperfectly taken into consideration in extant models, particularly in its qualitative aspects. Technological progress, on the other hand, is often treated as a sort of *deus ex machina*: while crucially important, its mechanisms somehow elude comprehension.[14] Technological developments in fact represent a mixture of factors underlying common measurement, embracing not only invention and application, but also quality of labour and capital, external economies, and economies of scale; such factors interact in a *cumulative process*, the rate of progress of which is, statistically speaking, ill defined (Nelson 1981). More recently, in work on the sectoral breakdown of growth, new factors such as energy consumption have been introduced into production functions.

The Integration of Demographic Variables in Growth Models

Integration of the labour factor (linked, in the long term, to demographic change) into a total production function of the Cobb–Douglas type is not an easy task, even when limited to the two factors of labour and capital. The question of heterogeneity of variables immediately arises: capital is subject to short- and longer-term fluctuations, whereas the effects of demographic

---

[14] Denison's account, in which growth may be broken down in a series of analytical deductions, concludes that the contribution made by technological progress embraces factors which are either omitted or badly measured in terms of capital or labour. Here, for example, is his breakdown of American growth from 1929 to 1969: Increase in production factor (labour (1.32) + capital (0.50) = 1.82); plus variation of output per unit of input (acquired skills (0.92) + economies of scale (0.36) + allocation of resources (0.30) + others (0.01) = 1.59); equals annual rate of growth of national income (3.41).

variations are perceptible only over the very long term.[15] There is insufficient articulation between the two because the method employed is suitable only for analysis of the short term. Moreover, in time series, the colinearity between labour and capital variables is generally strong, which means that it is impossible, in practical terms, to measure the particular contribution of one or the other's growth. Production functions are hardly used any more in studies of growth, except at the level of the sector or firm,[16] owing to the greater clarity with which causal processes can be perceived.

More generally, certain institutional, political, or social phenomena (such as legislation, government policy, relation between social groups, and the international environment), whose importance in creating long-term growth differentials is crucial, are omitted from the analytical framework. Theoretical models of growth, whether of the Harrod–Domar type or the neo-classical model, assume, moreover, that the economy is closed to foreign exchange. This is a major limitation, given the growing internationalization of economies; foreign competition is becoming a fundamental stake in the game. However, this is conditioned by differentials in production costs, which may involve the intervention of demographic factors such as the relative scarcity of young manpower in dynamic sectors, the ageing of the working population, and the proportion of the elderly. All these elements are in fact capable of affecting the cost of enterprises and the level of taxation and parafiscal economic agents.

At the present juncture there is no general framework which takes sufficient account of the existence of causes as multiple and complex as those characteristic of long-term macro-economic growth. Ideally, a theory of growth should be a theory of coefficients permitting substitution between components in the growth process. However, it has to be admitted that we are a long way from this goal. Before considering the possible influence of demographic variables on growth, therefore, it is not irrelevant to review the historical experience of the main industrial countries.

2. National Experience

Development is not a linear process; certain areas of Europe experienced phases of prosperity characterized by strong manufacturing industries and

---

[15] Whence the persistent tendency of macro-economic models linking the two to treat demographic factors as exogenous. Even in a recent model of the generation of capital such as the DMS (Dynamique Multi Sectoriel) in France, demographic variables only occupy a residual place, even though it has long been demonstrated (see Kuznets 1958, for the American series) that the linkage with rates of demographic growth, or fluctuations in the size of younger generations, is determinant for the two large portions of investment represented by housing, and public works and infrastructure.

[16] The production function gives the maximum possible production obtained by the use of given production factors. Many economists are now turning more towards the use of functions of demand factors.

considerable commercial growth during the Middle Ages (Tuscany, Lombardy, Venice, Flanders) and the Renaissance (The Netherlands), only to regress subsequently or fall into decline, whilst others in their turn took the lead. The question naturally arises of why certain societies emerged earlier, and to what extent demographic factors might have affected this development. Was this a matter of resources, administrative competence, political organization, or, more fundamentally, educational standards?[17]

Two conflicting theories exist with regard to this question. First, there is Boserup's thesis (1981), confirmed by long series (1500–1900) on European agricultural yields (Slicher van Bath 1963) and by long-term trends in Japanese agricultural production (Ohkawa 1970; Ohkawa et al. 1957); according to this theory, where resources are not used to their full extent, a population increase results in a rise in food prices, which in turn stimulates agricultural development through the extension of arable land and an intensification of labour (irrigation, increased number of harvests); population density and development tend to coincide. Secondly, there is the Malthusian line of reasoning, illustrated by McNeill (1976), according to which an increase in population density[18] can generate excess mortality of disastrous proportions: this view is equally well supported, in this case by European experience (in urban contexts, at least) up to the eighteenth century.

The following analysis aims to introduce new elements into this discussion. In increasingly diversified economies demographic growth exerts a complex influence on economic development, which extends well beyond the effects produced by increases in population density, and which varies according to the particular source of population increase (notably mortality decline, or the influx of immigrants) and its composition by age and sector.

Guide to Interpretation

Analysis of comparative rates of demographic and economic growth between countries and periods can only be usefully performed if two prior observations are taken into account. First, the limits of variability in each phenomenon are completely different: historically, over an 'average' period of, say, a quarter of a century, demographic growth in industrial countries never exceeded 2%, whereas the annual growth of per capita income could be as much as 8%. Secondly, differences in a country's initial condition confer very different

---

[17] Education increases receptiveness and adaptation to new ideas, encouraging a more rational approach to life, and thus appears indispensable to economic and demographic change. Countries with the highest education levels were the first to experience industrial revolution (Cipolla 1969). But the importance of education presupposes that the first three conditions, just mentioned, are present in a context of minimal density.

[18] In fact, the historical and geographical fields of the two authors are not strictly interchangeable, since McNeill's analysis applies more to the pre-modern period and to urban contexts, while Boserup's refers more to traditional and modern agricultural societies.

TABLE 17.1. *Distribution of world manufacturing, large industrial nations, 1870 and 1913* (%)

Country	Year	
	1870	1913
United Kingdom	31.8	14.0
France	10.3	6.4
Germany	13.2	15.7
United States	23.3	35.8
Italy	2.4	2.7
Japan	—	1.2
Russia	3.7	5.5

Source: Léon (1977: iv. 20).

meanings on the same rate of growth. Thus, high demographic growth in certain pre-nineteenth century European countries may be merely a recovery following particularly devastating wars (the Thirty Years War in Germany, and the Northern War in Scandinavia) or a stage in the process of colonizing virgin territory (eastern Europe). Similarly, the outstanding rate of Japanese economic growth is largely a matter of catching up, given the disadvantageous level from which it started: according to Kuznets (1971), real per capital income for 1874–79 was respectively 4 and 6 times below that of Germany and the United Sates at the equivalent stage of development—i.e. 1850–59 and 1834–43 respectively. Even if more recent studies have shown that this difference is heavily overestimated, the fact of Japan's relative backwardness is not disputed (Ohkawa 1979).

By 1870, four-fifths of the world's manufactured production is accounted for by 5 countries alone: the United Kingdom, France, Belgium, Germany, and the US. All are countries with a commercial outlook belonging to the most advanced part of the world: north-west Europe and its North American extension. All may be characterized by demographic transitions which are fairly mature, with low mortality, and fertility already declining (France and the US), or about to start. British supremacy was uncontested, but would not last. Just before the First World War, a handful of further countries entered the first stages of industrial transformation and experienced remarkable growth: the Scandinavian countries, Japan, Russia, Italy, and Spain.[19] The differences between England and the US in economic and demographic growth, especially, resulted in the former being overtaken entirely by the latter (see Table 17.1).

[19] From 1871–75 to 1909–13, real per capita income in the US rose 1.5, and in Germany 1.2, times faster than in Britain.

England

England was the cradle of the Industrial Revolution, and the uncontested model[20] of technological progress up to the third quarter of the nineteenth century. As early as 1688, according to Gregory King, 14% of the population was engaged in activities outside the productive sphere of material goods (trade, Church, State, liberal professions); the relative portion of national income derived from agriculture was only 40%, which testifies to a remarkably advanced level of social organization. Only Holland was then in a position to challenge England, still maintaining, through its geographical disposition and banking tradition, the clear superiority it had acquired at an earlier date (North and Thomas 1970). But Dutch superiority would be lost with the wars of Louis XIV and the French occupation. According to King (1696), average per capita income in Holland at the end of the seventeenth century remained 2% higher than the English figure, itself about 30% higher than the French.[21] France then occupied third position in the international hierarchy.[22] the difference in per capita growth over the long term up to the mid-twentieth century was, in fact, fairly slight: the English rise to power, compared with the French, owed essentially to differences in long-term population growth.[23] Despite considerable emigration, the population of the British Isles between 1700 and 1950 multiplied sixfold, whereas French population only managed to double. From 1735 to 1785 industrial progress was comparable in the two countries, and at the time of the French Revolution, France was even producing twice as much cast iron. This is, however, a question of scale, because France at the time numbered three times as many inhabitants; the difference is much smaller where the other chief industry, textiles, is concerned (Deane and Cole 1964).

But the really new factor was that English industrial progress was associated with unprecedented demographic increase: whereas from 1701 to 1741 the population tended towards stasis (an annual average increase of only 0.24%) and national production increased only slowly (+0.3% per year), the following period from 1741–71 witnessed a doubling of the rate of population growth (15.6% over 30 years, or 0.48% per year) and a 30% increase in production

[20] It is often pointed out that a start occurred in France after 1715 (with the return to peace), but it appears to have been more rural in character and not as strong as in England. This start was, moreover, interrupted by the Revolution and wars of the Empire. Whatever weightings are used, in 1851, for example, real per capita income in England was appreciably higher than in France: the difference varies from 17% to 25% (Kindleberger 1964).

[21] King's total estimates are difficult to swallow (Le Roy-Ladurie (1968) speaks of 'fantastic' figures), but the orders of magnitude still deserve respect.

[22] Various authors (Kuznets, Bairoch, Maddison, etc.) have attempted to classify average per capita income amongst industrialized countries for periods dating as far back as the mid-19th century. Their estimates agree only some of the time.

[23] The *Report of the Royal Commission on Population* (1949) clearly considers demographic growth to have been a prime factor in the country's wealth and power. From the 15th to the 18th century England is distinguished by a demographic growth considerably higher than that of other European countries.

(or 0.9% per year). The acceleration continued during the last decades of the eighteenth century, increases rising to 34% and 75% respectively over a thirty-year period from 1771 to 1801. Thus, in spite of an exceptional demographic growth of almost 1% per year, the increase in per capita income was three times the rate of the preceding period. Of course, these are only estimates—with very little claim, moreover, to accuracy. Wrigley and Schofield (1981) have also called into question a number of Deane and Cole's (1964) calculations. Nevertheless, in its main outlines the period does not appear to require reconsideration, particularly regarding the phase of acceleration.

Thus, at the very date at which Malthus's *Essay* was published in its first edition (1798), his propositions were no longer true for his own country. In the three last decades of the eighteenth century, cotton production increased tenfold, and steel production quadrupled. In only 20 years (1781–1801) the volume of exports went up 2.8 times. Progress was so considerable that food production employed only a minority of the working population; around 1800, the portion of the work-force employed in the primary sector was less than 40%:[24] England imported a large part of its food requirements.

These trends continued more or less uninterrupted up to the First World War (Fig. 17.1), although there was a slight inflexion after 1880. England lost its technological supremacy in the last quarter of the nineteenth century. It was as if, once economic success had been attained, England seemed incapable of adapting itself; subsequently, English growth was perceptibly less than in other industrial countries. This decline in comparative growth rates may be linked to many mechanisms, of which some may relate to the very fact that the process of industrialization began earlier: an ageing stock of capital goods, exhaustion of labour reserves necessary for transfer to more productive sectors.

France

After 1715, there was a long period of peace in France, and demographic growth resumed. Outbreaks of famine and epidemics became more rare. Pressure on the land mounted, but food production developed to the extent that some historians have advanced the hypothesis of an agricultural revolution in the eighteenth century. This argument is rejected by Morineau (1970): the country certainly had an obsession for agronomy, but not, properly speaking, real growth in agricultural productivity. But the question is far from settled. Indeed, population growth seems to have been the impulse behind agricultural progress rather than the reverse;[25] agricultural change was not noticeable until around 1840. A number of questions would arise, were this

---

[24] An equivalent percentage was not reached in other industrial countries for another century to a century and a half.

[25] Calling into question the view of certain authors, such as Bairoch.

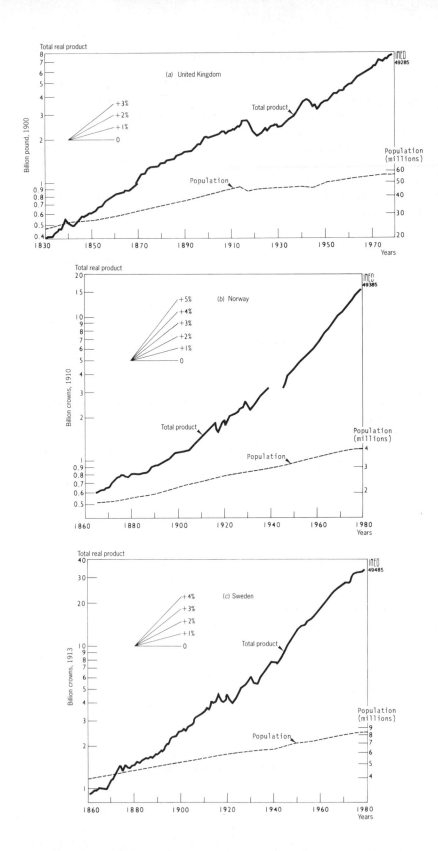

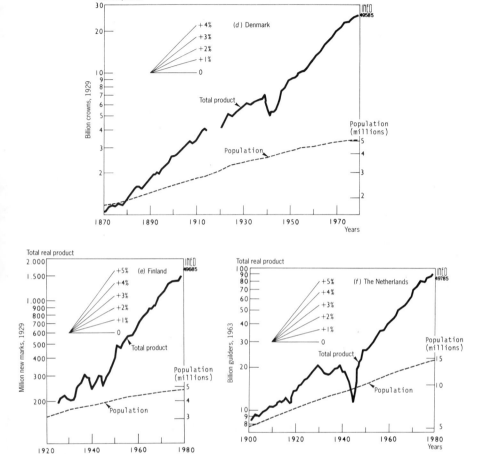

FIG. 17.1. Population and total real product, Nordic model of transition

not the case: How are the increase in prices and the notorious Corn War of 1775 to be explained? Why, moreover, were traditional Malthusian constraints characteristic of poor societies maintained? Delayed marriage remained the rule, and illegitimate births and pre-marital conception were common. Even prostitution developed, reaching a peak in the revolutionary period. Poverty still evidently persisted.

Aside from Belgium—for which, however, there are few reliable data— France was the first country to follow the British example: by the time of the Revolution, average productivity was only slightly lower than Britain's. Given their social and cultural heritage, the two countries were at more or less the

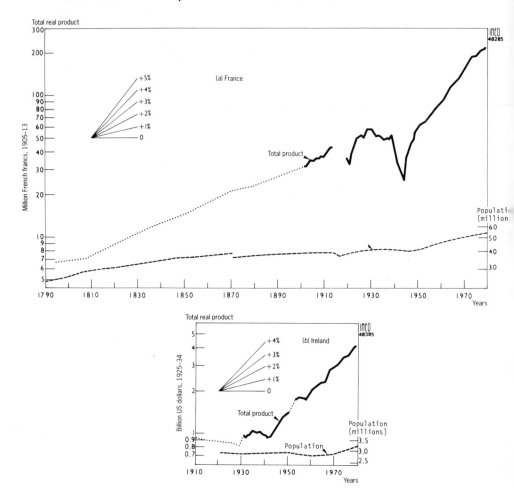

FIG. 17.2. Population and total real product in countries with flat or U-shaped transition profiles, France and Ireland

same stage of development. But with the Revolution and the long period of unrest that followed, England strengthened its lead. French progress was subsequently relatively slow, and whatever indicator is consulted—the total horse-power of steam engines, the number of kilometres of railway line built—France was considerably behind England in terms of industry by the middle of the nineteenth century. Despite a slight improvement between 1830 and 1860, the level of French industrialization was surpassed before the end of the nineteenth century by the US, Germany, and Belgium. In 1890, the portion of the national economy derived from agriculture was still 35%,[26] a level England had crossed at the turn of the century (33% in 1801).

[26] Compared with 59% in 1789 and 46.5% in 1845.

Demographic and economic growth were much slower than in neighbour-ing countries: between 1830 and 1930, for example, despite immigration, the population grew by only 27%, compared with Britain's 187% and Germany's 140% (even though the latter's territory had been reduced and both countries experienced high emigration). In the same period real per capita income increased by 1.1% annually in France, as opposed to 1.2% in Britain and 1.4% in Germany. The population of the United States at this time increased thirteenfold and the annual rate of growth in national per capita income was 1.6% (Carré *et al.* 1972). Thus, far from encouraging economic progress, demographic weakness appears to have inhibited it.[27] Of course, allowing for differences in the rate of growth of labour, French investment rates (in terms of the structure of gross fixed capital) were comparatively high,[28] but the whole question is precisely not that of the level, but the *structure*, of invest-ment: a large portion of the savings are uselessly hoarded or otherwise lost when capital is tied up inaccessibly outside national boundaries (Sauvy 1943). Here we return to one of the central points of the Coale–Hoover model: low fertility, as predicted, certainly went hand in hand with a high rate of invest-ment, but, contrary to the theory's prediction, growth did not ensue. This makes the post-war boom all the more remarkable: from 1946 to 1982, the population increased by 14 million (or by +35%), which is more than during the preceding century and a half; real per capita income tripled (Fig. 17.2); development, both of the population and of income, was more rapid than the average for OECD countries (excluding non-European countries).

This résumé of French experience suggests that the slow rate of demo-graphic growth over the period 1780–1940 did not produce the beneficial effects that certain theories might lead one to expect,[29] and that, conversely, the return to moderate rates of demographic growth may be linked to out-standing economic performance.

Germany

The main force behind changes in Germany seems to have been, above all, political. The first half of the nineteenth century was a period of great intellectual excitement, which prepared the way for the social and national

---

[27] In conformity with the Keynesian model.

[28] In conformity with the Harrod–Domar model of growth, based on investment. It is here that we encounter the uncertain status of demographic variables in economic theory; as each theory arises from a particular point of view, the same phenomenon assumes opposite implications.

[29] Co-determination is possible. Amongst the most frequent explanations for the comparative weakness of French growth is the prevalence of small family farms. The property division characteristic of such agriculture would have promoted an attachment to the land favourable to restriction of family size, resulting in reduced demand and a weak incentive for rural exodus; this, in turn, would have reinforced trends unfavourable to the emergence of a mobile and dynamic industrial proletariat necessary for the rise of industry. If this was the case, the only question remaining is that of the relation between mentalities and property structures.

revolution of 1848. Feudalism was gradually abolished, with the emancipation of peasants more or less complete by 1830 in the western part of the country, and by 1840 in the east. This process removed several obstacles to efficient production, resulting in a tremendous boost to the agricultural revolution— through both the extension of cultivated land and an intensification of crops and livestock. Between 1816 and 1865, animal production increased 213%; this in turn stimulated demographic growth, which in the same period increased by 59%. In the two decades following the adoption of *Zollverein*, in 1834, foreign trade doubled, whereas previously there had been stagnation. From 1850 onwards, the railway boom, stimulated by both the Prussian government and the increase in demographic density, gave a significant boost to an industrial system which, up to the mid-nineteenth century, had remained relatively archaic and dispersed. In 1851, there were only 6,053 km of road and railway; 20 years later this figure had tripled to 19,719 km. Germany then went through a phase of economic growth considerably greater than France, as well as England. Both the newly unified Germany and the United States overtook Great Britain's lead in the period 1870 to 1914. The comparative speed of German growth was thus not only a phenomenon of the 1950s and 1960s:[30] it may be observed from the mid-nineteenth century onwards (Fig. 17.3). As in England, it coincides more or less with the greatest phase of growth in the working-age population.[31]

The United States

The United States represents a special kind of European colony. It may be contrasted to tropical colonies (excepting Kenya), where employment was aimed at trade and the export of primary products, requiring only the development of a narrow coastal strip or a few interior enclaves. However, like other sparsely populated colonies of the temperate zone (Australia, Canada, and New Zealand), the US swiftly became an extension, and then a replica, of the motherland. It proceeded rapidly to independence and adopted all the institutions necessary to economic and political life. Emphasis was placed on food production, reflecting the need to establish migrants; and as the cost of long-distance travel became 10 times cheaper, immigration increased massively from the 1840s. In order to facilitate industrial development, large capital investments (mainly from England) were accepted, particularly before the

---

[30] However, the reasons may not be the same: the end of the 19th century corresponds with the beginnings of the movement, within a new political and institutional framework; and the 1950s with post-war reconstruction, which is characterized by an outstanding rate of accumulation and a massive immigration of qualified labour from the East.

[31] The notion of employment age has varied greatly over time: whilst the current span in Western countries is about 18–62 years, it was long much wider (around 5–75 years). The shift reflects two institutional changes: the introduction of compulsory schooling (in the second half of the 19th century) and social security systems (generally in the 1930s and 1940s).

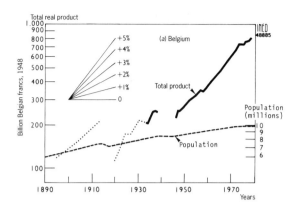

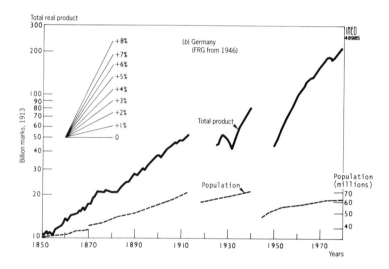

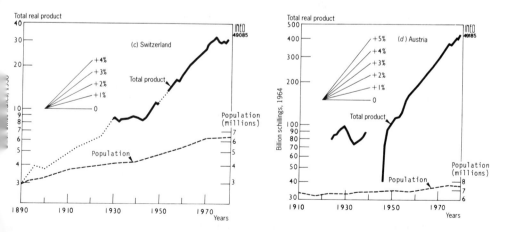

FIG. 17.3. Population and total real product, Western transition model

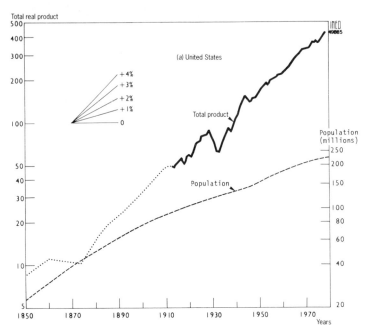

FIG. 17.4. Population and total real product, overseas immigration countries

First World War. Up to the last quarter of the nineteenth century, migrants came from the most advanced countries; hence, the first American towns were populated by Europeans who brought with them their skills, as well as a fabled spirit of enterprise which contrasted with the persecutions, regulations, and guilds of the Old World.

Under these conditions, the United States came to rank second in per capita income along with Belgium and The Netherlands, as early as 1840. At this stage it occupied a position about 25% higher than France. But it was really from the mid-nineteenth century, when European migration was wide open, and a certain demographic size had been reached, that the US began really to amass its power. Half a century later, in 1890, it had the highest living standards of all countries, including England, a position which would be strengthened by twentieth-century devastations in Europe. The 1930s depression was, however, more severe in the US than elsewhere. Some authors, following Hansen (1939), have associated its impact with the suspension of international migration, especially in 1921 and 1924, and the check this put on investment. America in the 1920s had enjoyed unheard-of prosperity, envied by the entire world; but in only four years (1929–33) this proved to be fragile, national income falling by over a third. In 1933 American unemployment figures had reached 14 million, or about a quarter of the working population. All this shook America's confidence: its model virtues

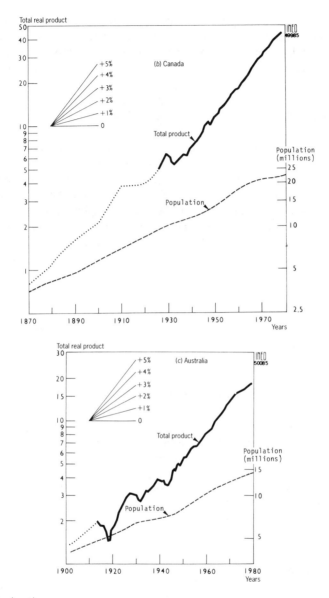

FIG. 17.4. (*cont.*)

had suddenly become vices. The depression and the war prompted a return to traditional moral values, centred upon social solidarity, religion, and the family. This resurgence of religious activity, and an extraordinary increase in fertility, took place in the context of economic recovery and a return to full employment stimulated by the arms industry.

In Kuznets's estimate (1977), the power of the US, measured by its total product, increased one thousandfold in the two centuries from 1775 to 1975. Demographic development played a chief role in this multiplication, given that the size of the population multiplied by a factor of 85, and average real per capita income by 11.5.[32] Fig. 17.4 illustrates the development since 1850. Over the period 1850–1980, the average annual population growth was 2%, as compared with 2.8% for the period 1775–1850, while real per capita income rose by 1.4%.

There are thus three points of view from which the demographic and economic history of the US may be seen as unusual: (1) its boundary changes, and progressive expansion of territory; (2) the role of international migration, which stimulated both economic growth (by acting as a check on *wage levels*, whilst increasing social mobility, etc.) and demographic growth (immigration played a more important role than natural increase in population growth up to the 1920s); and (3) the correlative and exceptional importance of foreign investment up to the First World War.

Italy

Along with Japan and Russia, Italy belongs to those countries in which change, although manifest in the late nineteenth century, did not truly emerge until the inter-war period. Setting aside the estimates for Russia, which are debatable and will be discussed below, Italy may be contrasted with the two others on two counts. It fails to confirm Gerschenkron's cherished hypothesis (1962), according to which less advanced countries experience faster rates of growth, particularly at the outset. In the period 1863–1914, production in man-hours only increased by an average of 0.7% per year. Nor does the Italian case support Rostow's thesis that growth divides into three stages: a rapid beginning, sustained growth, and then maturity. Labour productivity per hour increased by 1.7% per year[33] for the period 1913–59, that is, faster than in the initial phase. A further increase occurred in the 1960s. In fact, it was not until the 1950s and 1960s that really lively growth got going, and began to percolate into the south, which had long remained unaffected. It is thus reasonable to wonder whether this particular type of growth is not partly connected with the importance of emigration, as this would have reduced pressure towards modernization by encouraging the maintenance of traditional attitudes and dependence on the outside world.

---

[32] If structural changes are included in the evaluation, the demographic factor becomes even greater; improvements in labour inputs (owing to age structures and the relocation of the work-force) accounted in no small part for the fact that per capita incomes grew, for example, more than a third, in the 19th century.

[33] Given the amount of unreported labour (Fua 1965), these estimates should be taken as orders of magnitude only.

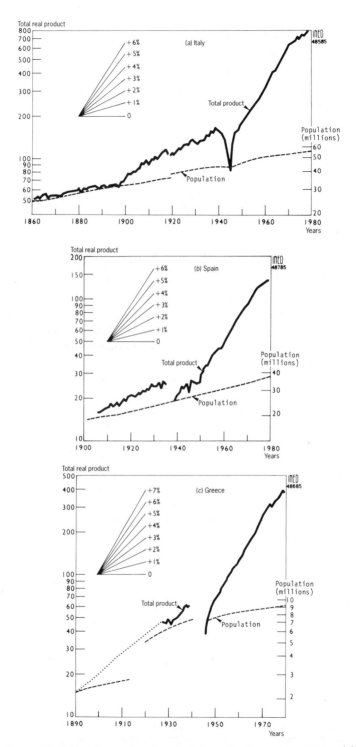

FIG. 17.5. Population and total real product, Southern transition model

Japan

After a century and a half of virtual demographic and economic stagnation (1720–1870), Japan, following the Meiji Restoration, responded to the
European challenge.[34] Its initial backwardness is manifest in its level of per
capita income, which was 2 to 3 times lower than that of western Europe at
the same stage of development; such levels would have been a handicap in
developing its consumer market, as well as in accumulating capital through
education and construction. Its institutional legacy of enormous landed properties, feudal traditions, and military dictatorship would likewise hardly seem
conducive to modernization.[35] Japan none the less experienced very rapid
development from the late nineteenth century on, with a growth peak of about
5% around 1890.[36] The abolition of feudalism and the introduction of foreign
techniques were encouraged by an imperial government which was eager to
free itself of tradition. The need to safeguard national independence doubtless played an important role in this: Japan's backwardness left it vulnerable to
foreign domination. China no longer being a model of technological progress,[37] Japan turned towards the West, borrowing its experts and methods in
a manner which resulted in intense modernization, both in agriculture and
industry.

Here, too, the nationalist reflex is at issue. Japan intended both to evade
foreign control and to become a great military power, using its superiority to
control access to raw material and rice. This was the start of its imperial
phase, which lasted up to the military defeat of 1945, characterized by the
colonization of Korea, Taiwan, and Manchuria, and a successful war against
the Russians (1905). For half a century, up to the 1920s, Japan was at the
height of a demographic boom in which the family model became large, and
infanticide and abortion receded. The resulting pressure on land, accentuated
by mortality decline, brought about an intensification of labour (including
irrigation and multiple annual harvests) and the adoption of new techniques
such as the use of chemical fertilizers.

No other country, even in Europe, matches the rapidity of this agricultural
transformation effected under the influence of demographic pressure. The
intensive application of fertilizers spread from the 1880s onwards, and by

---

[34] Contrary to accepted belief, the Meiji era does not represent a sudden break: it was in fact
part of a continuing process of slow secular maturation. The Tokugawa era was not properly
speaking one of stagnation, but a period of uneven growth exclusively benefiting the nobility and
urban bourgeoisie: trade developed rapidly, and towns flourished to some extent, but the peasants
were crippled by heavy taxes which discouraged production and lead to female infanticide, thus
inhibiting demographic growth.

[35] Curiously, this burdensome legacy seems to have become an advantage once
industrialization got under way: the acceptance of hierarchy, collective discipline, and unitary
ideology facilitated mobilization of the work-force.

[36] This progress is all the more remarkable for the fact that Japanese society was
predominantly agricultural—to an extent comparable with tsarist Russia.

[37] In the 19th century the Chinese government had opposed modernization.

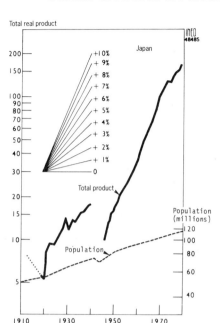

FIG. 17.6. Population and total real product, Japan

1915 the use of chemical fertilizers per hectare reached an average of 45 kg, which is similar to that of the US around 1960.[38] Paradoxically, the lack of land, rather than presenting an obstacle, served as a spur, stimulating research into seeds and methods of culture (Sinha 1975). Japan represents a type-case of creative pressure, clearly illustrated in Boserup's most recent study (1981). In 1880, the population of Japan stood at 36 million, despite a surface area of cultivable land of only around 60,000 km^2 (a sixth of the entire country). Progress in production was encouraged by the State, which revised property taxes in order to encourage landowners themselves to participate in the investment. Between 1894 and 1918–20, production relative to the number of persons in the agricultural labour force doubled; the labour of women and children increased,[39] more hours being put in on a more regular basis. Nineteenth-century Japan was unique in showing greater progress in agricultural than in industrial productivity.

The increase in the working population (Table 17.2), together with considerable progress in the agricultural sector, helped not only to create a new consumer market but to liberate labour for nascent industrialization. And the

[38] Where, however, its application was in extensive agriculture.
[39] These statistics are, however, incomplete. Here one runs up against the classic problem of evaluating the working agricultural population: flexibility relates to the role of women and children.

TABLE 17.2. *Development of the sectoral distribution of the working population since the mid-nineteenth century in the principal capitalist developed countries*

Country and years	Total working population not including women in agriculture (millions)	Numbers A		I	S	Proportions A	I	S
		Men	Women					
Germany								
1882	15,097	5,702	(2,535)	6,690	2,705	37.8	44.3	17.9
1895	18,019	5,540	(2,753)	8,707	3,772	30.7	48.3	20.9
1907	22,227	5,284	(4,599)	12,011	4,932	23.8	54.0	22.2
1925[a]	27,040	4,793	(4,969)	14,759	7,488	17.7	54.6	27.7
1933[a]	27,647	4,694	(4,685)	14,605	8,348	17.0	52.8	30.2
1939[b]	29,698	4,065	(4,920)	16,514	9,119	13.7	55.6	30.7
West Germany								
1946	16,302	2,735	(2,853)	8,545	5,022	16.8	52.4	30.8
1950	20,272	2,328	(2,806)	11,134	6,810	11.5	54.9	33.6
1961[c]	24,764	1,625	(1,959)	14,105	9,034	6.6	57.0	36.4
1970[c]	25,644	1,025	(966)	14,193	10,426	4.0	55.3	40.7
1980[c]	25,845	748	(—)	13,160	11,937	2.9	50.9	46.2
France								
1856	11,964	5,146	(2,159)	4,017	2,801	43.0	33.6	23.4
1866[d]	12,906	5,299	(2,237)	4,686	2,921	41.1	36.3	22.6
1886[e]	14,110	5,248	(2,598)	4,843	4,019	37.2	34.3	28.5
1896[e]	16,171	5,741	(2,760)	5,937	4,493	35.5	36.7	27.8
1901[e]	17,239	5,581	(2,664)	6,930	4,728	32.4	40.2	27.4
1906[e]	17,399	5,525	(3,330)	7,210	4,664	31.8	41.4	26.8
1911[e]	17,691	5,331	(3,241)	7,894	4,466	30.1	44.6	25.2
1921	17,756	5,062	(3,961)	7,884	4,810	28.5	44.4	27.1
1926	18,006	4,809	(3,391)	8,501	4,696	26.7	47.2	26.1
1931	18,420	4,510	(3,194)	8,725	5,185	24.5	47.4	28.1
1936	17,341	4,282	(2,922)	7,576	5,483	24.7	43.7	31.6
1946	17,531	4,221	(3,263)	8,081	5,229	24.1	46.1	29.8
1954	17,440	3,369	(1,826)	8,396	5,675	19.3	48.1	32.5
1962	18,220	2,634	(1,273)	8,809	6,777	14.5	48.3	37.2
1968	18,989	2,120	(1,013)	9,550	7,319	11.2	50.3	38.5
1975	20,311	1,475	(633)	9,346	9,489	7.3	46.0	46.7

custom of intensive labour for low pay, combined with an abundant and docile work-force, were to prove a decisive element in Japan's industrial competitiveness after the First World War, when it moved into international trade. On account of its structural characteristics, Japan has had little choice but to export its industrial product; but this factor has, in turn, become an agent of its growth, with well-known results. Between the two World Wars, the growth

TABLE 17.2. (*cont.*)

Country and years	Total working population not including women in agriculture (millions)	Numbers		I	S	Proportions		
		A				A	I	S
		Men	Women					
Great Britain								
1841[f]	6,825	1,458	(81)	3,257	2,110	21.4	47.7	30.9
1851	9,100	1,824	(230)	4,949	2,327	20.0	54.4	25.6
1861	10,354	1,818	(164)	5,712	2,824	17.6	55.2	27.3
1871	11,747	1,681	(136)	6,270	3,796	14.3	53.4	32.3
1881[g]	12,721	1,575	(119)	7,060	4,086	12.4	55.5	32.1
1891	14,417	1,475	(81)	8,192	4,750	10.2	56.8	32.9
1901	16,216	1,390	(86)	9,777	5,049	8.6	60.3	31.1
1911	18,227	1,489	(117)	11,082	5,656	8.2	60.8	31.0
1921	19,248	1,261	(111)	10,775	7,212	6.6	56.0	37.5
1931	20,997	1,181	(76)	11,389	8,427	5.6	54.2	40.1
1951	22,493	1,025	(117)	12,833	8,635	4.6	57.1	38.4
1961	23,917	777	(97)	13,105	10,035	3.2	54.8	42.0
1971	25,093	643	(97)	11,809	12,641	2.6	47.1	50.4
Italy								
1871	11,226	5,664	(3,036)	3,596	1,966	50.5	32.0	17.5
1881	13,640	5,498	(3,101)	4,559	3,583	40.3	33.4	26.3
1901	13,254	6,466	(3,200)	4,414	2,374	48.8	33.3	17.9
1911	12,777	6,112	(2,973)	4,912	1,753	47.8	38.4	13.7
1921	15,166	7,147	(3,117)	5,230	2,789	47.1	34.5	18.4
1931	14,621	6,650	(2,641)	6,023	1,948	45.5	41.2	13.3
1936	15,914	6,412	(2,431)	5,858	3,644	40.3	36.8	22.9
1951	17,544	6,228	(2,033)	7,075	4,241	35.5	40.3	24.2
1961	18,012	4,150	(1,507)	8,766	5,096	23.0	48.7	28.3
1971	18,862	2,299	(943)	9,341	7,222	12.2	49.5	38.3
1980	20,052	1,870	(—)	8,917	9,265	9.3	44.5	46.2
Japan								
1872	10,970	8,380	(6,115)	943	1,647	76.4	8.6	15.0
1887	14,650	9,815	(7,383)	2,198	2,637	67.0	15.0	18.0
1897	16,900	10,039	(7,292)	3,431	3,430	59.4	20.3	20.3
1912	19,500	9,360	(7,129)	5,577	4,563	48.0	28.6	23.4
1920	20,200	8,115	(6,326)	6,922	5,170	40.2	34.3	25.6
1930	23,000	8,250	(6,449)	7,153	7,581	35.9	31.1	33.0
1940	25,200	7,095	(7,290)	10,196	7,868	28.2	40.5	31.3
1950	27,800	9,063	(8,422)	9,619	9,118	32.6	34.6	32.8
1960	37,750	6,863	(7,374)	14,800	16,100	18.2	39.2	42.6
1970	46,520	4,440	(4,420)	21,440	20,640	9.5	46.1	44.4
1980	52,668	3,078	(2,692)	23,070	26,520	5.8	43.8	50.4

TABLE 17.2. (*cont.*)

Country and years	Total working population not including women in agriculture (millions)	Numbers A		I	S	Proportions A	I	S
		Men	Women					
United States								
1850	7,400	5,059		1,671	670	68.4	22.6	9.1
1860	10,100	6,458		2,583	1,059	63.9	25.6	10.5
1870	12,400	6,455	(455)	3,883	2,062	52.1	31.3	16.6
1880	16,800	8,056	(626)	5,220	3,524	48.0	31.1	21.0
1890	22,900	9,324	(796)	8,248	5,328	40.7	36.0	23.3
1900	28,100	11,112	(1,009)	11,029	5,959	39.5	39.2	21.2
1910	35,500	10,657	(1,176)	15,010	9,833	30.0	42.3	27.7
1920	40,400	10,549	(1,170)	18,678	11,173	26.1	46.2	27.7
1930	47,900	9,812	(910)	20,496	17,592	20.5	42.8	36.7
1940	52,300	8,628	(513)	20,203	23,469	16.5	38.6	44.9
1950	59,400	6,568	(612)	26,849	25,983	11.1	45.2	43.7
1960	67,600	4,069	(450)	28,767	34,923	5.8	42.6	51.7
1970	80,400	2,522	(601)	31,383	46,155	3.6	39.0	57.3
1980	100,900	2,704	(680)	38,118	59,400	2.7	36.2	58.9

Notes: A = farming, forestry, fishing; I = mining, manufacturing, construction, water, electricity; S = commerce, banking, services, and others. Data have been rendered as comparable as possible between countries and periods.

[a] Not incl. the Saar Basin.
[b] Boundaries as of 1937.
[c] Incl. West Berlin.
[d] Incl. Nice and Savoy.
[e] Not incl. Alsace-Lorraine.
[f] Number in active employ underestimated at this date.
[g] Retired persons were classified according to their last employ up to this date.

Sources: Population censuses (various sections) since 1960. Bairoch *et al.* (1968: 220), up to 1960, for European countries. Clark (1957: 516–20), for Japan and the United States up to 1950; ILO (1981).

in real per capita income was three times the Western average, and over twice as much in the post-war period—a phenomenon all the more striking in that Western growth achieved historically unequalled[40] levels in the period between 1950 and 1973.

Demographic pressure was one of the keys to the Japanese boom, but this

---

[40] The figure was 2.3% for 1913–38 compared with the European average of 0.8%, and 7% for 1950–75 compared with 3% for the entire capitalist developed world (excluding Japan).

condition, while necessary, was far from being sufficient in itself. Experience shows that different areas of China and India in the nineteenth century (see Chapter 18) were similar on a number of points. In the Japanese case, State intervention was crucial in turning to advantage what in other circumstances might have been an insurmountable obstacle. Other elements may also help to explain the uniqueness of the Japanese case. Japan was the only large country of non-European population to experience considerable growth in the nineteenth century. Its insular character and ethnic homogeneity gave it a greater ability, with sufficient numbers, to defend itself against foreign penetration and to recover from foreign challenge. And it had an urban tradition going back to the sixteenth century, when Tokyo already had half a million inhabitants. Such urbanization carries implications not only for social structure, in terms of an educated élite, but for occupational structures, in terms of craftsmen and tradesmen possessed of modern or proto-industrial qualifications. These are characteristics which evoke British history, and which, in both cases, greatly facilitated the transition to industrial civilization.

Russia

Russia will be considered only in the pre-revolutionary period, since data produced subsequently are unreliable.[41] Its performance requires complex reconstructions as, for example, have been carried out by Bergson (1961). In 1860, Russia was the least advanced of the great powers, having a per capita income a third to a half lower than the US. It was entirely dependent on foreign capital and techniques for its modernization, and hence represented a kind of extension of western Europe. The population employed in industry (860,000) was still small compared with the size of the total population (74 million).[42] The greater part of national income was derived from the agricultural population, which was emancipated from serfdom only in 1861. Industry, however, underwent a remarkable development, starting from a very low level in the second half of the nineteenth century. For the period 1845–63, the growth rate of industrial production has been estimated at an average of 3.5% to 4% per year, and this rise continued over the ensuing decades; according to Goldsmith (1961), the rate for the period around 1861–65 to 1911–13 would have been 5.2%. In other words, in half a century the volume of industrial production increased more than twelvefold: so much for the myth of the rise of industrialism brought about by Stalin! Russia's growth was in fact more rapid not only than England's in its initial

---

[41] For the period 1928–69, for example, the official measure of industrial production gives a coefficient of 33.6; according to Moorsteen and Powell, who are authorities on the matter, it should be only 11.

[42] For the period around 1860, the proportion of labour in industry was only about 2%, compared with 55% in England, and approximately 35%, 30%, and 20% in Germany, France, and the US respectively.

phase of acceleration, but also than the growth of Germany or the US, which were in precisely the same phase of industrial development over the period 1860–1913. In 1913, however, the country was still fundamentally rural (about 75% of the total population); two-thirds of the working population were employed in agriculture (which still produced half of the national income), and in this respect, it was in a similar position to France three-quarters of a century earlier. But given the speed of demographic growth, progress was all the more remarkable, since at the outbreak of the First World War agriculture supported an urban population of over 40 million, as opposed to only 7 million, around 1850. Apart from countries of immigration, in particular the US, Russia represented the country with the fastest demographic growth—an annual average of 1.43% for the period 1860–1910, according to Khromov's (1950) estimate. Demographic growth in no way impeded the rise of per capita income which, at +2% (Bergson and Kuznets 1976), represents one of the highest increases over this fifty-year period.

Other Countries

As Figs. 17.1 to 17.6 indicate, the basic situation of average or small countries is similar to what we have seen thus far: demographic and economic growth go hand in hand. The disadvantages associated with a size insufficient to create certain industrial sectors are compensated by recourse to international trade (Bairoch 1976).

This overview of the demographic and economic experience of the principal industrial countries shows that, aside from fluctuation in the world economy, there is no common type of economic growth related to a given model of demographic transition. Thus, Italy and Spain, for example, which both belong to the same transition model (see Chapter 7) experience very different patterns of economic development. The attempts at theorization or general formalization of growth so common in the 1950s and 1960s thus prove to be considerably qualified, not only in the light of recent experience (since 1973), but also by a simple historical overview.

3. Demographic Aspects of Modern Economic Growth

Kuznets has at times defined modern economic growth by one of its principal characteristics: sustained population growth unaccompanied by a decline in per capita income. The contrast here is to traditional conditions, in which any progress in levels of subsistence is systematically consumed by demographic expansion. Historically, as already seen, demographic transition is accompanied by an unprecedented improvement in living standards, and economic performance is largely independent of the type of transition and its associated population multiplier. Table 17.3 gives the results obtained for our series.

TABLE 17.3. *Population increase and growth of per capita income over the long term, industrial countries*

Country	Period	Annual average variation of the population (%)	Annual average variation of real per capita income
England	1830–1979	0.74	1.44
France	1795–1979	0.35	1.54
Germany	1850–1938	0.82	1.52
West Germany	1950–1979	0.64	4.79
United States	1850–1979	2.01	1.68
Italy	1861–1979	0.69	1.65
Japan	1876–1979	1.26	3.30
Russia	1870–1913	1.56	1.02
Austria	1913–1979	0.15	2.21
Belgium	1913–1979	0.38	1.70
Denmark	1870–1979	0.97	2.00
Spain	1906–1979	0.89	2.07
Finland	1926–1979	0.70	3.18
Greece	1913–1979	(0.90)	(3.05)
Ireland	1926–1979	0.18	2.80
Norway	1865–1979	0.77	2.10
Netherlands	1900–1979	1.27	1.67
Sweden	1861–1979	0.64	2.45
Switzerland	1913–1979	0.77	1.83
Australia	1865–1979	1.70	1.16
Canada	1872–1979	1.74	1.93

Sources: see Appendix 3.

If, then, over the very long term there is in each country a coincidence between the growth phases of the two phenomena (these being, *by nature*, interconnected), there is not any apparent relation between their *levels* or rates of growth. The coefficients of linear correlation, whether between series or between growth indices (base of 100 for the period or initial year), are not significant. This view conforms to what Kuznets put forward in 1956 for a sample of 11 smaller countries over a shorter period: only a slight—but not significant—positive correlation was observable.

Under these conditions, even if the rate of demographic growth hardly affects differences in the development of per capita income, it is a determining factor in the establishment of relations of power arising from the differential growth of the total product of nations.

The first part of this section will show to what extent demographic variations have contributed to the respective power of nations; the second part considers how demographic growth in economies with sustained technical progress is capable of stimulating an increase in productivity via the sectoral redeployment of the population; the final part will show how, even in a context of virtual demographic stagnation, other elements of population growth—in particular mortality decline—can serve to encourage economic growth.

Shifts in Power Relationships

The effect of differences in demographic growth only emerges in the *longue durée*. But it is already very noticeable over the course of a century. Between 1800 and 1950, the total product of France increased only sevenfold (in conditions of demographic stagnation) whereas other European capitalist countries had a multiplier of 14, and the US something between 30 and 35 (high demographic growth). The contrast between Europe and America is striking. One is confronted quite simply with a geometric progression which, over almost a century and a half, applied without interruption to the US, which experienced a growth rate close on 2% per year. The longer the duration, the wider the differences. As seen, the effect over two centuries (1775–1975) was extremely powerful, the population increasing by a factor of 85, while the multiplier for other countries of European population ranged from 3 to 7 (with the French exception of 2). Differences, on the other hand, in the development of real per capita income seem to have been relatively slight[43]—if, that is, they can be judged by available statistics for certain countries (and international comparability is not guaranteed). Thus, still referring to the period 1775–1975, the multiplier would have been around 14 in France, 10 in England, and 11.5 in the US. The greatest prudence is required in interpreting these differences, owing to both problems of statistical measurement and differences in starting levels. By 1775, England, for example, had already entered its phase of long-term economic growth.

This being the case, even if economic trends remain, as a general rule, fairly independent of demographic development, and if this hypothesis applies equally to less developed and developed countries, the decisive factor in the reorganization of the map of power on a world scale is quintessentially demographic: it is the differential secular growth of populations, through international migration, and the time lags and differences between transitions which basically determine changes in relations of power. What is being measured here is the wider economic significance of the transitional multipliers of population calculated in Chapter 10. The map of multipliers—still largely hypothetical for most of the world—would become the preferred index for the differential effect of demographic transitions on the economic growth of nations. This assumes, of course, that the observations can be generalized.

---

[43] The initial differences were relatively unpronounced (Bairoch 1979; Kuznets 1971), and, even today, the relative differences are slight (around 1 to 2); while the international hierarchy is no longer the same, the income effect has altered little.

TABLE 17.4. *Growth of the working population employed in non-agricultural sectors, and growth of real per capita income, 1950–1980*

Country	Annual average variation of the working population employed in non-agricultural sectors (%)	Annual average variation of real per capita income (GDP) (%)
France	+1.19	3.7
Italy	+1.72	4.1
United Kingdom	+0.38[a]	2.1
United States	+1.98	2.0
West Germany	+1.17	4.3
Japan	+3.37	6.6[b]

[a] 1951–80.
[b] 1952–80.

Sources: National statistical yearbooks; UN *Yearbook of National Accounts Statistics*.

Sectoral Redeployment of the Working Population

The decline in rural mortality, by slowing down the rate at which land became available, was related to rising demographic pressure: a large body of labour shifted from low-productivity agriculture to higher-productivity sectors, particularly industry. A considerable part of the growth in average per capita income arose from this transfer.

Consequently, the sectoral distribution of labour may be seen as an indicator of the growth potential of productivity: where the primary sector remains small it is possible to observe a tendency for progress in productivity to slow down, as the supply of transferable labour is gradually exhausted; conversely, a large agricultural labour reserve provides a potential for accelerating productivity. The rate of economic growth would thus be closely connected to the relative weight of rural supplies of labour. In England, for example, the fact that there was so small a work-force remaining for redeployment into new activities may account, at least partially, for the lower comparative growth in productivity which prevailed for a century. Japan represents the diametrical opposite, since around 1870 more than three-quarters of the working population were employed in agriculture.[44] The exceptional rise in post-war Japanese production is related to the very high growth of the non-agricultural work-force, which enabled large economies of scale.[45] Table 17.4 gives a few comparative data on this subject for the period since the Second World War.

[44] The proportion of the work-force employed in agriculture in 1851–61 was only 23% in Great Britain, compared with 48% in France (1856), 62% in Sweden (1860), and 76% in Japan (1872) (Clark 1957; Kuznets 1975).

[45] Or, put another way, a context of industrial growth encouraged rural exodus.

TABLE 17.5. *Growth of the working population and product in large industrial nations since the mid-nineteenth century: agricultural and non-agricultural sectors, in successive long-term periods*[a]

Country	Period	Average annual rate of increase			
		Agricultural sector		Non-agricultural sector	
		Working population[b]	Product[c]	Working population	Product
Germany	1882–1907	−0.30	(+1.86)	+2.39	+3.95
	1907–1938	−0.82	+0.14	+1.30	+2.27
FRG	1950–1970	−4.02	+1.02	+1.59	+7.00
	(1882–1970)	(−1.93)	(−0.33)	(+1.10)	+2.86
France	1856–1896	+0.27	+0.96	+1.07	+1.80
	1896–1946	−0.61	(−0.46)	+0.49	+1.13
	1946–1975	−3.56	+0.61	+1.20	+6.09
	1856–1975	−1.04	(+0.27)	+0.86	+2.54
Great Britain	1851–1911	−0.34	(+0.31)	+1.40	+2.55
	1911–1951	−0.93	(+0.79)	+0.62	+1.16
	1951–1971	−2.30	(+0.28)	+0.65	+2.94
	1851–1971	−0.87	(+0.47)	+1.02	+2.15
Italy	1871–1921	+0.47	+0.87	+0.73	+1.85
	1921–1951	−0.46	(+0.27)	+1.15	+2.76
	1951–1971	−4.86	(+0.44)	+1.92	+7.59
	1871–1971	−0.90	(+0.60)	+1.10	+3.25
United States	1870–1920	+0.99	+1.75	+3.48	+4.27
	1920–1950	−1.58	+1.02	+1.95	+3.33
	1950–1970	−4.67	+1.24	+2.00	+3.72
	1870–1970	−0.94	+1.43	+2.85	+3.88
Japan	1872–1897	+0.73	—	+3.97	—
	1897–1950	−0.19	—	+1.91	—
	1950–1980	−3.54	+2.10	+3.30	+9.03
	1872–1980	−0.92	—	+2.77	—

[a] Periods correspond to changes in the working agricultural population.
[b] As understood in Table 17.2, i.e. excl. female employ.
[c] Rough estimates, especially in parentheses.

The non-agricultural Japanese work-force increased from 18 to 49 million; it had a growth rate twice that of the US or Italy, and three times that of West Germany or France. The rate of growth in GDP per capita was considerably higher. In these conditions, the absence of a correlation between the respective increases in real per capita income and population (or the working population) could, in addition to the reasons mentioned above (see

Chapter 16), have arisen from the conjunction of opposing statistical factors. The first is a negative relation between the development of agricultural productivity and that of agricultural employment; and the second, a positive relation between the development of real productivity in the non-agricultural sector and that of its corresponding work-force.

Based on our reconstruction of long-term series of national product by sector, Table 17.5 gives a breakdown of the annual average increase in the working population,[46] and the corresponding product for the agricultural and non-agricultural sectors: it covers a lengthy period in the principal capitalist developed countries considered above.

The lowest growth recorded in non-agricultural working populations occurs in France and Great Britain, which also register the least improvement of non-agricultural production. Conversely, with an increase of almost 3% for over a century in their non-agricultural working populations, the US and Japan experienced a higher growth in product. Germany and Italy occupy an intermediate position.

Sources of Demographic Growth

A given demographic pattern may induce an infinite set of permutations, as possible combinations of mortality, fertility, and external migration are played out. Thus the same rate of demographic growth can assume different economic implications, for not only may diverse adjustments of age structure be related to it, but, at a given age, different demographic characteristics such as life expectation, the number of children, etc. may be more or less pronounced. These effects and their different implications are difficult to determine a priori, but it is not implausible that the effects of age (ageing) may be compensated by generational effects (changes in behaviour).

We shall confine ourselves here to illustrating two extreme cases: Ireland and France. In Ireland, despite relatively high sustained fertility and a continuous decline in mortality, mass emigration resulted in a decrease in population each decade for almost a century. This distinctive demographic trend did not prevent the country from participating in the general pattern of Western expansion. Was this conjunction of economic improvement and population decline due to its interdependence with the British economy? Or to remittances from emigrants? Or to an accumulation of capital achieved by delayed marriage and reduced pressure on resources? Or to the longer life

---

[46] Increase in the working population was accompanied by a considerable reduction in the numbers of hours worked per day, so that the relation of the growth rate of product to that of the actively employed population underestimates productivity returns per hour.

of generations? All these elements—which have a strongly demographic character—may have been at work, reversing the expected effects of certain simplistic models. The analysis of such demographic developments produces no conclusive economic effect, either positive or negative.

The French case is equally instructive, since there virtual demographic stagnation lasted for almost a century. And yet, as we have seen, even though economic growth in the period concerned was slightly below that of neighbouring countries, per capita income made a marked increase. Here, too, an analytical breakdown of demographic developments is capable of shedding light on historical facts. Let us take 1800 as our starting-point. The period from 1800 to the present may be divided into two distinct subperiods, each characterized by a roughly similar absolute population increase (13 to 14 million). The first covers almost a century and a half (1800–1940), and the second, a third of a century (1946–82). Let us examine the components of growth in each period. For 1800–1940, it has been calculated that immigration just sufficed to compensate for the size of the deficit from fertility decline (5 million inhabitants), whilst the growth of the population as a whole owed mainly to improvements in life expectation in successive generations. The latter added 16 million persons to the population; the difference between this figure and total growth over the period $(16 - 13 = 3$ million) corresponds to First World War losses (deaths + deficit of births) (Landry 1945).

Thus, even in this context of more or less zero demographic growth, we would be wrong to take away the impression of immobility, because such a population is capable of experiencing considerable spatial redistributions (i.e. internal migration), not to mention fundamental, if concealed, changes. The advantages brought about by immigration have been amply stressed in the specialist literature (Sauvy 1952), as has the effect of the reduction in family size on the supply of capital. The influence of mortality decline, however, which was crucial in this case—as indeed in most other countries—has been neglected, if not consistently overlooked. The entry into a modern mortality regime of sustained low levels represents an indispensable pre-condition to efforts to improve production and long-term savings. The low productive capacity of traditional populations—often assumed to be mere indolence—is in fact largely attributable to food shortages and the poor quality of health conditions. The few existing data on morbidity in the nineteenth century (see Quételet 1835, 1871; Mannewitz 1941, for example) or the beginning of the twentieth century (see Landry 1930, for example) demonstrate the primordial influence of this factor on the productive potential of the work-force. From the earliest age, and often from school age, a considerable fraction of the population contracts various infections which undermine—sometimes permanently—general health.

For the period following the Second World War (1946–82), the components of demographic growth may, as a first approximation, be given as follows (in millions):

Immigration (including repatriation as a result of decolonization)[47]	4.3
Fertility increase[48]	(5.0)
Mortality decline	(4.7)
TOTAL	14.0

Although considerably less than before the war, the contribution of mortality declines remains significant. While emphasis is now justly given to the recovery of fertility as a reflection of the stimulation of general demand, this factor needs to be placed in its precise position in the play of demographic variables. The effect of mortality declines on population increase was similar to that of the baby boom. In the context of an ageing population, the comparison of successive mortality tables is telling: it shows that the age structure of mortality decline was such that the fraction of the employable population surviving over most of the period has grown continually, especially amongst females; finally, it may be noted that the role of immigration in this estimate[49] also takes on a new significance.

Above all, it is the influence of mortality declines which should be stressed. This factor acted through the localization of its effects (for instance, the stronger decline in rural areas in the nineteenth century, which helped to swell the numbers leaving for the factories and industry), through its impact on demographic structure, and through its social and occupational distribution. In this respect the Japanese case remains remarkable. After the spectacular post-war fertility decline, population growth in the period 1955–82 totalled 28.5 million; this growth, which represents a 32% increase in the population of 90.1 million in 1955 owed, aside from the effects of age distribution, exclusively to the exceptionally rapid decline in mortality.

Conclusion

Modern population growth coincided with an economic breakthrough without historical precedent. Given that sustained declines in mortality could hardly have occurred without far-reaching improvements in the human condition, this fact is in itself hardly suprising. Yet it does not seem to have received a fully satisfactory explanation. The most frequently advanced arguments (e.g. Habbakuk 1971) refer implicitly to the creation, in the context of certain conditions, of a self-enhancing circle of factors intimately bound up with demographic growth. These factors include:

[47] Direct effects only (migratory balance).

[48] The excess in relation to replacement level, taking into account the average size of generations. Given its shape, the impact of the initial age structure of the population (which in 1946 was close to a stationary population) is assumed to be negligible.

[49] For the period 1946–79, approximately four-fifths of the growth of the labour force in West Germany is due to to migration.

1. an increase in total demand;
2. resulting economies of scale, advantageous both to business and reduced production costs;
3. a decline in per capita unit costs accompanying the establishment of certain goods and services, divisible and indivisible (schools, hospitals, government, the legal system, defence, etc.);
4. maintenance of a balance between wages and profits conducive to productive investment; and
5. a rate of renewal of the working population which supports the replacement of physical and human capital, both of which then assist the growth of real income, and help thereby to prolong demographic growth by lowering mortality.

But these general arguments are of an atemporal and universal nature, and the real question is why the force of such phenomena was incapable of manifesting itself in earlier societies. Why did this force suddenly manifest itself in the eighteenth century? To what extent did it require breaking the equilibrium of traditional systems? Such disequilibrium—a factor of growth— would have been closely related to long-term mortality decline. Of course, equally profound factors were involved, such as the rise of technological progress and the massive development in communications.

In directing our attention to the analysis of long-term growth in large industrial nations, we have focused more particularly on two generally over-looked aspects of this demographic dynamic: rural migration to sectors of high productivity; and, in a more general manner, the direct and indirect implications of mortality declines, according to the various forms they have taken historically. More detailed study of the connections between demographic and economic growth, based on long time series, would require—as in our treatment of the French case, only in greater detail—separating out the components not only of demographic increase but of variations in national product. The components of economic growth (consumption,[50] investment,[51] and foreign trade) could then be connected in their temporal variations to the components of demographic growth. But this is the subject of a more detailed analytical study than the ground-clearing task we have undertaken here.

---

[50] Consumption would be divided according to its degree of sensitivity to variations in population size (food supply) or age composition (education, health, etc.).
[51] Similarly, investment could be divided according to its flexibility in response to demographic change, using categories such as: (1) housing; (2) infrastructure; (3) others.

Bibliography to Chapter 17

ABRAMOVITZ, M. (1956), 'Resource and Output Trends in the US since 1870', *AER* (May), 5–23.

ADELMAN, I. (1963), 'An Econometric Analysis of Population Growth', *AER*, 53 (June), 314–39.

ASHTON, T. S. (1948), *The Industrial Revolution, 1760–1830* (London: Oxford University Press).

ASSELAIN, J. C. (1984), *Histoire économique de la France* (Paris: Seuil).

BAIROCH, P. (1963), *Révolution industrielle et sous-développement* (Paris: SEDES).

—— (1976), *Commerce extérieur et développement économique de l'Europe au xixe siècle* (Paris: Mouton).

—— (1979), 'Écarts internationaux des niveaux de vie avant la révolution industrielle', *Annales ESC*, (Jan.–Feb.), 145–71.

—— DELDYCKE, T., GELDERS, H., and LIMBOR, J. M. (1968), *La Population active et sa structure* (Brussels: Institut de Sociologie, Université Libre de Bruxelles).

BERGSON, A. (1961), *The Real National Income of Soviet Russia since 1928* (Cambridge, Mass.).

BJERKE, K., and USSING, N. (1958), *Studier over Danmark National produkt, 1870–1950* (Copenhagen).

BORCHARDT, K. (1973), *The Industrial Revolution in Germany 1700–1914*, in *FEHE*, vol. iv, pt. 1 (Glasgow: Collins), 76–160.

BOSERUP, E. (1965), *The Conditions of Agricultural Growth* (London: Allen & Unwin).

—— (1970), *Woman's Role in Economic Development* (London: Allen & Unwin).

—— (1981), *Population and Technology* (Oxford: Blackwell).

CAFAGNA, L. (1973), *The Industrial Revolution in Italy 1830–1914*, in *FEHE*, iv (1) (Glasgow: Collins), 279–328.

CARRE, J. J., DUBOIS, P., and MALINVAUD, E. (1972), *La Croissance française: un essai d'analyse économique causale de l'après-guerre* (Paris: Seuil).

CHAYANOV, A. V. (1966), 'The Theory of Peasant Economy', in D. Thorner *et al.*, (eds.), (Homewood, Ill.: Irwin).

CHENERY, H. B., and SYRQUIN, M. (1975), *Patterns of Development, 1950–1970* (Oxford: Oxford University Press).

CIPOLLA, C. M. (1962), *The Economic History of World Population* (Baltimore, Md.: Pelican).

—— (1969), *Literacy and Development in the West* (London: Penguin).

CLARK, C. (1957), *The Conditions of Economic Progress*, 3rd edn. (London: Macmillan).

DAVID, P. A. (1974), *Nations and Households in Economic Growth: Essay in Honor of Moses Abramovitz* (New York: Reder, Academic Press).

DEANE, P., and COLE, W. A. (1964), *British Economic Growth 1688–1959: Trends and Structure* (Cambridge).

DENISON, E. (1962), *Sources of Economic Growth in the US and the Alternatives Before Us* (New York: Committee for Economic Development).

—— (1967), *Why Growth Rates Differ: Post-war Experience in Nine Western Countries* (Washington, DC: Brookings Institution).

DOVRING, F. (1965), *The Tranformation of European Agriculture, CEHE*, vi (Cambridge).

DUPRÉEL, E. (1928), *Deux Essais sur le progrès* (Brussels: Lamertin).

FUA, G. (1965), *Notes on Italian Economic Growth 1861–1964* (Milan: Angelli).

—— (1978–81), *Lo sviluppo economico in Italia: storia dell'economia italiana negli ultimi cento anni*, 3 vols. (Milan: Angelli).

GERSCHENKRON, A. (1962), *Economic Backwardness in Historical Perspective* (Cambridge, Mass.).

GLOVER, D., and SIMON, J. L. (1975), 'The Effect of Population Density upon Infrastructure: The Case of Road-Building', *EDCC*, 23: 453–68.

GOLDSMITH, R. W. (1961), 'The Economic Growth of Tsarist Russia, 1860–1913', *EDCC*, 9 (Apr.).

HABAKKUK H. J. (1971), *Population Growth and Economic Development since 1750* (Leicester: Leicester University Press).

HAGEN, E. E. (1975), *The Economics of Development* (Homewood, Ill.: Irwin).

HANSEN, A. H. (1939), 'Economic Progress and Declining Population Growth', *AER*, 29: 1–15.

HARTWELL, R. M. (1965), 'The Causes of the Industrial Revolution: An Essay in Methodology', *EHR*, 18: 164–82.

HAYAMI, Y. (1968), 'Technological Progress in Agriculture', in L. Klein and K. Ohkawa (eds.), *Economic Growth* (Homewood, Ill.: Irwin).

—— and RUTTAN, V. W. (1971), *Agricultural Development: An International Perspective* (Baltimore, Md.: Johns Hopkins University Press).

HENRY, L., and BLAYO, Y. (1975), 'La Population de la France de 1740 à 1860', *Population*, Special Number, 71–122.

HOFFMAN, W. G. (1965), *Das Wachstum der deutschen Wirtschaft seit der Mitte des 19 ten Jahrhunderts* (Berlin).

ILO (1979, 1980, 1981), *Annuaire des statistiques du travail* (Geneva: ILO).

JORGENSON, D. W. (1967), 'Surplus Agricultural Labour and the Development of a Dual Economy', *OEP*, 19: 288–312.

KENDRICK, J. W. (1961), *Productivity Trends in the US*, NBER, General Series, no. 71 (Princeton, NJ).

KINDLEBERGER, C. P. (1964), *Economic Growth in France and Britain, 1851–1950* (Cambridge, Mass.: Harvard University Press).

KING, G. (1696), *Natural and Political Observations on the State of England.*

KUZNETS, S. (1952), 'Long-Term Changes in the National Income of the USA since 1870', *Income and Wealth*, Ser. 2 (Cambridge, Mass.).

—— (1954), 'Underdeveloped Countries and the Preindustrial Phase in the Advanced Countries', *Proceedings of the World Population Conference, Rome, 1954*, 947–70.

—— (1956–61), 'Quantitative Aspects of the Economic Growth of Nations (QAEGN)', pt. 1: 'Levels and Variability of Rates of Growth', *EDCC*, 5 (Oct. 1956), 5–94; pt. 2: 'Long-Term Trends in Capital Formation Proportions', *EDCC*, 9 (July 1961).

—— (1958), 'Long Swings in the Growth of Population and in Related Economic Variables', *Proceedings of the American Philosophical Society*, 25–52.

—— (1960), 'Population Change and Aggregate Output', in NBER, *Demographic and Economic Change in Developed Countries* (Princeton, NJ).

—— (1966), *Modern Economic Growth: Rate, Structure and Spread* (New Haven, Conn.: Yale University Press).

—— (1971), *Economic Growth of Nations: Total Output and Production Structure* (Cambridge, Mass.).

—— (1975), 'Population Trends and Modern Economic Growth: Notes towards an Historical Perspective', in UN, *The Population Debate: Dimensions and Perspectives*, World Population Conference, Bucharest, 1974, i (New York: UN).

—— (1977), 'Two Centuries of Economic Growth: Reflections on US Experience', *AER*, 67(1), 1–14.

LANDRY, A. (1930), *L'Hygiène publique en France* (Paris: Alcan).

—— (1949), *Traité de démographie* (Paris: Payot).

LEE, R. D. (1980), 'A Historical Perspective on Economic Aspects of the Population Explosion: The Case of Preindustial England', in R. Easterlin (ed.), *Population and Economic Change in Developing Countries* (Chicago, Ill.: University of Chicago Press), 517–66.

LEE, W. R. (ed.) (1979), *European Demography and Economic Growth 1750–1970* (London).

LÉON, P. (1977), *Histoire économique et sociale du monde* (Paris: Colin), iii–vi.

LE ROY-LADURIE, E. (1968), 'Les Comptes fantastiques de Gregory King', *Annales ESC* (Sept.–Oct.), 1086–102.

—— (1978), *Le Territoire de l'historien* (Paris: Gallimard), ii.

LÉVY-LEBOYER, M. (1968), 'La Croissance économique en France au XIXe siècle: résultats préliminaires', *Annales ESC* (July).

LOCKWOOD, W. W. (1954), *The Economic Development of Japan: Growth and Structural Change, 1868–1938* (Princeton, NJ).

MCNEILL, W. H. (1976), *Plagues and Peoples* (New York: Anchor Press).

MADDISON, A. (1964), *Economic Growth in the West: Comparative Experience in Europe and North America* (London: Allen & Unwin).

—— (1976), *Economic Policy and Performance in Europe 1913–1970*, in *FEHE*, vol. v, pt. 2 (Glasgow: Collins), 442–508.

MALINVAUD, E. (1984), 'La Science économique aujourd'hui', *Revue Économique et Sociale*, Lausanne (Jan.), 35–45.

MANNEWITZ, R. (1914), *Morbidität und Mortalität im deutschen Reich, ihre zeitliche Entwicklung und ihre räumlichen Unterschiede* (Dresden: Verlag Dittert).

MARCZEWSKI, J. (1961), 'Some Aspects of the Economic Growth of France, 1660–1958', *EDCC*, 9(3) (Apr.), 369–86.

—— (1963), 'The Take-Off Hypothesis and French Experience', in W. W. Rostow, *The Economics of Take-Off in Sustained Growth* (New York).

MARKOVITCH, T. J. (1966), *L'Industrie française de 1789 à 1964*, Cahiers de l'ISEA, AF7, no. 179 (Paris).

MEIER, G. M. (1964), *Leading Issues in Development Economics* (New York: Oxford University Press).

MULHALL, M. G. (1880), *The Progress of the World in Arts, Agriculture, Commerce, Manufactures, Instruction, Railways and Public Health since the Beginning of the Nineteenth Century* (London: Stanford).

—— (1896), *Industries and Wealth of Nations* (London: Longman).

NELSON, R. R. (1981), 'Research on Productivity Growth and Productivity Differences: Dead Ends and New Departures', *JEL*, 19 (Sept.), 1029–64.

NORTH, D. C., and THOMAS, R. P. (1970), 'An Economic Theory of the Growth of the Western World', *Economic History Review*, 2nd ser., 23: 1–19.

OECD (1981), *Comptes nationaux des pays de l'OCDE* (Paris: OECD).

OHKAWA, K. (1970), 'Phases of Agricultural Development and Economic Growth', in

K. Ohkawa, *et al.* (eds.), *Agriculture and Economic Growth* (Princeton, NJ: Princeton University Press).

—— and SHINOHARA, M. (1979), *Patterns of Japanese Economic Development* (New Haven, Conn.: Yale University Press).

—— UMEMURA, M., ITO, M., and NODA, T. (1957), *The Growth Rate of the Japanese Economy since 1878* (Tokyo: Kinokuniya Bookstore).

OLUWASEANMI, H. A. (1976), 'Socio-economic Aspects of Feeding People', in *Proceedings of the World Food Conference, Rome, 1976*, 96–97.

PATEL, S. J. (1961), 'Rates of Industrial Growth in the Last Century, 1868–1958', *EDCC*, 9(3).

—— (1964), 'The Economic Distance between Nations: Its Origin, Measurement and Outlook, *EJ* (Mar.), 122–29.

PERROUX, F. (1955), 'Prises de vue sur la croissance de l'économie française 1780–1850', *Income and Wealth*, Ser. 5 (Cambridge, Mass.), 41–78.

PHELPS-BROWN, E. H., and HOPKINS, S. V. (1959), 'Builders' Wage-Rates, Prices and Population: Some Further Evidence', *Economica*, 26(101) (Feb.), 18–38.

POLANYI, K. (1944), *The Great Transformation: The Political and Economic Origins of our Time* (New York: Rinehart).

QUÉTELET, A. (1835), *Sur l'homme et le développement de ses facultés* (Paris).

—— (1871), *Anthropométrie* (Brussels: Murquardt).

Report of the Royal Commission on Population (1949) (London: HMSO).

ROSTOW, W. W. (1960), *The Stages of Economic Growth: A Non-Communist Manifesto* (Cambridge).

SAUVY, A. (1943), *Richesse et population* (Paris: Payot).

—— (1952), *Théorie générale de la population* (Paris: PUF).

—— (1967–72), *Histoire économique de la France entre les deux guerres*, 3 vols. (Paris: Fayard).

SCHULTZ, T. W. (1961), 'Investment in Human Capital', *AER* (Mar.), 1–17.

SCHUMPETER, J. A. (1912), *Theorie der wirtschaftlichen Entwicklung* (Leipzig: Duncker und Humblot).

—— (1939), *Business Cycles* (New York: McGraw-Hill).

SIMON, J. L. (1977), *The Economics of Population Growth* (Princeton, NJ: Princeton University Press).

SINHA, J. H. (1975), 'Population and Agriculture', in L. Tabah (ed.), *Population and Economic Growth in the Third World*, i (Liège: IUSSP).

SLICHER VAN BATH, B. H. (1963), *The Agrarian History of Western Europe, AD 500–1850* (London: Arnold).

SOLOW, K. (1957), 'Technical Change and the Aggregate Production Function', *Review of Economics and Statistics*, Aug.

TINBERGEN, J. (1942), 'Zur Theorie der langfristigen Wirtschaftsentwicklung', *Westwirtschaftsliche Archiv*, 55.

TOUTAIN, J. C. (1961), 'Le Produit de l'agriculture française de 1700 à 1958', in *Histoire quantitative de l'économie française*, Cahiers de l'ISEA, no. 115 (Paris).

TOYNBEE, A. (1884), *Lectures on the Industrial Revolution of Eighteenth Century England* (London: Rivington).

WOYTINSKY, W. S. and E. S. (1953), *World Population and Production* (New York).

WRIGLEY, E. A., and SCHOFIELD, R. S. (1981), *The Population History of England, 1541–1871: A Reconstruction* (London: Edward Arnold).

18 Economic Breakthrough in Poor Countries

Real solutions to a people's problems cannot be drawn from other people's experiences.

(Nasser)

ALTHOUGH in most cases the demographic growth of less developed countries is in the process of slowing down, it is likely to continue for several decades yet. Aside from quasi-arithmetical constraints associated with number and structure, such as food requirements, educational costs, and the creation of employment opportunities—upon which it is easy to reach minimal agreement—the economic implications of this phenomenon are not only difficult to anticipate, but widely disputed. The usual theoretical postulates which serve as a frame of reference are in fact analytically debatable. Some may even be logically reversed. And they have the limitation of only very scant empirical testing.

Most assume that the continuation of rapid population growth in poor countries must—if it does not actually increase poverty—serve at least to perpetuate low standards of living. This general pessimism rests on a number of hypotheses, but also on historical observation of the widening difference between rich and poor countries since the industrial revolution. When measured by current levels converted to a common monetary unit,[1] and projected backwards from known real rates of growth, the differences in starting levels of development as of 1850 between countries of European population and others are of the order of 1 to 2 or 1 to 4, depending on the author (Patel 1961; Kuznets 1965). A century later, around 1960, these differences could be anything from 1 to 20 (Kuznets 1954, 1971). The economic boom in Europe and its overseas extensions during the second half of the nineteenth century saw real per capita income increase sevenfold (Patel 1964); in contrast, the less developed countries were in a state of virtual stagnation, while simultaneously experiencing an increase in demographic growth rates tending towards a much higher historical maximum. Russia's maximum decennial peak was 17.5%, compared with 40% in Kenya and Mexico; as an average,

---

[1] With the aid of exchange rates, or, better still, scales of equivalence for purchasing power which take into account international price differences, and patterns of consumption (estimates of purchasing-power parities).

the decennial growth peak was around 12.5% in Europe, as opposed to 25% to 35% in the less developed world.

Such comparisons, in our view, invite serious reservations[2] to which may be added the finding (Bairoch 1979) that evaluations which depend on direct comparisons of the purchasing power of money in the period under consideration give considerably smaller differences. Moreover, certain major historical facts remain to be considered:

1. In countries with completed demographic transition (excepting Ireland) the Malthusian model universally failed to be realized, for the population never attained its maximum 'biological' growth (3.5% to 4% per year): fertility reacted to the decline, and generally very swiftly. If one sets aside the post-war period, which certainly appears to constitute a digression (see Chapter 7), the transition from the average of 5 children characteristic of the *ancien régime* to 2 children per woman in the modern era generally took less than half a century to complete. With the decline in mortality, at the time of writing, the same process of adjustment has already begun in most of the less developed countries.

2. Over the entire period 1750–1980 (longer than the transition period as we have defined it), the population of countries of European origin increased almost sixfold; if the term 'demographic explosion' has a meaning, it would seem appropriate here. But then one should also speak of an 'economic explosion' since, at the same time, real per capita income was multiplied by over 10 (see Chapter 17). Everything suggests that, far from cancelling each other out, these two secular booms were mutually compatible, giving an extraordinary power to the Western world.

3. Post-war experience, in this respect, indicates that in the long term there is no reason why comparable developments should not come to characterize less developed countries. Contrary to the general view, although rates of demographic growth have been without historical precedent, they have in no way impeded economic growth—and, as we have seen in Chapter 16, there is no statistical connection between rates of population growth and real per capita income. Viewed in historical perspective this phase of demographic

---

[2] These reservations relate to the measurement of initial differences, which appear exaggerated. Available statistical data for the mid-19th century are not in fact adequate to permit comparison between advanced countries (Great Britain, the US, France, etc.) and colonies under British administration, such as India and Egypt. The latter were often amongst the least advanced. However, developed countries represented only a small fraction of Europe, and it is doubtful that much difference would be found in standards of living between the greater part of Europe (including southern, central, and eastern areas, and Russia) and the rest of the world. Existing data on infant mortality invite scepticism. Moreover, those less developed countries for which it is possible to draw comparisons for the 19th century were characterized by greater poverty amongst their rural masses. Finally, price structures are not taken into account. It is likely that initial differences in standards of living between European and non-European populations on the eve of the industrial 'revolution' were less pronounced than Kuznets's estimations would imply; but the thesis of Bairoch, which suggests that these differences were negligible (less developed countries possible even having a slight advantage) is not based on sufficiently solid reasoning to be useful.

development has tended, on the whole, to coincide with accelerating economic progress.[3] Furthermore, analysis of comparative economic performances over the last two decades shows that, for the first time in history, the growth of average per capita income in developing countries has caught up with and overtaken that of the rich countries:[4] 3.1% compared with 3.6% respectively during the years 1960–70, and 3.0% compared with 2.5% for 1970–80 (OECD 1981). This reversal has occurred at the very time that differences in demographic evolution have been at their most extreme, following the massive decline in fertility in rich countries. The usual paradigms of Malthusian or neoclassical theory, for example, relating to the presumed negative influence of demographic increase on the marginal productivity of labour, or on the availability of savings for capital formation, thus prove inappropriate to rendering a reality quite removed from what they anticipated.

These facts having been stated, we must try to interpret them; what we need to understand is why, finally, this extraordinary increase in population proved to be compatible with sustained growth in per capita income. The preceding chapter showed that exaggerated attention to high fertility resulted in neglect of the role of mortality declines in the modern demographic dynamic. The view that mortality declines were totally exogenous to economic development was largely disproved in the 1970s. Once accepted, this change of perspective has a decisive influence on economic interpretation, and is especially pertinent to less developed countries. Mortality decline liberated a great productive capacity; for example, in some countries three-fifths of the population had hitherto been affected by malaria. By removing the chief obstacle to investment—the permanent risk of death—it helped dispel ingrained fatalism. This argument need not be repeated here.

A second argument, relating to surplus labour generated by demographic growth in the traditional sector and employable in new, more productive areas, is, however, more difficult to work with. Indeed, it can prove ambiguous, given the enormous diversity of absorptive capacity in the modern industrial sector, from one country to another. We shall therefore leave this argument to one side.

Two fundamental questions, around which the same misunderstandings and errors of theoretical analysis have for decades arisen, strike us as meriting special attention: the food situation, and the accumulation of human and non-human capital.

A reconstruction will be undertaken, below, of long series of per capita

---

[3] One might, of course, wonder what would have happened if the demographic growth had been less, but there is no objective answer to this question.

[4] In the sense of *developed* capitalist countries which are members of the OECD (i.e. zoned OECD, excluding Turkey). This observation is based on OECD data, which differ fairly significantly from those of the World Bank, due mostly to different nomenclature. But in both cases the results cast doubt on the idea of an aggravation of relative differences in levels of development between 'developed' and 'less developed' countries, for the last decades at least.

product at constant prices, for the few rare large countries with early macro-economic estimates. This is necessary to bring into relief particular features of the period of demographic acceleration. It requires some unconventional methods of interpretation or, rather, data not easily adapted to the quantitative analysis of growth on account of its residual elements. But by these means, we clarify differences in the growth of productivity related to the following facts: the density of infrastructural and communications networks, and the importance of investment in human capital. Both of these factors reflect the crucial role of the State[5] and a necessary minimum population density (and thus, by implication, demographic growth).

1. Food

In most poor countries agriculture still employs almost two-thirds of the working population, and provides 30% to 40% of total production. Its pre-dominance is essential, not only because the lot of most people depends on it, but also because improvement in agricultural productivity conditions the rise of industrialization both by stimulating demand and by liberating additional supplies of labour.

But curiously, although its role is in all senses vital, it is one of the most difficult sectors to evaluate owing to the number of uncertainties and the powerful ideologies that surround it.

Myths and Ambiguities

There are two principal myths current on the effects of demographic pressure in poor countries: that of the constant aggravation of the food situation, and that of the increasing scarcity of cultivated land. The persistence of such myths is helped by the almost insurmountable difficulties of evaluation con-fronting any attempts at assessment in this field. Not only are production figures difficult to establish, but also food consumption and other uses, above all food quality in terms of calorific and protein content. Owing to the multiplicity of variables and difficulty of statistical observation, food pro-duction remains hard to quantify: the fraction consumed by society may also vary substantially according to shortcomings in harvesting, transport, and storage,[6] and the extent of waste. Human consumption also depends on

---

[5] Technological changes, together with institutional variables, are, in the long term, the major determinants of progress in productivity. This fact has been stressed on a number of occasions by Kuznets, particularly in recent studies. But with the exception of Boserup's thesis (1981) which connects technical innovation to the increase in population density on a world scale and over several centuries, the causes of technological change, on the long-term historical and national scale which concerns us, remain unknown.

[6] Destruction due to rats and other vermin is often far from negligible.

hygiene and the state of health, notably as regards intestinal bacteria and digestive illnesses. There is every reason to believe, however, that with improvements in agricultural organization and the decline of traditional diseases, the rate of wastage decreases with time. Enquiry into production—the first logical stage to tackle—remains blocked by insufficient information from the FAO: the greater part of the data arising from the first three world surveys on food have remained unpublished (Eberstadt 1981).

Even less is known about another aspect needing evaluation: energy requirements. These vary from one person to another, some needing as much as three times as others. It is not surprising, then, that the most contradictory reports may circulate, for instance, on the number of victims of severe malnutrition. Attempts at the conceptual or methodological refinement of estimates can give rise to profound alterations, of which the fluctuation in successive FAO evaluations, particularly during in 1970s, gives evidence (Klatzmann 1981).[7]

Long-Term Trends in Per Capita Food Production

According to the US Ministry of Agriculture, world food production per capita increased by 40% between 1950 and 1978. As debatable as this figure may be, this evaluation was not fundamentally questioned by the habitually alarmist FAO. In fact, they were aware that a considerable improvement had occurred, although their estimate was a little below 30%. Whilst progress was more pronounced in developed countries, with a rise in net exports, the increase in food production in less developed countries was, on average, greater than that of population over the last three decades. The considerable improvement in life expectation, linked very closely to the state of nutrition, together with the results of certain anthropometric tests such as the development of height by generation, also provide indirect indices of the progress achieved by these countries.

Improvement, however, was very uneven, from one country to another, yet the pattern which followed bears little resemblance to prevailing opinion on the subject. India, for example, experienced a more favourable development than Black Africa, with its small population and low standard of living. The annual average rate of increase in food production in most cases has been around 2% to 3%—close on that of population growth, or slightly above. In places with the highest increase, the improvements are attributable either to the green revolution, or to intensification of labour via irrigation systems, land clearance, and an increased number of harvests. In some cases, both factors have contributed. A quarter of the countries recorded increases of less than 1% in food production per capita, and over a third registered declines. In

---

[7] Thus, in 1974, as a result of an unexplained methodological revision, the proportion of people considered undernourished rose suddenly from a quarter to a third.

TABLE 18.1. *Currently cultivated and potentially cultivable land, by continent*
(millions of hectares)

Continent	Total surface area	Cultivated surface area	Potentially cultivable surface area	Percentage of cultivable land in use
North America	2,420	273.4	627.5	44
South America	1,780	78.3	595.6	13
Africa	3,030	157.5	711.3	22
Asia	4,390	684.8	886.9	77
Australia New Zealand	860	33.5	199.1	17
Europe	1,050	212.1	398.7	53
WORLD	13,530	1,439.6	3,419.1	42

Source: National Research Council (1977).

many cases, this reflects a voluntary policy which forms part of an economic strategy in which less costly importation is substituted for local production; some South-East Asian and oil-producing Arab countries are examples. In other cases no such policy applies, but a detailed examination shows in these cases that demographic causes in fact remain marginal to political upheavals (international conflicts, civil war) or to bad economic management.

Some Further Data and Explanation

It is often said that space is the principal factor limiting the growth of food production—in fact, it is more a question of water—and yet an examination of basic data shows that agricultural land is not a fixed resource, but that it has increased massively in the course of history, under demographic pressure. Less than half of the surface area of the globe that could be cultivated using current techniques is in fact under cultivation. Table 18.1 gives a synthesis, by continent, of this observation.

The cultivated surface of the world covers 1.4 billion hectares. The lowest estimate for the extent of potentially cultivable land (Mesarovic and Pestel 1974), which excludes pasture, is of the order of 2.4 billion; the highest—of the order of 3.4 billion hectares—derives from a detailed geographic survey conducted by Buringh (1975), which has been confirmed on an entirely independent basis by studies of the US Academy of Science (National Research Council 1977), whose figures have been used in the present study. In other words, the unexploited arable surface is about 1.5 times greater than that already under cultivation. Almost all the existing reserves form part of the underdeveloped world, especially in Africa and Latin America. Land is scarcer in Asia, but there is an enormous potential for increase in yields, given the land's fertility, which reflects a high proportion of alluvial and volcanic soils.

Over 50% of the increase in food production in less developed countries during the 1950s, and around 40% in the 1960s, is due to the extension of cultivated area (Murdoch 1980). The improvement in yields per hectare would therefore appear to be assuming a growing role in the progress of food production.

There is a considerably larger margin of variation where yields are concerned. A few brief considerations, either historical or geographical in bearing, suffice to illustrate this:

1. Before the war, according to the large-scale survey of 1933–38, there was on average little difference in yields per hectare between developed and less developed countries. Today, whatever product one considers (wheat, rice, maize), yields are two to three times higher in the developed world.

2. Japan, in the century 1880–1980, doubled its rice yield per hectare and tripled its wheat yield, despite its already comparatively high production, while experiencing a decline in unit costs of real production.

3. At the beginning of the 1980s, Japan's rice yield per hectare was close on 8 metric tonnes, compared with only 2 in less developed countries. The difference is due largely to chemical fertilizers, which are applied at a rate almost 30 times less (per hectare) in India than in Japan, and 10 times less in Asia than in Europe. In addition, fertilizer is differently used in these developing countries, being often less effective and reserved for commercial, non-food crops. Lesser production also relates to the insufficiency of irrigated land: the irrigated area in less developed countries amounts only to about a seventh, and this land produces as much in value as the unirrigated land. Thus, in Indian experimental agricultural stations, where optimum productivity conditions have been realized, yields are around 7 times higher than the average.

Consequently, the question is to establish the price behaviour of modern agricultural aids (fertilizers, pesticides, seeds, equipment, and related materials). Analysis of long-term trends since the war shows that these prices have risen considerably more slowly than those of other goods and services (Eberstadt 1981), which should therefore facilitate the introduction of new techniques. An examination of the food problem thus shows up the extraordinary elasticity of potential production. European history furnishes ample evidence of this: even before the introduction of modern techniques in the eighteenth century, the rhythms of labour (daily and seasonal), crop selection (introduction of the potato and fodder), and diet (greater emphasis on the potato as opposed to cereals, and on pork as opposed to beef) were adapting to the constraints of demographic pressure.

While the demographic transition is maturing in industrial countries and, in the absence of immigration, their populations stagnate or decline, their food supply will continue to increase, especially if the same policies of government subsidy continue on either side of the Atlantic. The real questions henceforth are not so much of a technical as of a political order: the control of international prices, the elimination of surpluses in Western countries, financing indebtedness, and revising investment options in the favour of agriculture in poor countries. Great famines are no longer, as in previous centuries, the result of bad harvests or economic crises; they are increasingly the fruit of errors, or even deliberate acts of government. The growing interdependence of nations and the emergence of modern administration are rapidly bringing the risk of such disasters to an end. The worst famines of this century were all directly related to political disorder or carelessness, when they were not officially planned (Russia in the 1930s: 6 million deaths; China during the Great Leap Forward, 1959–61: over 20 million; and Cambodia, 1975–80: approximately 2 million).

2. Savings

Amongst the negative effects generally attributed to rapid population growth, its influence on savings has without doubt been a principal subject. Two implicit postulates have directed research: (1) income growth is determined by the accumulation of capital; (2) demographic growth is an obstacle to the formation of capital.

Investment and Growth

According to the most recent econometric studies, the role of investment is far less important than it is still sometimes considered. Here is what Denison (1980) says: 'Contrary to current opinion, physical capital is not *the* source of growth, but *one* of its determinants among many others.' For the period 1948–73, only one-sixth of American growth can be attributed to the accumulation of material capital. Above all, analysis of time series proves that it is the rate of growth which tends to generate investment rather than the reverse. The few correlations that have been produced, when significant, are therefore misleading.

The idea of a systematic association between investment and growth was so compelling during the 1950s and 1960s that it dominated the first attempts at economic planning in many less developed countries. In order to predict growth rates in GDP, a given incremental capital–output ratio, ICOR,[8] was applied to the total rate of investment. However, reality is more complex. The analysis of long time series for the gross or net formation of fixed capital,

---

[8] This coefficient enjoyed such a vogue that it was even used as an acronym in France.

measured from average or marginal values, shows no correlation with corresponding GDP or national income. In other words, there is no firm connection between rates of accumulation in physical capital and rates of growth (Kuznets 1960). On the contrary, an extraordinary variety of ICORs has been observed, from one country to the next, and for the same country over time, with similar rates of growth. Thus, the order of magnitude for European countries in the second half of the nineteenth century ranges from 2.5 to 7; in the UK, the figure doubled between the beginning and end of the nineteenth century (6 compared with 3) whereas growth scarcely altered. In contrast, other variables such as the source and distribution of income, savings composition, and the sectoral distribution of investment seem to play a major role.

Savings and Demographic Growth

The usual argument, which we have observed already in the Coale–Hoover model, is based on the hypothesis that an increase in family size reduces savings, and that the disadvantages of having a smaller supply of capital outweigh the benefits of additional labour (the latter assumed automatically to be in excess of requirements).

The few empirical studies on this question show that, once again, economic reality squares badly with theoretical presupposition. Leff (1969) has compared savings rates and dependency rates for a large number of countries over a given period, establishing a negative correlation between them. His study, however, proves on examination to be unconvincing, since the elimination of certain atypical or statistically inadequate countries divests his results of all significance. Similarly, Kelley's work (1976) on the survey of American farming households (1889) results in a very ambiguous conclusion, owing to the tendency of fertility to vary with income and the influence of early child employment on family resources. Other studies, such as those of Sinha (1975) on India, or Kelley and Williamson (1968) on Indonesia, also tend to question the hypothesis of a linear negative relation between family size and savings capacity. The influence of family size and composition—very difficult to isolate on account of the number of interfering variables involved—ultimately remains obscure (Chernikovsky 1978).

Turning now from synchronic to diachronic analyses, an examination of long series of capital formation in the US (1855–1914) shows that, for certain components such as housing construction or infrastructure, there is a fairly close positive relation with long-term population trends, particularly with the flow of net migration or the intensity of internal migration. The US, however, appears to be a case unto itself, on account of both the predominant role of immigration in its population growth and the importance of inflows of foreign capital.

The connection between savings and population growth must appear, a priori, more tenuous where other countries are concerned. Let us therefore

TABLE 18.2. *Population growth and capital formation*

Country	Period	Average Rate of investment	Incremental capital output ratio (ICOR)	Rate of population increase (%)	Annual average rate of increase in product (%)
United Kingdom	1855–1914	9.0	4.1	0.84	2.22
Germany	1851–1913	19.8	7.4	1.15	2.69
Italy	1861–1915	12.5	9.6	0.65	1.30
Japan	1887–1916	10.9	2.9	0.90	3.75
Denmark	1870–1914	12.6	3.9	1.07	3.25
Norway	1865–1914	13.2	6.3	0.76	2.08
Sweden	1861–1915	12.2	4.1	0.72	2.95

Sources: Kuznets (1961: 5–17); Mitchell (1975).

consider available data (see Table 18.2) for several industrial nations over the same period, which more or less corresponds to the stage at which most developed countries currently stand.

The investment rate appears to possess neither a positive nor a negative link with the rate of demographic growth. Moreover the ICOR itself manifests no obvious relation to demographic development: there is therefore no evidence that, for a given level of economic growth, investment should increase automatically with the rate of population increase.

Indetermination: The True Nature of Savings

Such indeterminancy is not very surprising, but it is appropriate at this stage of the analysis to take account of the sources, determinants, and content of savings.

Sources. The household, business, and the State are the main sources of savings, the combinations of which may vary enormously from one country to another. Demographic growth affects each one differently: its influence is, a priori, more positive on the formation of capital by the State and business, and more negative on that of households (Leibenstein 1975). Household savings, while more frequently studied in relation to demographic factors, in reality do not always represent a dominant part of overall savings in poor countries.

Determinants. The savings rate is a function of income distribution and social structure—factors absent from Keynesian theory. There is, moreover, a much greater inequality of incomes in poor countries than in rich ones; according to Kuznets (1966), the 5% of richest families control 30% to 40%

of the total income in less developed countries, compared with 20% to 25% in developed ones. The volume of private savings depends above all on the behaviour of this small minority, which also often has low fertility. This inequality tends to increase in the first phases of modern economic growth. There is also a considerable likelihood that most families composed of small producers are more inclined to limit consumption than break into their savings when family size, owing to mortality decline, increases. But this issue remains to be studied, particularly in a dynamic perspective.

Content. If one takes into account non-monetary savings, in particular human capital, and if one assumes that demographic growth within certain limits does not impede progress in education and professional training down generations, then the rate of accumulation of human capital is positively linked to the rate of renewal of generations on the job market. Since the first studies by Schultz (1961), it has been known that the accumulation of human capital has played a greater role in secular growth than the accumulation of material capital.

3. Some Long-Term Series

The lack of basic data of sufficient historical depth remains an obstacle to correctly weighting the components of economic development during the last few decades. Precise statements for most countries await the availability of complete statistical series. Reasoning based on a few cases runs the risk of leading to erroneous conclusion; as far as we know, data for evaluating long-term growth exist for only four less developed countries. In proceeding to a reconstitution of demographic and economic series for these countries, we shall keep in mind that such cases should be taken for nothing more than what they are: examples, without any model value.

China is not amongst the four countries for which we have data. The same extreme views—sometimes alarmist, sometimes enthusiastic—have continued to prevail about its prospects. By way of example, here is an authoritative opinion, uttered half a century ago, when the country's population was about three times smaller than it is today: 'Observers are unanimous in the belief that the population of China is already redundant and that, with existing production capacities, a large increase in the population can only take place at the expense of a serious decline in the standard of living, which is already pitifully low' (Notestein, in Buck 1937). For some, the country has experienced a rapid development over recent decades much greater than that of India (Malenbaum 1982); others, like Étienne (1982), see the situation as more ambiguous; and still others, like Bergère (1981), regard recent developments as yet another failure following many previous ones, due to the same fundamental cause: a weakness of State structures. Gerschenkron (1962) has demonstrated the prime importance of the State's role in recently in-

TABLE 18.3. *Sectoral distribution of labour in four less developed countries, 1872–1979*

Country	Years	Workers (millions)				Proportions (%)		
		Total	A	I	S	A	I	S
Brazil	1872	5,316.8	3,261.3	810.5	1,245.0	(61.3)	15.2	13.6
	1900	8,123.5	5,332.5		(2,801.0)	(65.5)		(34.5)
	1920a	9,150.2	6,451.5	1,443.0	1,255.7	70.5	15.8	13.7
	1940a	14,020.1	9,453.5	2,264.4	2,302.3	67.4	16.2	16.4
	1950	17,117.4	10,369.9	2,928.3	3,819.2	60.6	17.1	22.3
	1960	22,651.3	11,697.8	4,453.0b	6,500.3b	51.6	19.7	28.7
	1970	29,787.1	12,878.3	5,895.0	11,013.8	43.2	19.8	37.0
	1976	39,717.9	14,388.6	10,766.2	14,563.1	36.2	27.1	36.7
Egypt	1907c	3,530.9	2,440.0	481.5	609.4	69.1	13.6	17.3
	1917c	5,846.5	4,044.4	652.1	1,159.0	69.2	11.1	19.8
	1927c	5,845.7	(3,525.2)	752.0	(1,568.5)	(60.3)	12.9	26.8
	1937	6,095.0	4,308.2	748.6	1,038.2	70.7	12.3	17.0
	1947	6,476.9	4,125.8	1,001.1	1,351.1	63.7	15.4	20.9
	1960	7,595.4	4,402.9	1,174.4	2,018.2	58.0	15.5	26.5
	1979	9,599.0	4,002.0	2,557.5	3,039.5	41.7	26.0	31.7
Mexico	1900d	8,675.5	3,157.5	912.8	4,605.3	(36.4)	(10.5)	(53.1)
	1910	5,618.2	3,581.4	800.0	1,236.8	63.7	14.2	22.0
	1921	5,535.2	3,490.0	735.5	1,309.8	63.0	13.3	23.7
	1930	5,352.2	3,626.3	850.5	875.4	67.8	15.9	16.4
	1940	5,858.1	3,830.9	895.8	1,131.5	65.4	15.3	19.3
	1950	8,272.1	4,823.9	1,529.7	1,918.5	58.3	18.5	23.2
	1960	11,332.0	6,143.5	2,504.2	2,684.2	54.2	22.1	23.7
	1970e	(10,488.8)	(4,836.9)	(2,841.3)	(2,810.5)	46.1	27.1	26.8
	1979	19,650.7	7,885.8	5,437.4	6,327.5	40.1	27.7	32.2

India							
1901[f]	135,520.0	90,894.0	15,194	29,433	67.1	11.2	21.7
1911[f]	143,762.0	103,355.0	20,219	20,189	71.9	14.1	14.0
1921[f]	140,648.0	101,962.0	18,043	20,644	72.5	12.8	14.7
1931[f]	148,817.0	100,037.0	18,040	30,740	67.2	12.1	20.7
1951[g]	139,712.0	102,879.0	13,230	23,603	73.6	9.5	16.9
1961	188,676.0	137,546.0	24,536	26,594	72.9	13.0	14.1
1971	180,049.0	130,058.0	25,149	25,278	72.2	14.0	14.0

Notes: A = Agriculture, forestry, hunting and fishing; I = Mining and manufacturing, building, electricity, gas, water and health services, transport, storage, and communications; S = Commerce, banking, insurance, real estate, armed forces, and other services (incl. ill-defined activities). These three general sectors reclassify the following branches of activity as defined by the ILO: A = 1; B = 2, 3, 4, 5, 7; C = 6, 8, 9, 0.

[a] Not incl. domestic work.
[b] Water, gas, electricity, health services, banking, insurance, and real estate are included in S.
[c] From the age of 5 years onwards.
[d] Incl. servants working in agriculture and housewives (4.318, 500 employed in 1910).
[e] Without adjustment for gaps in enumeration.
[f] British India, incl. Indian states and Burma.
[g] Not incl. Jammu, Kashmir, Jullundar, and tribal territories of Assam (5 m. inhabitants).

Sources: Bairoch *et al.* (1968), up to 1960; censuses and ILO *Yearbook of Labour Statistics*, 1979, 1980, 1981.

dustrialized countries, where it provides both impetus through infrastructural development and investment, and economic control through prices and incomes policies. Data such as produced by the 1982 census on the degree of literacy or the frequency of female infanticide, together with the relative silence surrounding the World Bank's big survey (the Bank had revised its economic projections considerably upwards some years previously), imply that Gerschenkron's judgement is fairly close to reality. (At least, this may hold up to the 1970s; a significant change seems to be currently in process.) This view is further strengthened by current awareness of the damage caused by political disorder, and of the fact that the backwardness of the country's infrastructure has not been overcome. In 1970, for instance, there were less than 3 metres of railway line per km^2, a figure 6 times less than India's, and scarcely higher than it was in India a century earlier. Nevertheless, according to official data, the level of per capita consumption, after adjustments for inflation, increased by 2.3 between 1952 and 1982. The only way of resolving the contradiction is to acknowledge that progress has on the whole been achieved in recent years, since the decollectivization of 1979.

The four countries we shall consider are Brazil, Mexico, Egypt, and India. For the latter, the recent re-examination of Chinese data enables us better to assess its relative performance. It should be recalled that all four of these countries experienced a significant mortality decline *before* the Second World War, sometimes from quite an early date: in Mexico and India declines occurred in the 1920s, and for Brazil and Egypt they were even earlier. Such developments represent one of the first signs of economic breakthrough, since it is not possible to have substantial improvements in general health without a minimum of openness to external influences and transformation of economic structures. But these changes have apparently not yet affected the sectoral distribution of labour, perhaps because they are related to differences in natural increase in the various population groups. In spite of difficult questions of comparability concerning the definition of agricultural employments, or possible gaps in the recording of marginal groups (the young, the old, and women), or, again, the presence of mixed activities, it is possible to observe a more or less constant level of around 70% of the population employed in agriculture.[9] With developments during the post-war period up to the late 1970s, this figure fell by almost half, except in India, which constitutes a striking exception, since its sectoral distribution has remained almost unchanged since the beginning of the century.

India: Slow and Irregular Growth

India's development remains a subject of great controversy; for many years, various purely fictitious estimates (Digby, for example) were produced, either

---

[9] According to Buck's survey (1937), the same order of magnitude prevailed in China in 1930.

TABLE 18.4. *Population and gross domestic product (GDP) per capita (at constant prices, 1970), India, 1861–1980*

Years	GDP (millions of rupees)	Population (millions)	GDP per inhabitant	Average annual rate of increase from one period to the next	
				Population	GDP per inhabitant
1861–1869	56.5	175.0	323	—	—
1881–1889	80.2	200.0	401	0.7	1.1
1901–1909	105.9	260.0	407	1.3	0.1
1921–1922	168.0	320.0	525	1.3	1.6
1925–1929	167.0	338.0	494	1.0	−0.9
1931–1934	221.5	352.0	629	0.8	4.5
1935–1939	231.7	370.0	626	1.0	−0.1
1940–1944	213.1	360.0	592	−0.6	−1.1
1945–1949	187.0	340.0	550	−1.1	−1.5
1950–1954	205.7	370.0	556	1.7	+0.2
1955–1959	242.7	410.0	592	2.1	+1.3
1960–1964	297.3	455.7	652	2.1	+1.9
1965–1969	344.4	506.8	680	2.1	+0.8
1970–1974	414.4	563.7	735	2.2	+1.6
1975–1979	502.8	625.8	803	2.1	+1.8
1980	552	663.6	832	2.0	+1.2

Note: Territorial boundaries vary.

Sources: Mukherjee (1969); UN *Yearbook of National Accounts Statistics*, and *Monthly Statistical Bulletin*.

to extol the merits of British colonialism, or, to the contrary, to condemn its practices. With time, available statistical data have been re-examined by different writers, in particular Mukherjee (1965), and Heston (1983), to name only recent studies. In spite of regular discrepancies on certain aspects, such as in evaluations of the weight of the government sector, or the development of agricultural production, these two authors agree on essentials and, moreover, do not appear to contradict earlier work on similar periods of observation by authors such as Rao (1940) and Desai (1948) (whose sources were fairly similar). Indian secular growth is very slow and irregular, with profound long-term fluctuations up to the mid-century. Between 1870 and 1970, real per capita income improved only by 75%, giving a long-term annual trend of only 0.56% (compared with America's 1.76%, for example). Development comprises several successive periods: expansion in the late nineteenth and early twentieth centuries; stagnation from 1925 to 1940; recession from 1940 to 1950; and a renewed and more sustained expansion of 3.6% per year, or

1.5% per capita per annum, from 1950 to 1980. On the basis of different retrospective series and estimates for the recent period, Table 18.4 reconstructs the development of population and real per capita product in rupeess at their 1970 value, since the 1860s.

Even if orders of magnitude present few problems, the interpretation of trends remains open to discussion. Feeble growth, and even a decline in rural employment in the first half of the century, have often been attributed to British administration. Rigid policies of regional specialization sometimes forbidding exportation are cited, as are revenue control policies which included dismantling traditional craft occupations without sufficient encouragement to put suitable infrastructures in their place. Certain areas which served British commercial interest, like the Punjab, escaped such policies. The importance of transport and communications networks in developing a national economy is well known: they convey products (fertilizers, seeds, medicines, etc.) and heavy goods; guarantee swift access to professional services (hospitals, schools, repairs), and open up populations to the many advantages of outside influences. India has never really overcome its structural handicap in this respect, which affects gains in agricultural productivity as well as the rate of industrialization. Even today, India still has a less extensive railway network than England or Germany in the mid-nineteenth century. The density of its road and railway network was 0.3 km per km^2 compared with 1.0 around 1970 in developed countries with a similar population density; this figure is 10 times below that of Japan (International Railway Union 1972; International Road Federation 1974). The network is also of a lower standard.

Between 1952 and 1972, food production per capita increased 0.5% per year; although tentative, the development was in positive contrast to the past, and became fully confirmed by the late 1970s. It was marked by a reorientation of priorities in development policies, resulting in a rapid increase in food production (the green revolution); by the beginning of the 1980s India had even begun to export cereals. Considerable progress may be envisaged for the future, as several constraints are overcome: antiquated irrigation systems and machinery; the low use of chemical fertilizers (India uses 30 times less per hectare of arable land than Japan, where yields are three times higher); strictures imposed by the caste system (agricultural labour being forbidden to many populations) or religion (sacred cows); and so forth. The low level of agricultural productivity helps, in turn, to explain the country's low degree of industrialization.

The role of the demographic growth which began in the 1920s was not clear, at least at the outset. While certain statistics suggested a reduction in food supply per capita over the period to the 1950s, paradoxically in the same period food prices increased no faster than those of other goods and services. This puzzle disappeared in the post-war period: the acceleration of demographic growth was accompanied by an improvement in living standards, contrary to all prognostications. As Swamy writes (1974), 'If it had been announced in 1941 that the population would increase from 350 to 700 million there would have been ... intellectual alarm.' Once again, Indian society proved its capacity for overcoming dearth. This is a phenomenon which should not surprise the experts, for two reasons:

1. As a general rule, where technical progress has begun more than two centuries earlier, the portion of non-renewable resources (such as land) in the creation of wealth continually decreases, while, contrary to this, the substitutability of inputs necessary to production increases considerably, to the point of becoming almost total.

2. More specifically, the plain of the Indus, the Ganges, and the Brahmaputra, which crosses Pakistan, North India, and Bangladesh, comprises 40 million naturally fertile hectares. It is one of the largest, if not the largest, agricultural basins in the world and, according to certain estimates, its annual yield could be increased tenfold without excessive cost (Murdoch 1980).

Brazil, or the New Frontier

The case of Brazil is like a graphic inversion of India. Endowed with rich natural resources of land and minerals, historically linked to the West in virtue of its population, institutional heritage, and trade, Brazil until recently officially encouraged demographic expansion. From a number of angles, its development recalls that of the US, with still more remarkable results, given that in a little over a century, from 1872 to 1980, the population increased twelvefold from 10 to 120 million; at the same time, GDP per capita increased by a coefficient of at least 10 (10.6 for the period 1900/1902–80 alone; see Table 18.5).

Generally speaking, there is no doubt about the existence of a positive relation between demographic increase and economic expansion in the Brazilian case. In the first half of the twentieth century, with a much higher rate of population growth than other less developed countries, Brazil recorded annual average growth rates in GDP per capita of 2.1%, quite exceptional for that period of world economic history. Moreover, up to mid-1970s, when a period of rising debt and falling employment intervened, the government was frankly hostile to the idea that high population growth impeded economic development. The desire to populate its immense territory and to extend the size of its market and job supply, and above all strong nationalist sentiments, encouraged a policy of demographic growth. However, there is no point in searching for a statistical link between demographic and economic growth in the detail of subperiods, since the sporadic nature of economic activity, dictated by the flow of primary materials, the price of oil, the rate of exchange, etc. obviously depended little on the demographic trend—which was characterized simply by its considerable inertia.

TABLE 18.5. *Population and gross domestic product (GDP) per capita (at constant prices, 1970), Brazil, 1900–1980*

Years	GDP (millions of cruzeiros)	Population (millions)	GDP per inhabitant	Average annual rate of increase from one period to the next	
				Population	GDP per inhabitant
1900–1902	7.12	18.58	383	—	—
1910–1912	10.50	22.84	460	2.1	1.8
1920–1922	15.50	28.06	552	2.1	1.8
1930–1932	23.04	34.33	671	2.0	2.0
1940–1942	36.50	42.13	866	2.1	2.6
1945–1947	47.68	47.33	1,007	2.4	3.1
1950–1954	75.87	55.16	1,375	2.6	(5.3)
1955–1959	98.77	64.08	1,541	3.0	2.3
1960–1964	131.80	74.22	1,776	3.0	2.9
1965–1969	164.50	84.68	1,943	2.7	1.7
1970–1974	267.70	97.30	2,752	2.8	7.2
1975–1979	397.10	110.27	3,601	2.5	5.5
1980	481.00	118.61	4,055	2.5	4.0

Sources: Haddad 1974; UN *Yearbook of National Accounts Statistics*, from 1957, and *Monthly Statistical Bulletin* (Jan. 1983). OECD (1981), Bulletin no. 14.

Mexico: Post-War Demographic and Economic Boom

The point of departure for Mexico's economic development is generally placed around 1890, when there was a boom in tropical exports. In short, the massive drop in shipping costs linked producing countries to the international economy. But development was for a long time hesitant and precarious, owing to the influence of the international climate: in 1934, at the height of the depression, per capita income in Mexico was barely higher than its average at the beginning of the nineteenth century. But the Second World War brought about a real breakthrough, Western markets being deprived of their usual sources by the hostilities. This situation gave rise to a development unprecedented in the annals of economic demography: population increased through its natural growth alone at a rate which was close to the highest known maximum in human history (Kenya excepted); but while this growth maintained a peak of almost 3.5% per year for 20 years, the standard of living tripled.

In a nation constrained by its resources in land, water, and raw materials, but already possessed of well-established State institutions, this sort of boom is not just a product of chance. Agricultural and industrial production together

TABLE 18.6. *Population and gross domestic product (GDP) per capita (at constant prices, 1950), Mexico, 1895–1980*

Years	GDP (millions of pesos)	Population (millions)	GDP per inhabitant	Average annual variation from one period to the next	
				Population	GDP per inhabitant
1895–1899	7,350	13,022	564	—	—
1900–1904	8,980	13,955	642	1.4	2.6
1905–1909	10,645	14,745	722	1.1	2.4
1910	11,650	15,160	768	0.9	2.1
1921–1924	11,986	14,689	816	−0.3	0.5
1925–1929	15,884	15,821	1,004	1.5	4.2
1930–1934	15,502	17,134	905	1.6	−2.1
1935–1939	20,313	18,669	1,087	1.7	3.7
1940–1944	26,368	21,087	1,248	2.5	2.8
1945–1949	33,883	24,242	1,396	2.8	2.3
1950–1954	45,541	27,895	1,634	2.7	3.2
1955–1959	62,695	32,656	1,917	3.2	3.3
1960–1964	82,490	38,596	2,134	3.4	2.2
1965–1969	118,064	45,744	2,581	3.5	3.9
1970–1974	163,334	54,279	3,009	3.5	3.1
1975–1979	218,937	63,912	3,426	3.3	2.6
1980	272,048	61,350	3,923	2.8	4.6

Sources: Perez-Lopez (1960: 587–89); UN *Yearbook of National Accounts Statistics*, from 1957, and *Monthly Statistical Bulletin* (Jan. 1983).

made enormous progress. The increase in agricultural production was related to a combination of factors: agrarian reform; price regulation; the introduction of new seed cultures and the use of chemical fertilizers (with the help of the Rockefeller Foundation); and, finally, an extension of the irrigation network and total surface area under cultivation, reflecting the pressure of increasing numbers. Industrial production benefited from the existence of oil reserves and the extension of the domestic market, which, in the course of agricultural development and urbanization, gave rise to an ample supply of cheap labour. Thus, population and development worked reciprocally.

Egypt: A Late Start

Egypt is a special case, entirely opposed on grounds of space and resources to Brazil and Mexico. It is a country of over 50 million inhabitants whose existence depends on the narrow alluvial strip of cultivated land which borders

TABLE 18.7. *Population and gross domestic product (GDP) per capita (at constant prices, 1970), Egypt, 1895–1980* (Egyptian pounds at 1975 value)

Years	GDP (millions of Egyptian pounds)	Population (millions)	GDP per inhabitant	Average annual variation from one period to the next	
				Population	GDP per inhabitant
1895–1899	761	9.69	78.5	—	—
1945–1949	1,335	19.00	70.3	1.4	−0.2
1950–1954	1,722	21.34	80.7	2.4	2.8
1955–1959	2,057	23.97	85.8	2.4	1.2
1960–1964	2,799	27.30	102.3	2.6	3.6
1965–1969	3,449	30.85	111.8	2.5	1.8
1970–1974	4,253	34.76	122.4	2.4	1.8
1975–1979	6,205	38.89	159.5	2.3	5.4
1980	8,108	42.29	191.7	2.8	6.3

Sources: Central Agency for Public Mobilisation and Statistics (1978: 243, 271); UN *Yearbook of National Accounts Statistics*, recent years, and *Monthly Statistical Bulletin* (Jan. 1983); OECD Development centre (1981), Bulletin no. 11.

the Nile. This strip has a density of over 1,000 inhabitants per km^2, but none the less yields over a quarter of the country's agricultural product. Land is scarce, but fertile. Agricultural development has had some difficulty in keeping up with population: between 1950–54 and 1970–74, cereal production per capita only increased by 7.5%. On the other hand, vast industrial progress has been made since the 1950s, brought about by the rise in exports: the portion of total product (GDP) derived from industry rose from 12.9% in 1954 to 26.8% in 1973 and 40.4% in 1979. Overall, despite accelerated demographic growth, average per capita income has risen considerably since 1950, increasing by more than 150%, after an initial phase of stagnation—or slight recession—during the first half of the century. In that earlier period, forced attempts at industrialization gave rise to a series of false starts. The balance between population and subsistence, however, looks precarious in the long term, given the lack of control over demographic growth; Egypt may be one of the first countries to run up against physical limits to growth (a risk of excessive urbanization).

Progress in agricultural productivity, although slow, is in itself already a great achievement, given that it has coincided with a doubling of the population since 1950. This accomplishment is doubtless closely connected to the conjunction of a number of positive policies, notably property reform (1952) and provision of agricultural credits and financial aid to the poorest peasants.

Similarly, efforts towards raising education standards have been remarkable: in 1937 only 15% of the population over 10 years of age could read and write (6% among women); this figure had risen to 42% by 1976 (29% among women). The importance of the role played by skilled Egyptian labour in the development of other Middle Eastern countries is a well-known fact, and this role has likewise assisted in the economic equilibrium in Egypt itself.

Conclusion

Several general observations arise from this comparative examination of long-term trends in real GDP per capita:

1. While remembering our caveat that the four countries studied are only individual cases, attention may be drawn to the considerable demographic weight of these countries, and the fact that in them international migration has generally been of marginal importance. This means that economic development is more closely connected with the characteristics peculiar to each national demographic transition. If we had, instead, examined relations between demographic and economic growth in smaller countries more subject to external influences, the results could only have had a very relative significance.

2. Beyond the shared fact of growth in real per capita income, there are clear differences in each country's experience of demographic and economic development: the broad types of demographic transition shared by India and Egypt, for example, are associated with very different patterns of economic development, not so much in their rates of growth in average per capita income as in institutional solutions adopted. Such variability calls for subtlety and caution in any attempt at theorizing. There are no economic recipes: the diversity of cultural history, of economic systems, and of attitudes does not lend itself to system-building or to the linear frameworks so favoured in the West.

3. Both the standard of living already achieved in certain countries and the results of recent long-term studies show that the starting date for economic development for several less developed countries belongs to a much earlier period than is generally admitted. These countries, above all in Latin America (Argentina, Brazil, Chile, Colombia, and Mexico) and Asia (in South and South-East Asia: Indonesia, Malaysia, Sri Lanka, Thailand, etc.—but not China, or India), registered their first surge of growth in the second half of the nineteenth century, in conjunction with developments in the dominant economies of the time. Although often confined to the modern sector, developments in this period none the less laid the foundations for sustained future growth, even if this growth for the most part awaited the post-war period on account of the stagnation of world trade in the inter-war years. The foundation included the establishment of infrastructures (roads, railway, ports, etc.), services (schools, hospitals, banks, postal services, communi-

cations, etc.), and above all an emergent educated élite. Certain of the new
industrial countries of Asia, however, appear to have made their real start
only in the inter-war period; this was the case with Korea and Taiwan,
then under Japanese administration, where transportation networks were
greatly improved.

This often-overlooked historical dimension is actually determinant of
certain current trends, both demographic and economic; the explanation of
trends characteristic of land-locked countries is a case in point.

4. The pessimism which has surrounded rapid population growth and its
implications in poor countries has been excessive. Concentration on the most
visible aspects of the problem has led to a preference for highly deterministic
arithmetical and statistical approaches. Two examples are the effect of fertility
levels on the cost of educating future generations, and the effect of the
increase in numbers on average standards of living (considered at a given level
of total income, taken as unchanging). Such approaches have been pursued to
the detriment of more reflective and sustained analyses, such as monographic
treatment of possible interactions in the long term. Population growth, often
considerably higher than that projected in the 1950s, has required a very
costly phase of adjustment (in the job market, for example), but it has not yet
proved to be an insurmountable obstacle to economic development. The
economic achievements of the four countries examined here are impressive
enough, given the handicaps they started with: a colonial legacy of dis-
industrialization and political subjugation up to as recently as the 1950s and
1960s; low income levels; demographic growth at 1.5 to 2.5 times higher than
in Europe at the same stage of transition; a lack of unpopulated continents
to which to emigrate; and so forth. Whilst the first steps in demographic
transition have been completed and a pattern of slower demographic growth
more or less successfully established, the standard of living in these countries
has, at a minimum, tripled.

5. Such a pattern of development is utterly contrary to the general run of
forecasts, necessitating a revision of long-accepted doctrines. The classic
demographic issue has long been described as a race between two rates of
growth. However, such a view hinders understanding, since population growth
and economic development not only share common structural origins, they
may interact dynamically with each other. Thus, policies for the improvement
of agricultural techniques or the construction of drainage and irrigation
systems may remove obstacles not only to economic but to demographic
growth. The latter, in its turn, is a force sufficiently powerful to eliminate
various traditional resistances to technological change and innovation. In all
developed countries, industrial revolution and rapid population growth have
consistently been associated over the long term. This is the very essence of
the theory of demographic transition.

6. The literature of population economics reveals, at certain points, a
crucial gap in relation to works on economic history. The fundamental ques-

tion of agriculture is ignored, and two aspects essential to long-term economic growth, and closely connected with the demographic dynamic, are neglected: the establishment of infrastructures and the formation of human capital. Most existing indicators of development are indicators of results and not of means. The differences which exist in the stock of available useful knowledge— which represents the principal factor in the growth of per capita income (Schultz 1961; Kuznets 1975)—have yet to be the object of a single statistical evaluation. While there is an astonishing paucity of retrospective data on this issue, as is true of anything pertaining to basic infrastructures, our knowledge of less determinant aspects of the growth of societies has greatly increased. Finally, only crude measures exist with which to describe anything relating to the effectiveness of State intervention. New indicators, based, for example, on the functional orientation of budgetary expenditure in relation to demographic parameters, must be established.

Bibliography to Chapter 18

BAIROCH, P. (1979), 'Écarts internationaux des niveaux de vie avant la révolution industrielle', *Annales ESC* (Jan.–Feb.), 145–71.

—— (1981), 'The Main Trends in National Economic Disparities since the Industrial Revolution', in P. Bairoch and M. Lévy-Leboyer (eds.), *Disparities in Economic Development since the Industrial Revolution* (London), 3–17.

Banco de Mexico, SA; Departemento de Estudios Economicos (1969), 'Producto bruto interno y series basicas, 1895–1967', mimeo, Mexico, 82.

BERGÈRE, M. C. (1981), 'Aux origines du sous-développement chinois', *Tiers-Monde*, 3 (Apr.–June), 467–76.

BINSWANGER, H. P., and RUTTAN, W. W., *Induced Innovation: Technology, Institutions and Development* (Baltimore, Md: Johns Hopkins University Press).

BOSERUP, E. (1970), *Women's Role in Economic Development* (London: Allen & Unwin).

—— (1981), *Population and Technology* (Oxford: Blackwell).

BUCK, J. L. (1937), *Land Utilization in China* (Nanking).

BURINGH, F. *et al.* (1975), *Computation of the Absolute Maximum Food Production of the World* (Wageningen).

Central Agency for Public Mobilisation and Statistics (1978), *Population and Development: A Study on the Population Increase and its Challenge to Development in Egypt* (Cairo: CAPMS).

CHERNIKOVSKY, D. (1978), 'Personal Savings and Family Size and Composition: The Unresolved Issue', in *Proceedings of the IUSSP Conference on Economic and Demographic Change: Perspectives for the Years 1980 Helsinki*, 345–59.

CLARK, C. (1971), *Population Growth and Land Use* (London: Macmillan).

DENISON, E. F. (1980), 'The Contribution of Capital to Economic Growth', *AER*, 70 (May), 220–24.

EBERSTADT, N. (1981), 'Hunger and Ideology', *Commentary* (July), 40–49.

ÉTIENNE, G. (1982), *Développement rural en Asie: Les Hommes, le grain et l'outil* (Paris: PUF).

FAO (1976), 'Population, Food Supply and Agricultural Development', in UN, *The Population Debate*, i (New York), 494–97.

—— (1977), *The Fourth World Food Survey*, Statistics Series, no. 11 (Rome).

GERSCHENKRON, A. (1962), *Economic Backwardness in Historical Perspective* (Cambridge, Mass.: Harvard University Press).

GILBERT, M., and KRAVIS, I. B. (1954), *An International Comparison of National Products and the Purchasing Power of Currencies: A Study of the US, the UK, France, Germany and Italy* (Paris: OECD).

GLOVER, D., and SIMON, J. L. (1975), 'The Effect of Population Density upon Infrastructure: The Case of Road-Building', *EDCC*, 23: 453–68.

HABBAKUK, J. (1963), 'Population Problems and European Economic Development in the Late Eighteenth and Nineteenth Centuries', *AER*, 53 (May), 607–18.

HADDAD, C. (1974), 'Crescimento do producto real Brasileiro 1900–1947', *Ensaios economicos da EPGE*, 14.

HAGEN, E. E. (1959), 'Population and Economic Growth', *AER*, 49 (June), 310–27.

HAYAMI, Y., and RUTTAN, V. W. (1971), *Agricultural Development: An International Perspective* (Baltimore, Md.: Johns Hopkins University Press).

HESTON, A. (1983), 'National Incomes', in *Cambridge Economic History of India* (Cambridge).

HICKS, J. R. (1936), 'Mr Keynes's Theory of Employment', *EJ* (June), 252.

International Railway Union (1972), *International Railway Statistics* (Paris).

International Road Federation (1974), *World Road Statistics* (Geneva).

ISSAWI, C. (1961), 'Egypt since 1800: A Study in Lop-Sided Development', *JEH* (Mar.), 1–25.

KELLEY, A. C. (1976), 'Saving, Demographic Change and Economic Development', *EDCC*, 24: 683–93.

KLATZMANN, J. (1981), 'Que sait-on de la situation alimentaire mondiale?', *JSSP*, 122(2), 91–98.

KUZNETS, S. (1949), 'National Income and Industrial Structure', *Econometrica*, 17 (July), suppl.

—— (1954), 'Underdeveloped Countries and the Preindustrial Phase in the Advanced Countries', in *Proceedings of the World Population Conference, Rome, 1954*.

—— (1960), 'Population Change and Aggregate Output', in *Demographic and Economic Change in Developed Countries* (Princeton, NJ: Princeton University Press).

—— (1965), 'Demographic Aspects of Modern Economic Growth', Paper presented at the *World Population Conference, Belgrade, Sept. 1964*.

—— (1966), *Modern Economic Growth* (New Haven, Conn.: Yale University Press).

—— (1971), *Economic Growth of Nations* (Cambridge, Mass.: Harvard University Press).

—— (1975), 'Population Trends and Modern Economic Growth: Notes towards an Historical Perspective', in *UN, The Population Debate: Dimensions and Perspectives, World Population Conference, Bucharest, 1974*, i (New York: UN).

—— MOORE, W. E., and SPENGLER, J. J. (eds.) (1955), *Economic Growth: Brazil, India, Japan* (Durham, NC: Duke University Press).

LEFF, N. H. (1969), 'Dependency Rates and Saving Rates', *AER*, 59 (Dec.), 886–96.

LEIBENSTEIN, H. (1975), 'Population Growth and Savings', in L. Tabah (ed.), *Population Growth and Economic Development in the Third World* (Paris: Ordina, IUSSP).

LEWIS, W. A. (1970), *Aspects of Tropical Trade 1863–1965*, Wicksell Lectures 1969 (Stockholm: Almqvist).

MCCLELLAND, D. C. (1966), 'Does Education Accelerate Economic Growth?', *EDCC*, 14 (Apr.), 257–78.

MALENBAUM, W. (1982), 'Modern Economic Growth in India and China: The Comparison Revisited, 1950–1980', *EDCC*, 31 (Oct.), 45–84.

MERRICK, T. W., and GRAHAM, D. H. (1979), *Population and Economic Development in Brazil: 1800 to the Present* (Baltimore, Md.: Johns Hopkins University Press).

MESAROVIC, M., and PESTEL, E. (1974), *Stratégie pour demain: Deuxième rapport au Club de Rome* (trans. from English; Paris: Seuil).

MUKHERJEE, M. (1965), 'A Preliminary Study of the Growth of National Income in India 1857–1957', *Asian Studies in Income and Wealth* (New York), 71–103.

MURDOCH, W. W. (1980), *The Poverty of Nations: The Political Economy of Hunger and Population* (Baltimore, Md.: Johns Hopkins University Press).

National Research Council (1977), *Supporting Papers: World Food and Nutrition Study*, ii, Study Team 4, *Resources for Agriculture* (Washington, DC: National Academy of Sciences).

NELSON, R. R. (1956), 'A Theory of the Low-Level Equilibrium Trap', *AER*, 46 (Dec.), 894–908.

OECD Development Centre (1968–), *Comptes nationaux des pays moins développés* (Paris).

—— (1981), *Informations récentes sur les comptes nationaux des pays en développement*, Bulletin nos. 11, 14 (Oct.) (Paris: OECD).

OLUWASEANMI, H. A. (1976), 'Socio-economic Aspects of Feeding People', in *Proceedings of the World Conference of 1976*, 96–97.

PAGLIN, M. (1965), 'Surplus Agricultural Labor and Development: Facts and Theories', *AER*, 55 (Sept.), 815–34.

PATEL, S. J. (1961), 'Rates of Industrial Growth in the Last Century, 1860–1958', *EDCC*, 9(3) (Apr.).

—— (1964), 'The Economic Distance between Nations: Its Origin, Measurement and Outlook', *EJ* (Mar.), 122–29.

PEREZ-LOPEZ, E. (1960), 'El producto national', in *50 Años de revolucion*, i (Mexico: Fondo de Cultura Economica).

Population and Development: A Study on the Population Increase and its Challenge to Development in Egypt (1973: 243, 1978: 271) (Cairo).

REVELLE, R. (ed.) (1971), *Rapid Population Growth: Consequences and Policy Implications* (Baltimore, Md.: Johns Hopkins University Press).

REYNOLDS, L. G. (1980), 'Economic Development in Historical Perspective', *AER*, 70 (May), 91–95.

SCHULTZ, R. (1961), 'Investment in Human Capital', *AER*, 51 (Mar.), 1–17.

SIMON, J. L. (1975), 'The Positive Effect of Population on Agricultural Savings in Irrigation Systems', *RES*, 57: 71–79.

SINHA, J. H. (1975), 'Population and Agriculture', in L. Tabah (ed.), *Population and Economic Growth in the Third World* (Paris: IUSSP), i. 251–305.

SPENGLER, J. J. (1966), 'The Economist and the Population Question', *AER*, 56(1), 9.

SWAMY, S. (1973), 'Economic Growth in China and India, 1952–1970: A Comparative Appraisal', *EDCC*, 21 (July).

—— (1974), 'Population Growth and Economic Development', in *Population in India's development* (Delhi: IASP), 211–15.

World Bank (1979), *Report on World Development, 1979* (Washington, DC).

General Conclusion

Women: soap bubbles; money: soap bubbles. The reflections in the bubbles are the world we live in.

(Mishima)

A certain number of provident husbands constitutes a nation without concern for the future.

(Valéry)

THE analysis of long time series in international perspective makes it possible to place national history in a world context. But in the twentieth century, with the abolition of distances, everything that touches upon changes in human life has become not only increasingly international, but a-national. The same applies to modern population history: the nature of demographic upheavals has evolved in an almost identical manner from country to country.

The Virtues of the Original Theory of Demographic Transition

As a descriptive account of the successive stages which lead from an early regime of high mortality and high fertility to a regime of low mortality and low fertility, the original theory of demographic transition has universal relevance. However, as already seen, similarity of trajectory does not preclude diversity of rates: the hierarchy of multipliers associated with the different types of transition is the statistical translation of this fact.

The theory is equally valid as an explanatory framework. There is a close relation between fertility and socio-economic development: at a given date the stage of development and degree to which the transition has advanced are, at an international level, clearly associated. Similarly, for a given country, the structural path followed by modern economic growth is accompanied by progressive declines in fertility. Improvements in living standards, bringing in train better nutrition and health conditions, may, via diverse mechanisms such as the longer survival of couples, higher fecundability, and lower fetal mortality, tend in the short term to promote fertility increase. This phenomenon is equally observable in Latin American and Africa, as in Europe. But this is only temporary. And durable growth in real income results, over the long term, in a decline in fertility.

But transition theory is ultimately concerned only with fertility. It ignores the role of international migration and neglects specific effects of mortality decline, not only on the long-term decline of fertility itself, but also on other aspects of development. As high mortality receded, the insurance effect connected with the need to replace children dying in infancy diminished; where the size of households increased, and structures and institutions remained unchanged, economic tension then called for adjustment. If the theory does present an undeniable robustness, it is only as a theory of fertility. There are few theories without significant exceptions; but in the present instance, cases where fertility declined in the context of relative under-development are extremely rare. France, Bulgaria, and Sri Lanka are the ones usually cited in the specialist literature. The theoretical strength of transition theory is doubtless a function of the fact that its original formulation rests on an empirical generalization (that of European experience): in other words, it was based from the beginning on duly tested postulates.

Even though recent developments have added to its value, the theory still seems devoid of any true predictive capacity. There have, of course, been modifications (still provisional where less developed countries are concerned), but a considerable diversity of observations remains because national trajectories are connected with fundamental differences of culture, regional characteristics, and long-term strategies of development. As we have seen, the process of development itself entails many components which behave differently depending on the country and period.

Peaks of Population and Civilization

If we now consider demographic transition as a fact of history, attending to its implications rather than its derivation, two weighty considerations must be taken into account: the time lags between countries, and the differences between their multipliers. The transition was accompanied by a considerable redistribution of populations to the advantage of certain countries in certain periods, but later to their detriment, with all the ensuing consequences.

First affected were western Europe and the United States, then gradually eastern Europe, Russia, Japan, and so forth. The world map of political and economic dominion was redraughted by these demographic upheavals; in a sense, a succession of imperialisms is inscribed in the history of demographic transition. The high point of civilizations has tended to coincide with peaks in population.

Eighteenth-century France may be taken as the starting-point of this process. Its demographic weight was at that time the heaviest Europe had ever known, and it dominated the old continent politically and intellectually. Louis XIV acted as treasurer to sovereigns in a state of need. France gave rise to the philosophy of the Enlightenment and inaugurated modern democracy. Napoleon I invaded Europe. And, of course, France led the way in fertility regulation, but in so doing committed itself to a period of demographic stagnation at precisely the time when most of its powerful rivals began rapid demographic growth.

England then took the lead, with an incomparable demographic expansion in the nineteenth century related to its comparatively low mortality level. Despite its small territory, the country gradually came to dominate entire continents. England on the eve of the First World War could claim to be the mistress of the world. It had become the universal banker, the first and by far the largest foreign investor, and the source of millions of colonists in the New World. Germany's period of influence came later, after its unification, but its rate of demographic and economic modernization was very rapid. This rise to power led to dreams of empire and the ensuing catastrophe. After Germany came the 'peri-European' imperialisms of North America and Russia, the demographic wave always moving on to sweep over other countries, like Japan and Brazil, which would emerge as powers in their own sphere of influence. At the same time, centres of much earlier civilizations long displaced by the technological domination of the West have begun to reassert their world importance: China, India, and the Maghreb.

Thus, European demographic growth came to be bound up in the history of colonial expansion. By the time of its culmination in the nineteenth century, the continents of America and Australia had been occupied, Siberia colonized, as also the main parts of Asia and Africa. In 1914, almost all of Africa and America, and much of Asia, Australia, and the Pacific Islands, were in the hands of Europeans or their descendants. The world belonged to the white man. The assassination at Sarajevo gave the signal for decline: war broke out, and from then on Europe's influence was replaced by that of the United States and Russia. Doubt emerged, self-confidence waned, and a sense of guilt gradually invaded people's minds. This, too, was accelerated by the ineluctable movement, the displacement of equilibriums, dictated by the course of demographic transition. The result was decolonization. In the 15 years following the Second World War, most of the dominated countries attained their independence; by the hundreds and thousands, colonial administrators returned to Europe.

Historical Interdependence

The era of European supremacy which began with Vasco da Gama in the end lasted only a few centuries, but it left a deep imprint on the history of most of the world. This was the great era of foreign investment. Two-thirds of these investments were in public services, particularly the infrastructure of canals, communications, roads, railways, ports, and the like. By virtue of the technological transfer they brought with them, they would play a major role in laying the foundations for demographic transition in many less developed countries. Even if the relative volume of these investments declined from the 1920s onwards, their structure, which laid greater stress on education, public works, health, and agriculture, contributed to the decline in mortality.

There is thus a close interdependence between the history of European transition and that of other continents. Intercontinental migration first led to the export of tens of millions of men; but from the 1930s onwards, Europe became a land of immigration, experiencing return migration from America in consequence of the Great Depression. The interdependence of transitions may also be traced to the movement of capital and technology, which influenced trends in natural increase. In the earlier stages of this history, such transfers served above all to accelerate demographic growth—although, as we have seen, economic growth proceeded at an even faster rate. In the later, contemporary period, the transfers have tended rather to have the opposite effect; and massive international aid, in the form of family planning, has also served to reinforce the effects of the modernization of economic structures.

The degree to which demographic transition has progressed in poor countries thus depends not only on their own historical heritage, but on their colonial legacy, their inclusion in networks of international aid, and, more generally, the circuitry of foreign trade. These factors are unlikely to be independent of each other. The countries in which secular fertility declines have not occurred are by now a select group, characterized by little contact with the outside world and intense poverty; it cannot be excluded that, in the future, demographic transition will occur for these cases, at least according to specific modalities. Even if, with the aid of experience, family planning programmes can be better integrated into world-wide planning policy, and so prove (theoretically at least) more effective than in the past, there are many matters to be resolved. In addition to the characteristics of these countries there are, for instance, factors such as the slowing down of world economic growth: the better part of the less developed countries with advanced transition have seen their fertility decline at precisely the moment most opportune for a period of expansion. Another issue is the present accentuation of the technological gap between rich and poor countries; if this has the effect of inhibiting demographic change in the most underprivileged areas, it would thereby exacerbate existing disequilibriums and delay the secular convergence of demographic development. Recent trends in the world economy, since 1986, together with the growing concentration of efforts by specialist development agencies such as the World Bank on less developed countries in Black Africa, suggest that such pessimism deserves to be tempered.

Appendix 1.   Crude Birth-Rates

TABLE A1.1. *Crude birth-rates, Europe, 1735–1799*

Year	England and Wales	Finland	France	Norway	Sweden
1735				29.4	—
1736				30.7	29.8
1737	} 35.5			30.5	30.5
1738				28.1	33.6
1739				30.9	36.4
1740			39.5	29.6	32.0
1741			40.3	27.1	31.9
1742	} 32.9		37.8	26.3	31.5
1743			40.6	28.5	30.1
1744			41.5	30.1	35.1
1745			41.0	32.8	36.9
1746			40.5	28.2	34.8
1747	} 33.5		38.6	33.0	34.6
1748			37.4	32.9	33.5
1749			39.6	33.0	33.8
1750			39.0	30.6	36.4
1751		44.3	39.7	35.0	38.7
1752		44.7	39.0	33.5	35.9
1753	} 33.8	44.1	40.4	34.8	36.1
1754		46.4	40.7	35.3	37.2
1755		46.9	40.6	33.5	37.5

Year	Czech countries	England and Wales	Finland	France	Norway	Sweden
1770			40.9	37.8	32.1	33.0
1771			38.0	36.5	31.6	32.2
1772		} 35.9	37.6	36.8	28.2	28.9
1773			37.9	36.8	25.0	25.5
1774			40.3	37.8	28.3	34.5
1775			40.4	37.8	33.8	35.6
1776			39.0	37.3	28.8	32.9
1777		} 36.3	40.1	39.5	31.3	33.0
1778			42.7	36.3	31.2	34.8
1779			43.2	37.3	31.5	36.7
1780			41.2	38.2	32.4	35.7
1781			37.7	38.1	31.4	33.5
1782		} 35.6	41.7	37.8	30.9	32.1
1783			40.0	37.2	27.6	30.3
1784			42.7	37.6	30.5	31.5
1785			39.8	38.9	28.9	31.4
1786			39.9	39.8	30.6	32.9
1787	} 44.2	} 37.6	40.4	39.2	29.2	31.5
1788			36.1	38.7	30.7	33.9
1789			34.2	37.5	30.6	32.0

Year					Group avg
1756	45.8	43.1	36.1	36.1	
1757	43.3	40.4	34.5	32.6	32.8
1758	42.3	40.4	33.6	33.4	
1759	44.5	39.9	32.3	33.6	
1760	46.6	39.2	35.0	35.7	
1761	45.8	40.7	35.9	34.8	33.9
1762	41.3	38.2	35.8	35.1	
1763	43.0	38.7	34.5	35.0	
1764	45.7	38.6	35.8	34.7	
1765	42.9	39.9	34.5	33.4	
1766	41.5	39.0	34.0	33.8	34.3
1767	40.7	39.5	35.1	35.4	
1768	42.9	37.4	32.8	33.6	
1769	42.4	39.8	33.7	33.1	

Year					Group avg
1790	37.0	37.4	32.0	30.5	
1791	36.0	35.9	32.7	32.6	
1792	42.2	36.7	34.7	36.6	43.6
1793	43.8	36.2	34.1	34.4	39.1
1794	41.4	38.3	33.7	33.8	
1795	42.1	36.7	32.3	32.0	
1796	39.7	35.8	31.5	34.7	43.1
1797	41.2	37.7	32.7	34.8	38.7
1798	38.6	37.2	32.3	33.7	
1799	38.7	36.3	32.5	32.0	

TABLE A1.2. *Crude birth-rates, Europe, 1800–1849*

Year	Austria	Belgium	Czech countries	Denmark	England and Wales	Finland	France	Germany	Netherlands	Norway	Sweden
1800				29.9		37.6	34.4			—	28.7
1801				31.1		39.6	32.9			22.7	30.0
1802			42.7	32.2		39.2	32.9			27.6	31.7
1803				33.1	37.7	35.6	32.2			28.9	31.4
1804				32.2		39.1	31.7			27.7	31.9
1805				32.8		38.4	33.0			29.2	31.7
1806			42.1	30.2		35.7	31.8			29.6	30.8
1807				31.0		36.2	31.9			29.0	31.2
1808				30.6		30.4	32.4			26.9	30.4
1809				29.3	40.5	28.6	32.7			22.2	26.7
1810				30.3		40.5	32.0			26.3	33.0
1811				30.5		36.4	32.0			26.7	35.3
1812			43.4	29.8		38.9	30.7			29.1	33.6
1813				29.1		35.6	32.7			25.6	29.7
1814				30.4	39.5	36.7	35.1			24.2	31.2
1815				34.1		37.5	33.4			29.9	34.8
1816				32.9		38.8	34.3			35.1	35.3
1817			43.2	32.8		39.0	31.9	39.5		32.5	33.4
1818				32.1		38.4	31.2	39.5		30.8	33.8
1819				32.5	41.9	36.1	33.4	41.5		31.9	33.0

Note: columns B and E consist of quinquennial averages shown with a brace spanning five years; the value is placed at the central year of its group.

Year	A	B	C	D	E	F	G	H	I	J	K	L
1820	43.0			31.5			36.6	32.4	39.9		33.3	33.0
1821	41.4			32.1			41.4	31.8	40.8		34.7	35.4
1822	38.5	42.1		33.7	40.8		35.6	32.1	39.8		32.9	35.9
1823	39.6			32.6			40.3	31.2	38.8		33.9	36.8
1824	40.1			31.3			37.8	31.9	38.6		32.5	34.6
1825	40.3			31.3			38.5	31.3	39.1		34.3	36.5
1826	39.6			31.4			37.6	31.8	38.9		34.8	34.8
1827	38.6	39.6		29.2	38.9		36.7	31.0	36.1		32.0	31.3
1828	37.6			30.3			39.3	30.6	36.1		31.8	33.6
1829	36.1			29.6			38.7	30.3	35.3		33.6	34.9
1830	38.0		32.3	28.9			36.6	30.2	35.5		32.3	32.9
1831	35.6		33.0	29.7			35.2	30.6	35.0		31.0	30.5
1832	36.6	38.9	31.5	27.0	35.7		34.5	28.9	34.1		29.9	30.9
1833	40.4		33.2	32.2			30.2	29.9	36.7		30.7	34.1
1834	39.3		33.3	33.0			36.6	30.2	37.6		31.7	33.7
1835	38.5		34.0	31.7			34.3	30.2	36.4		32.6	32.7
1836	37.8		34.0	30.5			31.1	29.6	36.7		29.4	31.8
1837	39.7	38.1	33.4	30.0	35.6		31.6	28.3	36.3		28.7	30.8
1838	37.9		35.2	29.8		30.3	31.8	28.8	36.3		27.7	29.4
1839	38.0		33.7	29.0		31.8	33.7	28.5	36.4		26.7	29.5
1840	38.6		34.2	30.4		32.0	34.7	27.9	36.4	35.0	27.8	31.4
1841	38.3		34.0	29.7		32.2	34.0	28.5	36.4	35.5	29.8	30.3
1842	41.2	38.8	32.6	30.1	35.9	32.1	37.2	28.5	37.6	34.2	30.7	31.7
1843	39.3		31.9	29.8		32.3	35.8	28.2	36.0	33.8	30.2	30.8
1844	39.7		31.8	30.3		32.7	35.0	27.5	35.9	34.4	29.9	32.2
1845	39.5		32.2	30.6		32.5	35.7	27.9	37.3	34.2	31.2	31.5
1846	37.0		27.8	30.1		33.8	33.2	27.3	36.0	31.4	31.1	29.9
1847	36.0	37.4	27.2	30.6	34.9	31.5	33.9	25.4	33.3	28.6	30.8	29.6
1848	32.7		27.7	30.6		32.5	36.5	26.5	33.3	30.1	29.8	30.3
1849	40.0		31.0	31.0		32.9	37.5	27.7	38.1	34.2	32.0	32.8

TABLE A1.3. *Crude birth-rates, Europe, 1850–1899*

Year	Austria	Belgium	Bulgaria	Denmark	England and Wales	Finland	France	Germany	Greece	Hungary	Scotland	Spain
1850	39.6	30.0		31.4	33.4	35.7	26.8	37.2				
1851	39.2	30.3		30.1	34.3	38.2	27.1	36.7				
1852	37.5	30.0		33.2	34.3	35.0	26.8	35.5				
1853	37.2	28.3		31.6	33.3	35.1	26.0	34.6				
1854	36.3	28.8		32.7	34.1	37.5	25.5	34.0				
1855	32.2	27.7		31.9	33.8	35.8	25.0	32.2			31.3	
1856	35.6	29.1		32.4	34.5	36.3	26.3	33.5			34.0	
1857	39.4	31.6		32.9	34.4	32.8	25.9	36.0			34.3	
1858	39.8	31.7		33.2	33.7	36.5	26.7	36.5			34.4	35.2
1859	40.7	32.4		33.6	35.0	35.8	27.9	37.5			35.0	38.4
1860	38.2	31.0		32.6	34.3	36.4	26.2	36.4	28.4	—	35.6	36.7
1861	37.4	31.1		31.6	34.6	37.8	26.9	35.7	29.5	39.7	34.9	39.0
1862	38.1	30.4		30.8	35.0	37.3	26.5	35.4	—	41.8	34.6	38.5
1863	40.6	32.2		30.9	35.3	36.2	26.9	37.5	—	44.3	35.0	37.8
1864	40.6	32.1		30.1	35.4	39.3	26.6	37.8	28.2	41.2	35.6	39.2
1865	38.0	31.6		31.1	35.4	34.2	26.5	37.6	29.4	41.8	35.5	38.6
1866	37.9	31.7		32.0	35.2	32.0	26.4	37.8	27.8	41.1	35.4	38.3
1867	36.8	32.6		30.3	35.4	32.3	26.2	36.8	30.1	38.0	35.1	38.5
1868	38.1	31.9		31.0	35.8	24.6	25.7	36.8	28.6	41.7	35.3	35.7
1869	39.6	32.0		29.3	34.8	33.7	26.0	37.8	28.8	41.9	34.3	37.0

Year												
1870	39.8	32.7		30.3	35.2	36.3	25.9	38.5	28.1	42.1	34.6	36.6
1871	38.7	31.2	—	30.1	35.0	37.3	22.9	34.5	28.4	42.8	34.5	—
1872	38.9	32.7	—	30.3	35.6	36.4	26.7	39.4	28.6	40.6	34.9	—
1873	39.6	33.0	—	30.8	35.4	37.0	26.0	39.7	27.6	42.4	34.8	—
1874	39.6	33.1	—	30.9	36.0	37.9	26.2	40.1	29.2	42.8	35.6	—
1875	39.8	32.9	—	31.9	35.4	36.6	25.9	40.6	28.2	45.4	35.2	—
1876	40.0	32.7	—	32.6	36.3	36.7	26.2	40.9	29.6	45.9	35.6	—
1877	38.5	32.8	—	32.3	36.0	38.2	25.5	40.6	28.5	43.3	35.3	—
1878	38.4	31.9	—	31.6	35.6	35.4	25.2	38.9	27.2	42.8	34.9	36.1
1879	39.1	31.9	—	31.9	34.7	37.8	25.1	38.9	24.8	45.7	34.3	35.8
1880	37.5	31.0		31.7	34.2	36.5	24.6	37.6	24.4	42.8	33.6	35.5
1881	37.5	31.8	33.7	32.2	33.9	35.0	24.9	37.0	24.5	43.2	33.7	37.1
1882	39.0	31.6	36.7	32.3	33.8	36.3	24.8	37.2	25.2	44.2	33.5	36.2
1883	38.1	30.9	38.5	31.8	33.5	35.9	24.8	36.6	25.0	45.0	32.8	35.6
1884	38.6	30.9	38.5	33.3	33.6	36.1	24.7	37.2	28.6	45.8	33.7	36.7
1885	37.5	30.3	37.6	32.5	32.9	34.2	24.3	37.0	28.5	44.9	32.7	36.3
1886	37.9	29.9	32.6	32.4	32.8	35.3	23.9	37.1	—	45.6	32.9	36.7
1887	38.2	29.7	38.4	31.7	31.9	36.2	23.5	36.9	—	44.3	31.8	36.1
1888	37.8	29.4	37.7	31.5	31.2	34.9	23.1	36.6	—	43.9	31.3	36.4
1889	37.8	29.4	36.7	31.2	31.1	33.4	23.0	36.4	34.1	43.8	30.9	36.4
1890	36.2	29.0	35.1	30.5	30.2	32.9	21.8	35.7	35.3	40.4	30.4	34.4
1891	38.2	30.0	39.1	31.0	31.4	34.3	22.6	37.0	—	42.6	31.2	35.3
1892	36.0	28.9	36.0	29.6	30.4	31.6	22.3	35.7	—	40.6	30.7	35.8
1893	37.9	29.5	35.0	30.8	30.7	30.1	22.6	36.8	—	43.0	30.8	35.6
1894	36.6	29.0	38.0	30.4	29.6	31.1	22.3	35.9	—	41.6	29.9	34.8
1895	37.9	28.5	40.7	30.3	30.3	32.9	21.7	36.1	—	41.8	30.0	35.0
1896	37.8	29.0	41.4	30.5	29.6	32.5	22.5	36.3	—	40.7	30.4	35.9
1897	37.2	29.0	42.5	29.8	29.6	32.3	22.2	36.0	—	40.5	30.0	34.1
1898	36.0	28.6	39.4	30.2	29.3	34.4	21.7	36.1	—	37.8	30.1	33.3
1899	36.8	28.8	40.7	29.7	29.1	33.7	21.8	35.8	—	39.2	29.8	34.2

TABLE A1.4. *Crude birth-rates, Europe and Japan, 1850–1899*

Year	Czech countries	Ireland	Italy	Netherlands	Norway	Portugal	Romania	Russia	Serbia	Sweden	Switzerland	Japan
1850				34.6	31.0					31.9		
1851				35.1	31.9					31.7		
1852	39.7			35.5	31.0					30.7		
1853				33.2	32.0					31.4		
1854				32.8	34.3					33.5		
1855				32.1	33.4					31.8		
1856				32.8	32.2					31.5		
1857	37.6			34.7	33.0					32.4		
1858				32.4	33.5					34.8		
1859				34.9	34.8		29.6			35.0		
1860				31.6	33.3		31.6	49.7		34.8		
1861				35.1	30.7		32.0	51.1		32.6		
1862	38.0		38.0	33.0	32.1		32.0	50.0	40.5	33.4		
1863			39.4	36.1	32.7		30.4	52.9	43.0	33.6		
1864		24.2	38.0	35.4	31.9		36.0	50.0	45.1	33.6		
1865		25.9	38.5	35.9	31.9		34.6	—	46.7	32.8		
1866		26.5	38.9	35.1	31.7		31.3	51.2	45.7	33.1		
1867	38.1	26.3	36.6	35.2	30.1		31.7	48.8	44.8	30.8		
1868		26.7	35.4	34.7	29.5		33.4	49.7	45.7	27.5		
1869		26.7	37.2	34.4	28.9		34.0		45.2	28.3		

Year	Group mean											
1870	39.7	27.7	36.8	35.8	29.2		34.4	49.2	44.8	28.8	29.8	
1871		28.1	37.0	35.2	29.3		33.5	51.0	43.2	30.4	29.0	
1872		27.8	38.0	35.8	30.0		32.0	50.0	39.1	30.0	29.8	
1873		27.1	36.4	36.1	29.9		32.5	52.3	42.4	30.8	29.7	
1874		26.6	35.0	36.2	31.0		34.3	51.4	41.7	30.9	30.4	25.3
1875	38.4	26.1	37.8	36.4	31.5		38.8	51.5	45.8	31.2	31.8	26.1
1876		26.4	39.3	37.1	31.6		37.0	50.6	41.6	30.8	32.8	25.5
1877		26.2	37.1	36.6	31.7		35.4	49.6	33.3	31.1	32.0	24.5
1878		25.1	36.3	36.1	31.5		31.5	47.3	38.1	29.8	31.3	24.4
1879		25.2	37.9	36.6	32.1		37.1	50.2	39.4	30.5	30.5	24.3
1880	37.6	24.7	33.9	35.6	30.9		37.7	49.7	40.7	29.4	29.6	25.6
1881		24.5	38.1	35.0	30.0		41.5	49.1	45.7	29.1	29.8	24.9
1882		24.0	37.2	35.3	30.6		40.4	51.6	44.4	29.4	28.9	26.8
1883		23.5	37.2	34.3	31.0		42.8	50.6	47.0	28.9	28.5	25.8
1884		23.9	39.0	34.9	31.6		41.4	51.5	47.6	30.0	28.3	26.9
1885		23.5	38.6	34.4	31.5	31.9	43.1	50.0	46.6	29.4	27.7	27.3
1886	37.0	23.2	37.0	34.6	30.9	33.7	42.2	49.0	42.0	29.8	27.8	27.1
1887		23.1	38.9	33.7	31.4	33.1	41.0	49.5	46.3	29.7	27.9	29.6
1888		22.8	37.5	33.7	30.4	33.7	42.4	49.9	45.7	28.8	27.7	30.2
1889		22.7	38.3	33.4	29.6	33.7	40.6	51.6	44.1	27.7	27.7	28.3
1890	35.8	22.3	35.8	32.9	30.4	32.6	38.5	50.3	40.3	28.0	26.6	26.7
1891		23.1	37.2	33.7	30.8	32.0	42.3	50.6	45.0	28.3	28.2	29.4
1892		22.5	36.2	32.0	29.6	31.2	39.0	46.0	42.4	27.0	27.7	28.5
1893		23.0	36.5	33.8	30.3	31.9	40.5	48.8	42.5	27.4	27.9	28.9
1894		22.9	35.5	32.5	29.6	29.7	40.9	49.2	42.5	27.1	27.3	29.5
1895	35.8	23.3	34.9	32.8	30.4	30.0	42.3	50.1	44.0	27.5	27.3	30.0
1896		23.7	34.8	32.7	30.0	30.0	40.7	50.4	41.2	27.2	28.1	30.9
1897		23.5	34.7	32.5	30.0	30.4	42.9	50.0	42.6	26.7	28.3	30.9
1898		23.3	33.5	31.9	30.3	30.2	36.7	48.6	35.1	27.1	28.5	31.3
1899		23.1	33.9	32.0	29.9	29.9	42.0	49.3	39.3	26.4	29.0	31.4

TABLE A1.5. *Crude birth-rates, Europe, 1900–1945*

Year	Albania	Austria	Belgium	Bulgaria	Czech countries (Czechoslovakia since 1919)	Denmark	England and Wales	Finland	France	Germany	Greece	Hungary
1900		35.0	28.9	42.3		29.7	28.7	32.6	21.3	35.6		39.4
1901		36.6	29.4	37.7		29.7	28.5	33.2	22.0	35.7		37.6
1902		37.0	28.4	39.1	34.6	29.2	28.5	32.4	21.6	35.1		38.6
1903		35.2	27.5	41.3		28.7	28.5	31.5	21.1	33.8		36.5
1904		35.6	27.1	42.8		28.9	28.0	33.0	20.9	34.1		37.0
1905		33.8	26.2	43.5		28.4	27.3	31.8	20.6	33.0		35.5
1906		35.0	25.6	43.7	31.5	28.5	27.2	32.8	20.5	33.1		36.1
1907		34.0	25.2	43.3		28.2	26.5	32.8	19.7	32.3		36.2
1908		33.7	24.8	40.3		28.6	26.7	32.2	20.1	32.1		36.7
1909		33.4	23.5	40.4		28.2	25.8	32.8	19.5	31.1		37.1
1910		32.5	23.7	41.4		27.5	25.1	31.7	19.6	29.8		35.4
1911		31.3	22.8	39.9		26.7	24.3	30.8	18.7	28.6		34.8
1912		31.3	22.5	41.7	27.8	26.6	23.9	30.8	18.9	28.3		36.0
1913		29.7	22.3	25.7		25.6	24.1	28.8	18.8	27.5		34.3
1914	—	20.4	45.1	—		25.6	23.8	28.7	18.1	26.8		34.5
1915	—	16.1	40.2			24.2	21.9	27.0	11.8	20.4		23.7
1916	—	12.9	21.3	14.2		24.4	20.9	25.7	9.5	15.2		16.8
1917	—	11.3	17.2			23.7	17.8	25.9	10.4	13.9		16.0
1918	14.1	11.3	21.2	—		24.1	17.7	25.4	12.1	14.3		15.3
1919	18.5	16.9	32.8	22.4		22.6	18.5	20.5	13.0	20.0		27.6
1920		22.7	22.2	39.9	26.7	25.4	25.5	27.0	21.4	25.9		31.4
1921		23.2	21.7	40.2	29.2	24.0	22.4	25.9	20.7	25.3	21.2	31.8
1922		23.1	20.4	40.5	28.2	22.2	20.4	25.0	19.3	23.0	21.5	30.8
1923		22.5	20.3	37.7	27.3	22.3	19.7	25.3	19.1	21.2	19.0	29.2
1924		21.7	19.8	39.8	25.8	21.8	18.8	23.8	18.7	20.6	19.5	26.9
1925		20.6	19.6	36.9	25.1	21.0	18.3	23.7	19.0	20.8	26.3	28.3
1926		19.3	18.9	37.4	24.6	20.5	17.8	23.0	18.8	19.6	30.0	27.4
1927		17.9	18.2	33.2	23.3	19.6	16.6	22.5	18.2	18.4	28.8	25.8
1928		17.6	18.2	33.1	23.3	19.6	16.7	22.8	18.3	18.6	30.5	26.4
1929		16.8	18.1	30.6	22.4	18.6	16.3	22.2	17.7	18.0	28.9	25.1
1930		16.8	18.6	31.4	22.7	18.7	16.3	21.8	18.0	17.6	31.3	25.4
1931		15.9	18.1	29.5	21.5	18.0	15.8	20.7	17.5	16.0	30.8	23.7
1932	25.1	15.2	17.5	31.5	21.0	18.0	15.3	19.8	17.3	15.1	28.5	23.4
1933	—	14.3	16.3	29.2	19.2	17.3	14.4	18.4	16.2	14.7	28.6	21.9
1934	—	13.6	15.9	30.1	18.7	17.8	14.8	19.1	16.2	18.0	31.1	21.8
1935	—	13.1	15.2	26.4	17.9	17.7	14.7	19.6	15.3	18.9	28.2	21.1
1936	—	13.1	15.1	25.9	17.4	17.8	14.8	19.1	15.0	19.0	27.9	20.3
1937	—	12.8	15.0	24.3	17.2	18.0	14.9	19.9	14.7	18.8	26.2	20.0
1938	34.3	13.9	15.5	22.8	16.8	18.1	15.1	21.0	14.6	19.7	25.9	19.9
1939	27.9	20.7	15.0	21.4	18.6	17.8	14.8	21.2	14.6	20.4	24.8	19.4
1940	31.3	—	13.3	22.2	20.6	18.3	14.1	17.8	13.6	20.1	24.5	20.0
1941	28.0	—	11.9	21.9	20.1	18.5	13.9	24.2	13.1	18.1	18.3	19.0
1942	32.9	—	12.8	22.7	19.7	20.4	15.6	16.6	14.5	14.9	18.1	19.9
1943	—	—	14.6	21.8	21.5	21.4	16.2	20.4	15.7	16.0	16.7	18.4
1944	—	—	15.0	22.0	22.1	22.7	17.7	21.3	16.1	—	20.0	—
1945	—	—	15.3	24.1	19.5	23.5	15.9	25.5	16.2	—	25.1	18.7

TABLE A1.5. (cont.)

Ireland	Italy	Netherland	N. Ireland	Norway	Poland	Portugal	Romania	Scotland	Spain	Sweden	Switzerland	USSR (Russia)	Yugoslavia Serbia
22.7	33.0	31.6		29.7		30.5	38.8	29.6	33.9	27.0	28.6	49.3	42.4
22.7	32.5	32.2		29.9		31.3	39.3	29.5	35.0	27.0	29.0	47.9	38.0
23.0	33.4	31.8		29.2		32.0	39.0	29.3	35.6	26.5	28.5	49.1	38.0
23.1	31.7	31.6		28.6		33.0	40.1	29.4	36.4	25.7	27.4	48.1	40.9
23.6	32.9	31.4		27.9		31.6	40.1	29.1	34.2	25.8	27.3	48.6	39.8
23.4	32.7	30.8		27.1		31.8	38.3	28.6	35.1	25.7	26.9	45.0	37.3
23.5	32.1	30.4		26.8		32.1	39.9	28.6	33.8	25.7	26.9	47.1	42.0
23.2	31.7	33.0		26.3		30.7	41.1	27.7	33.3	25.5	26.2	47.5	40.0
23.3	33.7	29.7		26.3		30.3	40.3	28.1	33.7	25.7	26.4	44.8	36.8
23.4	32.8	29.2		26.8		29.9	41.1	27.3	33.1	25.6	25.5	44.7	38.7
23.3	33.3	28.6		25.8		31.7	39.3	26.2	32.7	24.7	25.0	45.1	39.0
23.2	31.5	27.8		25.7		38.6	42.3	25.6	31.5	24.0	24.2	45.0	36.3
23.0	32.4	28.1		25.4		34.9	43.4	25.9	31.8	23.8	24.2	43.7	—
22.8	31.7	28.2		25.1		32.5	42.1	25.5	30.6	23.2	23.2	43.1	—
22.6	31.0	28.2		25.1		31.5	42.1	26.1	29.9	22.9	22.4	—	—
22.0	30.5	26.2		23.6		32.6	40.5	23.9	30.9	21.6	19.5	—	—
20.9	24.1	26.5		24.2		32.1	—	22.8	29.1	21.2	18.9	—	—
19.7	19.5	26.0		25.1		31.4	—	20.1	29.0	20.9	18.5	—	—
19.8	18.2	25.1		24.6		29.7	—	20.2	29.3	20.3	18.7	—	—
20.0	21.5	24.4		22.7		27.6	23.0	21.7	27.9	19.8	18.6	—	—
22.8	32.2	28.6		26.1		33.6	33.7	28.1	29.5	23.6	20.9	30.9	—
20.8	30.7	27.7		24.2	32.8	32.4	38.2	25.2	30.5	21.5	20.8	32.6	—
19.5	30.8	26.1	23.3	23.3	35.3	33.1	37.2	23.5	30.5	19.6	19.7	33.4	—
20.5	30.0	26.2	23.9	22.8	36.0	33.2	36.4	22.9	30.5	18.9	19.4	38.8	—
21.1	29.0	25.1	22.7	21.3	35.0	32.8	36.7	22.0	29.7	18.1	18.9	43.1	—
20.8	28.4	24.2	22.0	19.7	35.4	32.6	35.2	21.4	29.1	17.6	18.5	44.7	—
20.6	27.7	23.8	22.5	19.6	33.1	33.5	34.8	21.1	29.6	16.8	18.3	43.6	—
20.3	27.5	23.1	21.3	18.1	31.6	31.0	34.1	19.9	28.1	16.1	17.5	43.2	—
20.1	26.7	23.3	20.8	17.9	32.0	31.9	34.7	20.0	29.1	16.1	17.4	44.3	—
19.8	25.6	22.8	20.4	17.3	31.8	29.9	34.1	19.2	28.3	15.2	17.1	—	—
19.9	26.7	23.1	20.8	17.0	32.3	29.7	35.0	19.6	28.3	15.4	17.2	—	—
19.5	24.9	22.2	20.5	16.3	30.2	29.7	33.3	19.0	27.6	14.8	16.7	—	—
19.1	23.8	22.0	19.9	16.0	28.9	29.9	35.9	18.6	28.2	14.5	16.7	—	—
19.4	23.8	20.8	19.6	14.7	26.5	28.9	32.1	17.6	27.7	13.7	16.4	—	—
19.5	23.5	20.6	20.1	14.6	26.6	28.4	32.4	18.0	26.2	13.7	16.3	—	—
19.6	23.4	20.2	19.5	14.3	26.1	28.2	30.7	17.8	25.7	13.8	16.0	30.1	—
19.6	22.4	20.2	20.3	14.6	26.2	28.1	31.5	17.9	24.7	14.2	15.6	33.6	—
19.2	22.9	19.8	19.8	15.0	24.9	26.7	30.8	17.6	22.6	14.4	14.9	38.7	—
19.4	23.8	20.5	20.0	15.4	24.3	26.6	29.6	17.7	20.0	14.9	15.2	37.5	—
19.1	23.6	20.6	19.5	15.8	—	26.2	28.3	17.4	16.5	15.4	15.2	36.5	—
19.1	23.5	20.8	19.5	16.1	—	24.3	26.5	17.1	24.4	15.1	15.2	31.2	—
19.0	20.9	20.3	20.5	15.3	—	23.8	23.0	17.5	19.6	15.6	16.9	—	—
22.3	20.5	21.0	22.3	17.7	—	24.0	21.4	17.6	20.2	17.7	18.4	—	—
21.9	19.9	23.0	23.5	18.9	—	25.1	23.4	18.4	22.9	19.3	19.2	—	—
22.2	18.3	24.0	22.8	20.3	—	25.3	21.7	18.5	22.5	20.6	19.6	—	—
22.7	18.3	22.6	21.3	20.0	—	26.0	19.6	16.9	23.1	20.4	20.1	—	—

TABLE A16. *Crude birth-rates, overseas English-speaking countries and Japan, 1900–1945*

Year	Australia	Canada	New Zealand	United States	Japan
1900			25.6		31.7
1901	27.2		26.3		33.1
1902	26.7		25.9		32.9
1903	25.3		26.6		32.0
1904	26.4		26.9		30.6
1905	26.2		27.2		30.6
1906	26.6		27.1		29.0
1907	26.8		27.3		33.7
1908	26.6		27.5		33.7
1909	26.7		27.3	30.0	33.9
1910	26.7		26.2	30.1	33.9
1911	27.2		26.0	29.9	34.1
1912	28.6		26.5	29.8	33.4
1913	28.2		26.1	29.5	33.3
1914	27.9		26.0	29.9	33.8
1915	27.1		25.3	29.5	33.2
1916	26.6		25.9	29.1	32.9
1917	26.3		25.7	28.5	32.7
1918	25.0		23.4	28.2	32.2
1919	23.5		21.4	26.1	31.6
1920	25.5		25.1	27.7	36.2
1921	25.0	29.4	23.4	28.1	35.1
1922	24.7	28.3	23.2	26.2	34.3
1923	23.8	26.7	22.0	26.0	35.2
1924	23.2	26.8	21.6	26.1	33.9
1925	22.9	26.1	21.2	25.1	34.9
1926	22.0	24.7	21.1	24.2	34.6
1927	21.6	24.3	20.3	23.5	33.4
1928	21.3	24.1	19.6	22.2	34.1
1929	20.3	23.5	19.0	21.2	32.7
1930	19.9	23.9	18.8	21.3	32.4
1931	18.2	23.2	18.5	20.2	32.1
1932	16.9	22.5	17.1	19.5	32.9
1933	16.8	20.9	16.6	18.4	31.5
1934	16.4	20.5	16.5	19.0	29.9
1935	16.6	20.3	16.2	18.7	31.6
1936	17.1	20.0	16.6	18.4	30.0
1937	17.4	20.0	17.3	18.7	30.9
1938	17.4	20.6	17.9	19.2	27.2
1939	17.6	20.4	18.7	18.8	26.6
1940	17.9	21.5	21.2	19.4	29.4
1941	18.9	22.2	22.8	20.3	21.1
1942	19.0	23.4	21.7	22.2	30.3
1943	20.6	24.1	19.7	22.7	30.3
1944	21.0	23.8	21.6	21.3	29.2
1945	21.7	24.0	23.3	20.5	23.2

TABLE A1.7. *Crude birth-rates, Europe, 1946–1984*

Year	Albania	Austria	Belgium	Bulgaria	Czechoslovakia	Denmark	England and Wales	Finland	France	FRG	GDR	Greece
1946	27.1	15.9	18.3	25.6	22.7	23.4	19.2	27.9	20.9	16.1	10.4	28.2
1947	35.8	18.5	17.8	24.0	24.2	22.1	20.5	28.0	21.3	16.4	13.1	27.4
1948	36.1	17.7	17.6	24.6	23.4	20.3	17.8	27.6	21.1	16.5	12.8	27.0
1949	38.6	16.3	17.2	24.7	22.4	18.9	16.7	26.1	20.9	16.8	14.5	26.1
1950	38.8	15.6	16.9	25.1	23.3	18.6	15.8	24.5	20.5	16.2	16.5	20.0
1951	38.5	14.8	16.4	21.0	22.8	17.8	15.5	23.0	19.5	15.8	16.9	20.3
1952	35.2	14.8	16.7	21.2	22.2	17.8	15.3	23.1	19.4	16.0	16.7	19.2
1953	40.9	14.8	16.6	20.9	21.2	17.9	15.5	22.0	18.9	15.8	16.4	18.4
1954	40.8	14.9	16.8	20.2	20.6	17.3	15.2	21.5	18.9	16.1	16.3	19.2
1955	44.5	15.6	16.8	20.1	20.3	17.3	15.0	21.2	18.6	16.0	16.3	19.4
1956	41.9	16.7	16.8	19.5	19.8	17.2	15.7	20.8	18.4	16.1	15.9	19.4
1957	39.1	17.0	17.0	18.4	18.9	16.8	16.1	20.1	18.4	16.6	15.6	19.2
1958	41.8	17.1	17.1	17.9	17.4	16.5	16.4	18.6	18.1	16.7	15.6	19.0
1959	41.9	17.7	17.4	17.6	16.0	16.3	16.5	18.9	18.3	17.3	16.9	19.4
1960	43.4	17.9	16.9	17.8	15.9	16.6	17.1	18.5	17.9	17.5	17.0	18.9
1961	41.2	18.6	17.2	17.4	15.8	16.6	17.6	18.4	18.2	18.0	17.6	17.9
1962	39.3	18.7	16.8	16.7	15.7	16.7	18.0	18.1	17.7	18.6	17.4	18.0
1963	39.1	18.8	17.1	16.4	16.9	17.6	18.2	18.2	18.2	19.0	17.6	17.5
1964	37.8	18.5	17.1	16.1	17.2	17.7	18.5	17.7	18.2	19.0	17.2	18.0
1965	35.2	17.9	16.4	15.3	16.4	18.0	18.1	17.1	17.8	17.7	16.5	17.7
1966	34.0	17.6	15.9	14.9	15.6	18.4	17.7	17.0	17.6	17.6	15.7	17.9
1967	35.3	17.4	15.3	15.0	15.1	16.8	17.7	16.8	17.0	17.0	14.8	18.7
1968	35.6	17.2	14.8	16.3	14.9	15.3	16.9	15.9	16.7	16.1	14.3	18.3
1969	35.3	16.5	14.7	17.0	15.5	14.6	16.3	14.6	16.7	14.8	14.0	17.6
1970	32.5	15.2	14.7	16.3	15.9	14.4	16.1	14.0	16.8	13.4	13.9	16.5
1971	33.3	14.6	14.4	15.9	16.5	15.2	16.1	13.4	17.1	12.7	13.8	16.1
1972	—	13.9	14.0	15.3	17.4	15.1	14.8	12.7	17.0	11.4	11.8	15.9
1973	—	13.0	13.4	16.2	18.9	14.3	13.8	12.2	16.5	10.3	10.6	15.4
1974	—	12.9	12.7	17.2	19.8	14.1	13.0	13.3	15.2	10.1	10.6	16.1
1975	—	12.5	12.2	16.6	19.5	14.2	12.2	14.1	14.1	9.7	10.8	15.7
1976	—	11.6	12.3	16.5	19.2	12.9	11.9	14.1	13.6	9.8	11.6	16.0
1977	—	11.3	12.4	16.0	18.7	12.1	11.6	13.8	14.0	9.4	13.3	15.5
1978	—	11.3	12.4	15.4	18.4	12.1	12.1	13.4	13.8	9.4	13.8	15.7
1979	27.5	11.5	12.5	15.3	17.8	11.6	13.0	13.3	14.1	9.4	14.0	15.9
1980	26.5	12.1	12.6	14.4	16.2	11.1	13.3	13.2	14.9	10.0	14.6	15.4
1981	26.5	12.5	12.6	13.9	15.5	10.3	12.8	13.2	14.9	10.1	14.2	14.5
1982	27.8	12.4	12.2	13.9	15.1	10.2	12.6	13.7	14.7	10.0	14.4	14.0
1983	26.0	11.9	11.9	13.8	14.8	9.9	12.7	13.8	13.7	9.7	14.0	13.6
1984	26.0	11.5	11.7	13.6	14.7	10.1	12.8	13.3	13.8	9.5	13.7	12.7

TABLE A1.7. (*cont.*)

Hungary	Ireland	Italy	Netherlands	N. Ireland	Norway	Poland	Portugal	Romania	Scotland	Spain	Sweden	Switzerland	USSR
18.7	22.9	23.0	30.2	22.3	22.6	22.8	25.4	24.8	20.3	21.6	19.7	20.0	23.8
20.6	23.2	22.3	27.8	23.2	21.4	26.2	24.5	23.4	22.3	21.5	18.9	19.4	—
20.9	22.0	22.0	25.3	21.7	20.5	29.3	26.8	23.9	19.7	23.3	18.4	19.2	—
20.6	21.5	20.4	23.7	21.2	19.5	29.4	25,5	27.6	18.4	21.7	17.4	18.4	—
20.9	21.3	19.6	22.7	21.0	19.1	30.5	24.4	26.2	18.1	20.2	16.4	18.1	26.5
20.2	21.1	18.5	22.3	20.7	18.4	31.0	24.5	25.1	17.8	20.1	15.6	17.2	26.8
19.6	21.9	17.9	22.3	20.9	18.8	30.2	24.7	24.8	17.7	20.8	15.5	17.4	26.5
21.6	21.2	17.7	21.7	20.9	18.7	29.7	23.7	23.8	17.8	20.6	15.4	17.0	25.1
23.0	21.3	18.2	21.5	20.8	18.5	29.1	23.0	24.8	18.1	20.0	14.6	17.0	26.6
21.4	21.1	18.1	21.3	20.8	18.5	29.1	24.3	25.6	18.1	20.6	14.8	17.1	25.7
19.5	21.0	17.9	21.3	21.1	18.5	28.0	23.4	24.2	18.6	20.7	14.8	17.4	25.2
17.0	21.2	17.9	21.2	21.5	18.0	27.6	24.4	22.9	19.1	21.8	14.6	17.7	25.4
16.0	20.9	17.6	21.2	21.6	17.9	26.2	24.4	21.6	19.4	21.8	14.2	17.6	25.3
15.2	21.1	18.5	21.4	21.9	17.7	24.7	24.3	20.2	19.2	21.7	14.1	17.7	25.0
14.7	21.4	18.1	20.8	22.5	17.3	22.4	24.2	19.1	19.6	21.8	13.7	17.6	24.9
14.0	21.2	18.4	21.3	22.4	17.3	20.9	24.5	17.5	19.5	21.3	13.9	18.3	23.8
12.9	21.8	18.4	20.9	22.7	17.1	19.8	24.5	16.2	20.1	21.3	14.2	18.7	22.5
13.1	22.2	18.8	20.9	23.1	17.3	19.2	23.5	15.7	19.7	21.5	14.8	19.3	21.1
13.1	22.4	19.7	20.7	23.6	17.7	18.1	23.8	15.2	20.0	22.1	16.0	19.5	19.5
13.1	22.1	19.1	19.9	23.1	17.8	17.3	22.9	14.6	19.3	21.1	15.9	19.1	18.4
13.6	21.6	18.7	19.2	22.5	17.9	16.7	22.2	14.3	18.6	20.7	15.8	18.5	18.2
14.6	21.1	18.0	18.9	22.4	17.6	16.3	21.5	27.4	18.6	20.8	15.4	17.9	17.3
15.0	20.9	17.6	18.6	22.1	17.6	16.2	20.6	26.7	18.3	20.2	14.3	17.3	17.2
15.0	21.5	17.5	19.2	21.4	17.6	16.3	21.7	23.3	17.4	20.0	13.5	16.7	17.0
14.7	21.8	16.8	18.3	21.0	16.6	16.8	20.0	21.1	16.8	19.5	13.7	15.8	17.4
14.5	22.8	16.8	17.2	20.6	16.8	17.2	19.6	19.6	16.6	19.5	14.1	15.2	17.8
14.7	22.7	16.3	16.1	19.4	16.3	17.4	20.3	18.8	15.1	19.4	13.8	14.3	17.8
15.0	22.5	16.0	14.5	18.9	15.5	17.9	20.1	18.2	14.3	19.3	13.5	13.6	17.6
17.8	22.3	15.7	13.7	17.6	15.0	18.4	19.6	20.3	13.4	19.3	13.4	13.1	18.0
18.4	21.6	14.8	13.0	17.0	14.0	18.9	19.1	19.7	13.1	18.8	12.6	12.4	18.2
17.5	20.9	13.9	12.9	17.1	13.3	19.5	19.3	19.5	12.5	18.3	11.9	11.7	18.4
16.6	21.0	13.1	12.5	16.5	12.5	19.0	18.5	19.5	12.0	18.0	11.6	11.5	18.1
15.7	21.0	12.5	12.5	17.1	12.7	19.0	17.0	19.0	12.4	17.3	11.2	11.2	18.2
14.9	21.5	11.7	12.4	18.2	12.6	19.5	16.2	18.6	13.2	16.2	11.6	11.3	18.2
13.8	21.8	11.2	12.8	18.6	12.4	19.4	16.2	17.9	13.4	15.1	11.3	11.5	18.2
13.3	21.0	10.9	12.5	18.1	12.3	18.9	15.4	17.0	13.4	14.1	11.3	11.4	18.5
12.4	20.2	10.8	12.0	17.9	12.4	19.3	15.1	15.3	12.9	13.4	11.1	11.6	19.0
11.9	19.0	10.6	11.8	17.4	12.1	19.7	14.4	14.3	12.6	12.5	11.0	11.4	19.8
11.8	18.1	10.5	12.1	17.5	12.1	18.9	14.2	15.5	12.7	12.2	11.3	11.6	19.6

TABLE A1.8. *Crude birth-rates, Yugoslavia, overseas English-speaking countries, and Japan, 1946–1984*

Year	Yugoslavia	Australia	Canada	New Zealand	United States	Japan
1946	—	23.6	27.0	25.3	24.1	25.3
1947	26.6	24.1	28.7	26.5	26.5	34.3
1948	28.1	23.1	27.1	25.6	24.8	33.5
1949	30.0	22.9	27.1	25.0	24.5	33.0
1950	30.4	23.3	27.1	24.7	23.9	28.1
1951	26.9	22.9	27.2	24.4	24.8	25.3
1952	29.7	23.3	27.9	26.0	25.0	23.4
1953	28.4	22.9	28.2	25.4	24.8	21.5
1954	28.6	22.5	28.5	25.9	25.2	20.0
1955	26.9	22.6	28.2	26.1	24.9	19.4
1956	26.0	22.5	28.0	26.0	25.1	18.4
1957	23.9	22.9	28.1	26.2	25.2	17.2
1958	24.0	22.6	27.5	26.6	24.5	18.0
1959	23.3	22.6	27.4	26.5	24.3	17.5
1960	23.5	22.4	26.7	26.5	23.8	17.2
1961	22.7	22.8	26.0	27.1	23.5	16.9
1962	21.9	22.2	25.2	26.2	22.6	17.0
1963	21.4	21.6	24.6	25.5	21.9	17.3
1964	20.8	20.6	23.4	24.2	21.2	17.7
1965	21.0	19.6	21.3	22.9	19.6	18.6
1966	20.4	19.2	19.3	22.5	18.5	13.7
1967	19.6	19.4	18.7	22.5	17.9	19.4
1968	19.1	20.1	17.6	22.7	17.6	18.6
1969	18.9	20.4	17.6	22.6	17.8	18.5
1970	17.8	20.6	17.4	22.1	18.2	18.8
1971	18.3	21.6	16.8	22.6	17.3	19.0
1972	18.3	20.5	15.9	21.8	15.7	19.3
1973	18.0	18.9	15.5	20.5	15.0	19.4
1974	17.9	17.8	15.4	19.6	14.7	18.4
1975	18.1	16.7	15.8	18.3	14.5	17.1
1976	18.1	16.2	15.6	17.7	14.5	16.3
1977	17.6	15.9	15.5	17.3	15.1	15.5
1978	17.3	15.6	15.3	16.3	14.9	14.9
1979	17.1	15.3	15.5	16.8	15.5	14.2
1980	17.0	15.3	15.4	16.2	15.8	13.5
1981	16.7	15.7	15.2	16.2	15.7	13.0
1982	16.7	15.8	15.1	15.8	15.9	12.9
1983	16.6	15.8	15.0	15.8	15.5	12.7
1984	16.4	15.5	15.0	16.0	15.6	12.5

TABLE A1.9. *Crude birth-rates, Egypt, Mauritius, Réunion, and Tunisia, 1910–1984*

Year	Egypt	Mauritius	Réunion	Tunisia	Year	Egypt	Mauritius	Réunion	Tunisia
1910		24.4			1950	44.4	49.7	47.5	—
1911		39.2			1951	44.8	47.5	49.6	—
1912	42.4	35.5			1952	45.1	48.0	51.3	—
1913	41.8	40.8			1953	42.5	46.3	51.2	—
1914	41.4	40.8			1954	42.4	40.9	49.6	—
1915	41.8	34.8			1955	40.2	41.4	49.2	—
1916	40.2	35.0			1956	40.7	43.3	47.7	35.5
1917	40.3	36.9			1957	38.0	42.6	46.9	39.3
1918	39.0	34.8			1958	41.1	40.3	44.9	44.6
1919	38.3	35.2			1959	42.8	37.8	44.0	44.8
1920	42.8	35.1			1960	43.0	38.5	44.0	43.2
1921	42.3	38.1			1961	43.9	40.1	43.7	42.9
1922	43.2	37.0			1962	41.3	38.0	44.4	41.6
1923	43.0	36.8			9163	42.8	40.1	44.4	42.1
1924	43.3	41.1			1964	42.0	37.9	43.4	45.4
1925	42.7	42.6			1965	41.4	35.4	42.0	41.8
1926	43.2	39.4			1966	41.0	34.9	40.9	43.8
1927	44.0	34.5			1967	39.2	30.6	38.7	38.9
1928	43.8	37.9			1968	38.2	30.6	37.2	38.2
1929	44.5	34.0			1969	36.9	27.7	34.8	38.8
1930	45.8	31.6			1970	34.8	26.0	30.2	36.4
1931	44.9	29.7			1971	34.8	25.2	31.7	35.1
1932	43.0	26.3			1972	34.1	24.7	29.5	37.4
1933	44.8	34.6			1973	35.3	23.1	28.1	35.8
1934	42.8	33.7			1974	35.5	27.1	28.4	35.6
1935	42.0	32.8			1975	36.0	25.1	28.0	36.6
1936	45.0	34.1			1976	36.4	25.7	26.8	36.1
1937	43.4	34.4			1977	37.3	25.7	25.6	36.5
1938	43.2	32.6			1978	37.2	27.1	24.1	34.1
1939	42.0	35.2			1979	39.8	27.6	25.4	34.8
1940	41.3	29.1			1980	37.3	27.0	25.0	35.0
1941	40.4	32.2			1981	36.8	25.1	23.4	34.3
1942	37.6	32.5			1982	36.0	22.4	23.1	32.8
1943	38.7	32.6			1983	36.8	20.7	23.7	31.4
1944	39.8	43.4			1984		19.7	24.4	32.6
1945	42.7	38.4							
1946	41.2	38.4	} 44.3	40.3					
1947	43.6	43.7		36.8					
1948	42.7	43.4	40.0	33.1					
1949	41.8	45.6	41.1	—					

TABLE A1.10. *Crude birth-rates, Latin America, 1900–1949*

Year	Argentina	British Guiana	Chile	Costa Rica	Cuba	Jamaica	Mexico	Panama	Puerto Rico	Trinidad and Tobago	Uruguay	Venezuela
1900	36.2		34.6				36.2				32.6	
1901	35.8		35.9				35.8				33.9	
1902	34.8		35.7				34.8				33.2	
1903	35.3		34.0				35.3				33.8	
1904	34.0		35.4				34.0				27.6	
1905	34.0		35.1				34.0				33.9	
1906	33.1		36.8				32.2				32.3	
1907	—		38.8				32.8				32.9	
1908	—		39.7				34.3				34.2	
1909	—		39.1				34.0				33.3	
1910	38.3		38.8				32.0				32.4	
1911	37.9		39.4				—				32.6	
1912	38.6		39.5				—				33.1	
1913	38.0		40.4				—				33.0	
1914	36.7		39.0				—				30.7	
1915	35.3		38.6				—				29.5	
1916	35.3		40.3				—				27.9	
1917	33.6		41.1				—				27.0	
1918	32.9		39.9				—				27.8	
1919	32.7		39.2				—				27.4	
1920	32.3		39.1				—				26.7	
1921	32.7		39.2				—				26.2	
1922	33.1		38.7				31.4				26.0	
1923	34.0		39.5				32.0				25.4	

TABLE A1.10. (*cont.*)

Year	Argentina	British Guiana	Chile	Costa Rica	Cuba	Jamaica	Mexico	Panama	Puerto Rico	Trinidad and Tobago	Uruguay	Venezuela
1924	32.8		40.0				30.8				25.8	
1925	31.8		39.8				33.1				25.4	
1926	31.2		40.1				31.2				25.4	
1927	30.7		42.8				30.5				24.6	
1928	30.8		43.6				32.3				25.0	
1929	30.2		41.9				39.3				24.2	
1930	29.5		39.8			37.0	49.4				24.4	
1931	28.5		34.6			34.8	43.8				23.3	
1932	28.1	34.3	34.2	42.6	16.8	32.7	43.3	38.6	41.1	29.0	22.5	28.4
1933	26.6	32.7	33.4	43.2	17.4	33.4	42.2	33.6	37.4	31.1	21.0	27.9
1934	26.0	28.9	33.8	42.7	20.1	31.7	44.3	37.1	39.1	29.7	20.6	27.0
1935	25.8	34.6	34.1	43.6	20.5	34.1	42.3	32.0	39.5	32.9	20.4	27.8
1936	25.2	35.5	34.6	43.5	20.7	32.9	43.0	38.5	39.6	32.9	19.9	31.9
1937	24.8	33.5	32.3	42.8	24.4	31.5	44.1	38.0	38.2	31.5	19.9	33.7
1938	24.9	29.7	32.1	43.6	26.6	33.3	43.5	45.5	38.6	32.8	19.8	33.7
1939	24.9	28.3	33.3	42.8	15.5	32.3	44.6	27.9	39.6	31.0	20.1	35.9
1940	25.3	35.0	33.4	43.2	18.1	30.8	44.3	28.2	38.6	34.7	19.9	36.0
1941	25.0	35.8	32.6	43.4	16.9	31.4	43.5	37.6	39.8	33.5	20.4	35.3
1942	24.5	38.9	33.2	41.6	—	32.7	45.5	37.4	40.2	34.7	19.4	35.7
1943	25.6	33.6	33.1	43.7	33.3	31.5	45.5	38.2	38.7	38.5	19.6	36.3
1944	25.7	28.8	33.2	41.8	36.0	33.2	44.2	38.4	40.6	39.0	20.7	35.9
1945	25.2	36.6	33.3	44.2	—	30.0	44.9	38.4	41.9	39.5	—	36.2
1946	24.7	35.6	32.4	42.4	—	30.8	43.7	37.8	41.6	38.8	—	37.6
1947	25.0	39.4	33.8	44.5	—	32.6	46.1	37.2	42.2	38.3	—	38.2
1948	25.2	42.3	33.7	43.9	—	30.9	45.2	35.6	40.2	39.9	—	39.2
1949	25.0	42.3	33.2	43.2	—	31.9	44.7	32.8	39.0	37.2	—	41.2

TABLE A1.11. *Crude birth-rates, Latin America, 1950–1984*

Year	Argentina	British Guiana	Chile	Costa Rica	Cuba	Jamaica	Mexico	Panama	Puerto Rico	Trinidad and Tobago	Uruguay	Venezuela
1950	25.3	40.4	35.2	46.5	29.6	33.1	46.0	33.3	39.0	37.5	18.6	42.6
1951	24.9	42.5	36.1	47.6	25.4	33.9	44.2	32.4	37.5	36.7	18.5	45.0
1952	24.9	44.3	36.2	48.6	25.1	33.3	43.9	36.0	36.1	34.6	18.7	43.7
1953	25.2	44.1	36.7	49.6	28.2	34.4	45.0	37.9	35.1	37.7	18.7	45.3
1954	24.6	42.9	35.4	50.9	—	35.3	46.4	39.3	35.2	41.9	19.3	43.7
1955	24.3	43.2	36.3	49.8	—	36.2	46.4	39.4	34.6	41.9	21.4	45.5
1956	24.6	41.5	37.0	49.0	—	37.2	46.8	39.3	34.8	37.0	23.5	44.4
1957	24.4	42.8	38.1	47.7	29.3	37.9	47.3	40.5	33.7	37.7	23.1	43.2
1958	23.7	42.7	37.4	46.4	—	39.0	44.5	39.3	33.2	37.6	23.1	42.7
1959	23.5	42.7	36.9	48.2	30.5	40.0	45.1	40.8	32.4	37.4	22.6	45.8
1960	22.9	40.5	37.4	47.4	31.5	42.0	44.2	39.9	32.4	39.5	23.9	46.0
1961	22.8	40.0	37.6	47.9	33.8	40.2	43.8	40.4	31.4	37.9	25.0	45.3
1962	23.1	40.4	37.5	46.6	36.9	39.1	43.9	41.1	31.3	37.9	25.3	43.4
1963	22.8	40.1	36.9	48.0	35.2	39.0	44.5	40.2	31.0	35.6	23.8	43.4
1964	22.7	38.0	35.7	45.5	35.2	39.3	44.6	39.6	31.0	34.6	23.4	43.4
1965	21.7	39.4	34.7	44.9	34.2	39.6	44.1	39.2	30.7	32.8	22.2	43.6
1966	21.3	38.9	33.0	42.4	32.8	40.0	44.1	38.9	28.9	30.2	21.4	41.8
1967	21.1	33.4	31.2	40.2	31.7	37.3	43.2	38.8	26.7	28.2	21.7	43.8
1968	21.3	35.1	29.2	36.2	30.1	35.7	43.4	38.9	25.5	27.5	21.7	40.0
1969	24.8	29.8	27.5	34.4	29.2	35.1	41.6	38.0	24.9	24.4	21.3	39.9

TABLE A1.11. (cont.)

Year	Argentina	British Guiana	Chile	Costa Rica	Cuba	Jamaica	Mexico	Panama	Puerto Rico	Trinidad and Tobago	Uruguay	Venezuela
1970	22.9	33.4	27.0	33.4	27.7	34.4	42.1	37.2	24.8	26.2	22.4	38.2
1971	23.5	31.6	27.6	31.3	29.5	34.9	42.5	37.2	25.6	26.5	22.6	38.2
1972	22.9	—	27.9	31.2	28.0	34.3	43.2	36.0	24.0	28.2	20.9	37.1
1973	22.7	—	25.8	28.5	25.0	31.3	45.8	33.2	23.0	26.6	19.1	35.9
1974	—	—	26.2	29.5	22.3	30.8	43.4	31.3	23.2	26.2	21.1	37.3
1975	—	—	25.0	29.3	20.7	30.1	37.5	32.3	22.3	25.4	21.1	37.2
1976	25.5	26.3	23.3	29.6	19.8	29.8	38.0	30.8	22.7	26.5	20.9	37.4
1977	25.4	28.3	21.6	30.1	17.6	29.4	36.8	29.8	22.6	26.9	20.4	36.5
1978	25.2	—	21.4	32.1	15.1	28.9	35.6	29.1	22.4	27.0	19.9	36.3
1979	23.3	—	21.5	30.2	14.8	27.7	33.7	28.6	23.3	27.9	19.3	35.6
1980	24.7		22.2	29.4	14.1	26.9	35.3	26.9	22.8	27.6	18.6	35.4
1981	23.7		23.4	29.8	14.0	26.8	33.6	26.9	22.0	28.9	18.4	32.1
1982	22.8		23.9	30.7	16.3	26.9		26.7	21.3	28.8	18.5	32.0
1983	23.9		22.3	30.0	16.7	27.1		25.4	20.1	28.9	18.0	31.4
1984			22.3	32.7	16.6	23.4		26.5	19.3		17.7	29.9

TABLE A1.12. *Crude birth-rates, Latin America, 1870–1985 (UN estimates since 1950)*

Year	Chile	Uruguay	Year	Argentina	Chile	Mexico	Uruguay
1880	39.3		1890		37.6		40.7
1881	46.2		1891		34.3		40.6
1882	41.9	43.0	1892		38.3		39.6
1883	42.7	42.6	1893		37.7		37.6
1884	40.3	38.9	1894		39.5		38.1
1885	25.8	40.7	1895		36.2	30.5	39.2
1886	32.0	41.5	1896		34.6	31.8	37.8
1887	33.0	42.1	1897		34.8	28.9	32.1
1888	35.4	42.0	1898		33.1	37.1	33.6
1889	38.7	41.6	1899	38.3	33.5	37.7	34.3

Period	Argentina	Brazil	British Guiana	Chile	Costa Rica	Jamaica	Mexico	Panama	Trinidad and Tobago	Uruguay	Venezuela
1870–1874	49.1										
1875–1879	49.0										
1880–1884	48.9										
1885–1889	45.8				42.0					41.6	
1890–1894	44.0				37.1					39.3	
1895–1899	44.5			46.5	41.6		47.3			35.4	
1900–1904	44.3	43	32.9	47.3	37.7	38.6	46.5		35.5	32.2	
1905–1909	42.1	44	30.3	45.1	41.2	38.4	46.0		34.6	33.2	
1910–1914	39.2		32.1	46.0	43.7	38.6	43.2		33.4	32.4	
1915–1919	36.5		27.2	43.0	40.9	35.3	40.6		31.7	27.9	
1920–1924	34.9		31.7	42.4	38.8	37.6	45.3	37.4	32.5	26.0	29.9
1925–1929	32.5		32.3	41.9	44.6	35.6	44.3	38.4	31.5	24.9	31.4
1930–1934	29.0		32.3	40.5	45.8	33.6	44.6	36.5	30.3	22.3	28.2
1935–1939	25.7	44	32.4	36.6	45.0	32.2	43.5	36.4	32.4	20.0	32.7
1940–1944	25.5		34.5	36.4	44.9	32.0	44.6	37.5	36.2	20.0	35.7
1945–1949	26.3		40.3	35.7	45.0	31.7	45.0	36.0	38.7	—	38.6
1950–1955	25.4	44.6	48.1	35.8	47.6	34.8	46.7	40.3	38.2	21.2	47.0
1955–1960	24.3	43.3	43.9	37.7	48.3	39.2	45.8	41.0	38.0	21.9	45.3
1960–1965	23.2	42.1	40.4	36.4	45.3	39.6	44.9	40.8	38.0	21.9	44.2
1965–1970	22.6	36.4	35.4	30.4	38.3	37.3	44.2	39.3	30.3	20.5	40.6
1970–1975	23.4	33.6	32.5	27.0	31.0	32.5	42.7	35.7	26.6	21.1	36.1
1975–1980	25.0	32.0	31.5	22.4	30.7	28.2	37.6	31.0	26.3	20.3	34.4
1980–1985	24.6	30.6	28.5	22.7	30.5	28.1	33.9	28.0	25.4	19.5	33.0

TABLE A1.13. *Crude birth-rates, Asia and Oceania, 1900–1949*

Year	China (Taiwan)	Cyprus	Fiji	Hong Kong	India	Israel	Malaysia	Philippines	Singapore	Sri Lanka
1900										38.8
1901		30.6								37.5
1902		28.0								38.5
1903		28.6						37.3		40.0
1904		30.4						27.8		38.5
1905		29.6						30.9	—	28.7
1906	38.6	30.7						26.3	25.2	36.5
1907	39.1	31.4						31.4	25.7	33.6
1908	38.2	32.9						33.3	28.4	41.0
1909	40.2	29.8						28.6	26.4	37.5
1910	41.3	32.1						33.5	25.2	39.0
1911	41.8	31.6						34.3	25.0	37.9
1912	41.3	28.5						34.2	28.0	33.2
1913	40.8	30.7						34.5	27.0	38.5
1914	41.4	33.1						37.2	29.1	37.9
1915	40.0	34.3						34.4	29.3	37.3
1916	37.3	20.0						34.8	28.2	39.9
1917	40.9	29.5						35.1	30.7	41.4
1918	39.7	32.9						33.4	28.6	41.0
1919	38.5	29.2						29.8	30.3	35.9
1920	39.5	29.5						33.6	29.6	36.5
1921	42.8	26.8						34.4	32.6	40.6
1922	41.8	28.6	}32.0			32.7		34.7	30.5	39.1
1923	39.1	25.5				36.5		35.2	30.4	38.7
1924	41.4	27.3				38.2		—	32.5	37.5

Year										
1925	40.8	25.6	⎫		32.7			—	31.8	39.9
1926	43.7	25.9	⎪		35.5			33.6	32.9	42.0
1927	43.2	25.2	⎬ 32.5		34.6			35.3	35.1	41.0
1928	43.7	28.9	⎪		34.9			35.5	36.0	41.9
1929	44.0	30.4	⎭		33.6			35.5	37.2	38.3
1930	44.8	32.1	⎫ 35.0		33.0			32.8	36.0	39.0
1931	45.8	30.2	⎭		32.2			32.8	36.4	37.4
1932	44.8	28.6	35.8		29.2	33.6	36.1	32.6	35.8	37.0
1933	45.1	27.2	36.4		29.2	35.4	37.8	32.7	41.9	38.6
1934	45.4	29.7	36.8		30.2	33.4	37.1	31.1	43.3	37.2
1935	45.7	31.6	36.7		30.8	34.3	37.8	31.3	45.2	34.4
1936	44.2	33.7	37.9		29.7	34.8	40.4	32.2	46.6	34.1
1937	45.5	28.6	35.8		26.7	33.7	39.0	33.3	45.8	37.8
1938	43.9	30.2	38.4	⎫ 26.7	26.3	33.3	41.2	32.4	44.9	35.9
1939	44.4	31.0	36.9	⎭	23.1	32.7	42.0	—	47.6	36.0
1940	43.0	33.1	38.6	25.2	23.5	32.0	40.7	—	45.0	35.8
1941	41.1	27.9	40.9	—	20.4	32.1	38.0	—	44.7	36.5
1942	40.3	22.4	38.3	—	22.5	29.5	—	—	—	36.7
1943	40.1	29.8	39.0	—	28.6	26.1	—	—	—	40.6
1944	—	33.7	37.3	—	29.7	25.8	—	—	—	37.1
1945	—	30.5	39.9	—	29.9	28.0	—	—	—	35.7
1946	38.3	32.4	40.8	20.1	28.6	28.8	36.8	28.9	—	38.4
1947	39.7	33.2	39.9	24.3	30.1	26.4	43.2	30.5	45.9	39.4
1948	42.4	32.3	41.9	26.4	26.3	25.2	40.4	31.5	46.2	40.6
1949	—	27.8	38.6	29.5	29.9	26.4	43.8	30.9	47.1	39.9

TABLE A1.14. *Crude birth-rates, Asia and Oceania, 1950–1984*

Year	China (Taiwan)	Cyprus	Fiji	Hong Kong	Israel	Malaysia	Philippines	Singapore	Sri Lanka
1950	43.4	29.4	39.9	26.8	34.3	42.0	31.7	45.7	39.7
1951	50.0	28.7	38.4	34.0	34.1	43.6	30.5	46.2	39.8
1952	46.6	26.3	40.7	32.0	33.0	45.0	30.1	45.4	38.8
1953	45.2	26.1	40.7	33.6	32.1	44.4	29.8	45.8	38.7
1954	44.6	26.6	40.2	36.6	29.2	44.6	30.7	45.7	35.7
1955	45.3	25.9	38.5	36.3	29.2	44.0	31.2	44.3	37.3
1956	44.8	25.9	40.7	37.0	28.6	46.7	31.2	44.4	36.4
1957	41.4	25.8	41.9	35.8	28.2	46.1	30.0	43.3	36.5
1958	41.7	25.7	40.3	37.4	26.7	43.3	29.7	41.9	35.8
1959	41.2	25.4	41.8	35.2	26.8	42.2	30.4	40.1	36.9
1960	39.5	25.3	39.9	36.1	26.9	40.9	23.7	38.4	36.6
1961	38.3	25.8	40.9	34.3	25.1	41.9	23.0	36.2	35.9
1962	37.4	25.2	39.5	36.1	24.9	40.4	26.7	34.8	35.7
1963	36.3	24.9	38.0	34.6	25.0	40.5	26.3	34.3	34.4
1964	34.5	24.2	37.8	31.8	25.7	39.1	26.0	32.8	33.0
1965	32.7	24.5	35.9	29.6	25.8	37.7	25.0	30.7	33.1
1966	32.4	24.2	34.9	26.6	25.5	38.6	25.2	29.9	32.3
1967	28.5	23.7	34.5	25.3	24.3	36.6	24.9	26.6	31.6
1968	29.3	23.3	30.8	22.0	25.5	36.8	25.9	24.5	32.0
1969	27.9	19.8	29.7	21.3	26.2	34.7	26.5	22.8	30.4

Year									
1970	27.2	19.2	29.9	20.0	26.9	33.9	26.2	23.0	29.4
1971	25.6	18.8	30.3	19.7	28.9	34.3	25.5	22.8	30.4
1972	24.2	18.6	28.0	19.7	27.8	33.3	24.9	23.4	30.0
1973	23.8	18.3	28.2	19.8	27.6	31.9	26.3	22.3	27.0
1974	23.4	18.1	29.8	19.7	28.2	32.1	26.3	19.7	27.5
1975	23.0	16.9	29.0	18.1	27.7	31.3	28.2	17.8	27.7
1976	25.9	18.7	28.3	17.7	28.0	31.7	—	18.9	27.8
1977	23.8	18.5	27.0	17.7	26.4	30.7	— ⎫	16.6	27.9
1978	24.1	19.3	28.3	17.6	25.1	30.0	— ⎬ 33.9	16.9	28.5
1979	24.4	19.5	29.8	16.8	24.7	30.5	— ⎭	17.3	28.9
1980	23.4	20.0	29.6	16.9	24.1	30.2	—	17.3	28.4
1981	23.0	20.8	29.9	17.2	23.6	30.9		17.0	28.2
1982	22.1	22.1	30.6	16.5	24.0	30.6		17.3	26.8
1983	20.6	22.3		15.4	24.1	29.8		16.2	26.2
1984				14.4	23.7	30.7		16.4	24.8

Appendix 2. Total Fertility Rates

TABLE A2.1. *Total fertility rates, developed countries (populations over 10 million inhabitants), 1851–1980, per woman*

Period	Australia	Belgium	Canada	Czechoslovakia	France	Germany FRG	Germany GDR	Hungary	Italy	Japan	Netherlands	Poland	Romania	Spain	England and Wales	United States	USSR	Yugoslavia
1851–1855		4.18			3.38						4.60							
1856–1860		4.51			3.46						4.60				4.82			
1861–1865		4.63			3.50						4.98				4.91			
1866–1870		4.76			3.50						5.05				4.93			
1871–1875		4.87			3.42						5.23				4.94			
1876–1880		4.78			3.45						5.42				4.88			
1881–1885		4.61			3.38	5.29					5.25				4.55			
1886–1890		4.30			3.12	5.22					5.14				4.16			
1891–1895		4.17			2.97	5.16					4.97				3.90			
1896–1900		3.98			2.90	5.04					4.75				3.62			
1901–1905			4.82		2.79	4.77					4.48				3.40	3.83		
1906–1910	3.35		4.73		2.60	4.34					4.15				3.14	3.63		
1911–1915	3.51		4.54		2.25	3.52					3.82				2.84	3.45		
1916–1920	3.07		4.20		1.65	2.26					3.59				2.40	3.28		
1921–1925	3.03		3.72	3.13	2.42	2.62				5.18	3.48			3.96	2.39	3.11		
1926–1930	2.73		3.29	2.55	2.30	2.10		3.03		4.99	3.07			3.75	2.01	2.69	5.23	
1931–1935	2.19		2.94	2.13	2.16	1.84		2.63	3.06	4.65	2.73			3.50	1.79	2.24	3.52	
1936–1940	2.21		2.69	2.18	2.07	(2.24)	—	2.47	3.00	4.12	2.61			2.77	1.79	2.18	4.00	
1941–1945	2.54	2.43	2.97	2.69	2.11	(1.90)	—	2.48	2.56	3.94	2.88			2.72	1.98	2.56	2.55	
1946–1950	3.02		3.46	3.05	2.98	2.07	(1.84)	2.51	2.77	4.04	3.48			2.68	2.39	3.10	3.01	
1951–1955	3.18	2.34	3.70	2.91	2.72	2.10	2.38	2.71	2.30	2.75	3.04	3.64	3.00	2.54	2.19	3.43	2.87	3.36
1956–1960	3.41	2.50	3.90	2.59	2.70	2.33	2.27	2.24	2.32	2.08	3.11	3.31	2.59	2.76	2.51	3.70	2.83	2.82
1961–1965	3.29	2.64	3.58	2.42	2.84	2.50	2.45	1.84	2.50	2.01	3.15	2.67	2.02	2.90	2.83	3.31	2.59	2.68
1966–1970	2.87	2.35	2.52	2.09	2.60	2.33	2.29	1.99	2.43	2.02	2.75	2.29	3.05	2.92	2.55	2.55	2.42	2.48
1971–1975	2.55	1.96	1.97	2.34	2.24	1.63	1.72	2.09	2.31	2.10	1.98	2.26	2.60	2.85	2.06	1.99	2.43	2.31
1976–1980	2.00	1.70	1.79	2.33	1.87	1.42	1.84	2.06	1.85	1.79	1.59	2.26	2.51	2.49	1.79	1.83	2.32	2.14

TABLE A2.2. *Total fertility rates, Europe, 1855–1899, per woman*

Year	Finland	France	Norway	Sweden
1855		3.24	4.61	4.30
1856		3.40	4.42	4.23
1857		3.36	4.54	4.36
1858		3.46	4.62	4.66
1859		3.61	4.82	4.71
1860		3.40	4.63	4.71
1861		3.51	4.30	4.44
1862		3.46	4.52	4.59
1863		3.53	4.69	4.65
1864		3.51	4.55	4.69
1865		3.53	4.60	4.58
1866	4.38	3.53	4.61	4.68
1867	4.39	3.55	4.38	4.40
1868	3.31	3.49	4.30	3.93
1869	4.46	3.49	4.22	4.03
1870	4.79	3.44	4.26	4.11
1871	4.89	3.08	4.29	4.37
1872	4.79	3.59	4.40	4.34
1873	4.90	3.51	4.41	4.49
1874	5.03	3.53	4.59	4.54
1875	4.88	3.51	4.67	4.60
1876	4.90	3.57	4.68	4.57
1877	5.13	3.49	4.69	4.62
1878	4.75	3.44	4.64	4.44
1879	5.08	3.44	4.71	4.56
1880	4.95	3.36	4.53	4.36
1881	4.73	3.40	4.40	4.29
1882	4.92	3.40	4.47	4.32
1883	4.90	3.38	4.51	4.24
1884	4.96	3.38	4.59	4.40
1885	4.72	3.32	4.56	4.34
1886	4.92	3.26	4.48	4.39
1887	5.10	3.22	4.56	4.36
1888	4.99	3.16	4.42	4.24
1889	4.82	3.12	4.31	4.10
1890	4.77	2.95	4.43	4.15
1891	4.98	3.03	4.51	4.19
1892	4.60	2.96	4.35	3.99
1893	4.37	3.02	4.47	4.05
1894	4.54	2.94	4.38	4.04
1895	4.81	2.86	4.52	4.13
1896	4.74	2.96	4.47	4.09
1897	4.71	2.92	4.48	4.01
1898	5.01	2.87	4.53	4.07
1899	4.90	2.88	4.47	3.96

TABLE A2.3. *Total fertility rates, Europe, anglo-saxon overseas countries, and Japan, 1900–1939, per woman*

Year	Australia	Belgium	Bulgaria	Canada	Czechoslovakia	Denmark	England and Wales	Finland	France
1900									2.80
1901									2.89
1902									2.84
1903						4.04	3.40		2.77
1904									2.74
1905									2.70
1906				4.77				4.76	2.69
1907				4.75				4.72	2.57
1908				4.73		3.84	3.14	4.60	2.62
1909				4.71				4.66	2.54
1910				4.69				4.55	2.56
1911				4.65		3.60	2.92	4.41	2.45
1912				4.59		3.58	2.90	4.40	2.47
1913				4.53		3.43	2.93	4.11	2.49
1914				4.48		3.42	2.88	4.08	2.31
1915				4.45		3.23	2.59	3.85	1.50
1916				4.38		3.23	2.60	3.64	1.21
1917				4.29		3.11	2.10	3.67	1.32
1918				4.20		3.16	2.03	3.56	1.52
1919				4.11		2.96	2.31	2.84	1.55
1920			5.48	4.00	3.28	3.29	3.08	3.72	2.67
1921	3.12		—	3.98	3.45	3.11	2.69	3.54	2.58
1922	3.11		—	3.83	3.27	2.87	2.44	3.38	2.40
1923	3.02		—	3.65	3.16	2.86	2.38	3.40	2.38
1924	2.97		4.83	3.63	2.96	2.78	2.28	3.18	2.34
1925	2.95		4.86	3.53	2.82	2.66	2.20	3.13	2.38
1926	2.85		4.28	3.36	2.75	2.58	2.15	3.02	2.36
1927	2.80		4.25	3.32	2.58	2.44	2.01	2.92	2.28
1928	2.77		3.89	3.29	2.54	2.43	2.01	2.94	2.29
1929	2.63		3.96	3.22	2.43	2.30	1.95	2.83	2.22
1930	2.58	2.25	3.69	3.28	2.45	2.30	1.95	2.75	2.29
1931	2.36	2.22	3.91	3.20	2.32	2.20	1.89	2.59	2.26
1932	2.19	2.19	3.59	3.08	2.27	2.19	1.83	2.46	2.25
1933	2.17	2.08	3.70	2.86	2.09	2.10	1.72	2.27	2.13
1934	2.11	2.04	3.27	2.80	2.03	2.15	1.76	2.33	2.15
1935	2.11	1.94	3.24	2.76	1.95	2.12	1.75	2.37	2.05
1936	2.18	1.95	3.04	2.70	1.93	2.14	1.77	2.31	2.06
1937	2.21	1.99	2.87	2.65	1.95	2.16	1.79	2.40	2.08
1938	2.21	2.11	2.68	2.70	2.07	2.18	1.84	2.52	2.11
1939	2.22	2.09	2.75	2.65	2.30	2.16	1.84	2.56	2.15

TABLE A2.3. (*cont.*)

Hungary	Italy	Netherlands	Norway	Spain	Sweden	Switzerland	United States	USSR	West Germany*	Japan
					4.06					
		4.53	4.37		4.06					
		4.46	4.26		3.97					
	4.43	4.42	4.16		3.84	3.82			4.77	
		4.38	4.07		3.83					
		4.29	3.95	4.66	3.83					
		4.23	3.92		3.81		3.70			
		4.18	3.87		3.77		3.68			
	4.47	4.13	3.87		3.77	3.56	3.62		4.34	
		4.04	3.96		3.74		3.60			
		3.94	3.82	4.43	3.60		3.57			
		3.81	3.80		3.49		3.54			
		3.84	3.72		3.44		3.50			
	4.28	3.85	3.64		3.32	3.01	3.48		3.52	
		3.86	3.62		3.26		3.40			
		3.59	3.37		3.06		3.34			
		3.64	3.43	4.22	2.99		3.25			
		3.59	3.53		2.93		3.30			
	3.08	3.47	3.44		2.83	2.47	3.36		2.26	
		3.36	3.17		2.72		3.30			
		3.89	3.61	4.14	3.22		3.20			5.35
3.81		3.75	3.31		2.93		3.12			5.22
—		3.54	3.18	4.02	2.66		3.12			5.12
—	3.90	3.55	3.09	4.02	2.55	2.43	3.20		2.62	5.26
3.18		3.39	2.85	3.92	2.43		3.10			5.07
3.36		3.26	2.61	3.82	2.34		3.03		2.21	5.22
3.24		3.18	2.59	3.87	2.22		2.91	5.57	2.10	5.19
3.05		3.08	2.38	3.70	2.11		2.83	5.42	1.98	5.00
3.08	3.46	3.09	2.34	3.80	2.08	2.10	2.66	5.32	1.99	5.09
2.92		3.00	2.23	3.69	1.95		2.52	4.99	1.93	4.87
2.84	3.38	3.02	2.19	3.68	1.96		2.51	4.83	1.88	4.82
	3.21	2.88	2.08	3.58	1.88		2.38	4.26	1.71	4.76
2.72	3.06	2.85	2.04	3.64	1.83	1.96	2.29	3.57	1.62	4.86
2.57	3.04	2.69	1.86	3.59	1.72	1.91	2.15	3.62	1.58	4.63
2.55	3.00	2.67	1.82	3.38	1.70	1.89	2.20	2.90	1.93	4.39
2.48	2.98	2.57	1.78	3.31	1.70	1.86	2.16	3.26	2.03	4.59
2.42	2.87	2.57	1.80	3.18	1.75	1.82	2.12	3.65	2.07	4.34
2.46	2.93	2.53	1.84	2.89	1.77	1.76	2.15	4.31	2.09	4.45
2.50	3.05	2.63	1.88	2.56	1.84	1.80	2.20	4.35	2.25	3.88
2.47	3.07	2.64	1.91	2.12	1.90	1.81	2.15	3.96	2.39	3.80

* retrospective estimate

Total fertility rates, Europe, anglo-saxon overseas countries and Japan, 1940–1987, per woman

Year	Australia	Austria	Belgium	Bulgaria	Canada	Czechoslovakia	Denmark	England and Wales	Finland	France	FRG	GDR	Greece	Hungary
1940	2.25			2.75	2.77	2.64	2.22	1.74	2.16	1.98	2.40			
1941	2.36			2.72	2.83	2.57	2.24	1.72	2.90	1.82	2.25			2.48
1942	2.37			2.78	2.96	2.52	2.50	1.93	2.15	2.01	1.83			2.52
1943	2.57			2.66	3.04	2.75	2.65	2.03	2.46	2.19	2.00			2.40
1944	2.63			2.65	3.01	2.83	2.84	2.25	2.56	2.24	1.89			2.61
1945	2.74			2.88	3.02	2.78	2.98	2.35	3.07	2.30	1.53			2.37
1946	2.99		2.52	3.06	3.37	3.21	3.02	2.47	3.41	2.98	2.00			2.30
1947	3.08		2.46	2.84	3.60	3.10	2.90	2.70	3.37	3.02	2.03	1.69		2.54
1948	2.98		2.44	2.87	3.44	3.00	2.71	2.39	3.47	3.00	2.08	1.64		2.58
1949	2.99		2.38	2.86	3.46	2.89	2.58	2.26	3.33	3.00	2.15	1.93		2.54
1950	3.07		2.34	2.94	3.46	3.04	2.58	2.19	3.16	2.93	2.10	2.30	2.60	2.60
1951	3.06	2.06	2.29	2.45	3.50	3.02	2.50	2.14	3.01	2.79	2.06	2.41	2.46	2.53
1952	3.18	2.06	2.33	2.44	3.64	2.97	2.54	2.16	3.06	2.76	2.09	2.40	2.25	2.47
1953	3.19	2.07	2.33	2.41	3.72	2.87	2.60	2.22	2.96	2.69	2.08	2.37	2.30	2.76
1954	3.19	2.11	2.37	2.35	3.83	2.83	2.54	2.21	2.93	2.70	2.13	2.35	2.38	2.97
1955	3.28	2.23	2.38	2.41	3.83	2.85	2.58	2.22	2.93	2.67	2.13	2.35	2.37	2.81
1956	3.33	2.41	2.40	2.36	3.86	2.83	2.59	2.36	2.91	2.66	2.25	2.26	2.31	2.60
1957	3.42	2.49	2.45	2.26	3.93	2.75	2.56	2.45	2.86	2.68	2.33	2.21	2.25	2.30
1958	3.42	2.52	2.50	2.23	3.88	2.57	2.54	2.52	2.68	2.68	2.32	2.20	2.21	2.18
1959	3.44	2.61	2.57	2.23	3.94	2.39	2.49	2.54	2.75	2.74	2.40	2.35	2.25	2.09
1960	3.45	2.69	2.56	2.30	3.90	2.39	2.54	2.67	2.71	2.73	2.37	2.33	2.20	2.02
1961	3.55	2.79	2.62	2.28	3.84	2.38	2.55	2.77	2.70	2.81	2.46	2.40	2.13	1.94
1962	3.43	2.80	2.59	2.29	3.76	2.34	2.54	2.83	2.66	2.78	2.44	2.41	2.16	1.79
1963	3.34	2.81	2.68	2.19	3.67	2.50	2.64	2.87	2.67	2.88	2.52	2.47	2.13	1.81
1964	3.15	2.77	2.71	2.16	3.50	2.51	2.60	2.92	2.58	2.90	2.55	2.51	2.24	1.82
1965	2.97	2.68	2.61	2.08	3.15	2.37	2.61	2.85	2.47	2.84	2.51	2.48	2.23	1.82
1966	2.88	2.66	2.52	2.02	2.81	2.22	2.62	2.77	2.40	2.79	2.54	2.40	2.29	1.89
1967	2.85	2.63	2.42	2.03	2.60	2.09	2.35	2.66	2.32	2.66	2.49	2.33	2.40	2.01
1968	2.89	2.59	2.31	2.28	2.45	2.01	2.12	2.58	2.14	2.58	2.39	2.29	2.37	2.06
1969	2.88	2.50	2.25	2.27	2.41	2.04	2.00	2.49	1.93	2.52	2.22	2.23	2.31	2.03
1970	2.85	2.32	2.25	2.18	2.33	2.07	1.95	2.42	1.84	2.47	2.01	2.19	2.42	1.96
1971	2.94	2.23	2.18	2.10	2.19	2.13	2.04	2.40	1.70	2.48	1.92	2.13	2.30	1.92
1972	2.74	2.14	2.09	2.03	2.02	2.21	2.03	2.20	1.59	2.40	1.71	1.79	2.30	1.93
1973	2.49	1.98	1.96	2.16	1.93	2.39	1.92	2.03	1.50	2.29	1.54	1.58	2.23	1.95
1974	2.40	1.95	1.83	2.30	1.88	2.50	1.90	1.91	1.62	2.10	1.51	1.54	2.35	2.31
1975	2.17	1.84	1.73	2.24	1.85	2.46	1.92	1.79	1.69	1.93	1.45	1.54	2.28	2.35
1976	2.08	1.70	1.72	2.25	1.82	2.43	1.75	1.73	1.72	1.83	1.46	1.64	2.35	2.23
1977	2.03	1.65	1.71	2.20	1.81	2.38	1.66	1.68	1.69	1.87	1.40	1.85	2.27	2.15
1978	1.98	1.62	1.69	2.14	1.76	2.37	1.67	1.75	1.65	1.83	1.38	1.90	2.29	2.07
1979	1.96	1.62	1.69	2.15	1.75	2.33	1.60	1.86	1.64	1.87	1.38	1.88	2.28	2.01
1980	1.94	1.68	1.68	2.04	1.73	2.16	1.54	1.91	1.63	1.95	1.45	1.94	2.21	1.90
1981	1.91	1.71	1.66	2.01	1.70	2.10	1.44	1.82	1.64	1.95	1.44	1.85	2.10	1.88
1982	1.93	1.70	1.60	2.02	1.69	2.09	1.43	1.77	1.72	1.91	1.40	1.85	2.02	1.79
1983	1.88	1.56	1.56	2.00	1.68	2.07	1.38	1.76	1.74	1.79	1.32	1.79	1.94	1.72
1984	1.95	1.53	1.52	1.99	1.69	2.07	1.40	1.76	1.70	1.81	1.29	1.75	1.82	1.73
1985	1.90	1.47	1.50	1.95	1.67	2.07	1.45	1.78	1.65	1.82	1.27	1.74	1.68	1.83
1986	1.87	1.46	1.53	1.99	1.67	2.03	1.48	1.78	1.63	1.84	1.33	1.70	1.61	1.83
1987	—	1.43	1.54	1.96	1.66	1.98	1.50	1.81	1.59	1.82	1.37	1.74	1.52	1.82

TABLE A2.4. (*cont.*)

Ireland	Italy	Netherlands	Norway	Poland	Portugal	Romania	Spain	Sweden	Switzerland	United States	USSR	Yugoslavia	Japan
	3.07	2.67			3.22		3.09	1.86	1.83	2.30	3.75		4.14
	2.74	2.61			3.12		2.47	1.92	2.06	2.40	3.74		4.36
	2.69	2.71			3.14		2.53	2.19	2.28	2.63	2.93		4.18
	2.61	2.98			3.27		2.88	2.41	2.42	2.72	2.37		4.11
	2.39	3.13			3.28		2.84	2.61	2.51	2.57	1.94		3.95
	2.37	2.97			3.39		2.91	2.63	2.61	2.49	1.76		3.11
	3.01	3.97	2.77		3.29		2.70	2.57	2.62	2.94	2.87		3.37
	2.85	3.70	2.66		3.14		2.67	2.50	2.56	3.27	3.23		4.51
	2.83	3.41	2.60		3.42	2.89	2.88	2.47	2.54	3.11	3.08		4.38
	2.62	3.22	2.52		3.23	3.34	2.68	2.39	2.45	3.11	3.01	4.09	4.30
3.28	2.49	3.09	2.52	3.71	3.08	3.17	2.48	2.30	2.40	3.09	2.88	3.74	3.64
—	2.34	3.05	2.48	3.75	3.14	3.03	2.47	2.22	2.30	3.27	2.92	3.29	3.25
—	2.29	3.08	2.61	3.67	3.19	3.00	2.57	2.24	2.33	3.36	2.87	3.60	2.97
—	2.25	3.03	2.66	3.61	3.02	2.88	2.55	2.27	2.29	3.42	2.73	3.38	2.68
—	2.32	3.03	2.70	3.58	2.92	3.00	2.51	2.19	2.28	3.54	2.97	3.34	2.47
3.26	2.31	3.03	2.79	3.61	3.08	3.09	2.58	2.25	2.30	3.58	2.87	3.16	2.36
3.46	2.30	3.05	2.86	3.51	2.95	2.89	2.62	2.29	2.35	3.69	2.82	3.02	2.22
3.60	2.30	3.08	2.86	3.49	3.06	2.73	2.78	2.28	2.41	3.77	2.84	2.76	2.04
3.62	2.28	3.10	2.89	3.36	3.05	2.59	2.81	2.26	2.40	3.70	2.83	2.77	2.11
3.75	2.35	3.17	2.91	3.22	3.02	2.43	2.80	2.25	2.42	3.67	2.81	2.74	2.04
3.81	2.37	3.12	2.88	2.98	3.01	2.33	2.81	2.19	2.44	3.65	2.84	2.80	2.01
3.79	2.41	3.20	2.91	2.83	3.12	2.17	2.78	2.23	2.53	3.63	2.76	2.73	1.95
3.90	2.43	3.17	2.89	2.72	3.24	2.04	2.82	2.25	2.59	3.47	2.65	2.68	1.95
3.95	2.49	3.19	2.91	2.70	3.11	2.01	2.90	2.34	2.67	3.33	2.59	2.66	1.98
4.01	2.62	3.17	2.96	2.59	3.17	1.96	3.05	2.48	2.68	3.21	2.50	2.64	2.03
4.05	2.55	3.04	2.93	2.52	3.07	1.91	2.97	2.42	2.61	2.93	2.46	2.71	2.14
3.91	2.52	2.90	2.89	2.43	3.04	1.90	2.95	2.36	2.52	2.74	2.50	2.65	1.60
3.84	2.48	2.79	2.80	2.33	3.00	3.66	3.01	2.28	2.41	2.57	2.40	2.56	2.22
3.77	2.44	2.72	2.75	2.24	2.90	3.63	2.93	2.07	2.30	2.48	2.39	2.48	2.10
3.84	2.45	2.75	2.70	2.20	2.84	3.19	2.90	1.93	2.19	2.47	2.37	2.44	2.06
3.87	2.37	2.58	2.51	2.20	2.62	2.89	2.87	1.92	2.09	2.48	2.43	2.29	2.13
3.96	2.39	2.38	2.49	2.25	2.90	2.66	2.88	1.97	2.02	2.30	2.46	2.37	2.17
3.88	2.34	2.17	2.39	2.24	2.69	2.55	2.86	1.91	1.91	2.05	2.46	2.35	2.15
3.78	2.33	1.92	2.22	2.26	2.66	2.44	2.83	1.87	1.81	1.93	2.39	2.31	2.17
3.70	2.31	1.79	2.13	2.26	2.60	2.72	2.86	1.77	1.72	1.90	2.43	2.28	2.09
3.44	2.19	1.66	1.99	2.23	2.59	2.60	2.81	1.77	1.60	1.80	2.41	2.26	1.91
3.32	2.08	1.63	1.87	2.27	2.58	2.55	2.79	1.68	1.54	1.77	2.39	2.25	1.85
3.20	1.95	1.58	1.75	2.20	2.48	2.57	2.66	1.64	1.52	1.83	2.37	2.18	1.80
3.19	1.84	1.58	1.77	2.18	2.28	2.52	2.53	1.60	1.49	1.80	2.32	2.15	1.79
3.22	1.74	1.56	1.75	2.24	2.17	2.48	2.33	1.66	1.50	1.84	2.28	2.12	1.77
3.20	1.66	1.61	1.72	2.25	2.13	2.43	2.16	1.68	1.53	1.82	2.26	2.13	1.75
3.08	1.57	1.56	1.70	2.22	2.03	2.35	1.99	1.63	1.54	1.81	2.25	2.06	1.77
2.95	1.57	1.49	1.71	2.31	2.00	2.15	1.88	1.62	1.55	1.81	2.33	2.13	1.77
2.74	1.53	1.47	1.66	2.40	1.95	2.00	1.71	1.61	1.51	1.79	2.37	2.10	1.80
2.54	1.50	1.49	1.66	2.37	1.89	2.16	1.69	1.66	1.52	1.82	2.41	2.10	1.81
2.49	1.42	1.50	1.68	2.31	1.70	2.31	1.61	1.73	1.51	1.84	2.40	2.05	1.76
2.43	1.35	1.56	1.71	2.20	1.61		1.53	1.79	1.52	1.77	2.46	2.01	1.70
2.34	1.28	1.56	1.76	2.15	1.56			1.88	1.52		2.53	2.00	1.65

TABLE A2.5. *Total fertility rates, Europe, anglo-saxon overseas countries, and Japan, 1851–1985*

Period	Australia	Austria	Belgium	Bulgaria	Canada	Czechoslovakia	Denmark	England and Wales	Finland	France	Germany / FRG	GDR	Greece	Hungary	Italy	Netherlands
1851–1855			4.18						4.92	3.38						4.60
1856–1860			4.51				4.82		4.76	3.46						4.60
1861–1865			4.63				4.91		5.03	3.50						4.98
1866–1870		(5.09)	4.76				4.93		4.32	3.50					4.92	5.05
1871–1875			4.87				4.94		4.97	3.42					4.88	5.23
1876–1880			4.78				4.88		5.02	3.45					4.92	5.42
1881–1885		(5.07)	4.61					4.55	4.92	3.38	5.29				5.06	5.25
1886–1890			4.30					4.16	4.99	3.12	5.22				5.02	5.14
1891–1895		(5.11)	4.17				4.31	3.90	4.72	2.97	5.16				4.84	4.97
1896–1900		5.11	3.98				4.24	3.62	4.88	2.90	5.04				4.59	4.75
1901–1905		4.93		4.82			4.04	3.40	4.77	2.79	4.77				4.43	4.48
1906–1910	3.35	4.67		4.73			3.84	3.14	4.71	2.60	4.34				4.47	4.15
1911–1915	3.51			4.54			3.45	2.84	4.22	2.25	3.52				4.28	3.82
1916–1920	3.07			4.20			3.15	2.42	3.53	1.65	2.26				3.08	3.59
1921–1925	3.03			4.85*	3.72		2.85	2.40	3.37	2.42	2.62				3.90	3.48
1926–1930	2.73			4.06	3.29		2.41	2.01	2.89	2.30	2.10			3.04	3.46	3.07
1931–1935	2.19			3.63	2.94		2.15	1.79	2.40	2.16	1.84			2.62	3.06	2.73
1936–1940	2.21			2.92	2.69		2.17	1.80	2.39	2.07	2.24			2.47	3.00	2.61
1941–1945	2.54		1.96	2.74	2.97		2.64	2.00	2.60	2.11	1.90	—		2.48	2.56	2.88
1946–1950	3.02		2.43	2.91	3.46	3.05	2.75	2.40	3.37	2.98	2.05	1.89		2.51	2.77	3.48
1951–1955	3.18	2.10	2.34	2.41	3.70	2.91	2.55	2.19	2.98	2.72	2.10	2.41		2.71	2.30	3.04
1956–1960	3.41	2.54	2.50	2.28	3.90	2.59	2.54	2.51	2.78	2.70	2.33	2.29	2.24	2.24	2.32	3.11
1961–1965	3.29	2.77	2.64	2.19	3.58	2.42	2.59	2.85	2.58	2.84	2.50	2.46	2.18	1.84	2.50	3.15
1966–1970	2.87	2.54	2.35	2.16	2.52	2.09	2.21	2.58	2.06	2.60	2.33	2.29	2.36	1.99	2.43	2.75
1971–1975	2.55	2.03	1.96	2.17	1.97	2.34	1.96	2.07	1.62	2.24	1.63	1.71	2.29	2.09	2.31	1.98
1976–1980	2.00	1.65	1.70	2.16	1.79	2.33	1.64	1.79	1.66	1.87	1.42	1.85	2.28	2.07	1.85	1.59
1981–1985	1.92	1.59	1.57	2.00	1.69	2.08	1.42	1.78	1.69	1.86	1.34	1.80	1.91	1.79	1.53	1.60

* 1924–1925

T ABLE A2.5. (*cont.*)

New Zealand	N. Ireland	Norway	Poland	Portugal	Rep. of Ireland	Romania	Scotland	Spain	Sweden	Switzerland	United States	USSR	Yugoslavia	Japan
									4.27					
									4.53					
									4.58					
									4.22					
		4.46							4.49	4.03				
		4.67							4.51	4.31				
		4.47							4.34	4.03				
		4.41							4.25	3.86				
		4.36							4.09	3.84				
		4.35							4.05	3.92				
		4.13							3.91	3.32	3.83			
		3.85							3.76	3.56	3.63			
		3.60							3.31	3.01	3.45			
		3.43							2.94	2.47	3.28			
		3.00						3.96	2.58	2.43	3.11			5.18
		2.32						3.75	2.08	2.10	2.69	5.23		4.99
		1.91						3.50	1.77	1.91	2.24	3.52		4.65
		1.86						2.77	1.82	1.80	2.18	4.00		4.12
		2.21						2.72	2.35	2.38	2.56	2.55		3.94
		2.62		3.23			2.64	2.68	2.45	2.51	3.10	3.01		4.04
3.54		2.64	3.64	3.07		3.06	2.45	2.54	2.23	2.30	3.43	2.87	3.36	2.75
3.93	(3.50)	2.86	3.31	3.02	3.65	2.59	2.76	2.76	2.24	2.40	3.70	2.83	2.82	2.08
3.78		2.93	2.67	3.14	3.94	2.02	2.98	2.90	2.33	2.62	3.31	2.59	2.68	2.01
3.21		2.72	2.29	2.88	3.85	3.05	2.74	2.92	2.12	2.30	2.55	2.42	2.48	2.02
2.79	2.83	2.24	2.26	2.69	3.75	2.60	2.15	2.85	1.89	1.82	2.00	2.43	2.31	2.10
2.15	2.65	1.77	2.25	2.31	3.24	2.52	1.80	2.49	1.65	1.52	1.83	2.32	2.14	1.79
		1.68	2.36	1.91		2.19		1.78	1.65	1.53	1.82	2.35	2.09	1.78

TABLE A2.6. *Total fertility rates, less developed countries in advanced transition (populations over 10 million inhabitants), 1950–1986, per woman*

Year	Argentina	Brazil	Chile	Malaysia	Mexico	South Korea	Sri Lanka	Taiwan	Venezuela
1950	—	—	4.31	—	5.89	—	7.6	6.0	—
1951	—	—	—	—	5.95	—	—	7.0	—
1952	—	—	4.24	—	5.74	} 5.6	7.5	6.6	—
1953	—	—	—	—	5.95	—	5.1	6.5	6.36
1954	3.17	—	—	—	—	—	—	6.4	6.36
1955	—	—	4.51	—	—	—	5.1	6.5	—
1956	3.21	—	—	6.7	—	—	—	6.5	—
1957	3.20	—	—	6.1	5.95	} 6.3	—	6.0	6.36
1958	3.13	—	—	6.1	6.56	—	—	6.1	6.38
1959	3.12	—	4.42	6.1	—	—	5.3	6.0	6.45
1960	3.07	(5.59)	4.69	6.1	6.35	6.0	5.1	5.8	6.40
1961	3.05	—	4.71	6.2	—	} 6.0	—	5.6	6.16
1962	3.11	} 6.15	4.64	5.9	—	—	} 5.1	5.5	6.23
1963	3.09	—	4.96	5.9	—	—	—	5.4	—
1964	3.08	—	4.81	6.0	6.20	—	—	5.1	—
1965	3.08	(5.38)	4.90	5.5	—	—	—	4.8	5.17
1966	—	—	4.63	5.2	—	} 4.6	—	4.8	5.43
1967	} 3.01	} 5.66	4.16	5.2	—	—	} 4.7	4.2	5.00
1968	—	—	3.87	5.1	—	—	—	4.3	4.99
1969	—	—	3.63	4.8	—	—	—	4.1	—

TABLE A2.6. (*cont.*)

Year	Argentina	Brazil	Chile	Malaysia	Mexico	South Korea	Sri Lanka	Taiwan	Venezuela
1970	2.97	5.77	3.51	4.7	6.56	4.2	—	4.0	4.73
1971	—	—	3.57	4.7	—	—	—	3.7	4.73
1972	2.95	5.08	3.56	4.8	6.19	4.1	4.2	3.4	5.1
1973	—	—	3.43	4.6	—	—	—	3.2	4.83
1974	—	—	3.31	—	—	—	—	2.9	4.96
1975	2.91	—	3.06	4.2	5.39	—	—	2.8	4.90
1976	—	—	2.87	—	—	—	—	3.1	4.78
1977	2.87	4.51	2.62	3.9	—	3.4	—	2.7	4.66
1978	—	—	2.57	3.9	—	—	3.9	2.7	4.6
1979	—	—	2.54	3.9	—	—	—	2.7	4.50
1980	—	—	2.47	—	—	—	—	2.5	4.4
1981	—	—	—	—	—	—	—	2.5	4.0
1982	—	—	—	—	—	—	—	2.3	4.0
1983	—	—	—	—	—	—	—	2.1	3.9
1984	—	—	—	—	—	—	—	2.1	3.7
1985	—	—	—	—	—	—	—	1.9	3.6
1986	—	—	—	—	—	—	—	1.7	—

TABLE A2.7. *Total fertility rates, less developed countries in advanced transition, 1950–1985 (UN estimates, except Taiwan)*

Country	Period						
	1950–55	1955–60	1960–65	1965–70	1970–75	1975–80	1980–85
Europe							
Albania	5.57	5.95	5.74	5.09	4.63	4.18	3.60
Africa							
Egypt	6.56	6.97	7.07	6.56	5.53	5.27	4.82
Mauritius	6.28	5.98	5.73	4.25	3.25	3.07	2.76
Réunion	5.69	5.89	5.69	4.85	3.56	2.84	2.23
South Africa	5.55	5.59	5.62	5.61	5.33	5.07	5.07
Tunisia	6.87	6.97	7.17	6.83	6.15	5.64	4.82
Latin America							
Argentina	3.16	3.12	3.08	3.04	3.14	3.37	3.38
Brazil	6.15	6.15	6.15	5.31	4.69	4.20	3.81
British Guiana	6.64	6.73	6.01	5.30	4.52	3.91	3.26
Chile	4.90	5.25	5.10	4.12	3.48	2.69	2.59
Colombia	6.72	6.72	6.72	5.94	4.78	4.30	3.93
Costa Rica	6.72	7.11	6.95	5.80	4.26	3.73	3.50
Cuba	4.01	3.76	4.67	4.30	3.48	2.18	1.97
Dominican Republic	7.50	7.50	7.32	7.01	6.31	4.80	4.18
Jamaica	4.24	5.04	5.45	5.43	5.43	3.96	3.37
Mexico	6.74	6.74	6.74	6.70	6.40	5.39	4.61
Panama	5.68	5.88	5.92	5.62	4.94	4.06	3.46
Puerto Rico	5.02	4.82	4.37	3.40	2.99	2.75	2.54
Trinidad and Tobago	5.33	5.33	5.02	3.89	3.48	3.07	2.88
Uruguay	2.73	2.83	2.89	2.81	2.99	2.93	2.76
Venezuela	6.46	6.46	6.46	5.90	4.96	4.45	4.10

TABLE A2.7. (cont.)

Country	Period						
	1950–55	1955–60	1960–65	1965–70	1970–75	1975–80	1980–85
Asia							
Cyprus	3.69	3.48	3.42	2.78	2.32	2.31	2.43
Hong Kong	3.60	4.68	5.27	3.98	2.87	2.30	1.91
India	5.97	5.92	5.81	5.69	5.43	4.83	4.30
Indonesia	5.49	5.67	5.42	5.57	5.53	4.81	4.10
Israel	4.16	3.89	3.85	3.79	3.77	3.50	3.09
Lebanon	5.74	6.15	6.35	6.05	4.92	4.30	3.79
Mainland China	5.98	6.27	5.37	6.13	5.08	3.07	2.34
North Korea	5.15	5.77	5.57	5.64	5.21	4.53	4.02
Philippines	7.25	7.06	6.57	6.01	5.27	4.94	4.41
Singapore	6.32	5.93	4.87	3.42	2.60	1.84	1.69
South Korea	5.15	6.04	5.37	4.49	4.09	3.14	2.60
Sri Lanka	5.70	5.40	5.12	4.65	3.97	3.76	3.38
Taiwan	6.50	6.10	5.20	4.30	3.65	3.15	2.23
Thailand	6.62	6.42	6.42	6.14	5.01	4.27	3.52
Turkey	6.15	6.15	6.01	5.80	5.45	4.30	3.96
West Malaysia	6.80	6.91	6.69	5.91	5.13	4.14	3.91
Oceania							
Fiji	6.60	6.76	5.92	4.57	3.34	3.59	3.18

Appendix 3. Crude Death-Rates

TABLE A3.1. *Crude Death Rates, Europe, 1735–1799*

Year	England and Wales	Finland	France	Norway	Sweden
1735	⎫			19.3	—
1736	⎬ 27.7			20.9	27.0
1737	⎪			24.8	33.7
1738	⎪			23.2	30.5
1739	⎭			23.2	30.6
1740	⎫		38.7	26.1	35.5
1741	⎬		43.8	36.9	32.2
1742	⎪ 31.6		40.1	69.3	39.0
1743	⎪		43.9	29.2	43.7
1744	⎭		34.4	22.1	25.3
1745	⎫		32.3	18.8	25.3
1746	⎬		37.2	21.2	26.4
1747	⎪ 27.0		48.8	23.9	27.5
1748	⎪		42.8	33.1	26.0
1749	⎭		38.6	27.9	28.1

Year	Czech countries	England and Wales	Finland	France	Norway	Sweden
1770		⎫	30.2	29.8	24.0	26.1
1771		⎬	26.1	33.1	23.2	27.8
1772		⎪ 27.6	23.9	37.2	26.2	37.4
1773		⎪	21.5	35.7	48.1	52.5
1774		⎭	21.5	34.4	25.8	22.4
1775		⎫	25.6	34.6	23.6	24.8
1776		⎬	30.5	30.1	20.7	22.5
1777		⎪ 25.5	32.0	30.8	21.0	24.9
1778		⎪	25.0	30.6	20.2	26.7
1779		⎭	21.9	41.3	27.4	28.5
1780		⎫	21.1	36.4	25.6	21.7
1781		⎬	26.5	36.5	20.9	25.6
1782		⎪ 28.8	25.1	38.7	22.6	27.3
1783		⎪	31.2	38.0	24.8	28.1
1784		⎭	25.3	35.7	24.0	29.8

TABLE A3.1. (cont.)

Year	England and Wales	Finland	France	Norway	Sweden	Year	Czech countries	England and Wales	Finland	France	Norway	Sweden
1750			36.7	27.2	26.9	1785			30.3	37.7	33.3	28.3
1751		24.6	31.7	27.0	26.2	1786			26.3	36.7	24.4	25.9
1752	26.2	26.3	34.4	25.4	27.3	1787	31.4	27.0	23.7	35.0	22.8	24.0
1753		26.1	38.2	23.4	24.0	1788			33.3	34.9	26.1	26.7
1754		35.1	37.8	24.1	26.3	1789			37.7	33.4	30.6	33.1
1755		30.7	34.2	25.1	27.4	1790			38.1	32.3	23.0	30.5
1756		36.3	33.3	27.2	27.7	1791			40.9	34.7	23.0	25.5
1757	25.9	36.2	32.1	22.1	29.9	1792	33.1	26.2	25.0	36.2	24.0	23.9
1758		29.5	36.8	24.6	32.4	1793			25.6	36.5	22.1	24.3
1759		28.1	40.6	19.5	26.3	1794			32.0	45.2	20.8	23.6
1760		27.9	35.0	23.1	24.8	1795			23.6	34.2	22.6	27.9
1761		28.3	37.6	24.4	25.8	1796			23.4	29.9	21.5	24.7
1762	28.7	29.6	37.6	25.9	31.2	1797	32.7	26.7	20.2	28.4	22.4	23.8
1763		41.0	36.6	38.8	32.9	1798			22.0	27.1	22.6	23.1
1764		33.1	34.5	29.1	27.2	1799			27.6	28.0	20.9	25.2
1765		29.7	36.7	30.2	27.7							
1766	28.1	28.6	36.9	30.4	25.1							
1767		29.1	38.8	25.1	25.6							
1768		25.8	35.3	24.4	27.2							
1769		28.3	29.5	23.7	27.2							

TABLE A3.2. *Crude death-rates, Europe and Australia, 1800–1849*

Year	Belgium	Czech countries	Denmark	England and Wales	Finland	France	Germany	Netherlands	Norway	Sweden	Australia
1800			28.5		25.5	29.4			—	31.4	
1801			27.7		21.8	27.0			27.6	21.1	
1802		34.3	23.2		22.3	28.9			24.9	23.7	
1803			22.5	27.1	33.1	32.9			24.6	23.8	
1804			23.7		25.0	34.4			23.2	24.9	
1805			23.2		21.2	28.5			20.4	23.5	
1806			22.3		21.9	28.3			20.7	27.5	
1807		39.7	22.9	24.7	29.2	30.1			22.1	26.2	
1808			25.2		60.5	28.6			26.4	34.9	
1809			25.1		59.2	28.2			35.3	40.0	
1810			22.7		24.6	26.0			26.8	31.6	
1811			24.4		30.8	26.4			24.7	28.8	
1812		37.6	27.0		24.1	32.7			21.3	30.3	
1813			22.8	25.6	27.3	34.3			28.9	27.4	
1814			24.7		32.4	33.6			22.2	25.1	
1815			21.6		26.0	28.5			19.7	23.6	
1816			20.7		23.4	25.8			19.3	22.7	
1817		31.0	19.0		24.0	26.3	26.7		17.7	24.3	
1818			18.9		24.8	25.5	27.1		19.1	24.4	
1819			19.5	25.5	27.2	27.1	27.9		19.7	27.4	

Year	C1	C2	C3	C4	C5	C6	C7	C8	C9	C10	C11	C12
1820	26.6	24.5	18.9		24.4	25.6	25.3			20.9		
1821	25.7	25.6	20.5		22.9	24.4	22.9			24.0	27.4	
1822	27.2	22.6	19.5		24.6	25.6	27.8			20.3		
1823	28.8	21.0	17.7		24.5	24.0	24.2	24.1		17.7		
1824	26.4	20.8	18.5		24.2	25.1	27.3			18.6		
1825	26.9	20.5	17.4		24.5	25.1	26.1			19.2		
1826	27.7	22.6	18.5		26.1	25.6	25.2			21.1		
1827	28.9	23.1	18.0		26.4	24.8	21.5			20.0		
1828	32.7	26.7	19.4		26.6	25.6	22.6	23.4		23.6	29.0	
1829	31.4	29.0	19.4		27.8	24.8	26.3			28.8		
1830	30.3	24.1	19.7		27.4	24.8	25.4			25.3		25.6
1831	42.2	26.0	19.8		30.4	24.4	28.5			30.1		24.0
1832	35.6	23.4	18.5		28.9	28.5	33.8			26.3	31.0	28.0
1833	31.8	21.7	20.3		28.5	24.6	46.4	22.0		23.3		26.8
1834	30.9	25.7	22.4		29.4	27.7	23.9			23.5		27.8
1835	30.2	18.6	19.5		26.2	24.6	24.7			22.9		24.0
1836	33.1	20.0	19.2		25.9	22.4	31.9		22.3	22.3		23.9
1837	33.2	24.7	20.8		29.1	25.4	28.4			21.7	30.6	27.6
1838	28.3	24.1	19.9		26.0	24.2	22.5	22.4		20.0		25.5
1839	30.0	23.6	21.6		27.2	22.8	20.6	21.8		20.5		26.1
1840	30.4	20.4	19.8	23.5	26.5	23.7	22.1	22.9		21.0		25.0
1841	29.5	19.4	17.3	23.3	26.2	23.2	22.4	21.6		19.8		23.8
1842	30.8	21.1	28.0	25.8	27.1	24.0	21.9	21.7	22.3	20.2	28.2	24.9
1843	31.4	21.5	17.9	23.1	26.9	23.1	22.2	21.2		19.3		23.3
1844	28.9	20.3	17.1	24.1	24.5	22.0	21.8	21.6		19.3		22.5
1845	29.7	18.8	16.9	23.2	25.3	21.1	22.9	20.9		19.4		23.0
1846	28.9	21.8	17.9	28.5	27.1	23.2	25.1	23.0		21.5		25.1
1847	44.4	23.7	20.3	31.1	28.3	23.9	23.3	24.7	23.0	21.7	31.0	27.7
1848	41.3	19.7	20.5	29.2	29.0	23.6	23.8	23.0		21.1		24.0
1849	35.0	19.8	18.3	31.2	27.1	27.4	24.5	25.1		22.4		27.7

TABLE A3.3. *Crude death-rates, Europe, and Australia, 1850–1899*

Year	Belgium	Bulgaria	Czech countries	Denmark	England and Wales	Finland	France	Germany	Greece	Hungary	Italy
1850	21.2			19.1	20.8	26.3	21.4	25.6			
1851	21.4			18.4	22.0	23.7	22.3	25.0			
1852	21.5		29.5	19.6	22.4	30.0	22.6	28.4			
1853	22.2			25.0	22.9	29.3	22.0	27.2			
1854	20.5			18.4	23.5	25.9	27.4	27.0			
1855	24.7			20.0	22.6	32.0	26.0	28.1			
1856	24.1			18.7	20.5	34.0	23.1	25.2			
1857	22.8		29.5	21.8	21.8	32.5	23.7	27.2			
1858	23.6			23.2	23.1	29.7	24.1	26.8			
1859	24.2			20.3	22.4	25.0	26.8	25.7			
1860	19.9			20.2	21.2	24.8	21.4	23.2	20.4		
1861	22.5			18.4	21.6	23.8	23.2	25.6	20.9	32.2	
1862	20.9			18.3	21.4	28.1	21.7	24.7	—	32.3	30.9
1863	22.3		27.9	18.1	23.0	29.6	22.5	25.7	—	33.9	31.0
1864	23.7			23.2	23.7	22.6	22.7	27.6	20.6	30.9	29.8
1865	24.7			23.0	23.2	24.9	24.7	27.6	21.4	30.3	29.9
1866	30.3.			20.2	23.4	33.6	23.2	30.6	19.7	38.0	29.1
1867	21.9		31.4	19.8	21.7	38.1	22.7	26.1	20.0	32.8	34.2
1868	22.0			19.2	21.8	77.6	24.1	27.6	22.7	33.1	30.6
1869	22.1			19.0	22.3	25.2	23.6	26.9	22.6	31.3	27.9
1870	23.6			19.0	22.9	18.2	28.4	27.4	21.9	33.5	29.9
1871	28.1			19.4	22.6	17.9	35.1	29.6	20.0	40.1	30.0
1872	23.5		29.4	18.4	21.3	19.7	22.0	29.0	20.6	42.9	30.8
1873	21.8			18.6	21.0	23.6	23.3	28.3	24.1	62.9	30.1
1874	20.9			20.0	22.2	24.1	21.4	26.7	19.3	43.3	30.4
1875	22.9			21.0	22.7	22.9	23.0	27.6	19.7	37.7	30.8
1876	21.6			19.7	20.9	21.9	22.6	26.4	19.4	36.0	28.9
1877	21.4		28.6	18.7	20.3	24.2	21.6	26.4	19.2	36.9	28.4
1878	21.7			18.4	21.6	24.1	22.5	26.2	18.5	37.7	29.2
1879	22.1			19.7	20.7	19.6	22.5	25.6	18.2	36.3	29.8
1880	22.3			20.4	20.5	23.9	22.9	26.0	17.9	37.8	30.8
1881	21.2	16.4		18.3	18.9	25.0	22.0	25.5	18.9	35.1	27.6
1882	20.5	19.1	28.9	19.2	19.6	22.3	22.2	25.7	18.8	36.1	27.6
1883	21.1	19.8		18.4	19.6	20.8	22.2	25.9	20.1	32.2	27.6
1884	21.2	17.2		18.3	19.7	20.9	22.6	26.0	17.7	31.0	26.9
1885	21.4	16.7		17.8	19.2	22.0	22.0	25.7	19.9	32.3	27.0
1886	21.3	19.2		18.1	19.5	22.2	22.5	26.2	—	32.3	28.7
1887	19.3	18.2	28.5	18.2	19.1	19.0	22.0	24.2	—	34.5	28.0
1888	20.3	18.2		19.5	18.1	19.8	21.9	23.7	—	32.3	27.5
1889	19.8	18.5		18.5	18.2	19.6	20.7	23.7	24.5	29.9	25.6
1890	20.8	21.1		19.0	19.5	19.6	22.8	24.4	23.2	32.5	26.3
1891	21.2	26.7		20.0	20.2	21.2	22.9	23.4	—	33.4	26.1
1892	21.8	31.6	27.7	19.5	19.0	23.8	22.8	24.1	—	34.7	26.2
1893	20.3	27.6		19.0	19.2	21.0	22.5	24.4	—	31.1	25.2
1894	18.6	27.4		17.6	16.6	19.4	21.2	22.3	—	30.4	25.0
1895	19.5	26.5		16.9	18.7	17.9	22.2	22.1	—	29.7	25.0
1896	17.5	24.3		15.7	17.1	18.7	20.0	20.8	—	28.6	24.1
1897	17.2	25.6	25.0	16.6	17.4	17.7	19.4	21.3	—	28.1	21.9
1898	17.6	23.1		15.5	17.5	17.7	20.9	20.6	—	28.0	22.9
1899	18.8	24.8		17.3	18.2	20.2	21.0	21.5	—	27.3	21.9

TABLE A3.3. (*cont.*)

Netherlands	Norway	Portugal	Rep. of Ireland	Romania	Russia	Scotland	Serbia	Spain	Sweden	Switzerland	Australia
22.2	17.2								19.8		32.9
22.5	17.1								20.7		29.8
24.0	17.9								22.7		30.9
24.6	18.3								23.7		31.9
24.1	16.0								19.8		34.5
28.1	17.2					20.8			21.5		43.9
23.5	16.9					19.5			21.8		30.2
26.8	17.1					20.6			27.6		28.2
27.9	16.1					21.0		28.0	21.7		29.1
31.0	17.0		16.9			20.3		28.8	20.1		29.2
24.8	17.2			20.3		22.3		27.4	17.7		26.8
25.3	19.5			21.6	35.4	20.3		26.6	18.5		29.8
23.9	20.0			21.8	34.0	21.7	38.6	27.3	21.4		29.5
23.9	18.9			26.2	37.7	22.9	35.1	29.2	19.3		29.9
25.3	17.8	16.8		26.0	38.7	23.6	31.3	31.5	20.3		30.1
25.9	16.6	16.9		27.1	36.9	22.3	25.5	33.8	19.4		30.5
28.7	17.1	17.1		38.0	—	22.2	24.3	29.0	20.0		40.8
23.7	18.5	17.6		25.1	36.8	21.3	25.7	30.4	19.6		29.4
24.8	18.3	16.3		25.1	39.7	21.2	32.7	34.1	21.0		28.7
23.1	17.2	16.9		24.3	38.3	23.0	29.7	34.1	22.3		29.0
25.9	16.2	17.2		26.1	35.0	22.2	33.2	31.6	19.8	25.8	29.4
29.5	16.9	16.8		26.4	37.9	22.2	32.4	—	17.2	27.6	29.8
25.9	16.7	18.8		30.5	41.2	22.3	32.1	—	16.3	22.2	32.6
24.1	17.0	18.9		32.6	36.5	22.4	32.6	—	17.2	22.7	38.9
22.7	18.3	18.1		34.9	35.2	23.2	36.4	—	20.3	22.3	31.7
25.5	18.8	19.0		32.0	34.6	23.3	31.3	—	20.3	24.0	30.0
23.5	18.9	17.9		28.3	34.9	20.9	48.3	—	19.6	24.1	29.8
22.2	16.9	18.2		29.8	34.4	20.6	33.6	—	18.7	23.5	31.5
23.0	16.0	19.3		33.2	38.2	21.2	33.4	30.5	18.1	23.3	31.6
22.4	15.1	20.1		29.2	34.8	20.0	31.3	30.5	16.9	22.6	29.9
23.6	16.2		20.4	35.9	36.1	20.5	31.5	30.1	18.1	21.9	29.7
21.5	17.0		17.9	26.7	34.1	19.3	24.7	30.2	17.7	22.4	30.5
20.7	18.6		17.4	28.2	40.4	19.4	23.1	31.4	17.4	21.9	30.8
21.8	17.0		19.4	26.0	37.5	20.2	22.8	32.7	17.3	20.4	30.1
22.2	16.6		17.9	25.5	34.4	19.6	25.0	30.6	17.5	20.2	29.3
21.0	16.5		18.7	25.0	35.8	19.3	26.9	38.0	17.8	21.3	30.1
21.8	16.3	20.4	18.0	26.7	33.2	19.0	29.6	29.2	16.6	20.7	29.4
19.7	16.2	22.1	18.4	30.5	33.8	19.0	24.9	32.8	16.1	20.2	28.9
20.4	17.3	21.7	17.9	30.6	33.4	18.0	24.4	30.1	16.0	19.9	29.2
20.2	17.8	22.5	17.4	27.2	35.5	18.4	25.5	30.4	16.0	20.3	27.3
20.5	18.0	25.2	18.2	28.4	36.7	19.7	25.3	32.1	17.1	20.9	29.1
20.6	17.7	22.8	18.4	30.1	35.8	20.7	26.5	31.8	16.8	20.6	28.0
21.0	17.9	20.3	19.4	34.7	41.0	18.5	33.5	30.6	17.9	19.0	28.8
19.2	16.5	21.4	18.0	30.8	34.4	19.3	29.7	29.7	16.8	20.1	27.1
18.5	16.9	20.7	18.2	31.7	34.3	17.1	28.1	30.3	16.4	20.1	27.8
18.6	15.6	20.8	18.5	27.6	35.5	19.4	26.9	29.0	15.2	19.2	27.5
17.2	15.2	22.7	16.7	29.1	33.3	16.6	27.0	29.6	15.6	17.8	26.2
16.9	15.4	21.9	18.5	29.6	31.7	18.4	26.5	28.4	15.4	17.7	25.5
17.0	15.3	21.4	18.2	26.5	33.2	18.0	22.9	28.2	15.1	18.3	24.8
17.1	16.8	20.2	17.7	27.5	31.2	18.1	24.3	28.8	17.7	17.7	25.2

TABLE A3.4. *Crude death-rates, Europe, 1900–1945*

Year	Albania	Austria	Belgium	Bulgaria	Czechoslovakia	Denmark	England and Wales	Finland	France	Germany	Greece	Hungary
1900		25.2	19.3	22.6		16.8	18.2	21.9	21.9	22.1		27.0
1901		24.0	17.2	23.3		15.7	16.9	21.1	20.1	20.7		25.0
1902		24.7	17.3	24.0	23.7	14.6	16.3	19.0	19.5	19.4		26.9
1903		23.8	17.0	22.9		14.6	15.5	18.5	19.3	20.0		26.1
1904		23.8	16.9	21.4		14.1	16.3	18.4	19.4	19.6		24.8
1905		25.1	17.5	21.7		15.0	15.3	19.1	19.6	19.8		27.8
1906		22.6	16.0	22.2	21.9	13.5	15.5	18.2	19.9	18.2		24.9
1907		22.7	15.4	22.2		14.1	15.1	18.8	20.2	18.0		25.6
1908		22.5	16.1	24.2		14.6	14.8	19.3	18.9	18.1		25.0
1909		22.9	15.4	26.5		13.3	14.6	17.4	19.1	17.2		25.4
1910		21.2	14.9	23.0		12.9	13.5	17.4	17.8	16.2		23.4
1911		21.9	16.0	21.4		13.4	14.6	17.4	19.6	17.3		24.8
1912		20.5	14.5	20.6	9.5	13.0	13.3	17.2	17.5	15.6		23.0
1913		20.3	14.2	29.0		12.5	13.8	17.1	17.7	15.0		23.2
1914		—	14.2	20.7		12.5	14.0	16.6	18.5	19.0		23.4
1915		—	13.1	19.9		12.8	15.7	16.9	18.3	21.4		25.3
1916		—	13.1	20.8	20.0	13.4	14.3	17.6	17.3	19.2		20.9
1917		—	16.3	21.2		13.2	14.2	18.8	18.0	20.6		20.7
1918		26.4	20.8	32.0		13.0	17.3	30.4	22.3	24.8		25.7
1919		20.4	14.9	20.2	18.3	13.0	14.0	20.2	19.0	15.6		20.0
1920		19.0	13.9	21.4	19.0	12.9	12.4	17.0	17.2	15.1		21.4
1921		17.0	13.4	21.7	17.7	11.0	12.1	14.9	17.7	13.9	13.6	21.2
1922		17.4	13.9	23.6	17.4	11.9	12.7	15.3	17.5	14.4	16.0	21.4
1923		15.3	12.9	21.2	15.0	11.3	11.6	14.7	16.7	13.9	17.0	19.5
1924		14.0	12.7	20.7	15.3	11.2	12.2	16.3	16.9	12.2	15.6	20.4
1925		14.4	12.8	19.2	15.2	10.8	12.1	14.4	17.4	11.9	14.9	17.1
1926		15.0	12.8	17.2	15.6	11.0	11.6	14.2	17.4	11.7	13.9	16.7
1927		15.0	13.0	20.3	16.0	11.6	12.3	15.4	16.5	12.0	16.3	17.8
1928		14.5	12.8	17.7	15.1	11.0	11.7	14.3	16.4	11.6	17.0	17.2
1929		14.6	14.4	18.1	15.5	11.2	13.4	15.9	17.9	12.6	18.4	17.8
1930	16.3	13.5	12.8	16.2	14.2	10.8	11.4	14.0	15.6	11.0	16.3	15.5
1931	—	14.0	12.7	16.9	14.4	11.4	12.3	14.1	16.2	11.2	17.7	16.6
1932	17.9	13.9	12.7	16.3	14.1	11.0	12.0	13.3	15.8	10.8	18.0	17.9
1933	—	13.2	12.7	15.6	13.7	10.6	12.3	13.6	15.8	11.2	16.8	14.7
1934	—	12.7	11.7	14.1	13.2	10.4	11.8	13.1	15.1	10.9	15.0	14.5
1935	—	13.7	12.3	14.6	13.5	11.1	11.7	12.7	15.7	11.8	14.8	15.3
1936	16.6	13.2	12.2	14.3	13.3	11.0	12.1	13.6	15.3	11.8	15.1	14.3
1937	19.5	13.3	12.5	13.6	13.3	10.8	12.4	12.8	15.0	11.7	15.0	14.2
1938	17.7	14.0	12.5	13.7	12.8	10.3	11.6	12.8	15.4	11.7	13.2	14.3
1939	15.0	15.3	13.2	13.4	13.3	10.1	12.1	14.3	15.3	12.3	13.9	13.5
1940	16.4	—	15.1	13.4	14.0	10.4	14.4	19.4	18.0	12.7	12.8	14.3
1941	16.6	—	14.4	12.7	14.0	10.3	13.5	19.8	17.0	12.1	17.1	13.2
1942	14.2	—	14.2	13.0	14.3	9.6	12.3	15.1	16.6	12.0	26.0	14.6
1943	—	—	13.1	18.8	14.1	9.6	13.0	13.3	16.0	12.1	15.3	13.5
1944	—	—	15.1	18.4	15.0	10.2	12.7	18.9	17.1	—	15.2	—
1945	—	—	14.5	16.2	17.8	10.5	12.6	13.1	16.1	—	11.7	23.4

TABLE A3.4. (*cont.*)

Italy	Netherlands	North. Ireland	Norway	Poland	Portugal	Ireland	Romania	Scotland	Spain	Sweden	Switzerland	USSR	Yugoslavia
23.8	17.9		15.8		20.3	19.6	24.2	18.5	29.0	16.8	19.3	31.1	
22.0	17.2		15.0		20.9	17.8	26.2	17.9	27.8	16.1	18.0	32.1	
22.2	16.3		13.9		19.7	17.5	27.7	17.3	26.1	15.4	17.0	31.5	
22.4	15.6		14.8		20.1	17.5	24.8	16.8	25.0	15.1	17.4	30.0	
21.2	15.9		14.3		18.9	18.0	24.4	17.1	25.7	15.3	17.5	29.9	
22.0	15.3		14.8		20.0	17.1	24.7	16.2	25.7	15.6	17.6	31.7	
20.9	14.8		13.7		22.0	16.9	23.9	16.4	25.9	14.4	16.6	29.9	
20.9	14.6		14.3		19.7	17.6	26.3	16.6	24.4	14.6	16.4	28.4	
22.8	15.0		14.2		20.0	17.5	27.4	16.6	23.6	14.9	15.8	28.3	
21.7	13.7		13.6		19.2	17.1	27.4	15.8	23.7	13.7	16.1	29.5	
19.9	13.6		13.5		19.2	17.1	24.8	15.3	23.1	14.0	15.1	31.5	
21.4	14.5		13.2		22.0	16.5	25.3	15.1	23.4	13.8	15.8	27.4	
18.2	12.3		13.5		20.1	16.5	22.9	15.3	21.3	14.2	14.2	26.5	
18.7	12.3		13.3		20.6	17.1	26.1	15.5	22.3	13.7	14.3	27.4	
17.9	12.4		13.5		19.3	16.3	23.5	15.5	22.2	13.8	13.8	—	
22.3	12.5		13.4		20.5	17.6	24.5	17.1	22.1	14.7	13.3	—	
23.3	12.9		13.8		21.6	16.3	—	14.7	21.4	13.6	13.0	—	
26.0	13.1		13.6		22.3	16.6	—	14.4	22.5	13.4	13.7	—	
35.1	17.4		17.2		41.4	17.9	—	16.3	33.3	18.0	19.3	—	
18.9	13.4		13.8		25.4	17.6	20.6	15.6	23.0	14.5	14.2	—	
19.0	12.3		12.8		23.7	14.8	25.9	14.0	23.4	13.3	14.4	—	
17.7	11.4		11.5	20.9	20.8	14.2	22.9	13.6	21.4	12.4	12.8	—	20.9
18.1	11.7	15.4	12.1	19.9	20.4	14.7	22.8	14.9	20.5	12.8	13.0	—	20.8
17.0	10.2	14.7	11.6	17.5	22.7	14.0	22.1	12.9	20.7	11.4	11.8	—	20.3
17.1	9.8	15.9	11.3	18.2	20.0	15.0	22.5	14.5	19.6	12.0	12.6	—	20.2
17.1	9.8	15.7	11.1	16.8	18.4	14.6	21.1	13.5	19.2	11.7	12.2	—	18.7
17.2	9.8	15.0	10.8	17.8	19.8	14.1	21.4	13.1	18.8	11.8	11.8	19.9	18.8
16.1	10.2	14.6	11.2	17.3	18.8	14.8	22.2	13.6	18.6	12.7	12.4	20.8	21.0
16.1	9.6	14.4	10.9	16.4	18.7	14.2	19.6	13.5	18.1	12.0	12.0	23.3	20.4
16.5	10.7	15.9	11.5	16.7	17.7	14.6	21.4	14.7	17.6	12.2	12.5	—	21.0
14.1	9.1	13.8	10.6	15.6	17.1	14.3	19.4	13.3	16.9	11.7	11.6	—	19.0
14.8	9.6	14.4	10.9	15.5	16.8	14.6	20.8	13.3	17.4	12.5	12.1	—	19.8
14.7	9.0	14.1	10.6	15.0	17.1	14.6	21.7	13.5	16.4	11.6	12.2	—	19.2
13.7	8.8	14.3	10.1	14.2	17.2	13.7	18.7	13.2	16.4	11.2	11.4	—	17.0
13.3	8.4	13.9	9.9	14.4	16.6	13.2	20.7	12.9	16.0	11.2	11.3	—	17.1
14.0	8.7	14.6	10.3	14.0	17.0	14.0	21.1	13.2	15.7	11.7	12.1	—	16.9
13.8	8.7	14.4	10.4	14.2	16.3	14.4	19.8	13.4	16.7	12.0	11.4	—	16.1
14.3	8.8	15.1	10.4	14.0	15.8	15.3	19.3	13.9	18.9	12.0	11.3	18.9	16.0
14.1	8.5	13.7	10.0	13.7	15.4	13.6	19.2	12.6	19.2	11.5	11.6	17.5	15.6
13.4	8.6	13.5	10.1	—	15.3	14.2	18.6	12.9	18.4	11.5	11.8	17.3	15.0
13.6	9.9	14.6	10.8	—	15.6	14.2	19.1	14.9	16.5	11.4	12.0	18.3	—
13.9	10.0	15.2	10.8	—	17.4	14.6	19.3	14.7	18.6	11.3	11.1	—	—
14.3	9.5	13.3	10.7	—	16.1	14.1	19.5	13.3	14.7	9.9	10.9	—	—
15.2	10.0	13.4	10.4	—	15.3	14.8	18.1	14.0	13.2	10.2	11.0	—	—
15.3	11.8	12.8	10.7	—	14.8	15.3	19.6	13.6	13.0	11.0	12.0	—	—
13.6	15.3	12.3	9.7	—	14.2	14.5	20.0	13.2	12.2	10.8	11.6	—	—

TABLE A3.5. *Crude death-rates, overseas English-speaking countries and Japan, 1900–1945*

Year	Australia	Canada	New Zealand	United States	Japan
1900	12.2				20.8
1901	12.5				20.9
1902	12.2				21.3
1903	11.1				20.4
1904	10.9				20.7
1905	10.9				21.6
1906	11.0		9.3	15.7	20.3
1907	11.0		11.0	15.9	21.4
1908	11.1		9.6	14.7	21.5
1909	10.3		9.2	14.2	22.5
1910	10.4		9.7	14.7	21.6
1911	10.7		9.4	13.9	20.9
1912	11.2		8.9	13.6	20.5
1913	10.7		9.5	13.8	20.0
1914	10.5		9.3	13.3	21.2
1915	10.6		9.1	13.2	20.7
1916	11.0		9.6	13.8	22.2
1917	9.7		9.6	14.0	22.2
1918	10.0		14.8	18.1	27.3
1919	12.7		9.5	12.9	23.3
1920	10.5		10.2	13.0	25.4
1921	9.9	10.6	8.7	11.5	22.7
1922	9.2	10.6	8.8	11.7	22.5
1923	9.9	10.7	9.0	12.1	22.9
1924	9.5	9.9	8.3	11.6	21.3
1925	9.2	9.9	8.3	11.7	20.3
1926	9.4	10.3	8.7	12.1	19.1
1927	9.4	10.0	8.5	11.3	19.7
1928	9.4	10.3	8.5	12.0	19.8
1929	9.5	10.4	8.8	11.9	19.9
1930	8.6	10.0	8.6	11.5	18.2
1931	8.7	9.9	8.3	11.1	19.0
1932	8.6	9.9	8.0	10.9	17.7
1933	8.9	9.6	8.0	10.7	17.7
1934	9.3	9.5	8.5	11.1	18.1
1935	9.5	9.7	8.2	10.9	16.8
1936	9.4	9.8	8.7	11.6	17.5
1937	9.4	10.3	9.1	11.3	17.1
1938	9.6	9.6	9.7	10.6	17.7
1939	9.9	9.7	9.2	10.6	17.8
1940	9.8	9.8	9.2	10.8	16.5
1941	10.6	10.0	9.8	10.6	16.0
1942	12.0	9.7	10.6	10.3	16.1
1943	11.5	10.1	10.0	10.9	16.7
1944	10.3	9.7	9.9	11.4	17.4
1945	10.3	9.4	10.1	11.0	29.2

TABLE A3.6. *Crude death-rates, Europe, 1946–1984*

Year	Albania	Austria	Belgium	Bulgaria	Czechoslavakia	Denmark	England and Wales	Finland	France	FRG	GDR	Greece	Hungary
1946	—	13.4	13.2	12.2	14.1	10.2	12.0	11.8	13.5	13.0	22.9	9.9	15.0
1947	18.9	12.9	12.7	11.6	12.1	9.7	12.3	11.9	13.1	12.1	19.0	9.3	12.9
1948	16.1	12.1	12.0	11.4	11.5	8.6	11.0	11.2	12.4	10.5	15.2	12.4	11.6
1949	12.5	12.8	12.4	12.2	11.9	8.9	11.8	11.2	13.7	10.4	13.4	7.9	11.9
1950	14.1	12.4	12.0	11.5	11.5	9.2	11.6	10.2	12.7	10.5	11.9	7.1	11.5
1951	15.2	12.7	12.4	10.7	11.4	8.8	12.5	10.0	13.3	10.8	11.4	7.5	11.7
1952	15.6	12.0	11.8	11.6	10.6	9.0	11.3	9.5	12.3	10.7	12.1	6.9	11.3
1953	13.7	12.0	12.1	9.3	10.5	9.0	11.4	9.6	12.9	11.3	11.7	7.3	11.7
1954	13.1	12.2	11.9	9.2	10.4	9.1	11.3	9.1	12.0	10.7	12.2	7.0	11.0
1955	15.1	12.2	12.2	9.1	9.6	8.7	11.7	9.3	12.0	11.1	11.9	6.9	10.0
1956	11.5	12.5	12.1	9.4	9.6	8.9	11.7	9.0	12.4	11.3	12.0	7.4	10.5
1957	11.8	12.8	11.9	8.6	10.1	9.3	11.5	9.4	11.9	11.5	12.9	7.6	10.5
1958	9.3	12.3	11.7	7.9	9.3	9.2	11.7	8.9	11.1	11.0	12.7	7.1	9.9
1959	9.8	12.5	11.3	9.5	9.7	9.3	11.6	8.8	11.2	11.0	13.3	7.4	10.5
1960	10.4	12.7	12.3	8.1	9.2	9.5	11.5	9.0	11.3	11.6	13.6	7.3	10.2
1961	9.3	12.1	11.6	7.9	9.2	9.4	11.9	9.1	10.8	11.2	13.0	7.6	9.6
1962	10.7	12.7	12.1	8.7	10.0	9.7	11.9	9.5	11.4	11.3	13.7	7.9	10.8
1963	10.0	12.8	12.4	8.2	9.5	9.8	12.2	9.2	11.6	11.7	12.9	7.9	9.9
1964	8.7	12.3	11.6	7.9	9.6	9.9	11.3	9.3	10.7	11.0	13.3	8.2	10.0
1965	9.0	13.0	12.1	8.2	10.0	10.1	11.5	9.6	11.1	11.5	13.5	7.9	10.7
1966	8.6	12.5	12.1	8.3	10.0	10.3	11.7	9.4	10.7	11.5	13.2	7.9	10.0
1967	8.4	13.0	12.0	9.0	10.1	9.9	11.2	9.4	10.9	11.5	13.3	8.3	10.7
1968	8.0	13.1	12.6	8.6	10.7	9.7	11.9	9.6	11.0	12.2	14.2	8.3	11.2
1969	7.5	13.4	12.5	9.5	11.2	9.8	12.0	9.8	11.3	12.2	14.3	8.1	11.3
1970	9.3	13.4	12.3	9.1	11.6	9.8	11.8	9.6	10.6	12.1	14.1	8.4	11.6
1971	8.1	13.1	12.3	9.7	11.5	9.8	11.6	9.9	10.7	11.9	13.8	8.4	11.9
1972		12.7	12.1	9.8	11.1	10.1	12.1	9.5	10.6	11.8	13.8	8.6	11.4
1973		12.3	12.1	9.5	11.6	10.1	12.0	9.3	10.7	11.8	13.7	8.7	11.8
1974		12.5	11.9	9.8	11.7	10.2	11.9	9.5	10.5	11.7	13.5	8.5	12.0
1975		12.8	12.2	10.3	11.5	10.0	11.8	9.3	10.6	12.1	14.3	8.9	12.4
1976		12.7	12.1	10.1	11.4	10.7	12.2	9.4	10.5	11.9	13.9	8.9	12.5
1977		12.2	11.4	10.7	11.5	9.9	11.7	9.2	10.1	11.4	13.4	9.0	12.4
1978		12.6	11.7	10.4	11.5	10.3	11.9	9.1	10.3	11.7	13.8	8.7	13.1
1979	6.5	12.2	11.4	10.6	11.5	10.6	12.1	9.1	10.2	11.5	13.8	8.7	12.7
1980	6.2	12.2	11.6	11.0	12.2	10.9	11.8	9.2	10.2	11.6	14.2	9.0	13.5
1981	6.4	12.3	11.2	10.7	11.8	11.0	11.7	9.2	10.3	11.7	13.9	8.8	13.5
1982	5.8	12.1	11.6	11.2	11.8	10.8	11.7	9.0	10.1	11.6	13.7	8.7	13.4
1983		12.3	11.3	11.4	12.0	11.2	11.7	9.3	10.2	11.7	13.3	9.1	13.9
1984		11.6	11.2	11.3	11.8	11.2	11.4	9.2	9.9	11.3	13.3	8.9	13.8

TABLE A3.6. (*cont.*)

Italy	Netherlands	North. Ireland	Norway	Poland	Portugal	Rep. of Ireland	Romania	Scotland	Spain	Sweden	Switzerland	USSR
12.1	8.5	12.5	9.4	13.4	14.7	14.0	18.8	13.1	12.9	10.5	11.3	10.8
11.5	8.1	12.6	9.5	11.3	13.3	14.8	22.0	13.1	12.0	10.8	11.4	—
10.6	7.4	11.2	8.9	11.2	13.0	12.1	15.6	12.0	10.9	9.8	10.8	—
10.5	8.1	11.5	9.0	11.6	14.1	12.7	13.7	12.5	11.4	10.0	10.7	—
9.8	7.5	11.6	9.1	11.6	12.2	12.7	12.4	12.5	10.8	10.0	10.1	9.7
10.3	7.6	12.8	8.4	12.4	12.5	14.3	12.8	12.9	11.5	9.9	10.5	9.7
10.0	7.4	10.8	8.5	11.1	11.8	11.9	11.7	12.1	9.6	9.6	9.9	9.4
9.9	7.7	10.7	8.5	10.2	11.4	11.8	11.6	11.5	9.6	9.7	10.2	9.1
9.1	7.5	10.9	8.6	10.3	11.1	12.1	11.5	12.0	9.0	9.6	10.0	8.9
9.1	7.6	11.1	8.5	9.6	11.6	12.6	9.7	12.1	9.3	9.5	10.1	8.2
10.1	7.8	10.6	8.7	9.0	12.4	11.7	9.9	12.1	9.7	9.6	10.2	7.6
9.7	7.5	10.9	8.8	9.5	11.7	11.9	10.2	11.9	9.8	9.9	10.0	7.8
9.3	7.6	10.8	9.0	8.4	10.5	12.0	8.7	12.1	8.6	9.6	9.5	7.2
9.1	7.6	10.9	8.9	8.6	11.1	12.0	10.2	12.2	8.8	9.5	9.5	7.6
9.6	7.7	10.8	9.1	7.6	10.8	11.5	8.7	11.9	8.7	10.0	9.7	7.1
9.3	7.6	11.3	9.2	7.6	11.2	12.3	8.7	12.3	8.4	9.8	9.5	7.2
10.0	8.0	10.6	9.4	7.9	10.8	12.0	9.2	12.2	8.8	10.2	9.9	7.5
10.0	8.0	11.0	10.1	7.5	10.8	11.9	8.3	12.6	8.9	10.1	10.1	7.2
9.4	7.7	10.5	9.5	7.6	10.6	11.4	8.1	11.7	8.5	10.0	9.3	6.9
9.8	8.0	10.6	9.5	7.4	10.3	11.5	8.6	12.1	8.4	10.1	9.5	7.3
9.3	8.1	11.1	9.6	7.3	10.8	12.2	8.2	12.3	8.4	10.1	9.4	7.3
9.5	7.9	9.8	9.6	7.8	10.2	10.8	9.3	11.5	8.4	10.1	9.2	7.6
9.9	8.2	10.6	10.0	7.6	10.0	11.4	9.6	12.2	8.4	10.4	9.5	7.7
10.0	8.3	10.8	9.9	8.1	10.6	11.5	10.1	12.3	8.9	10.5	9.5	8.1
9.6	8.4	10.8	10.0	8.2	10.7	11.4	9.5	12.2	8.3	9.9	9.2	8.2
9.7	8.4	10.5	10.0	8.6	11.4	10.7	9.5	11.8	8.9	10.2	9.3	8.2
9.6	8.5	11.0	10.0	8.0	10.5	11.4	9.2	12.5	8.2	10.3	8.8	8.5
10.0	8.2	11.4	10.1	8.3	11.1	11.3	9.8	12.4	8.6	10.5	8.9	8.7
9.6	8.1	11.2	9.9	8.2	11.0	11.2	9.1	12.4	8.3	10.6	8.8	8.7
9.9	8.3	10.7	9.9	8.7	10.4	10.7	9.3	12.1	8.3	10.8	8.7	9.3
9.7	8.3	11.1	10.0	8.8	10.5	10.5	9.6	12.4	8.3	11.3	8.8	9.4
9.6	7.9	11.1	9.8	9.0	9.9	10.2	9.6	12.0	8.0	10.7	8.8	9.6
9.5	8.2	10.5	10.0	9.2	9.8	10.1	9.7	12.6	8.0	10.8	9.1	9.7
9.4	8.0	10.9	10.2	9.1	9.4	9.7	9.9	12.7	7.8	11.0	9.0	10.1
9.6	8.0	10.9	10.1	9.8	9.7	9.6	10.4	12.3	7.6	11.0	9.2	10.3
9.5	8.1	10.7	10.2	9.2	9.7	9.4	10.0	12.4	7.6	11.0	9.3	10.2
9.4	8.1	10.5	10.0	9.2	9.3	9.3	10.0	12.6	7.4	10.8	9.3	10.1
9.9	8.2	10.2	10.1	9.5	9.9	9.3	10.4	12.3	7.8	10.9	9.3	10.4
9.4	8.3	9.9	10.3	9.9	9.6	9.1	10.3	12.1	7.7	10.9	9.1	10.8

TABLE A3.7. *Crude death-rates, Yugoslavia, overseas English-speaking countries, and Japan 1946–1984*

Year	Yugoslavia	Australia	Canada	New Zealand	United States	Japan
1946	—	10.1	9.4	9.7	9.9	17.6
1947	12.8	9.7	9.4	9.4	10.1	14.6
1948	13.5	10.0	9.3	9.2	9.9	11.9
1949	13.5	9.5	9.3	9.1	9.7	11.6
1950	13.0	9.6	9.0	9.3	9.6	10.9
1951	14.1	9.7	9.0	9.7	9.7	9.9
1952	11.8	9.4	8.7	9.5	9.6	8.9
1953	12.4	9.1	8.6	9.0	9.6	8.9
1954	10.8	9.1	8.1	9.0	9.1	8.2
1955	11.4	8.9	8.2	9.0	9.3	7.8
1956	11.2	9.1	8.2	9.0	9.3	8.0
1957	10.7	8.8	8.2	9.4	9.5	8.3
1958	9.3	8.5	7.9	8.9	9.5	7.4
1959	9.9	8.9	8.0	9.1	9.4	7.4
1960	9.9	8.6	7.8	8.8	9.5	7.6
1961	9.0	8.5	7.7	9.0	9.3	7.4
1962	9.9	8.7	7.7	8.9	9.4	7.5
1963	8.9	8.7	7.8	8.8	9.6	7.0
1964	9.4	9.0	7.6	8.8	9.4	6.9
1965	8.8	8.8	7.6	8.7	9.4	7.1
1966	8.1	9.0	7.5	8.9	9.5	6.8
1967	8.8	8.7	7.4	8.4	9.4	6.8
1968	8.7	9.1	7.4	8.9	9.7	6.8
1969	9.3	8.7	7.3	8.7	9.5	6.8
1970	8.9	9.0	7.3	8.8	9.4	6.9
1971	8.7	8.7	7.3	8.5	9.3	6.6
1972	9.2	8.5	7.4	8.6	9.4	6.5
1973	8.6	8.4	7.4	8.6	9.4	6.6
1974	8.4	8.4	7.4	8.3	9.0	6.4
1975	8.7	7.8	7.3	8.1	8.7	6.2
1976	8.5	8.0	7.2	8.1	8.7	6.2
1977	8.4	7.6	7.1	8.3	8.6	6.1
1978	8.6	7.5	7.1	7.9	8.6	6.1
1979	8.5	7.3	7.0	8.1	8.5	6.0
1980	8.8	7.3	7.1	8.5	8.7	6.1
1981	9.0	7.3	7.0	8.0	8.6	6.1
1982	8.9	7.5	7.1	8.0	8.5	6.0
1983	9.6	7.3	7.0	8.1	8.6	6.2
1984	9.3	7.1	7.0	8.2	8.7	6.2

TABLE A3.8. *Crude death-rates, Egypt, Mauritius, Réunion, and Tunisia, 1910–1983*

Year	Egypt	Mauritius	Réunion	Tunisia
1910		36.9		
1911		32.8		
1912		38.8		
1913		35.5		
1914		32.5		
1915		34.8		
1916		30.4		
1917	29.4	32.5		
1918	39.6	33.9		
1919	29.4	64.9		
1920	28.0	32.3		
1921	25.0	40.3		
1922	25.1	34.5		
1923	25.8	28.5		
1924	24.9	28.1		
1925	26.0	24.9		
1926	26.9	25.3		
1927	25.2	25.1		
1928	26.4	28.2		
1929	27.7	30.7		

Year	Egypt	Mauritius	Réunion	Tunisia
1950	19.1	13.9	21.9	—
1951	19.3	14.9	18.6	—
1952	17.8	14.8	18.1	8.3
1953	19.6	15.9	16.7	8.3
1954	17.9	15.8	14.8	8.2
1955	17.6	12.8	15.4	7.4
1956	16.4	11.7	12.7	8.5
1957	17.8	12.8	14.3	9.2
1958	16.6	11.7	14.5	9.1
1959	16.3	10.8	13.6	10.2
1960	16.9	11.2	11.5	10.1
1961	15.8	9.8	11.5	10.8
1962	17.9	9.3	11.5	11.6
1963	15.4	9.6	10.9	10.4
1964	15.7	8.6	10.3	10.0
1965	14.0	8.6	9.5	11.7
1966	15.8	8.8	10.5	10.6
1967	14.2	8.5	8.7	—
1968	16.1	9.0	8.8	—
1969	14.4	8.0	8.9	—

Year			
1930	24.5	35.4	
1931	26.6	38.4	
1932	28.5	32.2	
1933	27.5	26.6	
1934	27.8	25.1	
1935	26.4	25.8	
1936	28.8	25.8	
1937	27.1	28.1	
1938	26.3	29.2	
1939	25.8	27.4	
1940	26.3	24.9	
1941	25.7	25.0	
1942	28.2	28.6	
1943	27.6	25.5	
1944	26.0	27.0	
1945	27.7	36.0	
1946	25.0	29.3	14.6
1947	21.3	20.0	14.8
1948	20.4	24.0	14.9
1949	20.6	16.4	—

(brace spanning 1945–1948: 23.5)

Year				
1970	15.0	7.8	8.2	
1971	13.1	7.6	7.7	
1972	14.3	7.9	7.3	
1973	12.9	7.8	7.2	
1974	12.5	7.3	6.5	
1975	12.1	8.1	6.7	
1976	11.7	7.8	6.4	
1977	11.7	7.9	6.3	
1978	10.4	7.1	6.2	
1979	10.8	7.3	6.1	
1980	—	7.2	6.6	—
1981	10.1	6.8		9.3
1982	10.2	6.7		7.5
1983		6.6		8.0

TABLE A3.9. Crude death-rates, Latin America, 1900–1984

Year	Argentina	British Guiana	Chile	Costa Rica	Cuba	Jamaica	Mexico	Panama	Puerto Rico	Trinidad and Tobago	Uruguay	Venezuela
1900											13.7	
1901											13.4	
1902	26.1			24.0							14.1	
1903											14.2	
1904											11.8	
1905											13.7	
1906				25.8			33.1				15.0	
1907	22.7						33.0				15.2	
1908							31.8				13.9	
1909							32.3				14.3	
1910							33.3				14.9	
1911							—				14.4	
1912	19.7			24.1			—			24.0	14.1	
1913							—				12.6	
1914							—				12.2	
1915							—				12.9	
1916						25.6	—				15.3	
1917				25.9			—				12.8	
1918	17.7						—				14.3	
1919							—				13.2	

Year												
1920	} 15.1						—				12.9	
1921							—				12.2	
1922				} 22.9	} 13.5	} 24.4	25.3	} 17.1	} 21.0		10.6	
1923							24.4				11.4	
1924							25.6				11.7	
1925							26.5			23.9	11.8	
1926	} 14.1			} 23.1	13.0	} 20.4	24.9	} 17.1	22.6		11.7	
1927					13.1		24.0		20.6		10.5	
1928					11.2		25.3		23.6		11.5	
1929					11.2		26.8		25.3		10.7	
1930	12.2	23.2	24.1	22.5	9.8	17.3	26.6	13.1	18.6	19.1	10.7	17.2
1931	11.9	22.0	21.5	24.7	10.3	18.9	25.9	16.4	20.4	20.1	11.0	18.4
1932	11.4	21.2	22.2	22.9	10.9	17.4	26.1	15.8	22.0	17.1	10.1	17.1
1933	11.3	24.6	26.0	21.7	12.4	19.7	25.7	15.6	22.3	19.6	10.3	18.5
1934	11.1	24.8	25.7	18.6	11.6	17.3	23.8	15.7	18.9	18.6	10.0	18.1
1935	12.5	20.8	23.9	22.9	12.0	18.0	22.6	11.9	18.0	17.5	10.6	16.6
1936	11.3	20.6	24.0	21.0	10.7	17.7	23.5	12.7	20.0	16.3	9.7	17.4
1937	11.5	22.1	22.7	19.2	10.2	15.6	24.4	13.1	20.9	17.3	10.4	18.1
1938	11.8	25.8	23.1	17.7	11.1	16.8	22.9	14.2	18.7	15.8	10.3	18.3
1939	10.7	19.8	22.9	19.3	9.8	15.1	23.0	11.4	17.7	16.0	9.1	18.7
1940	10.7	18.6	21.3	18.1	9.7	15.4	23.2	11.5	18.3	15.8	9.6	16.6
1941	10.4	15.7	19.4	18.1	9.3	14.4	22.1	13.3	18.3	16.1	9.4	16.4
1942	10.3	17.4	19.9	21.0	9.4	14.3	22.8	12.8	16.2	17.7	9.4	16.3
1943	10.1	24.8	19.3	17.7	10.5	14.1	22.4	13.0	14.3	16.6	9.3	15.9
1944	10.2	22.0	18.9	16.7	9.4	15.1	20.6	12.3	14.4	15.0	8.9	17.0
1945	10.3	17.9	19.3	15.5	9.7	14.9	19.5	11.8	13.7	14.5	8.7	15.0
1946	9.6	15.6	16.6	13.9	7.1	13.3	19.4	11.2	12.9	13.8	8.8	14.7
1947	9.9	14.8	16.1	14.9	7.1	14.1	16.6	11.7	11.8	13.4	9.0	13.5
1948	9.4	14.2	18.7	13.2	7.2	13.3	16.9	10.2	12.0	12.2	8.9	12.9
1949	9.1	13.3	17.3	12.7	7.5	12.2	17.7	9.8	10.6	12.2	8.6	12.0

TABLE A3.9. (cont.)

Year	Argentina	British Guiana	Chile	Costa Rica	Cuba	Jamaica	Mexico	Panama	Puerto Rico	Trinidad and Tobago	Uruguay	Venezuela
1950	9.1	14.6	15.7	12.2	7.1	11.8	16.2	9.6	9.9	12.1	8.0	11.0
1951	8.8	13.5	15.7	11.7	7.3	12.1	16.9	8.6	10.0	12.0	7.8	11.1
1952	8.6	13.5	13.0	11.6	6.5	11.5	14.7	8.4	9.2	12.1	7.7	10.8
1953	8.9	13.3	12.4	11.7	6.3	10.4	15.5	9.2	8.2	10.7	7.7	9.9
1954	8.4	12.4	12.8	10.6	5.9	10.7	12.8	8.8	7.6	9.8	7.4	10.1
1955	8.8	11.9	12.9	10.5	6.1	9.9	13.3	9.1	7.2	10.4	7.9	10.3
1956	8.3	11.2	12.1	9.6	5.8	9.4	11.7	9.2	7.4	9.6	7.7	9.9
1957	9.0	11.6	12.8	10.1	6.3	8.9	12.7	9.3	7.1	9.5	8.0	9.3
1958	8.3	10.2	12.2	9.0	6.5	9.1	12.0	9.3	7.0	9.2	7.6	8.7
1959	8.4	10.0	12.6	9.0	6.5	10.6	11.4	8.7	6.8	9.1	9.0	8.0
1960	8.2	9.5	12.4	8.6	6.2	8.9	11.2	8.3	6.7	7.8	8.1	7.2
1961	8.7	9.3	11.6	7.9	6.5	8.8	10.4	8.0	6.8	7.9	7.9	7.0
1962	8.6	8.0	11.7	8.5	7.2	9.0	10.5	7.2	6.7	8.1	7.8	7.3
1963	8.6	7.8	11.8	8.2	6.8	8.9	10.4	8.0	6.9	7.2	8.9	7.2
1964	8.7	7.9	11.1	8.5	6.4	7.6	9.9	7.4	7.2	7.0	9.0	7.2
1965	8.9	6.9	10.5	7.8	6.5	8.0	9.8	7.3	6.8	6.9	9.1	—
1966	8.6	7.3	10.2	7.4	6.5	8.0	9.8	—	6.7	7.1	9.0	—
1967	8.6	7.0	9.5	7.1	6.3	7.4	9.5	—	6.3	6.7	9.5	—
1968	9.2	7.0	9.0	6.5	6.6	7.9	9.9	—	6.5	7.0	9.2	—
1969	9.5	6.1	8.8	6.9	6.7	7.6	9.7	—	6.5	6.9	9.7	—

Year												
1970	9.4	6.8	8.5	6.7	6.3	7.7	9.9	—	6.7	6.8	9.2	—
1971	—	7.1	8.7	5.9	6.0	7.6	9.0	6.7	6.5	6.8	9.8	6.6
1972	—	—	8.2	5.9	5.5	7.2	8.8	6.0	6.7	6.6	9.6	6.7
1973	—	—	8.2	5.1	5.8	7.2	8.2	5.8	6.8	6.7	9.5	6.8
1974	—	8.0	7.8	5.0	5.6	7.2	7.5	5.3	6.8	6.5	10.2	6.3
1975	9.1	7.6	7.3	4.9	5.4	6.9	7.2	}	6.7	6.5	9.8	6.2
1976	8.7	7.9	7.4	4.7	5.6	7.0	7.4	}	6.6	6.7	10.1	6.1
1977	8.5	7.3	6.9	4.3	5.8	6.8	7.1	6.0	6.5	6.3	10.1	5.8
1978	8.5	7.3	6.7	4.1	5.6	5.9	6.4	}	6.4	6.3	9.8	5.5
1979	8.5	—	6.8	4.2	5.7	6.2	6.3	}	6.4	5.8	9.8	5.5
1980	8.5		6.7	4.1	5.7	5.8	6.3		6.4	6.0	10.3	
1981	8.4		6.2	4.0	6.0	6.1	6.0		6.5	6.2	9.4	5.5
1982			6.1	3.9	5.8	5.7	5.6		6.6	6.8	9.2	5.2
1983			6.4	3.9	5.9	5.5			6.6			4.8
1984			6.3		6.0							4.6

TABLE A3.10. *Crude death-rates, Latin America, 1870–1985*
(UN estimated for 1950–1985)

Year	Chile	Uruguay	Year	Argentina	Chile	Mexico	Uruguay
1880	32.1		1890		36.2		21.2
1881	28.6		1891		34.0		17.1
1882	29.2		1892		36.5		17.0
1883	27.0	16.3	1893		33.1		17.2
1884	23.8	17.3	1894		32.7		18.5
1885	30.6	16.7	1895		27.3	31.0	15.6
1886	32.4	18.3	1896		29.2	31.6	15.6
1887	37.1	20.2	1897		28.1	35.0	14.5
1888	37.3	18.8	1898		26.4	34.3	14.4
1889	32.5	19.1	1899	17.1	26.9	37.9	12.8

Period	Argentina	Brazil	British Guiana	Chile	Costa Rica	Jamaica	Mexico	Panama	Trinidad and Tobago	Venezuela
1870–1874	31.9	31.1				26				
1875–1879	29.6	30.2								
1880–1884	29.8	29.1		27.5						
1885–1889	29.7	28.0	33.1		22.3	23.1				
1890–1894	28.4	26.8		33.1	24.3					
1895–1899	28.9	25.7	27.9		25.3	23.5				
1900–1904	26.1	24.6		30.5	24.0					
1905–1909	22.7	23.6		32.5	25.8					
1910–1914	19.7	22.7		(31.0)	24.1	25.6				(22.0)
1915–1919	17.7	21.9		—	25.0					—
1920–1924	15.1		(28.5)	31.0	22.9		25.1	17.1	22.3	21.7
1925–1929	14.1	24.9	25.6	26.4	23.1	17.9	25.5	17.1	20.1	19.5
1930–1934	12.5		23.2	24.5	22.1		25.6	12.9	18.9	17.9
1935–1939	12.5		21.8	23.7	20.0		23.3	12.9	16.6	17.8
1940–1944	11.3	20.6	19.7	19.8	18.3		22.0	8.8	—	16.4
1945–1949	10.5		15.2	17.2	14.0		17.8	10.9	—	—
1950–1955	9.1	15.1	13.5	13.6	12.3	11.5	16.2	13.2	11.3	14.9
1955–1960	8.6	13.6	10.7	12.8	10.7	9.8	13.2	10.9	9.3	12.3
1960–1965	8.8	12.3	8.6	11.9	9.1	9.1	11.3	9.6	7.3	10.1
1965–1970	9.1	10.8	7.7	10.0	7.2	8.0	10.3	8.4	6.9	8.3
1970–1975	9.0	9.7	7.6	8.4	5.8	7.4	9.2	7.3	6.8	6.8
1975–1980	8.8	8.9	6.7	8.1	4.6	6.7	8.0	6.0	6.8	6.1
1980–1985	8.7	8.4	5.9	7.7	4.2	6.7	7.1	5.4	6.2	5.6

TABLE A3.11. *Crude death-rates, Asia and Oceania 1900–1984*

Year	China (Taiwan)	Cyprus	Israel	Hong Kong	India	Malaysia	Philippines	Singapore	Sri Lanka	Fiji
1900								40.0	28.7	
1901		18.1						43.0	27.6	
1902		14.6						39.4	27.5	
1903		14.6					43.2	39.0	25.9	
1904		14.8					18.9	40.5	24.9	
1905		17.7					21.0	—	27.7	
1906	33.4	15.8					17.8	37.8	35.1	
1907	32.4	17.7					16.9	38.5	30.7	
1908	31.9	19.7					22.8	42.5	30.1	
1909	31.1	16.9					21.1	37.1	31.0	
1910	27.5	15.2					22.1	38.5	27.3	} 32.4
1911	26.2	16.2					21.3	46.0	34.7	
1912	25.0	17.7					20.6	39.0	32.3	
1913	25.0	18.8					16.8	35.0	28.4	
1914	27.6	17.6					17.6	34.1	32.0	
1915	31.5	19.8					18.6	29.2	25.4	
1916	28.6	17.9					20.0	30.7	27.4	
1917	27.0	18.2					21.1	37.0	25.5	
1918	34.1	22.9					35.5	43.9	33.4	
1919	26.8	17.2					31.7	33.0	37.5	
1920	32.1	23.9					19.2	33.2	29.5	
1921	24.2	20.0					19.4	31.7	31.1	
1922	24.6	29.6	11.6				18.7	30.6	27.5	} 15.3
1923	21.3	18.0	14.7				18.5	27.8	30.3	
1924	24.5	17.4	12.7				—	27.4	25.8	

TABLE A3.11. (*cont.*)

Year	China (Taiwan)	Cyprus	Israel	Hong Kong	India	Malaysia	Philippines	Singapore	Sri Lanka	Fiji
1925	23.9	14.4	14.9				—	27.2	24.2	
1926	22.4	17.1	11.9				19.3	31.8	25.3	17.3
1927	22.1	15.6	13.3				18.8	33.5	22.6	
1928	22.0	15.2	11.9				18.3	28.8	26.0	
1929	21.6	13.5	11.6				19.7	26.1	26.2	
1930	19.4	16.4	9.5		26.9		19.3	27.6	25.5	22.3
1931	21.3	17.0	9.6		24.9		18.0	24.2	22.1	16.5
1932	20.4	16.3	9.7		21.4	20.1	15.4	20.4	20.5	13.6
1933	19.7	13.8	9.3		22.1	21.1	16.2	22.5	21.2	14.9
1934	20.5	13.2	9.5		24.5	23.4	16.7	24.1	22.9	15.6
1935	20.3	13.7	8.6		23.2	22.3	17.5	24.3	36.5	15.5
1936	19.8	12.7	8.8		22.2	22.0	15.9	24.2	21.8	20.1
1937	19.7	17.1	7.8		22.0	20.9	16.4	22.0	21.7	15.9
1938	19.7	14.5	8.1		23.7	20.4	16.5	21.4	21.0	16.3
1939	19.8	14.0	7.6	28.1	21.5	19.1	17.0	19.5	21.7	17.1
1940	19.4	11.7	8.1	29.9	21.1	20.7	16.6	20.9	20.6	12.1
1941	16.2	12.4	7.8	34.2	21.9	—	—	20.8	18.3	12.1
1942	17.7	16.4	8.5	37.4	21.4	—	—	—	18.1	11.4
1943	18.8	12.4	7.6	—	23.9	—	—	—	20.8	11.7
1944	—	10.0	7.0	—	24.5	—	—	—	20.8	13.0
1945	—	9.5	6.6	—	22.1	—	—	—	21.5	11.3
1946	—	8.5	6.2	10.7	18.7	20.0	15.1	—	19.8	13.1
1947	18.1	8.5	6.2	7.6	19.5	19.4	12.7	13.3	14.0	11.0
1948	14.3	8.5	6.7	7.5	17.0	16.3	12.2	12.4	12.9	12.1
1949	13.1	8.9	6.8	8.8	15.8	14.2	11.8	11.8	12.3	12.4

Year										
1950	11.5	8.2	6.9	8.2	16.1	15.8	11.1	12.1	12.4	11.2
1951	11.6	8.4	6.7	10.2	14.4	15.4	11.4	11.6	12.7	10.6
1952	9.9	7.6	7.3	8.6	13.6	13.8	11.2	10.7	11.8	11.7
1953	9.4	7.0	6.7	8.1		12.6	10.8	9.7	10.7	9.2
1954	8.2	7.2	6.8	8.5		12.4	9.5	8.6	10.2	9.5
1955	8.6	5.8	6.1	7.7		11.7	9.0	8.1	10.8	8.2
1956	8.0	6.3	6.6	7.4		11.6	9.0	7.5	9.8	7.4
1957	8.5	6.3	6.5	7.1		12.4	9.6	7.4	10.1	7.5
1958	7.6	6.3	5.8	7.2		11.0	8.5	7.0	9.7	7.0
1959	7.2	6.1	5.9	6.8		9.7	7.4	6.5	9.1	7.6
1960	7.0	5.7	5.7	6.2		9.5	7.2	6.3	8.6	6.6
1961	6.7	5.6	5.8	5.9		9.2	7.4	6.0	8.0	6.4
1962	6.4	5.9	6.0	6.0		9.4	5.8	5.9	8.5	6.3
1963	6.1	6.1	6.1	5.6		9.0	7.2	5.8	8.7	5.8
1964	5.7	6.6	6.3	5.0		8.1	7.4	5.8	8.8	6.1
1965	5.5	6.1	6.3	5.0		7.9	7.4	5.5	8.2	5.1
1966	5.5	5.8	6.3	5.3		7.6	7.2	5.5	8.3	5.2
1967	5.5	6.5	6.6	5.4		7.5	7.1	5.4	7.5	—
1968	5.5	7.2	6.8	5.1		7.6	7.5	5.5	7.9	—
1969	5.0	6.9	7.0	5.0		7.2	6.8	5.0	8.4	—

TABLE A3.11. (cont.)

Year	China (Taiwan)	Cyprus	Israel	Hong Kong	India	Malaysia	Philippines	Singapore	Sri Lanka	Fiji
1970	4.9	6.8	7.0	5.1		7.3	6.4	5.2	7.5	—
1971	4.8	9.6	6.9	5.0		7.1	6.6	5.4	7.7	5.9
1972	4.7	9.7	7.2	5.3		6.9	7.3	5.4	8.0	5.0
1973	4.8	9.5	7.2	5.1		6.9	7.1	5.5	7.7	5.0
1974	4.8	10.8	7.2	5.2		6.6	6.9	5.3	9.0	4.9
1975	4.7	9.8	7.1	4.9		6.4	6.4	5.1	8.5	6.9
1976	4.7	9.8	6.8	5.1		6.1	—	5.1	7.8	4.3
1977	4.8	9.0	6.9	5.2		6.2	—	5.2	7.4	3.8
1978	4.7	8.4	6.8	5.2		5.7	— ⎱ 7.7	5.2	6.6	4.1
1979	4.7	8.2	6.8	5.3		5.8	— ⎰	5.3	6.5	3.8
1980	4.8	—	6.8	5.1		5.8	—	5.2	6.1	6.3
1981	4.8	8.2	6.6	4.9				5.3	6.0	6.7
1982	4.8	8.3	6.9	4.8				5.2		5.7
1983	4.9	8.5	6.8	5.0						
1984				4.8						

Appendix 4. Infant Mortality Rates

TABLE A4.1. *Infant mortality, Europe, and Russia 1740–1900, per 1000 live births*

Period	Austria	Belgium	Bulgaria	Denmark	England and Wales	Finland	France	Germany	Hungary
1801–1805						196			
1806–1810	191					242			
1811–1815	189					211			
1816–1820	182					195			
1821–1825	191					204			
1826–1830	195					202	182		
1831–1835	258	180		152		214	183		
1836–1840	246	183		144	153	191	166	295	
1841–1845	246	149		137	147	178	156	296	
1846–1850	248	154		148	161	180	162	300	
1851–1855	252	150		134	156	176	166	289	256
1856–1860	244	157		136	150	186	179	287	249
1861–1865	259	165		136	151	180	179	309	240
1866–1870	255	142		132	157	222	180	302	
1871–1875	264	151		137	153	170	179	295	
1876–1880	249	155		139	144	164	166	227	
1881–1885	252	156		135	139	162	167	229	
1886–1890	248	161		136	145	143	165	224	
1891–1895	245	164	144	139	151	145	170	224	253
1896–1900	226	158	143	132	156	139	158	217	221

Sweden (S) and Finland (F)

Period	S	F	Period	S	F	Period	S	F
1751–55	206	227	1761–65	221	248	1771–75	218	201
1756–60	204	225	1766–70	211	235	1776–80	192	219

France

Period		Period		Period	
1740–49	297	1780–89	278	1800–09	209

TABLE A4.1. *(cont.)*

Ireland	Italy	Netherlands	Norway	Romania	Spain	Sweden	Switzerland	Russia
						186		
						213		
						192		
						176		
						159		
						176		
						168		
		164	140			167		
		174	118			154		
		192	112			153		
		190	106			149		
		204	101		180	144		
98	231	197	107	232	187	136		
95	224	203	114	198	197	143		266
95	221	211	107	190	—	133	198	272
99	210	197	101	205	192	126	188	275
94	195	181	99	180	193	116	171	272
95	195	175	97	195	186	105	159	264
102	185	165	98	219	—	103	155	275
106	168	151	96	212	—	101	143	261

Period		S	F		Period		S	F
1781–85		194	219		1791–95		193	216
1786–90		206	214		1796–1800		201	198
1820–29		181						

TABLE A4.2. *Infant mortality, Europe, 1900–1939, per 1000 live births*

Year	Austria	Belgium	Bulgaria	Czechoslovakia[a]	Denmark	Finland	France	Germany	Greece	Hungary	Ireland[b]	Italy
1900	231	172	132		128	153	162	229		223	109	174
1901	209	143	143		136	145	145	207		207	101	166
1902	216	144	143		114	129	137	183		219	100	172
1903	215	155	154		114	127	138	204		204	96	172
1904	210	152	142		113	120	146	196		197	100	161
1905	231	147	160		120	135	137	205		232	95	166
1906	202	154	154	205	109	119	146	185		207	93	161
1907	209	133	154	214	108	112	133	176		212	92	156
1908	199	148	169	207	123	125	130	178		201	97	148
1909	209	138	171	211	97.7	111	120	170		214	92	157
1910	189	135	159	190	102	118	112	162		195	95	140
1911	207	167	156	203	106	114	159	192		208	94	157
1912	181	120	132	187	93.2	109	106	147		186	86	128
1913	190	130	—	184	93.6	113	114	151		201	97	138
1914	172	130	—	179	98.3	104	112	164		197	87	130
1915	218	125	138	216	94.7	111	144	148		264	92	147
1916	192	116	161	190	99.9	110	126	140		219	83	166
1917	186	140	146	182	99.6	118	127	149		216	88	153
1918	193	134	146	194	74.2	115	140	158		217	86	187
1919	156	103	110	142	91.6	135	123	145		164	88	129

1920	157	110	146	178	90.2	96.7	99.2	131	—	200	83	127
1921	154	122	158	173	77.0	94.6	117	134	68	193	77	129
1922	144	114	155	166	85.4	99.2	86.6	130	82	198	69	126
1923	141	100	165	145	82.9	92.4	96.3	131	92	184	66	128
1924	127	95	150	148	84.5	107	84.8	108	98	193	72	126
1925	119	100	152	145	79.8	85.0	88.9	105	90	168	68	119
1926	123	104	127	154	84.4	85.6	97.0	102	75	168	74	127
1927	125	98	168	157	83.4	97.1	83.4	97.1	101	186	71	120
1928	120	94	149	146	80.8	84.0	91.5	89.2	94	177	68	120
1929	113	110	156	142	82.9	97.6	96.0	96.6	111	179	70	125
1930	104	100	138	137	80.0	75.1	78.2	84.7	99	153	68	106
1931	103	89.3	156	134	81.4	74.8	75.8	83.2	134	162	69	113
1932	106	93.6	150	137	72.3	70.9	77.0	79.4	129	184	72	111
1933	94.2	92.0	146	127	67.6	75.7	74.8	76.8	122	136	65	100
1934	91.6	82.5	131	128	64.4	73.0	69.4	66.0	112	148	63	99
1935	98.7	84.6	154	123	71.0	66.8	68.9	68.6	113	152	68	101
1936	93.1	86.1	144	124	67.3	65.9	67.0	66.2	114	139	74	100
1937	91.9	82.8	150	122	66.1	68.5	65.4	64.4	122	133	73	109
1938	80.1	81.3	144	121	58.7	67.8	65.6	59.8	99	131	67	106
1939	73.1	82.4	139	98	58.1	69.6	63.5	72.3	118	121	66	97

TABLE A4.2. (cont.)

Netherlands	Norway	Poland	Portugal	Romania	Spain	Sweden	Switzerland	United Kingdom			USSR[c]	Yugoslavia[d]
								England and Wales	Scotland	N. Ireland		
155	91			197	214	99	150	154	128		252	150
149	91			202	194	103	137	151	129		272	145
130	74			212	189	86	132	133	113		258	151
135	78			294	170	93	133	132	118		250	151
137	75			—	182	84	140	145	123		232	135
131	82			—	169	88	129	128	116		272	163
127	69.9		163	193	182	81.0	127	132	115		248	143
112	66.4		153	208	166	76.8	121	118	110		225	147
125	76.0		157	211	168	84.1	108	120	121		244	158
99.1	71.6		150	—	161	72.2	115	109	108		248	181
108	67.2		134	—	157	75.1	105	105	108		271	139
137	64.8		—	197	170	72.0	123	130	112		237	
87.0	67.5		—	186	144	70.9	93.8	94.8	105		—	
91.4	64.6		160	202	163	69.7	96.0	108	110	107	273	
94.8	67.9		149	187	159	72.9	91.5	105	111	102		
86.8	67.6		148	208	160	75.8	90.0	110	126	107		
84.5	64.0		154	—	154	69.7	78.5	91.2	97.1	88.5		
87.1	64.0		148	—	163	64.5	79.2	96.5	107	97.0		
92.8	63.1	186	209	301	192	64.6	88.2	97.2	100	101		
84.1	62.3	—	182	205	164	69.6	82.4	89.1	102	95.3		

72.8	57.9	—	164	222	174	63.3	83.7	79.9	92.0	94.3		
76.2	54.3	187	148	200	155	64.0	74.0	82.8	90.3	86.7		
67.3	54.9	167	144	207	149	62.5	69.6	77.1	101	77.2		
56.9	49.8	—	164	207	155	56.2	60.5	69.4	78.9	76.5		
51.2	50.3	—	144	201	147	60.3	62.0	75.1	97.7	84.6		145
58.4	50.4	—	132	192	143	55.7	58.4	75.0	90.6	86.4	198	143
61.1	48.3	—	148	195	124	56.0	56.5	70.2	83.1	84.9	172	143
58.7	51.1	151	144	209	133	59.8	56.8	69.7	88.7	77.7	190	163
52.3	49.3	145	—	184	132	58.8	53.6	65.1	85.7	77.9	155	150
59.0	54.4	149	151	197	129	58.5	52.1	74.4	86.8	85.6		147
50.9	45.6	143	144	176	123	54.7	50.8	60.0	83.0	67.8		153
49.6	46.3	142	141	180	122	56.6	49.4	66.4	81.8	73.4		165
46.3	46.8	144	147	185	118	50.7	51.0	65.0	86.2	83.0		167
43.9	47.6	128	149	174	118	49.5	47.8	63.7	81.1	79.7		140
42.6	39.3	141	144	182	119	47.2	45.7	58.6	77.7	69.7		150
40.0	44.2	127	149	192	115	45.9	47.9	56.9	76.8	86.3		149
38.9	42.0	141	140	175	114	43.4	46.5	58.5	82.3	76.9		137
38.1	42.0	136	151	178	135	45.2	46.7	57.6	80.3	77.5	170	141
36.5	37.3	140	137	183	124	42.5	42.8	52.7	69.5	75.1	161	140
33.7	37.2	—	120	176	140	39.5	42.6	52.7	68.5	70.5	167	132

c European Russia (50 provinces), not incl. Finland, Poland, Caucasus, until 1913.
d Serbia only until 1910.

TABLE A4.3. *Infant mortality, Europe, 1940–1986, (per 1000 live births)*

Year	Austria	Belgium	Bulgaria	Czechoslovakia	Denmark	Finland	France	Germany FRG	Germany GDR	Greece	Hungary	Ireland	Italy
1940	74.2	93.2	136	98.8	50.2	88.3	90.5	64.1		101	130	66	103
1941	69.8	91.6	125	99.9	55.0	59.2	72.7	—		—	116	74	115
1942	73.5	83.9	131	110.9	47.0	67.2	71.0	—		—	133	69	112
1943	79.0	74.5	130	108.8	44.8	49.5	75.4	—		—	116	83	113
1944	87.8	82.6	121	108.8	47.7	68.6	77.7	—		—	—	79	102
1945	161.7	99.6	145	137	48.3	63.2	112.7	FRG	GDR	—	169	71	103
1946	81.4	74.8	125	108.8	45.8	56.2	71.9	90.2	(131)	—	117	65	86.8
1947	78.3	68.7	130	88.9	40.4	58.5	70.6	83.8	(114)	—	103	67	84.2
1948	76.2	59.1	118	83.5	35.3	51.9	55.9	67.9	(89.0)	—	99.6	50	72.2
1949	77.3	57.2	116	32.4	34.5	48.3	60.2	58.4	(74.8)	(42)	91.0	53	74.0
1950	66.1	53.4	94.5	77.6	30.7	43.5	52.0	55.5	72.2	(36)	85.7	45.3	63.8
1951	61.3	50.0	108	73.4	28.9	35.4	46.2	53.4	64.0	(44)	83.9	45.4	66.6
1952	51.9	44.8	97.7	55.5	28.9	31.8	45.2	48.3	59.1	(41)	69.9	41.4	63.4
1953	49.9	41.9	80.8	45.0	27.2	34.2	41.9	46.4	53.5	(43)	70.8	39.4	58.4
1954	48.3	41.4	86.3	37.6	26.9	30.6	40.7	42.9	50.3	(42)	60.7	37.8	53.0
1955	45.6	40.7	82.4	34.1	25.2	29.7	38.6	41.7	48.9	(44)	60.0	36.7	50.9
1956	43.3	39.4	72.0	31.4	24.9	25.7	36.2	38.6	46.5	(39)	58.8	35.6	48.8
1957	44.2	35.9	66.3	33.5	23.4	27.9	33.7	36.4	45.5	(44)	63.1	33.1	50.0
1958	40.7	31.3	52.2	29.5	22.4	24.5	31.5	36.0	44.2	(39)	58.1	35.4	48.2
1959	39.8	30.4	55.9	25.7	22.5	23.6	29.5	34.3	40.7	(41)	52.4	32.0	45.4

Year														
1960	37.5	31.2	45.1	23.5		21.5	21.0	27.4	33.8	38.8	(40)	47.6	29.3	43.9
1961	32.7	28.1	37.8	22.7		21.8	20.8	25.6	31.7	33.7	39.8	44.1	30.5	40.7
1962	32.8	27.5	37.3	22.8		20.1	20.5	25.7	29.2	31.6	40.4	47.9	29.1	41.8
1963	31.3	27.2	35.7	22.1		19.1	18.2	25.4	26.9	31.2	39.3	42.9	26.6	40.1
1964	29.2	25.3	32.9	21.4		18.7	17.0	23.3	25.2	28.6	35.8	40.0	26.7	36.1
1965	28.3	23.7	30.8	25.5		18.7	17.6	21.9	23.9	24.8	34.3	38.8	25.2	36.0
1966	28.1	24.7	32.2	23.8		16.9	15.0	21.7	23.6	22.9	34.0	38.4	24.9	34.7
1967	26.4	22.9	33.1	22.9		15.8	14.8	20.7	22.9	21.4	34.3	37.0	24.4	33.2
1968	25.5	21.7	28.3	22.2		16.4	14.4	20.4	22.8	20.2	34.4	35.8	21.0	32.7
1969	25.4	21.2	30.5	23.1		14.8	14.3	19.7	23.4	20.3	31.8	35.7	20.6	30.8
1970	25.9	21.1	27.3	22.1		14.2	13.2	18.2	23.4	18.5	29.6	35.9	19.5	29.2
1971	26.1	20.4	24.9	21.7		13.5	12.7	17.1	23.1	18.0	26.9	35.1	18.0	28.5
1972	25.2	18.8	26.2	21.6		12.2	12.0	16.0	22.4	17.6	27.3	33.2	18.0	27.0
1973	23.8	16.9	26.2	21.2		11.5	10.6	15.4	22.7	15.6	24.1	33.8	18.0	25.7
1974	23.5	16.2	25.5	20.4		10.7	11.0	14.6	21.1	15.9	24.0	34.3	17.1	22.6
1975	20.5	14.6	22.9	20.9		10.4	9.6	13.6	19.7	15.9	24.0	32.6	17.5	21.2
1976	18.3	13.9	23.2	20.8		10.3	9.9	12.5	17.4	14.1	22.6	30.0	15.5	19.5
1977	16.8	13.6	24.0	21.0		8.7	9.1	11.4	15.5	13.1	20.4	26.2	15.7	18.1
1978	14.9	11.7	22.2	19.7		8.8	7.6	10.6	14.7	13.1	19.3	24.4	14.9	16.9
1979	14.8	11.2	19.8	18.7		8.8	7.7	10.0	13.5	13.0	18.7	23.7	12.8	15.7
1980	14.3	11.0	20.2	18.4		8.4	7.6	10.0	12.6	12.1	17.8	23.0	11.2	14.6
1981	12.7	11.7	19.5	16.8		8.0	6.3	9.7	11.6	12.3	16.3	20.6	10.3	14.1
1982	12.8	11.7	18.2	16.1		8.2	5.8	9.3	10.9	11.4	15.3	20.0	10.5	12.7
1983	12.0	11.3	16.8	15.7		7.7	6.1	9.0	10.2	10.7	15.1	19.0	10.1	12.2
1984	11.4	10.7	16.1	15.1		7.7	5.9	8.3	9.6	10.0	14.6	20.4	9.6	11.3
1985	11.2	9.4	15.4	13.9		7.9	6.5	8.3	9.0	9.6	14.3	20.4	8.9	10.9
1986	10.3	9.6	14.7	13.9		8.4	6.5	8.1	8.6	9.2	12.3	19.0	9.1	10.1

Table A4.3. (cont.)

Netherlands	Norway	Poland	Portugal	Romania	Spain	Sweden	Switzerland	United Kingdom			USSR	Yugoslavia
								England and Wales	Scotland	N. Ireland		
39.1	38.7	—	126	188	114	39.2	46.2	57.4	78.3	86	184	—
43.6	43.0	—	151	166	149	37.0	41.1	59.7	82.7	76.6	—	—
39.5	35.9	—	131	178	109	29.3	38.3	49.5	69.3	76.4	—	—
40.1	35.4	—	133	184	104	28.9	39.8	48.9	65.2	78.2	—	—
46.3	36.7	—	122	162	98.1	31.1	42.2	44.5	65.0	67.7	—	—
79.7	36.4	—	115	188	84.9	29.9	40.7	47.0	56.2	68.1	—	—
38.7	34.6	—	119	164	87.2	26.3	39.2	40.9	53.8	54.0	—	—
33.6	34.6	—	108	199	70.7	25.2	39.3	41.6	55.8	53.0	—	—
29.3	29.6	111	100	143	64.3	23.2	35.9	34.5	44.7	45.6	—	—
26.8	27.7	107	115	136	68.9	23.3	34.3	32.7	41.4	45.2	—	102
25.2	28.2	108	94.1	117	64.2	21.0	31.2	30.0	38.6	40.5	81	119
26.7	25.7	115	89.1	118	62.6	21.4	30.1	29.7	37.4	41.2	84	140
24.1	23.7	95.3	94.3	105	54.7	20.0	29.1	27.5	35.2	38.8	75	105
23.7	22.0	87.5	95.5	96.3	52.9	18.7	29.8	26.8	30.8	37.6	68	116
22.6	21.4	82.6	85.5	88.8	49.2	18.7	27.2	25.4	31.0	33.0	68	102
21.6	20.6	81.4	90.2	78.2	50.9	17.4	26.5	24.9	30.4	32.4	60	113
20.2	21.2	70.7	87.8	81.5	46.4	17.3	25.8	23.6	28.6	28.8	47	98.3
18.4	20.5	76.5	88.0	82.1	47.3	17.8	22.9	23.1	28.6	28.9	45	101.5
18.5	20.0	72.4	84.0	70.5	42.5	15.9	22.2	22.5	27.7	28.1	40.0	86.4
18.1	18.7	71.9	88.6	77.0	42.3	16.6	22.2	22.2	28.4	28.4	40.6	92.0

17.9	18.9	56.8	77.5	75.7	43.7	16.6	21.1	21.8	26.4	27.2	35.0	87.7
17.0	17.9	54.1	88.8	71.4	46.2	15.8	21.0	21.4	25.8	27.5	32.0	82.0
17.0	17.7	54.8	78.6	60.3	41.6	15.4	21.2	21.7	26.5	26.5	32.0	84.2
15.8	16.9	48.7	73.1	55.2	40.6	15.4	20.5	21.1	25.6	27.0	30.9	77.5
14.8	16.4	47.7	69.0	48.6	39.2	14.2	19.0	19.9	24.0	26.3	29.0	75.8
14.4	16.8	41.7	64.9	44.1	37.8	13.3	17.8	19.0	23.1	25.1	27.6	71.8
14.7	14.6	38.9	64.7	46.6	36.0	12.6	17.1	19.0	23.2	25.5	26.1	62.1
13.4	14.7	38.1	59.2	46.6	34.0	12.9	17.5	18.5	21.0	23.5	26.3	62.1
13.6	13.7	33.4	61.1	59.5	32.4	13.1	16.1	18.2	20.8	24.0	26.4	58.6
13.2	13.8	34.3	55.4	54.9	30.2	11.7	15.4	18.0	21.1	24.4	25.8	57.3
12.8	12.7	33.4	58.0	49.4	28.1	11.0	15.1	18.1	19.6	22.9	24.4	55.5
12.1	12.8	29.7	49.8	42.4	25.7	11.1	14.4	17.5	19.9	22.7	22.6	49.5
11.7	11.8	28.6	41.4	40.0	22.9	10.8	13.3	17.2	18.8	20.5	24.7	44.4
11.5	11.9	26.1	44.8	38.1	21.5	9.9	13.2	16.9	19.0	20.9	26.4	44.2
11.3	10.4	23.7	37.9	35.0	19.9	9.6	12.5	16.3	18.9	20.9	27.7	40.0
10.6	11.1	25.1	38.9	34.7	18.9	8.6	11.0	15.7	17.2	20.4	—	39.9
10.6	10.4	24.0	35.0	31.4	17.1	8.3	10.5	14.3	14.8	18.3	—	37.1
9.5	9.2	24.6	30.3	31.2	16.0	8.0	9.8	13.8	16.1	17.2	—	35.6
9.6	8.6	22.5	29.1	30.3	15.3	7.8	8.6	13.2	12.9	16.1	—	33.8
8.7	8.8	21.1	26.0	31.6	14.3	7.5	8.5	12.8	12.8	14.8	—	32.7
8.6	8.1	21.3	24.3	29.3	12.3	6.9	9.1	12.0	12.0	13.4	—	31.4
8.2	7.5	20.6	21.8	28.6	10.3	7.0	7.6	11.1	11.3	13.2	—	30.7
8.3	8.1	20.2	19.8	28.0	9.6	6.8	7.7	10.8	11.4	13.5	27.7	29.9
8.4	7.9	19.2	19.2	23.9	7.3	7.0	7.6	10.1	9.9	12.1	—	30.2
8.3	8.3	19.2	16.7	23.4	9.0	6.4	7.1	9.5	10.3	10.5	26.0	28.9
8.0	8.5	18.5	17.8	25.6	8.9	6.8	6.9	9.4	9.4	9.8	25.4	28.8
8.1	7.8	17.5	15.8		8.7	5.9	6.8	9.5	8.8	9.9		27.3

TABLE A4.4. *Infant mortality, overseas English-speaking countries, Japan, Latin America, Asia, Africa, 1900–1939, per 100 live births*

Year	Australia	Canada	New Zealand	United States	Japan	Argentina	Brazil	Chile	Costa Rica	Cuba	Mexico	Uruguay
1900					155.0							
1901					149.9							
1902				142.9	154.0						325.9	
1903					152.4							
1904					151.9							
1905					151.7							
1906	83.3		62.1	136.9	153.6		243	327			318.5	109.2
1907	81.1		88.8		151.3		173	298			310.6	108.8
1908	77.8		67.9		158.0		167	318			288.1	100.6
1909	71.6		61.6		167.3		169	315			294.3	100.5
1910	74.8		67.7	115.8	161.2		206	267			323.1	110.7
1911	68.5		56.5		158.4		—	333			—	109.4
1912	71.7		51.2		154.2		—	287			—	117.6
1913	72.2		59.2		152.1		—	286			—	93.3
1914	71.5		51.4		158.5	122	—	255			—	94.5
1915	67.5		50.1	99.9	160.4	124	—	254			—	111.3
1916	70.3		50.7	101.0	170.3	124	—	241			—	123.9
1917	55.9		48.2	93.8	173.2	128	—	269			—	106.9
1918	58.6		48.4	100.9	188.6	138	—	255			—	110.1
1919	69.2		45.3	86.6	170.5	134	—	306			—	100.5

Year												
1920	69.1		49.2	85.8	165.7	127	—	263			—	117.3
1921	65.7		47.8	75.6	168.3	116	204	278			—	107.1
1922	52.7		41.9	76.2	166.4	112	180	240			223.1	93.5
1923	60.5		43.8	77.1	163.4	112	—	283			222.4	101.0
1924	57.1		40.2	70.8	156.2	117	176	266			232.2	107.6
1925	53.4		40.0	71.7	142.4	125	168	258			215.9	115.2
1926	54.0	101.8	39.8	73.3	137.5	119	163	251			209.4	93.4
1927	54.5	94.0	38.7	64.6	141.7	126	168	226			193.0	106.1
1928	53.0	89.5	36.2	68.7	137.6	115	158	212			193.4	99.5
1929	51.1	92.1	34.1	67.6	142.1	103	—	224			167.6	92.7
1930	47.2	89.3	34.5	64.6	124.1	105	168	234	155.1		131.7	99.7
1931	42.1	84.7	32.2	61.6	131.5	101	169	232	163.7		137.7	109.6
1932	41.3	73.3	31.2	57.6	117.5	95.1	164	235	135.6	113.5	137.5	98.6
1933	39.5	73.1	31.6	58.1	121.3	86.6	184	258	157.0	131.6	139.3	92.8
1934	43.6	71.7	32.1	60.1	124.8	96.6	178	262	152.9	100.0	130.3	95.7
1935	39.8	71.0	32.3	55.7	106.7	105.6	175	251	141.7	127.2	125.7	102.0
1936	41.2	66.1	31.0	57.1	116.7	96.2	189	252	121.7	106.4	130.8	91.6
1937	38.1	75.8	31.2	54.1	105.8	95.4	—	241	140.1	86.8	130.8	96.2
1938	38.3	63.3	35.6	51.0	114.4	105.3	—	236		83.0	128.0	98.8
1939	38.2	60.7	31.1	48.0	106.2	91.7	—	225			122.6	82.1

TABLE A4.4. (cont.)

Year	Puerto Rico	Venezuela	Korea	India	Malaysia	Philippines	Singapore	Sri Lanka	Taiwan	Egypt	Mauritius
1900								—			
1901				⎫ 215				170			
1902				⎭				173			
1903								164			
1904								174			
1905								176			
1906				⎫ 228				198			
1907				⎭				186			
1908								183			
1909								202			
1910				⎫				176			
1911								218			
1912				204				215			
1913				⎭				189			
1914								213			
1915								171			
1916				⎫				184			
1917				219				174			
1918				⎭				188			
1919								223			

Year	A	B	C	D	E	F	G	H	I	J	K
1920								182			
1921								192			
1922								188			
1923								212			
1924								186			
1925		—						172			
1926		—				157		174	153		
1927		144				153		160	157		
1928		153				150		177	164		
1929		149				162		187	150		
1930	—	150			178	165	214	175	148		
1931	—	156			158	155	198	158	159	173.5	159.0
1932	132.3	134	97.0	168.1	149.7	138	177.1	162.3	153.7	162.5	131.5
1933	139.6	162.5	83.7	169.7	157.5	146	168.0	157.2	149.4	166.0	129.8
1934	113.7	158.3	82.9	185.4	173.9	161	169.4	173.0	155.4	160.6	139.4
1935	114.8	137.5	82.3	162.8	159.0	153	159.3	263.2	146.6	163.8	142.3
1936	128.2	133.7	80.7	161.0	159.9	134	171.6	165.5	145.8	165.5	154.4
1937	137.8	134.9	72.5	161.7	148.7	137	155.2	158.2	144.8	163.4	162.5
1938	121.0	138.7	101.0	167.1	149.4	139	158.9	151.4	145.7	161.2	157.5
1939	112.6	131.7	103.9	155.6	131.1	146	130.5	165.8	139.6		

Brace summary values: 149.7, 140.7, 126.5, 152.5, 229.7, 212.4, 174, 150.2, 163, 162.5, 163.1

TABLE A4.5. *Infant mortality, overseas English-speaking countries, Japan, Latin America, Asia, and Africa, 1940–1985, per 1000 live births*

Year	Australia	Canada	New Zealand	United States	Japan	Argentina	Brazil	Chile	Costa Rica	Cuba	Mexico	Uruguay
1940	38.4	56.4	30.2	47.0	90.4	90.2	—	192.8	134.4	—	—	86.5
1941	39.7	59.7	29.8	45.3	84.4	84.8	202.3	206.2	125.9	—	—	82.8
1942	39.5	53.8	28.7	40.4	85.8	86.1	190.2	194.7	161.3	—	—	92.7
1943	36.3	53.7	31.4	40.4	87.0	80.0	185.3	194.0	123.9	—	—	77.9
1944	31.3	54.7	30.1	39.8	—	80.7	188.6	180.8	127.5	—	—	65.7
1945	29.4	51.3	28.0	38.3	—	82.1	170.2	164.5	112.3	—	—	—
1946	29.0	46.7	32.0	33.8	—	74.0	162.7	159.5	110.7	—	110.6	—
1947	28.5	45.5	29.9	32.2	76.7	77.1	142.9	160.9	108.1	—	95.0	—
1948	27.8	43.7	27.7	32.0	61.7	69.7	145.4	160.4	93.3	—	99.7	60.6
1949	25.3	42.9	30.0	31.3	62.5	67.0	149.6	169.0	99.7	—	106.6	52.4
1950	24.5	41.3	27.6	29.2	60.1	68.2	136.6	136.2	90.2	—	95.8	64.2
1951	25.2	38.4	27.5	28.6	57.5	67.4	151.5	131.5	85.9	—	98.8	54.7
1952	23.8	38.2	28.4	28.4	49.4	64.9	160.1	117.8	89.5	—	89.8	51.0
1953	23.3	35.6	25.7	27.8	48.9	63.4	137.2	106.9	89.7	—	95.2	51.2
1954	22.5	31.9	24.1	26.6	44.6	60.4	140.0	120.7	81.0	—	80.5	49.3
1955	22.0	31.3	24.5	26.4	39.8	61.8	124.9	116.5	82.8	—	83.3	46.6
1956	21.7	31.9	23.2	26.0	40.6	57.0	144.1	108.1	73.9	—	71.0	43.9
1957	21.4	30.9	24.3	26.4	40.0	68.5	142.6	112.5	81.7	32.3	80.1	53.4
1958	20.5	30.2	23.4	27.1	34.5	61.4	131.3	118.1	72.3	32.5	80.1	48.6
1959	21.5	28.4	23.9	26.4	33.7	59.1	140.0	114.2	70.4	34.6	74.4	57.0

Year												
1960	20.2	27.3	22.6	26.0	30.7	62.4	118.7	120.3	70.8	36.5	74.2	47.4
1961	19.5	27.2	22.8	25.3	28.6	59.1	105.2	108.9	65.3	39.3	70.2	—
1962	20.4	27.6	20.4	25.3	26.4	58.7	102.6	108.0	70.7	43.4	69.9	—
1963	19.5	26.3	19.6	25.2	23.2	62.2	94.6	100.2	74.1	37.8	68.5	—
1964	19.1	24.7	19.1	24.8	20.4	60.1	109.4	102.9	86.1	36.7	64.5	49.8
1965	18.5	23.6	19.5	24.7	18.5	56.9	102.4	95.4	65.2	37.9	60.7	43.3
1966	18.2	23.1	17.7	23.7	19.3	54.2	101.1	97.7	62.8	37.2	62.9	58.8
1967	18.3	22.0	18.0	22.4	14.9	62.9	98.0	94.3	60.3	36.8	63.1	53.9
1968	17.8	20.8	18.7	21.8	15.3	59.6	105.9	83.5	59.7	39.0	64.2	48.7
1969	17.9	19.3	16.9	20.6	14.2	52.6	89.6	78.7	67.1	47.4	68.4	
1970	17.9	18.8	16.7	19.8	13.1	58.9	91.2	78.8	61.5	35.9	68.5	42.6
1971	17.3	17.6	16.5	19.2	12.4	—	108.7	77.8	56.5	37.4	63.3	40.4
1972	16.7	17.1	15.6	18.5	11.7	} 47.2	—	—	54.4	28.3	60.9	45.4
1973	16.5	15.6	16.2	17.7	11.3	—	— } 79.0	—	44.8	28.9	52.0	—
1974	16.1	15.0	15.5	16.7	10.8	—	—	65.2	37.6	29.0	46.9	48.1
1975	14.3	16.1	16.0	16.1	10.0	—	—	56.4	38.2	27.3	52.8	48.8
1976	14.3	15.1	13.9	15.1	9.3	—	—	56.6	33.2	23.3	54.7	45.9
1977	12.5	12.4	14.2	14.1	8.9	44.6	—	50.1	27.8	24.9	46.2	48.5
1978	12.2	12.0	13.8	13.8	8.4	40.8	—	40.1	23.8	22.4	60.2	43.8
1979	11.4	10.9	12.8	12.9	7.9	38.5	—	37.9	23.4	19.3	— } 59.8	39.6
1980	10.7	10.4	12.9	12.5	7.4	33.2		33.0	20.2	19.6		37.5
1981	10.0	9.6	11.7	11.7	7.1	33.6		27.0	19.1	18.5		33.4
1982	10.3	9.1	11.8	11.3	6.6	30.5		23.6	19.3	17.3		29.4
1983	9.6	8.5	12.5	10.9	6.2	35.3		21.9	18.6	16.8		30.0
1984	9.2	8.1	11.6	10.6	5.9			19.6	18.4	15.0		
1985	9.9	7.9	10.8	10.5	5.5			19.5		16.5		

TABLE A4.5. (*cont.*)

Year	Puerto Rico	Venezuela	Korea	India	Malaysia	Philippines	Singapore	Sri Lanka	Taiwan	Egypt	Mauritius
1940	113.6	121.7	106.9	159.8	138.5	136	142.6	148.9	135.5	161.8	162.0
1941	116.2	121.2	92.6	158.0	—	—	—	129.4	122.9	150.2	134.8
1942	103.3	115.1	88.9	162.6	—	—	—	120.5	126.1	168.4	163.4
1943	96.4	109.0	108.1	164.6	—	—	193.6	132.0	125.2	160.2	141.6
1944	99.3	116.8	115.6	169.3	—	—	284.9	135.1	—	152.3	141.0
1945	93.0	98.6	—	150.9	—	—	215.9	139.7	—	152.8	188.0
1946	83.7	102.1	—	136.4	91.7	126	89.7	140.5	77.4	140.8	145.2
1947	71.5	99.6	—	145.6	102.2	112	87.3	101.0	56.6	126.8	113.9
1948	78.3	97.8	48.9	130.1	89.6	114	80.8	92.1	47.9	138.6	186.2
1949	68.0	90.7	70.9	122.8	80.6	109	72.0	87.0		135.5	91.0
1950	67.5	80.9		127.1	101.6	102	82.2	81.6	39.8	129.6	76.3
1951	67.1	79.8		124.4	97.3	106	74.9	82.3	40.4	128.6	83.5
1952	66.4	79.5		116.3	90.0	102	70.0	78.4	37.2	127.1	80.8
1953	62.8	67.9	114	—	83.4	105	67.1	71.2	35.8	145.8	93.5
1954	57.6	69.2	(1950–59)	—	83.1	94	56.0	72.0	32.2	137.9	81.1
1955	55.8	69.9		—	78.4	84	49.6	71.5	36.9	135.7	67.2
1956	55.1	67.3		—	75.2	84	42.5	66.5	35.9	124.3	66.0
1957	50.3	65.8		—	75.5	93	41.1	67.5	37.3	130.5	75.1
1958	53.2	56.8		—	79.6	80	43.4	64.5	37.9	112.3	67.4
1959	47.6	60.9		—	66.0	72	35.8	57.5	35.9	109.3	62.5

(Korea, 1950–1959: combined value 114. India, 1953–1959: combined value 146.)

Year												
1960	43.3	53.9		—		68.9	85	34.8	56.8	32.4	109.3	69.5
1961	41.5	54.9		—		59.7	88	32.1	52.1	32.7	108.0	62.0
1962	41.7	47.0		—		59.4	59	31.0	52.8	31.3	133.8	60.1
1963	44.6	47.9		—		56.8	73	27.9	55.8	28.4	118.6	59.3
1964	51.6	48.7		—		48.4	71	29.3	57.0	25.5	117.3	56.7
1965	42.8	47.7		—		50.0	73	25.3	53.2	23.7	113.2	64.3
1966	35.7	46.5		—		47.9	72	24.7	54.0	22.1	127.1	64.9
1967	32.8	41.4		—		45.1	72	23.6	48.0	21.1	116.1	70.1
1968	29.2	45.5		—	129	42.2	71	22.4	50.3	21.3	131.3	70.0
1969	29.7	42.7		—		43.2	67	20.0	53.0	19.5	119.0	69.1
1970	28.6	49.3		—		40.8	60	19.7	50.0	17.4	116.3	58.5
1971	27.5	50.2	49	—	122	38.5	62	20.1	44.8	16.0	103.3	51.7
1972	27.1	—		—		37.9	68	19.2	45.6	16.4	116.0	63.8
1973	24.2	53.8		—		38.5	65	20.3	46.3	16.2	98.0	63.3
1974	23.0	46.0		—		35.4	59	16.8	51.2	14.1	101.3	45.6
1975	20.9	(43.7)		—		33.0	48	13.9	—	13.9	89.2	48.6
1976	20.2	(43.0)	45.0	—		28.6		11.6	43.7	12.9	87.5	40.4
1977	20.1	(39.4)		—	129.1	30.0		12.4	42.4	12.4	85.3	45.0
1978	18.5	(35.5)	34.0	—	59.0	26.7		12.6	37.1	11.3	73.5	33.9
1979	19.9	(33.7)		—		26.0		13.2	37.7	11.0	76.4	32.7
1980	19.0	—		—		24.9		11.7	34.4	11.0	76.0	33.0
1981	18.6					22.3		10.8	29.5	10.0	70.3	34.1
1982	17.2					20.5		10.7	30.7	9.0		29.4
1983	17.3					20.3		9.4		8.3		25.8
1984	15.6					17.5		8.8		7.5		23.1
1985						20.2		9.3		7.4		23.8

Appendix 5. Real Product

THE following series cover all the developed capitalist countries in our selection (i.e. 19 countries) for a period ranging from 66 (Finland) to 184 years (France). Each of the series has been compiled and standardized for the whole of the period covered according to the value of the appropriate national monetary unit in a given year. However, only in some countries, like the UK, Japan, and the USA, has it been possible to use the same definition of product for the whole series. Overall, a number of measures were used: NNP: net national product; GNP: gross national product; and GDP: gross domestic product.[1] In each case, both the measure and the corresponding period are specified. Wherever series have required adjustment, we have implicitly assumed that distortions between rates of growth consequent on the use of these different aggregate measures could be ignored; generally, for the periods concerned (before 1950 in all cases), this results in a satisfactory approximation. Since our aim is not so much to assess real comparative levels of product for different countries as to follow the general development of long-term growth in a given country in relation to its demographic trends, the potential inconvenience which may result from such a process of calculation appears relatively small. This is especially the case given the comparative data this approach makes possible between sometimes very distant periods.

However, it is necessary to bear in mind that the measurement of growth on the basis of changes in total product at constant prices over very long periods remains hazardous; retrospective evaluations made by different authors with reference to past times do not always agree. This variation relates to a number of factors: the concepts used, the nature of the data, methods of calculation, and the techniques employed in estimating production at constant prices (see Chapter 17). Series prior to the Second World War have often been the object of major revisions. We have therefore retained only those estimates reconsidered in the light of recent research in economic history. But it must be remembered that these are still only estimates, the precision of which is in no way comparable to that of current demographic figures. However, since the 1950s there has been greater international and intertemporal comparability owing both to more compatible procedures for keeping national accounts and to improvements in registration and statistical evaluation.

The following general works have been consulted:

CLARK, C. (1957), *The Conditions of Economic Progress* (London).

GOLDSMITH, R. (1955), 'Financial Structure and Economic Growth in Advanced Countries', in *Capital Formation and Economic Growth* (New York: NBER).

KUZNETS, S. (1966), *Modern Economic Growth, Rate, Structure and Spread* (New Haven, Conn.).

MADDISON, A (1964), *Economic Growth in the West* (London: Allen & Unwin).

For European data before 1970, we have used the annual series given in:

MITCHELL, B. R. (1975), *European Historical Statistics* (London: Macmillan).

Except for certain early estimates, for which we have used:

---

[1] At market price, unless specified otherwise.

CLARK, C. (1957), *Conditions of Economic Progress*, 3rd edn. (New York: Macmillan). For recent data, OECD publications have been used.

For countries situated outside Europe, the following additional sources have been consulted:

Japan
    1878–82. Quinquennial evaluations of NNP at constant prices of 1928–32, cited in OHKAWA, K. (1957), *The Growth Rate of the Japanese Economy since 1878* (Tokyo: Kinokynos Bookstore), 17.
    1885–1940. Evaluations of GDP at constant prices of 1934–36, in:
OHKAWA, K. *et al.* (1979), *Patterns of Japanese Economic Development: A Quantitative Appraisal* (New Haven, Conn.: Yale University Press), 278.
    1940–46 and 1946–53 in:
OHKAWA, K. *et al.* (1979: 8).
CLARK, C. (1957: 160–61).
    1953–70 in:
OKHAWA, K *et al.* (1979: 282).
    1970–79 in:
OECD Development Centre (1981), *Latest National Accounts of Developing Countries* (Paris: OECD).

United States
    1868–1908. Estimates are taken from those of Kendrick and Kuznets, published in:
KENDRICK, J. W. (1961), *Productivity Trends in the US* (New York: NBER).
    1909–70. Estimates in:
National Bureau of Economic Analysis (Ministry of Commerce) (1975), *Historical Statistics of the US* (Washington, DC: US Department of Commerce), pt. 1, p. 224.
    1970–80. Estimates in:
National Bureau of Economic Analysis (1981), *Statistical Abstract of the US* (Washington, DC: US Department of Commerce), 421.

Canada
    1867–1950:
FIRESTONE, O. J. (1958), *Canada's Economic Development, 1967–1953: Income and Wealth*, Ser. 7 (London: Bowes and Bowes).
    1959–70:
OECD (1981).

Australia
    1861–1950 in:
CLARK, C. (1957: 90–91).
    1950–79 in:
OECD (1981).

TABLE A5.1. *Real product, France, 1790–1979* (millions of francs, 1905–1913)

Years	GDP	Year	NNP
1791–1799	6,949	1936	48,436
1803–1812	7,324	1937	50,133
1815–1824	8,969	1938	49,611
1825–1834	10,977	1939	53,136
1835–1844	12,929		
1845–1854	14,628	1940	43,866
1855–1864	17,972	1941	34,728
1865–1874	21,199	1942	31,072
1875–1884	23,418	1943	29,505
1885–1894	27,541	1944	24,936
1895–1904	30,788	1945	27,025
1905–1914	38,035	1946	41,125
1915–1924	42,565	1947	44,519
1925–1934	62,529	1948	47,783
1935–1938	60,988	1949	54,050
	NNP		GNP
1901	31,333	1950	58,137
1902	31,333	1951	61,596
1903	32,247	1952	63,545
1904	34,858	1953	65,243
1905	34,466	1954	68,167
1906	35,250	1955	71,658
1907	36,164	1956	75,839
1908	36,425	1957	79,644
1909	37,600	1958	81,845
		1959	84,077
1910	37,600		
1911	39,166	1960	90,062
1912	42,822	1961	94,903
1913	42,822	1962	103,698
		1963	107,211
1920	35,250	1964	113,188
1921	32,639	1965	119,248
1922	39,689	1966	125,898
1923	42,953	1967	132,049
1924	49,741	1968	138,123
1925	50,133	1969	148,233
1926	52,353		
1927	50,525	1970	156,868
1928	53,528	1971	165,153
1929	59,141	1972	174,487
		1973	184,635
1930	58,358	1974	190,468
1931	55,878	1975	190,828
1932	51,961	1976	200,700
1933	52,222	1977	206,329
1934	51,178	1978	213,733
1935	48,958	1979	220,520

TABLE A5.2. *Real product, Ireland, 1911–1979* ($US millions, 1925–1934)

Year	NNP	Year	GNP
1911	922	1953	1,752
		1954	1,771
1926	865	1955	1,805
		1956	1,782
1929	921	1957	1,792
		1958	1,758
1930	—	1959	1,829
1931	983		
1932	943	1960	1,927
1933	962	1961	2,025
1934	994	1962	2,091
1935	1,037	1963	2,186
1936	1,033	1964	2,268
1937	1,005	1965	2,329
1938	1,009	1966	2,350
1939	999	1967	2,487
		1968	2,693
1940	967	1969	2,818
1941	938		
1942	940	1970	2,910
1943	981	1971	3,011
1944	1,003	1972	3,190
1945	1,092	1973	3,323
1946	1,184	1974	3,447
1947	1,254	1975	3,521
1948	1,314	1976	3,592
1949	1,357	1977	3,801
		1978	4,039
1950	1,383	1979	4,118
1951	1,425		
1952	1,611		

TABLE A5.3. *Real product, United Kingdom,*[a] *1830–1979* (£ millions, 1900)

Year	GNP	Year	GNP	Year	GNP	Year	GNP
1830	397	1870	1,021	1910	2,328	1950	3,659
1831	415	1871	1,190	1911	2,398	1951	3,758
1832	413	1872	1,182	1912	2,388	1952	3,739
1833	415	1873	1,182	1913	2,514	1953	3,910
1834	432	1874	1,253	1914	2,529	1954	4,060
1835	456	1875	1,271	1915	2,746	1955	4,186
1836	473	1876	1,285	1916	2,736	1956	4,268
1837	466	1877	1,296	1917	2,734	1957	4,351
1838	493	1878	1,305	1918	2,683	1958	4,374
1839	576	1879	1,281	1919	2,439	1959	4,543
1840	500	1880	1,379	1920	2,279	1960	4,750
1841	490	1881	1,377	1921	2,073	1961	4,912
1842	480	1882	1,400	1922	2,146	1962	4,966
1843	487	1883	1,461	1923	2,221	1963	5,177
1844	517	1884	1,452	1924	2,290	1964	5,487
1845	545	1885	1,449	1925	2,413	1965	5,619
1846	581	1886	1,465	1926	2,314	1966	5,730
1847	585	1887	1,536	1927	2,474	1967	5,872
1848	592	1888	1,561	1928	2,514	1968	6,091
1849	602	1889	1,592	1929	2,574	1969	6,211
1850	596	1890	1,615	1930	2,572	1970	6,359
1851	620	1891	1,670	1931	2,440	1971	6,530
1852	631	1892	1,645	1932	2,432	1972	6,675
1853	655	1893	1,637	1933	2,478	1973	7,174
1854	673	1894	1,724	1934	2,644	1974	7,090
1855	691	1895	1,776	1935	2,747	1975	7,036
1856	742	1896	1,857	1936	2,831	1976	7,328
1857	758	1897	1,862	1937	2,938	1977	7,400
1858	763	1898	1,966	1938	3,022	1978	7,667
1859	779	1899	2,069	1939	3,119	1979	7,738
1860	791	1900	2,032	1940	3,533		
1861	831	1901	2,113	1941	3,729		
1862	831	1902	2,126	1942	3,751		
1863	839	1903	2,127	1943	3,814		
1864	852	1904	2,140	1944	3,639		
1865	877	1905	2,184	1945	3,414		
1866	876	1906	2,236	1946	3,535		
1867	888	1907	2,243	1947	3,322		
1868	919	1908	2,180	1948	3,419		
1869	947	1909	2,252	1949	3,515		

[a] Not incl. Rep. of Ireland from 1920.

TABLE A5.4. *Real product, Norway, 1865–1979* (millions of kroner, 1910)

Year	GDP	Year	GDP	Year	GDP
1865	601	1904	1,194	1948	4,026
1866	613	1905	1,203	1949	4,128
1867	628	1906	1,253		
1868	627	1907	1,307	1950	4,333
1869	651	1908	1,349	1951	4,566
		1909	1,378	1952	4,729
1870	650			1953	4,916
1871	661	1910	1,435	1954	5,162
1872	704	1911	1,491	1955	5,280
1873	721	1912	1,564	1956	5,556
1874	748	1913	1,649	1957	5,728
1875	769	1914	1,683	1958	5,725
1876	792	1915	1,757	1959	5,971
1877	798	1916	1,825		
1878	770	1917	1,659	1960	6,320
1879	777	1918	1,592	1961	6,706
		1919	1,865	1962	7,227
1880	802			1963	7,603
1881	809	1920	1,987	1964	8,019
1882	808	1921	1,795	1965	8,433
1883	805	1922	1,957	1966	8,808
1884	819	1923	2,041	1967	9,301
1885	827	1924	2,040	1968	9,671
1886	831	1925	2,166	1969	10,097
1887	842	1926	2,198		
1888	881	1927	2,281	1970	10,452
1889	914	1928	2,382	1971	10,931
		1929	2,607	1972	11,496
1890	940			1973	11,969
1891	949	1930	2,468	1974	12,425
1892	967	1931	2,272	1975	13,115
1893	993	1932	2,390	1976	14,008
1894	999	1933	2,444	1977	14,509
1895	1,011	1934	2,533	1978	14,985
1896	1,040	1935	2,660	1979	15,457
1897	1,095	1936	2,839		
1898	1,104	1937	2,963		
1899	1,138	1938	3,030		
		1939	3,178		
1900	1,152				
1901	1,181	1945	—		
1902	1,199	1946	3,309		
1903	1,192	1947	3,762		

TABLE A5.5. *Real product, Sweden, 1861–1979* (millions of kronor, 1913)

Year	GDP	Year	GDP	Year	GDP
1861	924	1901	2,628	1941	7,644
1862	944	1902	2,540	1942	7,670
1863	984	1903	2,811	1943	8,181
1864	974	1904	2,856	1944	8,638
1865	1,006	1905	2,890	1945	9,416
1866	999	1906	3,234	1946	10,396
1867	991	1907	3,238	1947	11,013
1868	979	1908	3,262	1948	11,613
1869	966	1909	3,333	1949	12,099
1870	1,163	1910	3,543	1950	13,027
1871	1,192	1911	3,685	1951	13,417
1872	1,276	1912	3,603	1952	13,649
1873	1,362	1913	4,128	1953	14,090
1874	1,436	1914	4,028	1954	14,932
1875	1,335	1915	4,180	1955	15,381
1876	1,470	1916	4,718	1956	15,892
1877	1,440	1917	4,307	1957	16,267
1878	1,407	1918	4,025	1958	16,651
1879	1,467	1919	4,117	1959	17,519
1880	1,482	1920	4,686	1960	18,189
1881	1,538	1921	4,129	1961	19,226
1882	1,501	1922	3,912	1962	20,051
1883	1,579	1923	4,237	1963	21,096
1884	1,591	1924	4,558	1964	22,533
1885	1,671	1925	4,995	1965	23,480
1886	1,647	1926	5,205	1966	24,172
1887	1,670	1927	5,447	1967	24,853
1888	1,693	1928	5,463	1968	25,853
1889	1,798	1929	5,920	1969	27,164
1890	1,821	1930	6,121	1970	28,515
1891	1,888	1931	5,537	1971	28,808
1892	1,870	1932	5,394	1972	28,393
1893	1,923	1933	5,463	1973	30,522
1894	2,104	1934	5,995	1974	31,770
1895	2,045	1935	6,292	1975	32,564
1896	2,315	1936	6,743	1976	33,081
1897	2,365	1937	7,192	1977	32,290
1898	2,376	1938	7,458	1978	32,730
1899	2,439	1939	7,868	1979	34,048
1900	2,569	1940	7,789		

TABLE   A5.6. *Real   product,   Denmark,   1870–1979*
(millions of kroner, 1929)

Year	GNP	Year	GNP	Year	GNP
1870	1,022	1910	3,351	1954	10,025
1871	1,106	1911	3,555	1955	10,050
1872	1,133	1912	3,877	1956	10,247
1873	1,165	1913	4,044	1957	10,769
1874	1,183	1914	3,904	1958	11,051
1875	1,164			1959	11,761
1876	1,203	1920	—		
1877	1,172	1921	4,067	1960	12,507
1878	1,197	1922	4,462	1961	13,242
1879	1,239	1923	5,081	1962	13,973
		1924	5,054	1963	14,037
1880	1,316	1925	4,883	1964	15,291
1881	1,393	1926	5,035	1965	15,938
1882	1,446	1927	5,208	1966	16,403
1883	1,547	1928	5,402	1967	17,038
1884	1,573	1929	5,556	1968	17,767
1885	1,565			1969	19,222
1886	1,511	1930	5,871		
1887	1,578	1931	6,005	1970	19,751
1888	1,664	1932	5,737	1971	20,232
1889	1,757	1933	5,844	1972	21,327
		1934	6,144	1973	22,443
1890	1,828	1935	6,170	1974	22,248
1891	1,902	1936	6,431	1975	22,112
1892	1,906	1937	6,563	1976	23,869
1893	1,939	1938	6,592	1977	24,296
1894	1,967	1939	7,022	1978	24,607
1895	2,121			1979	25,473
1896	2,216	1940	5,542		
1897	2,257	1941	5,016		
1898	2,484	1942	5,267		
1899	2,544	1943	5,273		
		1944	5,377		
1900	2,591	1945	5,899		
1901	2,605	1946	7,653		
1902	2,638	1947	7,689		
1903	2,786	1948	7,877		
1904	2,909	1949	8,298		
1905	2,980				
1906	3,161	1950	9,110		
1907	3,328	1951	9,090		
1908	3,219	1952	9,202		
1909	3,273	1953	9,744		

TABLE A5.7. *Real product, Finland, 1926–1979* (millions of new marks, 1929), *and The Netherlands, 1900–1979* (millions of guilders, 1963)

Year	Finland	Netherlands	Year	Finland	Netherlands
1900	—	8,980	1940	243	18,418
1901	—	8,468	1941	264	18,732
1902	—	9,052	1942	278	17,110
1903	—	9,295	1943	302	16,639
1094	—	9,059	1944	298	11,250
1905	—	9,355	1945	254	11,407
1906	—	9,800	1946	284	19,935
1907	—	9,977	1947	303	23,022
1908	—	10,250	1948	325	25,362
1909	—	10,555	1949	344	26,287
				GNP	GNP
1910	—	10,470	1950	388	26,109
1911	—	10,463	1951	486	26,396
1912	—	11,200	1952	483	26,979
1913	—	11,696	1953	472	29,401
1914	—	11,375	1954	516	30,823
1915	—	11,952	1955	555	33,623
1916	—	12,307	1956	566	34,881
1917	—	11,456	1957	574	35,874
1918	—	10,789	1958	574	35,763
1919	—	13,488	1959	616	37,518
1920	—	13,663	1960	677	40,660
1921	—	14,821	1961	731	42,039
1922	—	14,944	1962	762	43,631
1923	—	15,600	1963	780	42,258
1924	NNP	16,301	1964	831	49,291
1925	—	16,835	1965	873	51,953
1926	196	17,742	1966	893	53,289
1927	213	18,646	1967	913	56,371
1928	219	19,267	1968	936	59,788
1929	216	19,685	1969	1,034	63,204
1930	213	20,119	1970	1,118	68,101
1931	200	18,931	1971	1,139	71,010
1932	202	18,252	1972	1,225	73,438
1933	219	17,700	1973	1,305	77,627
1934	251	17,607	1974	1,346	80,374
1935	259	18,008	1975	1,354	79,546
1936	278	18,488	1976	1,357	83,777
1937	306	19,666	1977	1,362	85,763
1938	294	19,981	1978	1,394	87,887
1939	293	20,511	1979	1,494	89,817

TABLE A5.8. *Real product, Belgium, 1846–1979* (billions of francs, 1948)

Year	NNP	Year	GNP
1846	37	1950	270
		1951	284
1895	118	1952	296
		1953	300
1913	205	1954	312
		1955	327
1920	111	1956	337
		1957	345
	GNP	1958	342
1924	176	1959	351
1927	173	1960	370
		1961	388
1930	215	1962	411
		1963	429
1934	209	1964	458
1935	219	1965	476
1936	246	1966	489
1937	250	1967	508
1938	241	1968	530
1939	—	1969	568
1941	—	1970	602
		1971	625
1943	—	1972	658
		1973	699
1946	219	1974	730
1947	250	1975	716
1948	248	1976	754
1949	262	1977	760
		1978	783
		1979	801

TABLE A5.9. *Real product, Germany, 1850–1979*
(millions of marks, 1913)

Year	NNP	Year	NNP	Year	NNP
1850	10,534	1888	25,840	1934	52,102
1851	10,568	1889	26,478	1935	58,658
1852	11,121			1936	66,226
1853	10,630	1890	27,754	1937	73,167
1854	10,961	1891	26,822	1938	81,335
1855	10,316	1892	28,390		
1856	11,553	1893	30,606		GNP, FRG
1857	11,845	1894	30,196	1950	44,904
1858	12,053	1895	32,079	1951	49,717
1859	12,219	1896	33,377	1952	53,854
		1897	34,739	1953	57,910
1860	13,604	1898	36,813	1954	62,603
1861	13,002	1899	36,860	1955	69,365
1862	13,731			1956	74,137
1863	14,639	1900	36,466	1957	78,154
1864	14,677	1901	36,197	1958	82,251
1865	14,858	1902	36,918	1959	87,899
1866	15,106	1903	40,132		
1867	15,108	1904	42,263	1960	95,615
1868	16,621	1905	43,346	1961	101,382
1869	15,660	1906	44,299	1962	111,168
		1907	46,181	1963	114,996
1870	16,706	1908	46,410	1964	122,652
1871	17,395	1909	47,512	1965	128,889
1872	19,133			1966	132,377
1873	19,768	1910	47,457	1967	132,500
1874	21,316	1911	49,648	1968	141,453
1875	21,070	1912	51,914	1969	152,567
1876	20,890	1913	52,440		
1877	20,705			1970	161,859
1878	21,803	1924	—	1971	167,087
1879	21,193	1925	46,897	1972	173,202
		1926	46,587	1973	181,671
1880	20,576	1927	53,108	1974	182,649
1881	20,616	1928	53,950	1975	179,286
1882	20,444	1929	51,694	1976	188,520
1883	21,909			1977	194,237
1884	22,712	1930	49,289	1978	200,680
1885	23,452	1931	43,913	1979	209,891
1886	24,142	1932	41,760		
1887	24,558	1933	47,375		

TABLE A5.10. *Real product, Switzerland, 1890–1979*
(millions of francs, 1938)

Year	NNP	Year	GNP
1890	3,123	1952	—
		1953	13,230
1895	3,836	1954	13,687
		1955	14,719
1899	3,747	1956	15,604
		1957	16,049
1913	5,390	1958	15,757
		1959	16,899
1924	6,580		
		1960	17,881
1929	8,470	1961	19,191
		1962	20,163
1930	8,560	1963	21,090
1931	8,310	1964	22,160
1932	8,060	1965	23,123
1933	8,510	1966	23,787
1934	8,560	1967	24,212
1935	8,560	1968	25,225
1936	8,580	1969	26,579
1937	8,780		
1938	8,870	1970	28,077
1939	8,950	1971	29,221
		1972	30,156
1940	8,780	1973	31,076
1941	8,400	1974	31,528
1942	8,170	1975	29,232
1943	8,410	1976	28,822
1944	8,560	1977	29,523
1945	9,100	1978	29,619
1946	10,210	1979	30,275
1947	11,000		
1948	11,090		
1949	10,840		
1950	11,620		
1951	—		

TABLE A5.11. *Real product, Austria, 1913–1979* (billions of schillings, 1964)

Year	GNP	Year	GNP	Year	GNP
1913	91.24	1946	40.82	1965	234.94
		1947	78.49	1966	246.68
1921	—	1948	94.65	1967	252.56
1922	—	1949	95.59	1968	263.78
1923	—			1969	279.22
1924	80,85	1950	106.09		
1925	86.25	1951	113.33	1970	300.89
1926	87.69	1952	113.39	1971	317.80
1927	90.39	1953	118.39	1972	336.95
1928	94.53	1954	130.45	1973	354.67
1929	95.97	1955	144.89	1974	369.85
		1956	154.84	1975	363.59
1930	93.26	1957	164.32	1976	384.56
1931	85.75	1958	170.34	1977	401.32
1932	76.96	1959	175.17	1978	405.47
1933	73.34			1979	425.98
1934	75.02	1960	189.61		
1935	76.54	1961	200.14		
1936	78.73	1962	205.38		
1937	82.96	1963	213.91		
1938	89.08	1964	227.14		

TABLE A5.12. *Real product, Italy, 1861–1979* (millions of lire, 1938)

Year	GNP	Year	GNP	Year	GNP
1861	51.398	1900	73.149	1940	156.1
1862	52.710	1901	77.949	1941	150.5
1863	51.738	1902	76.307	1942	144.4
1864	53.999	1903	79.851	1943	129.8
1865	55.712	1904	79.579	1944	99.5
1866	56.857	1905	83.193	1945	83.2
1867	52.249	1906	84.637	1946	126.3
1868	53.368	1907	92.926	1947	152.5
1869	55.087	1908	90.985	1948	152.7
		1909	97.323	1949	162.9
1870	54.767				
1871	54.973	1910	90.407	1950	173.3
1872	54.654	1911	97.483	1951	183.4
1873	57.269	1912	99.738	1952	192.3
1874	56.802	1913	101.948	1953	207.8
1875	58.209	1914	99.238	1954	215.9
1876	57.694	1915	105.584	1955	230.4
1877	58.440	1916	113.498	1956	242.6
1878	58.477	1917	114.803	1957	257.0
1879	58.894	1918	109.070	1958	269.4
		1919	104.646	1959	288.1
1880	60.894				
1881	57.542	1920	110.800	1960	314.6
1882	60.583	1921	106.700	1961	341.7
1883	60.024	1922	113.000	1962	367.2
1884	61.130	1923	118.900	1963	395.8
1885	62.703	1924	118.300	1964	402.1
1886	64.555	1925	125.800	1965	428.7
1887	65.261	1926	126.800	1966	458.6
1888	63.084	1927	125.500	1967	494.0
1889	60.872	1928	137.500	1968	526.4
		1929	139.500	1969	569.5
1890	65.079				
1891	65.677	1930	130.000	1970	608.6
1892	62.576	1931	127.200	1971	618.6
1893	64.570	1932	132.300	1972	638.4
1894	64.059	1933	133.200	1973	683.2
1895	65.234	1934	132.500	1974	711.6
1896	66.373	1935	146.100	1975	685.7
1897	63.815	1936	142.500	1976	748.2
1898	68.667	1937	155.100	1977	739.7
1899	69.544	1938	153.700	1978	758.7
		1939	162.700	1979	796.3

TABLE A5.13. *Real product, Spain, 1906–1979* (millions of pesetas, 1929)

Year	NNP	Year	NNP
1906	15.840	1947	25.6
1907	16.026	1948	25.3
1908	16.755	1949	24.7
1909	16.935	1950	25.8
		1951	31.9
1910	16.983	1952	34.1
1911	18.571	1953	34.1
1912	17.224	1954	37.0
1913	17.776		
1914	18.425		GNP
1915	17.247	1955	38.9
1916	18.798	1956	41.7
1917	19.607	1957	43.5
1918	19.070	1958	45.4
1919	20.358	1959	44.6
1920	21.807	1960	45.6
1921	20.884	1961	51.0
1922	20.394	1962	55.8
1923	21.476	1963	60.7
1924	21.214	1964	64.4
1925	22.662	1965	69.0
1926	22.188	1966	74.6
1927	23.781	1967	77.8
1928	22.570	1968	82.2
1929	25.213	1969	88.5
1930	24.104	1970	93.7
1931	24.028	1971	98.4
1932	25.742	1972	106.3
1933	23.196	1973	114.7
1934	26.146	1974	121.3
1935	25.289	1975	122.6
		1976	126.3
1939	18.800	1977	130.4
		1978	134.0
1940	21.200	1979	135.0
1941	21.700		
1942	23.900		
1943	23.500		
1944	24.800		
1945	22.000		
1946	26.200		

TABLE A5.14. *Real product, Greece, 1891–1979* (millions of drachmas, 1929)

Year	NNP	Year	GNP
1891	15	1953	84
		1954	86
1912	30	1955	93
		1956	101
1927	47	1957	108
1928	47	1958	113
1929	45	1959	117
1930	49	1960	122
1931	45	1961	135
1932	48	1962	138
1933	49	1963	151
1934	52	1964	164
1935	54	1965	179
1936	56	1966	190
1937	61	1967	201
1938	59	1968	214
1939	60	1969	235
1946	39	1970	254
1947	52	1971	272
1948	57	1972	297
1949	66	1973	318
		1974	306
	GNP	1975	325
1950	67	1976	346
1951	73	1977	357
1952	74	1978	397
		1979	394

TABLE A5.15. *Real product, Japan, 1878–1979* (millions of yen, 1934–1936)

Year	GDP	Year	GDP	Year	GDP
1878–1882	(2,986)	1914	8,190	1949	16,605
		1915	8,953		
1885	3,850	1916	10,338	1950	17,474
1886	4,178	1917	10,688	1951	19,210
1887	4,354	1918	10,799	1952	20,730
1888	4,164	1919	11,898	1953	22,256
1889	4,385			1954	23,483
		1920	11,155	1955	26,373
1890	4,783	1921	12,386	1956	28,364
1891	4,555	1922	12,347	1957	30,596
1892	4,861	1923	12,362	1958	31,877
1893	4,876	1924	12,707	1959	36,270
1894	5,454	1925	13,227		
1895	5,529	1926	13,348	1960	41,452
1896	5,228	1927	13,541	1961	46,741
1897	5,337	1928	14,644	1962	50,882
1898	6,354	1929	15,106	1963	53,968
1899	5,883			1964	61,967
		1930	14,006	1965	64,822
1900	6,131	1931	14,126	1966	72,441
1901	6,348	1932	15,309	1967	82,271
1902	6,023	1933	16,813	1968	94,059
1903	6,447	1934	16,844	1969	103,480
1904	6,494	1935	17,304		
1905	6,389	1936	18,567	1970	115,166
1906	7,224	1937	19,454	1971	121,048
1907	7,454	1938	20,752	1972	132,350
1908	7,504	1939	24,023	1973	145,523
1909	7,490			1974	145,024
		1940	24,727	1975	147,012
1910	7,608			1976	156,515
1911	8,022	1946	10,745	1977	164,957
1912	8,313	1947	12,807	1978	174,647
1913	8,447	1948	14,652	1979	184,957

TABLE A5.16. *Real product, United States, 1850–1980*
(millions of dollars, 1958)

Year	GNP	Year	GNP	Year	GNP
1850	19.4	1918	151.8	1953	412.8
		1919	146.4	1954	407.0
1860	25.6			1955	438.0
		1920	140.0	1956	446.1
1869–1878	23.1	1921	127.8	1957	452.5
		1922	148.0	1958	447.3
1879–1888	42.4	1923	165.9	1959	475.9
1889	49.1	1924	165.5		
		1925	179.4	1960	487.7
1890	52.7	1926	190.0	1961	497.2
1891	55.1	1927	189.8	1962	529.8
1892	60.4	1928	190.9	1963	551.0
1893	57.5	1929	203.6	1964	581.1
1894	55.9			1965	617.8
1895	62.6	1930	183.5	1966	658.1
1896	61.3	1931	169.3	1967	675.2
1897	67.1	1932	144.2	1968	706.6
1898	68.6	1933	141.5	1969	725.6
1899	74.8	1934	154.3		
		1935	169.5	1970	722.5
1900	76.9	1936	193.0	1971	747.0
1901	85.7	1937	203.2	1972	789.0
1902	86.5	1938	192.9	1973	834.9
1903	90.8	1939	209.4	1974	830.3
1904	89.7			1975	821.0
1905	96.3	1940	227.2	1976	864.9
1906	107.5	1941	263.7	1977	912.8
1907	109.2	1942	297.8	1978	956.0
1908	100.2	1943	337.1	1979	986.6
1909	116.8	1944	361.3		
		1945	355.2	1980	985.3
1910	120.1	1946	312.6		
1911	123.2	1947	309.9		
1912	130.2	1948	323.7		
1913	131.4	1949	324.1		
1914	125.6				
1915	124.5	1950	355.3		
1916	134.3	1951	383.4		
1917	135.2	1952	395.1		

TABLE A5.17. *Real product, Canada, 1870–1979* (millions of Canadian dollars, 1949); *Real product, Australia, 1900–1979* (millions of US dollars, 1925–1934)

Year	Canada NNP	Australia NNP	Year	Canada NNP	Australia NNP
1870	831	—	1942	7,692	3,902
			1943	7,902	3,595
1880	1,083	—	1944	8,444	3,617
			1945	9,267	3,870
1890	1,616	—	1946	10,323	4,586
			1947	10,657	4,490
1900	2,145	1,370	1948	10,451	5,027
			1949	10,923	4,846
1910	3,959	—		PIB	PIB
			1950	11,642	5,270
1914	4,273	1,955	1951	11,817	5,608
1915	4,215	1,869	1952	12,633	5,522
1916	3,960	1,863	1953	13,338	5,870
1917	3,801	1,710	1954	13,650	6,224
1918	3,827	1,435	1955	14,662	6,534
1919	3,709	1,463	1956	15,603	6,658
			1957	16,083	6,803
1920	4,106	1,737	1958	16,585	7,305
1921	—	1,849	1959	17,392	7,698
1922	—	2,149			
1923	—	2,350	1960	17,945	7,964
1924	—	2,547	1961	18,410	8,059
1925	—	2,719	1962	19,656	8,608
1926	5,010	2,825	1963	20,745	9,220
1927	5,557	3,027	1964	22,068	9,880
1928	6,128	3,090	1965	23,562	10,087
1929	6,490	3,151	1966	25,219	10,740
			1967	26,086	11,119
1930	6,203	3,106	1968	27,544	12,179
1931	5,877	2,893	1969	28,976	12,865
1932	5,414	2,746			
1933	5,272	2,936	1970	29,736	13,527
1934	5,534	3,025	1971	31,804	14,137
1935	5,775	3,189	1972	33,663	14,642
1936	6,036	3,173	1973	36,199	15,390
1937	6,420	3,326	1974	37,481	15,644
1938	6,337	3,410	1975	37,900	16,056
1939	6,510	3,887	1976	40,100	16,564
			1977	42,077	16,615
1940	7,034	3,931	1978	42,566	17,271
1941	7,471	3,838	1979	43,811	17,646

General Bibliography

The Original Theory of Demographic Transition

DAVIS, K. (1945), 'The World Demographic Transition', *The Annals of the American Academy of Political and Social Sciences* 237 (Jan.), 1–11.

KIRK, D. (1944), 'Population Change and the Postwar World', *American Sociological Review* (Feb.), 28–35.

—— (1946), *Europe's Population in the Interwar Years* (New York).

LANDRY, A. (1909), 'Les Trois Théories principales de la population', *Scientia*, Paris, 3–29.

—— (1934), *La Révolution démographique* (Paris: Librairie Sirey).

—— (1945), *Traité de démographie* (Paris: Payot).

MOORE, W. E. (1945), *Economic Demography of Eastern and Southern Europe* (Geneva: Society of Nations).

NOTESTEIN, F. W. (1945), 'Population: The Long View', in T. Schultz (ed.), *Food for the World* (Chicago: University of Chicago Press), 36–57.

—— (1953), 'Economic Problems of Population Change', *Proceedings of the Eighth International Conference of Agricultural Economists* (New York: Oxford University Press), 13–31.

THOMPSON, W. (1929), 'Population', *American Journal of Sociology* (May), 959–75.

—— (1946), *Population and Peace in the Pacific* (Chicago: University of Chicago Press), 22–35, 251–318.

Demographic Data

International Retrospective Summary (Civil Registration)

The primary documents consulted are produced by the following bodies: CICRED, ISI, INED, UN, SGF, and the University of Columbia.

CICRED. National monographs on population for 44 countries out of our selection. These monographs were published on the occasion of World Population Year (1974). As they were all written according to the same plan, they facilitate the point-by-point comparison of countries.

Europe: Austria, Belgium, Bulgaria, Czechoslovakia, Denmark, Finland, France, FRG, Greece, Hungary, Italy, Poland, Portugal, Romania, Spain, Switzerland, Yugoslavia.

North America: Canada, United States.

Latin America: Argentina, Brazil, Chile, Colombia, Costa Rica, Cuba, Jamaica, Mexico, Panama, Trinidad and Tobago, Venezuela.

Africa: Egypt, Tunisia.

Asia: Hong Kong, India, Indonesia, Israel, South Korea, Lebanon, Malaysia, Philippines, Sri Lanka, Thailand, Turkey.

Oceania: New Zealand.

ISI permanent office (1917), *Annuaire international de statistique*, ii: *Mouvement de la population (Europe)* (La Haye: ISI).

—— (1920), *Annuaire international de statistique*, iv: *Mouvement de la population (Amérique)* (La Haye: ISI).

—— (1921), *Annuaire international de statistique*, v: *Mouvement de la population (Afrique, Asie, Océanie)* (La Haye: ISI).

—— (1932), *Aperçu de démographie, 1931*.

—— (1939), *Aperçu de la démographie des divers pays du monde* (La Haye: ISI).

INED (1954), *Le Mouvement naturel de la population dans le monde de 1906 à 1936* (Paris: Imprimerie Nationale), 156 ff.

UN (1949–1985), *Demographic Yearbooks*, 1948–1984 (New York: UN).

—— (1963), *Population Bulletin, with Special Reference to the Situation and Recent Trends of Mortality in the World, 1962*, no. 6 (New York: UN).

—— (1965), *Population Bulletin, with Special Reference to the Situation and Recent Trends of Fertility in the World, 1963*, no. 7 (New York: UN).

SGF (1907), *Statistique internationale du mouvement de la population jusqu'en 1905: résumé rétrospectif depuis l'origine des statistiques d'état civil jusqu'en 1905* (Paris: Imprimerie Nationale).

—— (1913), *Statistique internationale du mouvement de la population (2ᵉ volume, années 1901 à 1910) d'après les registres de l'état civil* (Paris: Imprimerie Nationale).

UNIVERSITY OF COLUMBIA (1975), *European Historical Statistics, 1750–1970*, ed. B. R. Mitchell (New York: Columbia University Press), 104–49.

Data and Additional Estimates, by Country

Estimates provided by the CICRED monograph series, national statistical yearbooks, and United Nations demographic yearbooks have been used, These apply to countries where civil registration was defective for a long time (or still is) but for which corrected rates exist based on census results, on the comparison of successive censuses, or on sample surveys intended to fill in registration gaps (or simply to measure its degree of completeness).

For periods prior to the establishment of civil registration, retrospective reconstructions of rates of natural increase (sometimes including a breakdown for fertility and mortality) have been produced, using either parish registers (as in France), retrospective projection, or other methods.

The following list indicates the countries referred to in this study, accompanied by the corresponding periods and sources for which available data exist:

Europe

Belgium

Estimates beginning 1803, from birth and death registration:

DUCHÈNE, J., and LESTHAEGHE, R. (1975), 'Essai de reconstitution de la population belge sous le régime français', *Population et famille*, 3: 1–47.

Czechoslovakia

Quinquennial estimates of birth- and mortality rates from 1785, based on annual

abstracts of births and deaths, and on censuses and local surveys, for Czech
populations only:
Atlas pohyb obyvatelstva ČSSR (1962) (retrospective yearbook).
'Dlouhobé populačni trendy na vzemi ČSR' (1981), *Acta demographica*, iv (Prague).

England and Wales
Decennial estimates of birth- and mortality rates, 1701–1840:
BROWNLEE, J. R. (1916), 'The History of the Birth and Death Rates in England and
Wales Taken as a Whole, from 1750 to the Present Time', *Public Health*, 20.
KRAUSE, J. T. (1965), 'The Changing Adequacy of English Registration, 1690–1837',
in D. V. Glass and D. E. C. Eversley, *Population in History: Essays in Historical
Demography* (London: Edward Arnold).
OHLIN, G. (1955), *The Positive and the Preventive Check: A Study of the Rate of Growth of
the Preindustrial Population* (Cambridge, Mass.: Harvard University Press).
Quinquennial estimates of birth- and mortality rates, and net and gross reproduction
rates, 1541–1871:
WRIGLEY, E. A., and SCHOFIELD, R. S. (1981), *The Population History of England,
1541–1871: A Reconstruction* (London: Edward Arnold).

France
Survey of parish registers for the whole of France, quinquennial estimates of birth-
and death-rates:
HENRY, L., and BLAYO, Y. (1975), 'La Population de la France de 1740 à 1860',
Population, special number: 'Démographique historique' (Nov.).

Greece
Decennial estimates of birth and mortality, from 1821:
SIAMPOS, G. (1973), *Demographic evolution of modern Greece* (in Greek; Athens), 20.

Ireland
Estimates of total population growth for extended periods, 1725–1821:
CONNELL, K. H. (1950), *The Population of Ireland, 1750–1845* (Oxford: Clarendon
Press).

Italy
Evaluations indicative of total population growth for extended periods, 1700–1860:
CIPOLLA, C. M. (1965), 'Four Centuries of Italian Demographic Development', in
D. V. Glass and D. E. C. Eversley, *Population in History: Essays in Historical
Demography* (London: Edward Arnold).

Soviet Union (or Russia only)
Estimates of total intercensal population growth from 1721 (first census) and annual
estimates of population growth based on civil registration and various documents:
BIRABEN, J. -N. (1958), 'Essai sur l'évolution démographique de l'URSS', *Population*,
special number (June), 41–44.
COALE, A. J., ANDERSON, B. A., and HARM, E. (1979), *Human Fertility in Russia since
the Nineteenth Century* (Princeton, NJ: Princeton University Press).
KABOUSANE, V. (1963), *La Population de la Russie du XVIII* siècle et dans la première
moitié du XIX siècle d'après les recensements* (in Russian; Moscow: USSR Academy of
Sciences, Institute of History).

Spain
Estimates of intercensal demographic growth, 1723–1858:

NADAL, J. (1966), *Historia de la Poblacion Española* (Barcelona).
VILAR, P. (1965), 'Quelques Problèmes de démographie historique en Catalogne et en Espagne', *Annales de Démographie Historique*.

Overseas English-Speaking Countries

Australia
Aggregate estimates of total, natural, and migratory increase for the entire period 1788–1861 without distinction, based on the censuses of 1788 and 1869 and population growth:
BORRIE, W. D. (1948), *Population Trends and Policies: A Study in Australian and World Demography* (Sydney: Australasian Publishing Company).

Canada (Quebec only)
Decennial estimates of fertility and mortality rates, 1711–60, using censuses and parish registers:
HENRIPIN, J. (1954), *La Population canadienne au début du XVIIIe siècle: nuptialité, fécondité, mortalité infantile* (Paris: PUF).
CHARBONNEAU, H. (1973), *La Population du Québec: études rétrospectives* (Montréal, Éd. du Boréal Express).

United States
Estimates of fertility in 1800 (white population only), 1820, 1840, 1860, 1880, and 1900; general mortality, 1865–1900, and infant mortality, 1851–1900, for the state of Massachusetts:
Historical Statistics of the U.S. Colonial Times to 1970 (1976), pt. 1, Bicentennial Edition (Washington, DC: US Department of Commerce, Bureau of the Census).
COALE, A. J., and ZELNIK, M. (1963), *New Estimates of Fertility and Population in the United States* (Princeton, NJ: Princeton University Press).

Latin America

Brazil
Estimates of the parameters of demographic growth, extended periods from 1800:
MORTARA, G. (1954), 'The Development and Structure of Brazil's Population', *Population Studies*, 8.

Asia

Mainland China
Evaluation of total demographic growth, year by year, 1931–57:
SPENCER, A. E. C. W. (1959), 'Agriculture and Population in Relation to Economic Planning', *The Annals* (Jan.).
CALOT, G. (1984), 'Données nouvelles sur l'évolution démographique chinoise', *Population*, 4–5: 897–936, and 6: 1045–62.

Long-Range Macro-Economic Time-Series

International Data

CLARK, C. (1957), *The Conditions of Economic Progress*, 3rd edn. (London: Macmillan).
KUZNETS, S. (1956), 'Levels and Variability of Rates of Growth', *EDCC*, 5 (Oct.), 5–94.
—— (1957), 'Industrial Distribution of National Product and Labor Force', *EDCC*, 5 (July), 5.
—— (1961), 'Long-Term Trends in Capital Formation Proportions', *EDCC*, 9 (July), 9.
MADDISON, A. (1964), *Economic Growth in the West, Comparative Experience in Europe and North America* (London: Allen & Unwin).
MULHALL, M. G. (1896), *Industries and Wealth of Nations* (London: Longman).
OECD (1981), *Comptes nationaux des pays de l'OCDE* (Paris: OECD).

National Data, Principal Developed Countries

DEANE, P., and COLE, W. A. (1962), *British Economic Growth 1688–1959: Trends and Structure* (Cambridge).
FUA, G. (1965), *Notes on Italian Economic Growth 1861–1964* (Milan).
—— (1978–81), *Lo Sviluppo Economico in Italia*, 3 vols. (Milan: Angeli).
HOFFMANN, W. G. (1965), *Das Wachstum der deutschen Wirtschaft seit der Mitte des 19. Jahrhunderts* (Berlin).
KUZNETS, S. (1952), 'Long-Term Changes in the National Income of the USA since 1870', *Income and Wealth*, ser. 2 (Cambridge, Mass.).
LOCKWOOD, W. W. (1954), *The Economic Development of Japan: Growth and Structural Change, 1868–1938* (Princeton, NJ: Princeton University Press).
MARKOVITCH, T. J. (1966), *L'Industrie française de 1789 à 1964*, Cahiers de l'ISEA, AF7 (Paris).
OHKAWA, K., *et al.* (1979), *Patterns of Japanese Economic Development: A Quantitative Appraisal* (New Haven, Conn.: Yale University Press).

Index of Names

Index of Subjects

117, 120, 153, 177, 254–6, 258,
261–3, 279, 280, 282, 293, 303,
311–13, 335, 344, 371, 376, 377,
383–6, 389, 390, 414, 468, 473,
494, 497, 500, 507, 515
civil registration:
  births 91–5
  deaths 49–53
Cocos-Keeling Islands 99
Colombia 19, 22, 33, 37, 38, 51, 60, 65,
  88, 94, 100, 103, 114, 119, 223,
  261, 262, 282, 371, 378, 382, 384,
  385, 388, 392, 435, 507
context of transition 17–19
Costa Rica 19, 22, 33, 37, 38, 44, 52, 60,
  78, 84, 94, 98, 100, 114, 117, 119,
  223, 261, 262, 269, 278, 282, 371,
  378, 384, 385, 435
Cuba 19, 22, 30, 33, 35, 37, 38, 44, 51,
  52, 60, 78, 83, 84, 94, 95, 98, 103,
  114, 117, 119, 120, 165, 223, 261–
  3, 282, 371, 379, 435
cultural change 4, 11, 12, 17, 18, 333–5,
  398–407
Cyprus 19, 22, 30, 33, 35, 37, 61, 78,
  93, 94, 98, 113, 117, 223, 254, 255,
  261, 262, 282, 371
Czechoslovakia 19, 22, 32, 36, 54, 58,
  67, 90, 102, 112, 117–19, 121, 126,
  127, 131, 143, 146, 147, 176, 178,
  223, 239, 240, 282, 351, 374, 376,
  403

death rates (crude) 32, 33, 55, 75, 262,
  556–78
Denmark 19, 22, 32, 36, 45, 54, 58, 65,
  73–5, 102, 111, 113, 117, 118, 120,
  131, 142, 146, 147, 176, 178, 194,
  203, 214, 215, 223, 227, 282, 354,
  375, 403, 406, 475, 496
development (socio-economic) 3, 18, 79,
  80; see also economic development;
  modernization
diffusionism 362, 363
disequilibrium (population) 115, 190,
  346, 399
Dominican Republic 19, 22, 33, 37, 38,
  51, 60, 114, 119, 224, 261, 262,
  282, 371, 378, 385, 435

economic development 17, 378–86, 400,
  433–6, 460–9

Ecuador 33, 37
education 359–60, 386–90
Egypt 20, 22, 32, 36, 40, 41, 43, 50, 51,
  56, 67, 74, 92, 109, 112, 114, 147,
  223, 261–3, 280, 282, 287–9, 303,
  311–13, 371, 377, 378, 383–90,
  435, 488, 498, 500, 505–7
El Salvador 33, 37, 114
emigration (rates of) 167–75
England 18, 54, 65, 67, 73, 75, 77, 90,
  102, 112, 117, 120, 122, 143, 145,
  146, 190, 192, 194, 200, 203, 210,
  214, 215, 219, 226, 252, 310, 326,
  355–9, 375, 401–3, 406, 415, 447,
  451, 458–62, 464, 475, 476, 502,
  515; see also United Kingdom
environment 221, 440
equilibrium (pre-transitional or post-
  transitional) 2, 3, 8, 191, 287
Ethiopia 32, 36, 43
Europe 16, 19, 20–2, 55, 58, 62, 73,
  101, 118, 123–7, 141, 166–8, 171,
  172, 174, 175, 178, 197, 226, 232,
  241, 291, 375, 376, 513, 514

family planning 393, 394, 399–401
Fiji 20, 22, 33, 37, 41, 114, 117, 261,
  262, 282
fertility (total fertility rate) 104–10, 124–
  31, 148, 323, 543–54
fertility transition 7, 10
Finland 19, 22, 32, 36, 54, 58, 65, 73,
  75, 77, 82, 102, 112, 117–20, 131,
  139, 140, 143, 147, 148, 176, 178,
  194, 197, 203, 210, 214, 215, 223,
  224, 226, 282, 375, 475, 598
food production 490–4
France 18, 19, 22, 32, 36, 45, 54, 58, 65,
  73, 75, 90, 112, 117–23, 125, 130–
  2, 139–48, 150, 157, 161, 163–7,
  171, 173, 176, 178, 179, 182–4,
  194, 197, 203, 210, 214, 215, 219,
  220, 223–5, 280, 287–90, 294–8,
  303, 305, 306, 309, 310, 313, 319,
  320, 321–43, 345, 350, 351, 353,
  355–7, 359, 375, 382, 383, 393,
  398, 400–3, 405, 406, 417–19, 447,
  448, 451, 453, 455, 458–62, 464,
  470, 475–82, 488, 494, 514, 598

Gabon 32, 34, 36
Galicia 175

Portugal (*cont.*)
217, 222, 223, 250, 282, 310, 344, 356, 375
post-transitional fertility 190–217
pre-transitional fertility 15, 98–111, 148
pre-transitional mortality 73–5
product:
Gross Domestic Product (GDP/GNP) 501, 504–6, 598–616
Prussia 336, 338, 350
Puerto Rico 19, 22, 33, 35, 37, 38, 44, 45, 52, 60, 94, 95, 98, 117, 119, 223, 261–3, 282, 371, 379, 384

Quebec 98

registration of births/deaths, *see* civil registration
religious change 404, 405, 407
Renaissance 11, 100, 116, 344, 354, 363
reproduction rates:
gross 35–8, 121, 122
net 121, 122, 201–17
reproductive transition 7, 14
reunion 20, 22, 32, 36, 40, 51, 56, 92, 98, 109, 113, 117, 223, 261, 262, 278, 282
Romania 19, 22, 32, 36, 55, 58, 67, 90, 91, 101, 103, 113, 117–19, 121, 125–7, 131, 145, 146, 175, 176, 178, 223, 250, 251, 282, 356, 362, 374, 376
Ruanda 32, 36
Russia 55, 58, 73–5, 77, 98, 101, 103, 113, 128, 163–7, 169, 175, 176, 224, 251, 252, 288, 289, 304, 306, 310, 336, 356, 362, 369, 376, 455, 466, 468, 473–5, 487, 494, 514, 515

Saudi Arabia 33, 37, 40, 41, 432
savings 494–7
Scandinavia 77, 90, 103, 116, 157, 158, 173, 176, 185, 224, 240, 401, 455
Scotland 117, 163, 308, 375
Senegal 32, 36
Serbia 58, 101, 113, 125, 175
Sierra Leone 32, 36
Singapore 20, 22, 30, 33, 35, 37, 38, 43, 52, 61, 65, 76, 78, 79, 84, 93, 94, 96, 107, 113, 117, 120, 223, 261, 262, 278, 282, 311, 371, 376, 377, 384, 388, 389, 434, 435

Somalia 32, 36, 43
South Africa 20, 22, 32, 36, 40, 43, 51, 92, 109, 115, 165, 261, 262, 282, 371, 377, 378, 384–6, 393, 432
Spain 19, 22, 32, 34, 36, 45, 55, 58, 67, 90, 103, 113, 117–19, 121, 125, 131, 132, 146, 147, 156, 163, 164, 166–8, 174, 176, 178, 203, 213, 216, 217, 222, 223, 240, 250, 282, 310, 356, 359, 360, 373, 375, 382, 455, 474, 475
Sri Lanka 20, 22, 30, 33, 36–8, 48, 52, 57, 61, 67, 74, 78, 84, 85, 93, 94, 98, 100, 107, 111, 113, 117, 222, 223, 261, 262, 265, 266, 282, 311–13, 316, 371, 372, 376, 377, 379, 381–5, 388–90, 434, 435, 507, 514
stages of demographic transition 2, 7, 11, 13, 14, 27–9
Sudan 32, 36
Surinam 33, 37
Syria 33, 37, 40, 43, 378
Swaziland 32, 36
Sweden 19, 22, 32, 36, 43, 45, 54, 58, 65, 73, 75, 102, 111–13, 116–18, 120–2, 124, 130, 131, 134, 139, 142–8, 156, 163, 164, 166–71, 176, 180, 194, 197, 203, 216, 217, 223, 224, 226, 227, 280, 282, 283, 287–90, 294, 303–6, 309, 319, 344, 345, 351, 354, 355, 375, 407, 475, 477, 496
Switzerland 19, 22, 32, 36, 45, 54, 58, 65, 73, 75, 102, 103, 111, 112, 117, 118, 120, 123, 128, 130, 131, 139, 145–8, 166–8, 176, 178, 193, 194, 203, 210, 216, 217, 223, 228, 230, 282, 344, 375, 403, 475

Taiwan 20, 22, 30, 33, 35, 37, 56, 61, 65, 67, 74, 76, 78, 79, 83, 84, 93, 94, 96, 107, 113, 116, 117, 147, 222, 223, 261, 278, 282, 311–13, 371, 372, 376, 377, 379, 385, 434–6, 468, 508
Tanzania 30, 32
Thailand 20, 22, 33, 34, 37, 40, 88, 93, 107, 114, 261, 262, 282, 371, 377, 382–5, 389, 390, 507
theory of demographic transition 1–9, 12–13
Togo 32, 36